PHOTOJOURNALISM
THE PROFESSIONALS' APPROACH

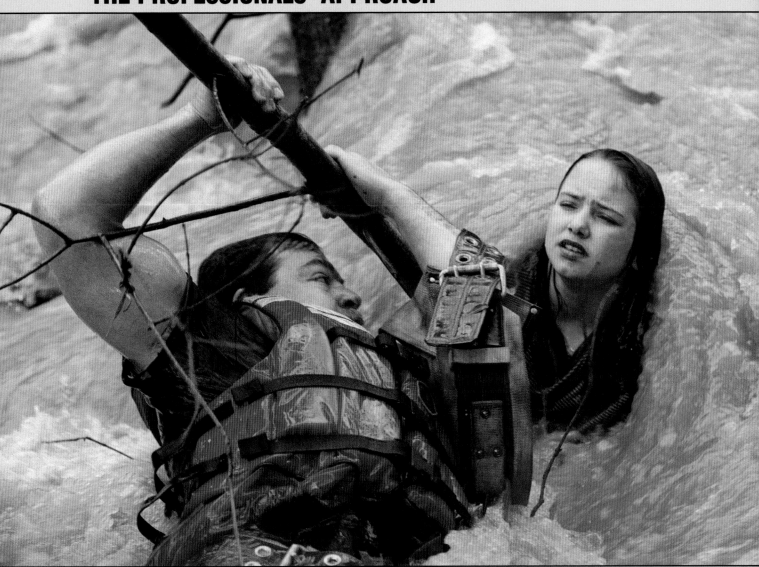

The exhausted rescuer was making his third and final attempt to save the girl. The rescue was successful. Annie Wells, for the *Press Democrat* [Santa Rosa, California]

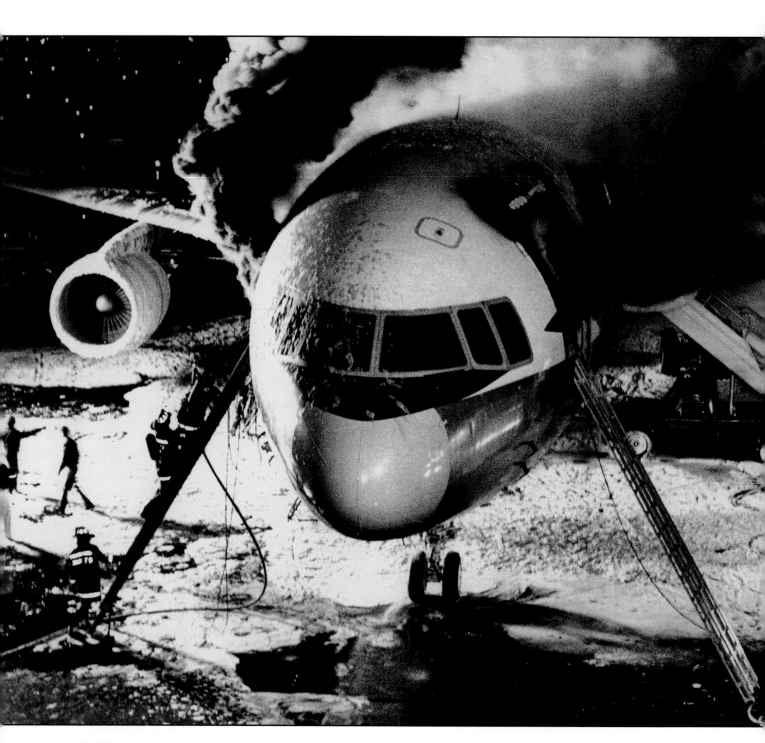

**Firefighters snuff an electrical fire aboard an
airplane parked on a Boston runway.** George Rizer, *Boston Globe*

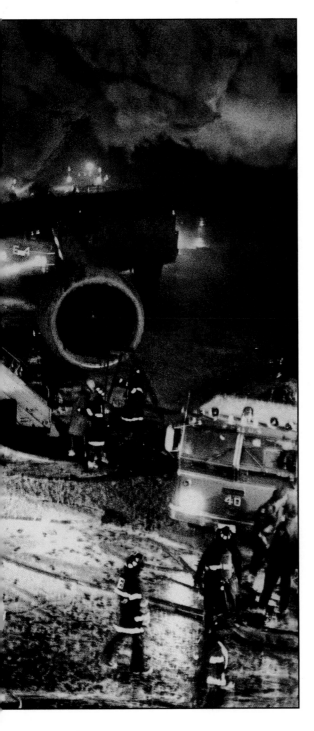

PHOTOJOURNALISM
THE PROFESSIONALS' APPROACH
fifth edition

Kenneth Kobré
Editing & Design by Betsy Brill

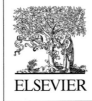

ELSEVIER

AMSTERDAM • BOSTON • HEIDELBERG • LONDON
NEW YORK • OXFORD • PARIS • SAN DIEGO
SAN FRANCISCO • SINGAPORE • SYDNEY • TOKYO

Focal Press is an imprint of Elsevier

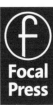

Focal Press

Focal Press is an imprint of Elsevier
200 Wheeler Road, Burlington, MA 01803, USA
Linacre House, Jordan Hill, Oxford OX2 8DP, UK

Permissions may be sought directly from Elsevier's Science and Technology
Rights Department in Oxford, UK. Phone: (44) 1865 843830, Fax: (44) 1865
853333, e-mail: permissions@elsevier.co.uk. You may also complete your
request on-line via the Elsevier homepage: http://www.elsevier.com by
selecting "Customer Support" and then "Obtaining Permissions".

 Recognizing the importance of preserving what has been written, Elsevier
prints its books on acid-free paper whenever possible.

Cover design and interior design:
      Betsy Brill, San Francisco
Cover photography:
      © Tom McKitterick, New York

This photograph is a moving tribute to the courage of Bill Biggart, a photojournalist who was killed while photographing the World Trade Center as it collapsed following terrorist attacks on September 11, 2001. Tom McKitterick, who took the still life of what was left of Biggart's equipment, was not only the slain photographer's colleague but his close friend. The photograph symbolizes the courage of the man and is a reminder of the dangers many photojournalists around the world face on a daily basis.

Line art illustrations & design of Digital Darkroom special section:
      Ben Barbante, San Francisco.

Library of Congress Cataloging-in-Publication Data
Application Submitted

British Library Cataloguing-in-Publication Data
A catalogue record for this book is available from the British Library.

ISBN-13: 978-0-240-80610-5
ISBN-10: 0-240-80610-7

For information on all Focal Press publications
visit our website at www.focalpress.com

06 07 08 10 9 8 7 6 5 4

Print in China

Dedication

This book is dedicated
to my parents, Reva and Sidney Kobre.

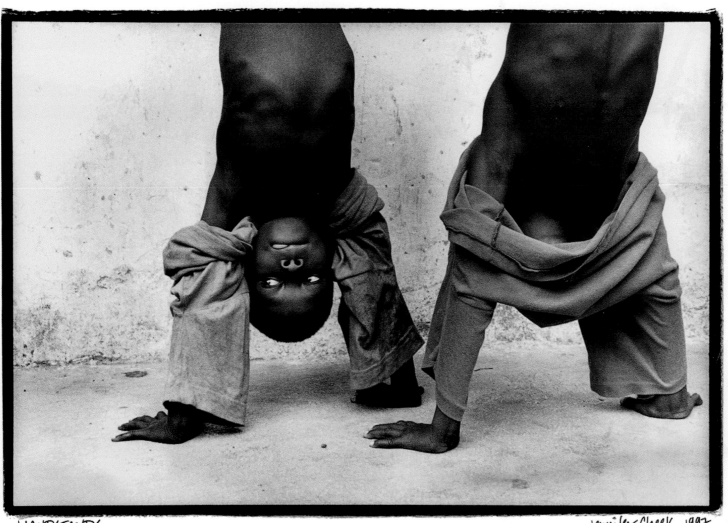

HANDSTANDS

Jennifer Cheek 1997

**Children perform handstands at the Lafanmi Selavi, a home for 350 street kids
in Haiti.** Jennifer Cheek Pantaléon, Pacifica, California

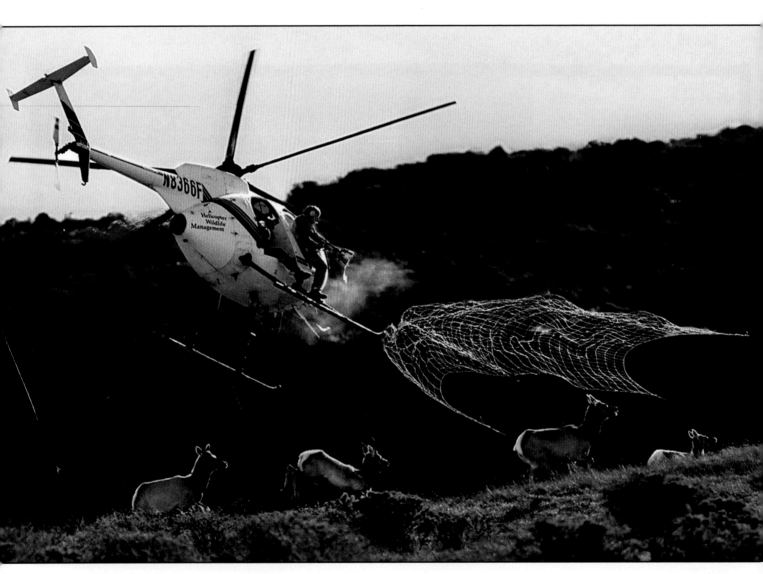

A net fired from a helicopter envelops a female tule elk. Scientists take specimens and measurements from the elk and attach a radio collar to track the movement and habits of the 270 animals in the area. John Burgess, *Press Democrat* [Santa Rosa, California]

Contents

Preface

Can anyone predict the future of photojournalism? The death of the field has been announced numerous times. With the advent of television in the early 1950s, Robert Capa, the famous war photographer and founding member of Magnum (pages 19 and 359–360), stated that photojournalism was finished. He was wrong.

Others predicted the demise of photojournalism with the end of the weekly *Life* magazine (page 356). They were wrong.

Doomsayers predicted the field's final chapter when a number of large afternoon newspapers closed. So far, they have been mistaken.

Other futurists anticipate that photographers will simultaneously shoot both stills and digital moving pictures (pages 254–255). Some even say that with the expansion of the World Wide Web, streaming video will supplant the need for still photojournalism.

So far, the prophecies have not materialized. More than fifty years after Capa's prediction of its death, photojournalism is alive and well.

In fact, the World Wide Web has resulted in an explosion of easily available information. Most sites use words and still pictures to present that information. Just as on the printed page, words need still pictures to attract and hold the readers.

Traditional news outlets like the *Washington Post*, *Newsweek*, *New York Times*, NBC, and CNN all have Web sites providing up-to-date news and pictures. The marriage of still images and words remains the most efficient way to report the news.

Perhaps the most hopeful trend is the rapid growth of personal Web pages. Today's photojournalists no longer need a printing press to circulate their work. They can use the Web to distribute every picture and story they produce. Photographers no longer are limited to one or two pictures per story (as in print) but can offer ten or even 100 pictures of floods in India or football in Indiana.

Thanks to growing access to the World Wide Web, millions of people around the world will be stimulated by powerful images transmitted to their computer screens—images not always preselected or filtered by conventional news agencies. The potential for quality photojournalism to affect change is greater than ever. ∎

A first-time bull rider takes a spill at the annual rodeo at the Howard County Fairgrounds. Rich Riggins, Patuxent [Maryland] Publishing Co.

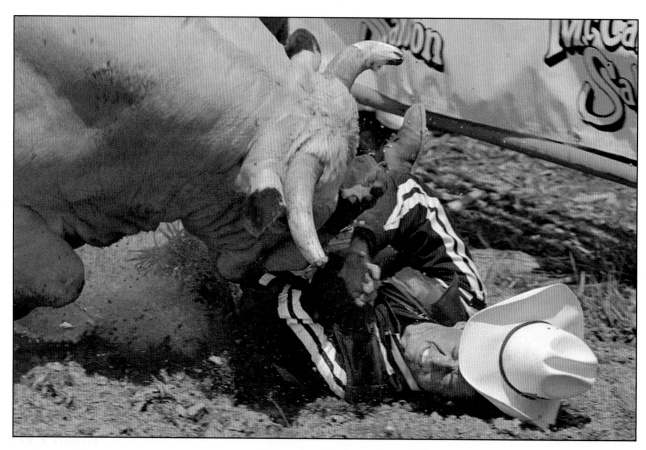

Acknowledgments

I would like to thank my parents, Dr. and Mrs. Sidney Kobré. Without their advice and guidance, I would never have written the first edition of this book. My father, who was a reporter, editor, and professor of journalism, helped give the book its clear journalistic focus. His specialty was the history of journalism. My mother, also a writer, suggested many ways to improve the prose of the original manuscript.

This edition of the book would have never obtained its look nor even been completed without the devotion and love of Betsy Brill, my wife. For nearly a year, through many alterations, including rewrites during the final layout, she helped guide the revision from initial idea to the final design of the printed page. Her experience as a professional photojournalist, writer, editor, and designer helped bring my abstract ideas into reality.

For some books, the author goes to the mountaintop and writes. That is not how I developed this book or its earlier editions. From the beginning, I have based the text on interviews—both formal and informal—with working pros on newspapers, magazines, wire services, and now Web sites. I have mentioned their names in the text whenever possible. Without their expertise and time, this book would not be complete.

In addition, numerous photographers, photo editors, academics, teachers, students, and lawyers have read parts of all the editions of **Photojournalism: The Professionals' Approach** and made a myriad of suggestions that have improved each revision. I greatly appreciate their time and effort. Many new photographers and editors generously shared the stories behind their work for this edition.

A second wave of people helped research the pictures that give the book its wide diversity of images. Almost all the photos have been lent to me by photographers, some of whom I know and others I've not had the honor to meet; some former students and some current ones. Their credits appear next to each of their pictures. I thank them all for their generous contribution to this project. A book of this scope and quality would be impossible without their collaboration.

In fact, many photographers who shared images for this edition have told me they used the book when they were students or were just starting out. I also hear from more photographers every year who not only used an earlier edition when they were students but who now are teaching and assigning the text to their own students. They and their images reach a new generation.

David Weintraub, a writer, editor, and contributor to *Photo District News* as well as a freelance shooter with more than twenty years in the business, copy edited the manuscript and contributed the freelancing section of a new chapter, "Turning Pro" (Chapter 16). John Kaplan of the University of Florida contributed an excerpt from his book, **Photo Portfolio Success**, for that chapter. Jim McNay at the Brooks Institute of Photography shared material from his *SportsShooter.com* column. Kenny Irby of the Poynter Institute for Media Studies allowed republication of his piece on digital manipulation at the *Los Angeles Times* in Chapter 14, "Ethics."

Behind-the-scenes heroes include Zach Link, a Stanford University history scholar, who conducted computer-assisted searches for the bibliography. He and Naomi Brookner tracked down bibliographic references. Barbara Oleksiw saved the day with crucial editing during layout. Carolyn Mackin helped prepare the more than 500 images for publication. Ben Barbante's skills in explaining technical situations with clear drawings are formidable. He also helped design the new special section, "Digital Darkroom."

My editor at Elsevier/Focal Press, Diane Wurzel, encouraged me to undertake this revision and chaperoned it to completion. The chairman of my department at San Francisco State University, John Burks, was supportive of the project, as was our new dean, Paul Sherwin. My assistant, Scot Tucker, helped me hold the pieces of the puzzle together.

Finally, like a chemist's research lab, my classes at SFSU have allowed me the opportunity to experiment on new approaches to photojournalism, particularly the picture story and the portrait. I thank my students for going through the trials and tribulations of trying new ways to tell stories photographically. These experiments have resulted in several extensive photo and writing projects, parts of which appear in this book. ∎

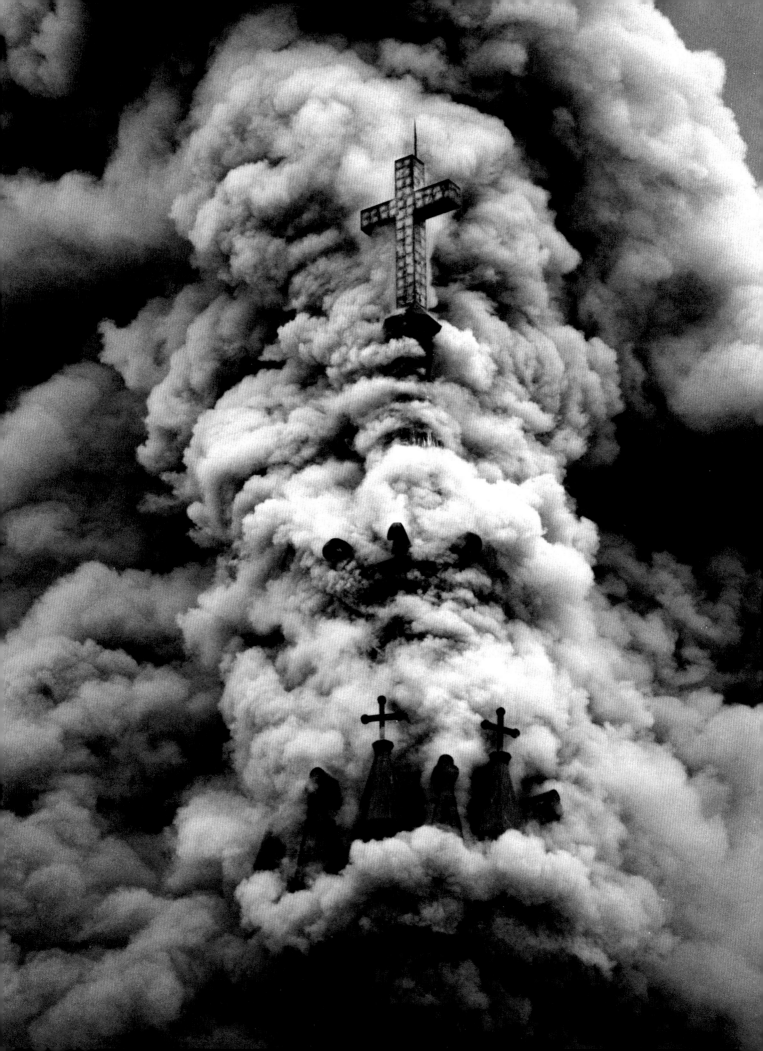

Chapter 1

Assignment

WHERE TO FIND NEWS: LOOKING FOR SCOOPS

Steve Linsenmayer, of the *Fort Wayne* (Indiana) *News-Sentinel*, heard the darkroom's emergency band scanner cackle "structure fire." Looking out the window of the newsroom, he saw black rain clouds covering a sky broken by distant lightning. Linsenmayer hesitated to race out into the storm until his boss, Keith Hitchens, came running down the hall yelling "church fire." Hitchens had heard the second call on the radio asking for additional fire companies and identifying the burning structure as St. Mary's Church. "Oh shit," Linsenmayer gasped as he raced by the darkroom to grab his camera bag on the way to his car.

The photographer heard about this out-of-control fire at a nearby church by monitoring the emergency scanner radio. Steve Linsenmayer, *Fort Wayne* [Indiana] *News-Sentinel*

When he got to St. Mary's, the lightning storm that had started the blaze was still in full glory. Within minutes of starting to shoot, Linsenmayer's umbrella blew out, so he radioed back to the office to send more film, more photographers—and dry towels.

About an hour later, heavy smoke started to billow out of the rear steeple. Linsenmayer kept shooting as he captured the shot of the church's crosses enveloped by smoke. The photo filled nearly the entire front page of the next day's edition. (See page 2.)

SCANNER RADIO SIGNALS FIRES AND ACCIDENTS

Most dramatic news photographs result not from city desk assignments but from vigilant photographers who monitor scanner radios to learn about breaking news situations. Police, fire, and other emergency agencies communicate with cops and firefighters in the field via low frequency, very high frequency (VHF), and ultra-high frequency (UHF) radio wave bands. Each agency—the police, the highway patrol, the coast guard—broadcasts on a different frequency. A scanner radio automatically switches from one frequency to another, stopping whenever a transmission is occurring. The scanner continually rotates through the frequencies it is programmed to listen for. By monitoring a scanner radio, a photographer can listen to transmissions from all the emergency agencies in an area. If a warehouse fire takes place, the dispatcher will call for fire engines and give a location. By noting the number of the alarms (indicating the size of

the fire), the number of engines called, and the location, a photographer can determine the magnitude of a blaze, its news value, and whether it will be burning by the time the photojournalist arrives on the scene.

Jim MacMillan, who covers spot news for the *Philadelphia Daily News*, says that he gets 90 percent of his tips from listening to the scanner radio—make that four scanners, all of which he monitors simultaneously. One scanner is tuned to the citywide police, one to local police, one to the fire department, and one to pick up transmissions from the local TV news desk, as well as the coast guard and airport.

Sam Costanza, on contract with the *New York Post*, spends six nights a week parked near the intersection of three main highways that lead to New York's boroughs—all the while monitoring the transmissions of the New York Police Department's special operations section. "I'm a listener," he says. "There aren't many listeners. Other photographers respond to assignments. By the time they arrive, I'm already leaving the scene."

Kent Porter of Santa Rosa's *Press Democrat*, covers spot news in rural Northern California. He tracks the action with five antennae on his Nissan truck as well as a scanner inside his house.

Not only does he monitor scanner transmissions, but he also carries a cellular phone and stays tuned to local news radio. He says all the antennae make his truck look like a centipede.

Political groups like this one demonstrating in front of an abortion clinic in Wichita, Kansas, often tip off the media about the time and place of their protests. Kim Johnson, for the Wichita [Kansas] *Eagle*

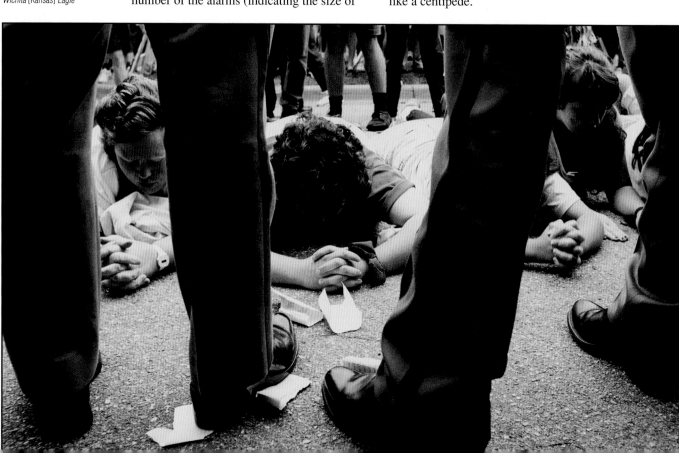

Different agencies use their own special codes when talking on the air. Porter knows he is heading out for a strong-arm robbery or assault with a weapon when he hears "211." He also knows to "be on the lookout" when he hears "B-O-L," and that "code 20" means an officer needs immediate assistance. In New York, Costanza knows that a "1045, code one," means a fire-related death.

Although there are no uniform codes from one city to another, stores that sell scanner radios usually have printed copies of local codes available.

The codes tell photographers what is taking place, but they don't always indicate the importance of the action. Every photographer interviewed for this chapter said that the tension in a dispatcher's voice reveals an emergency's significance. "I listen for the voices on the scanner," says Santa Rosa's Porter. "The stress in their voices will tell you so

much." The *Post*'s Costanza puts it this way. "The dispatchers have distinctive voices— you can tell when they are alarmed. Listen hard and quick. You might only get one shot at it."

OTHER SOURCES FOR NEWS

What else do photographers use to keep in touch with the news pulse of the city or the country or the world, especially when they can't monitor a scanner radio all day?

STAY TUNED TO ALL-NEWS RADIO, TELEVISION, AND WEB SITES

Alternatives include all-news-radio stations, television stations that provide frequently updated news reports, and Web sites that post the latest information as soon as it comes across the wires.

An all-news radio station or a cable network like Cable News Network (CNN)

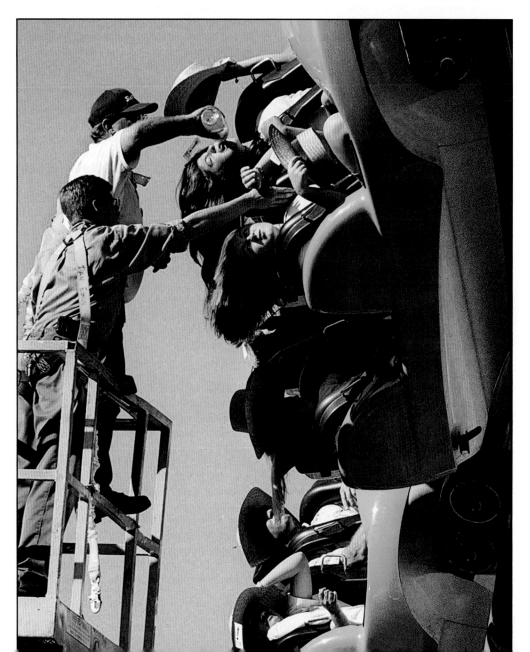

In 100-degree heat at Marine World, staff members distribute hats and water to stranded riders after a cable broke on the thrill ride Boomerang. The photographer heard the tip on an all-news-radio station while driving home. Dean Coppola, *Contra Costa* [California] *Times*

interrupts in-progress programming immediately if an emergency arises. These stations monitor several scanner channels, including the fire and police departments, and will announce when a major fire alarm or multi-car accident occurs. Radio alerted Dean Coppola to riders trapped on a stalled roller coaster at a local theme park. He was the first still shooter on the scene. With temperatures nearing 100 degrees, park workers started distributing water and hats to the people on the ride. Shooting with a 400mm lens, Coppola took a page-one picture based on a tip from the all-news-radio station.

The all-news channel's weather forecaster monitors natural disasters such as hurricanes or tornadoes. The information provided by all-news stations isn't as immediate as what you'll learn on a scanner, but their reports often will suffice.

For magazine and freelance photographers working overseas, CNN as well as the BBC and MSNBC provide around-the-clock news updates. Even photographers covering huge, breaking, international stories turn to one of the twenty-four-hour outlets to get news in English and see how the rest of the world is receiving the story.

Today, many photojournalists on foreign assignments carry laptop computers with modems for connecting to local telephone outlets or their mobile telephones. Once connected, they can track developing stories on the Web and, of course, transmit pictures and stay in touch with editors.

USE CONTACTS
Michael Meinhardt of the *Chicago Tribune* has developed his own system of finding out about local spot news as it happens. Using a system of pagers, two-way radios, cellular phones, and a network of sources and contacts, he stays abreast of news as it breaks in the Chicago and greater-Chicago area.

Firefighters, police officers, dispatchers, and even air-traffic controllers at surrounding airports notify Meinhardt of news events via a voice-message pager that he carries twenty-four hours a day. He has befriended these contacts at other news events, where he introduced himself, left a business card, and followed up by giving them photographs of themselves at work.

"You'd be surprised how many of them remember me when the news breaks," he says.

"Additionally," he explains, "I belong to a network of contacts led by a local radio news reporter who is considered the dean of spot news. . . . We all have two-way radios on our own frequency that we monitor around the clock. . . . Once the closest person arrives on the scene, I can usually ascertain whether it's worth traveling to shoot pictures. They can also let me know how urgently I need to get there before the scene clears up."

Not surprisingly, Meinhardt is considered a great source of information by his colleagues in the newsroom and also by the newspaper's city desk.

TIPS HELP
News organizations often get leads on top news stories when people call or write with tips. In fact, some newspapers and a few magazines offer monetary rewards for tips. The desk editor sizes up the event; then, if the decision is to respond, the editor or an assistant may send out a reporter and photographer or call a local freelancer.

Special-interest groups also notify news outlets if group members think publicity will do them some good. If minorities, mothers on welfare, gays, or antinuclear groups, for example, are going to stage a protest for which they want coverage, they might contact local and national outlets with the time and place of their planned demonstration.

BEAT REPORTER KNOWS THE TERRITORY
Most news outlets assign reporters to cover a certain beat: city hall, hospitals, or police headquarters for a city newspaper, or the White House, education, or medicine for a national magazine. These specialists keep up with the news and events in their area; consequently, they know when to expect a major story to break. The city hall reporter may call in to the city desk to say, "The mayor is greeting some astronauts today. It will be worth a good picture." The editor will probably assign a photographer. A magazine writer working on a story about education in America may need pictures of a school for the gifted. The magazine's photo editor, often in New York or Washington, will assign a photographer who is under contract with the publication or will call a local freelancer.

PR OFFICE IS THERE TO AID YOU
The senator will arrive at her office at 9:00 a.m. She leaves for the airport at 10:15 a.m. to dedicate a new runway. She will be at the Golden Age Senior Citizens' Home from 11:30 a.m. to 12:30 p.m. Then, during a 1:00 p.m. lunch at Parker House, the senator will meet with the Committee for State Beautification.

If you want to know the whereabouts of the senator at practically any minute of the day, just consult the politician's schedule. The senator's personal or press secretary arranges the itinerary weeks in advance.

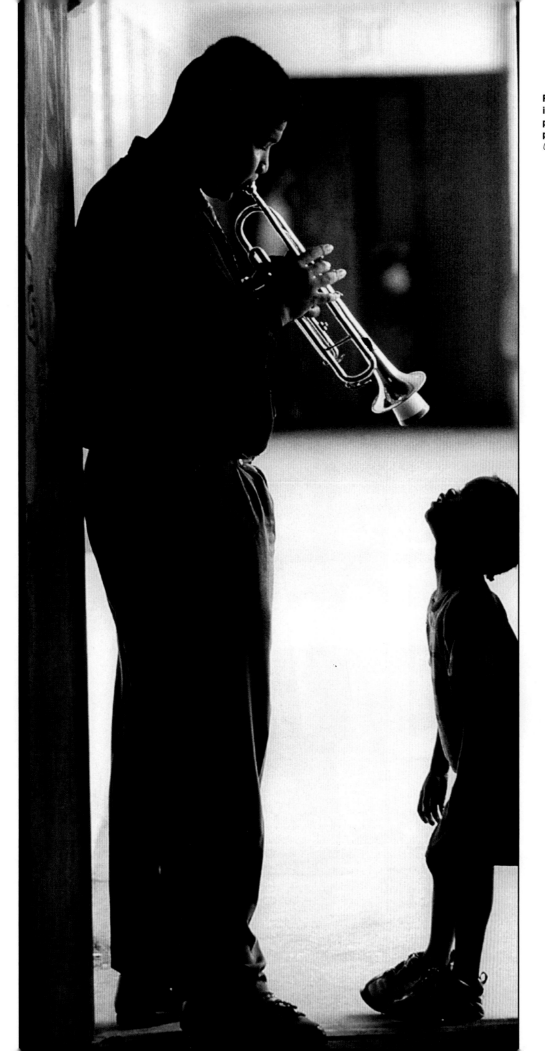

Photograph people in action. Whenever possible, avoid the office portrait. Milbert Brown, *Chicago Tribune*

PHILADELPHIA'S HOMELESS: HOW THEY SURVIVE

Tom Gralish of the *Philadelphia Inquirer* recalls that when he received an assignment to photograph the homeless, editors suggested he "might do portraits of the street people, each standing in front of their grates or cardboard boxes or whatever else they called home. At that point, I wasn't sure what I would do, but I decided then and there that whatever it was, it would be the most honest photography I'd ever done. I was determined to do something as true as possible to the traditional ideals of documentary photojournalism."

Consequently, Gralish did not set up portraits. Instead, he followed street people with names like Hammerman, Spoon, and Redbeard through the ups and downs of their barren, subsistence lives. He photographed them staying warm atop steam grates on a frozen street, drinking wine, and panhandling. He showed them sleeping in boxes. Rather than a series of formulated, posed portraits, Gralish photographed the nitty gritty of these men's lives. For his efforts, he won both the Pulitzer Prize and the Robert F. Kennedy Memorial Prize.

Tom Gralish, *Philadelphia Inquirer*

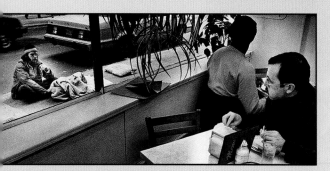

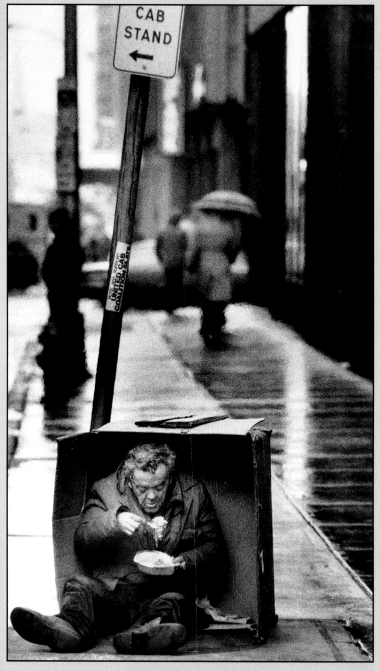

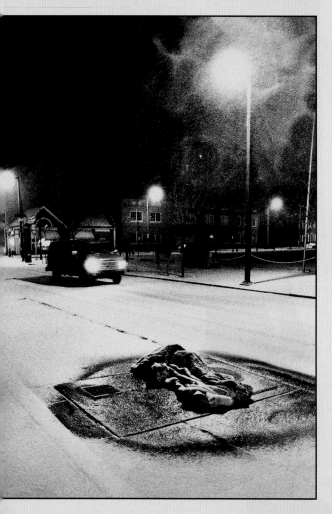

Politicians, from the mayor to the president of the United States, have carefully planned schedules, usually handled by press officers.

Companies, schools, hospitals, prisons, and governmental departments also have press or public relations offices. Sometimes called public affairs or public information departments, they generate a steady stream of news releases announcing the opening of a new college campus, the invention of a long-lasting light bulb, or the start of a new special-education program. Many of these PR releases suggest good picture possibilities. See Chapter 5, "Features," for more on working with PR professionals.

SCHEDULES IN PRINT OR ONLINE
Another source for upcoming news events comes daily to your doorstep rolled and held with a rubber band. The daily newspaper carries birth, wedding, and death announcements. It prints schedules of local theaters, sports events, parades, and festivals. When the circus arrives in your town, the newspaper is where you'll find the time and place of the big-top show.

Web sites also offer lists of upcoming events. Many organizations and sports facilities list activities on their own sites. Surf the Web for updated schedules.

UNUSUAL LEADS IN TRADE MAGAZINES AND ON SPECIALIZED WEBSITES
For more unusual activities, check special-interest newspapers, magazines, and special-interest groups on the Web. Dog and cat lovers, cyclists, plumbers, skateboarders, mental health professionals, and environmental groups all publish magazines or newsletters, and most have Web sites that announce special events.

To track upcoming happenings with visual possibilities, newspapers, wire services, and magazines maintain log books listing the time, place, and date of activities that might turn into stories. The notation in the book includes a telephone number for the sponsoring organization in case the photographer needs more information. Freelancers can adapt this idea to track events for themselves.

WORKING WITH REPORTERS: CLICKERS MEET SCRIBBLERS
PHOTO REQUEST STARTS THE PROCESS
Whether it's *Time* magazine or the *New York Times*, most news organizations have many more staff reporters than photographers. From their sources, these newshounds generate potential stories. When an editor approves a story proposal, the reporter makes out a photo request.

For the photographer, the key to great photo coverage depends on the information and arrangements on the photo request. Typical assignment requests include the name of the person or event to be photographed, as well as the time, date, and place. The editor usually assigns a slug—a one- or two-word designation for the story that serves as the story's name until the copy desk writes a final headline. The assignment sheet often includes a brief description of the proposed article, as well as a telephone number with which to contact the key subject if anything needs to be changed.

PHOTOGRAPHER AND REPORTER IN ADVANCE
Under the best of circumstances, the reporter, photographer, and assigning editors meet or talk on the telephone or by E-mail at this point in the story's development to discuss the team's approach or define the story's thrust. Here, the photojournalist can suggest visual ways to tell the story that correspond to the reporter's written approach. The photographer can recommend candids, a portrait, or a photo illustration—and also can estimate the amount of time needed for the shoot, or identify props and necessary clearances.

At some outlets, unfortunately, the photographer never meets with the reporter and assigning editor. Instead, the shooter receives the information from an intermediary editor, or is briefed by notes on the assignment sheet. In these circumstances the photographer plays a reduced role in determining the story's final outcome. Located at the end of the assigning chain, the photographer has little say in determining the best approach to the story.

BEST TIME FOR AN ASSIGNMENT
At many news organizations, the reporter calls the subject and makes shooting arrangements for the photographer. Sometimes this saves the photographer time. In most cases, though, the reporter will probably overlook great picture opportunities.

The reporter, for example, may decide to do a story about the controversial principal at Lincoln High.

The writer asks when the principal is free for an interview and pictures. The principal responds: "Well, I'm busy all day. I greet the kids as they get off the bus. Then I meet with parents and teachers. Next I observe classes and eat lunch with the kids. Then I usually work with student discipline problems in the afternoon. All the teachers and students are gone by four. How about meeting me in my office after four?"

From the reporter's point of view, four

From a writer's point of view
Reporter Ellie Brecher of the *Miami Herald* shared the following suggestions to photographers in 4Sight, a newsletter published by Region 4 of the National Press Photographers Association:

Understand the assignment by talking to the reporter ahead of time.

Don't barge into an interview.

Share information with the reporter.

Bring ideas to the reporter.

Have your technical act together.

o'clock is fine. The principal is free to answer questions and chat in a quiet environment in her office. From the photojournalist's perspective, four o'clock is okay if formal portraits or headshots are all that are sought. But four o'clock is a disaster if the photojournalist wants to shoot revealing candids.

The shooter should be at school at 7:30 a.m. as the principal greets the kids, again at noon when she eats with her teachers and students. Ideally, the photographer will later observe the principal's work with disciplinary problems. These pictures would show whether the principal is stern or kind, friendly or tough, or a little of each. Were the photographer to shoot when the writer originally planned, the resulting pictures would probably be of the subject standing in front of the building, in a hallway, or inside a classroom. The environmental portrait would show what the principal looked like but would hardly reveal her character.

PHOTOGRAPHERS MAKE THEIR OWN ARRANGEMENTS

Although reporters can hold a telephone interview or call back later for more facts, photographers need to be present when the subject is engaged in work. Photographers and photo editors need to educate those who report, or assign reporting, about this need if pictures are ever to go beyond the routine.

Photographers usually find that they can make better arrangements than a reporter or editor because they know the kinds of pictures they are looking for. Photographers are mindful of both the subject's activities and the quality of light at different times of the day. High noon outside rarely provides attractive light for an outdoors portrait, for example. Ideally, photographers would get names and phone numbers of subjects and then make the appointment, or decide what other pictures might go with the story. The reporter might tape the interview at four o'clock, and the photographer might arrange to shoot the subject from dawn until dusk on a different day.

When scheduling a shoot with a subject it's always good to ask, "What is your typical day like?" As the subject describes a normal day's activities, you can note which hours the person is sitting behind a desk talking and which hours he or she is doing something active and therefore photogenic. You also should find out if anything unusual is coming up that would lend itself to revealing photos.

ON THE SCENE: WORKING IN TANDEM

For some types of news, the photographer and reporter must cover the event together.

Sometimes it's the reporter who knows the important players. Sometimes the photographer needs a second set of eyes to help provide protection, such as at a violent street protest. "You be my extra ears," says Ellie Brecher, a photographer-friendly reporter for the *Miami Herald*, "and I'll be your extra eyes." (See Chapter 3, "General News," pages 47–48, for special situations where photographers must not share information.)

Even at dangerous breaking-news events like street riots, when the situation calls for all available eyes and ears, the photographer and reporter should not become wedded at the hip. Each has different needs. One is following the action as it flows down a street, while the other is checking a quote and making sure the name is spelled correctly. However, while the photographer and reporter each need independence, the two also need to reconnect every once in a while to confirm they are developing the story in parallel ways.

Although the photographer and writer don't shoot and interview at the same moment, they should coordinate the message of their words and pictures. Photographers should pass on their observations about the subject or event to the writers. Writers can explain to photographers how their story might lead.

In the end, the reader will be looking at both the picture and the accompanying story. If the writer describes the subject as drab, yet the picture shows a smiling person wearing a peacock-colored shirt, the reader is left to resolve the conflict. Writers and photographers should resolve conflicts between words and pictures before the story goes to press.

PICTURE POLITICS

With good planning, editors avoid poor use of photo resources. However, many news outlets continue to operate in a traditional structure long unfriendly to the effective use of photography.

Traditionally, news organizations have been organized to handle assignments proposed by either reporters or editors. Photographers rarely originated story ideas. And even if they did, the photo-reporters received little in the way of picture play for their efforts.

The old-style process (still widely used today) works this way: once the reporter gets the green light, research begins. The reporter might interview subjects, check the publication's library for related articles, do a Web search, call authorities, and, finally, write the copy over a period of days or even weeks. Only when the story is nearly completed and ready for publication does the reporter fill out a photo request. Finally, the photo department becomes aware of the issue.

With the story written and the publication date set, the photographer has little room to maneuver. While the reporter took days and weeks to develop the story, the photographer may have only hours to produce photos. While juggling three or four other assignments for the day, the photojournalist is unlikely to be able to shoot in the best light, have time to wait for a candid moment, or to reshoot.

THE BUDGET MEETING

At most news organizations, the decision about how much space to allocate to a story as well as where it will play takes place at a daily, weekly, or monthly conference often known as a budget meeting. Representing each section of a publication, different editors pitch their best stories to the managing editor, who ultimately decides which stories get cover display and which will run inside. While the photo editor speaks up for pictures at this meeting, the word editors always outnumber the lonely representative from the photography department. (See Chapter 10, "Photo Editing.")

Here, each editor represents a part of the paper or magazine. Individual editors defend their turf. On a large newspaper, the sports editor, fashion editor, city editor, and foreign desk editor might each have an entire section. On a news magazine, the national editor, political editor, and music editor each might have a minimum number of pages to cover the most important topics in a specific area. Too often, the photo editor has no designated turf: there is no space assigned solely to photo stories. Though seated at the table with other decision makers, the picture editor has no formally reserved space.

Furthermore, the picture editor is up against colleagues who think that their sections cover the most important news, contain the best writers, and ought to have the most space. And, because more and bigger photos mean fewer words, few editors see the advantages of storytelling pictures that eclipse longer stories. Furthermore, managing editors, most of whom move up from the writing rather than the visual side of the publication, make the final decisions about the use of space. The upshot at most publications: even a very outspoken photo editor can rarely counterbalance these inherent structural biases toward words.

The World Wide Web, on the other hand, because it can present an unlimited number of pictures without incurring additional cost,

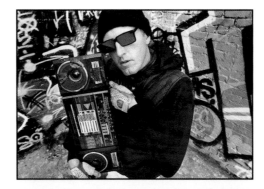

→ To avoid being attacked during his forays into San Francisco's Tenderloin neighborhood, Fred Larson dressed unobtrusively and hid his camera inside a portable stereo. Scott Sommerdorf, *San Francisco Chronicle*

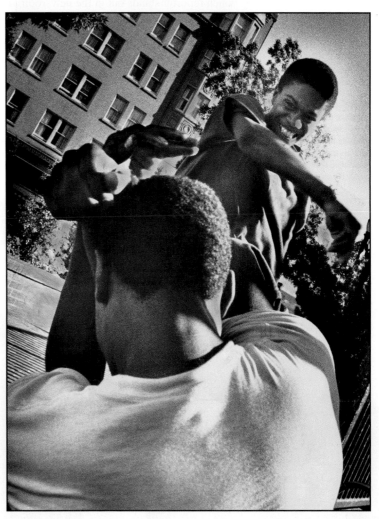

↑ Street fighters continued their battle while an unobtrusive Larson moved in close with his camera-in-a-boombox. Frederic Larson, *San Francisco Chronicle*

has inherent capacity advantages over print publications. On Web sites, you might think, having space for pictures should not be an issue.

Think again.

The "splash" or "home" page provides the reader with an essential guide to a Web site. The demand for space by section editors on the home page means that pictures are often run the size of postage stamps. In addition, because of download-speed considerations, Web meisters often reduce the number of pictures on the opening page as well as their size so the pages will load quickly. Just when photographers thought they had found a photo-friendly medium on the Web, they discovered their work squeezed again. Technology advances may change this, but for now, it's the same old battle for space.

TAKE A REPORTER TO LUNCH

To avoid the trap of being the last one to know about important stories—and having your pictures played poorly—try this. If you are a new staffer, ask the managing editor which reporter stands out in the newsroom. If you have been on staff for a while, you already know the names of the best writers.

Start by introducing yourself to one reporter and asking what he or she is working on. If the story sounds interesting, talk about picture possibilities. If you know that an event is coming up that would help explain the story, suggest to your photo editor or managing editor an assignment that will help illustrate the story. On your own, start reading about the issue. If you notice a picture that might support the story, shoot it.

Look for as many ways as you can to photograph the writer's story even before the wordsmith has finished the masterpiece.

When the story results in a formal photo request, your editor will likely assign the job to you because you already have started on the photos. By now you have a clear idea of the possible pictures that would help the story. Also, because a story was written by a top writer, it will probably receive prominent play in the paper.

If you continue to look for good writers, anticipate photo requests, and build alliances with the word side, you will probably find writers agreeable to listening to your story ideas. A writing/photography partnership is likely to claim more space than your proposal alone.

GENERATE YOUR OWN ASSIGNMENT

Sometimes a photographer pulls over next to an overturned car, jumps out, and shoots. No written assignment at all. Usually, a photographer receives a verbal or written assignment from an editor. But many shooters

Israeli soldiers fire at a rock-throwing demonstrator during a confrontation on the street marking the divide between Israeli- and Palestinian-controlled Hebron.
Wendy Sue Lamm, Contrasto

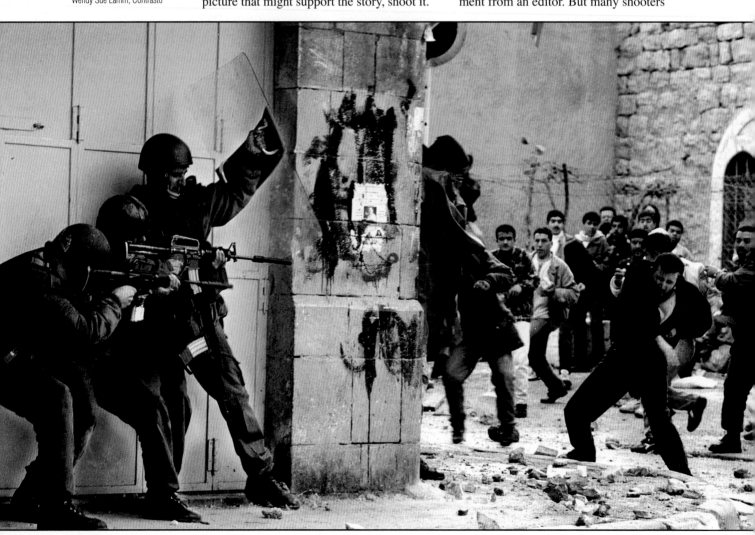

report that their best assignments are those they proposed themselves. Self-generated assignments allow the photographer to pick exciting topics that lend themselves to visuals. When a photographer has researched a good story, the next step is to request a reporter to provide the needed text. The more stories photographers propose, the more control they will have over their work. Fred Larson of the *San Francisco Chronicle* spent weeks photographing the city's tough neighborhood known as the Tenderloin (page 11). Chapter 4, "Covering the Issues," features other successful self-generated assignments.

INTERNATIONAL ASSIGNMENTS

Many of today's newspapers have expanded their beats to include the world. From covering earthquakes in India to uprisings in Rwanda, newspaper photographers are literally on the move. Photographers who covered high school football on Friday night may find themselves boarding a plane for Iraq on Sunday morning. Never has the mastery of foreign languages or knowledge of international affairs been more important to photojournalists.

Michael Kodas, who has covered international news for the *Hartford Courant*, reads voraciously: the *Wall Street Journal*, the *Christian Science Monitor*, and the *New York Times*, among others. National Public Radio is also a good source of international news for car-bound photographers. If an intensive

language course is out of your budget, try substituting language tapes for your favorite rock groups when you're stuck in traffic.

And don't forget the most basic preparations of all, as recommended by freelancer Keith Philpott, who shoots for *Time* and *People*. Keep a current passport in your camera bag, and make sure your inoculations are current for travel in developing countries.

Carol Guzy, who covered the Ethiopian famine for the *Miami Herald* and the tumbling of the Berlin Wall for the *Washington Post*, says to pack light for international assignments. She carries as little photo gear as she feels she can get away with, she says, but does bring an extra camera body—and film, lots of film.

Other photographers are stocking extra memory cards and more batteries than ever for their digital cameras.

ASSURING VISUAL VARIETY
OVERALL SHOT SETS THE SCENE

If readers themselves were at a news event, they would stand in the crowd and move their eyes from side to side to survey the entire panorama. The overall photo gives readers at home the same perspective. A good overall allows viewers to orient themselves to the scene.

For some stories, an overall might include just a long shot of a room. For others, the overall might cover a city block, a neighborhood, or even a whole town. The scope of the

GET HIGH

Gene Pepi knew the shot he wanted at a peace march in San Francisco couldn't be taken from ground level. He rented a 12-foot-tall ladder so he could photograph over the heads of the marchers for an overall shot of demonstrators filling the length of the Market Street, with the city's Ferry Building in the background.
Gene Pepi, *Frontlines*

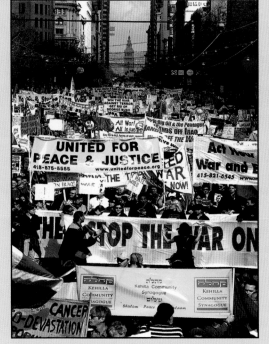

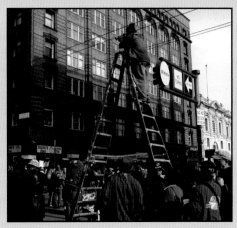

Gene Pepi gets the picture from atop a ladder he rented for the occasion. © Ken Kobré

shot depends on the size of the event. The overall shows where the event took place: inside, outside, country, city, land, sea, day, night, and so on. The shot defines the relative position of the participants. In a confrontation, for example, the overall angle would show whether the demonstrators and police were a block apart, or across the street from one another. The overall shot also allows the reader, by judging crowd size, to evaluate the magnitude of the event.

Margaret Bourke-White, a member of the original *Life* magazine staff, always shot overalls on each assignment, even if she didn't think they would be published. She explained that she wanted her New York editor to see the shooting location so that he could interpret the rest of the pictures she had taken.

Generally the overall requires a high angle. Knowing this, Pepi Gino rented a 12-foot-tall ladder and stationed it right in the middle of San Francisco's Market Street to photograph the crowd participating in a peace demonstration. His ladder and position provided the best location to capture the historic size of the crowd.

When you arrive at a news event, quickly survey the scene to determine what is happening. Then search for a way to elevate yourself above the crowd. In a room, a chair will suffice. But outside, a telephone pole, a leafless tree, or a nearby building will give you the high vantage you need for an effective overall. When caught in a flat area, even the roof of your car will add some height to your view.

The wider-angle lens you have, obviously, the less distance from the scene you will need. However, on a major news story that encompasses a vast area, such as a flood, hurricane, or conflagration, you may need to work with your editors to rent a helicopter or small airplane to get high enough to capture the dimensions of the destruction.

MEDIUM SHOT TELLS THE STORY

The medium shot should "tell the story" in one photograph. Shoot the picture close enough to see the participants' action, yet far enough away to show their relationship to one another and to the environment. The medium shot contains all the storytelling elements of the scene. Like a news story lead, the photo must tell the whole story quickly by compressing the important elements into one image.

An accident photo might show the victims in the foreground, the wrecked car in the background. Without the car, the photo would omit an essential detail—the

cause of the victims' injuries. With only the crumpled car, the reader would wonder if anyone had been hurt. The combination of elements—car plus victims—briefly tells the basic story.

A medium shot gains dramatic impact when the photograph captures action. Although the camera can catch fast action on film, you may still have difficulty: action often happens so quickly that you have no time to prepare. Shooting news action is like shooting sports action (Chapter 7, "Sports"). For both, you must anticipate when and where the action will take place. If a man starts a heated argument with a police officer, you might predict that fists will fly and an arrest will follow. You must aim your camera when the argument starts and not wait until a punch is thrown. If you hesitate, the quarrel might end while you're still fiddling with your equipment.

For the medium shot, a wide-angle lens such as a 24mm or 28mm works well, although a normal 50mm will do.

CLOSE-UP ADDS DRAMA

Nothing beats a close-up for drama. The close-up slams the reader into eyeball-to-eyeball contact with the subject. At this intimate distance, a subject's face, contorted in pain or beaming happily, elicits empathy in readers.

How close is close?

A close-up should isolate and emphasize one element. And not all close-ups include a person's face. Rich Abrahamson photographed only the hands of a 92-year-old organist who has played the organ at her church for more than three-quarters of a century. The aged hands tell the woman's story without showing her face.

Sometimes objects can tell the story even when the story involves tragedy. A close-up of a child's doll covered with mud might tell the story of a flood better than an aerial view of the disaster.

Longer lenses enable photographers to be less conspicuous when shooting close-ups. With a 200mm lens, you can stand ten feet away and still get a tight facial close-up.

The telephoto lens decreases the depth-of-field and thus blurs the foreground and background. This effect isolates the subject from unwanted distractions.

Rather than using a telephoto for close-up work, some photographers employ a macro lens or a standard lens with an extension tube. With either of these lenses, the camera can take a picture of a small object such as a contact lens and enlarge it until it is easily seen (page 214).

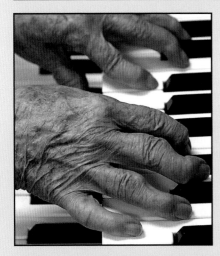

CLOSE-UP
A musician's hands resting on her church's organ keys shows the reader the curvature of the woman's fingers and the texture of her skin. The 92-year-old organist has played at her church since 1927. Rich Abrahamson, *Fort Collins Coloradoan*

OVERALL
Using a 17mm lens on a digital camera, the photographer took this overall of a Bikram Yoga class from atop a ladder she brought from home. The overall helps establish the size of the class. Naomi Brookner, for ***America 24/7***

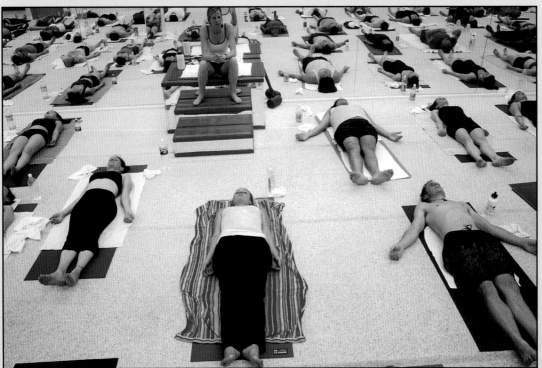

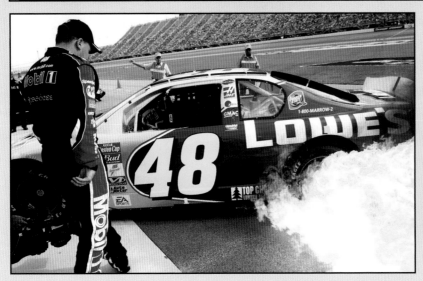

MEDIUM
When published alone, a medium shot must tell a complete story. Ryan Newman (left) jumps back as the last challenger's car erupts into fire while heading into the garage at the NASCAR Winston Cup Tropicana 400 at Chicagoland Speedway. Scott Strazzante, *Chicago Tribune*

HIGH/LOW ANGLES BRING NEW PERSPECTIVE

Since most people see the world from a sitting or standing vantage, a photojournalist can add instant interest to pictures simply by shooting from a unique elevation. Shoot down from a thirty-story building or up from a manhole cover. Either way, the viewer will get a new, sometimes jarring, but almost always refreshing look at a subject. Even when covering a meeting in a standard-sized room, standing on a chair or taking pictures while sitting on the floor can add interest to your pictures.

Avoid the "5'7" syndrome." On every assignment, avoid taking all your pictures at eye level. When you start shooting, look around for ways to take the high ground. Whether going out on a catwalk or shooting from the balcony, find some way to look down on the scene you are shooting. Digital cameras with flip-up LCD screens on the back allow shooting from (literally) ground level.

GOING WIDE

Walter Green, who worked for the Associated Press for many years, noted that he took most medium shots with a 24mm lens. With this lens, Green got extremely close to the subject and filled the entire frame. The resulting pictures, he said, tended to project a more intimate feeling between the subject and the viewer.

Because Green worked close to his subjects, few distracting elements intervened in front of his camera. Also, at this close distance, Green could emphasize the subject. Finally, Green's wide-angle took in a large area of the background, thus establishing the relationship of the subject to his or her surroundings.

Eugene Richards, a photographer who has won numerous awards, is master of the wide-angle lens. His lens is like a mother spreading her arms to include all her children in an embrace. Richards's wide-angle lens encompasses his subjects, often bringing together two elements into one picture to tell a more comprehensive story in a single image. His subjects, which also have appeared in books, have ranged from drug addicts (*Cocaine True, Cocaine Blue*) to emergency room personnel (*The Knife and Gun Club*). One of his award-winning pictures includes, to the right of the frame, a tiny coffin in the front seat of a hearse; in the middle, open car doors; and, at the extreme left, a young child. Richards brought together the widely

High angles such as this shot from above the net in a volleyball game help to give the reader a new perspective on the story. Charlie Riedel, *Hays* [Kansas] *Daily News*

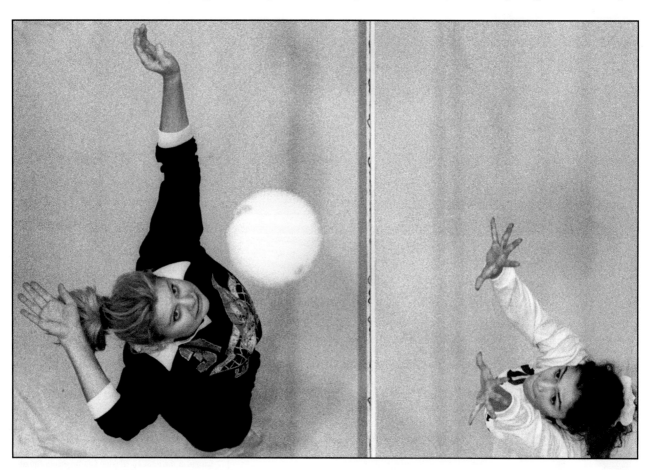

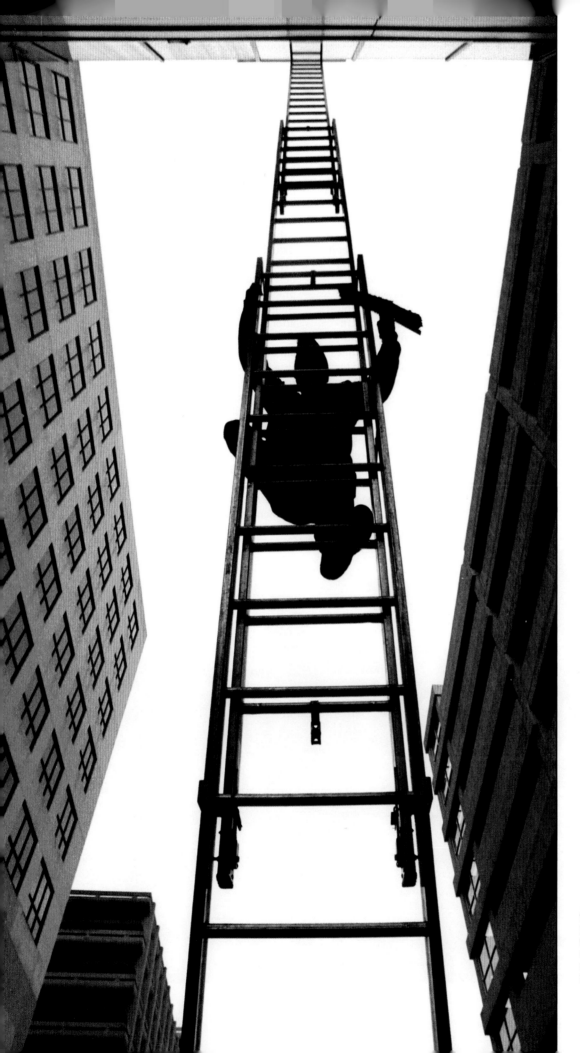

The photographer's
low angle turned what could
have been a routine picture
of a window washer into a
new view of the activity.
Doug Kapustin, *Baltimore Sun*

separated elements of the child-sized coffin and the youngster in one visual whole. For more on shooting with wide-angle lenses, see Chapter 11, "Camera Bag."

SHOOTING STYLES DIFFER

Photographers stay on location until they get the best picture possible within their time limits. Amateurs take a few snaps and hope for the best. Professionals search for the decisive moment and know when they get it. A pro might take a hundred or even a thousand frames to get the perfect moment.

As former *New York Times* photographer George Tames, once said, "If you see a picture, you should take it—period. It is difficult, if not impossible, to recreate a picture, so do not wait for it to improve. Sometimes the action gets better, and you will take that picture also, but if you hesitate and don't click the shutter, you've lost the moment, and you can't go back."

A contact sheet from a novice shows thirty-six frames of thirty-six different scenes. Professionals visually explore each scene, taking a number of pictures of essentially the same thing but at different moments or from different angles. (See a variety of one pro's images on page 194.) Usually this means that

they will take a few shots, then move to a different position and shoot the same thing from a fresh vantage. They might shoot six frames from one location and then walk around the subject and shoot six more. By watching the subject as well as the background, photographers are trying to find the perfect balance of a picture's elements while capturing a revealing expression or telling body position.

Each photographer's shooting style differs, though. Russell Miller, in his book, ***Magnum, Fifty Years at the Front Line of History***, described a wide range of shooting styles practiced by the diverse members of the Magnum picture agency, which was founded after World War II.

ERNST HAAS

Ernst Haas, a Magnum photographer known for his exquisite color work, always began shooting before the action occurred, according to Eve Arnold, another Magnum photographer. Haas, she said, followed through to the peak of the action, then tapered off.

HENRI CARTIER-BRESSON

On the other hand, Magnum's Henri Cartier-Bresson is famous for capturing one decisive moment in an image. In fact, his 1952 book

The photographer captured this candid "decisive moment" of fans checking out the action off the field at the Chicago Cubs' Wrigley Field.
Aristide Economopoulos, *State Journal-Register*

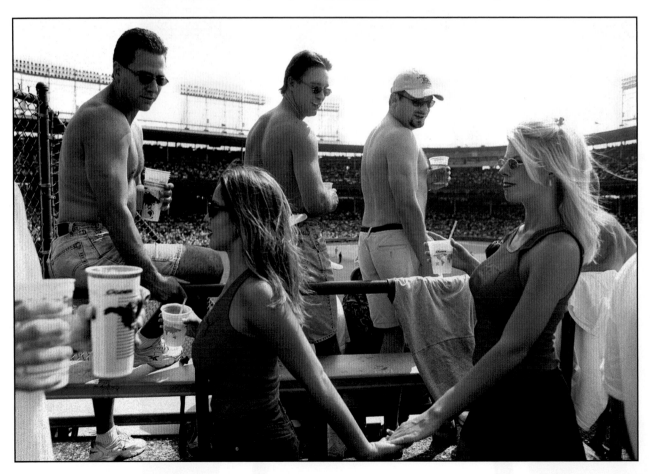

was published in the United States under the title *The Decisive Moment*.

The decisive moment suggests a sense of perfect shutter timing to freeze action at its peak. But Cartier-Bresson also looked for balanced composition. He wrote: "To me, photography is the simultaneous recognition, in a fraction of a second, of the significance of an event as well as of a precise organization of forms which give that event its proper expression. . . . Inside movement, there is one moment at which the elements in motion are in balance. Photography must seize upon this moment and hold immobile the equilibrium of it." For Cartier-Bresson, a photograph must not only freeze an instant of time, but it must also capture that instant within a well-designed composition. See pages 359–360. (Cartier-Bresson, however, did shoot some 15,000 rolls of film during his active career—not all of which caught decisive moments—according to Claude Cookman's dissertation, "The Photographic Reportage of Henri Cartier-Bresson, 1933–1973.")

ROBERT CAPA

Robert Capa, whose real name was André Friedmann, was perhaps the world's greatest war photographer and the founder of Magnum (pages 359–360). He had a yet different approach to shooting.

According to Magnum colleague Eve Arnold, Capa's contact sheets did not show Haas's persistence in pursuing a sequence. Nor were Capa's individual pictures as well designed as Cartier-Bresson's. Yet Capa took some of history's most memorable images. During the Spanish Civil War, he photographed a soldier, arms flung wide, falling backward at the moment of death (page 358). Capa also took the classic World War II D-day landing pictures. Capa was killed while covering the war in Vietnam.

When Eve Arnold told *New Yorker* writer Janet Flanner that Capa's pictures were not well designed, the reporter shot back, "History doesn't design well, either." After that, Arnold said, "I began to understand that the strength of Capa's work was that just by being there, where the action was, he was opening new areas of vision.

"He was aware that it is the essence of a picture, not necessarily its form, which is important."

CATCHING CANDIDS

What sets photojournalistic pictures apart from other types of photography? The photojournalistic style depends on catching candid moments. Good photojournalists have developed the instinct to be at the right place, at the right time, with the right lens and camera. Often, they can steal images like a pickpocket, without anyone ever knowing that photographic sleight-of-hand has taken place.

Photojournalists must catch their subjects as unaware as possible to record real emotions. Rather than stage-managing pictures, photographers observe but do not direct. The results depend on their ability to capture intimate moments without interrupting.

With good candid pictures, subjects are never caught gazing at the camera. Eye contact tips off the reader that the picture is not candid and suggests that the subject was at least aware of the photographer and might even be performing for the lens.

TECHNICAL STRATEGIES FOR CANDIDS
Preset Your Camera

Prepare your camera before you point the camera. If you're fiddling with the camera's dials, you might catch the subject's attention instead of a candid moment.

Select the appropriate lens before you bring the camera to your eye. With a manual focus camera, swing the lens once by the subject and stop just long enough to focus. As an alternative, you might focus on an object exactly the same distance away as your subject. With a telephoto lens, which requires critical focusing, you must focus on the subject, not on a nearby equivalent.

Some photographers prefer the wide-angle lens for candids, even though they must come closer to the subject. Prefocused at ten feet with a small aperture like f/16, you can use a 28mm lens to snap away happily without ever touching the focusing ring.

Finally, take your light meter reading without alerting your subject by pointing your camera toward an area that is receiving the same amount of light as the subject, and then adjusting your f-stop/shutter speed combination accordingly.

Watch your subject. You've preset your camera and now you must concentrate on your subject's expression and, when it's right, swing the lens, frame, and snap away.

Alternatively, use your camera's autofocus option: with autofocus selected, you are free to concentrate on action, not on hardware. With autofocus cameras, you can work at wide apertures like f/2.8 or f/3.5 but still get sharp pictures, even close to the subject.

If you see an interesting situation under way, you can swing the camera up, and frame, pressing the release at the same time. The lens will focus automatically to catch a natural moment. (See pages 126–127 and 228–229 for more about autofocus.)

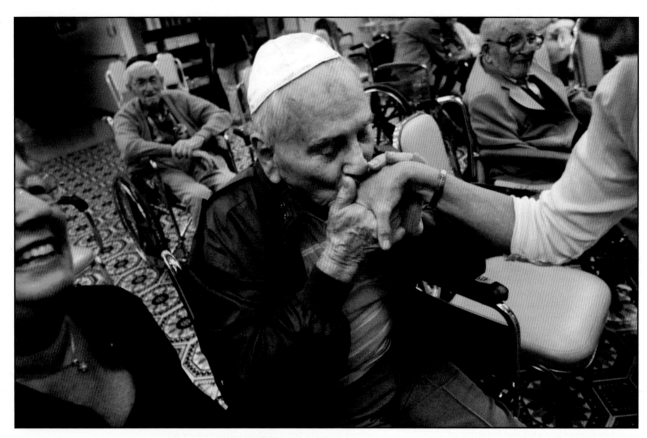

Everyone was aware of the photographer's presence during a Yom Kippur service at a retirement home. The subject was more involved in kissing the hand of the female rabbi than in the photographer. Robert Cohen, *St. Louis Post-Dispatch*

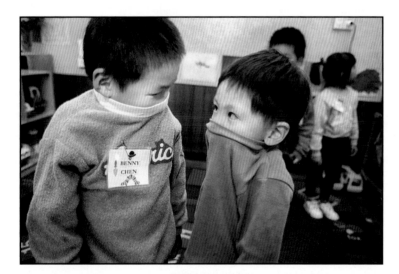

The photographer moved in quickly with a wide-angle lens for this candid shot. The moment was over in one frame. Julie Stupsker, *San Francisco Examiner*

Anticipation and Timing

Catching candids requires photographers to have the skills of the weather forecaster. They must guess what is going to happen based on how they see a situation developing. If two kids have their fists up, they are likely to fight. A couple holding hands might kiss. Sometimes the photographer, like the meteorologist, judges the evidence correctly and is prepared with the right lens, film, shutter

speed, and f-stop. At other times, like the weather person, the photographer misinterprets the data.

A photographer's timing to release the shutter at the optimum moment is as important as anticipation. Even with motor drives and autofocus, photographers must "get into the flow of the action." Most action builds to a peak and then settles down again. Almost every event has a crucial moment.

FOUR APPROACHES TO CANDIDS
Out in the Open

An out-in-the-open approach works when subjects, engaged in an engrossing activity, forget that a photographer is present.

Robert Cohen arrived at a Jewish nursing home early for the high holy days of Yom Kippur. He introduced himself to everyone and asked whether anyone in the room either didn't want to be photographed or could not be photographed for legal reasons.

"With elderly people I tend to stick with those who are with their family members or those who I am convinced are lucid enough to make decisions on their own," he says.

As the service proceeded, the female rabbi visited with residents. Cohen anticipated that a special spark might take place between the religious leader and one of the congregants. Just as an elderly man reached out and kissed the rabbi's hand, Cohen moved in close and

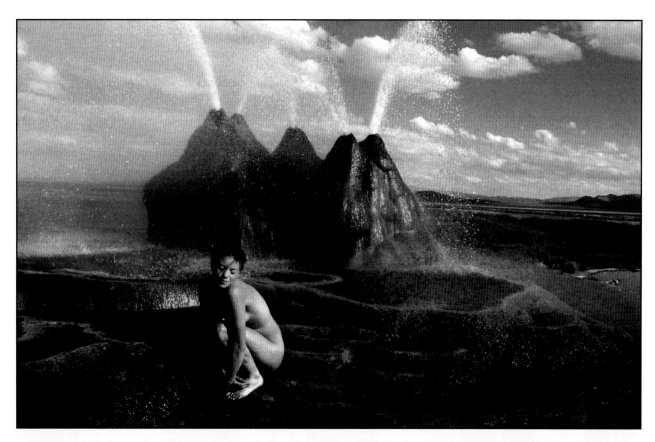

A woman enjoying a hot spring in the California desert was aware of the photographer who, by the way, also was naked. The subject returned to her own reverie after the photographer told her to ignore the camera. Julie Stupsker, *San Francisco Examiner*

grabbed a candid with his 17–35mm zoom lens. The elderly fellow was far more engaged in his own act of courtliness than the nearby photographer snapping the candid moment. After taking the picture, Cohen slipped away so as not to interfere with the event's natural flow.

Big Game Hunter

Like a hunter stalking prey, a photojournalist studies his or her subject. Sighting through a rifle-like telephoto lens, 100mm to 300mm long, the photographer stands across the room or across the street—watching, waiting, and trying to anticipate what might happen next.

Patience. Patience. Patience.

Bryan Patrick had been covering the "Gathering of Honored Elders" at the Indian Museum for two hours when he noticed an elderly woman playing with a young child. Using a 70–200mm f/2.8 zoom lens, he focused on the pair and watched from afar as the woman held up the child.

Just as she pinched the child's cheek and rubbed his nose, the *Sacramento Bee* photographer snapped the shutter. Only after he approached her for caption information did the centenarian realize she and her great-great grandson had been photographed.

When hunting features, many photographers carry a 70–200mm zoom lens or a 300mm telephoto lens.

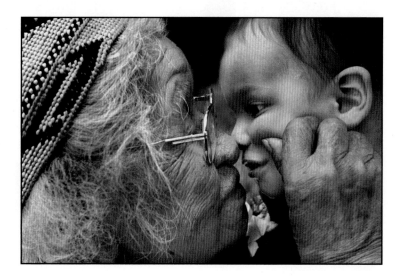

Click and Run

Rather than trying to operate unobserved, some photographers use the hit-and-run approach. They catch candids by walking past the subject, shooting quickly with a wide-angle lens, and then moving on. Observers have described Henri Cartier-Bresson's technique in this way. The French candid-catcher would pause in front of his subject and, with one fluid motion, raise his Leica, focus, and

With his telephoto lens, the photographer could shoot unobserved from a distance when the 101-year-old grandmother gave a kiss and a pinch to her great-great grandson. Bryan Patrick, *Sacramento Bee*

click several frames using. By the time the subject turned toward the photographer, Cartier-Bresson had gone his way.

Julie Stupsker saw two children at a day-care center about to duck into their sweat-shirts. She moved in close with her wide-angle lens and bounce flash just in time to grab one frame as they partially disappeared into their clothing. With the flash ready and the camera preset, Stupsker shot quickly and caught the candid moment (page 20).

Introduce Yourself
Even when someone is engaged in another activity, the sight of a photographer loaded with gear can bring all action to a stop. The advantage of stealth is gone. The simplest solution is to ask the person to continue, "Go on about your business and ignore me." If the person returns to work or fun, you may be forgotten altogether in the moments that pass.

Spotting a woman bathing in a hot spring in the California desert, Stupsker climbed a fence to get closer for the scenic shot. Then, following the ancient advice to do as the Romans when in Rome, the photographer stripped for action and joined the woman.

Having watched the photographer climb the fence with her gear and then take off her clothes, the woman was curious, of course.

MARKETING SPOT NEWS: A CASE STUDY

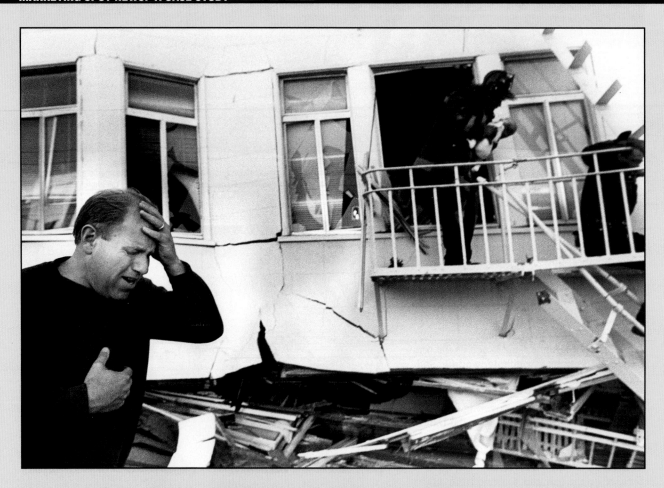

A few minutes after the 1989 San Francisco earthquake, a father reacts as his dead baby is removed from a collapsed apart-ment building. The photographer sold the picture to *Life* magazine. photo by Kaia Means, Oslo Norway

After the earthquake that rocked San Francisco in 1989, journalism student Kaia Means was one of thousands who initially thought the quake was "just another" shaker. Visiting friends atop Russian Hill, however, the San Francisco State University student noted, moments after the quake, a huge cloud of dust rising above the Marina District. She said her good-byes and left for a 5:30 p.m. meeting, thinking she'd drive by the Marina first to see what the dust was all about.

"I knew I had to turn in a spot news assignment sometime during the semester," recalls Means, who was a news-editorial major taking her second semester of photography. "So I thought I'd drive by to see if there was anything to take a picture of." Means found more than fallen bricks and broken glass. The first

When Stupsker explained she was taking pictures for the *San Francisco Examiner*, the woman resumed her respite and ignored the photographer. Stupsker was able to capture a natural moment before the arrival of a group of teenage boys quickly brought the shooting session to an end. (See page 21.)

Diana Walker, who shoots behind-the-scene photos at the White House for *Time* magazine, must catch candids in private areas almost every day. She says she tries to avoid conversation with her subjects so they will forget she is there. (For more on Walker's technique, see page 47, Chapter 3, "General News.")

SAVE THE LAST FRAME

Most photographers stop shooting before the end of the roll. They have been caught with only one frame left just as something spectacular takes place—such as a person leaping out of a building. They raised their cameras and ran out of film.

By changing film—or memory cards in the case of digital photojournalists—photographers build in some insurance. Having blank film or extra storage space at the end of an assignment is like having money in the bank. You may never need it, but it might save you in an emergency—and reduce your own anxiety, as well. ■

photographer on the scene, the 22-year-old student from Norway photographed a distraught father awaiting the rescue of his wife and baby.

In addition to the father in the crowd, Means photographed firefighters carrying the baby from the building, its father grieving in the foreground.

Later, in tears from the realization that the baby was dead, Means photographed the mother's rescue and reunion with her husband.

Although Means was "shaking all over" by the time she finished shooting the tragedy, the young photojournalist's real-life midterm exam was just beginning.

DETERMINING POSSIBLE OUTLETS

The photo student's pictures certainly had wide local and national interest. And Means was in a good bargaining position because she had exclusive images. However, the earthquake had shaken local news outlets as well as buildings and bridges.

Means took the film to the *San Francisco Examiner*, which had lost all electricity and phone capabilities, and was conducting its photo operation out of a van in the paper's parking lot. Having told the photo chief about the pictures, she helped out for a while and then left the film, marked "DEAD BABY" on the canister.

In less chaotic circumstances, Means could have bargained for the sale of the pictures. Having gotten a bid from the *Examiner*, she could have contacted local TV stations to see how much they would offer for rights to the photos. With the story's national impact, she could have offered the film to the wire services, either the Associated Press (AP), Agence France-Presse (AFP), or Reuters—all of which depend a great deal on stringers and freelancers.

None of the services maintains a large enough photo staff to cover the country—or the world—thoroughly. Many photos appearing in print and carrying the AP, AFP, or Reuters credit line are taken by independent photographers.

Alternatively, Means could have called other large dailies around the country. Today, newspapers want their own photos of a major story to augment those supplied by the wires, and many send staff photographers. However, none would have had this series of pictures.

But with phone lines down and chaos around her, Means left the film with the *Examiner*. Naturally, she was surprised when she opened the paper the following day and did not see the dramatic pictures. She called to see what had happened and learned that, in the confusion, the film had never even been processed.

Following more confusion at the newspaper, the young photojournalist finally got her film back—still unprocessed two days after the event. Under normal circumstances, this series of faux pas would have spelled photographic disaster for the fledgling photojournalist. The pictures' timeliness would have dissipated.

However, once the film was processed, it was easy to see that these were no ordinary pictures. It was time to seek a national market. The news magazines were already closing by the time the film had been processed, and they rarely buy anything but color. Her photo teacher, this author, gave her the number of Peter Howe, picture editor at *Life* magazine at the time. Means took over from there. Howe was out of town, but editors at *Life* wanted to see the prints.

After viewing the pictures, *Life* editors purchased first North American rights for six months and sent a reporter to San Francisco to interview Means and the parents she had photographed. When an order for a follow-up story came in, the second-semester photo student received the five-day *Life* assignment.

In the year-end issue of the magazine, Means' photo of the distraught father in addition to two of the follow-up pictures she shot on assignment ran as a two-page spread. ■

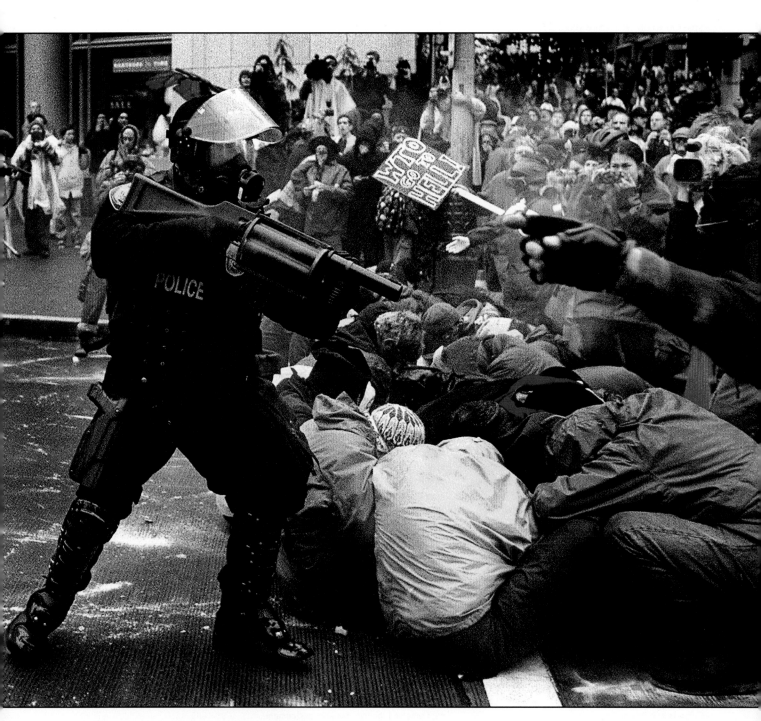

You can predict some crime news. The photographer expected
violence on the first day of World Trade Organization meetings
in Seattle. Paul Joseph Brown, *Seattle Post-Intellingencer*

Chapter 2

Spot News

CRIMES MAKE HEADLINES

Crime, whether it's a riot in Seattle or a hostage situation in Arlington, Texas, is costly to society. Crime can be a deep human tragedy for criminals and their families, as well as for victims and theirs. Almost any kind of crime makes a printable story in newsrooms across the country. The cub reporter soon learns that whether it's an atrocious murder or a $100 hold-up of a gas station, the event is considered news in city rooms from coast to coast.

Depending upon the crime's violence, the amount of money involved, the prominence of the people involved, or the crime's humorous or unusual aspects, the news is featured with varying amounts of emphasis.

ARMING FOR ACTION

Most spot news photographers have worked out the exact combination of cameras, lenses, and strobes that they need to work in the particular area they cover. Those who mainly shoot mayhem at night carry different hardware than those on the day shift. Photographers covering murder in the big city pack differently than those covering wildfires in the countryside.

DAYTIME ARSENALS

The *Philadelphia Daily News*'s Jim MacMillan, who usually works daylight hours, never leaves home without three cameras, including one mounted to a 500mm f/4

lens and connected to a monopod. As if that weren't enough glass power, he carries a 1.4X and a 2X tele-extender. "In Philly, the police keep us far away from the crime scene," MacMillan says. "I've gotten some of my best pictures from a block away." To carry all three cameras and lenses at one time, MacMillan hangs his 20–35mm zoom around his neck, slings an 80–200mm zoom on his shoulder, and hauls his 500mm lens, pointing backwards, over his left shoulder. "I can put two hands on any one of the cameras at any time," he points out.

On the fire watch for most of the dry season in Northern California, Kent Porter of Santa Rosa's *Press Democrat*, uses the full complement of lenses. "At a working fire I try to get pictures of the weary firemen. I also use a 20mm so I can get close to my

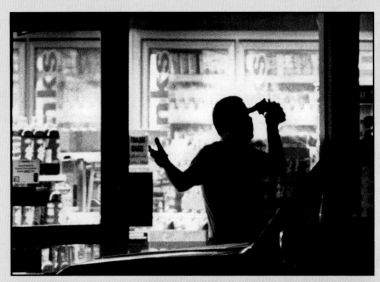

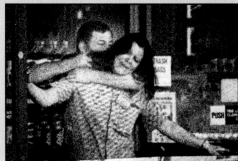

From daylight until dark, Joyce Marshall waited seven hours while a tense hostage situation played itself out. The stand-off finally ended (ABOVE) when the man took his own life. His wife, whom he had been holding hostage, escaped (RIGHT).
Joyce Marshall, *Fort Worth Star-Telegram*

At home early one morning, *Fort Worth Star-Telegram* staffer Joyce Marshall received a call from her paper's city desk. A man was holding his wife hostage at a 7–Eleven convenience store in nearby Arlington, Texas. Joyce threw on her clothes and, without brushing her teeth or combing her hair, jumped into her car, thinking, "This is probably a false alarm. Most of them are." With her cameras already in the trunk, she sped the five miles to the store in her two-door Subaru. As soon as she got to the store's parking lot, she got out of her car, grabbed her gear, and checked with the police officer in charge for an update. After determining that this standoff was for real, she called her office for backup equipment, including a 600mm lens and a two-way portable radio.

She knew the man had already shot and possibly killed someone inside the store. Later, she learned that the gunman's name was Thomas Stephens. His wife had left him because of his continued physical abuse during their seventeen-year marriage. When the divorce papers had arrived the day before, he snapped. He left the drug treatment center he was in and tracked down his wife, at work in the store. While taking her hostage, he killed several of her coworkers.

Knowing already there had been gunfire at the store, Marshall used a car in a nearby driveway as protection. She had a clear view of the store window. Her telephoto lens and radio arrived via another staffer who took up a position behind the store.

"I was inside the police barrier," Marshall recalls. "That area was cordoned off. The time dragged on interminably. I had not eaten, I could not get a drink of water. I had not brushed my teeth or my hair, and there was no bathroom."

Marshall knew that if she left she wouldn't be allowed to get across the police barrier again. "I had to stay."

subjects and incorporate the area the people are working in. I use a 300mm quite a bit," he says.

NIGHT ON THE STREETS

Sam Costanza, shooting mostly at night for the *New York Post*, rarely gets to use a long lens. He does most of his work with the Vivitar 283 or 285 flash, which he prefers over the more expensive dedicated flashes made by Nikon and Canon. "When you're running around on the scene, you're banging your cameras around. There's a good chance that the foot of the strobe will break off. Why take a chance of breaking a $400 Nikon flash?" The Vivitar usually costs less than a fourth of that price.

Costanza cranks his lens to infinity, sets his camera's shutter speed to 1/60 sec., and leaves the Vivitar's auto setting on "yellow."

"With those settings, I know everything will be in focus," he explains.

Costanza sets up his camera and strobe like a point-and-shoot so that he can concentrate on the scene and not worry about technical details.

At night, usually working around a hostile crowd, anxious police, or upset relatives, the New York newshound often gets off just one shot with his strobe. No need for a motor drive, either, he says. It's got to be right. No second chances here.

Porter in California, though, warns against using the strobe in some night news situations. The strobe light can be dangerous in a hostage situation, he cautions, especially when a confrontation involves guns. "You can also blind the police with the strobe," he says.

As the sun was setting directly into Marshall's lens, police went in to remove the victims. Marshall constructed a homemade sunshade on her lens barrel with some cardboard she found nearby and tape she kept wrapped around one leg of her tripod.

When removing the victims, the officers left the front door open. With her eye glued to her viewfinder, Marshall noticed Stephens coming to the front of the store while holding a gun to his wife's head. Marshall snapped off several frames.

By this time, a crowd had gathered behind the police lines. The neighborhood audience drank pop and beer and watched the situation in the 7–Eleven unfold like a movie playing in a theater. When the SWAT team arrived, the crowd started to yell, "Shoot them, shoot them. Hurry up and get this thing over with."

Marshall began switching to more sensitive film. She went from color print film rated at ISO 200 to 400 then to 800. When she could see no color at all in the scene, she threaded in a roll of ISO 400 black-and-white, which she rated at 1600. Only the lights in the store illuminated the site. Just then, Marshall could make out movement at the front of the store—a shadowy figure so low to the ground she could not photograph it. It was Stephens's wife.

Marshall learned later that when the gunman allowed his wife to go to the bathroom, she slipped out of the store.

Within minutes, Stephens, holding a gun to his head, walked out of the store. He said he would shoot himself at the count of thirty.

"Surely they will do something about it," Marshall thought. In the silhouette against the store's window she could see that the gun's hammer was pulled back, ready to fire. When he got to thirty, Stephens paused a few seconds. Marshall quickly took a few frames.

Then the gunman fired a bullet into his own head. He slumped to the ground. The crowd rushed forward.

"I'm not sure I shot a photo of the body," Marshall says now. "My mind was on getting the film back to the paper."

After racing back to the newspaper's darkroom and processing the film, Marshall quickly printed the frame of Stephens pointing the gun to his own head. She found the negative of Stephens holding his wife hostage, which was difficult to print because of the sun's flare. Also, because the subjects occupied only a small part of the negative, she had to enlarge the image extensively. The paper's editors felt the suicide picture was too graphic for the front page and ran it inside, but they played the hostage photo as the lead picture on page one for the following day. ■

During a tense hostage situation, Porter sticks to shooting available light with his long lenses—even at night.

Police Sergeant Carl Yates, who works with the media in Louisville, Kentucky, agrees. "Never underestimate the potential impact of a sudden flash of bright light at a night scene. It can anger officers; in some cases, escalate the incident; or worse, light up officers and others, making them potential targets."

GETTING ALONG WITH THE COPS

When Sam Costanza approaches a crime scene at night, the first thing he does is shout "New York Post photographer." But he doesn't wait to begin taking pictures. "By the time the 'New York' comes out, I've fired the first picture," he says. On the nighttime crime beat, Costanza must be within fifteen to thirty feet of his subject to get a well-exposed picture. Otherwise, the light from his strobe just won't be bright enough.

When faced with police at a crime scene, Costanza advances confidently but will walk away instead of confronting police if they are hostile. Jim MacMillan, who covers at least thirty murders a year for the *Philadelphia Daily News*, says that he goes in with confidence. "If I am going to get in a dispute with them over my rights, I have already lost," he says. Like Costanza, MacMillan will try to find the path of least resistance, but he has still faced everything from special treatment to harassment. The cops are especially pro-

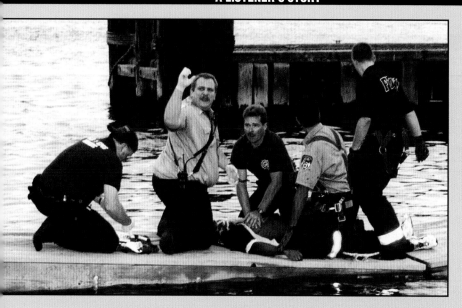

A LISTENER'S STORY

Medics frantically try to revive one of two drowning victims. To arrive in time to cover this kind of spot news, Sam Costanza carefully monitors two scanners in his car and an additional portable scanner that he carries with him. Sam Costanza, *New York Post*

The hour was sneaking up on midnight in Manhattan. Sam Costanza was sitting behind the wheel of his 1976 Ford Maverick, casually listening to the crackling sound of his scanner radio. So far, the evening was business as usual for the veteran contract photographer for the *New York Post*. Then he heard the New York City Police Department's special operations dispatcher: "10-10 shots fired on Wheeler Avenue in the Bronx."

Costanza didn't budge, but he continued listening.

A shooting on Wheeler Avenue was not news. Just another of many weekly shootings in that rough section of the Bronx. Definitely not page-one news for the next day's *Post*. There was no payoff for Costanza, a contract photographer, to cover "another routine shooting."

But, the next transmission from the special operations dispatcher alerted Costanza that a "newsworthy condition" was shaping up.

The disembodied voice over the radio said, "Three men to Jacobi Hospital for trauma."

From years of listening to the police department, Costanza knew that the second transmission meant that three officers were involved in a situation involving the death of a civilian but that no officers had been injured. According to police procedure, a New York officer always goes to a city hospital following situations involving the death of a civilian—"trauma." Putting the first and second transmissions together, Costanza figured that police had been involved with the "10-10 shots fired."

"Now my wheels are turning," Costanza recalls. "I begin to head for the Bronx from my current position on the upper Westside of Manhattan."

Pushing his powder blue Maverick at eighty miles per hour down the Sheridan Expressway, the photographer heard the crucial third transmission by the Special Operations Division, but by now the dispatcher's voice was tense. "Perp down. DOA, 1157 Wheeler Avenue, Bronx."

Costanza's experienced ears translated the facts. At least three officers had been involved in shooting another person—and that person was now dead at 1157 Wheeler Avenue, Bronx.

The photographer arrived at Wheeler Avenue, parked, jumped out of his car, and slung his two Nikons, mounted with Vivitar 283s, over his shoulder. Starting toward the crime scene, which was halfway down the block, he was accosted by no fewer than four officers who, seeing the cameras, told him he could proceed no further because an active crime scene had been set up.

Faced with tough, big-city cops attempting to block his access to crime scenes nearly every night of his working life, Costanza wasn't discouraged. Rather than waste time, he returned to his car, and drove around the block. This time, he knew he'd need a ruse to get near the scene.

Now, wearing a black military fatigue jacket, he left the car and headed out with just one Nikon and flash

tective of the scene if children are involved or if a cop has been hurt, he says. Under those circumstances, "I know I am going to run into problems," he notes.

WHEN THE POLICE SAY NO PICTURES

The police cite a number of reasons for pushing the media away from crime, accident, or disaster scenes. They sometimes feel (mistakenly) that they must protect the privacy of citizens from the press, says Donald Middlebrooks, who has written about police and photojournalistic access. Sometimes police claim to be pushing the media away to prevent interference with rescue efforts or to avoid pretrial problems that will prevent them from successfully prosecuting their case.

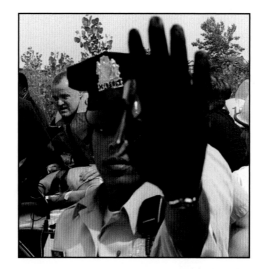

A police officer attempts to block the photographer's camera with her hand as rescuers hurry a drowning victim to an ambulance. Unfortunately, photographers have no more rights than the general public when it comes to access to crime, accident, or disaster scenes. Police may tell you to leave, they may limit your access to an outer perimeter, but they may not take your film.
Jim MacMillan, *Philadelphia Daily News*

unit tucked under his arm and out of view of the officers. He placed his hand radio, cranked up to full volume, in his upper jacket pocket. Perhaps, he hoped, the uniformed cops on this end of Wheeler would mistake him for a detective.

The ruse worked. The uniformed cops, he recalls, "neglected to accost me." Costanza got to within twenty-five feet of the crime scene, where he noticed styrofoam cups, at least thirty by his first count, placed upside down on the sidewalk. From past experience, he knew that the police use the cups to mark the location of spent bullet rounds or bullet casings. From the number of cups, he also realized that an incredible orgy of gunfire had taken place. He had never seen so many cups at a crime scene.

"As soon as I spotted the cups, I knew that this was the picture," Costanza says. "The cups would immediately show that multiple rounds had been fired in this area no larger than forty square feet."

Costanza also knew that once he pulled out his camera and shot off a picture, the cops would shut him down. He knew he could get off one—and only one—shot before he was out.

From under his arm, Costanza picked up the camera and flash. He had pre-focused the camera on infinity, set the f-stop at 5.6 on his 35mm lens, the shutter speed at 1/60 sec., and the strobe on "auto-yellow" to mirror the aperture setting on his lens. Just as a pair of plainclothes investigators walked by the overturned marking cups, he fired off three frames.

"All hell broke loose," he says. The police surrounded him and "escorted" him away. The first thing Costanza did when he got back to his waiting Maverick was call the city desk of the *New York Post*. "At least thirty shots appear to have been fired by N.Y.P.D., and there's a dead perp in the vestibule at 1157 Washington Avenue," he reported.

The editor responded, "I'm only interested if it's a cop that gets shot, not a perp."

Despite the editor's bad call, Costanza had left the scene with incredibly important pictures, he later learned. Four members of N.Y.P.D.'s elite Street Crimes Unit had fired forty-one—not just thirty—bullets at Amadou Diallo, an unarmed immigrant from Guinea, West Africa.

Nineteen bullets riddled the man's body. Diallo's death set off an intense racial conflict in New York and a review of New York police policies. When the four officers were found not guilty of second-degree murder, a new round of protests erupted—not just in New York but around the country.

While the *Post* never ran Costanza's picture, his agency, Sipa Press, sold the image to publications around the world. For Costanza, it was just another night in the life of a spot-news photographer. ∎

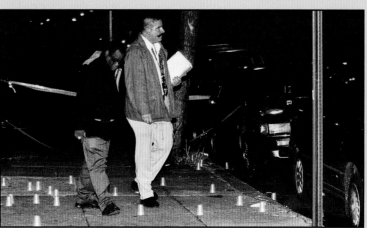

To get this exclusive picture of cups marking dozens of bullet casings after New York police officers shot an unarmed man, Costanza had to sneak up to the crime scene. He was able to fire only three quick frames before the police hustled him away.
Sam Costanza, *New York Post*

Too often, these reasons are an easy dodge for getting reporters and photographers out of law enforcement's hair at a time when the police are excited and sometimes overwhelmed by a disaster or a crime scene in which they are working. But that doesn't mean you can ignore the police when they don't want you around.

KNOW YOUR BOUNDS

Many police agencies today are using the two-perimeter system in dealing with the media, says Sergeant Yates of the Louisville, Kentucky, Police Department. They first establish an outer perimeter as a barrier for the general public. Once the scene has been secured, they create an inner perimeter for the news media.

One way to avoid some problems is to be aware of the crime scene perimeter. If you get there before the police put up the yellow tape, you do not want to contaminate the scene—by stepping on a bullet, for example. Kent Porter recounts the time he arrived before police when a man had been bludgeoned with a tire iron twenty-seven times. "My shoe prints got all over the crime scene," he recalls. "I had blood on my shoes. 'We have to make sure you are not the murderer,' the cops said. And then they took my shoes. The only thing I had to wear were my spiked baseball shoes."

The outer perimeter is designed to keep away curiosity-seekers. Photographers with media credentials should be able to cross the outer perimeter but not the inner perimeter. The inside yellow tape, known as the "hot zone," is where the crime scene is located.

Sergeant Yates suggests that photographers look for an officer (preferably a commanding officer), identify themselves, and then ask, "Could you direct me to where you want the news media?"

If this fails, ask if there is anyone on the scene in charge of public information.

The Sergeant cautions photographers not to violate the inner perimeter. You actually have no more legal right of access than the general public. What you do have, and what you hope the police will recognize, is a more significant reason to be there than the general public does. (See Chapter 13, "The Law.")

Yates recommends that, unless an immediate photo is necessary, you should take time to talk to officers before shooting. Try to get a feel for the mood of the scene.

Police are particularly on edge when a fellow officer has been injured or killed and may overreact. "These are times to ask first and shoot later," Yates points out. "Express regrets and ease into the situation."

In the rare instances when you arrive at the scene of a crime in progress, the police do not have the right to evict you even for your own safety. Of course, don't get in their way. They definitely have enough problems without trying to protect you.

Finally, Yates observes, don't argue with a police officer. "You can argue until you're blue in the face," he says, "and all you will usually be left with is a blue face."

ON THE SCENE

Once the police have set up their perimeter, you often have to shoot with a long lens and even add the tele-extender. Jim MacMillan's 500mm lens and extenders come in handy at times like this.

Sometimes the problem is not the length of lens but of time. You just have to wait.

Sam Costanza has done a lot of waiting in his time. He puts it this way: "Wait for the chief medical examiner to get there. Wait for the crime scene detectives to arrive. Wait for the medical examiner to check the wounds. Wait for the police photographer to photograph the body. And, finally, wait for the crime scene detectives to look to see if there are any weapons on the ground." While shooting spot news can produce an adrenaline rush, it can also result in fallen arches and tired legs.

Kent Porter in Santa Rosa says he tries to be as thorough as the detectives themselves. "I check to see if I have all the evidence on the film," he says. "Do I have all the names I need? If it is a shooting, do I have a picture of the gun? Do I have the picture of the main investigator? Do I have all the players the reporter has talked to? Do I have a photo of the surrounding scene? Did I get low and shoot the tape?" To ensure complete coverage, Porter says that he always shoots the crime scene like it was a picture story with a beginning, middle, and end.

PHOTOGRAPHING A CRIME IN PROGRESS

Unlike reporters who can reconstruct the details of a mugging from police reports and eyewitness accounts, the photographer must be at the crime scene to get action pictures. Robbers, kidnappers, rapists, and murderers tend to shy away from the harsh glare of public exposure.

PREDICTING VIOLENCE

A photographer with a good news sense, however, can learn to predict some situations that might erupt into violence.

For instance, tension was running high during the National Basketball Playoffs in Los Angeles. Stan Lim of the *Inland Valley*

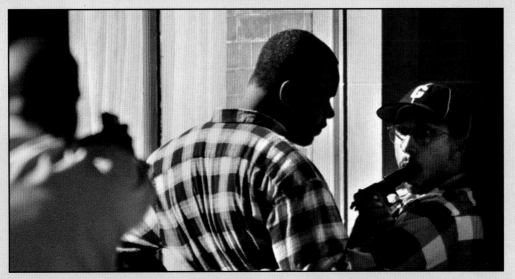

↓ After a high-speed chase into the center of Philadelphia, a triple-murder suspect bailed out of his car and led police on a brief foot-chase. As officers closed in, guns drawn, the suspect takes a hostage (the man in the middle), and places the barrel of his gun into his own mouth. Jim MacMillan shot this part of the sequence with a 500mm lens plus a 1.4 tele-extender, giving him an effective 700mm telephoto. The long lens allowed him to stay back and avoid the possibility of taking a bullet himself.

◄ The hostage wrestles away his attacker's gun.

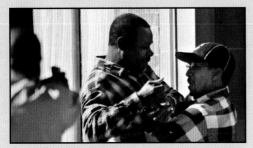

◄ After the hostage tries to pulls the gun away, police open fire, hitting their suspect twice. Police carry the wounded suspect to the paddy wagon. Using a second camera body, MacMillan rushed in and shot this photo with a wide-angle lens.

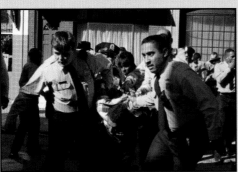

◄ The relieved hostage sits alone for a moment, giving a prayer of thanks while police arrest the gunman. The hostage was unharmed, and hailed as a hero by police for his cool demeanor under pressure. MacMillan, using his 80–200mm zoom on his third camera body, took this candid portrait. The whole incident lasted only thirty seconds.
Jim MacMillan, *Philadelphia Daily News*

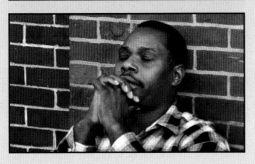

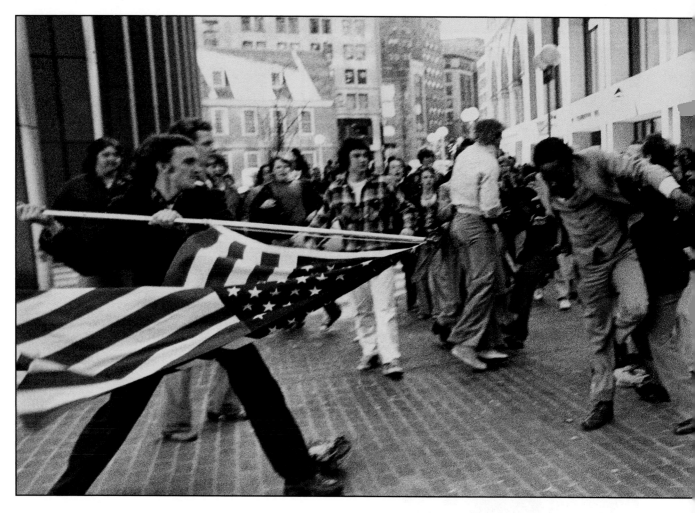

Daily Bulletin knew, based on fans' behavior after previous tight games, to expect rowdiness after the sixth game of the series. Lim's news sense led him to stick around after the game rather than going straight back to the newsroom.

When the final horn signaled a win by the Lakers, Lim headed for the streets. The crowd went wild, even torching a media truck parked outside the coliseum. Using a strobe and slow shutter speed, Lim photographed one of the rioters carrying a cardboard cut-out of the Lakers's Shaquille O'Neal as fire consumed the truck in the background. Anticipating what was about to happen had put Lim in the right place at the right time.

Be aware that demonstrations and marches can also become crime scenes. Even the police can overreact. Paul Brown was covering protests against the World Trade Organization for the *Seattle Post-Intelligencer* when police began firing rubber bullets at point-blank range into a group of demonstrators (page 24). Seattle police initially denied doing so, but Brown's photos clearly showed police bearing down on the

crowd with the menacing weapons. The photographer himself was hit by one of the bullets. After one of Brown's photos appeared on the newspaper's front page, the police were forced to admit that they had been firing the weapons. The picture eventually ran on the cover of *Time* magazine.

STAYING ALIVE: A CASE STUDY
Whether anticipating violence or racing into it on assignment, photographers must stay mentally alert to protect themselves while covering the story.

With the acquittal of white police officers who had been videotaped beating Rodney King, an African-American man, Los Angeles erupted into riots. By the second day of the riots, the Associated Press had called in John Gaps III, at the time one of the photographers the AP flies in when the agency needs an extra shooter to hit the ground running. They call this breed of photojournalist a photographic "fireman." Gaps was on the AP's photographic emergency squad.

"They told me to get to L.A.," Gaps recalls of receiving the assignment as the riots started to unfold. He landed at LAX, rented a car, and, after picking up another AP staffer (who had never covered a riot), headed for 18th and Broadway—the heart of the violence.

The photographers drove up to a blazing electronics warehouse, where looters were still hauling out the expensive goods.

"It didn't seem like a violent crowd," Gaps recalls. "I told the other photographer that I was going to park the car. If I could get on the ground, we wouldn't look like a drive-by." Gaps knew that by taking pictures from the car, he could be mistaken for an under-cover policeman.

Gaps's less experienced partner, however, started photographing through the windshield.

Almost immediately, a young Latino came to the driver's side of the car and aimed a gun at Gaps. Gaps picks up the story:

"I put my hands up, opened the car door, and said 'Here.' I showed him the camera, a Nikon 8008 with a 35–70mm zoom and strobe on it, and held it out the car door.

"Here, take the camera," Gaps told the man. "He lowered the gun, reached across, and took the camera from me.

"He had the camera in his hand, and I began to pull out. He raised the gun and aimed at me through the [closed] window," Gaps recalls. "Then he pulled the trigger right by my head. The car window just exploded.

"Fortunately, the glass deflected the bullet. He was standing right beside me when he pulled the trigger. He tried to blow my head off.

"Then I looked up, and traffic had cleared in front of the car. I hit the accelerator and drove like a bat out of hell down the street with my head down.

"I got about two blocks away before I stopped to see if anyone was hit. The bullet was lodged in the back seat.

"I guess we looked like cops taking pictures from the car. That set people off. We're just lucky we got out alive."

Of course, no flak jacket or bulletproof vest would have saved Gaps had the shooter's aim been slightly more accurate.

The moral to the story is this: take care when covering news. Even an automobile provides no real protection.

A fan hoists a life-size cutout of the LA Lakers's Shaquille O'Neal outside the Staples Center in Los Angeles. The team had just defeated the Indiana Pacers in the NBA Finals. In the background is a burning news media truck, set ablaze by out-of-control fans. The photographer combined flash and a slow shutter to get both the riot-er and the burning truck.
Stan Lim, *Inland Valley* [California] *Daily Bulletin*

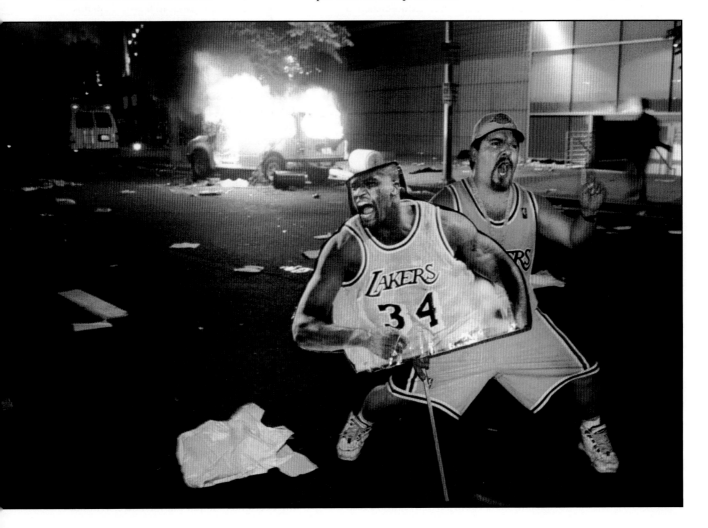

WHY SHOOT FIRES?

Reporting fires is an important part of the photojournalist's job. More than 500,000 homes catch fire each year. Fires also destroy apartment houses, stores, office buildings, and factories. Fires sweep through schools where children are having classes. Autos and trucks burn up, and fires devour forests in all parts of the country.

Altogether, 2 million fires are reported annually, costing more than $12 billion in property damage, according to the National Board of Fire Underwriters. Still more serious than monetary loss, thousands of people die in fires each year.

A photo can show not only the emotion of the participants but also the size of the fire better than words can. If a fire breaks out on the twenty-third story of a building from which an occupant might jump, a photo can indicate just how high twenty-three stories really is. The reader can quickly grasp the danger of jumping. If a wooden warehouse catches fire, requiring four companies to halt the spread of the flames, a photo can give the reader an idea of the vastness of the blaze.

After the fire has been extinguished, a photo of the charred aftermath carries impact beyond a mere statistical description of the loss. A photo of a house burning or an office worker trapped in a building ignites an empathetic reaction in the viewer, who thinks, "that could be my house . . . that could be me in that building."

FINDING AND FLEEING FIRES

Scanner radios, of course, provide one key means of learning about fires, but you can also develop a sense for when fires might occur. Kent Porter of Santa Rosa, California, has become an amateur meteorologist. By watching for low humidity and high winds, he is aware of the kinds of days when Northern California will be susceptible to wild fires. These fires might start in a field of dry grass, a grove of trees, or in someone's backyard. When conditions are right, such fires escalate quickly—which is exactly what happened in Oakland, California.

Porter described it this way. "It was windy and really warm. The humidity was down. I told my girlfriend, 'There's going to be a fire today.' I called my boss while I was driving down the road. I knew I was supposed to cover the football game, but I knew there was going to be a big fire. I turned on my car radio and heard the first reports coming from Oakland: 'Oakland Hills on fire.' The Oakland Hills fire turned out to be the biggest urban fire in history . . . more than 3,000 buildings and twenty-five lives were lost."

(See the documentary "Fire Photojournalist" on the enclosed DVD for more on covering fires and assessing their dangers.)

Plan for Traffic

While good news photographers know their hometowns extremely well, they also use their town's Thomas Brothers maps, a series of maps available nationwide. These maps provide the most accurate and complete road guides for different areas. The latest high-tech navigational tool is GPS (Global Positioning System), which uses sensors and satellites to pinpoint locations.

Jim MacMillan in Philadelphia notes that as he nears the location of a fire, he can find the flames by following the trail of water that fire trucks leave. At night, he says, smoke will be evident in the glow of streetlights if a fire is in the area. To avoid the possibility of colliding with fire trucks, shut off your radio, open your windows, and listen for fire engine sirens. When you arrive, find a parking spot that doesn't block fire hydrants—and plan for your escape.

"Get your film back to the office before the firefighters are prepared to leave," explains the *Boston Globe*'s George Rizer. "If they're parked in back of you, you'll be stuck until the fire is over and they've packed up their equipment. You'll miss your deadline."

OVERALL SHOT SETS THE SCENE

Once you have arrived at a fire and parked, you will want to start taking pictures. "The first thing I do," says Kent Porter, "whether it is a house fire or brush fire, is take a picture through the car window. I always shoot an overall of the whole scene, at the moment I drive up to the scene."

When you first see a fire, you should take a record shot since you don't know if the fire will flare up or die down. Later, to establish the size of the blaze, the location of the trucks, and the type of building that is burning, you might look for a high vantage from which you can shoot another overall.

WATCH FOR THE HUMAN SIDE

Once you have your overall shot, look for the human side of the tragedy. Are people trapped in the building? Will the firefighters bring up ladders to rescue the occupants, or have they already escaped? Do the firefighters have to administer mouth-to-mouth resuscitation or other kinds of first aid?

"Look for people's reactions," advises Jim MacMillan. "Play their ordinary lives against the crisis they are going through."

Meanwhile, don't overlook the efforts of the firefighters to put out the blaze. Without

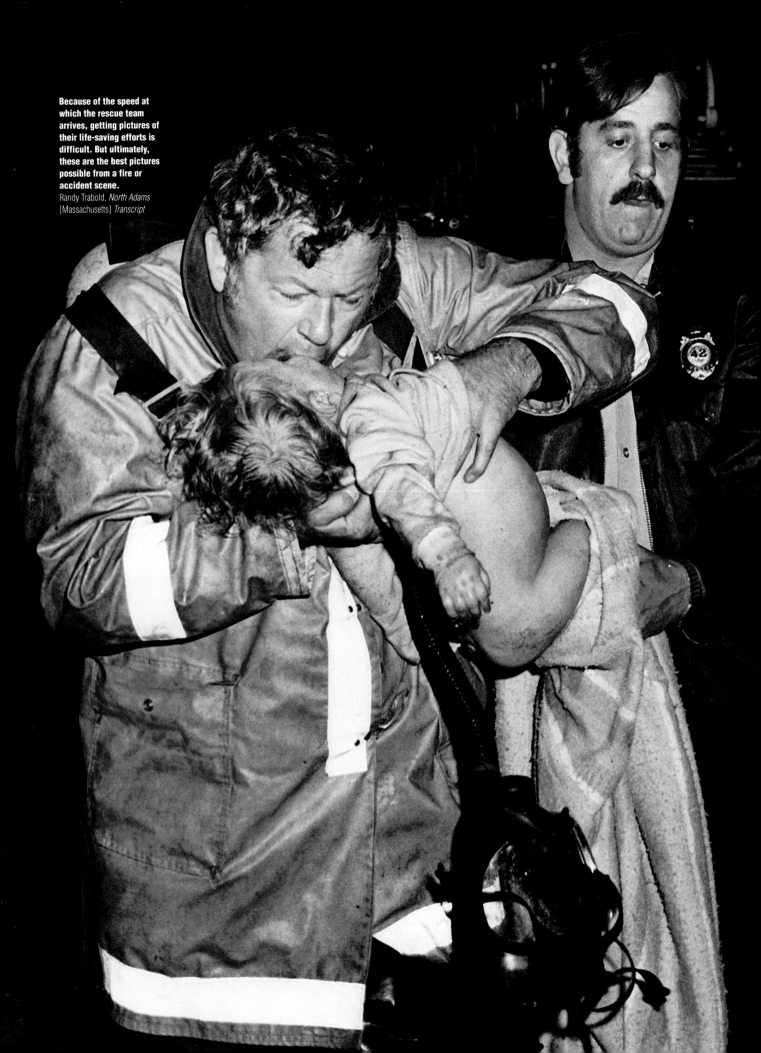

Because of the speed at which the rescue team arrives, getting pictures of their life-saving efforts is difficult. But ultimately, these are the best pictures possible from a fire or accident scene.
Randy Trabold, *North Adams* [Massachusetts] *Transcript*

LEAP FOR LIFE: A FIRE IN BOSTON

Stanley Forman, three-time Pulitzer Prize-winning photographer, knows Boston like the back of his hand. In this instance, he was cruising when he actually smelled smoke and pulled up to the burning house along with police. Trapped on the roof, the man in the pictures first handed down the child. When the woman froze, the man pushed her off before he jumped. The woman suffered minor injuries, but everyone else was okay. Forman approached the fire as if shooting a picture story. He takes the reader through the danger to the trapped residents on the roof, follows up with pictures of the rescue, and comes in tight to end with a close-up of the officer holding the child. Photos by Stanley Forman

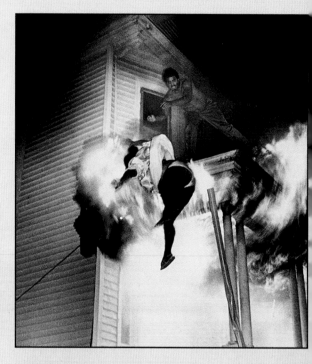

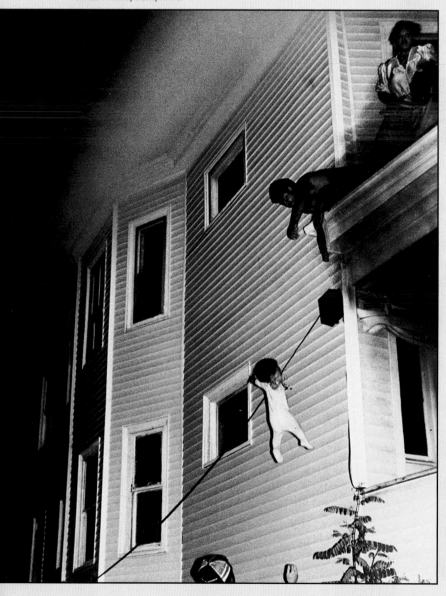

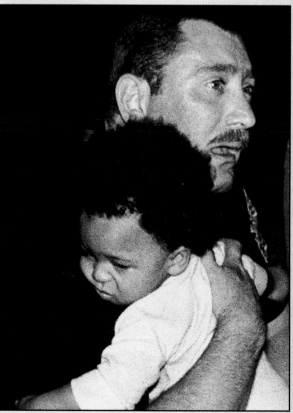

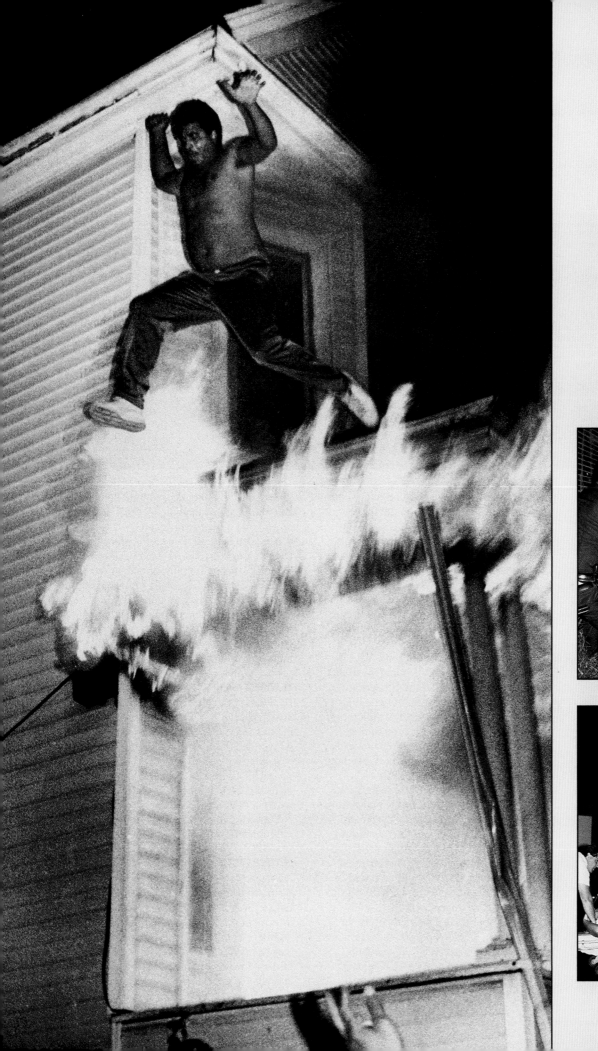
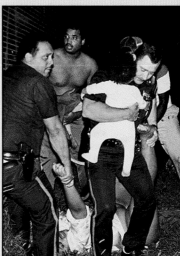
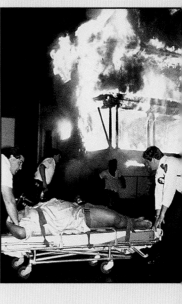

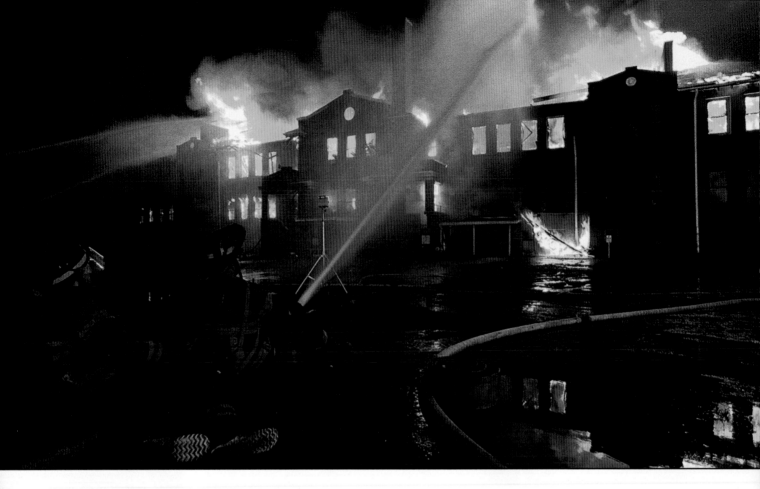

interfering, shoot the ladder and pump companies as they spray water on the flames. Keep an eye out for people overcome by smoke or exhaustion. Kent Porter recommends using a 300mm lens to get tight on the firefighters' faces.

Fires attract people. Whether in a big city or a rural town, a fire brings out an audience—whether neighbors or just passersby. Try to capture this psychological attraction.

LOOK FOR THE ECONOMIC ANGLE

Show the dimensions of the incident so that the reader learns whether the fire was a minor one or a major conflagration. Take a picture that indicates the kind of structure burned—single-family home, apartment house, business, or factory. Show how near the burned building was to other threatened structures in the neighborhood.

As the fire subsides, seek out a location where you can shoot a summary photo showing the extent of the damage. If you can accompany a fire inspector into a building, you might be able to photograph the actual cause of the blaze. When the fire marshal suspects arson, detectives will be called in to investigate. Investigators at work supply additional photo opportunities.

You might return to the scene of the fire the following day to photograph the remains of the charred building. Often, residents return to salvage their property. The next day's photo of a woman carrying out her water-soaked photo album might communicate more pathos than the pictures of flames and smoke of the night before.

You also can follow up a fire story by checking to see whether there has been a series of fires in the same area over the past year. If you find that certain blocks of houses or stores tend to have an unusually large number of fires, suggest that the editor run a group of fire pictures on one page, demonstrating the persistence of the fire hazard in that neighborhood.

FEATURES HIGHLIGHT THE SIDELIGHTS

Besides spot news, photographers can find good material for feature photos at fires. A picture story about the Red Cross worker who attends every fire might provide a sensitive sidebar. A small town may have an all-volunteer company, including a dentist who drills teeth and a mechanic who repairs cars when not battling flames.

Capturing this split life in pictures offers your readers a unique photo feature story.

GET THE FACTS

Always try to get factual data such as the firefighters' names and companies. Interview both the fire and police chiefs for cutline information: the exact location of the fire, the number of alarms sounded, the companies that responded, an estimate about the extent of the damage, and the names of the injured and what hospitals they were taken to.

NIGHT FIRES ARE DIFFICULT

Night fires tend to flare up between midnight and 6:00 a.m., when people are sleeping and smoke goes unnoticed. Arsonists choose nighttime for this reason. Because nighttime fires are not reported quickly, they tend to be larger and more frequent.

Photographically, night fires pose difficulties. The *Boston Globe*'s George Rizer, for example, does not take a reflected light-meter reading at nighttime fires.

"Why bother?" he asks. "A meter reading will be misled by the light from the flames and will not give an accurate indication of the amount of light reflected off the sides of the building."

For night fires, Rizer puts his camera on manual, uses a slow shutter speed, and adds flash. At faster shutter speeds, the flames still appear in the image, but the building goes black. Rizer is balancing the light from the strobe with the available light from the fire, the streetlights, and the portable working lights set up by the fire department. Within fifty feet, the flash also helps to light up the building.

With Fuji's ISO 800 color negative film, Kent Porter uses the same basic technique as Rizer in Boston. Porter puts his flash on 1/8 power. Using a 20mm or 24mm lens, he shoots at f/5.6, usually at a 1/30 sec. He warns against using this technique with a long lens, though, lest you give your subjects "red eye." (See Chapter 12, "Strobe.")

Besides lighting up the foreground, the strobe has an additional benefit. If the fire-fighters have brought in portable lights to work by, the spots will give off an orange color. The light from your strobe will help to counterbalance this orange cast from the tungsten lights. (See Chapter 12, "Strobe.")

But with the slow shutter speed, you must avoid even slight camera movement during the exposure. Rizer recommends resting the camera on a car, a fire hydrant, or holding the camera tightly and leaning against a lamppost to cut down camera movement.

Philadelphia's Jim MacMillan finds that he can even use his longer lenses at night if he braces himself carefully. He will shoot at 1/15 or 1/8 sec. with a 200mm lens when he is leaning securely against a car or utility pole.

He tries to wedge the camera lens against a stationary object and then "hammer off a number of frames to try to get one that's sharp."

But he puts away the strobe when flames start shooting out of every window in the building. "If it looks like a Christmas tree," he says, "you can shoot in available light, and you'll get great, action-packed fire pictures."

COVERING ACCIDENTS AND DISASTERS: GRIM BUT NECESSARY

(Dateline Baltimore) One Dead, 21 Hurt in Bethlehem Steel Blast
(Dateline Houston) Fatal Accident on Southwest Freeway Kills Six

So read the daily headlines, as accidents

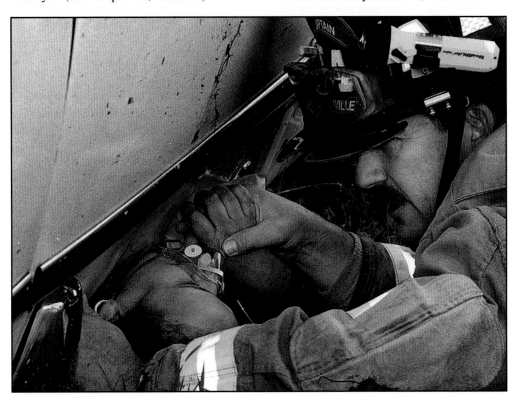

A close-up perspective adds intimacy to this photo of a fire captain comforting a woman trapped beneath a pickup truck in which she had been riding. Rick Roach, *Vacaville* [California] *Reporter*

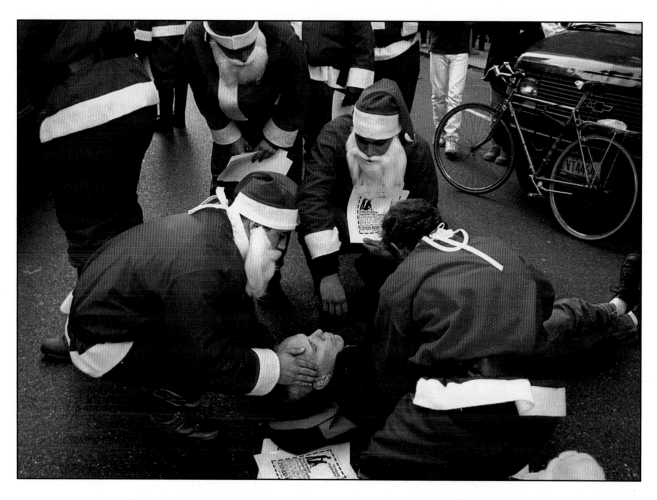

A bicycle accident might not merit photographic coverage–except when Sidewalk Santas come to the aide of the cyclist. This minor accident takes on the properties of a feature photo. Marty Lederhandler, Associated Press

take their toll of more than 100,000 lives and 10 million injuries each year (according to the National Safety Council). Almost half the accidents in the United States involve motor vehicles.

But people also die from falls, burns, drowning, gunshot wounds, poisonings, and work-related accidents.

Accidents make news. If one million Bay Area residents drive home safely on the freeway Friday night, that's not news. But if two people die in an auto crash on the Golden Gate Bridge, readers want to read a story and see a picture of the accident.

PHOTO POSSIBILITIES: FROM TRAGIC TO BIZARRE
If one hundred accidents take place daily in a typical city, no two will be identical. However, all accidents have certain points in common for the photographer.

CHECK HUMAN TRAGEDY FIRST
Concentrate on the human element of any tragedy. Readers relate to people pictures. Rick Roach of the *Vacaville Reporter* knew this when he came in close to photograph an emergency worker attempting to comfort a woman trapped beneath her car (page 39).

MAKE A RECORD
Make a straightforward record of what happened. The viewer, who doesn't know how the two cars hit or where they landed on the street, wants to see the cars' relationship to one another and to the highway.

SYMBOLIC PICTURES IMPLY RATHER THAN TELL
In some situations, the accident story is better told with a symbolic rather than a literal picture. A bent wagon lying in the street carries its own silent message. There is no need to show the body of the dead child.

PHOTOGRAPH THE CAUSE
In many news events such as riots or murders, there is no way of photographing the cause of the disturbance. At an accident, however, you can sometimes show clearly what caused the collision. For instance, if a car failed to stop on a slippery street, you might show the wet pavement in the foreground and the damaged vehicle in the background.

On a dry day, you might photograph skid marks left by the car as it screeched to a halt. Perhaps the accident was caused by the poor visibility of street signs. In that situation, a picture that showed the confusing array of flashing lights and fluorescent billboards that distracted the driver would be effective.

SHOW THE IMPACT

Accidents affect more than the drivers of the involved vehicles. Look in both directions for long lines of blocked traffic and drivers slowing down to gaze as they pass the site.

FOLLOW UP

If accidents keep occurring at one particular intersection, you might follow up to see if the highway department does anything to correct the hazard. A time exposure showing the traffic congestion might help to spur the highway department into action.

FEATURE ONE ASPECT

Notice how people adapt to their misfortune. Record the kinds of items people save from their wrecked vehicles. Note whether they act angry, sad, or frustrated. Catch the distress on the face of an owner of a new Mini Cooper as she views for the first time her crumpled fender. See if an owner of a thirteen-year-old Toyota reacts the same way when he sees the damage to his clunker.

Don't become hardened, however. No matter the size of the mishap, the accident usually is still a tragedy, or at least a traumatic experience, to the people involved. Even a bicycle accident can result in a telling picture, especially if several Santas stop to aid the victim.

GETTING THERE MAY BE THE BIGGEST PROBLEM

Taking pictures at the scene of a spot-news event requires a photographer with a cool head, someone who can work under pressure and adverse conditions. You need no unusual equipment or techniques—just nerves of steel and an unruffled disposition. However, before you arrive at the accident scene, you must be prepared. Load your camera and charge up your electronic flash so you will be ready to start clicking the minute you get out of the car.

In fact, getting to an accident in time is often the biggest challenge for the spot-news photographer. If you're stuck on the North Loop and two cars crash on the South Loop, you might find only a few glass shards from a broken windshield by the time you get to the scene. The ambulance has come and gone. Removed by the wrecker, even the

The oil tanker Argo Merchant went aground and broke up off the coast of Nantucket. Thousands of gallons of heavy fuel oil soiled the water. The Coast Guard provided journalists transportation by helicopter to the wreck site. Ken Kobré, for the *Boston Phoenix*

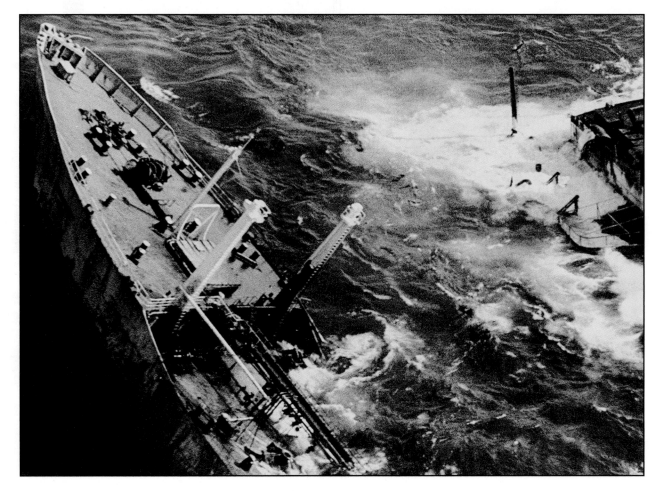

smashed vehicles are already on their way to the garage.

Consequently, a spot-news photographer's three most important pieces of equipment—after camera gear and a car, of course—are a scanner radio, a cell phone, and a Thomas map or GPS device. The radio provides the first report of the accident, the cell phone allows the photographer to check the location, and the detailed map or GPS shows the quickest way to get to the scene.

However, Stanley Forman attributes his success in winning three Pulitzer Prizes to old-fashioned, low-tech brainpower—knowing his city like the back of his hand. (See Forman's dramatic fire coverage on pages 36–37 and on page 322.)

A spot-news photographer finds hardest to cover the story in which all forms of transportation are down. During a flood, hurricane, tornado, or blizzard, you often can't drive a car or take public transportation.

Faced with a major natural disaster, you can sometimes get assistance from one of the public agencies such as the police department, fire department, Red Cross, civil defense headquarters, or the National Guard. In case of disasters at sea, you can telephone the Coast Guard.

Each of these agencies has a public information officer who handles problems and requests from the media. When a major disaster occurs, many of these agencies provide not only facts and figures but transportation, as well, for the photojournalist.

When the oil tanker Argo Merchant ran aground, cracked in half, sank off Nantucket Island, and leaked thousands of barrels of oil into the sea, the author contacted the U.S. Coast Guard on Cape Cod in Massachusetts.

Just one month before a tornado ripped the roof from this home, it had been featured in an architectural magazine. Using the magazine spread in the photograph helps tell the before as well as the after of this disaster. Robert Cohen, for the *Memphis* [Tennessee] *Commercial Appeal*

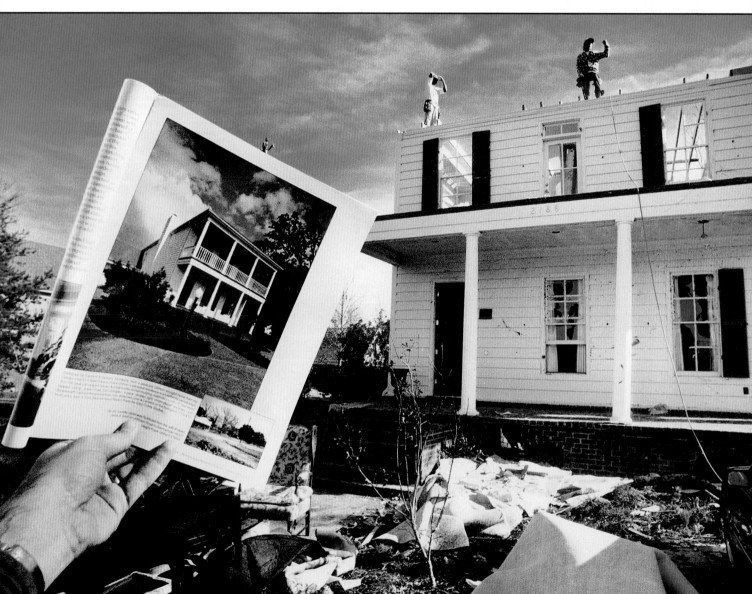

The Coast Guard arranged for the author to fly in one of its planes to take pictures over the site (page 41)

In another instance, when all of New England was buried under four-foot drifts during a major blizzard, the author contacted the National Guard, which provided a four-wheeled-drive vehicle and a driver so the photographer could shoot outlying areas hit by the storm.

As Dave Wurzel, the former New England photo bureau chief for United Press International, once said, "When a big storm breaks and everyone else heads for home, that's when the spot-news photographer goes to work."

WEATHER: NEWS EVERYBODY TALKS ABOUT

A photographer doesn't cover a blinding snowstorm or raging hurricane on every shift. However, even the slightest change in weather, from sunny and hot to cloudy and cool, interests and affects readers. The weather forecast is one of the most highly read sections of a Web site or newspaper.

On a slow news day, editors often call for "weather art"—regardless of the forecast.

DON'T SHOOT THE LAST FRAME

News photographers use multiple camera bodies so that they don't have to change film when the action is coming down. Some carry two or three bodies. Sam Costanza even carries a point-and-shoot automatic camera just in case he needs a backup.

One piece of advice worth repeating: don't shoot to the end of the roll or the last megabyte on a digital memory card.

"I change film like crazy," says newshound Jim MacMillan.

Annie Wells, now with the *Los Angeles Times*, attributes her Pulitzer Prize to conserving film while photographing the heroic rescue of a young woman in a flooded river (page i). (Wells shot the picture while at the *Press Democrat* in Santa Rosa, California.)

The last thing you want is to have to change film—or memory cards—at the most dramatic moment. ■

Weather is a constant news topic, and photographers are often assigned to find "weather art." The photographer captured this brilliant rainbow at sunset as fast-moving showers were leaving the area.
John Tlumacki, *Boston Globe*

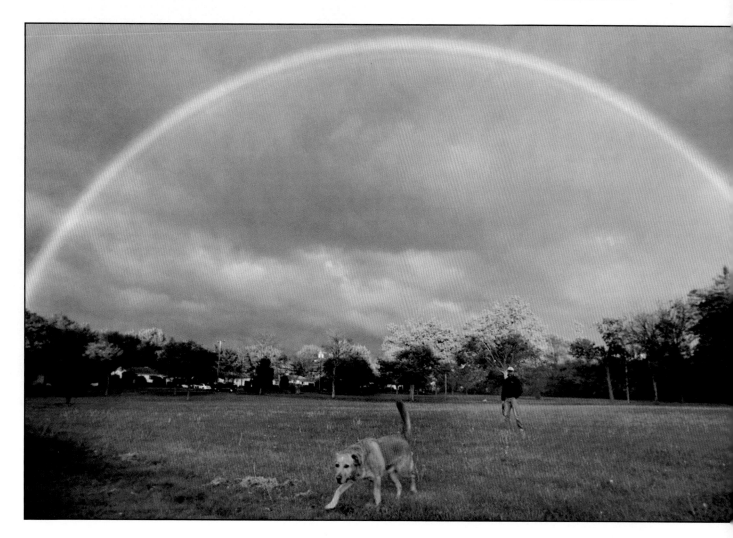

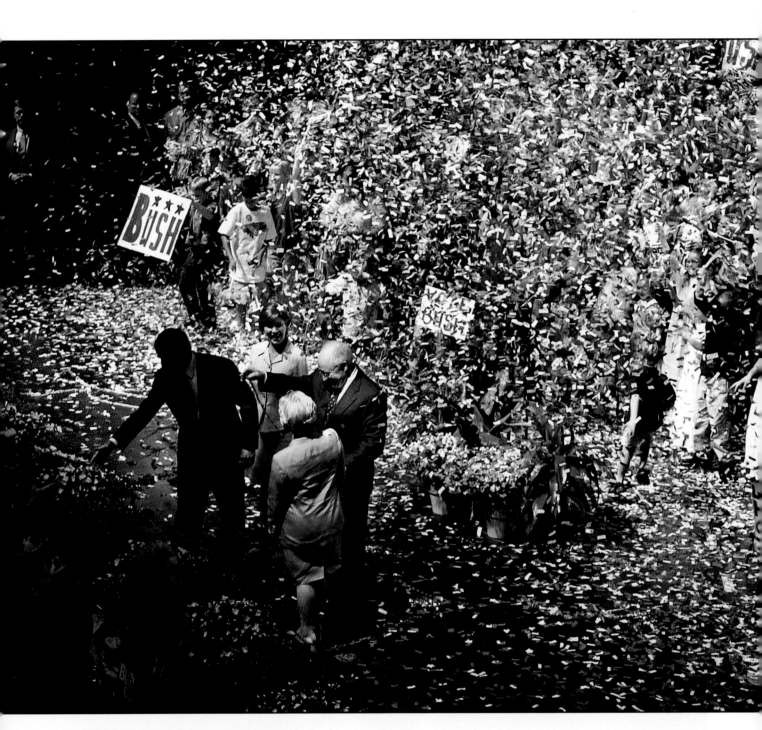

Using a digital camera from a high angle, the photographer
captured this pre-convention photo op of then-candidate
George W. Bush, Jr., left, reaching into the crowds. Tom Gralish,
Philadelphia Inquirer

Chapter 3

General News

POLITICS, POLITICIANS, AND MEDIA EVENTS

Politicians seek interviews and photographs. Press aides dream up news events and organize news conferences to attract coverage. Astute politicians know that reelection depends on good media coverage. The monetary worth of a page-one photo is inestimable—most newspapers and magazines will not sell front-page space for any kind of advertising.

A politician plans media events that attract the camera, even if the events themselves have little news value. Called "photo opportunities or photo ops" these non-events, often filled with balloons and confetti, have been designed for the camera journalist.

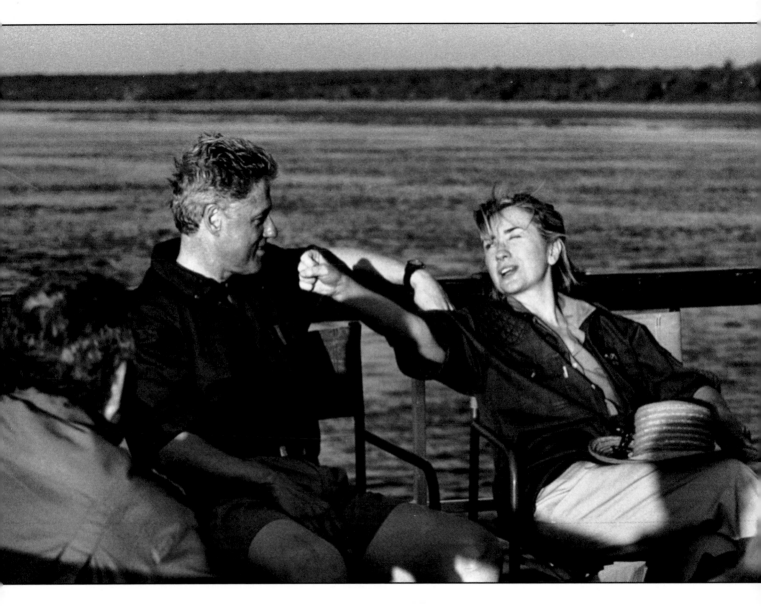

Diana Walker, who covers the White House for *Time* magazine, had behind-the-scenes access to Bill and Hillary Clinton during a trip to Africa. Walker was able to catch this rare, unguarded moment of President Clinton and his wife joking together. Diana Walker, *Time* magazine

If the president puts on a stupid hat for a photo, editors can't resist the picture. Politicians and photographers manipulate each other, to their mutual benefit. Politicians look for free publicity and photographers want visual events. Editors think readers want to see politicians in costume. The picture of the senator wearing a cowboy hat is not wrong. It's just not good journalism.

Politicians come alive at election time. The old "pol" leaves the desk in his plush office and starts pressing the flesh at ward meetings, cultural parades, and organizations for the elderly. The young challenger, by contrast, walks the streets of the ghetto with her suit jacket thrown over her shoulder. Both candidates plaster stickers on cars, erect billboards, appear in "I promise" TV ads, and attend massive rallies.

A photographer can take two sets of campaign pictures.

One would show the candidate's public life—shaking hands, giving speeches, and greeting party workers.

The other would reveal the candidate's private life—grabbing a few minutes alone with the family, planning strategy behind closed doors, pepping up the staff, and collapsing at the end of a fourteen-hour day.

All too often, news outlets present their readers with a one-sided visual portrait of the candidate—the public side, planned and orchestrated by the candidate's campaign directors. Editors tend to publish only upbeat, never downbeat, pictures; only happy, never sad, moments. Photographers continue to churn out photos of the candidate shaking hands and smiling—photos that reveal little about the person who wants to run the city, state, or federal government.

GOING BEHIND THE SCENES

The major U.S. news magazines have done a much better job of behind-the-scenes coverage than most of the country's newspapers and news Web sites. To capture insightful pictures of politicians, some magazine photographers and their news organizations have developed special access to high-level officials. While these photojournalists have uncommon access, their techniques are still useful for photographing people whose lives seem to be one long "photo op."

Diana Walker, contract photographer for *Time* magazine, has been covering the White House since the last year of the Carter administration. Presidents come and go at the White House. Walker remains. Walker says she is afforded access behind the scenes at the White House to show readers what the president is about when he is offstage. "I can show you relationships and atmosphere," she says, "how these people look when they are not in front of the lights and microphones."

Walker tries to be a "fly on the wall" when photographing private moments in a president's life. "My whole approach is for the president not to know I am there. I try not to engage with him—ever. I don't talk unless he talks to me," she says.

By becoming as familiar—and as unobtrusive—as the wallpaper in the Oval Office, Walker quietly records intimate moments inside the White House. The night before President Clinton's impeachment trial began, she recalls, "The President turned to his wife, suddenly put his arms around her neck and held on to her just for a quick second." That photograph, she says, captures a personal moment and an emotion that the President would not necessarily reveal in public.

While the president knows that Walker is in the room, neither he nor his staff can control how the people in the Oval Office will behave, she points out. "The scene is set, but the characters are themselves."

Walker, by the way, shoots only black-and-white film when photographing inside the White House. *Time* now signals its behind-the-scenes access by publishing these kinds of stories in black and white.

P.F. Bentley has covered every presidential election since 1980. Shooting solely in black and white all these years, Bentley has followed the campaigns of George W. Bush, Sr., Bill Clinton, Robert Dole, and Newt Gingrich for up to a year at a time. As Bentley says, the campaign stops are just the tip of the iceberg. "In the hotel room is your picture."

At the 1992 Democratic convention, Bentley's picture of Bill Clinton warming up his vocal cords in the steam room before going onstage was more revealing than any picture of the candidate at the podium.

STRATEGIES FROM THE PROS

Not every photographer has the chance to shadow presidential candidates for months at a time or to document the president of the United States on a daily basis. However, the experiences of shooters like Bentley, Walker, and other magazine professionals provide insights into how to cover any official—from governor to mayor to local supervisor.

Watch but Don't Talk

Diana Walker has developed several techniques for avoiding conversation with her subjects. If someone looks at her, she immediately breaks eye contact by looking at her watch. If they try to start a conversation, she adjusts her camera or changes film.

"Of course, if the president begins to talk to me," she admits, "I have no choice but to answer back." She describes her working manner as "trying to be as discrete, quiet, out-of-the-way, and unobtrusive" as she can. "Of course, he knows I am in the room," she continues, "but it is the closest I can get to the way people really are."

Covering politicians on the campaign trail has taught P.F. Bentley flexibility. The observer should remain unobserved, he says.

"You have to become a chameleon," he explains. "You have to adjust to who they (the politicians) are and to their routine. After awhile, you kind of know their moods. You know when to go in tight, when to back off, and, finally, when to lay low." If things aren't going on, for example, he will usually walk out of a room and check in later. "I don't hover all the time," he notes.

Newsweek photographer David Hume Kennerly is a well-known raconteur when he is not working, but he finds it advantageous not to chat when he is trying to catch candids. "Usually I am in a place where there is no reason for me to talk," he observes.

Zip Your Lips

All the photographers interviewed for this book who work behind the scenes have made tacit agreements with their subjects not to reveal what they overhear. "I don't talk about what I hear, and my writers never ask me," says *Time*'s Walker. P.F. Bentley, agrees: "Of course, there is a trust that I won't ever talk about anything I hear."

David Kennerly points out that still photographers have a real advantage over their television counterparts. Politicians can be themselves and say what is on their minds with still photographers in the room. They know their comments will stay off the record.

With video cameras rolling, he observes, politicians are unlikely to be their usual loquacious selves. "If you introduce sound into the situation, politicians will not talk naturally," he says.

No Gear You Can Hear

To accomplish this unobtrusive kind of photography, photographers rely on fast lenses and sensitive film to avoid using flash. Bentley's mantra is "No gear that you can hear." He shoots with Leicas and a Canon EOS A-2, using 24mm f/1.4, 35mm f/1.4, and 100mm f/2 lenses.

Walker, too, shoots with Leicas and a Canon, using 24mm, 35mm, and 50mm lenses and a longer lens—"just in case."

In each frame, she explains, she tries to include the president and other players who are in the Oval Office. "I am not doing tight head shots," she points out. Walker is looking

for relationships not portraits. But if a portrait is appropriate, she has that longer lens in her bag.

Sell Yourself

You can have the right approach, the right film, and the best cameras, but without access to politicians, you can't make revealing pictures. P.F. Bentley talks to politicians ahead of time about recording their entire campaigns from the inside. "I tell them about the type of pictures I will take and the type I won't take. They know they are part of history." Bentley assures the politicians that he is not out to ridicule them by taking "cheap-shot" pictures. No photos of scratching or adjusting, no images of people eating, he assures potential subjects. "I have been in the hotel room where the candidate is in his underwear," he says. "That is not the kind of picture I care to take. It is not a picture that has any meaning."

Kennerly, who has been on the inside as

The *Time* photographer caught this moment between President Clinton and his daughter, Chelsea, during his second inauguration. Diana Walker, *Time* magazine

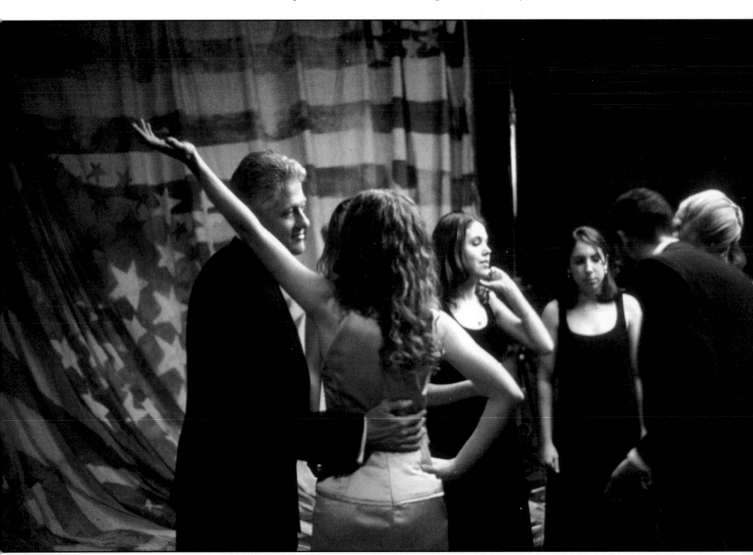

the White House photographer for President Ford and on the outside as the *Newsweek* photographer covering Clinton, has learned about getting access under difficult conditions. "The picture is only a small part of what I do. I am a salesman first and foremost. I have to sell myself to people to come into their lives."

Members of the House and the Senate are, for the most part, easy to deal with, he says. They have to be reelected and they have to get along. "Photographers are not considered to be the enemy," he says. "Reporters fall into that category."

Having worked in Washington on and off since the Ford administration, Kennerly has excellent connections. "I actually know a lot of senators," he says. "I would count ten senators that I am well acquainted with and could call on a moment's notice."

During President Clinton's impeachment trial, photographers were denied access to the Senate chambers during the proceedings.

Kennerly likens the situation to covering a bullfight when you can't see the bull or the matador. He wanted to take exclusive photographs at a high-level meeting of the representatives who were bringing the ominous charges against the President. He called on an old friend for whom he had done a favor twenty years ago. The friend was now a representative—and one of the managers of the impeachment trial. The twenty-year-old favor paid off, and Kennerly got exclusive access for *Newsweek*.

MEETINGS GENERATE NEWS

In large cities and small towns, journalists cover the news of governmental meetings because the results of those meetings are important to readers. Meetings possess the same news value as fires and accidents. Often, the results of a governmental meeting—those involving changes in the tax rate, for instance—directly bear on readers' lives even more than yesterday's fender-bender.

The photographer, who shot an extensive behind-the-scenes essay, caught this revealing moment of Bob Dole crying after he resigned from the Senate to concentrate on his presidential bid. P.F. Bentley, for *Time* magazine

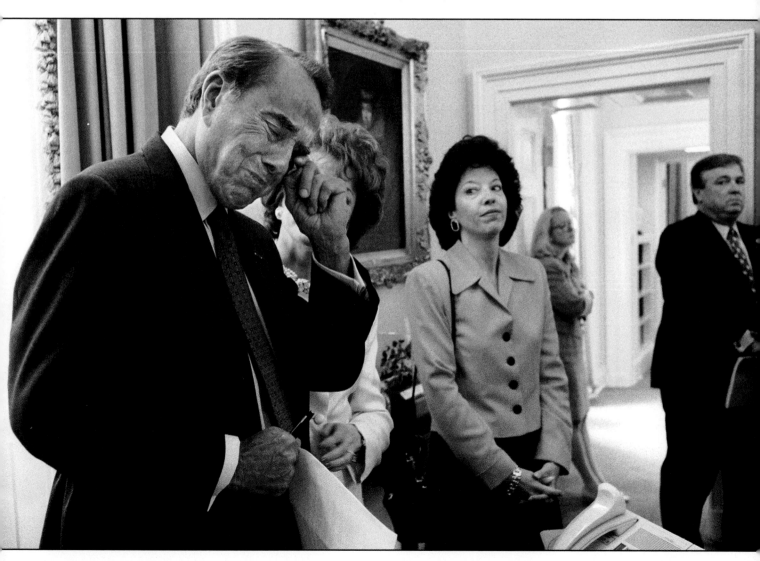

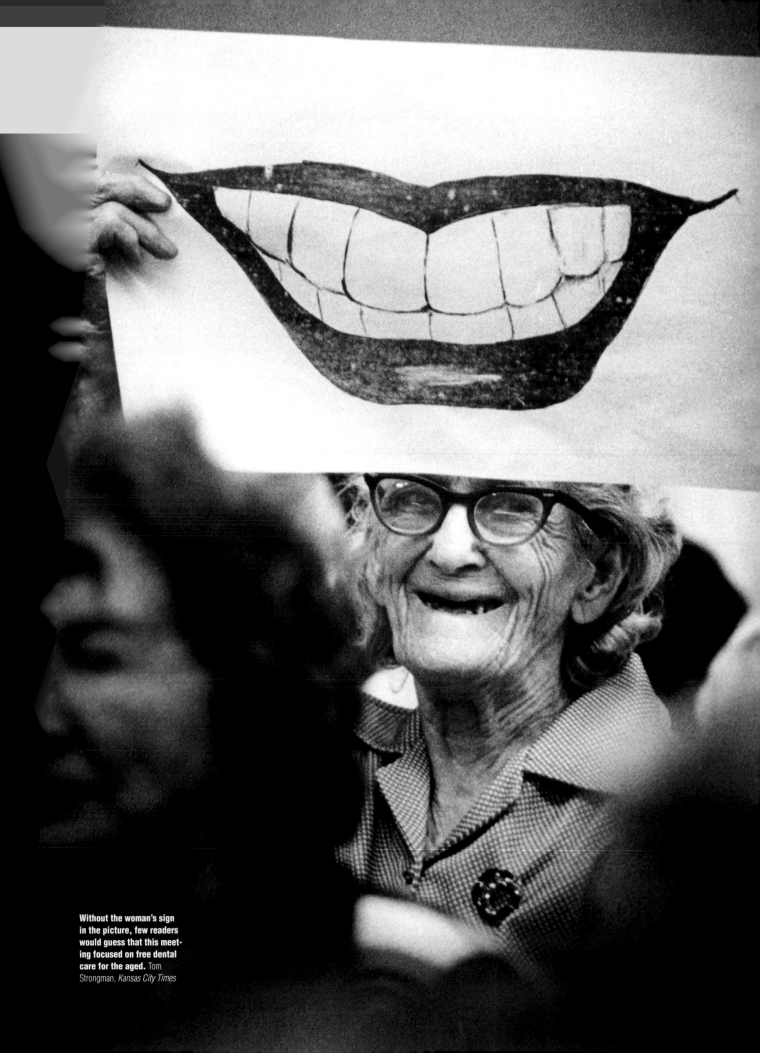

Without the woman's sign in the picture, few readers would guess that this meeting focused on free dental care for the aged. Tom Strongman, *Kansas City Times*

Meetings and press conferences carry a challenge: they test the photographer's creativity. Unfortunately, a critical meeting of the Senate Armed Services Committee looks very much like an ordinary meeting of the local zoning board.

If the pictures remained uncaptioned, readers could easily be confused. Press conferences as well as awards ceremonies all tend to look identical after a while.

Sometimes, through the creative application of framing techniques, catching the moment, and using long lenses and light, the photographer can help portray the excitement, the tension, the opposition, and the resolution of the meeting.

Face and Hands Reveal Emotion
Ray Lustig of the *Washington Post* has covered some of the most momentous as well as some of the most trivial political moments in the country's recent history. He works Capitol Hill on his beat as the *Post*'s chief political photographer. When Lustig raises his 70–210mm f/2.8 zoom lens at a committee hearing or press conference, he looks for expressive faces. "A wrinkled brow, a grin, or a curled lip can add life to a routine meeting picture," Lustig says. "Hands, too, reveal a speaker's emotion." Readers, of course, understand the meaning of a clenched fist or a jabbing finger.

Revealing vs. Accidental Photos
A speaker's facial expressions and hand gestures can be accidental and misleading. They might have nothing to do with the personality of the individual or the thrust of the message. Suppose that during a luncheon the governor is discussing closing the border to illegal immigrants. You take 100 to 200 frames. You might catch a shot while he is eating—showing him with his mouth screwed into a knot. This picture, although an actual moment, reflects nothing about the nature of the topic or even the speaker's character. The misleading picture, in fact, tends to distort the news rather than reveal it.

As *Time*'s P.F. Bentley points out, "I don't care who it is, eating pictures are ugly. Once people start to eat, it is not a picture I care to have."

Who's Who Is Important
Meetings, speeches, or press conferences in a town take on news value based on the personalities involved and on the importance of the subject debated.

The photographer must know or be able to recognize the players in the game without a scorecard. If you are not familiar with the

participants in a meeting, ask someone for information about the speakers. What are their names? Which ones are elected officials? Who is best known? With this information, you can zero in on the most newsworthy individuals.

Here is how Ray Lustig prepares for a day on Capitol Hill. "When I am preparing to go to the Hill, I first review the Reuters daybook. (The daybook lists all the upcoming activities, including Congressional caucuses, press conferences, speeches, etc.) If I have questions, I try to meet with the appropriate editors—national or defense, for example. When I get to the Hill in the morning, I check the Web for committee schedules. I read the *Washington Post* thoroughly before I arrive, and when I get to the pressroom I take a look at the *New York Times* and the *Washington Times*. I also will do a quick scan of our newspaper's Web sites. I also carry a pager that gives me information from both Houses' radio/TV gallery of events. I am doing my homework. I've got to know what is going on. That's my business."

The advantage of all this reading and preparation is that Lustig has a broad grasp of all the day's planned news. This allows him to select the most visual or most newsworthy events to cover.

Finally, his complete preparation allows him to be the first to arrive at a packed hearing or overcrowded press conference. He gets there early and stakes out a spot. His meticulous forethought gives Lustig the edge on his competition.

Props Add Meaning
Props can add meaning to a routine meeting photo. If someone holds up a prop, the reader will have an easier time understanding the point of the photo. If the speaker who denounces the lack of gun control laws brings to the meeting a few "Saturday Night Specials," the photographer can photograph the person examining or displaying the guns. A photo of an elderly woman, minus a few teeth yet holding aloft a poster of a toothy smile, helped summarize a meeting on free dental care for the aged (opposite).

SURVIVAL TACTICS
When Ray Lustig covers an important committee meeting on Capitol Hill for the *Washington Post*, his gear bag contains two strobes and two Nikon camera bodies: one with a 28–70mm zoom lens and the other with a 70–210mm zoom lens. He uses the short zoom for overalls of the conference room but saves the telephoto zoom for close-up portraits. The close-up brings the viewer

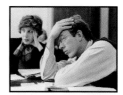
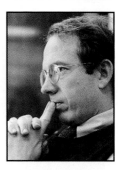
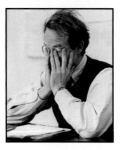
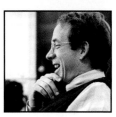

The hands of former Massachusetts Secretary of Human Services Jerald Stevens reveal the pressure, the pleasure, the tension, and the ease of this powerful state official.
Bill Collins

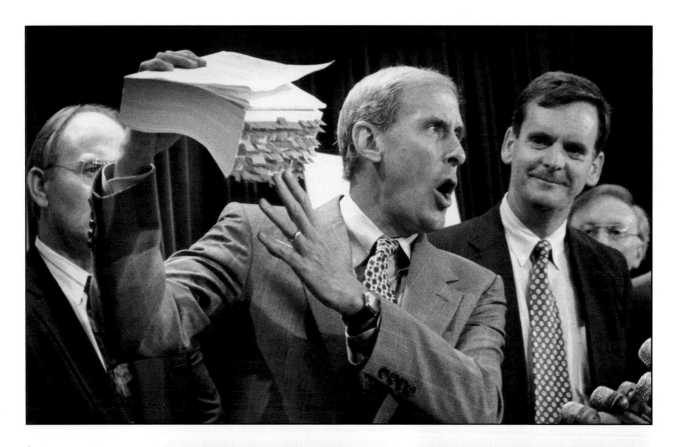

Republican Senator Dan
Coates (Indiana) holds legislation that would create a
comprehensive health care
package. Republicans critical of the plan claimed it was
too big, complicated, and
bureaucratic. Both the
Senator and the photographer
know that props help visualize the story behind a meeting or press conference.
Ray Lustig, *Washington Post*

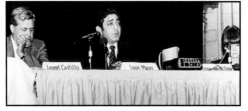

Avoid shooting perpendicular to the line of speakers.
The perspective results in a picture with large blank spaces
between each person, and each face appears quite small.
Jan Ragland

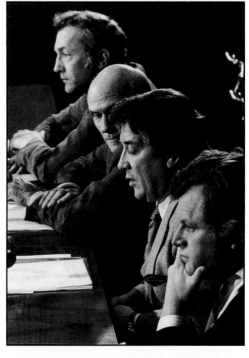

Shooting these dignitaries from the side eliminated dead
space between subjects. Photographing with a telephoto lens
appears to bring the subjects closer together.
James K.W. Atherton, *Washington Post*

and the subject nearer than they normally would meet in public.

Lustig also carries a small aluminum stool, which allows him to sit rather than kneel while waiting for a picture. "You need it," he says, "because it saves wear and tear on your body." He also carries a monopod and cable release.

Seated on his stool, his camera mounted on the monopod, and his cable release at the ready, Lustig can shoot at slower shutter speeds when necessary and also keep his lens aimed at his subject during those long, drawn-out meetings. Without tiring his arm or having to keep his eye glued to the viewfinder, Lustig can train the lens on his target and look for gestures, mannerisms, and expressions—all the way through each politician's speech.

PHOTOGRAPH THE ISSUES

Most political issues can be translated into pictures. If the mayor says city education is poor and should be improved, the photographer must search for supporting evidence of the claim. Are schools overcrowded? Do students hang around in the halls with nothing to do after class? If racial tension exists between white and African-American students, can the journalist photograph the situation?

A set of realistic photos will transform rhetoric into observable issues.

Photographers spend too much time shooting political mug shots and too little time digging up visuals that either confirm or deny the claims of politicians.

When covering a campaign, election, or any other contested issue, photographers have the same responsibility to objectivity as reporters. Like reporters, photographers can directly distort a scene.

An ultra-wide-angle lens can make a small room look large. Strong lighting and harsh shadows can transform, in Jekyll-and-Hyde fashion, a mild-mannered speaker into a tyrannical orator. Even more damaging, photographers, like writers, can report one side of an issue and, intentionally or not, leave the other side uncovered.

Because papers often run only one or two pictures, such biased photo reporting creeps into the paper easily. Honest photographers, however, try to select the lens, light, and camera angle as well as a representative moment or scene to present a fair view of a complicated topic.

Unfortunately, few newspaper photographers receive adequate time for investigative political photography. An editor finds it easy to send a staffer to cover a press conference. The editor knows the time and place of the

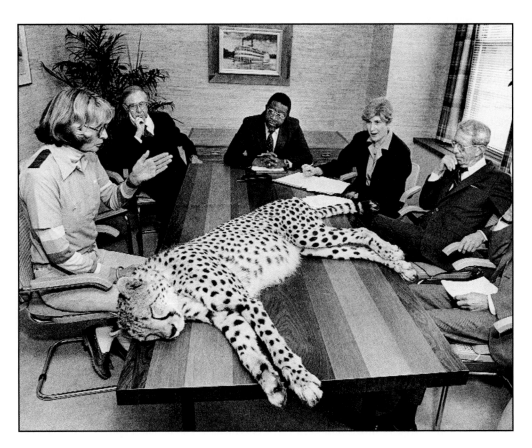

You will find it hard to come across a meeting situation with supporting visuals as strong as this fund-raising meeting for the Cincinnati Zoo—complete with cat-napping cheetah.
Patrick Reddy, *Cincinnati Enquirer*

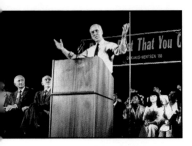

Enterprising photographers can avoid standard speaker pictures by moving away from the pack and looking for an interesting way to combine storytelling elements in one picture, such as the one on the right of former Senator Lloyd Bentsen. Kathy Strauss

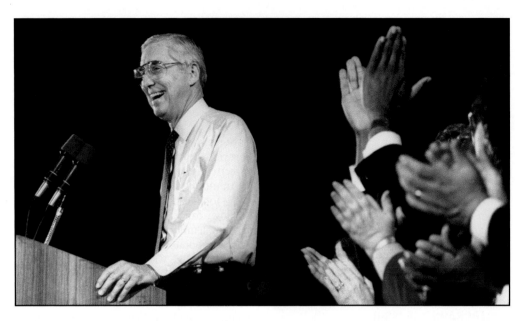

gathering and can guarantee that some usable "art" will result. But readers don't want to see another "mayor talking" picture. They already know what the mayor looks like. They want to determine if the mayor is telling the truth about the school system. Pictures can help substantiate or negate the mayor's assertions.

STEER CLEAR OF THE PACK

Even if you're out conducting photographic political investigations, your editor in all likelihood will continue to assign you to rallies, speeches, and photo opportunities. Cover these events if you must, but resist the PR-packaged photos politicians hope to see in tomorrow's paper. At the most, look where the packaging has peeled away—but don't be surprised if you can't find reality. At the least, turn your camera toward the crowd to find unusual political boosters. And, photographically, struggle to avoid the cliché of simply recording the routine picture.

Sometimes you will have to shoot next to other photographers. The *Washington Post*'s Lustig, who sometimes has to vie for position among twenty other still and video shooters, warns that you should avoid using a 20mm lens in this situation. To get close enough to your subject with a 20mm lens, you will have to walk in front of all your fellow shooters—and block their shots. The best solution to herd journalism, he points out, is to avoid the pack and find another angle for the shot.

Without doubt, all political rallies start to look alike. But, by angling for a new view, like the one of clapping hands and Lloyd Bentsen (above), perhaps you can at least bring back a photo you and your readers haven't seen thousands of times before.

COME EARLY—STAY LATE

Alex Burrows, director of photography at the *Norfolk Virginian Pilot*, tells this story about several of his photographers who were assigned to cover a funeral. "One of our young photographers was assigned the grave site. He thought his work was over after the service, but one of our pros stayed really late and got a shot of one of the funeral directors putting a final flower on the covered grave site. It was a great ending photo for the two-page spread. The younger photographer learned a lesson."

The advice "come early and stay late" will serve you well whether you are covering a funeral or other events like rallies, parades, or fairs. The best parade pictures often occur when the performers are waiting to begin. They are loose, natural, and relaxed. They often are kidding one another and joking around. You are more likely to get candid moments at this point than after the parade begins and the participants go into performing mode. Likewise, at the parade's end, the tuba player might be feeling goofy enough to put his head in the horn, or the majorette might be energized enough to turn flips.

Don't leave even after the principals have gone home. The leftover signs and banners forlornly festooning a trash barrel might tell more about the event than the staged moments earlier in the day.

Julie Stupsker, shooting for the *San Francisco Examiner*, hung around long after the lead competitors had passed to make her funny picture of a nude runner in the infamous Bay to Breakers footrace in San Francisco.

Photographers cover many pre-arranged events, from an annual Founders' Day parade to the bicentennial celebrations. Statues are unveiled. Old-timers wear costumes. Politicians give speeches. A photographer's real assignment is to look beyond the stage-managed elements for something surprising, revealing, or out of place. Robert Cohen, shooting for the *St. Louis Post Dispatch*, found just such a situation when he noticed a veteran wheeling his own oxygen tank and positioned between two well-built young soldiers at a war memorial dedication (page 56).

When covering events like street fairs, isolating your subject within the crowd is difficult. You can't use a long lens and let a wide aperture blur the background because foreground elements will interfere with your picture. You can dramatize your main target if you can get near enough with a wide-angle lens, but you will still have to contend with a bothersome busy background. Of course, you can use a low angle with the sky as your background, or perhaps shoot with a telephoto from a high perch and let the ground serve as a nondistracting background. You can also try working the edges of the crowd. Here you will find most of the same characters you were targeting before, but you can more easily—with any length lens—visually isolate them from the distracting crowd.

IN-DEPTH PHOTOJOURNALISM
PHOTOGRAPH THE TOPIC, NOT THE TALKER

Even with the best lens technique and a keen sensitivity to light, photographers still have trouble distinguishing for readers the difference between a city council meeting called to increase taxes and a meeting convened to decrease the number of district schools.

The difference between these meetings lies in what the council members said verbally, not what they did visually. The photojournalist must translate speakers' words into pictures that portray the underlying controversy.

Arthur Perfal, a former associate editor of *Newsday*, gave his view of the problem at a conference of editors. "Remember that people talking often supply material for good stories," Perfal said, "but they seldom supply material for good pictures. Particularly when

When you cover a parade or other event like the San Francisco Bay to Breakers footrace, it pays to stay to the end. Sometimes the funniest pictures occur after the main affair is over. Julie Stupsker, *San Francisco Examiner*

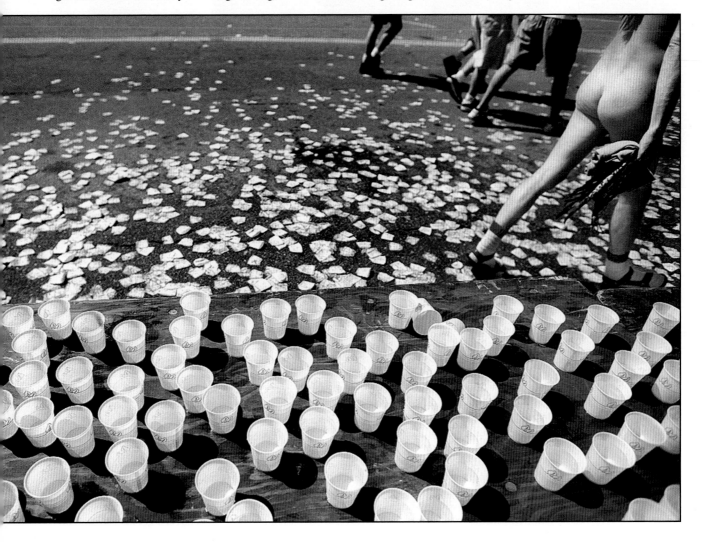

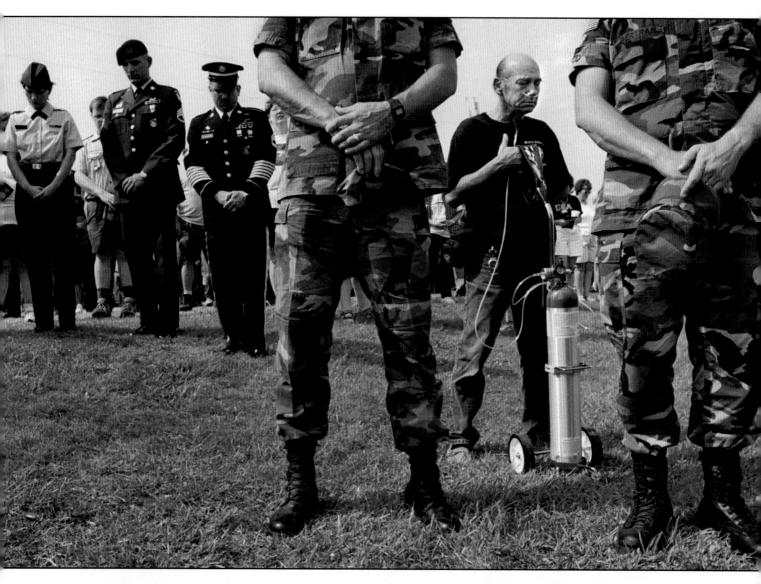

Although events like this dedication of a Vietnam veterans memorial are preplanned, the photojournalist cannot predict when something unusual or revealing will take place. A veteran wheeling his own oxygen tank and standing behind two robust soldiers adds poignancy to the scene. Robert Cohen, *St. Louis Post Dispatch*

the same officials or the same chairmen are doing the talking. Let the photographer go where the action is—shoot what they're talking about."

Although studies and news releases announced the decline of the small farm, Scott Strazzante actually documented how cattle farmers Harlow Cagwin and his wife confronted age and suburban sprawl. Because Strazzante had followed the story over several years, he was there on the day the couple moved out of their house and saw it demolished by a land developer (opposite).

Media Events and Photo Ops

After news conferences, meetings, and public events, the awards ceremony ranks as one of the most common of planned news events.

Some photographers argue that pictures of staged situations like awards ceremonies and news conferences simply should not run. Greg Mironchuk, a photographer in Revere,

Massachusetts, spoke for many colleagues in his comments to the National Press Photographers Association online discussion list, NPPA-L.

"It doesn't matter if [a press conference] was set up by the president, the World Health Organization, your local police department, Demi Moore's press agent, or the Maharishi Mahesh Yogi," he wrote.

"It's still a set-up and still something that wouldn't exist without a press presence . . . . We [the press] are in tacit collusion with every flack, hack, and terrorist that calls a press conference. If we didn't come, there'd be no reason to do it."

Many news outlets, however, especially in smaller communities, continue to publish such pictures. In his column for *News Photographer* magazine, Bryan Grigsby, photo editor at the *Philadelphia Inquirer*, discussed his strategy for dealing with such assignments. "Whenever I get an assignment to cover something that is obviously being staged for the media, I ask the photographer to step back and record the staged quality of that event rather than go along with the intended charade of the event's sponsors."

If you polled professional photojournalists, they would vote overwhelmingly to eliminate awards pictures. Some news outlets, in fact, have policies forbidding awards photos except for special circumstances. Most editors, nevertheless, continue to assign handshaking, check-passing pictures.

The Story Behind the Award

As with meeting pictures and political pictures, the real secret to covering press conferences and awards lies in searching out the reason for the event and bringing out this fact in your picture. Sometimes you only have to arrange a portrait to point out the meaning of an event. If a woman wins an award for most valuable player on the softball team, her uniform and equipment in the portrait cues the reader to the nature of the award.

In some cases, an award might even be a peg for a picture story. For example, the ceremony at which Annemarie Madison received an award for her work with people dying from AIDS was, as most of these stiff ceremonies are, a visual zero.

However, her dedication and compassion became the subject of a moving photo story that was part of a photo project that won awards of its own—"Helpers in the War on AIDS." (See pages 68–72. "Developing a Feature Beat" in Chapter 4, "Covering the Issues.") ∎

A former cattle farmer can't bear to watch as his house is demolished. The cleared land will be transformed into a subdivision. The photographer was present at this emotional moment because he had followed the plight of the family over a period of several years.
© Scott Strazzante

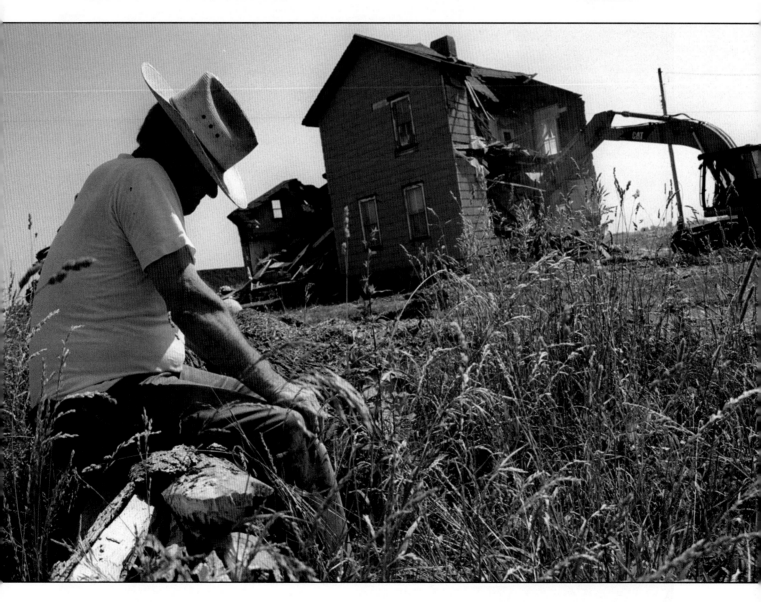

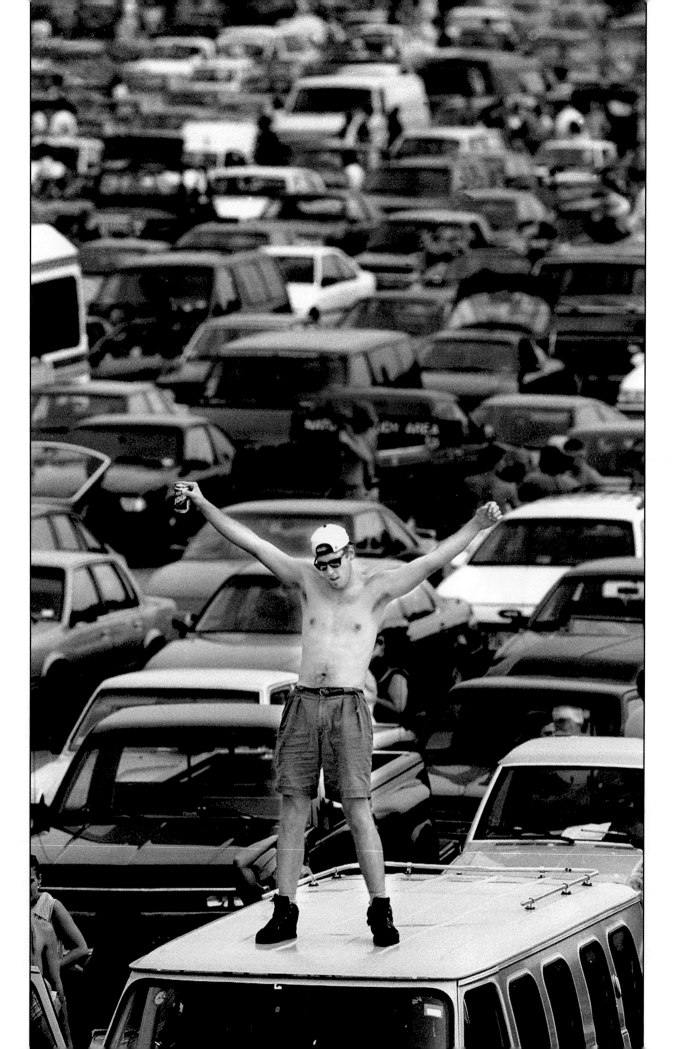

Covering the Issues

Photojournalism can bring about change. Since the turn of the century, on every continent on the globe, concerned photographers have brought to public awareness issues ranging from hunger and poverty to repression and torture. In the early twentieth century, Jacob Riis (page 343) exposed slum conditions suffered by new immigrants in New York City. Lewis Hine (page 345) sneaked into American factories to document industry's abusive use of children as laborers. During America's Great Depression, Dorothea Lang recorded bread lines and crop failures for the Farm Security Administration (FSA).

The combination of Pearl Jam, booze and teenagers equals one big party. "It's what everybody does, and it brings us together," says one concert fan. Research shows first use of alcohol usually begins around age 13. Drunken driving is the leading cause of death among young Americans. Brian Plonka, [Spokane, Washington] *Spokesman-Review*

More recently, David Peterson updated the farm story with pictures depicting farm crises in Iowa. Stephanie Welsh photographed controversial female genital mutilation rites in Africa. David and Peter Turnley documented the horrors of apartheid in South Africa, and Sebastiao Salgado showed the horrific working conditions endured by gold mine laborers in South America.

These are all examples of passionate photographers who believed that the world might care if the visual truth were told. They were all willing to find a way to shoot their stories and then to share their work with the public.

Not all of these projects righted the social wrongs they documented. But in **The Power of Photography**, Vicki Goldberg does track down cases where photography played a direct role in solving a social problem or even changing a country's policies. She attributes the passage of the Civil Rights Act, in part, to photos by Charles Moore that appeared in *Life* magazine. Moore covered demonstrations and sit-ins in Birmingham, Alabama, in the early 1960s. His pictures showed African Americans being attacked by snarling police dogs and blasted by water canons. Moore's unforgettable images helped put public opinion solidly behind the Civil Rights movement.

Malcolm Browne's picture of a Buddhist monk setting himself afire to protest repression of Buddhism in Vietnam (page 199); Eddie Adams' photo of a public execution by the Saigon police chief (page 326); and Nick Ut's photo of a napalm-burned little girl screaming in pain all had a cumulative effect on American policy in Vietnam. These and other images helped build an opposition to the Vietnam War that eventually led to U.S. withdrawal.

Today, some progressive news organizations give photographers time to cover stories. Carol Guzy (pages 78–83) spent weeks in Haiti, the Sudan, Somalia, and Ethiopia for in-depth stories for the *Washington Post*. Melanie Stetson Freeman traveled around the world photographing a series on the exploitation of children (below) for the *Christian Science Monitor*. Eugene Richards shot for months while covering the cocaine epidemic for *Life*.

When assignments fail to materialize, photographers often turn to grants to help underwrite their projects. Alan Berner received a grant from the National Press Photographers

The photographer traveled around the world to produce a series titled "Children in Darkness, the Exploitation of Innocence." These children in India are forced to beg for money.
Melanie Stetson Freeman, *Christian Science Monitor*

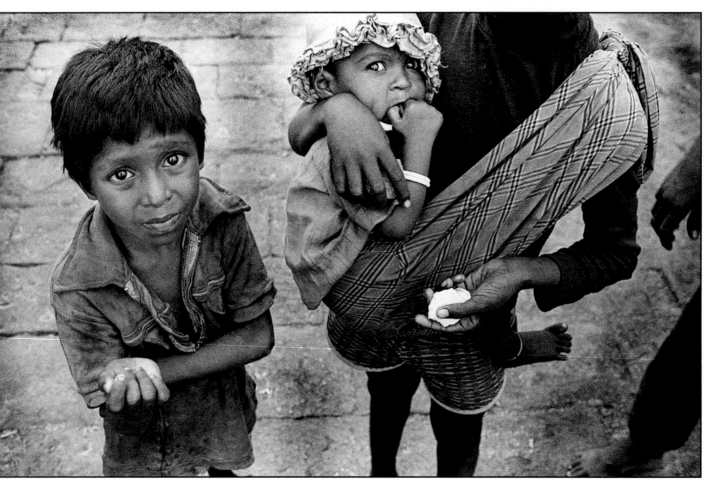

Association and Nikon to explore the changing face of the West (pages 76–77). John Kaplan's powerful story on torture in Africa (pages 74–75) was largely self-funded, but he did receive help from a University of Florida summer research grant.

This author received a Freedom Forum stipend to partially underwrite a project on children born to crack-addicted mothers (pages 72–73). The Guggenheim, the Alexia Foundation, and Fifty Crows Foundation are among other grantmakers that support photojournalists.

Other photographers have undertaken projects on their own time and dime. David Guralnick flew to Bucaramanga, Colombia, in South America, at his own expense, to photograph American plastic surgeons providing free medical help to children born with harelips and other disfigurements. Without backing or assurance of publication, Ken Light photographed the Mississippi Delta region of the United States (page 140). Andrea Hoyer self-funded a five-year project documenting the remains of Stalinist Russia. In addition to shooting, the project involved learning several languages while living in and traveling throughout the country (page 379).

Some photographers work alone. The *Boston Globe*'s Stan Grossfeld, a former winner of the Pulitzer Prize, shoots his own picture stories and often writes the accompanying text. Other photographers work in teams. The entire staff of the *Long Beach Press-Telegram*, for example, followed the path of a killer bullet from its use in a murder through the accused killers' trial. See pages 68–72, "Developing a Feature Beat," for how one group developed a beat to tackle a large project.

Some photographers like collaborating with a writer. Photographer Michael Williamson worked with writer Dale Maharidge on projects including *Journey to Nowhere: The Saga of the New Underclass*, which documented the effects of lost jobs.

The photographer/writer team also coauthored *The Last Great American Hobo*, about riding the rails in America. And the team produced a book called *And Their Children After Them*, a follow-up to the famous book from the 1930s, *Let Us Now Praise Famous Men*, which itself was a collaboration between a writer, James Agee, and Walker Evans, a Farm Security Administration (FSA) photographer.

Williamson and Maharidge published their extensive projects as books. While only a few documentary photojournalism projects wind up in bookstores, many are published as special sections or multipart series in newspapers, as a series of double-truck layouts in magazines, or as online slide shows.

While some newspapers and magazines make room for these projects, others won't give up the space for photo-driven stories. Fortunately, the World Wide Web is an excellent outlet for in-depth projects. Still other photographers have found ways to share their stories with the public by exhibiting their pictures in cafés and art galleries.

Perhaps as important as how photojournalists choose to work on and share their projects is how they identify the topics to pursue. Here is where their journalistic skills come in.

ISSUE REPORTING
NURSING HOMES: A CASE STUDY
Translating numbers into people
In California, investigators determined that over a three-year period, poor care in state nursing homes was a factor in 126 deaths. San Jose's *Mercury News* decided to investigate the findings.

Mercury News reporters discovered that "An aide shook a 74-year-old man in Long Beach so violently, an investigator said, that his brain was slammed against his skull 'like a clapper in a bell.'" Nurses diligently charted the progression of bedsores on an 81-year-old woman in Los Gatos until there was "black stuff oozing from her body"—but failed to save her life.

Photographing Statistics
The paper's graphics editor assigned Judy Griesedieck to illustrate the series.

PROBLEM ONE: The subjects of the story, the abused elderly, were dead and buried.

THE SOLUTION: Photograph current treatment of the elderly in nursing homes.

PROBLEM TWO: Nursing home owners and managers, aware of the stories the paper had already published, did not want a *Mercury News* photographer anywhere near their nursing homes.

THE SOLUTION: Griesedieck started the assignment by calling twenty nursing homes. Only two said she could come in and look around. The paper's lawyer pointed out that while nursing homes were private property, Griesedieck could enter and photograph with an invitation from one of the residents. She could photograph the person who invited her without being evicted by the management.

Gaining Access
To meet people in the homes, Griesedieck attended meetings of Bay Area Advocates of

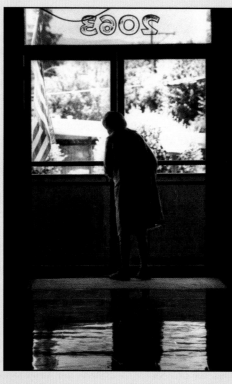

CALIFORNIA'S NURSING HOMES: NO PLACE TO DIE

Judy Griesedieck bypassed nursing home officials to develop relationships with families and doctors who allowed her to photograph the conditions of neglect in the nursing homes. She balanced her hard-hitting pictures of neglect with pictures showing love and care by staffers as well as by family. Judy Griesedieck, for the [San Jose, California] *Mercury News*

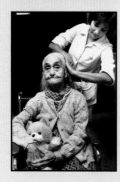

(ABOVE) Awilda Olmoa, a nurse's aide, combs the hair of 100-year-old Gregoria Santos.

(BELOW) A nursing home resident sits alone and neglected for hours.

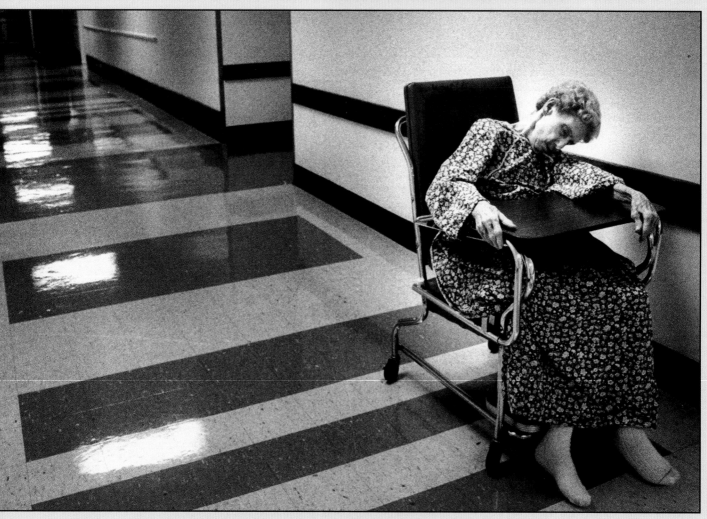

Nursing Home Reform. Most members were relatives of people in nursing homes. They were happy to introduce the *Mercury News* photographer to their mothers, fathers, wives, and husbands who were living with inadequate care. With invitations from people she met through the Advocates, Griesedieck began to shoot the story.

In one home, a daughter brought Griesedieck to see her mother. The older woman had bedsores because of neglect. In another home, a patient would be in bed at 9:00 a.m. and would still be there—undressed, unattended, with no outside stimulation—when the photographer left at 5:00 p.m.

But Griesedieck also found evidence of love and compassion at the nursing homes. The *Mercury News* photographer watched a man who visited his wife daily, bringing his spouse a rose on each visit. The husband said to Griesedieck, "I don't think she knows who I am," and started crying.

Griesedieck also entered nursing homes by accompanying a doctor who treated Alzheimer's disease. Here, too, she had to get permission from every patient or guardian before she could take pictures.

The photographer also made arrangements with the California Department of Health Services, which carries out unannounced inspections of nursing homes. The inspectors called Griesedieck on the mornings of surprise visits and, when possible, she followed the health service employees on their investigative raids.

Results

The four-part series in the *Mercury News* ran with Griesedieck's powerful pictures illustrating each day's stories. Under the headline "A Requiem of Neglect," reporters described the lack of care that caused each of the 126 deaths that had occurred over the previous three years. The series prompted the state to relaunch an investigation of California's nursing homes and its system for policing them. The series was a runner-up for the Pictures of the Year Canon Photo Essayist Award.

Griesedieck, however, continued to have nightmares about what she saw. Until leaving California, she continued to visit the people in several of the homes. "What I saw made me sad," she says. "I might be here some day. People in these homes had great careers—doctors, models—and now. . . ."

And now, at least, people do know about the situation in these homes and can take action because of solid investigative reporting and photography by Griesedieck and her fellow journalists.

INGREDIENTS FOR IN-DEPTH COVERAGE

Important issues

Griesedieck started with an important issue. Her paper had published a number of spot-news stories about deaths due to neglect in nursing homes and about official investigations. The paper had given each of the stories only inside play. In seeing the pattern generated by the numbers—noting the repetition of deaths due to neglect—the paper went beyond the individual news story.

The pictures and story attempted not only to document the phenomenon of needless death but also to show the cause of the problem—neglect.

Over the year-long project, Griesedieck tried to bring the statistics—126 deaths in state nursing homes caused by neglect—to light. She zeroed in on individual stories that provided examples of the larger trend.

She showed Carrie Chelucci being checked for bedsores. She showed Lucille Dennison, who has Alzheimer's disease, asleep in her wheelchair in the hallway of a locked wing in the home. Equally important, Griesedieck balanced these hard-hitting images with those showing tenderness and care on the part of some attendants and doctors.

Time

Like most investigative projects, Griesedieck's took time. The paper made a commitment of resources—a commitment of one photographer's time. Although she did not work full-time shooting this story alone, the paper gave her sufficient time from her daily shift to research the issue, make contacts, telephone possible subjects, and wait for their responses. Many news outlets think nothing of assigning a reporter for weeks or even months on an investigative story. Unfortunately, most fail to provide sufficient time for good visual reportage.

Display

Obviously, the photographer needed to make powerful images for the series, and Griesedieck's pictures were superb. Equally important, however, the images needed a showcase. The *Mercury News* featured a large lead picture on page one each day the series ran. Its editors also used photos extensively inside.

CONTINUED, PAGE 68

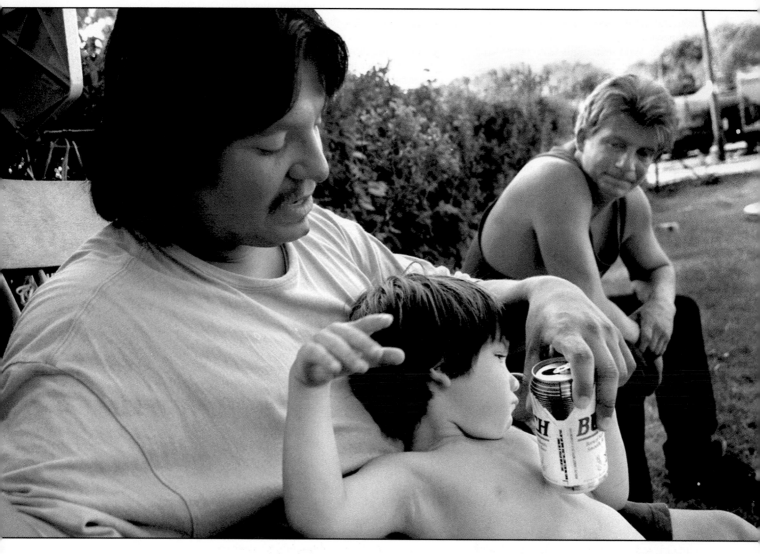

ALCOHOL: BRINGING US TOGETHER

Photos by Brian Plonka
[Spokane, Washington]
Spokesman-Review

(ABOVE) For some, the introduction to alcohol comes early. Three-year-old James Donato Ramirez rebuffs his father's attempt to share a beer. "It doesn't smell good," says James.

"**A**lcohol can be a legitimate and joyous influence in our everyday lives," writes photographer Brian Plonka, of the *Spokesman-Review* in Spokane, Washington. "It is with us in the locker room when we toast championships. It joins us at the dining room table for family celebrations."

Plonka spent more than two years focusing his camera on the impact of alcohol on American society. He calls his project "an attempt to put faces on an issue that is so tightly woven into society's tapestry that we often don't realize when it is causing our own lives to unravel."

Plonka and his editors laid out the package to show alcohol "bringing us together" and "tearing us apart." The sixteen-page special edition also showed alcohol's influence on the young, on adults, on one family, and on a single person undergoing therapy. These four pages include but a few photographs from the extensive investigation.

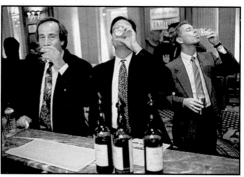

(ABOVE) For many, like these businessmen at the Scotch Malt Whiskey Society in Chicago, tasting alcohol loosens the tongue and tightens the bonds of friendship. Some 26,000 members strong, the Scotch Malt Whiskey Society is the world's largest drinking club.

(BELOW) "Come on, man. Do it!" says a buddy prompting his friend to guzzle from a beer bong at a Northern Illinois University party. The friend sucks beer from a tube attached to a funnel: total consumption time for 12 ounces—less than 10 seconds.

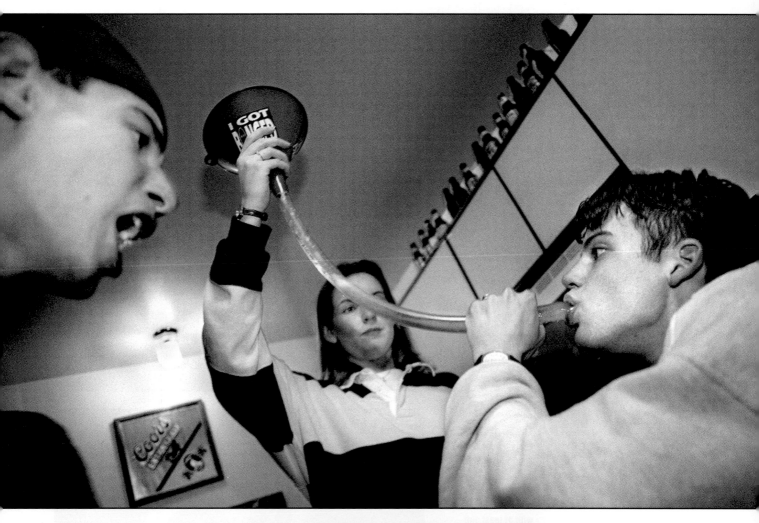

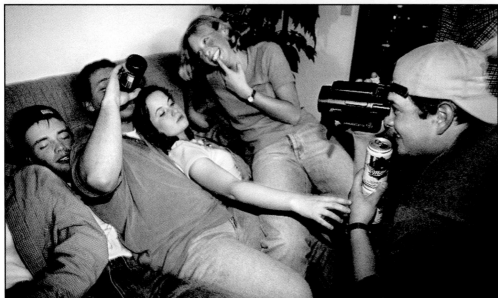

(LEFT) Students "wind down" after a week of classes with beer and liquor. Some say they like the carefree mood alcohol gives them; others say they like the way it allows them to let down their guard.

ALCOHOL:
TEARING
US APART

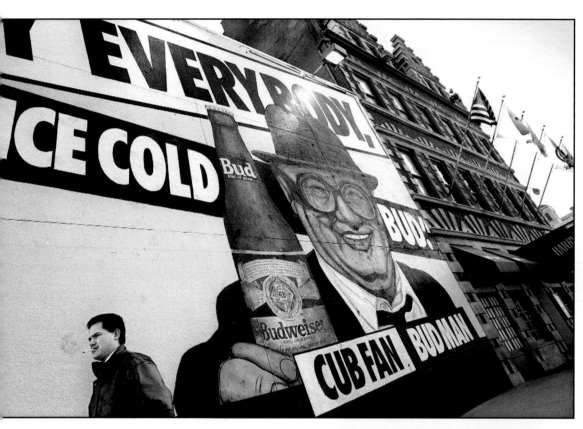

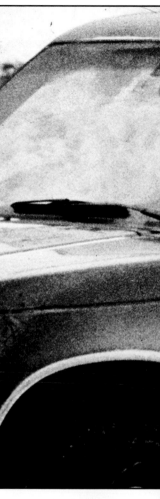

(ABOVE) In an effort to reach potential customers, alcohol companies spend hundreds of millions of dollars a year promoting their products.

SOBERING STATISTICS

- Alcohol abuse costs society an estimated $116 billion a year.

- As many as 6.6 million children live with at least one alcoholic parent.

- Alcohol is associated with up to half of all traffic fatalities.

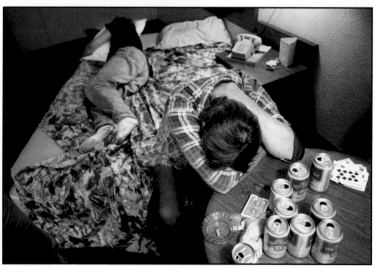

(ABOVE) Three cases of beer take a toll on men at a poker party at a cheap motel. After several hours of drinking, card playing becomes impossible.

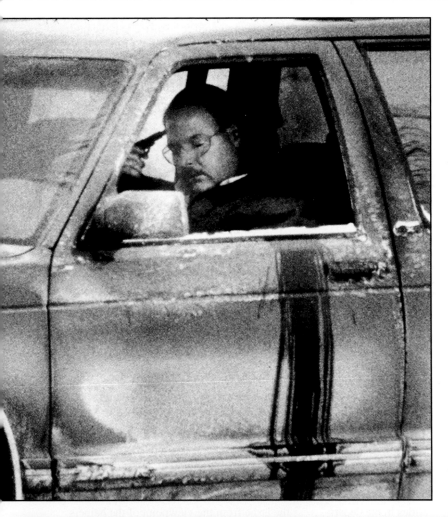

(LEFT) After Virgil Carmichael lost his job, he began drinking heavily in his car. After failing to get attention by smashing a bottle of booze against his door, he placed a pistol to his head. The incident was resolved peacefully.

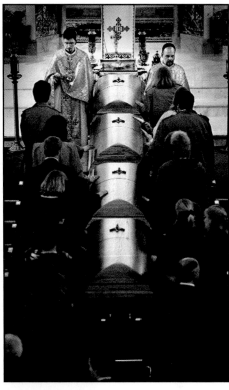

(ABOVE)
Friends and family pay their last respects to Peter Sawczuk, his wife, Sharon, and their daughters, Elizabeth and Kathryn. The entire family was killed by an 18-year-old alleged drunk driver as they drove to their summer home.

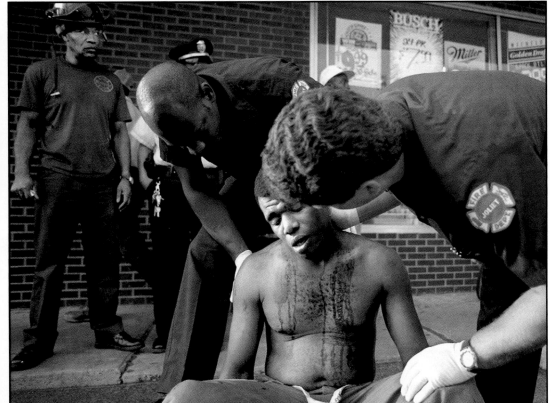

(LEFT) A dispute over the rationing of a six-pack results in a companion shoving this man's head through a liquor-store window.

BACKGROUNDING THE NEWS

"No Place to Die: California's Nursing Homes" is an outstanding example of "backgrounding" the news, a term Sidney Kobré, the author's father, a journalist and journalism professor, coined in a book by that name written in 1939.

Backgrounding means explaining the cause of a news story. Backgrounding means applying psychology, sociology, and economics to a news event to put it into perspective. While photography is an excellent medium for recording the immediate—the fire, the accident—photos can also explain. In the future, with television's instant reportage of breaking news, still photography will find an increasingly important role in providing in-depth coverage that identifies patterns and explains causes.

DEVELOPING A FEATURE BEAT

Another way to produce meaningful photojournalism projects is to develop your own specialty area—a beat.

For years writers have pried loose news by covering a beat. Typical beats include police, hospital, and courts. Reporters on police beats check the precinct headquarters each day to see what is going on. They look over the police blotter and talk to the sergeant to find out if anyone reported a major or unusual crime during the night.

Getting the inside track on current investigations, reporters find out about possible suspects. They know when the police plan to carry out a gambling raid or drug bust. They also get to know personalities in the department—the seasoned police officer as well as the new rookie fresh from the police academy. From these contacts and observations, beat reporters don't just react to the news; they also can interpret and anticipate it.

If the police go on strike, they can explain why. If a cop dies in the line of duty, they can write a story based on personal knowledge of the officer.

Feature photographers—whether they work on the staff of a news outlet or work independently as freelancers—can also cover a beat. Rather than choosing the police, hospital, or courts, they might select education, science, medicine, or religion.

GETTING THE IDEA

Sometimes a beat can grow out of one story. In the mid-1980s, the author happened upon volunteers assembling panels of the AIDS quilt: each piece a memorial to a person who had died of the disease, and the whole a testimony to the collective toll that the disease had taken.

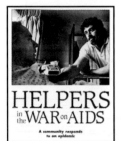

Magazine about those who helped people with AIDS. (Cover photo by Annie Wells.)

Though "The Names Project" since has been displayed in venues around the world, only its volunteers knew about it at the time. After photographing a story about the quilt and the people working on it for *People* magazine, the author did another story about an AIDS volunteer, entertainer Rita Rockett, who threw catered brunches and performed every other Sunday for AIDS patients on Ward 5A of San Francisco General Hospital.

It turned out that there were many unsung volunteers at work in San Francisco to help the growing number of people afflicted with the deadly disease.

PAST STORIES ON THE TOPIC

By 1987, there had been several excellent photo stories on people with AIDS. Steve Ringman, who was with the *San Francisco Chronicle* at the time, Cheryl Nuss at San Jose's *Mercury News*, and Alon Reininger for Contact Press Images had all photographed moving stories. Each had concentrated on patients' battles against the agonizing deaths they faced.

A new angle would focus on the outpouring of support in the San Francisco Bay Area to provide emotional, physical, and economic help to people with the incurable disease. The resulting photo project, produced by journalism students at San Francisco State University (SFSU), was eventually called "Helpers in the War on AIDS."

While the original identification and later unraveling of the cause of AIDS provided the basis of important news stories, approaching the issue from the viewpoint of the helpers gave the story a new twist.

ORGANIZATION

One photographer could photograph the AIDS "beat." However, in this instance, "Helpers in the War on AIDS" became a group project at SFSU's journalism department. Each student photographer researched, developed, and photographed three stories over a fourteen-week period. In addition to taking pictures, all group members either worked with writers or provided the text for the project's stories themselves.

RESEARCH

Before photography began on the project, the group brought in experts in order to learn about AIDS and to get story leads. Specialists ranged from San Francisco's Health Department expert on AIDS to journalists who had been tracking the story for several years. All group members read ***And the Band Played On***, a book by gay journalist Randy Shilts that analyzed the government's delayed and inadequate response to the growing epidemic. Other leads came from classified listings in local gay newspapers. Chris Adams, a student writer in the group who has since died from the AIDS virus, provided a key link to the gay community.

Having a beat gives a focus to research, and research directs you beyond the facts to investigate a problem's causes, solutions,

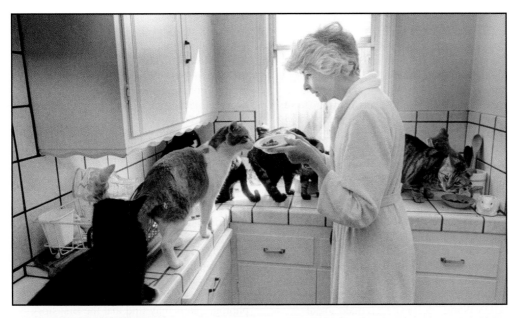

◄ **Knowing how much people love their pets, volunteers for PAWS (Pets Are Wonderful Support) care for pets when their owners, who have AIDS, are in the hospital. The volunteers then help find new homes when the owners die.** Mary Calvert, from *Helpers in the War on AIDS*

▼ **When a group of photojournalists collaborated on a beat focusing on helpers in the war on AIDS, a host of stories unfurled, including one about volunteers who bring food to people too sick to cook.** Mary Calvert, from *Helpers in the War on AIDS*

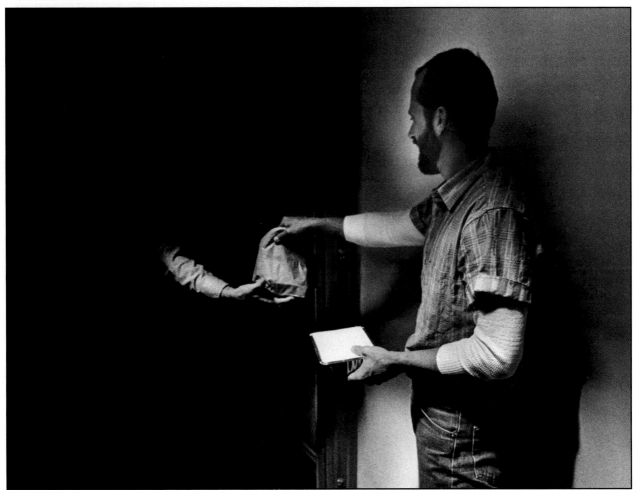

and, usually, stories that other journalists have not covered extensively.

INITIAL STORIES
To get a handle on such a large subject, the SFSU photographers divided the topic into sections, including medicine, religion, alternative healing approaches, minorities, physical support, and emotional support. Once the photographers selected subject areas, they began making telephone calls, and telephone calls, and more telephone calls. Then the photojournalists arranged for meetings with the subjects. Often these meetings involved no photography at all. For one story, photographer Annie Wells started by volunteering at the first private nursing home for people with AIDS on the West Coast.

Another of Wells's stories was called "The Godfather," about a man who raised money and then made wishes come true for hospital-bound AIDS patients. If someone needed a TV, The Godfather would provide it. If a bathrobe was lacking, The Godfather would bring one.

Kim Gerbich's story, "Mamacita of the AIDS World," followed a female social worker who cared for homeless people with AIDS living in a rundown transients' hotel.

Mary Calvert photographed a woman who cared for the pets of people with AIDS. Calvert also followed the work of volunteers for "Project Open Hand," an organization that provides meals for people shut in with AIDS. (See previous page.)

In the AIDS Ward at San Francisco General Hospital, one nurse allowed herself to be the subject of a story. Photographer Yvonne Soy tried to capture the life of a nurse who worked with people day after day knowing they would not live much longer.

The project's story list included a makeup artist who helped camouflage the ugly purple scars of Kaposi's Sarcoma that sometimes afflict people with AIDS. The list also featured a story about a faith healer and her work with the sick.

The list grew as the photographers dug deeper into the subject. Everyone knew someone who was helping out in the AIDS community.

Soon the photographers started to learn about people who helped prisoners with AIDS and volunteers who helped teen-age prostitutes avoid the disease.

START-UP PROBLEMS
After the photographers uncovered the initial leads for their stories, problems started to crop up. While many of the helpers were happy to have their pictures taken, sometimes their friends with AIDS did not want photos of themselves published. Some didn't want out-of-town friends to see them scarred by Kaposi's. Others didn't want people to know they were gay. Sometimes, the photographer would start on a topic, begin photographing the relationship between a helper and a patient, and, suddenly, the patient would die. The story would end before it began. Hospitals worried about lawsuits if the photos were published—even though the photographers obtained photo release forms from every subject.

"Helpers in the War on AIDS" was a difficult project to photograph.

ONE STORY LEADS TO ANOTHER
For good beat coverage, besides reading the daily papers and the special-interest gay newspapers, the photographers returned to their primary sources week after week for new leads. Sources such as research experts, specialized doctors, hotline workers, counselors, and friends with AIDS supplied suggestions for new stories.

Sometimes when working on a beat, photographers may find that the first story doesn't pan out. But it may lead to another, even better, opportunity—an opportunity a photographer might not have had without developing contacts in the field.

For example, while researching one story, photographer Sibylla Herbrich spoke at length with Ernie, who had AIDS. She asked him if he knew anyone doing extraordinary work with people who had the disease. He told the photographer that she must meet Annemarie.

Annemarie Madison, a striking woman with long silver hair and the smile of a saint, took the photographer with her as she went day after day to see her "boys." Annemarie's boys were men who, a few months earlier, had been in the prime of their lives. Now they were near death.

As a volunteer with the San Francisco Home and Health Care Hospice, Annemarie changed the men's beds, listened to their complaints and fears, and wiped saliva from their mouths. Whatever they needed, she provided. She was both a substitute mother and a father confessor. She was there to ease their pain and to provide dignity to their deaths. No pictures at first.

In the beginning, Herbrich came to know Annemarie and her "boys" before she brought out her camera. Then the photographer obtained permission to photograph from each person with whom Annemarie was working. Soon Herbrich was photographing everything.

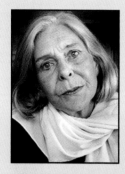

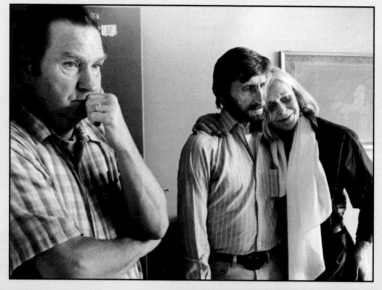

Annemarie Madison (FAR LEFT) is a volunteer hospice worker. (NEAR LEFT) Annemarie provides emotional support to the friends and relatives of Ernie, one of hundreds of her "boys" to die of AIDS. (BELOW) She comforts Ernie during his dying moments. These pictures are part of a story that was the product of a photographer's beat.

Sibylla Herbrich, from *Helpers in the War on AIDS*

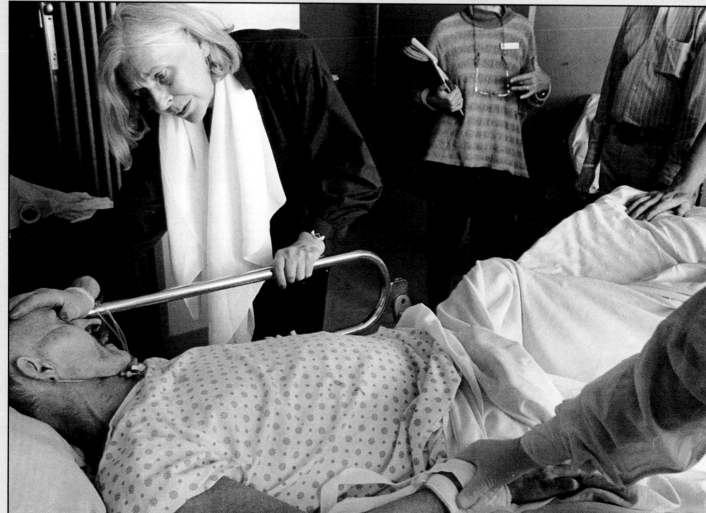

One Monday, the photographer accompanied Annemarie to the hospital to see Ernie, the man who had told Herbrich about Annemarie in the first place. On Wednesday, when Herbrich returned with the hospice worker, Ernie looked much worse. His friends were in the hospital room. Herbrich later wrote about that day:

"On the afternoon of June 9, for the first time I saw someone die. Ernie Smith died of AIDS at the age of 56. I photographed the hours of his dying and for two days I could not process the film. I stared at the one little roll that contained him in life and also in death. He died in the moment of the 'black space' between two frames. . . . I didn't sleep for a long time."

Herbrich's story, along with others in the project, was published in a seventy-six-page magazine named *Helpers in the War on AIDS*. The project won the national Sigma Delta Chi Award for feature photography and tied for first place in the college division of the Robert F. Kennedy Awards for Coverage of the Disadvantaged.

INFORMATIVE FEATURES REQUIRE EXTENSIVE RESEARCH

For more informative features, such as those produced in the "Helpers" project, you will need to perfect your skills as a reporter:
1) Pick an area of specialization.
2) Make contacts with experts in the field.
3) Become familiar with the issues and new trends on the subject.

Once you hear about a story that sounds interesting, arrange to photograph it. Often you will need to return several times to secure complete coverage. After shooting the pictures, you can write the captions and submit the feature series. You might suggest to your editor that a more detailed story by a reporter would amplify your series of pictures. To assure future stories on the subject, stay in touch with your sources. These contacts will tell you when something new happens that might make striking pictures.

Few news outlets will release photographers to work full time on their beats. You will probably need to work your special beat around routine assignments. Developing a feature area rarely produces great pictures on the first day. You need time for research. In the long run, though, a beat will generate meaningful feature pictures that will remain permanently in the viewer's memory. ∎

CRACK: THE NEXT GENERATION

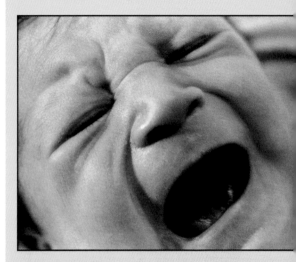

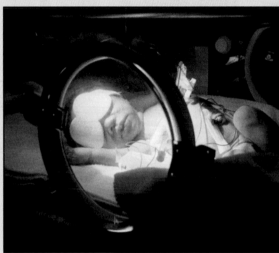

This project began as the first wave of children with what came to be known as Crack Baby Syndrome were entering the nation's public schools. At first, a prenatally drug-exposed child's prognosis was grim. Born prematurely to crack-addicted mothers, these children were thought by researchers to be living time-bombs—damaged mentally and physically and perhaps even a threat to society once they were grown. At one time, this group of children was even called the "lost generation." Recent research, however, shows that, with intervention, some prenatally drug-exposed babies can grow up healthy—emotionally, physically, and mentally. Reproduced here in part, this story looked at various stages of the lives of children born to crack-addicted mothers.

Conservative estimates suggest that at least 11 percent of all newborns in the United States today have been exposed in the womb to one or more illicit drugs. ∎

ADDRESSING THE PROBLEM
Ken Kobré

(LEFT ABOVE) Exposed to crack cocaine in the womb and born addicted, this newborn experiences severe withdrawal symptoms.
(LEFT BELOW) Addicted newborns are extremely sensitive to light. Covering their eyes helps them rest.

(BELOW) Bathing is one of the few ways nurses have found to comfort drug-exposed newborns. Soap and warm water soothe the frantic babies. The bath also removes the sweat that envelopes them as they go through withdrawal.

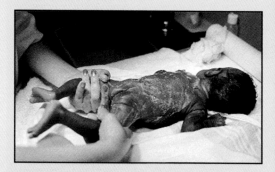

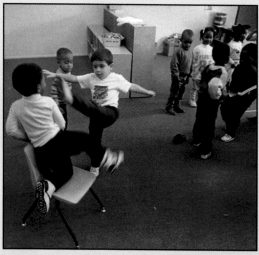

(LEFT) For some at-risk children, the slightest disruption sets off a temper tantrum, like this one. These children exhibit extreme mood swings. Researchers have learned that early intervention focusing on interaction with other children, individual work on children's problem areas, and parent counseling can help at-risk children improve significantly. These children are part of the Parent Child Intervention Program preschool in East Palo Alto, California.

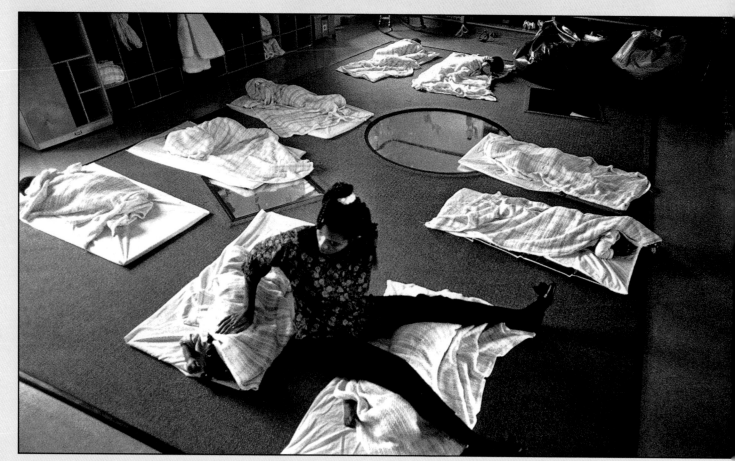

(ABOVE) To calm some of the at-risk children at nap time, a teacher stretches her legs across one child, holding the youngster down while massaging the back of another. The first group of students in the early intervention programs now being "mainstreamed" into classes with average children are showing signs of success.

John Sahr, 40 •Tongoma, Kailahun district, Sierra Leone

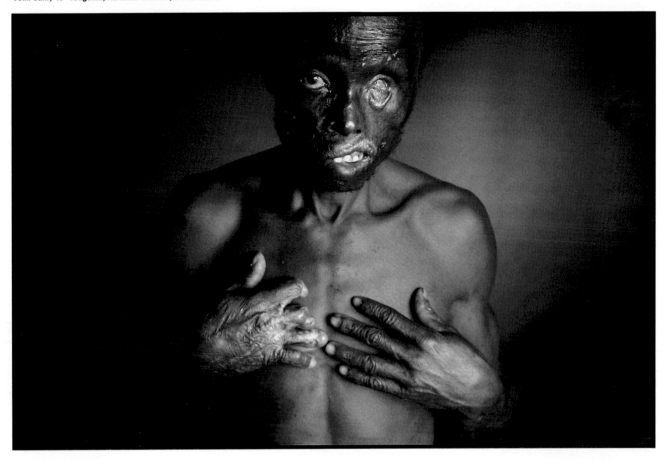

"I was captured in my village. They beat me mercilessly. I was tied and they pushed my head into boiling water. . . . They did not believe I would survive . . . . My message is, 'anything that comes your way as a human being, your condition should not lead you to feel you are not important. As long as you are alive, God has a plan for you.'"

•••

John Sahr was a farmer when his village was attacked in April 1991. He languishes in the Telikoro refugee camp and is unable to afford antibiotics and painkillers. Although physically able to work, he often is shunned by other refugees, who feel uncomfortable working alongside him.

LIVING TESTIMONY

Photos by John Kaplan

"Although the civil wars of Sierra Leone and Liberia have received coverage in the press, the increasingly relevant issue of torture has been largely under-reported," says photographer John Kaplan, who is a professor at the University of Florida.

Rebel warlords in Sierra Leone spread terror across this small West African nation by using mutilation as a weapon of war. In an attempt to terrify the population from joining the opposition, the rebels hacked off the hands, arms, and legs of ordinary civilians.

Kaplan, who previously won the Pulitzer Prize for feature photography, documented the aftermath of this brutality with portraits and first-person accounts from victims. The project was published over three pages in the *St. Petersburg Times*.

**Fayia Mondeh, 51
Seima, Kono district, Sierra Leone**

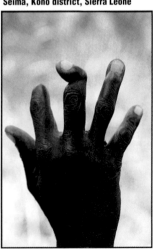

"'Lay down your hand,' they said. . . . Five were killed in my presence, as if normalcy."

•••

Fayia Mondeh was accosted on April 25th, 1998, when he was stabbed with a bayonet, hit on the head with a rifle, had his arm broken and two fingers hacked off his right hand. He had been a farmer in his village.

Fallah Mbayoh, 20 • Ylebema, Kailahun district, Sierra Leone

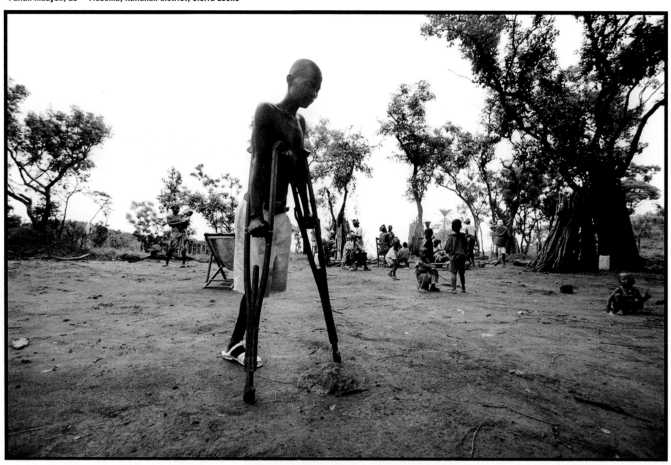

"When the rebels came, they said, 'We are freedom fighters. We have not come to destroy lives. Feel free to join us.'. . . I was 10 or 11."

●●●

After he was transported across the border to Guinea, Fallah Mbayoh was in and out of the hospital for five years. He dreams of a prosthetic leg or at least a tricycle that would allow him greater mobility. He now lives in the Telikoro refugee camp with his father, mother, and sisters. When the war ends in Sierra Leone, he hopes that his family will be able to return to its former home.

Tamba Saidu, 10 • Koidu, Kono district, Sierra Leone

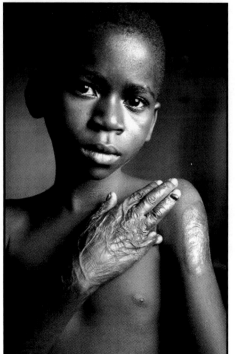

"What we should do is to learn to forgive those who have done this act. If we do not learn to forgive the war, it will continue to the next generation."

●●●

Tamba Saidu was 7 years old when his village was attacked by Revolutionary United Front rebels in February 1998. He ran to his grandmother's house but was grabbed by rebels. Tamba lives with his grandmother at the Kountaya refugee camp along with two uncles. His father and mother have found shelter in the nearby Boreah camp. He is now in grade four, taking classes at a makeshift refugee camp school. He dreams of being able to get a school uniform, shoes, and books.

PICTURES FROM A STRANGE & ORDINARY LAND

Photos by Alan Berner ©
Seattle Times

Alan Berner, who works for the *Seattle Times*, received a Nikon/NPPA Sabbatical grant to photograph "The West." His goal, he told *Seattle Times* writer Terry McDermott, was to photograph the West in the 1990s as Arthur Rothstein had done in the 1930s.

Rothstein had photographed the region for the Farm Security Administration (FSA) during the Great Depression. His assignment had been to document disaster. Berner's six-month photographic journey took place during the 1990s, a period of broad prosperity.

Berner's juxtapositions of the artificiality of modern life with the region's natural grandeur resulted in a variety of ironic images that capture late 20th-century Americans' relationship with the vast area known simply as the West.

As McDermott wrote in the story that accompanied the *Times*'s publication of Berner's images, "We once thought the West was so grand, so heroic, the landscape would automatically make heroes of those who strode it. No more. We have moved from being heroes to being almost inconsequential. Don't ever forget, these photographs warn, you're just a visitor. You're left with the overwhelming impression that people don't belong out here. The land is too powerful." ■

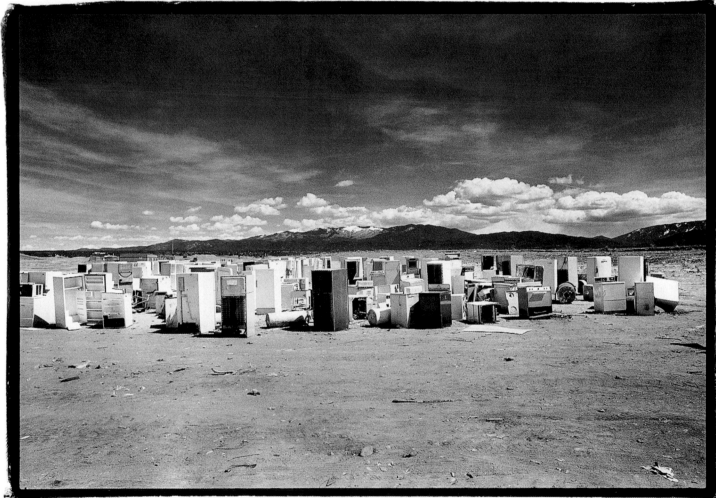

Santa Fe, New Mexico

(ABOVE) At this dump with a view, discarded refrigerators form their own artificial ridge line near Santa Fe, New Mexico. The Sangre de Cristo Mountains are in the background.

(BELOW) Chief Nelson Wallulatum of the Wasco Tribe and Col. Tim Wood of the U.S. Army Corps of Engineers break ground for new fishing sites being built where Bonneville Dam flooded traditional sites on the Columbia River. The sites were promised 56 years ago.

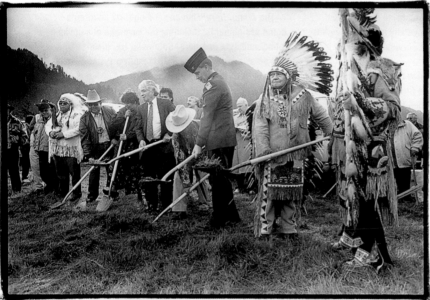

BREAKING GROUND

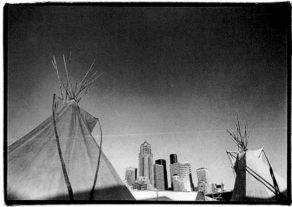

(BELOW) Tepees forming their own skyline at the annual Salmon Homecoming Celebration frame Seattle in the background.

Seattle, Washington

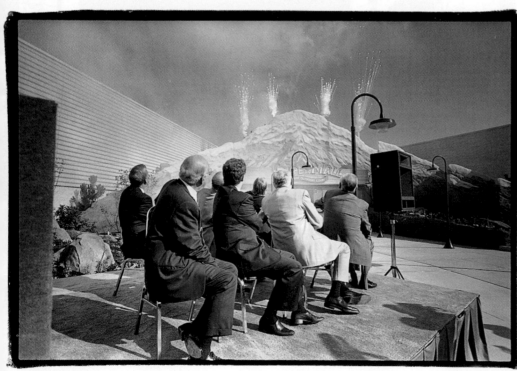

SuperMall
Auburn, Washington

(LEFT) Investors and dignitaries watch the "eruption" of the fake Mount Rainier front facade of the SuperMall at the mall's grand opening in Auburn, Washington, in 1995.

(This material is based on the author's interview with Carol Guzy and an article in *News Photographer Magazine* by Pete Souza.)

People who think of photojournalists in terms of the stereotypical movie version—hard-bitten, cynical, neurotically driven, competitive, and macho—miss the boat when it comes to one of the most celebrated news photographers of our time, the petite, unassuming *Washington Post* photographer Carol Guzy.

Guzy has covered some of the worst disasters, wars, famines, and conflicts occurring in the last decade of the twentieth century. From mud slides in Amero, Colombia, to the exodus in Rwanda, to famine in Ethiopia, to lawlessness and anarchy in Haiti, Guzy has photographed misery, murder, survival, and even moments of joy.

She has won the Pulitzer Prize twice, been selected Photographer of the Year three times by the National Press Photographers Association (NPPA), and been chosen White House Photographer of the Year seven times. These are but a few of her many awards.

This decorated photojournalist had set out to be a nurse, but an art school photography class pursued with her boyfriend's 35mm camera changed her life. Instead of applying for nursing positions, Guzy applied for an internship at the *Miami Herald*. Her work there led to a job in one the newspaper's suburban bureaus.

Independent of her regular assignments, she covered Miami's Haitian community during a time in which most media attention focused on Cuban immigrants. Guzy describes herself as working "twenty-four hours a day" on that project for a year.

Her commitment paid off. Based on her research and photos, the paper ran a special section on Miami's Haitian community. The pictures took top honors at the Atlanta photojournalism seminar and served as a springboard for her career.

The *Miami Herald* began sending Guzy on international assignments, including the coverage of a devastating mudslide in Amero, Colombia. Her pictures of that disaster earned her her first Pulitzer Prize, which she shared with Michel duCille.

After a burnout period that led to depression, she left the *Miami Herald* and went to work for the *Washington Post*, where she has covered everything from a homeless couple attending the first President Bush's inauguration to the U.S. Marines landing in Haiti to the crisis in Kosovo.

What's her secret?

"I really try to stay open—a childlike-wonder thing—trying to see it for the first time," she says. "I have a tremendous empathy. I imagine how someone else is feeling."

HAITIAN STREET JUSTICE

Photos by Carol Guzy
Washington Post

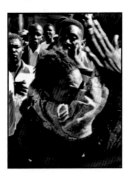

(ABOVE) There is no shelter for the man whom the crowd believes was part of a band of thieves that killed their beloved community leader.

(RIGHT) The man pleads for his life at the hands of the angry crowd of mourners who had just left the funeral of their community leader.

This can be a blessing and curse for a photographer, she observes. Guzy theorizes that her innate compassion might result from her own father's death when she was only six.

Guzy expresses her compassion both on assignment and in person in a thoughtful, subdued way. "I'm quiet by nature," she observes. "I'm horrible in social situations. I'm not the life of the party. But I think it helps in photo situations to be the way I am because they forget about me."

But Guzy also has incredible tenacity. "I have tremendous patience," she admits. "If you just wait a little while longer, something touching will take place."

The crash of TWA Flight 800 off Long Island, New York, tested Guzy's staying power. Dozens of photographers flew in to cover the tragedy's aftermath. Grieving families came to the beach to express their pain and leave mementos. For Guzy, the story was not over until the last family left.

She returned to the beach day after day to take pictures. On what turned out to be the last day family members came to the shore, one woman sat alone with a rose. That picture told the whole story. Other photographers shot one or two families on the first day and moved on to the next big news story, but Guzy stayed until she got the photo she was looking for. "Good enough is never enough," she says. She advises young photographers to stay a little longer and go the extra mile.

Whenever possible, Guzy tries to shoot "off" the main event. Covering the 1996 Democratic Convention, for example, she shot demonstrators outside more than the politicians inside the convention hall. "I tend to shoot the fringe as opposed to the mainstream stuff," she says.

Guzy's pictures run the gamut from intense violence to quiet, intimate moments. Her pictures in Haiti show a vigilante mob beating a man to death in the streets. Yet she maintains the ability to look for—and find—intimacy, as well.

Guzy spent a week in Mali photographing the nomads there. "It was a grueling week," she recalls. "The light and heat were brutal. The land was so stretched out it took me forever to go from one family to another. One morning was magical, however."

On that morning, the photographer saw two women walking together, their backs to her and her camera. One woman draped her arm over the other's shoulders. The tiny rear end of a naked baby appeared to be

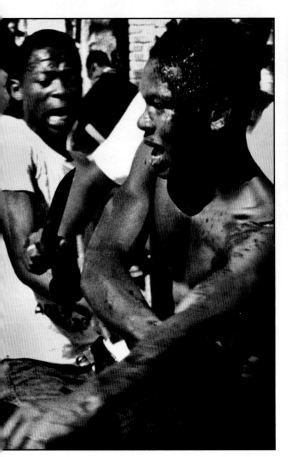

(LEFT) A knife finally ends the life of the suspected thief and murderer.

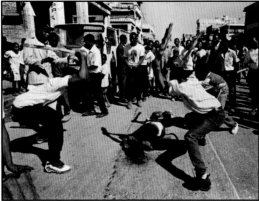

(ABOVE) The angry crowd continues to beat the man's lifeless body.

"I didn't look at these pictures for a long time . . .because I just couldn't deal with it. It was horrifying and there was a lot of guilt in thinking maybe I could have done something. I am sure in my heart that this man would have died no matter what I would have done. At first I was also not sure if I should show anyone these pictures, but I think they should be shown because the worst thing I could do would be to hide what is actually happening down there." — Carol Guzy, interview with Pete Souza, *News Photographer Magazine*

Photos by Carol Guzy
© *The Washington Post*

almost suspended between them. Guzy photographed the women as they continued on their way. At first glance, the viewer almost can't tell which woman carries the baby. Friendship, motherhood—it's all there in this one image, with nary a face to be seen. The magic was in "the moment" she seeks in all her pictures.

"I'm looking for little pictures. Moments of tenderness mean a lot," she explains. The response from editors, readers, and contest judges to the picture of the women and the baby was overwhelming. But perhaps Guzy's own mother puts it all into perspective. Examining the prize-winning picture, Guzy's typically American mother observed, "I can't understand it. It's a really cute picture, but why don't they have diapers on that baby?" "Everyone sees something different," Guzy says. "My mother looked at the picture like a mother, not as a photographer." ■

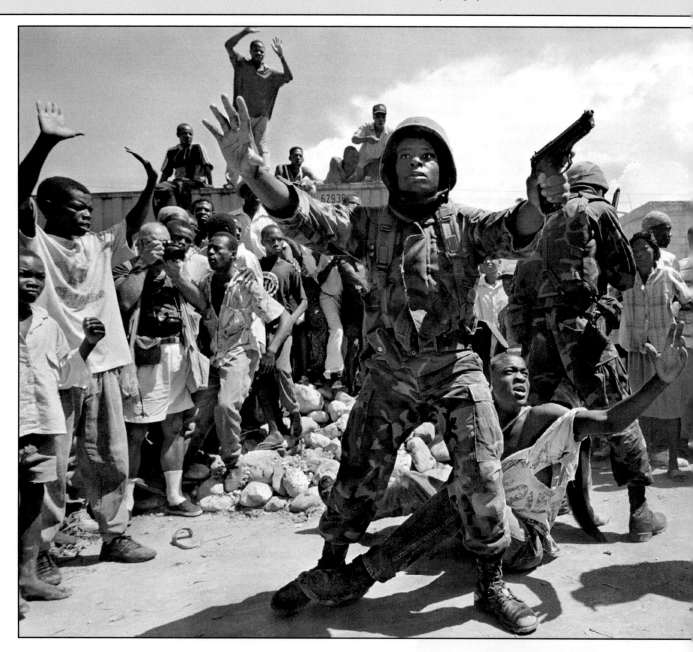

(ABOVE) A U.S. soldier orders the crowd to stand back after they tried to kill a man they thought had thrown a lethal grenade into a demonstration. U.S. troops had been sent to Haiti to restore some semblance of law and order. Guzy photographed from the front—an angle no other photographer got of this particular moment.

(RIGHT) Desert wanderers, the Nomadic Tuareg people of Mali live isolated lives. They roam the Saharan desert by camel with their meager belongings. Two friends walk from their tent with a child.

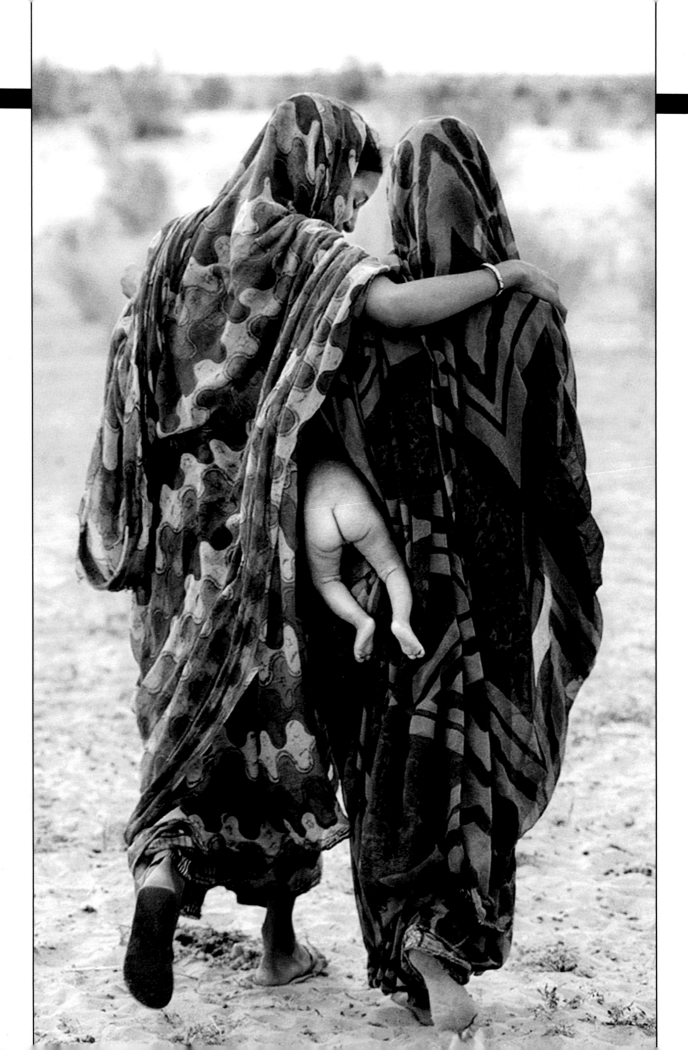

RWANDAN EXODUS

Photos by Carol Guzy
© *Washington Post*

Rwandan Hutu refugees began an exodus of biblical proportions as they left their camps in Zaire to return home after more than two years. The rebel movement in Eastern Zaire had used intimidation and fear to control the refugees' movements. Although apprehensive about returning to their country following the Tutsi genocide, the estimated one million refugees began their long trek. Along the way, the sick fell, people died, children were lost, and babies were born. Aid workers cared for people as they could and sent in trucks to move people home. Rwanda welcomed the refugees as joyful laughter of reunions with family and friends echoed in the land. — Carol Guzy

(BELOW) A young refugee walks past the body of a woman killed before she could return to her village.
"I saw the dead body, and I set up and waited for people to react," Guzy explains. "I used a telephoto to isolate. I cropped it in the camera to cut off distracting elements like a person's head because I wanted the focus to be on the kid."

(BELOW) Volunteer "body pickers" had poured lime on a mass grave in Mugunga camp in Zaire. Fierce fighting by rebels had released the hold on refugees by Hutu extremists. Many were killed as the exodus began.

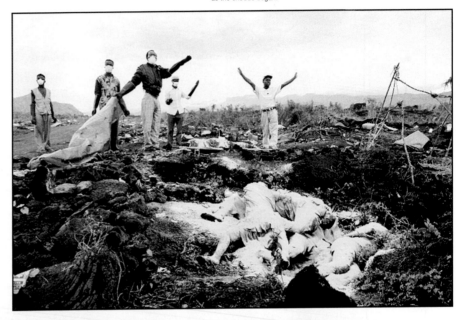

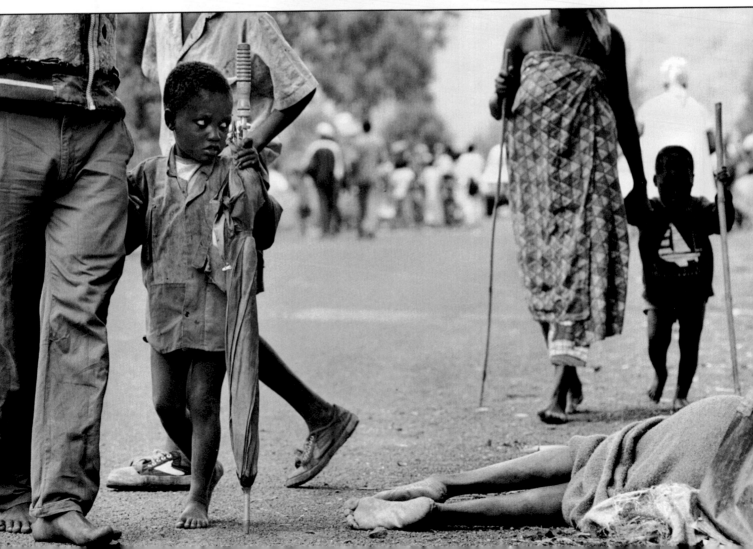

(BELOW) A baby lies near his gravely ill mother on the road from Gisenyl to Kigali, Rwanda. *"I watched for the child's eyes. They are the* *windows to his soul," says Guzy. "After I took the picture, I went to the Red Cross care center and told them to come and save the mother."*

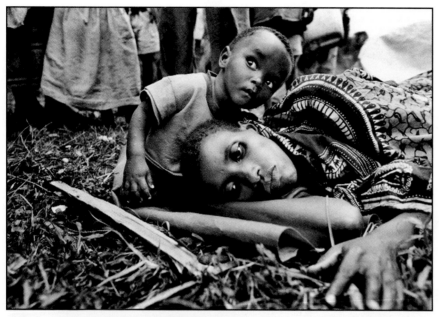

(BELOW) This exhausted Rwandan refugee breaks into tears when she is unable to scramble aboard a truck going to her home village.

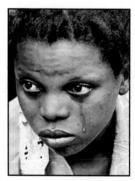

(BELOW) A refugee sees his father for the first time in more than two years as he returns to his village in Rwanda. *"I used a wide-angle lens in this situation,"* Guzy recalls. *"With so many people around, someone would block my view with a telephoto."*

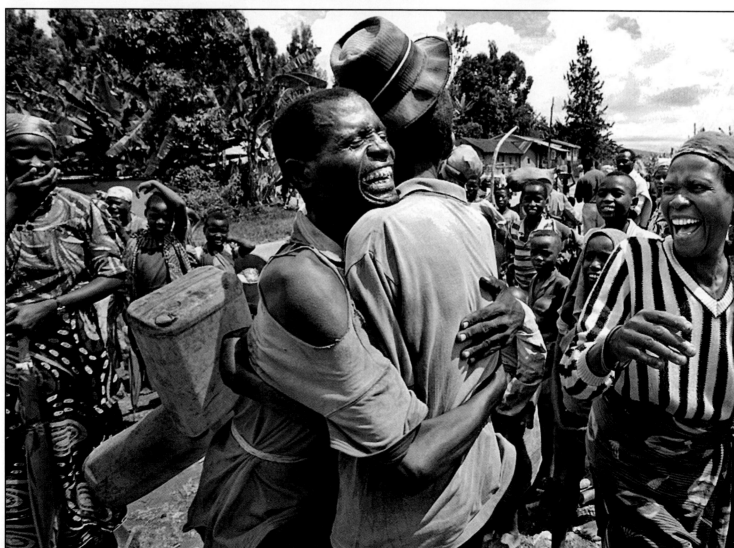

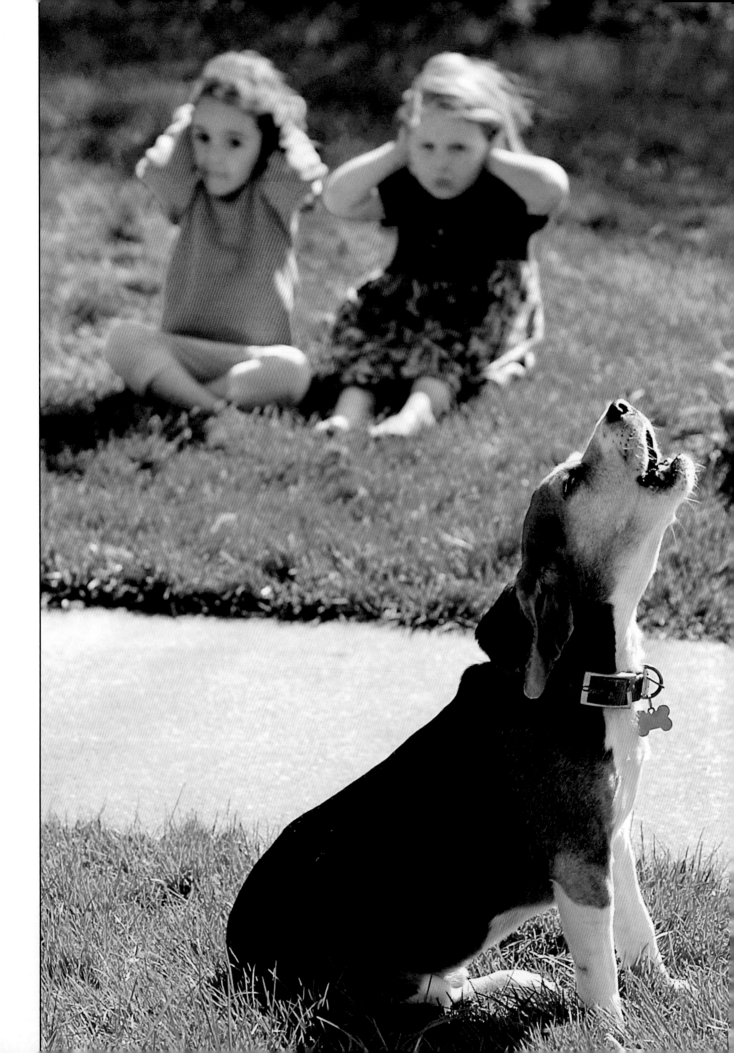

Chapter 5

Features

WHAT ARE FEATURES?

Feature photos provide a visual dessert to subscribers who digest a daily diet of accident, fire, political, and economic news. Many newspaper editors argue that because readers receive so much depressing news in the gray columns of type, subscribers deserve a break when they look at pictures. For some papers, feature pictures not only provide a diversion from the news and also have become the mainstay of the front page. Consistently, reader surveys show that people respond favorably to feature pictures. (See pages 198–201, Chapter 10, "Photo Editing," for more on reader preferences.)

Feature pictures provide a visual break from routine news. Two children cover their ears against the whistle of a passing train as Ruger, a 10-year-old beagle, howls in protest. Jennifer Jones, *Corvallis [Oregon] Gazette-Times*

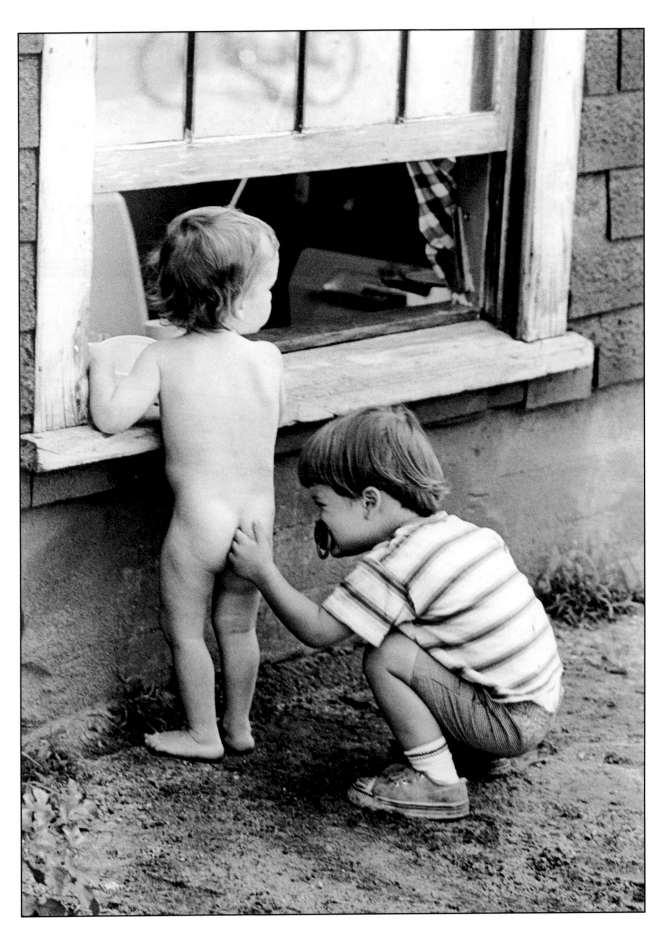

Cammie Toloui, an online photo editor for the *San Francisco Chronicle*'s *SFGate.com*, scouts the wire services everyday for fresh and funny features. Her gallery on the site, which contains lots of feature pictures, attracts nearly a million hits a day.

Features also allow newspapers to play up average citizens in circumstances other than accidents and other tragedies. Mark Johnson, a Massachusetts freelancer, argues that most feature pictures are interesting only to the people in the pictures. By contrast, Charlie Riedel, who shot for many years at the *Daily News* in Hays, Kansas, says feature pictures "freeze experiences in time so others can scrutinize them." Gordon Converse, who worked for the *Christian Science Monitor* for more than twenty years, described feature photography as the "search for moments in time that are worth preserving forever."

For Mark Hertzberg, director of photography at the *Journal Times*, in Racine, Wisconsin, "the measure of a newspaper's success is how many of these moments are in clippings held onto readers' refrigerator doors with magnets."

HOW FEATURES AND NEWS DIFFER
TIMELESSNESS
Feature photos differ from news photos in several respects. A news picture portrays something new. Because news is timely, news pictures get stale quickly. Many feature pictures, on the other hand, are timeless. Feature pictures don't improve with time, as good wine does, but neither do they turn sour. Some newspapers, in fact, refer to features as evergreens. Like evergreen trees, feature photos never turn brown. Wire service photos showing President Bush giving his inaugural speech carry little interest today. Yet feature pictures like those in this chapter will long retain their holding power.

SLICE OF LIFE
A news picture accrues value when (1) its subject is famous, (2) the event is of large magnitude, or (3) the outcome is tragic.

A feature picture, by contrast, records the commonplace, the everyday, the slice of life. The feature photograph, sometimes called "wild art," "stand-alone art," or "evergreen," tells an old story in a new way, with a new slant. Two children playing games at a day-care center will not change the state of world politics, but the photo might

◄
A feature picture records the commonplace, an everyday happening, or a slice of life. A child's curiosity at the Harvard day-care center is a natural feature subject. Ken Kobré, for *Boston Phoenix*

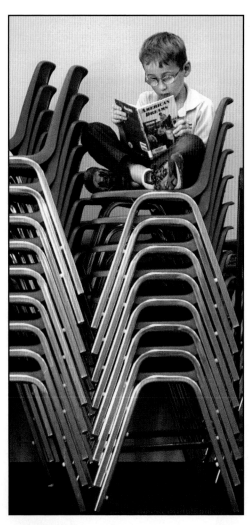

The photographer recognized the commonplace act of reading as a feature when he noticed the child atop a stack of chairs. Michael Wilson, *Ledger* [Lincoln, Illinois]

capture a funny moment and provide a feature picture. A child reading a book atop a stack of chairs provides the reader with a refreshing look at ingenuity.

With hard news, the event controls the photographer. Photojournalists jump into action when their editor assigns them to cover a plane crash or a train wreck. When they reach the scene, they limit their involvement to recording the tragedy.

As a feature photographer, on the other hand, you often can generate your own assignments. In fact, many newspapers call features "enterprise pictures."

What kind of enterprise might you employ to find great features? You might arrange to spend the day shooting photos of a man who makes artificial arms and legs. Or you might head to a school for dog groomers to find a student learning how to clip a poodle.

"FEATURIZING" THE NEWS
News does not stop with fires and accidents, and features don't begin with parks and kids. The division between these two types of pictures is not that clear-cut. The sensitive

photographer, for instance, could uncover features even at a major catastrophe. This is called "featurizing the news." The main story might describe a fire's damage to an apartment house, and give a list of the injured and dead. The news photo might show the firefighter rescuing the victims with the building burning in the background.

For a news feature, the photographer might take a photo of a firefighter being kind to a dog. This picture, along with a caption about the canine rescue, might be printed as a sidebar alongside the main story and photos, which would concentrate on the residents' injuries and the general damage to the building. Likewise, a picture of a driving school student in a wrecked car bearing the school's name straddles the line between news and features.

UNIVERSAL EMOTIONS

Great feature pictures, and there are few, evoke a reaction in the viewer. When viewers look at a powerful feature photo they might laugh, cry, stand back in amazement, or peer more closely for another inspection. If so, the photo has succeeded.

Some features are even universal in their appeal. They will get a response no matter in which country they are shown. When individuals in Europe, Asia, and Africa respond to the same photo, then the photographer has tapped into the universally understood language of feature pictures.

The term feature picture tends to serve as a catchall category. In fact, some writers define features as "anything that's not news."

Yet many pictures fit into neither the news nor the feature category. Snapshots from a family album, for example, don't really belong in either pigeonhole.

GOOD FEATURE SUBJECTS

Years back, each time a new photographer was hired by Florida's *St. Petersburg Times and Independent*, a veteran staffer would draw the newcomer aside to explain the secret ingredients of the feature picture.

"Friend," he would say, "if you need a feature picture for today's edition, you can't go wrong by taking photos of kids, animals, or nuns wearing habits."

These were not bad words of advice because a large percentage of published

Few fender benders merit photographic coverage—except when the driver is a trainee at the Easy Method Driving School. While serious to the student driver, this minor accident takes on the properties of a funny feature photo. J.M. Eddins, Jr., Patuxent [Maryland] Publishing Co.

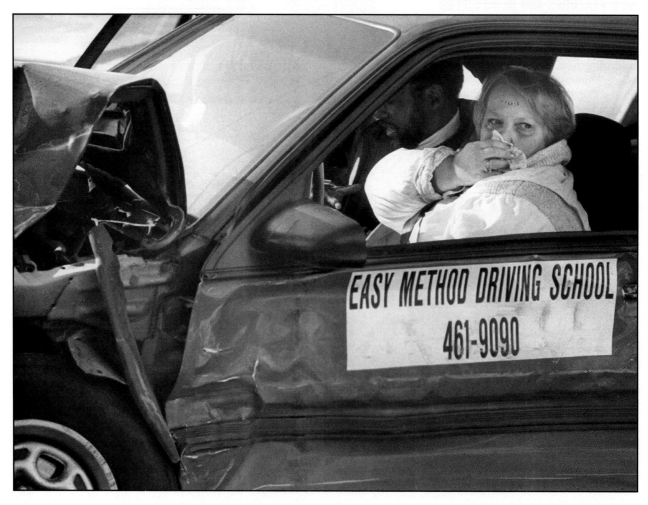

feature pictures includes kids, animals, and, sometimes, even nuns.

Kids Imitating Adults

Photographers find children to be relatively easy and willing subjects because they act in natural ways, play spontaneously, and look cute. "Kids are good subjects for features because they are uninhibited," says Charlie Riedel in Kansas. "They tend to be themselves. They don't have anything to prove to anyone." To grownups, children seem particularly funny when they imitate adult behavior. The child often acts as a mirror, showing the adult how grown-up behavior appears to the younger generation.

Ulrike Welsch, a specialist in photographing children when she worked for the *Boston Globe*, always asked permission of parents before photographing youngsters. "That way the parent does not become suspicious and does not interrupt the shooting," Welsch explains. If a parent is not around, Welsch would ask the child to lead the way to the adult, giving Welsch the opportunity to secure the permission. Although asking permission interrupts the child's activity,

Welsch notes that, as soon as the parent gives the go-ahead, the child almost always quickly resumes his or her natural play.

Given the unhappy reality of today's headlines of child molestation and kidnapping, this advice has never been more on target.

The Incongruous

A photo of a revolutionary soldier making a telephone call looks incongruous because revolutionary soldiers and modern telephones don't seem to go together. These kinds of features often have an ironic twist. And a picture of a technician appearing to be peering into the posterior of a prehistoric predator will always provoke a chuckle. Such photos provide eye-catching features. (See page 90.)

People Like People

Clearly, the feature does not restrict photographers to picturing only kids, animals, and nuns, although whenever you can include these elements in a picture, the photo has a greater chance for publication. People of any age prove fascinating when they labor or learn, play or pray.

A technician readies a robotic dinosaur for a tail connection. Even extinct animals make for fun features. Robert Cohen, for the *Memphis Commercial Appeal*

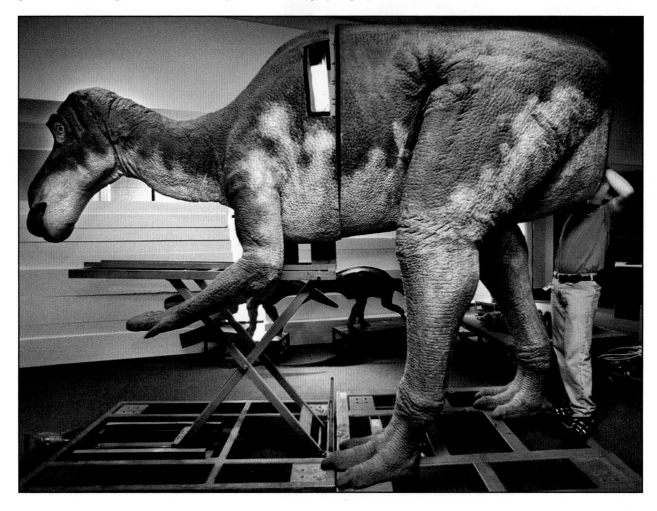

Animals Acting Like People

People commonly attribute human traits to animals. People respond to pictures in which pigs seem to smile or chimps look bored—and camels kiss cute little girls. Pet lovers often believe their animals exhibit human

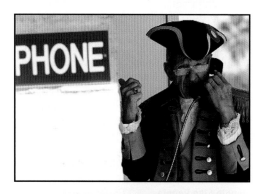

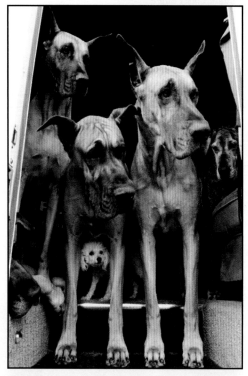

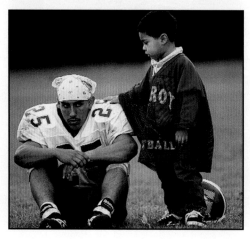

emotions and treat their animals as if they were little human beings. Dog fanciers feed their pooches at the dinner table, dress them in sweaters for walks, and at night tuck them in velvet beds. Such idiosyncrasies supply the material for good features.

DISCOVERING FEATURES
KEEP A FRESH EYE

To keep a fresh eye for features, Ulrike Welsch drives to an area she's never seen before. The experience is similar to traveling to a new country, even though the place might be only a few miles away. Whenever you live in the same place for awhile and see the same things daily, you grow accustomed to your surroundings.

Psychologists call this phenomena "habituation." Feature photographers face the same problem. They come to accept as commonplace the unique aspects of the areas they live in and cover.

"Whenever I go to a new place, even if it's just a little way down the road, everything is novel," Welsch points out. She notices and photographs the differences between the new environment and her familiar territory. When she first arrives, her eye is sharpest.

Those first impressions usually lead to her best photos. "I take pictures I might have overlooked if the subjects were in my backyard," she says.

When called on for a feature picture by 5:00 p.m. for the next day's metro section cover, many photographers jump in their cars and head to their favorite neighborhoods.

Like a fisherman returning to a fondly remembered fishing hole, they go back, hoping for one more catch of the day.

Other photographers start cruising. Charlie Riedel, who has spent almost his entire life photographing in the small town of Hays, Kansas, says that he finds 95 percent of his features by driving around.

Alan Berner of the *Seattle Times* says to stop your car and shoot if you see a feature while driving. "In general, you can't go back and get it again." Doug Kapustin of the *Baltimore Sun* agrees: "If you think you should, stop. If you don't, you will regret it later."

Some photographers, however, shun the car altogether. Even if they are on their way to an assignment, they prefer to walk if they have the time. They point out that if you are in a car whizzing through a neighborhood, you miss seeing how the residents respond to one another. This interchange provides the basis for good features. As Greg Locke, chairman of the Photojournalism Caucus of the Canadian Association of Journalists, told

News Photographer magazine, "Talk to people you meet. Sometimes keeping moving means you are never in one place long enough to see what's going on."

TAKE A CANDID

Constantine Manos, an outstanding freelance feature photographer for Magnum picture agency, looked for candid features during the year he spent shooting 500 rolls of black-and-white and color film for a forty-projector slide show called "Where's Boston?"

He says that he never posed or arranged any of the pictures contained in the show. Manos explored each area of the city on foot, introducing himself to the residents. "If you sneak up on people," he explains, "they have a right to resent you. Instead, if you say 'Hello,' and talk a bit about what you are doing, people will let you continue with your work. All my subjects are aware of me."

Henri Cartier-Bresson, a founding member of Magnum who is often referred to as the father of candid photography, used a different approach for taking street pictures. According to Russell Miller in his book

The photographer saw these boxes stacked on the sidewalk and anticipated that the mover would try to transport all of them at once, so he waited until the man returned and got this dramatic shot. The boxes, filled with styrofoam hats, were actually quite light.
©Paul Miller, San Francisco

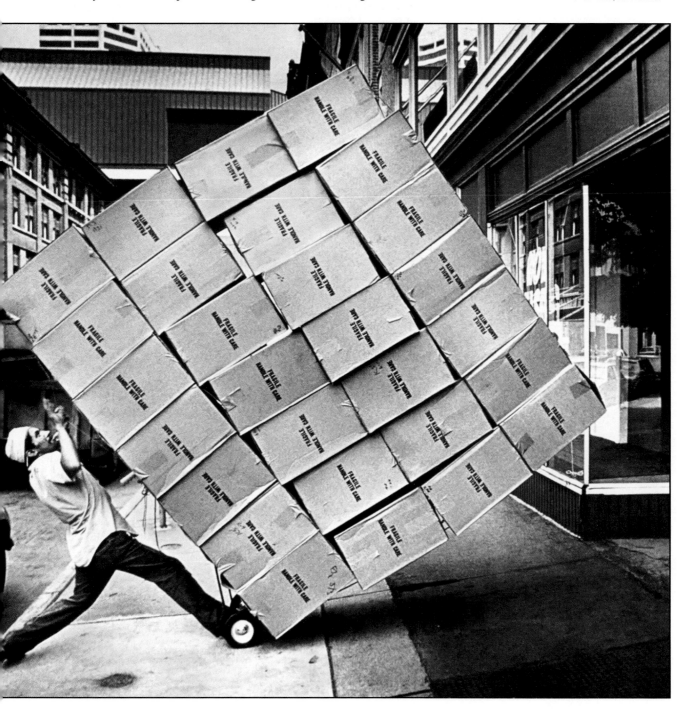

Magnum: The Story of the Legendary Photo Agency, Cartier-Bresson liked to pop up, as if out of nowhere, take a picture, and then innocently walk on as if nothing had happened.

Many photographers are fearful of photographing strangers on the street. Going up to someone you do not know and sticking a camera in his or her face is not a natural act for everyone.

Emily Nottingham studied the brief relationship formed between feature photographers and their subjects in her doctoral dissertation, "From Both Sides of the Lens: Street Photojournalism and Personal Space." While it might last only a few seconds or minutes, the relationship greatly affects the outcome of the picture, as well as how the subject and the photographer feel about the encounter.

Nottingham found that 86 percent of the time people were approached by photographers on the streets of Bloomington, Indiana, they agreed to be photographed, cooperated with the photographer, and even gave their names and addresses. The high percentage of cooperative—and satisfied—subjects reported in the study should put at ease those photographers fearful of street photography.

Nottingham also found that photographers who emphasized forming a relationship with the subjects as people rather than simply as subjects received a more favorable response from the individuals they were photographing.

"Those photographers tended to take more time with the subjects than the other photographers, spent a larger percentage of that time in conversation, and exchanged more personal information with the subjects," she observed.

While the photographer/subject bond does not indicate the quality of the final image, the study clearly shows that sensitive, caring photographers will find their subjects more receptive.

Keep in mind, however, the differences between what Nottingham observed in Indiana and Cartier-Bresson's approach to street photography.

Just as the photographer made this shot, the "Lineman's Rodeo," a competition for electrical workers, ended for the morning. The "unusual," like this surprising scene, always makes good feature material.
Terry Barner, *Independence Examiner* [Eastern Jackson County, Missouri]

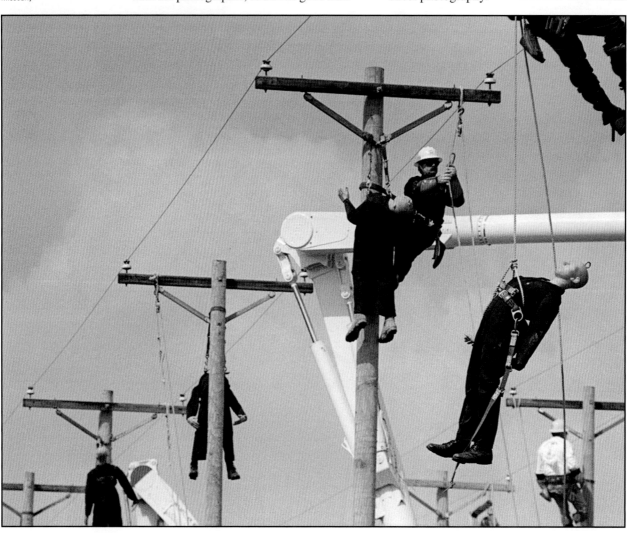

The Indiana approach involves an introduction by the photographer before taking a picture. The Cartier-Bresson approach depends on a photographer taking pictures without engaging the subject.

In fact, Cartier-Bresson's method, when executed in the style of the master himself, means that the photographer will shoot so fast that subjects may not realize they have been photographed at all.

Of course, photographers must decide which approach will work best and be most comfortable for them.

CALL A PR PERSON

Almost any city has more PR pros than journalists. While these professionals have many roles, one of their important functions is helping their organizations get coverage in the media. They are there, in part, to help photographers. In fact, they love photographers. The relationship can be mutual.

Ken James, a freelancer in San Francisco producing a weekly picture page for the *Examiner*, needed a continuous supply of story leads. With a call to Pier 39's Aquarium by the Bay, he discovered that divers would be cleaning the tank's underside on the day he needed to shoot. "Perfect," he said to himself.

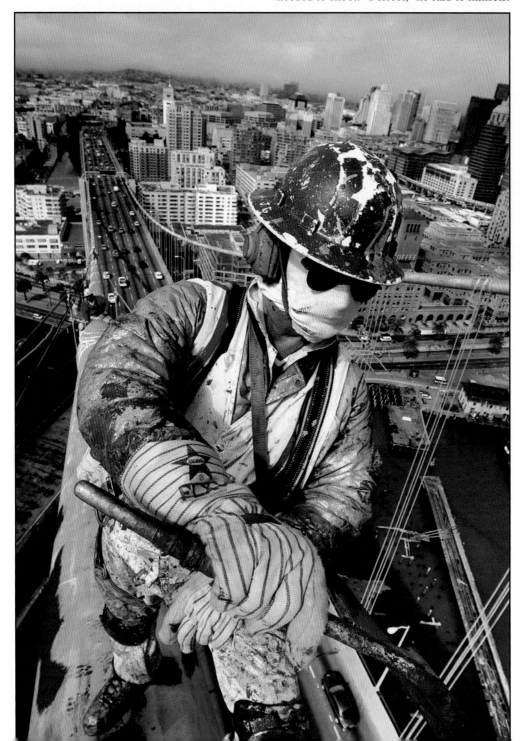

A call to the highway department's public affairs office gained the photographer access atop San Francisco's Bay Bridge along with a painter applying primer to one of its cables. The high-angle perspective adds drama to this feature picture. Ken James, for the *Examiner* [San Francisco]

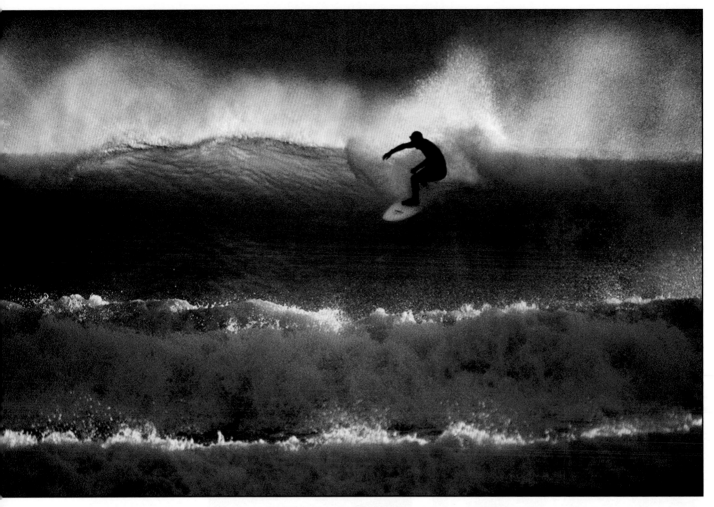

The photographer shot this feature as part of an essay about surfing. The waves were big that day, but it was overcast and drizzly, Tehan recalls. "I almost gave up because the light was so dull, and I was cold and tired. But I noticed that there was a break in the clouds near the horizon, and I figured if I waited long enough I might get some sun." The setting sun broke through the clouds, acted as a backlight, and helped isolate the surfer and rim the waves. Pat Tehan, *Mercury News* [San Jose, California]

Next, he called the public affairs office of the Post Office. He learned that a mail carrier would be testing the new single-person people mover, the Segway, at a specific location the following Thursday. James would never have known about this test if he had not called the Post Office's public affairs department. The chance of happening upon the right spot at the right time would have been slim to none.

With these successes behind him, James began contacting all sorts of PR people. He wanted to take a picture from the Bay Bridge. Three calls later, he had permission to shoot high above the bay while standing on one of the cables that holds up the span between Oakland and San Francisco. Going down the cable was his most frightening moment, he says.

James advises calling for feature pictures long in advance. He says PR pros prefer to make arrangements for the media several weeks before a shoot. Patience pays off in the long run.

"Once you start making the calls, they self-generate. One story leads to another," he says.

UNIQUE ANGLE

Sometimes the key to the feature photo is not a candid moment found on the street but rather taking the viewer to see a common event from a unique vantage point. "I try to show people what they would not normally see," says Charlie Riedel, who climbed a radio tower to show someone changing a light bulb atop it. Such an ordinary act seen at ground level certainly wasn't interesting, but from the tower, where few people ever get to go, readers saw an everyday activity from a fresh perspective.

Riedel—who exhibits no symptoms of vertigo—has climbed radio towers, mounted his cameras on bikes, airplanes, parachutes, and Gyrocopters. Not only does he go up but he climbs down manholes and even under trampolines to bring the readers in his small town a unique perspective. More commonly, he just climbs a tree or takes the prism off his camera and lies flat on the ground to give his readers a new view of their world.

Pat Tehan of San Jose's *Mercury News* used a combination of a long lens, the right light, perfect time of day, and favorable weather

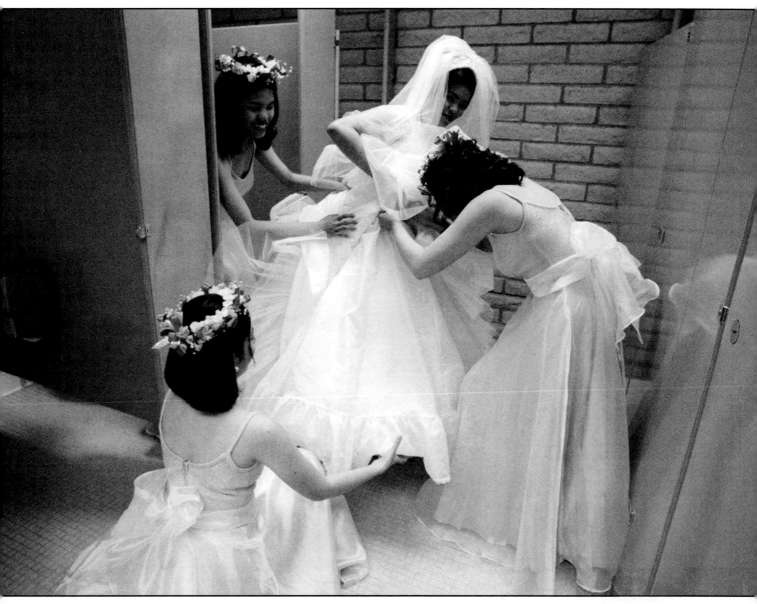

conditions to take a dramatic surfing picture. He had been shooting a series on surfing on the northern coast of California, so he already knew the location of the best waves and the lenses he would need. He waited for the kind of weather conditions that would produce giant rollers, and then waited even longer for the dramatic light of late afternoon.

PHOTO-DRIVEN COLUMN

A photo-driven feature column allows the photographer latitude to take pictures as well as to write. These regularly appearing columns often explore an overlooked area of a town or city or an aspect of city life. Originated in 1975 by Charlie Nye at *The Missourian* (Columbia, Missouri), the idea has been emulated in different incarnations

by a number of photographers at newspapers from the San Jose, California, to Concord, New Hampshire. Some columns have a consistent theme. Luci S. Houston of San Jose's *Mercury News* called her weekly look at weddings in the San Francisco Bay Area "From This Day Forward."

Column themes run from marriage to mayhem. After nine months of memos and meetings, the police allowed the *Boston Globe*'s Susan Kreiter to ride along with them during patrols. Her column was called "Cops."

Some columns, like those of Tom Burton of the *Orlando Sentinel*, seek quiet moments that typically don't earn news coverage. Tom Gralish of the *Philadelphia Inquirer* initially used his photographic platform to focus attention

Photo-driven columns often allow photographers to cover subjects overlooked on routine news assignments. For her *Mercury News* column, Luci Williams Houston regularly covered weddings in search of moments unlikely to appear in a typical wedding album.
Luci S. Williams Houston, *Mercury News* [San Jose, California]

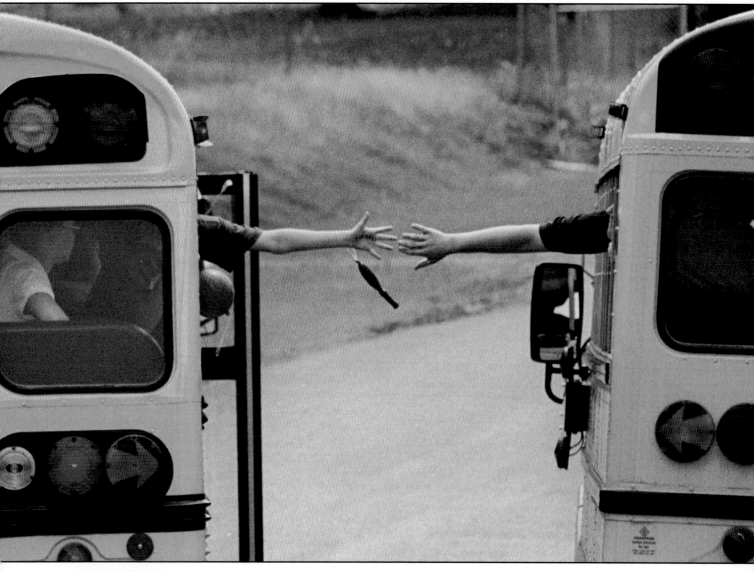

on each of one hundred neighborhoods in his city.

A few of columns contain strictly photos with a brief headline or short caption. Sylvia Plachy's weekly column in the *Village Voice* ran with just the title "Unguided Tour." Typically, though, photo columns include a short text block, usually written by the photographer.

David Reese, now head of the photojournalism program at the University of Missouri, was an early photo columnist. He outlined several tips for getting started in *News Photographer* magazine. Identify a niche in your paper that might be receptive to photo-driven columns—perhaps in the style or the metro section, he advises. Shoot a prototype before proposing the idea to the section editor. Emphasize the importance of building reader anticipation by featuring the column in the same position on a regular basis. Maintain photos as the column's priority.

AVOID THE TRITE

The bread-and-butter feature in today's newspaper is still the pretty child playing in the park or the chimp clowning at the zoo.

Photographers take pictures of kids and animals so often that these topics can become trite. *SFGate.com* editor Cammie Toloui views thousands of images daily while searching the AP wire.

"I see dozens of pictures of buildings reflected in puddles of water every day," she says.

Robert Garvin, writing in *Journalism Quarterly*, explained the genesis of the unsubstantial feature picture. "I have known picture editors (including myself up until ten years ago) who, on a dull afternoon, assign a photographer to walk around town and photograph anything he sees. What does he see? On an August day, he sees a small boy in the spray of a fire hydrant, or a group of tenement dwellers sitting on a fire escape.

"These are so obvious that every passerby has seen them in the newspaper for the last forty years. If there is no thought and preparation, one cannot expect striking pictures with more lasting merit."

When Arthur Goldsmith, an editor for *Popular Photography* magazine, judged the Pictures of the Year Contest, he concluded that pictures in the feature category tended to be hackneyed that year.

He wrote, "Feature pictures often mean space fillers for a slow news day. Here are the visual puns, the cornball, the humorous, the sentimental, the offbeat. (Greased pigs and belly dancers were especially big during this year's competition.)"

Goldsmith said editors divide the photo world into two camps. "Either an event is hard news, which usually means violence, death, horror, confrontation, etc., or the event is a 'feature,' meaning something that appeals to our warm, furry sentimentality. But between the two extremes—the agony of the spot-news disaster and the ecstasy of the feature picture—lies that great amorphous zone that is most of our life." ■

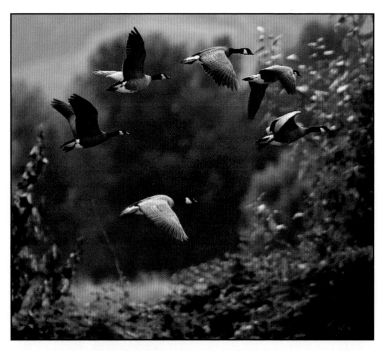

▲ **Dramatic features don't always require people. Here, geese rise from a field near the Port of Vancouver in Washington State.** Janet L. Mathews, *Columbian* [Vancouver, Washington]

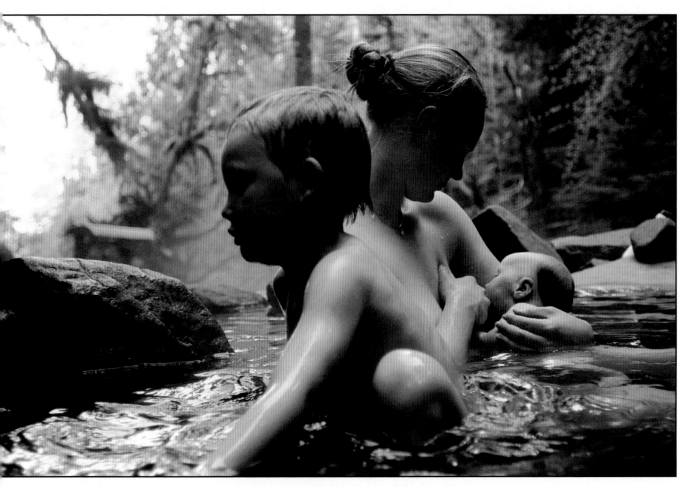

▲ **A quiet moment can become a timeless feature to give readers a respite from the news of the day.**
Sol Neelman, *Oregonian*

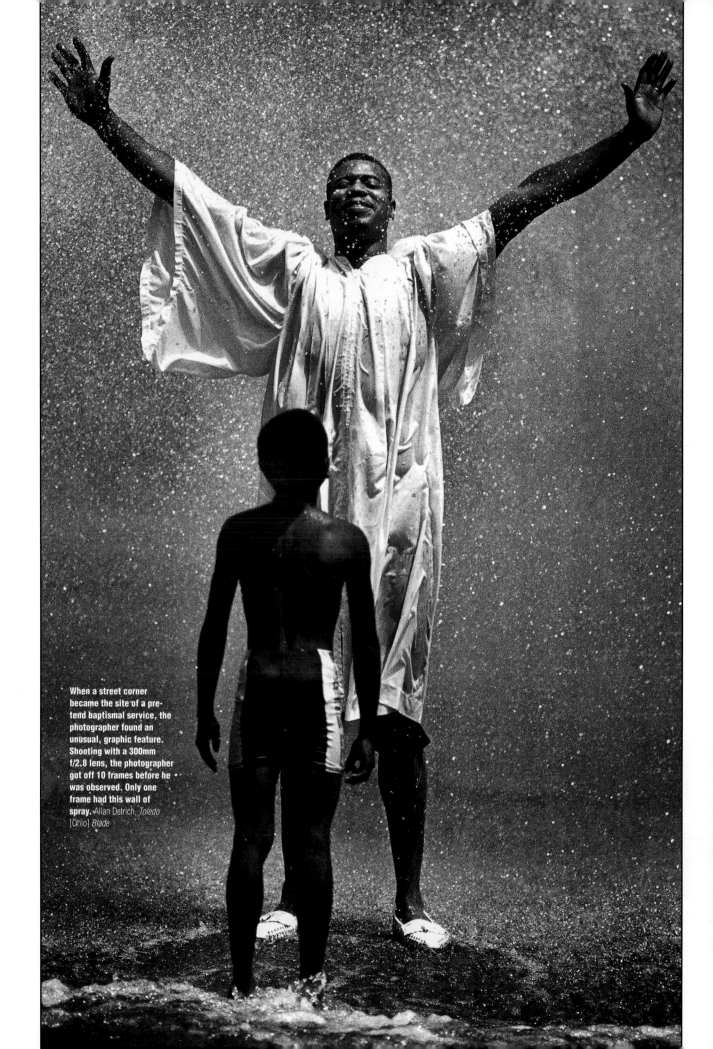

When a street corner became the site of a pretend baptismal service, the photographer found an unusual, graphic feature. Shooting with a 300mm f/2.8 lens, the photographer got off 10 frames before he was observed. Only one frame had this wall of spray. Allan Detrich, *Toledo [Ohio] Blade*

You can make the most of the amorphous—and possibly have your image displayed on your readers' refrigerators—by having an organized approach to looking for features. Here are some suggestions to send you on your way.

1) Head for a good cruising location such as the old part of town or a special neighborhood like Chinatown or Little Italy, where people are out and about.

2) Keep an idea book containing pictures you admire as reminders to yourself of places or people that can make good subjects.

3) Watch the calendar for upcoming topical days like the first day of summer, Flag Day, Secretaries Day, Martin Luther King Day.

4) Shoot from a unique vantage such as the top of City Hall's dome, underwater at the town's pool, or beneath a trampoline.

5) Collect news releases about upcoming events and activities that individuals or organizations are trying to promote.

6) Give out your business cards and ask people to fax, call, or E-mail you with story suggestions or picture possibilities.

7) Check the classified ads for people who are trying to sell belongings. You will find for sale everything from trained chimpanzees to antique art collections.

8) Peruse events calendars for listings ranging from the opening of a science fair to the Gay Pride Parade.

9) Get on the mailing lists of organizations—the more obscure the better. Ask them to send you newsletters and press releases.

10) Localize a national story or trend. If swing dancing is the rage in New York and San Francisco, is it happening on your campus or in your hometown?

11) Walk around a new neighborhood you have never been to before.

12) Select a word like "love" to capture in a picture. Then look for examples that reflect the word. A couple holding hands might come to mind, but see what other examples of this emotion you can find. Other words to try: contrast (see page 111), old and young, friendship.

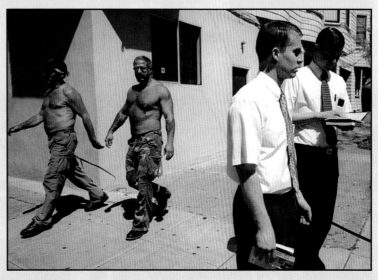

13) "Firsts" can be funny. Time your arrival to catch the first day of school, the first time off the diving board at swimming lessons, or the first time to dissect a frog in biology class.

14) Seek out striking scenics. From Ansel Adams's "Moonrise Over Hernandez" to the *National Geographic*'s sunsets in Saudi Arabia, scenics can be scintillating.

15) Dig out dangerous professions like high-wire walkers, test pilots, or lion tamers. You should also check out unusual if not dangerous professions: tea tasters or flagpole painters come to mind.

16) Study the students at vocational schools. What's in the curricula at the mortuary academy, the hairdressing school, or the clown college, all listed in the yellow pages?

17) Simplify the world by looking for graphic photos like silhouettes, patterns, or shadows.

18) On your way to an assignment, take the time to stop if you see a situation that lends itself to a feature.

19) Experiment using unusual lenses like a fish eye, 600mm telephoto, or close-up macro lens.

20) Develop a feature beat. (See Chapter 4, "Covering the Issues," pages 68–72.) ■

Contrasts in lifestyles make interesting features. Here, neatly attired Mormon missionaries waiting for a bus in San Francisco draw the attention of two locals wearing nipple rings and little else. The photographer was doing a story about the missionary life when this contrasting moment took place. © Martin Jimenez

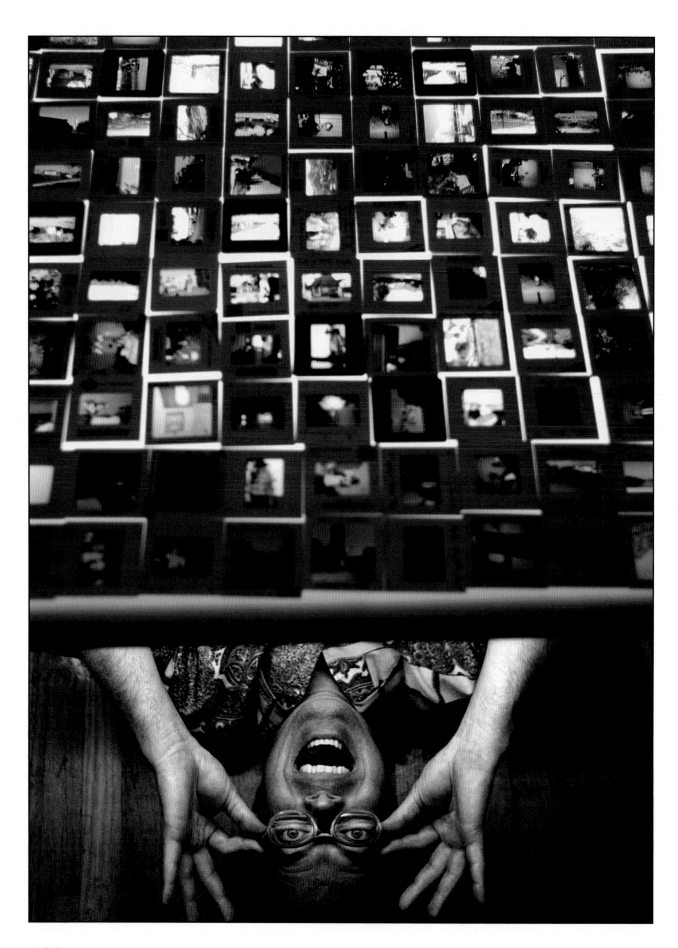

Chapter 6

Portraits

THE JOURNALISTIC PORTRAIT

The journalistic portrait of a scientist shouldn't look like that of a steelworker. An aggressive personality deserves a different portrait from the shy and retiring type. To tell each person's story, photojournalists shoot both posed and candid portraits. Candid photography can produce honest, believable portraits without a lot of elaborate prompting, staging, or lighting, says Steve Raymer, the longtime staff photographer for the *National Geographic* who now teaches at Indiana University. "It's a matter of knowing the subject, using the light, and waiting for the moment," he observes.

Charles Phoenix uses old slides in his theatrical productions. By photographing the artist under his slide table, the photographer conveys the artist's outgoing personality as well as an aspect of his profession. Genaro Molina, *Los Angeles Times*

Even when they arrange elements for a portrait, photojournalists look for honest, candid moments. Nicole Bengiveno, who shoots for the *New York Times*, expresses the sentiment of many of her colleagues. "My favorite pictures are real moments when the subjects have forgotten you are there," she says. Indeed, shooting posed portraits is not a natural activity for many news photographers, whose instincts are to observe—not control.

However, photojournalists often are assigned to shoot posed portraits that reveal both why the person is in the news and something about the person's personality.

PUTTING YOUR SUBJECT AT EASE

If someone doesn't feel comfortable in front of the camera, the best photojournalistic techniques in the world won't produce a revealing portrait. When a photographer disappears behind the camera, even if it is a relatively small 35mm, the shooter loses eye contact with the subject, who is left alone to respond to a piece of coated glass and a black

mechanical box—not exactly a situation conducive to stimulating conversation.

Bengiveno of the *New York Times* can relate to people who freeze when faced down by a camera. "All photographers should have a camera pointed at them," she says. "It is a scary feeling."

To understand the mindset of "the subject," Richard Koci Hernandez of San Jose's *Mercury News* photographed himself. "I took a lot of self-portraits so that I would know how uncomfortable it is to have your picture taken," he says.

Photographers develop different techniques to loosen up and relax their subjects. Keep in mind that an approach that works for one photographer might not work for you. Here are some choices to consider.

TALK IT OVER

One of the most enjoyable aspects of photojournalism is meeting different kinds of people. The most successful photojournalists research why their portrait subjects are in the headlines. During a shooting session, the talk usually turns to the person's involvement in the story. When people become engrossed in conversation, they often forget about the camera, which allows those candid moments in otherwise controlled situations.

"Ideally, I will talk to the subjects for fifteen to twenty minutes to find out what in their life might relate to the picture assignment," Koci Hernandez says.

He asks subjects where they feel most comfortable. "I take advice if people are willing to give it."

Smiley Pool of the *Houston Chronicle* enlists his subjects as collaborators. "How do you want to have your picture made?" he asks. "It's your picture."

The best ideas often come from his subjects, Pool says. "Other times, you have to dream something up."

LOOK 'EM IN THE EYE

"When we put the camera to our eye it blocks our face," says David Leeson of the *Dallas Morning News*. "It's like staring down a gun barrel. I find it unnerving." Leeson solved the problem in a unique way. "I'm still using Nikon F2s and F3s [older camera models]," he explains. "I take the prism off. The camera is at waist level 75 percent of the time I am shooting portraits. This way, I can maintain eye contact."

Photographers shooting with some digital cameras can use the LCD monitor to accomplish the same intimacy.

Alfred Eisenstaedt, an original *Life* magazine staffer, avoided the disruption of picking

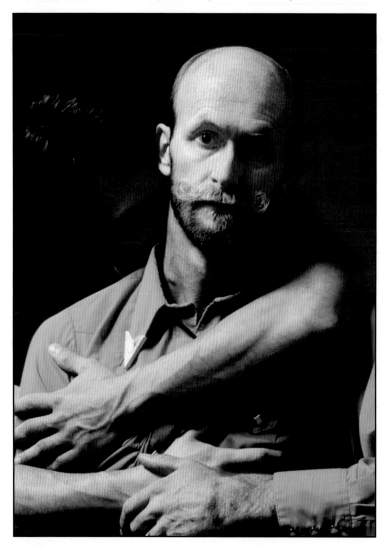

A real moment that developed during the shooting session gives intimacy to this portrait of a person with AIDs. Nicole Bengiveno, for *Newsweek*

up and putting down the camera by using a tripod and cable release. He put his camera on a tripod and focused, which freed him to talk directly and keep eye contact with his subject while taking pictures with the cable release. "For me," he said, "this method often gives the most relaxed pictures."

LET PEOPLE BE THEMSELVES

The secret to posing is to study your subjects, says Sibylla Herbrich. As photographer and photo editor of the *San Francisco Daily Journal*, her job for more than five years was to cajole fifteen minutes or so of the billable hours from busy attorneys to take their portraits for the legal newspaper.

"During the time you initially meet them and while you are setting up the lights or arranging the background, you can watch for the subject's natural body language," she says.

How do they hold themselves, erect or relaxed? Do they point with their fingers or make a fist? Which way do they tip their head? When they are relaxed, do they use one hand or two to hold up their head?

"Look to see how comfortable they are with their own body," Herbrich recommends. "Start by shooting the way they are naturally standing. Then, if they are frozen, hands rigidly at their sides and face pointed straight ahead, remind them of a gesture that you had seen them use earlier." Although you are directing the person, the body position you suggest will be natural, not something you've imagined.

BE A BORE (BUT NOT A BOOR)

When you have time, the boredom technique works well; if you wait long enough, the subject often gets tired of posing, and you can shoot natural-looking photos that result in casual, relaxed portraits.

Arthur Grace, who has been a staffer for both *Time* and *Newsweek* and photographer for the book **The Comedians**, says, "Once you put people in a location, you just wait, and they will get lost in their own thoughts." Grace just sits there. "Maybe I'll take one frame to make them think that I've started, but I haven't." Eventually, the subjects get so bored they forget they are having their

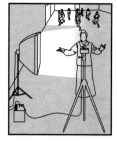

The director of the Ethnic Dance program was stiff and formal in her office. With the music playing in the rehearsal hall, she began to relax and started to move to the beat. The photographer aimed a strobe in a softbox at the teacher's left side and adjusted its output to match the window light falling on the students in the background. For more on using the strobe, see Chapter 12, "Strobe."
Ken Kobré, for *San Francisco State University Annual Report*

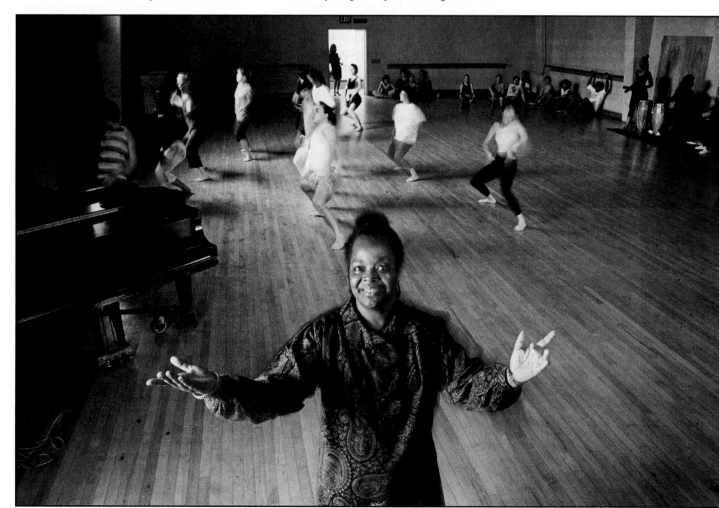

picture taken and they relax. That's when Grace goes to work.

As the photo shoot seems to be coming to an end, the thoughtful photojournalist often looks for one more frame. The *New York Times*'s Bengiveno says that sometimes when people think the picture session is over they let their guard down. "They might put their hand over their head," she says. "Then the real shooting session begins."

LET SOMEONE ELSE DO THE TALKING

Because it's often difficult to work the camera and carry on a meaningful conversation simultaneously, some photographers find it valuable to shoot pictures while the subject is being interviewed. If an interviewer doesn't accompany you on an assignment, take a friend along. When no outsider is available, look for someone on location, like the subject's colleague, to whom he or she might enjoy talking. Involved in conversation, the subject thaws and becomes animated— and the resulting photograph is natural and not contrived.

LIGHT AS A STORY-TELLING ELEMENT

Whether soft from the side or streaming in from above, light in all its various incarnations usually determines the picture's mood. When photographers shoot a picture that is lit brightly yet has only a few shadows, the photo is called "high key" (below). They often employ high-key lighting for pictures of brides, for example, because they want the photo to have an upbeat mood.

When a more moody effect is desired, however, photographers often choose lighting that will leave large areas of the

A writer (left) and his subject were on a book tour together. The photographer took the pair to the newspaper's studio and managed to get this lively reaction by kidding around with the subjects during the photo and interview sessions. The portrait's lighting and light background give it a "high-key" feel. Julie Stupsker, *San Francisco Examiner*

picture in shadow. The photo's dominant tones are dark gray and black. At night, a tough police chief might be photographed with the available light of a street lamp. The moody lighting called "low key" will support the story's thrust. For many photographers, the atmosphere created by light in a portrait is more important than any other element.

UNDERSTAND LIGHT

To add depth to a subject's face, arrange the person so that the main light, whether it is from flood, flash, or window, falls toward the side of his or her face. Unlike direct frontal light, side light adds a roundness and three-dimensionality to the portrait.

Side light also emphasizes the textural details of the face—a technique especially suited for bringing out the character lines in a person's features (pages 102, 105, and 112).

Saw the hot shoe off your camera was the advice the *Miami Herald*'s Jeffrey Salter gave to *Sporting News* staffer Robert Seale when he was starting out. Portraits are almost always more interesting when the light comes from any angle other than head on.

Alternatively, glamour photographers often light people with a large flat light located near the camera's lens to eliminate shadows. Shadowless light, sometimes called "butterfly" lighting, tends to eliminate wrinkles, giving a youthful look to the portrait sitter. See more on lighting in Chapter 12, "Strobe."

Not all light has to come from a strobe or even a window. Jeff Vendsel, working for the *Marin* [California] *Independent Journal* used the light of an overhead projector to illuminate his portrait of two members of a multimedia association (page 108).

LOOK FOR LIGHT

"I arrive fifteen minutes early to a portrait session," says Koci Hernandez of the *Mercury News*. "I look for a beautiful shaft of light in the hallway. Then I put the subject in it, and hope and pray for a candid moment to occur."

The San Jose photographer goes on to point out that "you can have everything working against you—background, uptight person. But if you have great light, everything will work out."

Like Koci Hernandez, Nicole Bengiveno will use any light she can find. "There have been times I have used the headlight of a car, street lamps, or a table lamp," she says. The *New York Times* provides Bengiveno with fast Fujicolor ISO 800 film, so the quantity of light is not as important as its quality.

To find the right light and to catch her subjects in a more relaxed atmosphere,

is multidimensional. Even the most sedate face reflects a surprising number of variations. Take a thirty-six-exposure roll of film of one person's face as she talks about her favorite topic. Note the number of distinctly different expressions the person exhibits. Is one frame of those thirty-six pictures true to the nature of the person? Have the others missed the essence of the person's underlying character?

The great portraitist Arnold Newman says in his book *One Mind's Eye*, "I'm convinced that any photographic attempt to show the complete man is nonsense. We can only show what the man reveals."

The photojournalist usually selects an image of the subject talking, laughing, or frowning, an action coinciding with the thrust of the news story. When a recently appointed city manager expresses fear about his new job, the photo might show him with his hand massaging his wrinkled brow. A year later, a story in which the city manager talks about his accomplishments might show him talking and smiling. The photojournalist's portrait doesn't reveal a person's "true inner nature" as much as it reflects the subject's immediate response to the current situation.

The respected magazine portrait photographer Mary Ellen Mark never asks her subjects to smile for the camera. A smile, she says, can be a person's defense mechanism against the discomfort of being the focus of a camera's lens. On the other hand, she doesn't hesitate to photograph a person's spontaneous laughter or glee.

EYES

Where should the subject look? Early journalism portraits taken around the turn of the century showed the sitter staring into the camera's lens during the prolonged time exposures. During the Depression, Farm Security Administration subjects seemed always to gaze into space. Portraits taken during the 1960s and 1970s often showed the subjects looking as if they were in action, never noticing the camera's presence. Through the 1980s, portraits tended to return to the direct gaze.

Photographers felt that the viewer would be most involved with a portrait's subject when the two made eye contact. David Leeson of the *Dallas Morning News* continues to ask the subject to look into the camera. "I don't want any doubt in the reader's mind that this is a portrait," he says, echoing the sentiment of many photojournalists.

This convention—subject looking directly into the lens—is in the process of yielding to another. Confronted with so many subjects staring into the lens, some photographers in the late 1990s began returning to the

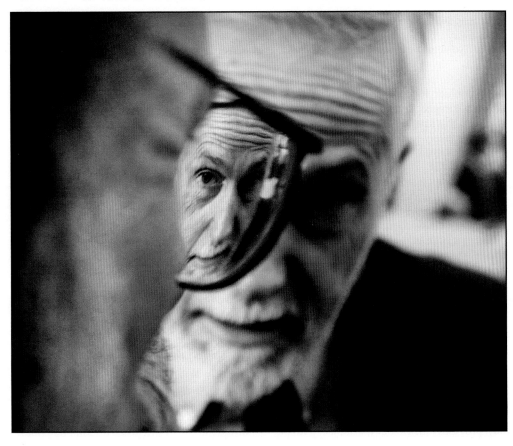

While you can't really see the world through someone else's eyes, this picture allows you to see it through one person's glasses. The photographer used the glasses as a compositional device to direct the viewer's attention. John Burgess, [Santa Rosa, California] *Press Democrat*

The mission of "Clowns Without Borders" is to bring comic relief to war-ravaged and developing countries. The photographer conceived the idea of the performer juggling the world and brought the inflatable globes to the photo session. The photographer "blew out" the background with two strobes bounced into umbrellas that he aimed at the white seamless paper. A third strobe/umbrella lit the juggler and also caught all three balls in the air. For more on using the strobe, see Chapter 12, "Strobe."
Paolo Vescia, *SF Weekly* [San Francisco]

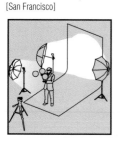

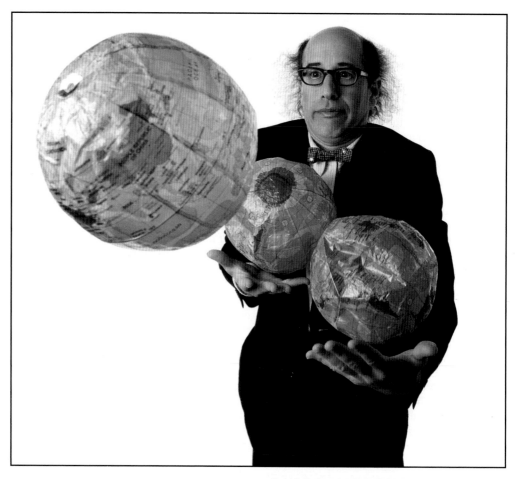

Depression-era approach in which the subject looks away from the camera into the distance. "Sometimes I have the subjects looking away," says Bengiveno of the *New York Times*. "Sometimes I have them looking over their shoulder. It depends on what feeling I want." Like other stylistic variables that contribute to this kind of picture, this new convention is likely to change as well.

BODY LANGUAGE
Hands help tell a story in a nonverbal way. A news photographer covering a speech won't even bother to click the shutter until the lecturer raises a hand to make a point. When shooting a portrait, watch the individual's hands as she toys with her hair, holds her chin, or pushes up her cheek. A person chewing his fingernails reveals a certain tension about the situation in which he finds himself.

Desmond Morris's excellent book, ***Manwatching: A Field Guide to Human Behavior***, is a terrific tool for improving your observational skills. Morris documented various types of gestures and signals that people use to express inner feelings. The way an individual stands, whether as straight as a West Point cadet or as bowlegged as a cowboy, provides clues about the subject's mood,

way of life, or even upbringing. Studying ways people communicate nonverbally can sensitize you to good picture possibilities in portrait sessions and beyond.

PRECONCEIVING THE PHOTO
When assigned to shoot a portrait, many photo journalists go to great lengths to imagine how a picture might look before they ever arrive on the scene.

Richard Koci Hernandez of the *Mercury News* says he almost always has some kind of preconceived notion when he approaches a portrait. "Sometimes you have to illustrate a point," he says. "If a scientist has invented a new baseball bat, I know I am going to need the bat in the picture."

To stay fresh, Koci Hernandez maintains an idea book. "I clip out portraits from magazine and newspapers," he explains. "I keep the pictures in a binder and flip through the book before I go into a portrait session."

Paolo Vescia's assignment was to take a portrait of Moshe Cohen, a member of "Clowns Without Borders." The group aims to bring comic relief to war-ravaged and underdeveloped countries. Cohen came with the humor, but Vescia came up with the idea of integrating clown and world in one photo.

Vescia bought several blowup plastic globes and after setting up the lights, asked his subject to juggle. The preconceived picture captures the spirit of clowning while differentiating this jester's story from any other.

The *Los Angeles Times* assigned Genaro Molina to photograph actor Laurence Fishburne after he directed his first movie. Molina preconceived a picture. "I told him that I wanted to photograph him holding a mirror in his hand as a symbol that he was taking control of his own fate by directing his first feature film," Molina says.

Molina's portrait of the actor goes past a record of the subject's face and tries to imply something about why Fishburne was in the news at the time.

Even if you have a great idea for a picture, don't hesitate to throw it away if something better comes along. Be flexible. Your

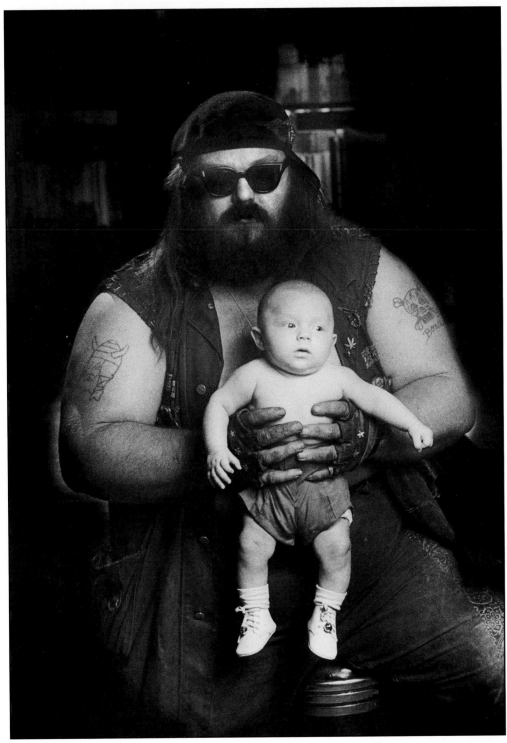

The father-son portrait of "Bones" Kah and his young offspring, Harley Davidson, resulted from a series of self-assignments created by the photographer. This personal assignment was to illustrate the word "contrast."
Rob Goebel, *Indianapolis Star*

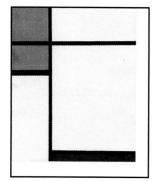

This piece by Piet Mondrian, "Composition," shows the distinctive lines and rectangular blocks the painter used to compose his paintings. The Museum of Modern Art, New York, The Sidney and Harriet Janis Collection

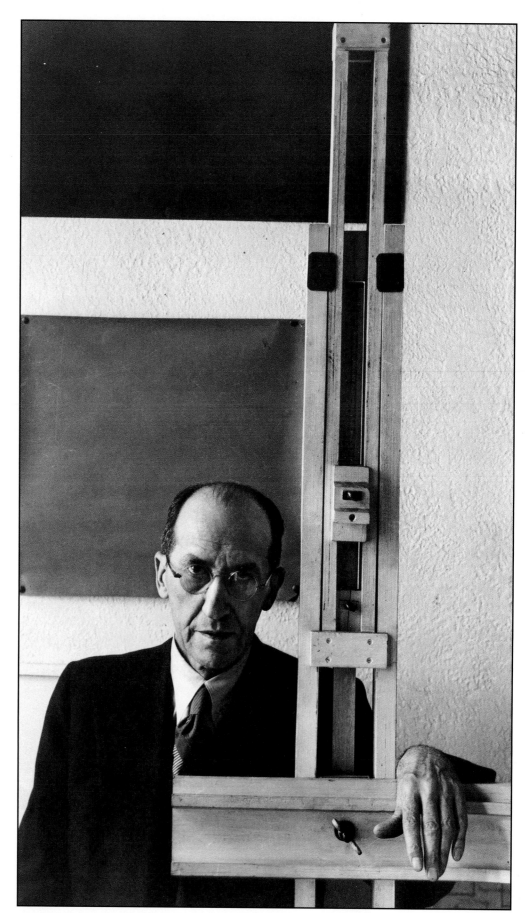

For this portrait of Piet Mondrian, the photographer used sheets of paper and a painter's easel to reflect the artist's painting style. A comparison of the artist's work (ABOVE) shows the inspiration for the photographic portrait. © Arnold Newman

preconceived idea/location/pose for a shoot may be great, but it helps to be open to new ideas presented by the subject or the setting.

"You might get to a location and find a great window, or a great architectural detail, or a great colored wall, or sky that you can build a great photo out of. Don't be afraid to chuck your original idea and go with something that your environment provides," advises Robert Seale, who spends approximately forty percent of his time at the *Sporting News* shooting portraits.

ENVIRONMENTAL DETAILS TELL THE STORY

From a studio portrait, or even from a photograph of an individual engaged animatedly in conversation, the viewer can't tell a banker from a bandit, a president from a prisoner. The wrinkles of a brow or the set of the eyes reveal little about a subject's past, profession, or newsworthiness. An environmental portrait, however, supplies enough details with props, choice of dress, and choice of background to let the reader know something about the lifestyle of the sitter.

Alfred Eisenstaedt wrote, "By now I've learned that the most important thing to do when you photograph somebody in a room or outside is not to look at the subject but at the background." Background details help report the story. A sharecropper's rundown shack relates the farmer's problems. The plush office of a new corporate executive suggests one of the job's perks.

In an environmental portrait, the subject is photographed at home, at the office, or on location, whichever place best reflects the story's theme. As in a traditional studio portrait, the subject typically looks directly into the camera. But rather than sitting before a plain seamless paper background, as in a studio portrait, the person in an environmental portrait is seen amid the everyday objects of his or her life.

Technically, the environmental portrait does not differ from any other portrait. The photographer can use a normal or, if necessary, a wide-angle lens. To record the environmental background sharply, maximum depth of field is necessary. You can increase the depth of field by stopping down the aperture to a smaller opening. This requires a longer shutter speed. Using the camera on a tripod gives the photographer freedom to use longer exposures—if the subject can hold still.

Arnold Newman, a master of the environmental portrait who has taken the official photographs of U.S. presidents, legendary artists, and corporate executives, often arranges his portraits so the background dominates. The subject in the foreground is relatively small. In fact, a famous portrait of Professor Walter Rosenblith of the Massachusetts Institute of Technology shows him wearing headphones with an oscilloscope in the foreground and a mazelike baffle system in the background. His face takes up a small percentage of the picture with the lines of the experimental chamber occupying the rest of the area.

Newman says that the subject's image is important, "but alone it is not enough. We must also show the subject's relationship to the world."

The power of Newman's photos lies in his choice of symbolic environmental details that show not only the sitter's profession but also the style of the sitter's work. For example, Newman photographed the modern artist Piet Mondrian at his easel. The artist is known for his exploration of pure shape and color (see opposite page). By creating a composition with the vertical bar of the easel juxtaposed against rectangular shapes on the wall, Newman's portrait of Mondrian suggested the artist's own style.

PSYCHOLOGICAL PORTRAITS
ANNIE LEIBOVITZ: BUILDING A PORTRAIT

For portraits of actors like Tom Cruise or Meg Ryan, the reader has a frame of reference—the famous face has been on television, in the movies, and on magazine covers. By the time Annie Leibovitz, who has shot many covers for *Rolling Stone* and *Vanity Fair*, photographs a celebrity, the viewer probably has read about the person in magazines or heard interviews on talk shows.

Leibovitz tries to go past a topographic map of the face. Her pictures ask the questions: What makes this person famous? What is the psychological factor that separates this individual from others in the field?

Leibovitz is not interested in showing the viewer details of the subject's life or lifestyle. She does not depend on found items in a celebrity's house or office on which to build the picture like Arnold Newman. She is not waiting and watching for a candid moment in the style of Cartier-Bresson. Rather, she imagines what the picture ought to look like. Then she creates that look.

For instance, Leibovitz photographed Dennis Connor, captain of the winning America's Cup racing team, wearing a red, white, and blue shirt, wading in a pond, sailing a toy boat. Although the America's Cup challenge represents millions of dollars in investments and winnings, the picture caught Connor's little-boy spirit. Leibovitz did not happen upon Connor wading one afternoon in the pond. She and her stylist bought the props, selected the clothes, and located the perfect pond.

Leibovitz builds rather than takes a picture. In conjunction with the subject, she dreams up a visually startling way to portray that individual. Leibovitz, for example, photographed the African-American comic Whoopi Goldberg in a white bathtub filled with milk. She persuaded John Lennon to lie, nude, curled in a fetal position around his wife, Yoko Ono. Leibovitz's pictures lie somewhere between psychological portraits and photo illustrations.

Her stylized approach has influenced many magazine and newspaper photographers.

GROUP PORTRAITS
Show all the Faces
A prime requirement of a formal group picture is that it shows, as clearly as possible, each person's face. This takes careful planning.

Arranging people shoulder-to-shoulder might work, but with more than a few people, the line becomes excessively long.

Each person's face will be quite small in the final image.

Instead, arrange people in rows, one row behind the other. Typically, you want to have the short people in the front and the taller ones in back. With an extremely large group like a band or a football team, you have little choice but to arrange them, military style, at different levels but in a fixed formation.

Soft Light is Best
For group portraits, soft light that creates the minimum of shadows is usually the most effective. If you can, avoid lighting that creates strong, well-defined shadows typical of a bright, sunny day. When you must take a large group portrait on a perfectly clear day, look for the open shade of a tree or large building to provide even lighting.

Add Zest to Small-Group Portraits
Try different levels. When the assembly is limited to between three and eight members, creativity is possible. Try to keep each

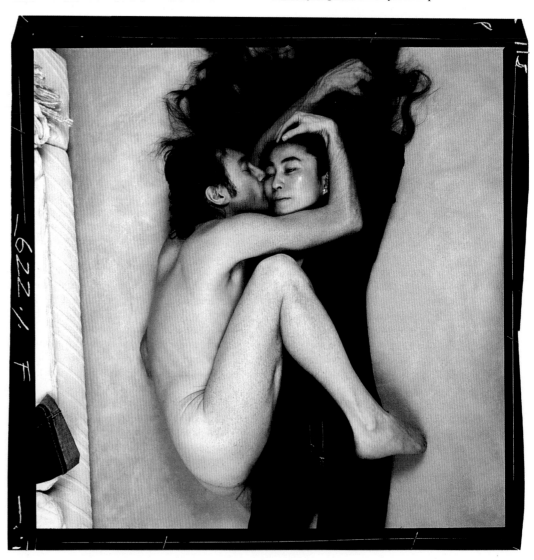

In this daring and stylistically original portrait of the Beatles' John Lennon and his wife, Yoko Ono, the photographer explored the couple's intense psychological relationship.
Annie Leibovitz, for *Rolling Stone*

person's head on a different level. With a combination of kneeling, sitting, and standing, you usually can arrange an attractive juxtaposition of heads so that each is spatially located on a different elevation. The closeness of the bodies holds the picture together as a unit; the staggered arrangement adds visual interest.

Dress them alike. A group of clowns in costume lightens up a graduation picture at the Ringling Brothers Clown School.

Hand 'em props. A cooking class holding spatulas and saucepans serves up a picture of their activities.

Watch the background. Women welders posed in front of a foundry reinforces the viewer's understanding of their profession.

Pose to carry information. A group of teenagers slouching in front of a low-slung car tells a different story than the same group posed sitting in classroom chairs.

TIMING IS EVERYTHING

Henri Cartier-Bresson told this story to Russell Miller for Miller's book *Magnum: The Story of the Legendary Photo Agency*. Cartier-Bresson had been asked to photograph Simone de Beauvior, the French writer, philosopher, and author of *The Second Sex*. "She wanted me to take the photo, and she said to me, 'I am rather in a hurry, how long will you be?' And I said just what came into my head: 'A bit longer than a dentist, but not as long as a psychoanalyst.'"

Apparently, that was the wrong length of time for a portrait because Cartier-Bresson never got the picture.

Knowing the location of the door is just as important as knowing the location of the shutter. With a few frames left at the end of the roll (just in case), you should pack your gear before you wear out your welcome.

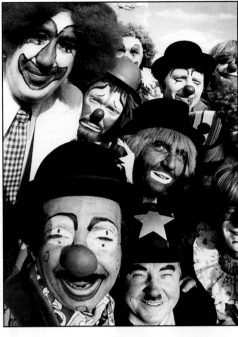

In a group portrait, try to stagger the placement of heads to allow each to occupy a different level. This arrangement maximizes the size of each face.
Vincent S. D'Addario, Springfield [Massachusetts] Newspapers

Photographers have a bad reputation for asking for just one more picture.

Leave in good standing with your subjects because you never know when they will be in the news again and you will need to make a new portrait. ■

(You can accompany photographers on assignment by viewing the DVD included with this book. "Shooting Stars: Photojournalists at the Cannes Film Festival" follows two shooters, Larry Laszlo, on assignment for *Entertainment Weekly*, and Al Seib, a *Los Angeles Times* staffer, as they photograph press conferences, photo calls, and private portrait sessions at the festival. "The Big Picture: The 20"x24" Polaroid" documents a portrait session with a photographer using Polaroid's huge instant camera.)

For a creative group portrait of San Jose State University's *Daily Spartan* photo staff, everyone jumped into the university's long-awaited new pool for an underwater picture. After many tries, the photographer was able to get a photo of the whole staff.
Michael Burke, Redding [California] *Record Searchlight*

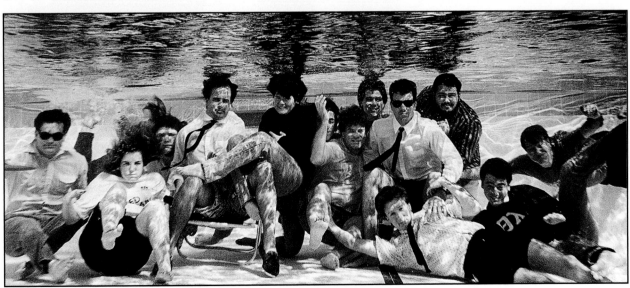

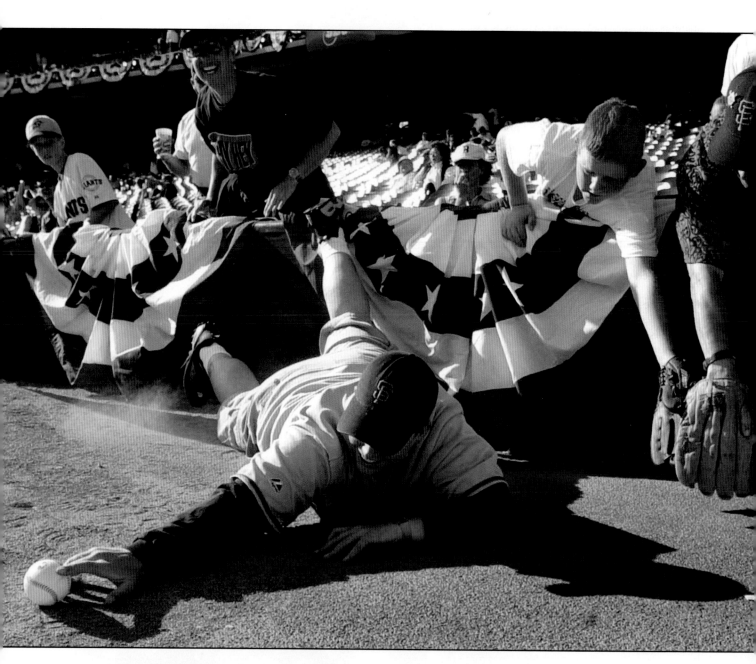

The photographer positioned himself along the third base line and waited for fans to catch foul balls during batting practice at the National League Championships. By keeping his eye on the fans as well as the batters, the photographer captured this over-eager future star spilling out of the bleachers in pursuit of a ball. Jeff Vendsel, *Marin* [California] *Independent Journal*

Chapter 7

Sports

SPORTS AS NEWS

Sports photographers are like athletes. They must have the aim of a football quarterback, the reflexes of a basketball guard, and the concentration of a tennis player. Sports photographers talk about getting in slumps just as baseball players who are having trouble at the plate get into ruts.

"At the beginning of the season I'm rusty," says Brad Mangin, a freelancer whose clients include *Sports Illustrated* and Major League Baseball. "After a few games I get into the groove."

Finding a groove isn't always easy for non-specialist photographers, who often are assigned different rotations every few weeks.

Just as players on the field cannot afford to lose their concentration, so photographers on the sidelines must be aware of every subtle movement in the game. Mangin tries to avoid talking to other photographers on the sidelines but sometimes slips up. "I enjoy talking with other photographers, but there is a balance between talking and keeping your head in the game. It's easy to get distracted," he says. Pam Schuyler, who photographed for the Associated Press and produced a book about the Celtics basketball team, says that she won't even sit next to other photographers when she is shooting basketball because the other photographers distract her too much.

TIMELY PHOTOS PARAMOUNT

Sports photographers strive to capture in a unique way the fast-paced action and drama of competition. A good sports photo and a well-written news story have similar characteristics: both are timely and both have high reader interest.

Timeliness in a sports picture is essential. Nobody cares about a week-old game score,

but millions of viewers stay up to see scores on the eleven o'clock newscast. Interest is so high in sports that millions of people watch the World Series on television, and even more see the summer and winter Olympics.

Sports is big business, and the financial side of football or baseball rates as much attention as any other business story. Players are bought, sold, and traded for millions of dollars: clubs approach the bidding block, ready to spend millions for promising superstars. Readers want to see pictures of these superstars sinking a basket, knocking a home run, or winning a marathon. Editors are aware of this star-gazing. "A paper is more likely to run a picture of a top star hitting a home run than a lesser player doing the same thing, even if the pictures are equally good," George Riley, a longtime wire service photographer once observed.

So sports photographers have to become sports fans; they must read about sports regularly to know the top stars, and what newsy things have happened to them lately. Frank O'Brien, who shot for the *Boston Globe* for many years, would comb the paper's sports

Barry Bonds connects for his 600th home run, an obvious news event in sports. The photographer left his camera shutter open one second, long enough to pick up the light of flash units fired by fans in the stands. Notice the slight blur of the moving players.

John Burgess, *Press Democrat* [Santa Rosa, California]

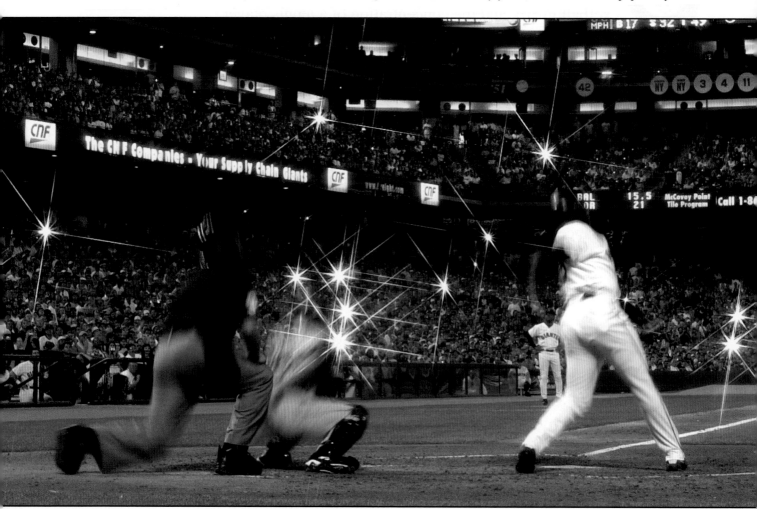

pages every day to learn about a player he might cover. He looked for stories about injured players and major trades, about fights and feuds among players and between players and coaches, about impending records, and about disputes over money. Before shooting for *Sports Illustrated*, Brad Mangin checks out the Web for pictures of the player he is covering. It's a good idea to find out which players are having hot streaks. A news angle like this adds an extra dimension to a sports photo. Also, if a player is making news on the sidelines, readers want to see how the athlete is performing on the court or the field.

A broken record is history in the making. As sportswriter George Sullivan once said, "One job of the newspaper is to record history." In baseball, especially, there seems to be an almost endless array of records to break. Surely, the record book has listed the left-hander who had the most hits during an out-of-town night game pitched by a southpaw.

Knowing that Barry Bonds was about to break a record, John Burgess mounted a camera on a tripod and set the shutter for a 1-sec. shutter speed, ready to fire with a remote trigger. Burgess wanted an unusual picture of Bonds's 600th career homer. A very slow shutter speed would pick up all the flashes firing in the stands as fans snapped their souvenir shots. Bonds needed just one swing that night to change history. Burgess needed just one frame to capture the swing. "The camera only fired this one frame before the remote failed," Burgess recalls.

Photographers can't memorize the record book, so they should check with the team statistician before every game to see if any new records are likely to be broken. A record-breaking home run or free-throw might be the most newsworthy moment of the game, and an editor will want to see a picture of it.

SUMMARIZING THE GAME IN ONE PHOTO

A sports story's lead usually contains the names of each team, key players, and the outcome of the game. It also describes the game's highlights—the turning point or winning goal, the star of the game, and injuries to important players. Knowledgeable sports photographers follow the game closely enough that their photos complement the story's lead.

"I always try to develop the lead picture that will parallel the thrust of our wire story," explains George Riley. "The wire service will often play up the top scorer in the game, so I will need a picture of him in action." If a particular play changes the course of the game, the photographer should have a shot of this play. As Tommy Metthe, a staffer for the

Abilene Reporter-News, observed on *SportsShooter.com*, "I think the biggest thing I've learned since starting my professional career is a great shot is not as important as getting the shot that tells the story."

A good sports photographer watches the action but doesn't stop when the final whistle blows. Sometimes the expressions on the athletes' faces after a tense meet tell the story better than an action shot.

Sports shooter Mangin knows the assignment doesn't end with the game. The crowd's reaction or anything else that will characterize the game's emotional flavor is often key. "If you are working for the hometown paper, you need to photograph the jubilation or dejection or just reaction at the end of the game," Mangin says.

Smiley Pool, shooting for the *Houston Chronicle*, caught Rulon Gardner's surprising reaction when the wrestler celebrated his Olympic gold medal with a cartwheel. Until that moment, the losing athlete in the background had been undefeated for thirteen years. Staying alert after the match ended, Pool caught the moment.

These pictures will often tell more about the outcome of the game than the peak action. With the action picture, you don't know who won unless you have the key play, Mangin points out. Mangin tells the story of the time he shot a San Francisco Giants victory over Chicago Cubs. "I got a great picture of the Giants celebrating, but I missed a potentially better photo of the Cubs in the dugout looking sad." Shooters sometimes run

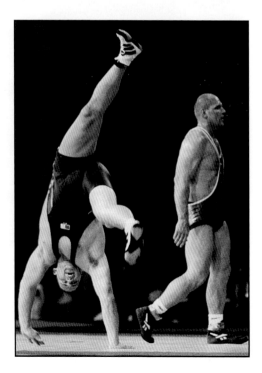

Sometimes a reaction after the competition can summarize the outcome better than an action shot. The burly wrestler celebrating his victory with a cartwheel had just defeated a thirteen-year champion. By staying alert even after the match was finished, the photographer caught victory and defeat in one frame. Smiley N. Pool, *Houston Chronicle*

onto the field after the game shooting with a wide-angle lens in order to be in the middle of the players' jubilation or dejection. Others stand back with a long lens, an approach that usually works only when all the photographers covering the game agree to "shoot long" and not get in each other's way.

CATCHING REACTIONS ON AND OFF THE FIELD

Sports photographers look for the interesting, the unusual, the emotional, and the unexpected, both on and off the field. What's happening on the bench can be as interesting as what's happening on the field. Watch the field and the sidelines simultaneously. You might lose some action plays sometimes, but you will get great emotional, storytelling pictures this way.

Coaches are under tremendous pressure because their jobs are on the line every time the team takes the field.

A picture of a coach pacing the sidelines, yelling at the referees, or jamming his finger at other coaches can reveal his underlying tension. Players feel that same pressure.

The clenched jaw of a player sitting on the sidelines or the frown of an athlete wearing a cast could also tell the evening's story.

Often but not always off-limits, the locker room can provide a venue for revealing pictures. Aristide Economopoulos of the *Jasper* (Indiana) *Herald* caught a basketball coach trying to inspire a less-than-intense player under a sign that reads "Intensity." Scott

Heckel photographed a member of the girls' swimteam reacting to the boys shaving their bodies before a meet (page 268).

Not all coaches permit this kind of access, especially for professional sports, but ask for permission anyway. Locker rooms are where the confident, pumped-up heroes are likely to reveal their more private emotions.

CAPTIONS NEEDED

Whether the picture shows critical action on the field or reactions off, photographers must have complete caption information. The caption, as it is called in a magazine, or cutline, as it is known in a newspaper, is the explanatory line of type usually found below the printed photograph. (See Chapter 10, "Photo Editing," for more on caption writing.)

If it is not obvious from the picture, a caption should answer the five Ws plus the H: Who? What? When? Where? Why? and How? Readers will know whether the photo depicts a basketball game. But they might not know when in the game the picture was taken, the identity of the players, or the significance of the play.

A photographer's nightmare is to bring back 200 shots of a game, select one frame with excellent action, and then not know the players' names, what happened, or when the action took place. Fortunately, players wear large numbers on their uniforms. If the numbers are visible in the print, identify the player by matching the number against the roster

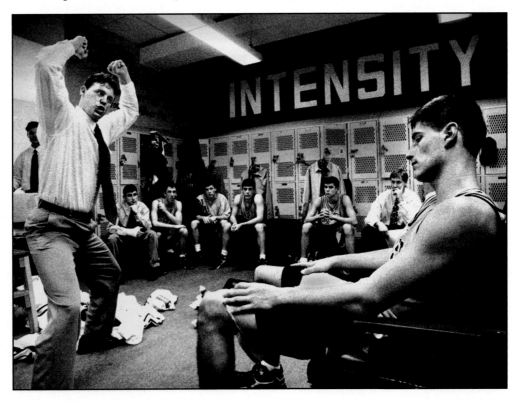

Sometimes a photographer will find the contest's revealing photo in the locker room rather than on the court. This rookie coach tries to inspire his starting center during a half-time pep talk. Despite the seeming lack of "intensity," the pep talk worked, and the team broke its five-game losing streak. Aristide Economopoulos, *Jasper* [Indiana] *Herald*

list in the program. To determine when the play occurred, take a picture of the score-board after each major play or at the end of each quarter. By working backward with your set of pictures, you can tell when each shot was taken and which plays led to which scores.

Play-by-play statistics sheets, available from officials after the game, also help photographers write accurate captions. Besides shooting frames of the scoreboard, sophisticated sports photographers usually take notes during the game. In baseball, there is time to record each play if you use a shorthand notation (for example, FB = first base, HR = home run). In football, jot down a short description after each play. Advises sports veteran George Riley, "Keeping track of the plays can get tricky at times. This is where newcomers usually have the most trouble in sports photography."

SPORTS AS FEATURES

Sports might be as timely and may command as much reader interest as any story in the newspaper. But sports events aren't hard news—they're entertainment. A football game, no matter who wins or loses, is still a game. You might have a side bet resting on the World Series, but the outcome of the game will not affect your life beyond giving a moment's elation or depression (unless, of course, you've staked your savings on your favorite team).

When looking for features, draw your lens away from the field action to view the fans in the stands. Die-hard fans go to great lengths to show their support for the hometown team. From funny signs to outrageous outfits, fans come prepared to root or rout the players of their choice.

Tommy Metthe describes the job of the sports photographer as "the epitome of

To beat the oppressive heat, these teammates are cooling off in an ice machine. Feature pictures like this one add spice to a steady diet of sports action.
Alan Hawes, *Post and Courier* [Charleston, South Carolina]

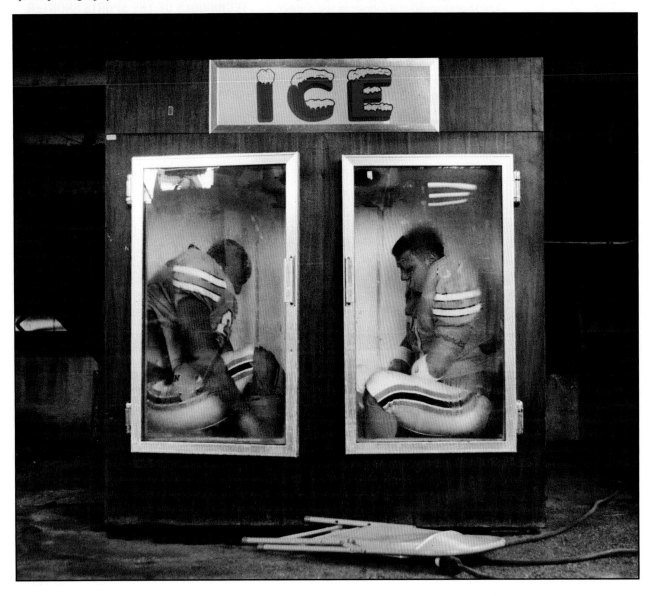

multi-tasking. While you constantly have to watch the game looking for the "peak action," you also are keeping an eye on the sidelines for reaction and feature stuff."

Players themselves can also provide grist for funny pictures. For many athletes, the pleasure of playing has never been lost. During the game, keep your eye on the dugout or the bench.

The news approach to sports usually involves getting sharp, freeze-frame action shots of players hanging suspended in midair, grasping for the ball. Sometimes this literal approach robs the sports photo of its most vital element—the illusion of motion.

A more impressionistic feature approach can add drama and reinforce motion in a still photograph. Certain camera techniques can heighten the effect.

A sports photographer might pan a cyclist's action by setting the camera on a slow shutter speed and following the subject with the lens, intentionally blurring the background while keeping the subject fairly sharp. (See page 124.) Such a picture can have more impact than would a traditional news photo of the winner of a race, in razor-sharp detail, crossing the finish line.

Also, the shooter might use a slow shutter speed but keep the camera rock solid. This technique lets the moving athlete blur but leaves the background sharp. (See opposite page.)

In a sports feature photo, photographers ignore the critical winning moment in favor of capturing the atmosphere of the event. Impressionistic pictures of this kind transcend the actual event and become a universal statement about the sport.

A bone-crushing tackle by a football player may resemble a delicate pirouette when captured by a skilled photographer. In "Man and Sports," a photo exhibit and catalogue produced by the Baltimore Art Museum, the outstanding sports photographer Horst Baumann said that there is an increasing appreciation for the impressionistic, nonfactual but visually elegant portrayal of sports.

TECHNIQUES OF THE SPORTS SHOOTER
FREEZING ACTION

Sports photography requires specialized technical skills because of the speed at which athletes move and because of the limitations of position imposed on the photographer. To stop motion in action sports like baseball, football,

SHUTTER SPEEDS FOR ACTION PARALLEL TO THE FILM PLANE

Type of Motion	Speed	Camera-to-Subject Distance		
		25 feet	50 feet	100 feet
Very fast walker	(5 mph)	1/125	1/60	1/30
Children running	(10 mph)	1/250	1/125	1/60
Good sprinter	(20 mph)	1/500	1/250	1/125
Speeding cars	(50 mph)	1/1000	1/500	1/250
Airplanes		———	———	1/500

MINIMUM SHUTTER SPEEDS REQUIRED TO FREEZE ACTION

Speed of Car (mph)	Speed of Car			Distance to Car			Direction of Car			Lens Focal Length		
	25 mph	50 mph	100 mph	50 mph	50 mph	50 mph	50 mph	50 mph	50 mph	50 mph	50 mph	50 mph
DISTANCE FROM CAR TO CAMERA 100' 50' 25'										Wide	Normal	Tele
Shutter Speed	1/250	1/500	1/1000	1/250	1/500	1/1000	1/500	1/250	1/125	1/250	1/500	1/1000

and basketball, photographers try to shoot with a shutter speed of at least 1/500 sec.

Says Eric Risberg, a top sports shooter for the Associated Press, "The slowest I ever shoot is at 1/500 sec. At 1/1000 sec., things get a lot sharper."

Four factors affect the apparent speed of a subject and therefore determine the minimum shutter speed to stop motion:

1) the actual speed of the subject;
2) the apparent distance between subject and camera;
3) the angle of movement relative to the camera's axis; and
4) the focal length of the lens.

Speed

You will need a faster shutter speed to stop or freeze the action of a track star running a 100-yard dash than you will to stop the action of a Sunday afternoon jogger.

To freeze a sprinter, the shutter must open and close before the image of the runner perceptibly changes position on the camera's image plane. Therefore, the faster the subject runs, the faster the shutter speed you will need to stop the action and avoid a blurred image.

Distance

A second factor affecting the final image is the camera-to-subject distance. If you stand by the highway watching speeding cars go by, you may observe them zoom rapidly past you; but when you move back from the edge of the highway 100 feet or so, the apparent speed of the cars is considerably less. Speeding cars on the horizon may appear to be almost motionless. Translated into shutter settings, a general guideline for this effect is that the closer the camera is to the moving subject, the faster the shutter speed needed to stop or freeze its movement.

Lens Length

Whether you get the camera closer by physically moving it toward the subject or remaining stationary and attaching a telephoto lens, thereby bringing the subject apparently closer, you must increase your shutter speed to freeze the action. Suppose you are 50 feet

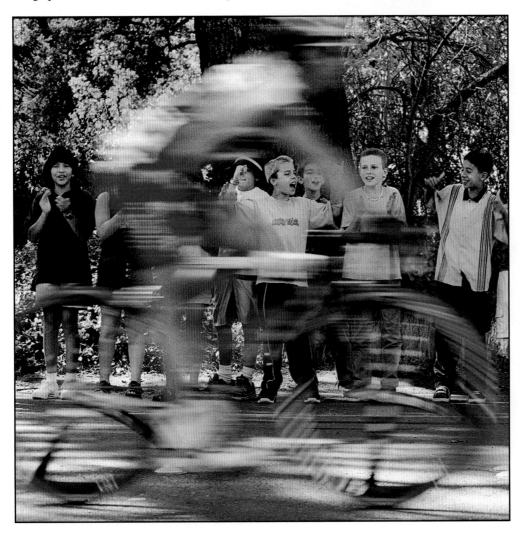

For this impressionistic sports image, the photographer focused on the young spectators on the opposite side of the road and held the camera steady at 1/125 sec. Because the cyclist passed so close to the camera, the action blurred even at 1/125 sec. See chart, opposite.
Todd Rasmussen, *Vacaville* [California] *Reporter*

away from the track with a normal (50mm) lens. A shutter speed of 1/500 sec. is adequate to get a sharp picture of a car going 50 miles per hour at this distance.

Using the same lens but at half the distance (25 feet) you must set the shutter speed twice as fast (1/1000) to stop the car's movement. If you remain at the original 50-foot distance but change from the normal lens to a 105mm telephoto lens, you also need 1/1000 sec. to stop the car (see chart, page 122).

The rule is this: if you halve either the real or apparent camera-to-subject distance, the shutter speed must be twice as fast—1/1000 is twice as fast as 1/500.

Angle

The angle of the subject's movement relative to the axis of the camera also affects your

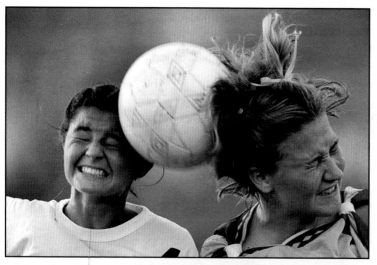

⊥ To freeze the action for this head-to-head soccer shot, the photographer needed a shutter speed of at least 1/500 second. Pete Erickson, *Dubuque* [Iowa] *Telegraph Herald*

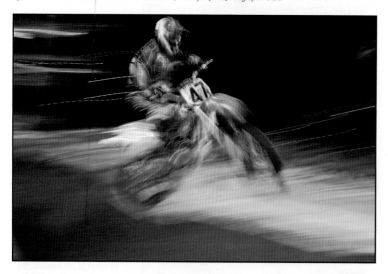

⊥ To retain a sense of movement in this still photo of a supercross moto race, the photographer panned the camera as the bikers passed in front of him. He kept the shutter open for 1/15 sec. as the cyclists zoomed by. Scot Tucker, *San Francisco Independent*

choice of shutter speed. A car moving directly toward you may appear to be nearly stopped because its image moves very little on the image plane in the camera.

Yet the same car—moving at the same speed, but this time moving across your line of vision—appears to be traveling quite rapidly. This phenomenon means that if you position yourself to photograph a car 50 feet away going 50 mph moving directly toward you, you would need only 1/125 sec. shutter speed to stop the action. From the same distance, the same car moving across your line of vision would require 1/500 sec. to stop the motion.

Peak Action

With some movements, it is possible to stop the action at a relatively slow shutter speed by timing the shot to coincide with a momentary pause in the subject's motion.

Athletes in some sports come to an almost complete stop at the peak of their movement.

Consequently, you can use a relatively slow shutter speed and still get a sharp picture. In track, for example, when a high jumper reaches the apex of his leap directly above the bar, his vertical motion is over. He can't go any higher, and, for a split second, his vertical motion ceases before gravity pulls him back to earth.

A basketball player shooting a jump shot follows the same pattern: he leaps into the air, reaches his peak, hesitates, and then shoots the ball before he begins dropping back to the floor.

You can use a slower shutter speed to stop action at the peak of the vault by anticipating where the peak will occur and waiting for the athlete to reach the apex of the arc.

ALERT: When photographing golf, never shoot until the club has struck the ball. The sound of a shutter can ruin a player's concentration. Quips Robert Beck, "If you do shoot during the back swing, at least wait for noise from the crowd—or under the worst of circumstances, look at the photographers next to you and hope that everyone will think that one of them took the picture and not you."

PANNING

While a fast shutter speed allows you to catch the action of the play, the resulting frozen figure may not capture the essence of a sport. Freezing a player in midair can rob the photo of any illusion of movement.

To solve this problem, use a technique known as panning.

Select a slow shutter speed and move the camera to follow the subject during the exposure. This technique produces a picture with a relatively sharp subject but a blurred and streaked background. A pan shot is dramatic and can make even the proverbial "old gray mare" look like a Triple Crown winner galloping at breakneck speed.

On sports assignments for *Life* magazine and *Sports Illustrated*, Mark Kauffman has used the panning technique on several different events. In **Photographing Sports**, a book about his work, Kauffman said, "Panning is something like shooting in the dark. It's practically impossible to predict the final result. Background colors will move and blend together giving shades and tones and creating hues which we cannot predict."

If you don't follow the subject smoothly, the image won't be sharp enough. Many photographers can't afford to risk a pan shot because editors count on having at least one tack-sharp photo of the key contestants in the event. Therefore, it's wise never to gamble solely on an impressionistic pan shot for an important assignment.

"When on assignment," Kauffman cautions, "get the picture the editor needs first—then, if you have time, experiment with a pan."

Lens choice is critical in panning. A long lens allows you to back off from the subject. The farther the camera is from the subject, the slower you can pan—thus achieving more control.

The lens, however, must allow a field of view that is wide enough to accommodate the anticipated action.

When panning, use your viewfinder to spot the subject as it moves into view. Pivot your head and shoulders so that you keep the subject in the viewfinder at all times.

When your subject is in front of you, release the shutter without interrupting your pivot. Be sure to follow through after you snap the shutter. The trick is to have the camera moving at the same speed and in the same direction as the subject.

FOCUSING: HOW TO GET SHARP IMAGES
MANUAL FOCUS
Whether you use a slow shutter speed to pan or a fast shutter speed to freeze the action, your subject will not be sharp unless the lens is critically focused. Focusing a lens on a rapidly moving subject takes practice.

Follow-focusing requires eye-hand coordination. As the runner moves down the field, you must move the lens's focusing ring to maintain a sharp image in the viewfinder. When the runner is near, you must completely rotate the focus ring to keep the subject sharp. When the runner speeds into the

distance, a minor twist of the ring suffices to pop the runner in or out of focus.

To follow-focus, use the ground glass on the edges of your viewfinder, not the split image or micro screen in the center. For most shooters, these focusing aids are too slow for the continuous movement of sports action.

Photographers must adapt eye-hand coordination to each lens length and camera brand. Each lens requires a different amount of movement to achieve sharpness. Like a musician playing the same note on a base fiddle, cello, or violin, the photographer must learn different eye-hand motor skills, depending on whether he or she is using a 100mm, 400mm, or 600mm lens. Even more confusing is the difficulty of switching among brands of cameras. Some focus clockwise, others counterclockwise. Whenever possible, try to stick to one camera brand to avoid this confusion.

One veteran shooter always advised new photographers to practice follow-focusing on cars coming down a highway. Select a car, he

TOP. The photographer has selectively focused on the batter and, with a wide aperture of f/2.8, let the crowd in the background blur. Selective focus helps separate the silhouetted batter from the potentially distracting background.

BOTTOM. Here, the focus is on the crowd watching batter San Francisco Giants's Barry Bonds. Because the crowd is both sharper and brighter than the batter, the reader's attention is drawn to this part of the picture. The photographer used a 400mm lens with internal stabilization, which allowed him to shoot at f/22. This approach recorded the crowd in sharp detail. The small aperture prevented the batter from dissolving completely. The shot appeared as a two-page spread in *Sports Illustrated*.
Brad Mangin, for *Sports Illustrated*

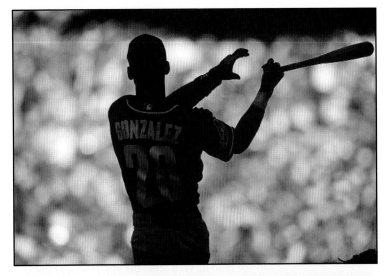

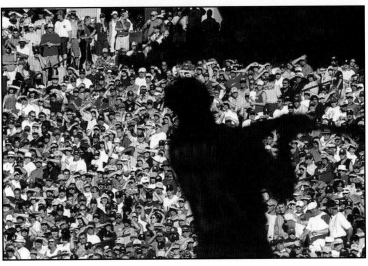

said, and try to keep its license plate in focus as it moves down the road. Track car after car, and soon, without thinking about it, your hand will move the lens barrel the exact amount necessary to hold focus as the speeding car passes in front of you, zooms down the highway, and recedes from view.

Don't be discouraged if every shot of your sports action is not tack sharp. Few sports photographers bring back thirty-six perfectly focused exposures. However, with practice, the number of razor-sharp frames will increase.

For many assignments, sports shooters use lenses in the 200mm to 600mm range. In terms of sharpness, the bad news is that long lenses have limited depth of field even at small apertures. This means that unless the lenses are exactly focused, the pictures will look blurry.

The good news is that when you peer through long lenses, the image pops in and out of focus very cleanly and dramatically on the viewfinder's ground glass. Critically focusing a long lens is actually easier than focusing a wide-angle lens. (See Chapter 11, "Camera Bag.")

ZONE-FOCUSING

In sports like auto racing or track and field, when photographers can predict exactly where the subject will be—at a finish line or a specific hurdle—they use a method called zone-focusing. To zone-focus, manually prefocus the lens for the point at which you expect the action to take place, and let your lens's depth of field do the rest. As the subject crosses the predetermined mark, frame and shoot your picture. Your picture will be sharp not only at the point at which you have focused but for several feet in front of and behind that point—depending on the depth of field of your lens, the aperture, and the distance from the subject.

AUTOFOCUS

With most camera-lens combinations, the equipment's autofocus option can outperform the most practiced photographer's eyes and hands.

Once you've set the camera and lens on autofocus, you can frame a runner within the etched lines in the viewfinder that indicate where you can autofocus. Now that you've aimed at the moving target, activate the autofocus feature on most cameras by partially depressing the shutter release. As the runner moves toward the camera, the lens will automatically focus, and the athlete will remain sharp. A good autofocus system will follow the runner without searching hesitantly.

Advanced autofocus lenses and motor-driven cameras were devised to fire and continuously advance at many frames per second while tracking a fast-moving subject.

Manual follow-focusing is easy when you're not firing off many frames. But when you want to shoot a rapid sequence of shots, the mirror is up more than down, which interrupts viewing and makes it difficult to manually follow-focus.

Some autofocus systems allow manual follow-focusing even while in autofocus mode. This manual override comes in handy when the auto feature misses the mark.

You should be aware, though, that you must center the athlete in the middle of the viewfinder for autofocus to work with some systems. But systems with multiple focusing sensors in the viewfinder allow the primary subject to be off-center while the camera lens stays on track. With these models, the photographer can select the designated off-center areas—the left portion of the viewfinder, for example, to follow-focus a runner who is on the left side of the frame. To shift to a runner on the right-hand side, readjust the target autofocus area. Other camera systems advertise a wide-area autofocus sensor that allows for continuous autofocus without any need for sensor selection. Some cameras have a "lock-on" feature that assures that the player will stay in focus.

If you are tracking a halfback running down the field and a ref gets in the way, some cameras will switch focus to the interloper and lose track of the halfback. When the halfback appears again, the lens has to search for the new point of focus.

However, with the "lock-on" feature and faster motors in some systems, the ref's momentary interruption won't cause focus to shift. Even if the player briefly moves out of the autofocus sensor's zone, the system will recognize when the athlete returns to view.

Even shooters who cover only sports—and who are accustomed to bringing back sharp images of swiftly moving athletes—claim to get even better results using autofocus.

"In a sequence of eight to ten frames, I get seven or eight that are sharp," says George Tiedemann, a contract photographer with *Sports Illustrated*, in describing his conversion to the technology. "That's better than the four or five I used to get."

Tiedemann says that the technology has dramatically increased his odds even when shooting car races. "I was shooting cars coming diagonally across, flying by me at speeds well over 100 miles per hour. I put the 600mm on autofocus and just nailed those guys."

While not a necessity, autofocus lenses and cameras seem like the best tools for those who don't want to miss a sharp picture of the critical play. (See also Chapter 11, "Camera Bag.")

THE SPORTS PHOTOGRAPHER'S BAG OF SOLUTIONS
FIXED-FOCAL-LENGTH TELEPHOTOS

A sports photographer can't just run onto the playing field with a wide-angle 20mm lens and snap a picture of the action. To get an image large enough to see clearly, the sports specialist usually must use long telephoto lenses. The telephoto adds drama to the photo and heightens impact. With these long lenses, whether manual or autofocus, you magnify what you want to show by eliminating all distractions.

In addition, using these lenses helps to pop the key player out of the pack, leaving a distracting background lost in an out-of-focus blur. In fact, most sports photographers always use the widest lens aperture to achieve minimum depth of field, therefore knocking out, as much as possible, the distracting background. (See pages 127, 130, 132, 133, and 136.)

Long lenses also can be creative tools because they pull things together in a way the human eye never sees. Because a telephoto lens appears to compress space, objects appear much closer together in depth than they really are. (See page 119.)

Using autofocus, the photographer captured members of the Anaheim Angels celebrating the winning play of the World Series. A wide aperture on a 400 telephoto lens blurred the background so that the victors stand out against the crowd. Bryan Patrick, *Sacramento Bee*

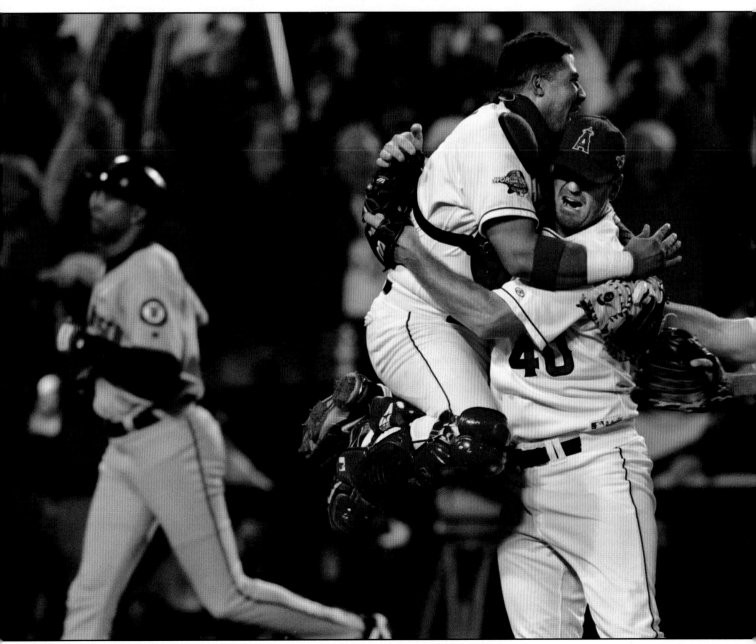

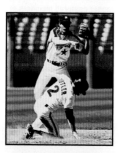

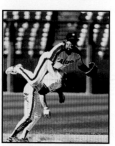

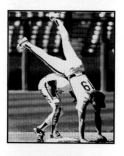

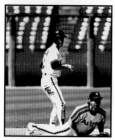

When using a motor drive, start shooting before the action starts and keep shooting until the play is completed. © Brad Mangin

ZOOM LENSES

Rather than carry a satchel of different lenses, some sports photographers prefer to use zoom lenses. With the zoom, you can continually change the focal length of the lens, so that one lens is doing the work of several. Because you can zoom to any millimeter within the range of the lens, your framing can be exact. Sports photographers also like the zoom because it lets them follow a player running toward the camera while it keeps the player's image size constant in the viewfinder. Another advantage of the zoom is that you can get several shots from a single vantage without moving. For instance, you can zoom back and catch all the horses at the starting line of a race; then, after the horses leave the gate, you can zoom in to isolate the leader of the pack—all this by just a twist or push of the lens barrel.

This versatile type of lens does have drawbacks. First, a zoom is usually heavier than a single-length telephoto lens. You can balance this increased weight, however, against not having to carry as many lenses to get the same effect.

Second, the zoom lens's widest apertures are sometimes smaller than the maximum aperture on an equally long fixed-focal-length lens, so the zoom is less useful in low-light situations such as in indoor arenas or at night games. Manufacturers, on the other hand, have introduced midrange zoom lenses (80–200mm), relatively fast (f/2.8) telephotos, but the lenses are still fairly expensive.

Third, manually focusing and zooming simultaneously as the subject moves can be difficult to coordinate. You can develop this skill with practice, of course, but it does take time. Autofocus cameras help a lot in this situation.

Although zoom lenses aren't a cure-all, the Associated Press's Risberg maintains that they are "one of the best tools for sports photography."

Iacono of *Sports Illustrated* uses both fixed-length and zoom lenses. He mounts a fixed-length 300mm, a 400mm, and a 600mm on monopods, slings an 80–200mm zoom on his shoulder, and hangs a 55mm on his chest. He keeps the 55mm handy in case a play develops right in front of him. If it does, he quickly grabs the camera with the 55mm and gets off a couple of quick one-handed "Hail Mary" shots. (Here, the photographer lets the lens focus without looking through the viewfinder and prays that the picture is sharp.)

FINDING A NEW LOCATION

Sports photographers are always looking for a different way to capture action since the daily and weekly games themselves look so similar. Instead of shooting from the sidelines, photographers will mount cameras behind the backboard of a basketball net or shoot from the rafters of a gymnasium. Brad Mangin shot a *Sports Illustrated* cover from a position he took in the stands with the fans. His high angle allowed him a clear shot of the Raiders's quarterback with little distracting background. Photographing from the first deck of the stadium, he was able to look almost directly into the eyes of the winning player.

THE MOTORIZED CAMERA FOR SHOOTING SPORTS

A motor drive allows you to fire a series of frames without manually advancing the film between each shot. Every sports photographer interviewed for this book uses a motor drive, but several mentioned that, in some instances, the dependence on a motor drive caused them to miss the peak action of a play.

As sports photographer George Riley points out, "Motors can throw your timing off, and sometimes the best pictures come between the frames." However, Riley quickly adds that, on a controversial play, you need the motor drive to fire off a sequence that shows how the play developed.

The motor drive trips the shutter, advances the frame, and cocks the shutter again for the next picture faster than you can blink an eye. If you use the motor drive semi-automatically—one frame at a time—you need not remove the camera from your eye to advance the film. Or you can shoot rapid-sequence pictures, depending on the make of the camera, at a rate of eight or more frames per second—or even faster with some cameras—without taking your finger off the shutter. This rapid-fire pace increases your chances of capturing peak action.

As in working with all photographic equipment, you must learn the technique of using a motor drive. With the motor drive set on "continuous," you should begin shooting before the action starts and continue holding down the shutter release until after it stops. This will expose a series of frames that encompasses the complete play. From the sequence, you can choose the best frame, one you might have missed had you advanced the film manually.

Because no sane photographer wants to be subjected to a barrage of speeding hockey pucks or powerful slam-dunks, a motor-driven camera also can be placed in a remote location such as inside a hockey goal or behind the plastic of a backboard. The camera can be activated either by an electrical wire or by a wireless remote. Firing the camera remotely can give you a unique vantage, almost in the middle of the melee.

SHOOTING IN POOR LIGHT
Developing Film for Poorly Lit Sports

Outdoor daytime sporting events present few lighting difficulties, but late afternoon and night sports can be tricky to shoot because of low light. First, poor light means that you must set your lens on its widest aperture. Unfortunately, this narrows the depth of field and reduces the chances for a sharp picture. You also might have to turn your shutter dial to a slower speed to compensate for the low light conditions, but this, too, may blur the image in the final picture.

Sports photographers shooting in poorly lit gyms, dark hockey arenas, or unevenly lit outdoor stadiums at night, select the fastest film available. The introduction of 1600 ISO color and 3200 ISO black-and-white film has saved the day for many sports shooters. Many sports photographers use a slower color film and push it one or two stops to achieve better quality and less grain. But sometimes even these fast films are not sensitive enough for shooting high school football, where half the stadium's light bulbs are burned out, or in dungeon-like basketball gyms. In these situations, photographers overrate their film, effectively underexposing it, and then partially compensate for the lack of exposure by increasing development. (See Chapter 11, "Camera Bag.")

Don't Hock Your Strobe Yet!

A few sports situations demand electronic flash, whereas others merely benefit from the use of this lighting source. The electronic flash from a strobe begins and ends so fast that the flash will stop just about any action you might encounter.

Although the lighting effect from a single strobe on camera can look harsh and unnatural, the resulting image will be sharper than a blurred shot taken with available light at a shutter speed too slow to stop motion.

Doug Duran, who shoots for Contra Costa (California) Newspapers, has found that by putting his flash on manual and dialing it to 1/16 power he can take well-exposed pictures at 1/250 sec.

His digital camera is set at 800 ISO and an aperture of f/2.8. Discussing his approach on *SportsShooter.com*, he noted that he sometimes encounters the "red eye" effect. "Red eye" occurs when the flash and lens are near enough to each other that the light from the strobe goes directly into the subject's eyes, hits the retina (which is filled with red blood vessels), and bounces back into the lens. In addition to repairing the image in Photoshop®, another solution is to shoot with the flash as far away from the lens as possible. Duran sometimes recruits a fan in the stands to hold the flash off-camera.

Some photographers like to set up strobes for a spectacular multilight photo at indoor and night sports events. Scot Tucker shoots a lot of high school basketball games in extremely dark gyms for the *San Francisco Independent*. He lights the gym two different ways. Because the gyms are often small, they tend to have low ceilings, enabling him to bounce his strobe.

Tucker uses a 400-watt battery-powered Dynalite aimed at the ceiling. This provides a flat, even light that is just a little brighter than the gym's available light. Alternatively, he sets up two portable, battery-operated strobe lights on either side of the gym and fires them remotely. The two lights can be synchronized with a connecting or wireless sensor that fires both units at the same time. This set-up provides more dramatic light than the bounce-flash approach, but, he cautions, "You have to be careful not to get a shadow from the backboard in the final image."

Some large newspapers and several major magazines such as *Sports Illustrated* light entire sports arenas with a series of huge strobes. When Darren Carroll, a freelancer for *Sports Illustrated*, photographed the national rodeo finals in Las Vegas, he set up twelve Speedotrons in the rafters in order to light an arena as big as a hockey rink.

Photographers connected to these systems can shoot with slow, fine-grain color film and still get outstanding results. The elaborate

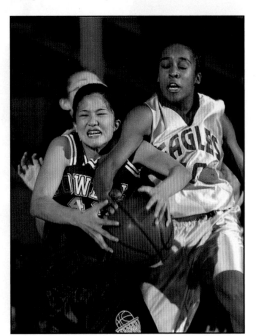

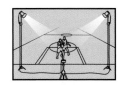

For sports played in poorly lit indoor arenas, you can supplement the available light with strobes mounted on light stands. Here, two battery-powered strobes were located off-court, behind the basket at the corners of the arena. The two strobes were fired with a radio remote slave that sends a signal from the camera to the strobes when the shutter is released. The strobes light up the subjects and also freeze the action at one end of the court. Scot Tucker, for the *San Francisco Independent*

multilight installations require a great deal of money and time but provide photographers enormous flexibility and increase the number of quality images. However, the photographer shooting with a bank of overhead strobes must wait up to three seconds for lights to recycle between pictures, limiting the usefulness of a motor drive to capture action. (See Chapter 12, "Strobe.")

KNOWING WHERE THE BALL WILL BE BEFORE IT GETS THERE
ANTICIPATION IN FOOTBALL

Anticipation in football means that knowing the kind of play to expect—run, pass, or kick. Then you must predict who will be involved in the play—quarterback, running back, or pass-receiver. And finally, you must guess where the play will take place—at the line of scrimmage, behind the line, or downfield.

Basing your position on these predictions, station yourself along the sidelines, usually at the point nearest the expected action. Choose the appropriate lens and follow-focus the player you expect to get the ball. Then wait—and hope your instincts are on target.

ANTICIPATION IN BASEBALL

At one time, photographers actually were allowed to work on the field of major league baseball games. But this freedom was curtailed because of the antics of photographers like Hy Peskin. An outstanding photographer, Peskin was covering a close game between the Giants and the Dodgers from a spot behind first base when he saw a ball hit into right field. He realized there would be a close play at third base.

With the volatile Leo Durocher coaching at third, Peskin knew there would be a scene. As the right-fielder chased down the ball, Peskin took the shortest route to third base—over the pitcher's mound and across the infield. Peskin, the runner, and the ball all arrived at third base at the same moment.

Peskin got his pictures, but after similar incidents, photographers were barred from the playing field of major league games.

Had Peskin anticipated third-base action before the play began, he could have positioned himself near that baseline, or he could have focused with a long lens on third.

The key to getting great sports photographs is anticipation. Anticipation means predicting not only what's going to happen but where it's going to happen. You must base these predictions on knowledge of the game, the players, and the coaches.

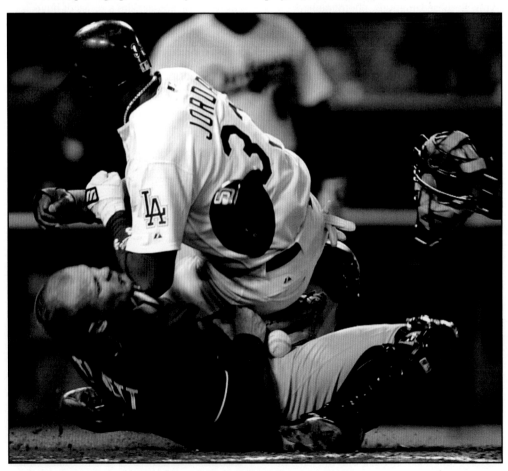

Anticipating that the next play would take place at home plate, the photographer had programmed his camera to prefocus there. Still, he tracked the runner from first to second before swinging his lens to home. As the runner arrived, the photographer adjusted the lens slightly with manual focus just at the right moment. The photo was taken with at f/2.8 with a 400mm lens on a digital camera, effectively making the lens a 600mm. Keith Birmingham, *Pasadena Star-News*

Keith Birmingham of the *Pasadena Star-News* was tracking Brian Jordan of the Los Angeles Dodgers as the player rounded second base. Birmingham quickly surmised that the important play would take place at home plate. The photographer swung his long telephoto, a 400mm f/2.8 on a digital camera, toward home, focused, and waited. He used a slight manual lens adjustment as the runner knocked the ball of the San Diego Padre catcher's hands on the way to the third run of the game (page 130).

Counteracting Reaction Time

Besides anticipating the action of key players, you must also press the shutter before the action reaches its peak. In baseball, for instance, if you hit the trigger of your camera when you hear the crack of the bat against the ball, your final picture will show a swinging batter but no ball. You would swear that you squeezed the shutter at the same instant the bat met the ball, yet the picture clearly demonstrates the shutter was delayed. Why?

As David Guralnick, who shoots sports for the *Detroit News*, points out, "If you saw it, you missed it." A lag-time occurs between the crack of the bat and the moment you press the shutter. Psychologists call this lag period "reaction time" and they are able to measure precisely its duration.

Reaction time is the period the brain takes to 1) recognize an important play in progress; 2) decide whether to take the picture; 3) send a positive signal to the proper muscle group, in this case the index finger; and 4) contract the forefinger muscles to release the camera's shutter.

Even after the shutter trigger is depressed, there's another delay while the camera itself responds. Even the most sensitive shutter still takes time to function. This shutter reaction time is the fifth element in reaction time. All five steps added together account for the reaction time between seeing the action and capturing the picture.

Your brain runs through these same steps every time you take any picture, but the

Because of the inherent delay caused by a photographer's reaction time, a shooter could have missed a key moment like this one without realizing it.

John Coley, *Palm Beach Post*

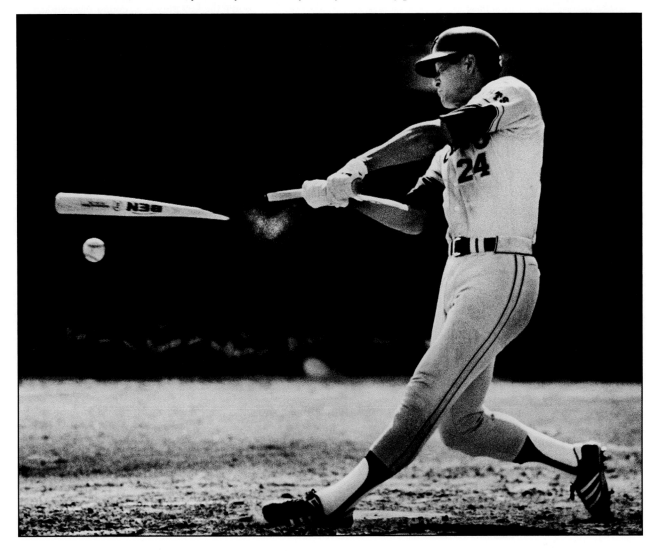

cumulative length of reaction time becomes critical when the subject is a baseball moving at 90 mph.

WAITING 'TIL "ALL HELL BREAKS LOOSE"

The AP's Pam Schuyler describes baseball as a "Zen sport" that requires infinite patience to photograph because the action erupts in spurts, and instant response is needed. "You wait and wait, and nothing happens. Then, all of a sudden, all hell breaks loose," says Schuyler. "I get bored easily at a baseball game and then I lose my concentration. That's when the big action always seems to occur!"

It does appear sometimes that nothing ever happens in baseball. In fact, the perfect game from the standpoint of a baseball aficionado is a "no-hitter." Sports writers still refer to the "great" game in the 1956 World Series when Don Larsen of the Yankees pitched a no-hitter. Not only were there no hits but there were also no walks and no errors. Twenty-seven Dodgers went from the dugout to the plate and back again without reaching first base.

Unfortunately, there was no action for the photographer to shoot in this "perfect" baseball game. The picture that is remembered shows Larsen pitching his last ball, with a row of Dodger zeroes on the scoreboard in the background.

SLIDING SECOND

Luckily for photographers, a no-hitter is rare. Most games have at least some action at the bases, and baseball, like all sports, has its standard action shot. In baseball, the standard photo is the second-base slide.

When the play is going to take place at second base, train your telephoto lens on the base, focus, and wait for the action. With a motor drive, the timing does not have to be so exact because the camera fires several frames per second. If you press the release as the slide begins and hold it until the umpire makes the call, one frame is likely to coincide with the peak of the action.

Often a good series of pictures results. Any photos from the series showing intense expressions on the players' faces will have additional human interest.

STEALING BASE

When the key play is a second-base slide, photographers simply zero-in on the base and concentrate. By watching second base, Michael Doherty of the *Utica* (New York) *Observer-Dispatch* caught the moment as a

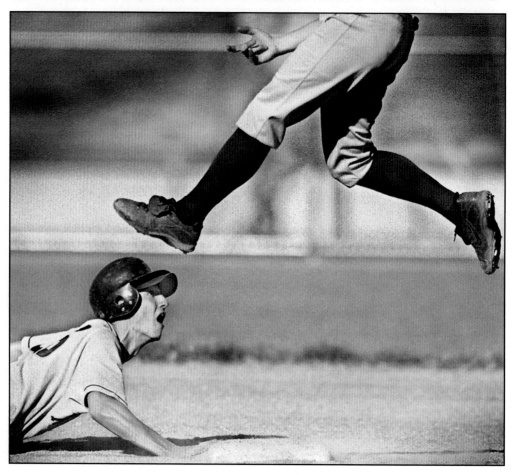

Watch for players trying to steal bases. Leaping to catch the ball, the infielder missed the catch and, fortunately, also missed landing atop the sliding runner.
Michael Doherty, *Utica Observer-Dispatch* [New York]

runner slid his hands under the cleated feet of a fielder leaping for a fly ball (page 132).

A more difficult situation occurs when a notorious base-stealer ventures into no-man's land between first and second. The pitcher could try to pick off the runner at first if he thinks the runner has too daring a lead-off, or the catcher could peg the runner if he breaks for second. Unfortunately, in the major leagues, players steal bases less often than they used to.

Cover this split action by prefocusing one camera on second base and setting this camera aside; then focus another camera on first base and keep the camera to your eye. You can snap a picture of the pick-off on first, or, if the runner heads for second base, you'll have time to raise your other, prefocused, camera and catch the slide at second.

When a runner gets to second base and is officially "in scoring position," you should prefocus on home plate. On the next fair play, the runner might try to score.

RUNNER VS. THE BALL

One general rule is to follow the runner, not the ball, with your lens. A routine catch in the outfield makes a routine picture. Except with a short fly, when either the infielder has to catch the ball in back of him, or the outfielder has to dive for it, keep your camera focused on the base runners.

AP's Risberg, however, says he has taken exciting pictures of outfield play with an extremely long telephoto lens. With the ball headed long, the outfielder could drop it or collide with another outfielder. "Ninety percent of the time nothing interesting happens," agrees freelancer Brad Mangin. "He just catches the ball. The other ten percent can provide a memorable picture."

If the ball is headed for a home run you can tell where it is likely to land by the excited reaction of the fans as they scramble to snag a souvenir.

Risberg also points out that, during slow games, shooters should watch the reactions of batters. For games without much action, he says, the dugout provides good picture opportunities.

Photographers position themselves several yards back from the base path between home and first base, home and third, or in the press gallery. From these positions, especially when shooting high school, college, and professional baseball, sports photographers prefer a 300mm or 400mm lens to cover the infield and a 600mm or 800mm to cover the outfield. A sandlot or Little League playing field measures a shorter distance, hence a 135mm lens covers the infield easily.

If you are trying to photograph a shortstop diving for the ball, focus on this player and wait. There's not enough time to shift focus from the batter to a shortstop hurtling toward a line drive. By the time you find and focus on the infielder, the play will be over.

THE UNUSUAL

Baseball is a team sport played by individuals, each with his own strengths and his own repertoire of favorite stunts. One ballplayer might hold the season's record in stolen bases, while a pitcher might lead the league in pick-offs at first.

With this combination, the smart photographer has the camera lens focused and aimed squarely at first. One batter might be a consistent bunter; another might consider a bunt below his dignity under any circumstances. The more you know about the idiosyncrasies of the players, the better your forecasts and your pictures will be.

Although the dust-swirling second-base slide is a sports photographer's guaranteed bread-and-butter shot, sometimes the shot can be overworked. "You can almost take the

Anticipating who is likely to receive a pass increases the photographer's chance of recording a critical play. Here, the photographer tracked the San Francisco 49ers's Jerry Rice off the scrimmage line through a 400mm lens with a 1.4 tele-extender to capture this successful pass. An aperture of f/2.8 blurred the background. © Brad Mangin

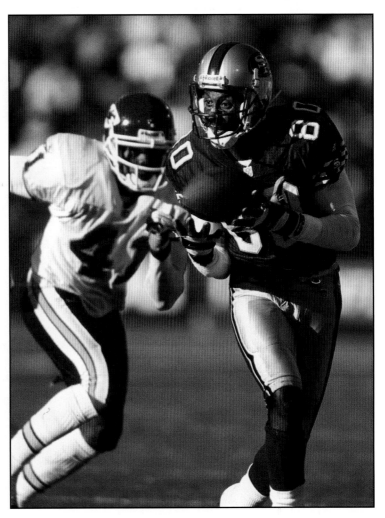

slide shot out of the files, the situation starts to look so similar," says one shooter.

When shooting for *Sports Illustrated*, Brad Mangin positions himself in the photographers' box behind first base and shoot with either a 600mm lens or a 400mm f/2.8 with a teleconverter. "This is a basic, good, safe angle for shooting second base, home, and the outfield," he says.

For a different shot, he sets up a remote camera before the game. He clamps it on the backstop behind home plate, points it toward third base, and prefocuses a little past home to anticipate the slide at the plate. He connects the remote camera to his box position with a long wire, uses either a foot switch or a button to trip the remote camera, and reloads between innings. When a play occurs, he activates the remote but also shoots with his long telephoto because the batter in the on-deck circle can block the camera.

"You can go ten games with no play at the plate," Mangin says, "but when you get the head-on shot, it's got impact."

The antics of the team manager also may provide a rich source of photographic material. When he strides onto the field, you can bet sparks will fly whether he harangues the umpire or yanks out the losing pitcher.

You can shoot baseball without being a Zen master. Just remember that you will never go hungry if you consistently catch your bread-and-butter action picture, the second-base slide. But you are more likely to be eating steak and lobster if you cover all the important action on the field.

FINDING THE FOOTBALL

When you cover a football game, you face some of the same problems as a 250-pound defensive tackle. Before each down, you and the football player have to predict which way the quarterback will move on the next play.

After the center hikes the ball, you and the tackle must react quickly and make adjustments as the play unfolds.

Will the quarterback hand off to a speedster for an end-run or to a powerful halfback for a bruising plunge through the center? Or will the quarterback throw a quick spike for short yardage or a long bomb to the end zone?

As the defensive player considers the options, sports photographers likewise anticipate the call and prepare for the play. You must be in the right place at the right time, with the right equipment, ready and waiting for the action: runs, passes, and punts.

Plays in which something goes wrong, like this assistant coach intercepting a pass, are often more interesting than plays executed successfully.
Scott D. Weaver, *Independence* [Missouri] *Examiner*

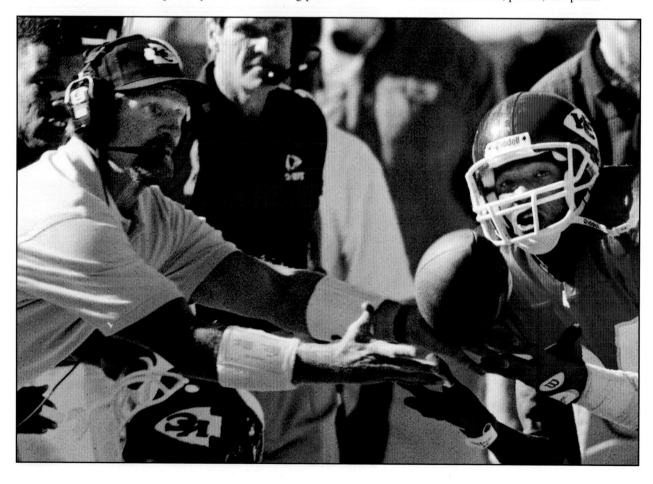

WATCHING FOR THE RUN

On a run, photographers track the football as it is snapped by the center and either carried by the quarterback or handed to another backfield player.

Most teams tend to run the ball on the first down because a run is generally considered a safer play than a pass. Or as former Ohio State coach Woody Hayes put it, "Only three things can happen when you pass, and two of them are bad." Therefore, cautious quarterbacks like to keep the ball on the ground on the first down, less a pass get intercepted or dropped. Caution also dictates the use of a running play on a third down when the team is just one or two yards shy of a first down. Some teams, particularly the Big Ten power squads with their strong running backs and blockers, carry the football not only on the first and third downs, but are very likely to run on the second down as well.

SHOOTING THE "BOMB"

Photographers can anticipate a pass on the first down instead of a run only if the team is behind on the scoreboard, needs long yardage on the play, or wants to stop the clock. A quarterback might go to the air on the second down if the team is just a few yards short of first down; he knows he still has two more downs to pick up the necessary ground. You can bet with good odds on a third-down pass if the team has lost ground or failed to advance the ball on the first two downs.

You can predict the "big bomb" by noting the score and watching the quarterback's body language. If the quarterback drops back far behind the line of scrimmage, firmly plants his feet, pumps the ball a few times, and then cocks his arm way back behind his head, he is very likely winding up for a long throw.

Once you read these cues and see a "bomb" in the making, you should immediately swing the barrel of your telephoto lens downfield, focus on the expected receiver, and follow his pass pattern.

Observe the direction of the quarterback's gaze for a tip-off on which downfield receiver will get the ball. Good sports photographers know that even the best quarterback has to look where he's throwing the ball. If you can predict ahead of time which receiver might catch the pass, you can train your lens on him and follow him as the play develops. You will have a higher probability of capturing the ball at the tips of a receiver's fingers if you have tracked him throughout the play.

ADJUSTING YOUR POSITION

At each down, station yourself a few yards ahead of the scrimmage line. Then, when the play begins, wait for a clear, unobstructed view of the ball carrier before you press the shutter release. At most stadiums, photographers are permitted to roam freely from the end zone to about the 25-yard line for National Football League games or the 35-yard line for other leagues. To avoid distracting the coaches and sidelined players, photographers are prohibited from moving in front of the benches at the center of the field.

Photographers must stay behind the sideline boundary strip at all times and never get between the player on the field and the yardage marker poles. If you had to jump back quickly as the thundering pack of players heads toward the sidelines, you could trip on the marking chain and get trampled—a high price to pay, even for the most dramatic action shot. Mickey Phleger, a freelancer for *Sports Illustrated*, suffered a concussion when a player ran out of bounds and took Mickey along with him.

Some photographers like shooting with a long lens from the end zone. They like that fact that they are looking directly into the face of the quarterback. Although linemen can block the shot, the photographer situated in the end zone can have a clear shot of a quarterback who rolls out.

All 50,000 pairs of eyes in the stadium are searching for the pigskin. The ball itself is the center of interest because everyone wants to know who has the ball and what's happening to it. Therefore, you have an obligation to get the brown leather ball in your picture as often as you can. The players, trained by their coaches to protect the ball at all times, will make your task difficult.

Not every picture must involve the ball carrier. After all, when one 250-pounder, with an indestructible frame and shoulder pads, meets another human impasse capped by an impact-resistant helmet, something has to give. The confrontation scene might be spectacular—even if it occurs ten yards away from the ball.

A 400mm lens will cover the action. If you try to cover midfield action with a shorter lens, the final image size will be too small for a high-quality enlargement. With a versatile 80–200mm zoom, you can photograph from the end zone when the team is on the ten-yard line and goal to go. In addition to the 200mm and 400mm lenses, some photographers carry an extra body with a 50mm or 35mm wide-angle attached for moments when the play runs toward them. Also, the wide-angle comes in handy when, at the end of the game, the team carries the coach on their shoulders or slumps off in defeat.

Avoiding the "Standard Stuff"
When Pam Schuyler covered football for the AP, she looked for dramatic catches, fumbles, collisions, and flagrant penalties such as face-masking or illegal holdings. She always searches for the unusual football picture. "You get only a half-dozen super pictures a year if you are lucky," she says. "The remainder is standard stuff."

DON'T BE FAKED OUT IN BASKETBALL
The ball travels so lightning-fast in basketball that following the ball is like keeping your eye on the pea in the old shell game. Unlike football with its discreet downs, and baseball with its clearly defined plays, the basketball game rolls on at full speed until a point has been scored, a foul called, or the ball goes out of bounds.

The basketball might be bigger than a baseball or a football, but keeping track of it can be just as tough.

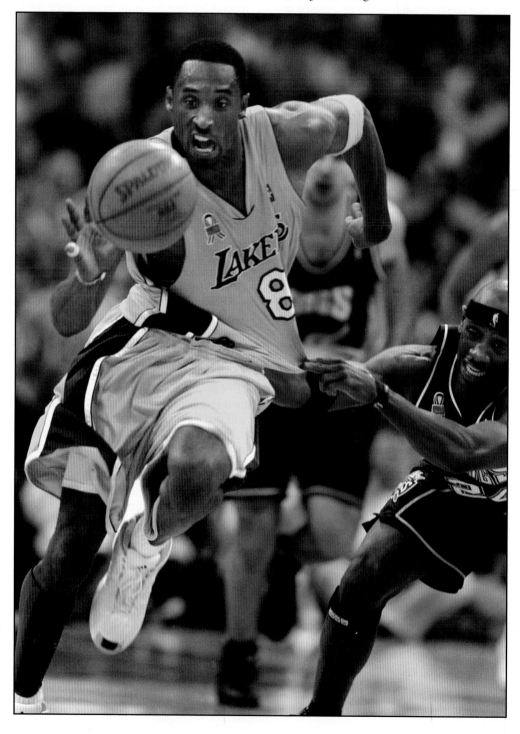

Watch for players to commit fouls. This frequently occurs when they try to steal the ball at midcourt. Here, Bobby Jackson tries everything to keep Kobe Bryant from making a basket on a fast break in the fourth quarter of game six of the NBA Western Conference Finals between the Sacramento Kings and the Los Angeles Lakers.
Bryan Patrick, *Sacramento Bee*

The AP's Risberg says that he concentrates on watching the ball and the players' arms. They tip him off when he is trying to anticipate action.

Pam Schuyler spent two intensive years covering the world-champion Boston Celtics for a picture book she photographed and wrote called *Through the Hoop: A Season with the Celtics*. She says that the key problem in photographing basketball is learning to read the "fake," the quick twisting and jerking movements that players use to deceive their opponents and get a clear shot at the basket. As Schuyler says, "They often fake out the photographer as well."

SIDELINE POSITIONS

Many basketball photographers sit on small stools or kneel on the floor behind and a little to either side of the basket. Then they shoot with a 50mm or 85mm lens, focusing about ten to fifteen feet into the court and wait. Even in the days before autofocus, Schuyler preferred to gamble on more unusual shots by follow-focusing the ball being tossed around the court. "You get more bad, out-of-focus shots when you follow-focus, but your good shots are usually worth it," Schuyler says.

After the first few minutes of the game, Schuyler identifies the key players and notes where they execute most of their plays: under the backboard, to the right of the foul line, and so on. She then positions herself as near as possible to this focal spot. If the action spot changes as the game progresses, she shifts her sideline position.

With her two favorite basketball lenses, the 85mm and the 180mm, Schuyler covers the entire court. From under the basket, she shoots with the 85mm; from midcourt, she works with the 180mm. She always sets the shutter speed at 1/500 sec. to freeze movement. "At slower speeds, I've found the players' hands move so fast they tend to blur." Detroit's David Guralnick prefers an 80–200mm zoom under the basket and a 300mm f/2.8 to cover the far court.

THE "ARMPIT" SHOT

The bread-and-butter basketball photo, nicknamed the "armpit" shot, shows a leaping player with arms extended over his head, pumping the ball toward the basket. Pro players use the jump shot so often that conscientious photographers actually have to work hard to avoid taking this standard photo.

SKIPPING THE CLICHÉ

For unique basketball pictures, watch for loose basketballs on the court. "You can bet when a ball's free, there will be a scramble for it, and then a fight to gain possession of it," Schuyler explains. "Players fouling one another always look funny in pictures, and these seem to be the pictures people remember longest. When a ball bounces loose or a foul is committed, the rhythm of the game is broken. A mistake was made. The game gets interesting, and so do the pictures."

When you can't attend practice sessions, or when you don't have time to learn the team's basic patterns, concentrate your coverage on the player with the star reputation. Stars tend to score the most points and snag the majority of rebounds.

Also, stars don't sink baskets like regular folk; they exhibit individual styles and almost choreographed moves. Michael Jordan, for example, would seem to counteract gravity as he floated through the air, passed the basket, and, as if it were an afterthought, changed direction in mid-flight to sink a hoop. A good sports photographer tries to capture in pictures the style of the star. ∎

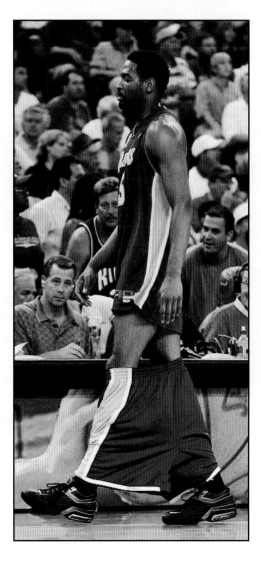

Keep a sharp eye on the sidelines for surprising features like this moment when Robert Horry lost his pants during the NBA Western Conference Finals between the Sacramento Kings and the Los Angeles Lakers.
Jose Luis Villegas, *Sacramento Bee*

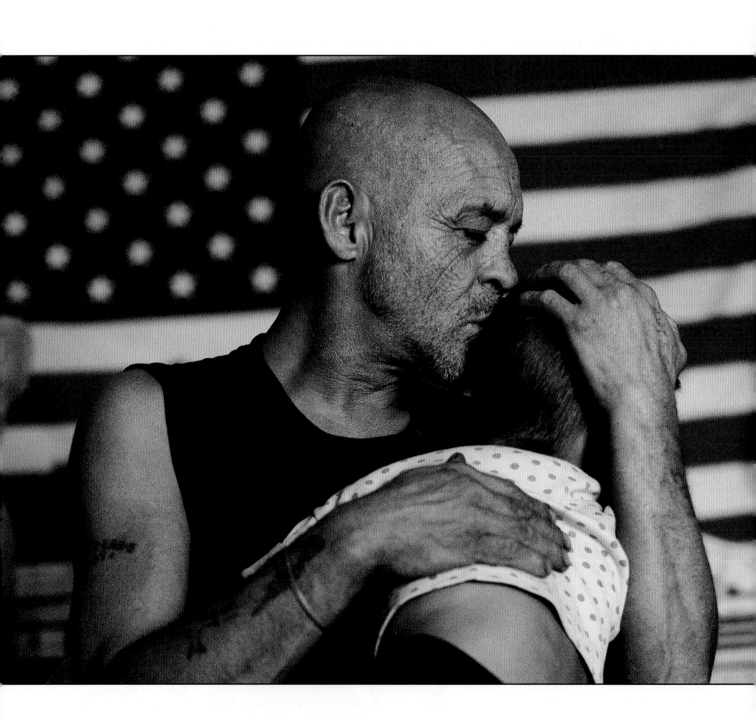

Chapter 8

Photo Story

TELLING STORIES WITH PICTURES

For many photojournalists, telling whole stories with pictures is the ultimate professional experience.

Sometimes stories can be built in a matter of minutes; sometimes storytelling can take years. Whereas Jim MacMillan of the *Philadelphia Daily News* photographed his story about a hostage situation in fewer than five minutes (see page 31), Alan Berner shot his essay about the New West (pages 76–77) during a six-month sabbatical from the *Seattle Times*.

Brian Plonka, of the Spokane (Washington)

Spokesman Review, spent two years documenting

When his girlfriend was sent to jail, Henry Guiliante was left with their four children in a single motel room. Having already abandoned six other children by three other women, would Henry find the strength to be a real father? Kari René Hall, Los Angeles

A PLACE UNSEEN

Photos by Ken Light

His curiosity aroused by African-American colleagues at the University of California, Berkeley, where he teaches, documentary photographer Ken Light began traveling to the Mississippi Delta region of the South in 1989.

"It seemed to me to be a place unseen by newspapers, magazines, and television," Light says. By networking in the community, Light met various people who acted as guides, introduced him into people's homes and helped him to understand the political and social workings of the area.

Light emphasized his role as professional photographer by shooting with the medium-format Hasselblad camera so that people would not mistake him for a tourist.

Completely self-supported, Light pursued the project for three years. Smithsonian Institution Press published his work as a book, *Delta Time*.

After the book's publication, Light says, he sold many original prints. The book and those sales have allowed him to continue working on independent projects. ∎

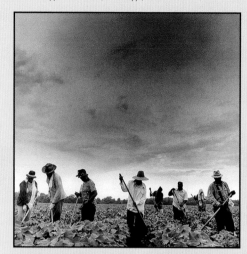

Cotton choppers in Sherard, Mississippi, 1992.

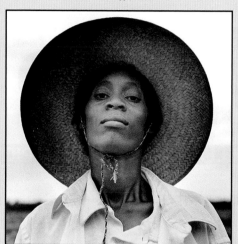

Shirley Clark, 30, on Sherard Plantation, has been chopping cotton since she was 13. Sherard, Mississippi, 1992.

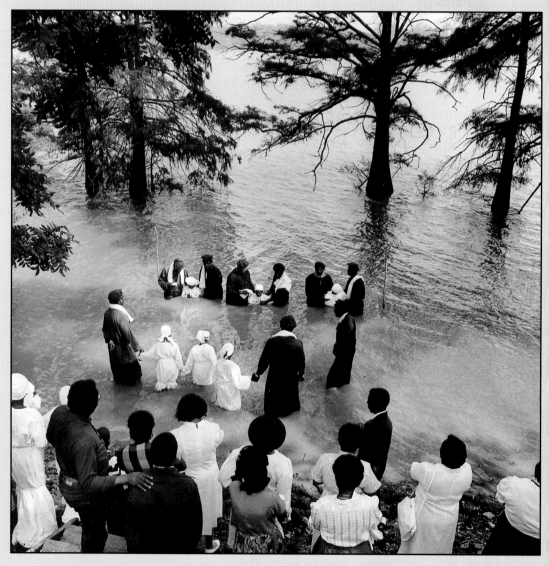

Baptism, Moon Lake, Coahoma County, Mississippi, 1989.

how alcoholism is passed from one generation to another (pages 64–67). Kari René Hall, while employed at the *Los Angeles Times*, followed the story of a single welfare father for five years on her own time and with her own funds (pages 166–171).

Why do photographers spend such time, effort, and money to shoot photo stories, essays, and documentaries? Whether personally financed, grant-supported, or underwritten by a newspaper or magazine, these sets of pictures are the avenues through which photographers document ways of life, explore topics in depth, present a point of view, or show with pictures the many sides of an issue.

THE ERA OF THE MODERN PHOTO STORY

With the advent of high-speed presses that could quickly dry the ink on glossy, coated paper, Henry Luce published the first issue of *Life* in 1936. Inspired by the success of *Life*, other large picture-dominated magazines with names like *Look, Click, Scoop, Peek, Pix,* and *Picture* hit the stands. (See Chapter 15, "History," page 357.) These magazines also ran pages of pictures on a single topic.

FOLLOWING A SCRIPT

Though some picture stories in these competing magazines were candid, most were heavily scripted. Even after World War II, magazines continued to produce highly scripted picture stories. *Look* magazine, for example, published on January 8, 1946, a story on quick-frozen, precooked, ready-to-serve meals (today's TV dinners). The opening picture featured a "family" in their living room reading and playing records. The following overly lit pictures show "mom" taking a frozen meal from the refrigerator, putting it in the oven, and then taking the food out after fifteen minutes. The final shot in the six-image series depicts "family members" seated around the table and prepared to eat the new cuisine. The photographer's shooting script, which specified opening and closing shots as well as a record of the preparatory steps in between, obviously left no room for real people or candid moments to interfere with the slick look of the pictures. The photos look like stills from an advertisement.

SMITH INTRODUCES THE MODERN PHOTO STORY

Toward the end of the 1940s, photographers began experimenting with a freer form of picture story development. W. Eugene Smith, working for *Life* magazine, broke with the typical pre-scripted story line. Smith's pictures of country doctor Ernest Ceriani of Kremmling, Colorado (population 1,000),

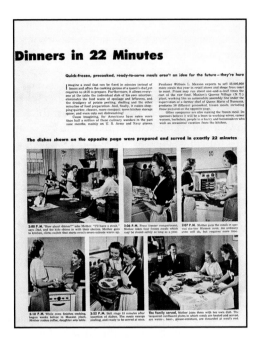

Picture magazines in the 1940s often published highly scripted stories like this one. The editor and photographer preplanned each photo as if it were a scene from a movie.
Look magazine

actually documented the physician's life—without a New York editor predetermining the story's look and point of view (*Life*, September 20, 1948). By staying with the doctor for six weeks in all, and by recording the doctor's everyday activities as well as the emergencies and traumas he faced, Smith built a realistic story about the dedicated health worker. The story still had cohesion, but was based on Smith's observations, not the preconceived idea of a New York editor who demanded an overall and a close-up for the script. Staying close to his subject and observing carefully, Smith fashioned a revealing story about the life of the rural doctor.

Today, though they usually work independently and not for magazines, some photographers follow in Smith's tradition in pursuing long-term photo projects. (For more on W. Eugene Smith, see pages 361–362.)

FINDING STORIES
PERSONAL EXPERIENCE

Sometimes a picture story comes from the photographer's own experience. When Brian Plonka's father, an alcoholic, celebrated ten years of sobriety, Plonka decided to explore alcoholism with his camera (pages 64–67).

Talking with other people also alerts you to good picture story ideas. In a casual conversation with the author, a professor of special education at San Francisco State University described the effects of crack cocaine on children exposed to the drug while still in the womb. The professor pointed out that a behavioral epidemic was brewing in public education as these crack-exposed children started to enter the schools. More questions and additional research led to a story about the impact of "crack kids" in the classroom. (See pages 72–73.)

ASSIGNMENTS

Some stories develop when the photographer takes an assignment from an editor or follows a call on the scanner radio. Jim MacMillan responded to a scanner exchange about a car chase that ended in a hostage situation. When MacMillan arrived at the scene, he found that the gunman had grabbed a bystander and was holding him hostage as cops with drawn pistols surrounded the two. While MacMillan was documenting the action, the hostage managed to grab the gun, the cops arrested the "perp," and the hostage sank down in relief for a moment of prayer. Within minutes, MacMillan had recorded an entire story (page 31).

Carol Guzy's previous trips to Africa made her the logical choice for the *Washington Post* to send to cover the return of Rwandan Hutus to their home villages; they had fled Rwanda to Zaire when their people were being slaughtered by their enemies, the Tutsis. Guzy sent back daily photographs for the paper, but she also accumulated images for a powerful story about the population's mass return (pages 82–83).

TOPICAL TRENDS

A trend story identifies a gradual but demonstrably real change that might include shifts in the public's buying preferences, lifestyles, or a technological shift in an industry. For example, a news story might read, "First National Bank Bankrupt." By comparison, a trend story might announce, "Increase in Number of Two-income Families over 10-Year Period." A trend doesn't start in one day; it occurs gradually over time.

Perhaps an issue addressed in a topical book or movie might stimulate a photographer's interest to investigate the subject with his or her camera. A trend story can be localized for a photographer's particular area. Judy Griesedieck, who worked for the San Jose's *Mercury News* at the time, used her camera as an investigative tool to expose the conditions in nursing homes in her area (page 62).

Like any good journalist, the photo reporter must rely on basic journalistic research, a highly sensitized nose for news, and a trained sense of whether what smells like news can be reported visually as well.

SPOTTING TRENDS

Surprisingly enough, the *Wall Street Journal*, which rarely runs a photograph, is an excellent source for picture story ideas. The *Journal* reports on interesting trends in the business world that photographers can translate into highly visual photo stories. Not only are the *Journal* reports often the first to spot a trend, but the stories are well researched. For major trend stories, which appear in the left and middle columns of the front page, *Journal* staffers spend months researching and gathering data before they begin to write.

After reading a *Wall Street Journal* story, you must find visual verification of the trend. Your job is to transform economic charts and abstract statistics from the *Journal*'s article into eye-catching pictures.

TELLING STORIES WITH PICTURES

How does a picture story differ from a collection of pictures on a topic? A picture story has a theme. Not only are the individual pictures in the story about one subject, but they also help to support one central point.

TEST YOUR THEME WITH A HEADLINE

Headlines for stories without a theme might begin in the following ways:
• "All you ever want to know about . . ."
• "A day in the life of . . ."
• "Aspects of . . ."
• "Scenes from . . ."

Stories with these headlines might contain beautiful or even powerful pictures, but the pictures don't add up to a story. They remain the photographer's observations without a story line or central message.

On the other hand, a theme story such as crack cocaine's lasting effect on children (pages 72-73) tries to visually identify only the specific behavioral reactions that the drug has on children who were exposed to crack in their mother's womb. This set of pictures does not tell the reader everything about crack or how to take care of newborns. Rather, the story tries to show the special behaviors crack-addicted infants and children exhibit—such as constant crying, painful expressions, the need for soothing massage, and disruption in the classroom. The headline for this story might read, "Crack: The Next Generation."

Here are some headlines for stories with a theme:
• "Every Day is Father's Day," a story about a single dad.
• "Generation Under the Influence," a story about how alcoholism is passed from one generation to the next.

Each of these headlines suggests a specific story with a defined theme.

Once you decide on a story and started to shoot it, try writing a headline for it. Nailing down a headline indicates that you have a clear focus for the story. Make sure your headline is specific to the story and differentiates your point of view from other stories on the same topic.

"Generations under the Influence" (pages 64–67) helped to define Brian Plonka's project on alcoholism. His story investigated not only excessive drinking but also how this problem affects different age groups as well as how it is passed from one generation to another.

Once you have a headline, see if you can include or reject pictures on the basis of whether the photos fit the story's headline. If the headline is so encompassing that all the photos fit, your theme is probably too broad and the headline not specific enough.

You can devise many themes and therefore many headlines from a single situation. Even after you have finished shooting, you might find that by rewriting a headline and then reediting your pictures, you could produce a different story line. Each theme or headline demands a different edit, for the opener and all the pictures that follow. Just for fun, try changing the titles on any of the stories in this book, and see how you might change the pictures that you would include in the edit.

FIND A NEWSPEG
Whether you are an employee or a freelancer, an editor is more likely to use your picture story if it has a newspeg, also known as a hook. A newspeg tells the reader why the story is being seen now instead of six months ago or six months in the future. If you can tie your picture story into a front-page news item, then your story will take on more immediacy.

Suppose your story centers on the life of a family doctor. You might peg your pictures on a recent study showing that the number of general practitioners is decreasing nationally. Or suppose your story concerns your town's emergency medical squad. If a squad member died last month while trying to save a child's life, your timeless story about the unit's general operations can be pegged to this recent news event.

Some editors assign stories and hold them until a related news event takes place. The news sections of the daily newspaper, therefore, provide excellent sources for story ideas because the news leads are timely. Dave Yoder, now a staffer for the *Orange County Register*, followed the dangerous lives of several bounty hunters (pages 156–157). Photos like these might find a home in the paper when a reporter writes about the high number of bail jumpers.

TYPES OF PEOPLE STORIES
Maitland Edey, who was an editor at *Life* magazine, once observed, "Great photo essays have to do with people: with human dilemmas, with human challenges, with human suffering." People's lives, even if they are not in crisis situations, still provide the basis for most of the best photo stories.

Photo stories about people usually break down into three categories: the well known, the little known but interesting, and the little known who serve as an example of a trend.

THE WELL KNOWN
Photo stories about well-known personalities provide the primary content for several larger circulation magazines. The best-read section of *Time* magazine, called "People," gave *Time*, Inc., editors the idea for a picture magazine featuring personalities as the sole subject. Naturally, the editors called the magazine *People*. This popular weekly publishes a steady diet of photos showing the lives of the famous and the infamous. Not only *People* but also an assortment of other magazines—from *Vanity Fair* to *Esquire*—publish an endless variety of stories about movie stars, TV personalities, media moguls, and politicians. (See behind-the-scenes photos of politicians by Diana Walker, pages 46, 48, and 202, and P.F. Bentley, pages 49 and 290, for *Time* magazine; also see Hollywood portraits by Michael Grecco, pages 270 and 273, and by Annie Leibovitz, page 114). Today, in fact, celebrity stories dominate the contents of most mass-circulation magazines.

THE LITTLE KNOWN BUT INTERESTING
In addition to the famous, *People* magazine prints photo stories about little-known people who either do something interesting or exhibit eccentric characteristics.

Hero or not, the person must do something to fascinate readers. The stuntman who climbed the outside of the World Trade Center and the champion stacker of bowling balls are examples of people with unusual accomplishments. The young Goths Warren Hsu photographed qualify as an example of a group of people living an unusual lifestyle (pages 164–165). Dave Yoder's in-depth look at bounty hunters reveals, to say the least, an unusual occupation (pages 156–157).

THE LITTLE KNOWN BUT REPRESENTATIVE
One Person as an Example of a Trend
Another type of personality story investigates the life of a little-known person who is an example of a new trend or developing style. For example, a growing number of children in America live with only one parent.

Mose Vinson
Piano Player

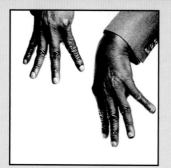

Bored during a long press conference, Robert Cohen found himself watching the hands of the mayor of Memphis. "I thought about the concept of people's hands and the stories they might tell, and I filed the idea away."

Later, he decided to follow through. "I wanted to photograph a myriad of folks. Well-known people, unknown people, and those in between were fair game." ■

Photos by Robert Cohen
The Commercial Appeal
[Memphis, Tennessee]

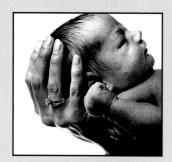

Diane Long, Obstetrician

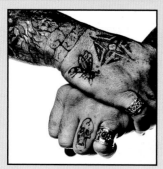

Larry Wright, Tattoo Artist

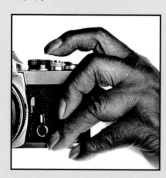

Ernest Withers, Photographer

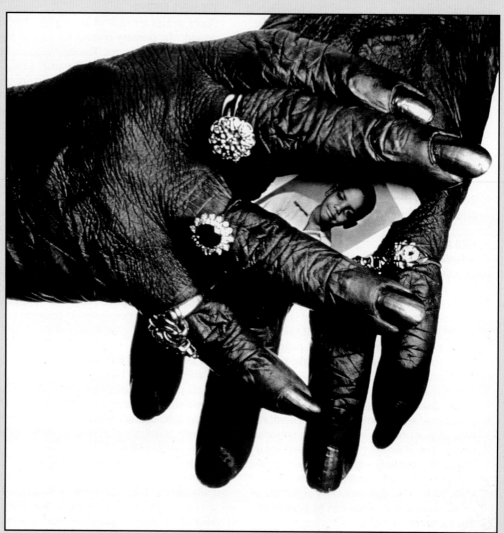

➤ Farris Hodges, Jr.
Purple Heart

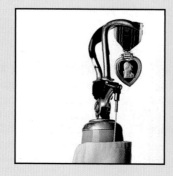

▲ Louise Hardaway
Grandmother of
Penny Hardaway,
basketball star

Nancy Andrews explored this trend in her story about single fatherhood. At the same time, she countered the conventional image of the absent African-American father. (See page 195 for one photo from the story.) "Never Too Old for Love" (pages 162–163) is the story of an otherwise ordinary 85-year-old widower who has decided to start dating again. He mirrors the future for Baby Boomers now approaching 60.

One Person Representing an Abstract Topic

At times, photographers want to explore abstract topics. But abstract topics often don't lend themselves to pictures. Again, photographers can use one person who is not famous to personify an abstract topic. Focusing on one person affected by atomic radiation or on one person living on the streets dramatizes the general problems of nuclear power or homelessness. Readers identify with the woes of an individual much more than with the problems of a political group or a sociological class.

For photographers, converting a topic into human terms provides a visual clothesline on which to hang the individual points of the picture story.

Annie Wells's story about one "average" woman—herself—facing cancer helps tell the story of many women who are living with the potentially deadly disease (pages 148–151). Kari René Hall visually explores the economic problems of welfare. She leads readers into the complicated lives of a struggling welfare family by concentrating on one father in one family (pages 166–171).

VISUAL CONSISTENCY TO HOLD PHOTOS TOGETHER

Regardless of their subject matter, pictures can take on greater power on a printed page. What suggests to the reader that a group of pictures interacts as a story rather than functions independently as individual images, such as the ones you see on a gallery wall?

In a successful layout, the photos interact with one another and form an eye-catching, compelling picture story. When the layout is unsuccessful, the pictures remain separate units simply coexisting on the page. To link pictures together visually, photographers use pictorial devices. With a visually unified essay, the viewer sees in almost every picture the same

1) person,
2) object,
3) mood,
4) theme,
5) perspective, or
6) camera technique.

SAME PERSON

The easiest way to tie pictures together into a photo story is to concentrate on one person. Restricting the scope to one individual helps to define the focus of the series. The person's identity, repeated in each photo, threads the story together and gives the layout continuity. (See "Face to Face with Breast Cancer" pages 148–151; "Never Too Old for Love," pages 162–163; "She's a Lady Boxer," page 153; and "Motel Dad," pages 166–167.)

Like a microscope, the camera magnifies the subject's daily routine in a picture story. The results of the visual probe depend on the subject's accessibility and cooperation. The photographer shadows the subject as long as the person doesn't object, and as long as the paper or magazine will allow.

In the heyday of the big glossy picture magazines and their lavish photo budgets, photographers were given considerably more time to shoot personality stories than they are today. When John Dominis was on the staff of *Life* magazine, he worked on his story about Frank Sinatra for four months before the story was finished. Later, as picture editor of *People* magazine, with its much smaller photo budget, Dominis assigned photographers to personality profiles and expected the job done in half a day.

Using one person as the continuous thread holds individual pictures together like beads on a necklace. Annie Wells's first-person story of her own breast cancer is the ultimate example. When Wells felt a lump in her breast that her own family history told her was malignant, she responded with the purchase of a Nikon Coolpix camera with a swivel lens that would allow her to photograph herself and what she was going through. Her face appears in almost every picture—during surgery, chemotherapy, hair loss, radiation therapy, and recovery. The diary approach is unusually riveting and personal with this set of photos.

Mary Calvert, of the *Washington Times*, wanted to explore the love lives of people over 60. She could have told the story by finding the most famous, the most outstanding, or the wildest senior lovers with a "hitting-the-highlights" approach. (See page 159 for more about hitting the highlights.) Instead, Calvert followed the life of one man, 85-year-old Charlie Thunell, whose wife had died four years earlier (pages 162–163).

The story sets up the widower's problem with a shot of Thunell holding a picture of his wife of 60 years. Calvert then accompanies the still-spry Thunell on outings and dates and even captures an intimate moment that ends the story.

Scott Strazzante's story about a female boxer follows the trials and tribulations of one athlete (page 153). His story is unified because it focuses on one central character. This is not a story about women boxers in general or about the sport of boxing or even about other parts of this boxer's life. By concentrating on one subject and one theme, the images form a unified package when presented on the page—pictures of this young woman that relate to her involvement in boxing.

SAME OBJECT OR PLACE

Sometimes the same object appears in all the pictures. In a story about rats, photographed by James Stanfield for *National Geographic* (July 1977), each photo featured a rat of some kind—a trained rat, rats as objects of worship, rats as lunch. These types of stories tend to document the most amazing or most photographic aspects of a subject. The story does not detail a day in one rat's life. Nor does it show the impact of rats on one family or town. Rather, it tries to portray interesting aspects of rats around the world.

Place stories often fall into this category. A travelogue that shows the most interesting stops on a visit to Paris would be held together by the visual consistency of the city even if no other connecting device were used.

John Burgess's essay about a hospice for animals is a story that sticks to its theme (pages 218–219). Each picture portrays a different aspect of the home, yet all demonstrate how the sick or injured animals are cared for. One photo shows a dog using a unique wheelchair after back surgery. Another picture shows a cat receiving an IV drip. The theme of helping injured animals is played out in each successive image. Like a *National Geographic* essay, each selection in Burgess's package adds information. Burgess includes pictures not because they are sweet or cute or pretty but to the reportage and ultimately provide a complete portrait of the unusual home.

Brian Plonka's powerful essay, "Generations Under the Influence" (pages 64–67) goes beyond documenting the problem of drinking to excess. His story attempts to show how young people get started on the path to alcohol and how, as adults, they pass the habit on to their children. The essay tries to show both the camaraderie of drinking and its after-effects. The pictures in the essay visually lock together because most contain beer cans, beer bottles, liquor ads, beer cups, or other alcohol-related paraphernalia. While some of the images—such as the photo of a line of coffins—don't show the beverage, these photos make sense in the essay because of their close association with other

supporting images that hammer home the visual theme of alcohol abuse.

Sometimes a group of pictures attempts to compare and contrast an aspect of life. André Kertesz compiled an entire book, ***On Reading***, showing all the ways people approach reading. He photographed people reading on benches, while lying down, and while standing up. The pictures documented people reading in a library, in a park, and on rooftops. Each picture added an element to the central theme. Kertesz provided the visual link between the pictures by showing a book, magazine, or newspaper in almost all the images.

CONSISTENT TECHNIQUE, PERSPECTIVE, OR VISUAL MOOD

A uniform technical approach can also add a coherent thread to a picture story. Robert Cohen's essay "Show of Hands" (page 144) gives attention to a common but often overlooked and forgotten subject—hands. Cohen photographed a Marine holding up a medal. All the viewer sees in the picture is the Marine's metal, two-pronged prosthetic gripping the Purple Heart. Other pictures in the essay show a tattoo artist's hands, an obstetrician's hands gently holding an infant's head, a grandmother's hands holding a photo of her grandson, a piano player's hands, and even a photographer's hands. Cohen not only omitted the subjects' faces and bodies, but he photographed his subjects' hands against a stark white background, which further stylized the images. The consistent technique, hands alone against a white, shadowless background, visually cemented the elements of the essay.

To capture a child's view of the world, a photographer might shoot the pictures from two feet above the ground. The same perspective in each picture interlocks the images. Other photographers have shot photo stories from the air. The unique view gives the pictures a consistent look. W. Eugene Smith took a series of pictures from the window of his downtown New York loft. The pictures of the street below were connected not just by the fact that they were all taken in the same place, but also by the restricted view of the camera.

A consistent mood holds together the images in Warren Hsu's pictures of San Francisco's Goth clubs. Each image has an otherworld feel. While the pictures are not about one place or one person, the images feel connected through this consistent sense of atmosphere. Hsu combines strobe and a long shutter speed to pick up the atmosphere in almost every image.

Holding a topic together with a series of portraits also provides a consistent perspective, whether the people are the royalty of Europe or the homeless of America. Sometimes, photographers use a consistent background—perhaps just seamless paper or a portable piece of painted canvas. Irving Penn, the famous fashion photographer, shot portraits of indigenous peoples in remote areas of the world against a gray backdrop—regardless of how exotic the locale. The resulting series of photographs lock together as a united whole.

Of course, sometimes photographers shoot each subject in his or her environment. Even an environmental portrait, however, requires consistent lighting and subject placement for the photographs to coalesce into a unified story. *San Francisco Business* assigned the author to photograph unique hotel rooms. Providing visual consistency, a white-faced mime representing a hotel guest appears in each picture. While each room in the series was distinctly different, each image shared the mime, which gave cohesion to the essay. (See page 244 for one picture from the series.)

NARRATIVE STORYTELLING

Multiple pictures remain individual images unless they are integrated into a cohesive narrative in which the selection, theme, and order of presentation transforms the individual photographs into stories that grab and then hold a reader's attention.

All short stories share a common structure, argues Pulitzer Prize-winning author Jon Franklin, in his book **Writing for Story**. Franklin, who twice won the prestigious award for feature writing, says that stories revolve around a complication and its resolution. He defines a complication as any problem that a person encounters. Being threatened by a bully is a complication. Having a car stolen or being diagnosed with cancer is a complication.

Complications are not all bad, Franklin says. Falling in love is a complication because you may not know whether the other person is in love with you. Winning the lottery means you have to figure out how to spend the money—but still pay the taxes.

Complications that lend themselves to journalism must tap into a problem basic enough and significant enough that most people can relate to it. When a mosquito bites you, you have a complication, but one that reflects neither a basic human dilemma nor a significant problem. Discovering you have malaria and might die, on the other hand, is a fundamental complication that would be significant to most readers.

The second part of a good story involves a resolution, which, Franklin says, "is any change in the character or situation that resolves the complication."

Whether you are cured of malaria or die from the disease, the complication is resolved. (See "Face to Face with Breast Cancer," pages 148–151.) Franklin points out that most daily problems don't have resolutions and therefore don't lend themselves to good stories.

COMPLICATION ALONE

Photojournalists sometimes concentrate on the complication but frequently present no resolution. While they document a social ill like poverty or drug addiction, their documentaries don't turn into narratives. Tom Gralish's moving photographs of homeless men sleeping on the streets of Philadelphia highlight a social problem but don't suggest a cure. (See page 8.) Without a resolution to the homeless problem, the group of photos does not have a narrative thread.

Photographs like the sad pictures of the homeless men legitimately document the complication of living on the streets, but they don't show how someone finally earns money to survive or kicks a drug or alcohol habit—how someone resolves the problem.

RESOLUTION ALONE

Sometimes photographers shoot the resolution without ever showing the complication. Pictures of awards ceremonies record someone's success without showing why they received the award or what they went through to deserve the medal. A cheering politician doesn't make a picture story.

A photograph of the outcome (resolution) of a campaign doesn't show the trials and tribulations (complications) it took a candidate to reach this goal.

While complications often don't have resolutions, resolutions almost always have complications. When Sally Smith wins the Olympic track and field award, you know that she faced many hurdles to get there. The photos become a narrative story only when the photographer shows both the challenges on the way to the top (the complication) as well as the final victory or defeat (the resolution).

EXTERNAL ACTION FOR PHOTO NARRATIVE

Unlike a written story, a compelling photo story requires not only complication and resolution but also action that can be photographed. The complication must be visual and not just internal. The subject must try to resolve the complication with action.

A woman sitting in a wheelchair presents a complication. The reader can see that the

CONTINUED, page 152 ►

Life Formula, continued

Life photographers who took all eight types of photos for a story had a high probability of bringing back a set of pictures worth publishing. Because the formula helped to assure visual variety, the designer had many layout options.

But keep in mind that following the *Life* formula does not necessarily produce a newsworthy or narrative story. Instead, the formula helps assure that all the pictures a photographer takes won't just be portraits or medium shots. The *Life* formula does not guide the photographer in the content or the structure of a story. ■

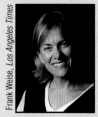

Frank Weise, Los Angeles Times

A PHOTO-JOURNALIST'S DIARY

© Photos by Annie Wells, Los Angeles

Annie Wells, a Pulitzer Prize-winning photographer and staffer at the *Los Angeles Times*, discovered she had breast cancer quite by accident. While lying in bed on her back, she bent her left arm and lightly brushed the bottom of her right breast. "I drew my left hand over my rib cage and my middle finger lightly brushed the bottom edge of my right breast. I felt something like a small grape under my skin. It was a malignant tumor. I knew it as well as I know my eyes are blue. For a moment all I felt was the sensation on the pad of that finger, and it stilled me."

Annie didn't "freak out," though. She knew she had time to make decisions.

Wells bought a Nikon Coolpix digital camera with a swivel lens, added a wide-angle adapter lens, and began photographing her own experiences as she underwent further diagnosis, surgery, chemotherapy, and then radiation treatment. Wells held the camera at arm's length, and with the swivel lens,

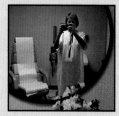

Over more than a year, Annie Wells documented her own confrontation with breast cancer using a swivel-lens digital camera. Here, she takes a self-portrait in a mirror in the doctor's examination room.

pointed it back at herself and everything else the wide-angle lens enveloped.

Her images include the doctor examining her, a nurse administering otherwise deadly chemicals into her veins, and X-rays targeting her breast.

Wells even had the presence of mind to photograph her own reactions: bleary-eyed from drugs as she waited to learn the results of the surgery, disbelief as she watched her hairdresser shaving her head, laughter when she saw herself in a wig. For over a year, Wells's camera accompanied her as she rode the emotional roller coaster of a new cancer patient. ■

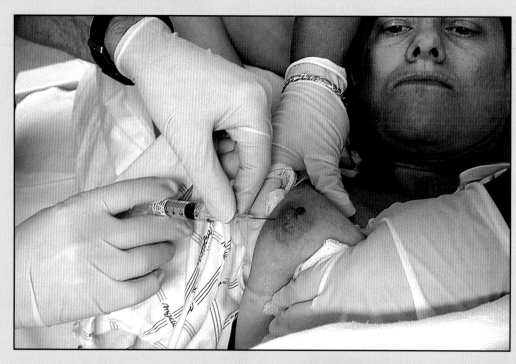

On April 3rd, 2002, I went to the hospital to have a cancerous tumor removed from my right breast. The morning began in nuclear medicine where I was injected with a radioactive isotope so the doctors could map lymph nodes.

I was disturbed to see my breast so swollen. But the incision on my breast didn't hurt as much as the incision in my armpit that was made to find my lymph nodes.

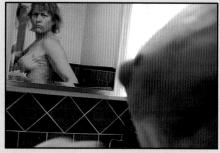

The chemotherapy is so vile that the nurses who administer it wear thick rubber gloves and cover themselves with a gown. They don't want it to touch their skin or clothes. This is what is coursing through my body—killing me to keep me alive.

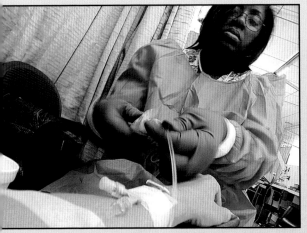

A couple of weeks after my first chemotherapy treatment I had my head shaved. I was going to lose it, or most of it and I didn't want to wake up with it on my pillow, or have it blow away with the hair dryer. So Allen, who, with tongue-in-cheek, calls himself a glamour technician, shaved off my hair.

During chemo, you don't just lose the hair on your head. So Allen taught me how to draw on eyebrows.

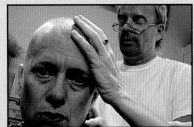

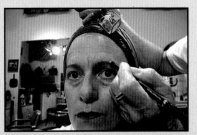

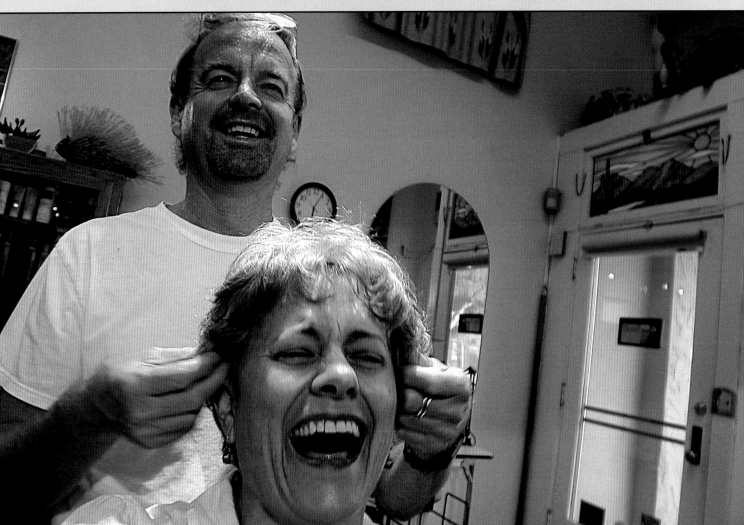

I just couldn't wear a wig. I actually had one that looked okay. But as my sister says, "It's like putting a hairdo on your head." I wore one once, dancing. The entire time I was afraid a guy would hit me in the head and knock it askew, or that the taller guys were looking down and saying, "Eeew, she's wearing a wig!"

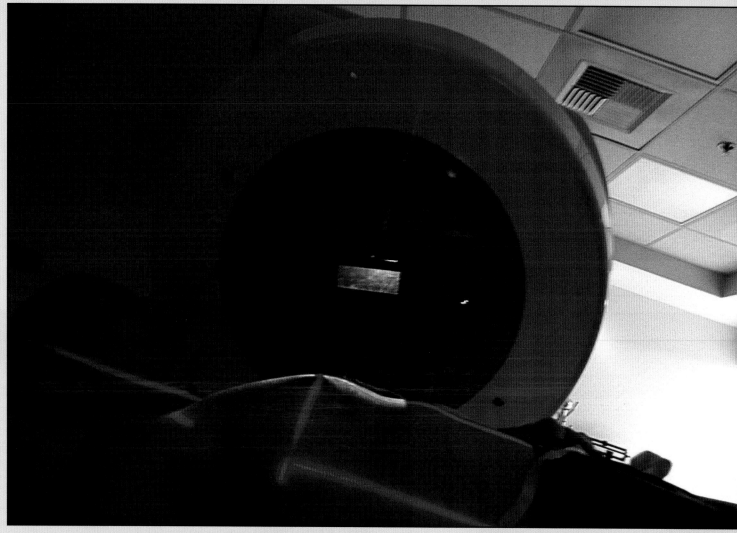

(ABOVE AND RIGHT) The radiation treatments were easy compared to chemotherapy. But after about a month they fatigued me. They obviously burned my breast, too. There wasn't much I could do except to apply aloe. After awhile the aloe didn't help, but since I kept fresh leaves in the refrigerator, they were at least cool.

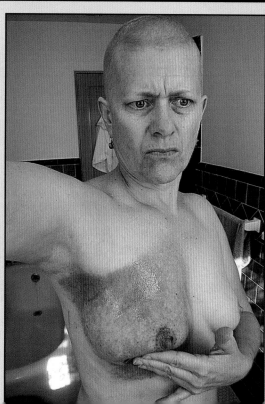

SHE'S A LADY BOXER

FROM PROM TO A POUNDING

Photos by Scott Strazzante
Herald News [Joliet, Illinois]

Scott Strazzante first got the idea for shooting a story about Maricella Rodriguez from a column in his own newspaper, the *Herald News*.

Maricella is a 17-year-old honors student who took up boxing as a way to get in shape and wound up in a local Golden Gloves bout. After first photographing Maricella, Strazzante followed her through spring and summer of that same year.

When she decided to compete at the National Golden Gloves contest in August, he traveled with a reporter to Georgia for that event.

His young boxing subject was totally at ease in front of the camera, Strazzante says. "That made my job description very simple—hang out and document."

His pictures recording Rodriquez's drive for success follows the natural arc of many sports stories. First, the photographer sets up the narrative's complication. In this series, the opening picture shows a young woman dressed for the prom but assuming a boxing stance. The contrast between the feminine attire and typically masculine body language signals that this story is unique. The photographer moves the story along by revealing through the photos the athlete's pain and determination in preparation for each match.

A successful story like this also reveals something of the subject's personality, maturity, and economic conditions. Finally, the story reaches its zenith with the contest itself. A natural ending shows how the athlete handles victory or defeat. ∎

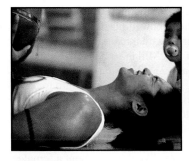

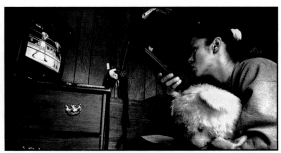

(FAR LEFT) While working out in the mornings, Maricella often babysits her nieces and nephews. Here, Juanito watches a medicine-ball workout at the gym.

(LEFT) Two days prior to her fight, Maricella clutches a teddy bear while studying a videotape tape of Latin boxers. Her favorite professional fighter is Julio Cesar Chavez.

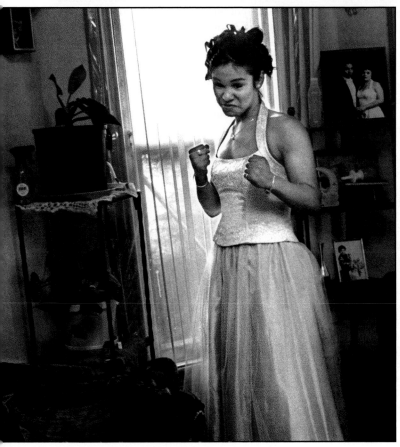

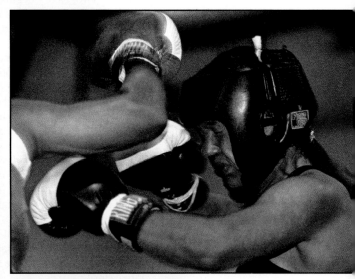

(ABOVE) Maricella receives a pounding in the first round of the National Golden Gloves.

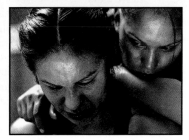

After losing her opening bout, Maricella is comforted by her sister Daria in the locker room of the Augusta Boxing Club.

One day after winning the Indiana Golden Gloves title, her second to go with the Chicago championship, Maricella hams it up for her sister's camera by striking a familiar pose as she prepares for senior prom.

with three other women. His pattern had been to abandon the mothers and their babies as he drifted off to the next relationship. The complication for Hall's story centers on whether Henry, the former deadbeat dad, would change his ways and assume the role of a parent once the children's mother was jailed. Would he cut and run this time, too?

Hall's pictures do not just document a randomly chosen poor family as an example of living on welfare. Hall attempts to tell a more universal tale, one about a man faced with life-altering choices and their consequences. The power of the project lies in the moral dilemma Henry faces, and the fact that the outcome was never obvious.

At the time she made these images, Hall was taking screenwriting courses. This influence is evident in her final project. Hall has grouped the pictures into a story with three acts, a structure used by traditional playwrights as well as screenplay authors.

Act One sets up the story with the family living in the crowded motel room. The mother's arrest provides the story's first complication—the father faced with dependent children and a filthy home.

In Act Two, Henry begins to clean up the family's motel room and to nurture his children. In the past, Henry had fled parental responsibilities.

Act Three brings the story to a resolution. Henry not only stays around, but he organizes other residents of the motel to demand better living conditions and ultimately takes the motel to court. Although he loses the court case, he goes to job training, and looks for work.

Conclusion: Motel Dad rose to the moral challenge presented by the complication of having dependent children in his life and found a resolution by changing his behavior.

Hall stayed with the story long enough to see all three acts played out in real life. Hall's story stands in contrast to most sets of pictures that don't meet the test of a real narrative story.

Many picture packages either document one end of the arc or the other. In a situation like this, the photographs might document a poor community in blighted section of town (complication) or the announcement of a new job training center or welfare office (resolution). These photos are necessary and can be powerful, but they don't have the emotional power that comes with a story that unveils a real-life continuum with its twists, turns, and unknown outcome.

Hall produced a set of photos that captured readers' hearts. Few readers who saw the first picture in the *Los Angeles Times Magazine*

or the opening image on MSNBC, *www.msnbc.com/modules/ps/henry/splash.asp*, did not want to know how the story ended.

NATURAL NARRATIVES
Some stories lend themselves to the narrative approach. Many adventure stories have a built-in complication as well as a resolution. Keith Philpott photographed an exploratory raft trip down Africa's Omo River for *National Geographic*. Starting in the Omo's headwaters near Ethiopia's capital city of Addis Ababa, the trip ended 600 miles later at the river's destination, Lake Turkana. The built-in complication involved overcoming the river's perils, including fighting off hippos. The rafters also witnessed the lives of people living near the river. The story's natural resolution showed placid Lake Turkana.

Other stories with a natural narrative include Jim MacMillan's photos of a hostage situation (page 31). The story of a hostage overcoming the gunman holding him makes for an obvious narrative, with complication and resolution taking place within a few minutes. Stanley Forman's "Leap for Life" (pages 36–37) also has this natural narrative.

A sports story, like the one about a female boxer photographed by Scott Strazzante (page 153), also has a natural narrative. Like many sports stories, the subject faces a complication: how to win. And like most sports stories, this one provides an obvious resolution involving an important match or game. Most athletes go through an intense practice period getting ready to face a challenger. These workouts, practice sessions, and test matches show how the subject faces the challenge of competing to win. The resolution, of course, climaxes with the big match, the big game—from a match on the local playground to the Olympics, the Super Bowl, the World Series, or the World Cup.

COMPRESSING NARRATIVE TIME
Writers can reconstruct past events with an interview. For photographers, the biggest problem with shooting narrative stories is that many complications faced by potential subjects simply don't take place in the relatively short time allotted for most assignments. Sometimes, months or even years pass before a person resolves a complication. Kari René Hall followed "Motel Dad" for more than five years. Editors sometimes allot photojournalists just a few days to work on stories.

Following are various methods for compressing time in a narrative story.

Resolution Near at Hand

Pick a story in which the resolution is near at hand. To shoot a story about a political newcomer running for mayor, zero in on the subject a few weeks before the primaries or before the actual election. At this time, you will be able to show how the candidate grapples with the complication of getting into office: glad-handing potential voters, strategizing, chain-smoking, meeting late at night, prepping for television interviews.

The narrative story will resolve itself on election eve or perhaps on the mayor's first day in office. Starting too early or too late, however, means you may miss the complication or resolution.

Strazzante's female boxer story delivers a complication and resolution, and the photographer knew from the beginning when this resolution would take place. Sports stories typically have the advantage of a built-in complication with a clear resolution that will occur at fixed time. These kinds of projects allow advance planning for timely publication. (See page 153.)

A Small Resolution

Within a story, you might zero in on a small resolution to the complication rather than its ultimate resolution. Annie Wells's breast cancer journal presents a small resolution. While the story follows her confrontation with the disease over the course of a year, an excellent prognosis—the story's end—is not a cure. Although Wells cannot yet report the ultimate victory over death, she has told a unified story (pages 148–151).

Existing Pictures

Investigate photo albums or archives to show what your subject or location used to look like. If your story is about a successful banker who has overcome a poverty-stricken past, can you show the complication with photos of the person as a youngster living in a cold-water flat or a run-down shack? Without these pictures, the banker's success (resolution) may seem unearned.

If your story is about a neighborhood, can you find old pictures from the historical society or your paper's morgue that indicate whether the neighborhood used to be wealthy or poor, or perhaps even farmland or forests?

Different Developmental Stages

Photographing a narrative story about the long-term impact of crack cocaine on newborns does not require following one child from birth through preschool. To address this issue at different critical stages, the author photographed infants suffering withdrawal at San Francisco General Hospital, (complication) toddlers in a testing program (partial resolution), and then crack-affected youngsters in an early intervention program in an East Palo Alto school (partial resolution.) Part of the project is reproduced on pages 72–73.

THE INHERENT APPEAL OF A NARRATIVE STORY

Narrative stories often require the research skills of a librarian, the patience of Job, and the planning of an air-traffic controller. Often, the end is not predictable. However, the difficulties are worth it. Rather than presenting a collection of pictures that holds readers' attention for a few minutes, a narrative story draws the viewer into the subject's predicament.

With a narrative story, readers start to care about the subject and want to know how the person is going to solve the dilemma. What is going to happen? When picture stories are done well, readers want to see the last picture that reveals the story's outcome. The story has a plot line—not an invented, preplanned script typical of early picture magazines but a real story line in which people face problems and overcome them in some honest way.

Most important, the reader comes to care about the story's protagonist. Whether the story is about Annie Wells, who has cancer, or Henry, the motel dad, the subject is not shown just once but is repeated in picture after picture. The reader gets involved in the subject's life. What will happen to Annie? Will Henry abandon this set of children, too? And, perhaps, if the story has merit and is well-photographed, the reader won't just give a passing glance to the pictures and move on, but will remember the story, repeat it, and show it to others.

COMPARING THE DOCUMENTARY AND THE PHOTO ESSAY TO THE NARRATIVE STORY

Editors, photographers, writers, and readers apply the term "picture story" to just about any group of pictures. One can divide the picture story into several categories.

EDITORIAL ESSAYS: A POINT OF VIEW

Some groups of photos don't set out to tell a narrative story. Rather, like a magazine opinion piece or newspaper editorial, they seek to make a point. These editorial photo essays clearly have a point of view. For instance, Brian Plonka does not tell the tale of one alcoholic in a narrative style (pages 64–67). Rather he exposes the highs and lows of alcohol addiction. He has a clear point of view. He is certainly not an advocate of alcohol consumption. His pictures look nothing like the ones shown in beer ads. Nor is he

CONTINUED, page 158 ►

OUTSIDE THE LAW

Photos by Dave Yoder
Orange County [California]
Register

Bounty hunters are, literally, hired guns. They pursue indicted fugitives who flee before their trial dates. When an accused person fails to appear in court, bail bondsmen, who actually loan the money for defendants to make bail, often hire bounty hunters to find and arrest the "skip," as a fugitive is known.

Unlike law enforcement officers who work for the government, bounty hunters are free agents—unlicensed and often untrained—who have the right to carry firearms, enter private homes without a specific search warrant, and arrest fugitives. In California, they don't even need a license for their guns as long as they can show they are pursuing a fugitive. There is no recourse, either, for the citizen whose home the bounty hunter enters by mistake. A nineteenth-century law (*Taylor v Taintor*) even gives bounty hunters the right to travel anywhere within the United States to capture fugitives, something ordinary police cannot do.

Luckily, though his subjects did draw their guns, no shots were ever fired while photographer Dave Yoder accompanied different bounty hunters in Indiana and California over a four-year period.

While still a student at the University of Indiana, Bloomington, Yoder began photographing the story after seeing several bounty hunters interviewed on television. A few phone calls later, and he was accompanying a "skip tracer," as they like to be called, on a stake-out of a fugitive's home. This was the first of more than 150 nights that Yoder spent with bounty hunters.

Often, nothing happened. Just a lot of sitting in the car, eating donuts, and drinking coffee. Sometimes, Yoder went three or four nights in a row without taking a picture. But then, he says, "All hell would break loose."

Photographically, Yoder learned when to shoot and when not to. He didn't want to make life more dangerous for his subjects, he says. In return, he got full access. During arrests, he followed the bounty hunters as they broke down doors or pushed their way into houses.

"You can't wait until they have the situation all calmed down," he explains. "You have to be there ready, anticipating. You have to be in the right position to get the photo."

Yoder says that only on one occasion did a property owner ask him to leave. He complied. With the Supreme Court having decided that police cannot invite journalists to enter a house while a warrant is being served, (pages 286–287), it is likely that few photographers will enjoy the kind of access Yoder had on this project—even though bounty hunters are almost a law unto themselves. ∎

(BELOW) Bounty hunter Ray Meredith readies his revolver .

(BELOW) Brian Uptgraft kicks in the door of an East Los Angeles apartment where he thinks a skip is hiding. As it turns out, he has mistaken the light from a partner's flashlight as someone being inside the empty dwelling. After finding no one inside he walks away, leaving the wrecked front door as it is.

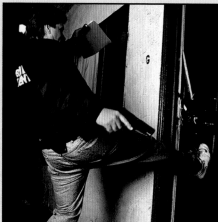

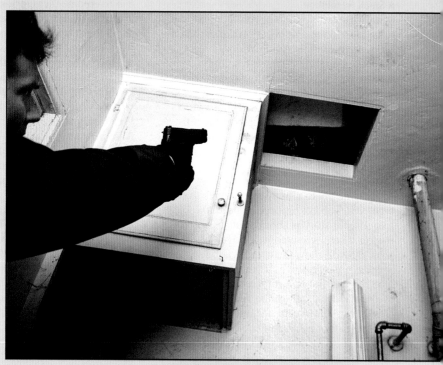

(ABOVE) Brian Uptgraft orders a skip out of the man's East Los Angeles attic where he was hiding. Uptgraft takes no chances, as the man had earlier been convicted of homicide for a drive-by shooting.

(RIGHT) Al "Colt" Schlegal interrogates the father of a skip at 3:00 a.m. in South Central Los Angeles. The questioning, which took more than two hours, scares and confuses the man, who is not the subject of the search.

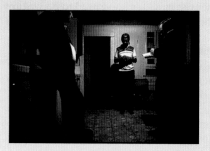

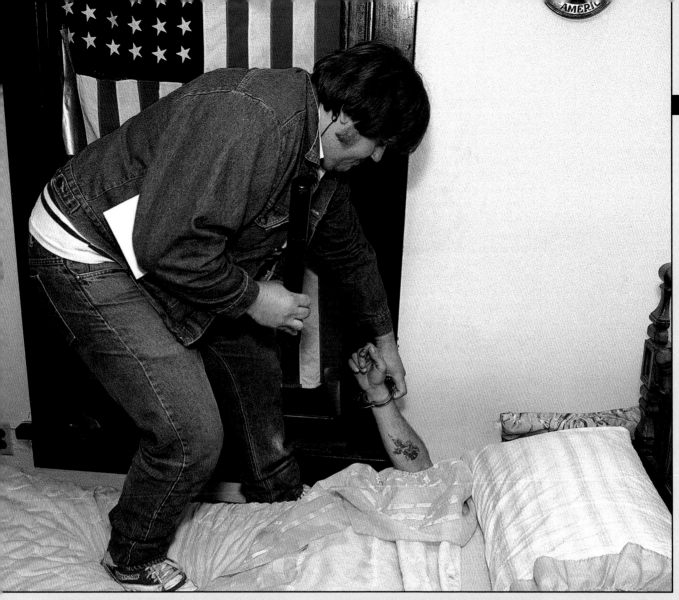

(ABOVE) Benny Hoppes finds a skip hiding underneath a bed in Indianapolis.

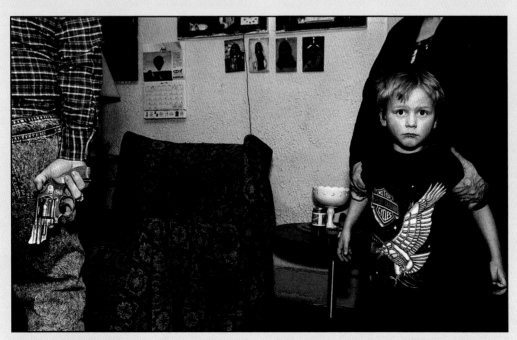

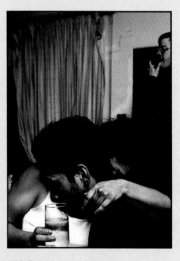

(ABOVE) A skip gets a final hug and some water from his girlfriend before he is taken to jail from his East Los Angeles home.

(ABOVE) A boy is witness to the rushed search of an Indianapolis home by Ray Meredith, who is sure the fugitive he seeks is hiding somewhere in the house because of how long it took for someone to answer the door. He is right; the man is upstairs hiding in a shower.

neutral, just recording everything about the beer industry from growing hops to bottling the product. Rather, his pictures all have a clear point of view. His photo of a father trying to get his son to taste beer makes some readers want to recoil. Plonka is not making an impartial statement about drinking. He is presenting an editorial essay with a clear point of view.

Likewise, Alan Berner has some interesting observations about development in the western United States (pages 76–77). Ironic juxtapositions in his photographs force readers to think. His picture of a line of abandoned refrigerators in front of a mountain range contrasts the ugly, disposable world of modern society against the naturally beautiful vista of the West. The line of appliances in the foreground and the mountains in the background share eerily similar silhouettes.

Berner finds another ironic contrast when he combines a city skyline and the tops of Native American tepees. He makes readers confront the old and the new. His picture of a mall opening, complete with dignitaries sitting outside in folding chairs to watch the eruption of a fake Mt. Ranier, pokes fun at the artificiality not only of this event but of development in general. Each picture in Berner's essay, to a greater or lesser extent, conveys his distinctive sensibility and point of view.

DOCUMENTARIES

Photographers don't always have a point of view about their subjects. They don't always want to tell a narrative tale with a complication and resolution. Sometimes photographers just want to show their readers something that they find fascinating. Often they want to remain neutral, to present a range of unfiltered observations that let viewers judge for themselves.

Documenting a Lifestyle

After meeting some Gypsies while traveling abroad, Cristina Salvador set out to document the life of Gypsies in America. Her documentary presented an even-handed view of this usually private, closed-off culture. She photographed the familial joy of Gypsies dancing and singing at a wedding, but she also photographed one of the men threatening his children with a belt. The variety and intimacy of Salvador's images provided a glimpse at the lifestyle of this rarely seen subculture.

Documenting a Place

Other photographers document a whole country, a region, or perhaps a single building in a city. Steve Raymer documented many aspects of Russia for a story titled "Mother Russia on a New Course" for *National Geographic*. Raymer's pictures included a retired colonel confronting a demonstrator at a May Day rally in Red Square (page 206), a late afternoon picture of Leningrad (the cradle of the Russian Revolution), as well as a group of elders at the Pskov-Pechory monastery sharing a meal.

Raymer did not try to tell a narrative story or photograph with an editorial point of view. Rather he tried to accurately describe in pictures what was happening in the country at the time.

Documentarian Ken Light photographed the Mississippi Delta, an often forgotten, impoverished region in the United States. During a series of trips to the area, Light photographed an outdoor baptism as well as laborers bent at work in the fields. He photographed a range of activities that give a sense of the area and its inhabitants. His pictures, published in his book *Delta Time*, also document for future generations a way of life that is likely to disappear. A small part of the project is reproduced on page 140.

John Burgess documented the life and times of a single place—Brighthaven, a rest home of infirm animals (pages 218–219.) Every picture, loaded with information, reveals another aspect of the range of care provided in this unusual home for animals. From pictures of cats being administered IVs to a toad who has lost his legs to gangrene, the images take the viewer behind the scenes of holistic healing place for critters. The pictures show the animals' injuries and illnesses as well as their caretakers' concern.

Documenting an Issue

Farm Security Administration (FSA) photographers documented the severe poverty resulting from the Great Depression. They also photographed government aid in the form of work programs and housing provided by President Franklin Roosevelt's Works Progress Administration (WPA).

Roy Stryker, director of the FSA photo project, never intended to tell a narrative story. FSA photographers did not follow one family or even a set of families through their difficulties on the way to economic self-sufficiency. Rather, Stryker's photographic corps created an important record of the times.

More recently, Pulitzer-Prize winner-turned-professor John Kaplan traveled to Sierra Leone to document the use of torture as a weapon of war. His portraits of and interviews with torture survivors provide a powerful record of brutality against civilians and its continuing impact. (See pages 74–75.)

Melanie Stetson Freeman's project for the *Christian Science Monitor*, "In Darkness: The Exploitation of Innocence," shows how children around the world work as beggars, as laborers in factories, or as conscripted soldiers even before they reach their teens. Taken in countries all over the world, her pictures provide irrefutable evidence of this tragic abuse of children's lives. (See one picture from this project on page 60.)

Documenting the Highlights of a Topic

In a documentary about diamonds, *National Geographic* might include the largest diamond mine in the world as well as photograph the biggest diamond ever found. In a "hitting-the-highlights" approach, the magazine searches for the most amazing aspects of its topic—from finding the stone to wearing it.

The article and accompanying pictures do not follow one diamond, the life of a diamond dealer, or that of one specialist who cuts and polishes diamonds. The report seeks out the biggest, the best, and the brightest the topic has to offer.

And *National Geographic* has the resources to send a photographer around the world looking for the best examples of the diamond trade to build its piece.

A documentary, of course, does not have to feature diamonds to use a "hitting-the-highlights" approach. Nor does a photographer have to fly from one continent to another to follow its subjects. Mike Stocker, a staffer on the *Sun-Sentinel* in Ft. Lauderdale, chose to hit the highlights for his photo reportage of a "Dog's Life" (pages 160–161).

"I got started on this story when I saw a segment on the local news about the dogs riding on the yellow school bus going to doggie day camp," says Stocker. "After riding on the school bus with the dogs, I started to do some research on other outlandish things people did for their dogs."

Stocker found every example possible of extraordinary, over-the-top, hard-to-believe luxuries for dogs in his area.

For a story that hits the highlights, the yellow pages, the library, and the Internet are good sources for leads. After a few calls, the persistent photographer is likely to discover an expert who knows everything about the subject. Tips on whom to call for more information will follow. Sometimes shooting one situation provides leads to other relevant aspects of the story.

"A Dog's Life" took Stocker eight months to shoot. The essay works because he did his research. He uncovered a range of places each with its own visual twist and all providing an assortment of possibilities.

No individual dog in south Florida benefits from all these luxuries, but every dog could.

One way to know when you have exhausted your research is when you begin to receive tips about places and situations you already have photographed. This is the time to put the story to bed.

ORGANIZING THE PICTURE ORDER

Written narratives typically have a fixed story line that proceeds from one moment in time to another. With a photo narrative, you don't know the end when you start, so the story line determines the sequence of pictures in the layout. Annie Wells's story about her confrontation with cancer has a natural order (pages 148–151).

On the other hand, Alan Berner's essay about the West (pages 76–77) does not have a natural order, nor does it need one. An editor can organize those pictures in many ways, starting with almost any of them. The last picture that Berner shot could be the first in the essay.

In general, the lead picture in a documentary is not necessarily the first or last one that was taken but rather the one that best summarizes the story. Steve Raymer's picture of a retired Russian colonel holding a Soviet flag while arguing with anti-Communist demonstrators during May Day celebrations in Red Square captured the country's old and new attitudes and provided a visual synopsis for his story "Mother Russia on a New Course." No timeline determined that this picture needed to lead the article. Rather, the editors felt that this image (page 206) best encompassed the story that would follow.

SELECTING AN APPROACH

Some stories lend themselves to the narrative form with a complication and resolution. For others, the documentary approach best conveys an objective record of a place or lifestyle. Still other stories lend themselves to the editorial photo essay—a story that has a clear point of view. Each way of shooting and packaging a photo story is difficult in its own right. Selecting the best approach is the first step in producing a powerful package. ■

More photo stories follow ►

A DOG'S LIFE

PAMPERED POOCHES

Photos by Mike Stocker
South Florida Sun–Sentinel

Mike Stocker searched out the best examples he could find for this amusing photo package about over-the-top treatment of dogs. His project is a good example of "hitting the highlights" of a topic. He plowed the yellow pages, sought out newspaper assignments, called on old contacts, and pounced on pure chance to find dogs living the good life. While the individual pictures are fun, the package shows the extremes people go to in order to pamper their four-legged friends. Stocker has created an essay that carries its own punch without the need of a great deal of text. While readers don't get to know any individual dog or owner, most might envy a "Dog's Life." ■

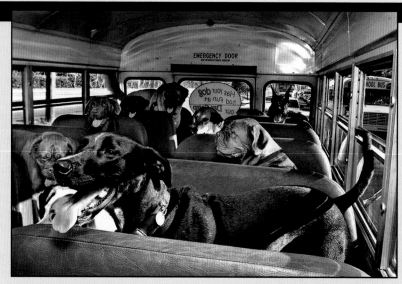

A yellow school bus picks up dogs each day for Planet Dog, a training and day camp in Homestead, Florida. The dogs receive training in English and Spanish and also enjoy playgroups, cageless sleepovers, and swimming in a bone-shaped pool.

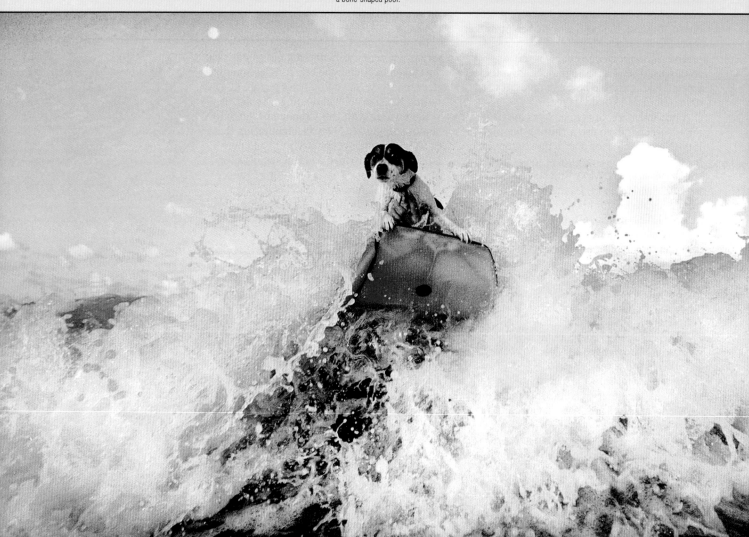

Toto goes surfing on a boogie board.

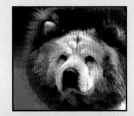

Smiley is an entertainer. His human, Miss Klown, dyes his hair with food coloring and Jello®.

Sheba and Truman await cake at Truman's second birthday party at the Three Dog Bakery. Their humans own the bakery.

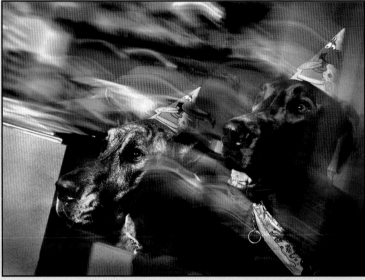

Doctors perform an in vitro fertilization on Champion Celtics Starstruck Sabrina, an English Mastiff.

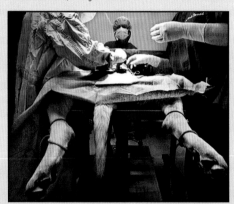

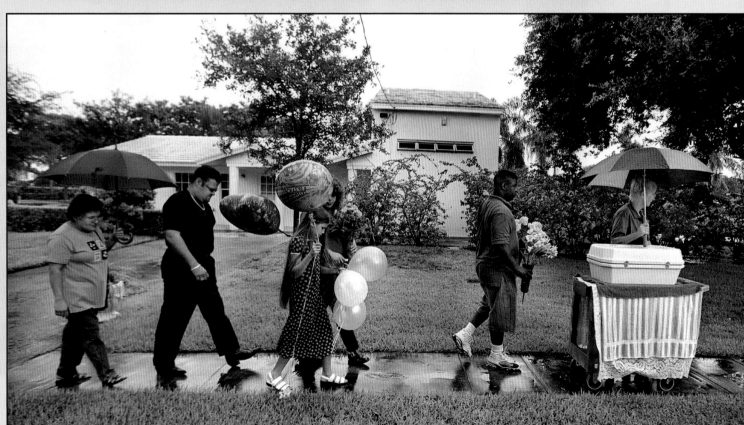

At the Broward Pet Cemetery, a family holds a funeral for Nicholas Sebastian, their Shih Tzu.

CASANOVA AT 85

Photos by Mary Calvert
Washington Times

Because they live longer, women outnumber men in later life—good news for guys over 80 who are still in the game of love. An energetic elder is hot property among the femmes fatales of his generation.

Recognizing that love among the elderly was a rarely examined but increasingly relevant topic to millions of maturing baby boomers, Mary Calvert set out to do a story about dating during life's sunset years.

During a routine newspaper assignment, Calvert found her silver-haired Casanova, 85-year-old Charlie Thunell, whose wife of 60 years had died four years earlier.

By following Thunell's life and recent loves, Calvert tells the story of one man's quest for companionship while opening a window on the world of romance and dating among the elderly.

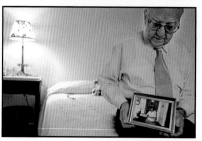

Following the death of his wife of sixty years, Charlie Thunell is lonely.

Calvert's narrative story introduces the reader to Thunell's problem—his wife's death and his resulting loneliness. The opening photo of the solitary Thunell holding his wife's portrait in their bedroom sets the stage for the rest of the story.

The story continues with a set of exposition pictures laying out some of Thunell's options for finding female companionship. The pictures demonstrate that a single man, even at 85, is a desirable commodity in a world abundant with unattached women. The story comes to a temporary resolution with a tender moment between Thunell and his date for the evening.

While the story has a narrative flow, the pictures were not necessarily taken in the order that they are presented. By carefully choosing the serial position of the pictures, the photographer presents Thunell's search for happiness as a narrative story with a complication and resolution, rather than just a collection of pictures about a lovelorn man. The pictures don't document "everything you ever wanted to know" about Charlie Thunell. Instead, they explore one aspect of his life. The pictures go beyond a documentary and try to tell a story with a bigger message. They help to explain why a man might be searching for love and, perhaps, eventually finding it in some of the right places. The images help demonstrate everyone's need for love and companionship, regardless of their age. ∎

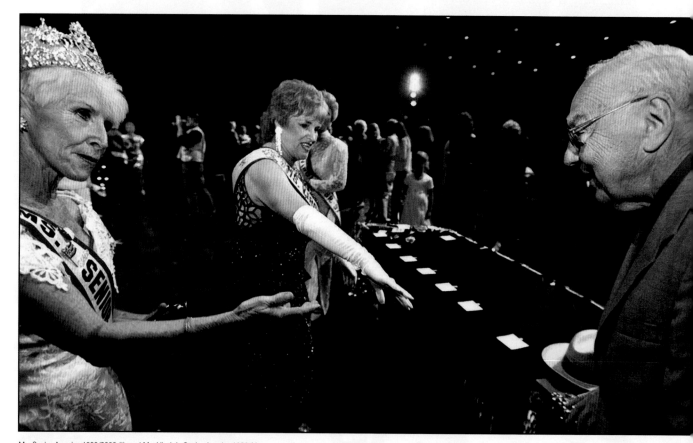

Ms. Senior America 1999/2000 (l), and Ms. Virginia Senior America 1996 (r), greet Thunell backstage at the state pageant. Thunell went behind the scenes to meet the beauty queens after the competition.

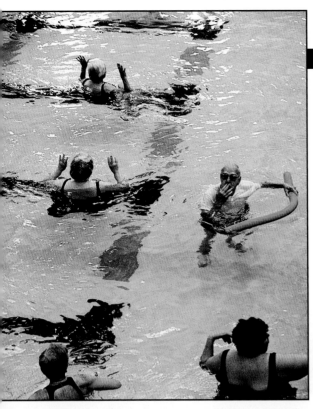

Thunell is often the only man in his water aerobics class.

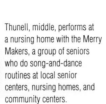

Thunell, middle, performs at a nursing home with the Merry Makers, a group of seniors who do song-and-dance routines at local senior centers, nursing homes, and community centers.

(BELOW, TOP) One of the women in the group looks to Thunell for help with her music during a Merry Makers rehearsal.

(BELOW, MIDDLE) Always the life of the party, Thunell, middle, flirts with two friends at a widow and widowers group that meets monthly for potluck dinner parties. He meets lots of ladies there, he says.

(BELOW, BOTTOM) Grabbing his coat and his hat, Thunell leaves his worries on the doorstep and prepares to step out for a night on the town with a favorite lady.

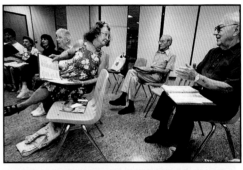

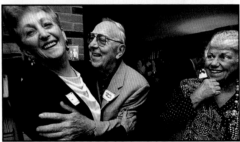

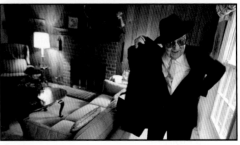

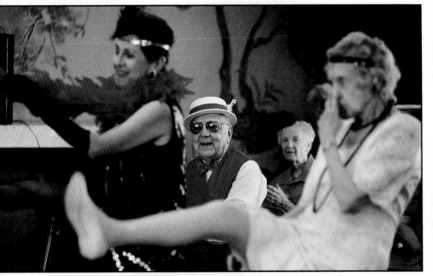

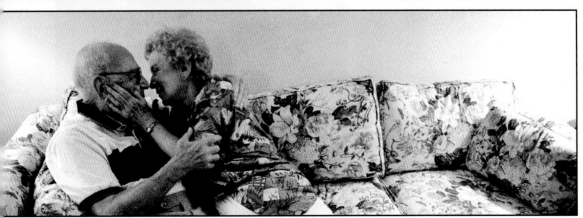

Thunell shares a tender moment with his date during her visit to the townhouse he shares with his son and daughter-in-law.

LIFESTYLE OF THE NIGHT

© Warren Hsu, San Francisco

Warren Hsu's photos take readers to places most newspaper readers never venture—San Francisco's Goth clubs. Devotees of the Goth (short for Gothic) subculture dress in often elegant, vampire-like outfits before hitting the club scene. They congregate in bars with names like House of Voodoo and the Deathguild.

Black is the dominant color of the night's attire. Colored contact lenses, spiked collars, and dark lipstick help transform people as diverse as computer programmers and other professionals into their semi-cult, bar-scene personas. Many like the nightstyle for its fashion and visual aesthetic. Industrial Techno, Death Rock, and 80s Rock are common sounds at the clubs. Far from new, Goth has been around since the 70s, when rocker Marilyn Manson established the scene.

"Something as simple yet universal as death isn't normally discussed or displayed in society," says Hsu of his subjects' attitude toward their lifestyle, "where in the Goth community, it is the underlying theme." While their dress may suggest otherwise, he says few are interested in Satan worship or Wiccan rituals.

Hsu became intrigued with the Goth scene through his brother, a clubber. When the photographer decided to explore the clubs through pictures, he knew his own clothing choices would be important. First impressions are especially critical in a world where the main theme is attire. Hsu began by wearing a preacher-like black coat, black boot-legged dress pants, and black boots with spikes protruding out the back. Eventually, he even donned the white, pasty make-up favored by the denizens of the Goth clubs, male and female alike.

"How you dress will determine how someone will react to you," Hsu says. "As long as you look clean and professional, you are showing respect to the people you are photographing and not just running in wearing a football jersey to take snapshots. Snapshots are easy, but try to get a straight answer if you need names and quotes for captions."

Hsu's photos work together because they share the same dark sensibility. Viewers looking at the images know they aren't in a piano bar at the Hilton. The photographs do not try to tell the story of one Goth clubber or even reflect the entire world of all Goths. Instead, they show the range of costumes and activities in this nighttime netherworld of San Francisco clubs.

(TOP) Typical darkness is infrequently punctuated by stroboscopic lights, which illuminate a temporary path.

(MIDDLE) "Sid Id" (left) and "Switchblade Suicide" live it up at Deathguild's bar.

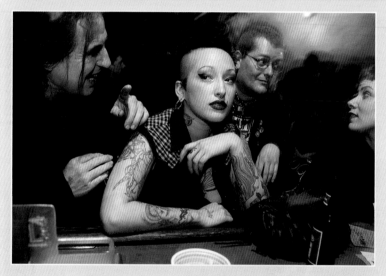

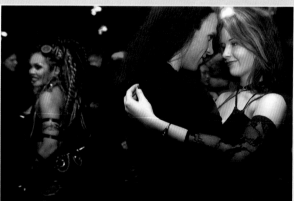

Dance-floor romance at Café du Nord's Dark Sparkle.

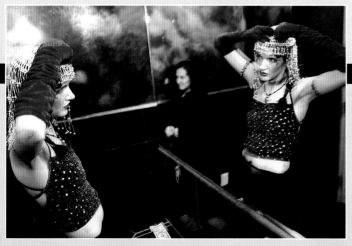

Wearing velvet gloves, a patron adjusts her headdress in the women's restroom at the Manhattan Lounge.

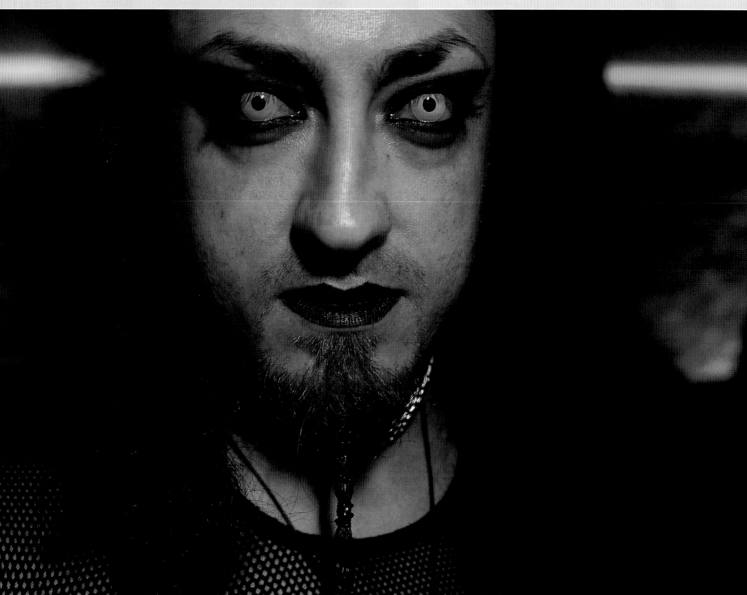

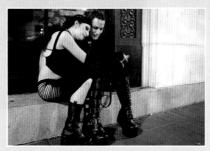

(LEFT) A tender moment away from the crowds at Deathguild.

(ABOVE) For his Goth look, Tom Steward wears gray contact lenses.

STRUGGLING WELFARE FAMILY

Photos by
Kari René Hall, Los Angeles

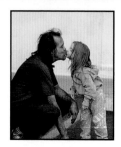

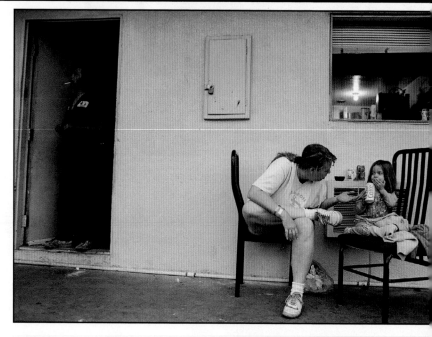

Kari René Hall was working for the *Los Angeles Times* when she began investigating photo projects to pursue. On her first visit to the roach-infested Ha' Penny Inn, the photographer was seeking a methamphetamine addict for a possible story. She found something quite different.

"As I was leaving, a little girl named Cailee, dressed in pink, dashes through the motel parking lot yelling 'Daddy! Daddy!' A scraggly, tattooed little man, Henry Guiliante, wearing a greasy mechanic's uniform, kneels down to kiss her. This moment seemed out of place in such a harsh environment," says Hall. "I didn't know it at the time, but the photo was the beginning of a five-year documentary project."

The original subject of Hall's project was to become Michelle Harig, the mother of the little girl in pink. Because editors at the *Times* weren't interested in pursuing the story, Hall began visiting the Guiliante family at the motel after her shift ended. The photographer anticipated that through Michelle and her family, the pictures would tell the story of the ongoing struggles of a mother who had become pregnant as a teenager. A 26-year-old former heroin addict, Michelle had given birth to the first of her four children at 16.

"I wanted to build a relationship, for them to trust me and to allow me into their life," Hall told *Photo District News* (May 2001). "I didn't come in with cameras blazing." Hall told the family she didn't want any posing, just life as normal. Michelle, Henry, and the kids discussed it and agreed.

All went smoothly until Michelle was convicted of welfare fraud and sent to jail. Henry already had fathered six children with three other women and abandoned them all. Now, Henry had been left with children needing care. At first Hall thought her story was gone. After all, Michelle was gone, and Henry was likely to leave, as he always had. Or would he become a responsible father? ▬

Michelle Harig first became pregnant at 16. Ten years later, in 1996, she shares a soda with Cailee, the youngest of her four children. In the doorway is the children's father, Henry Guiliante, a mechanic who works only sporadically. Though Henry is sweet with his children, Michelle handles all the family responsibilities, including looking after the children, cooking, and cleaning the one room they all share at the roach-infested Ha' Penny Inn as they struggle to get by on welfare and food stamps.

Henry, who has abandoned three other women and six other children, thinks of child care and housework as woman's work. These four children know he has left the others and fear he will leave them, too.

(RIGHT, BOTH.) Michelle and Henry do not allow the children to leave the motel room without supervision for fear of exposing them to the unsavory lifestyles at the Ha' Penny Inn.

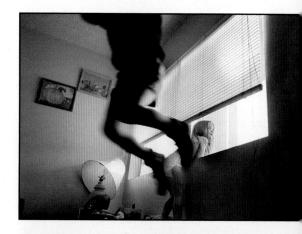

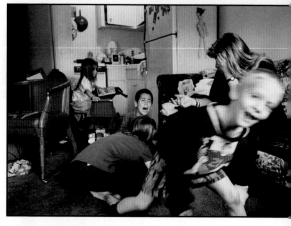

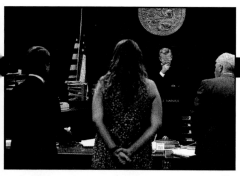

Charged with welfare fraud for not disclosing that Henry lives with her, Michelle pleads "no contest" in hopes that she will get little or no jail time. Instead, the judge sentences her to six months in jail and orders her to pay $25,000 in restitution. She must surrender in one week to serve her sentence.

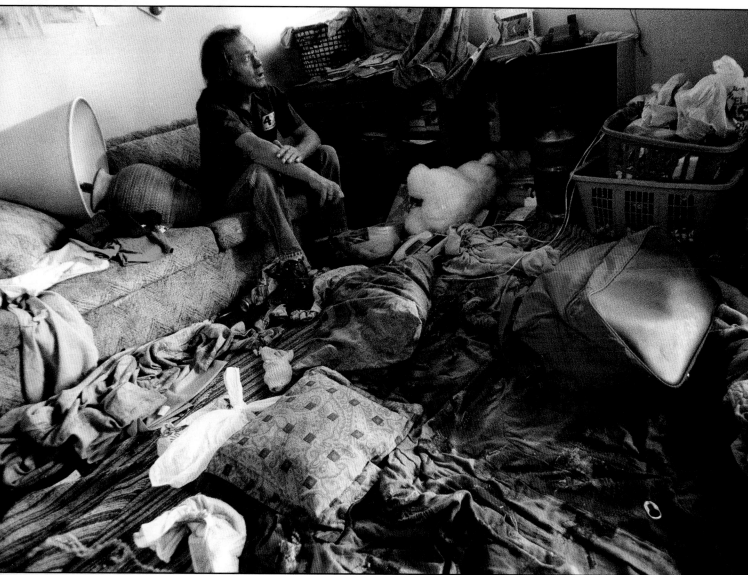

Without Michelle, Henry manages to feed his kids and get them off to school, but he is overwhelmed by all his other parental duties. How long can a man who had disparaged "woman's work" put up with this? Will he leave these four children as he has left his six others?

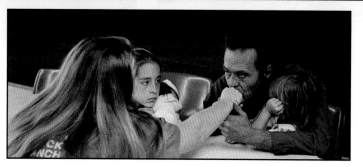

"Are you going home, Mommy?" asks Cailee, seated in her father's lap. Michelle answers, "No. No, sweetie." After Michelle's release, the children's mother returns briefly but then leaves for good.

ABANDONED DAD & KIDS

To Hall's surprise, the ex-biker, former addict, ex-con, stayed on.

"That's the difficulty and joy of documentary work," Hall says. "You have no idea what's going to happen. You just hold on for the ride."

Hall's story is a good example of a true narrative. Starting out, the photographer did not know which way the story would evolve. When the lives of her subjects shifted, with mom going to jail, Hall shifted, too, to a story about the dad. She searched through earlier negatives to find pictures of Henry, who often had been in the background of pictures tracking the mom's life. She stayed the course and over five years recorded the fateful changes in the life of one family.

As the story evolves, it is evident that life as a single dad isn't easy for Henry. "I want to spend prime time with the kids," he laments. "But I can't do that 'cause I gutta be mom and dad. If I'm not giving' 'em a bath, I'm washin' clothes. If I ain't wash' clothes, I'm cooking' dinner. If I ain't cooking' dinner, I'm cleaning' house. When you're doing it completely on your own, it's really, really hard. No matter how many times I clean it, it never stays clean. But I'll eventually figure that one out."

Another twist occurs when Michelle is released from jail, and she, not Henry, abandons the family. Henry seeks and receives custody of his four children. He continues to work occasionally on cars in the motel parking lot, but the family just scrapes by on Aid to Families with Dependent Children and food stamps. Henry tries to help the children with their homework, but he is a high-school dropout himself. He tries to guide his teenage daughter away from the path her mother had taken. ►

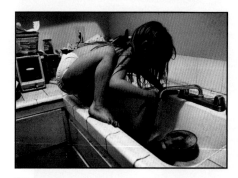

With her mother in jail and the housework piling up, Cailee, the youngest, pitches in to wash dishes.

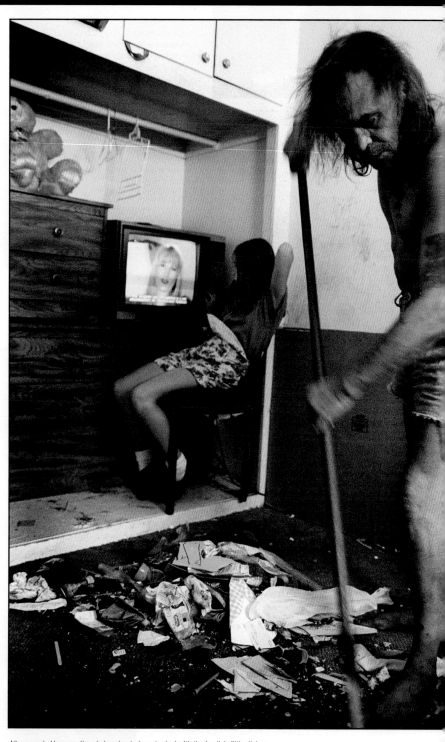

After a week, Henry realizes he's going to have to deal with the family's filthy living quarters. He begins to take charge. In the past, he had left all house-cleaning and parental responsibilities to Michelle. "When Michelle was here," he admits, "when I came home, the house was clean."

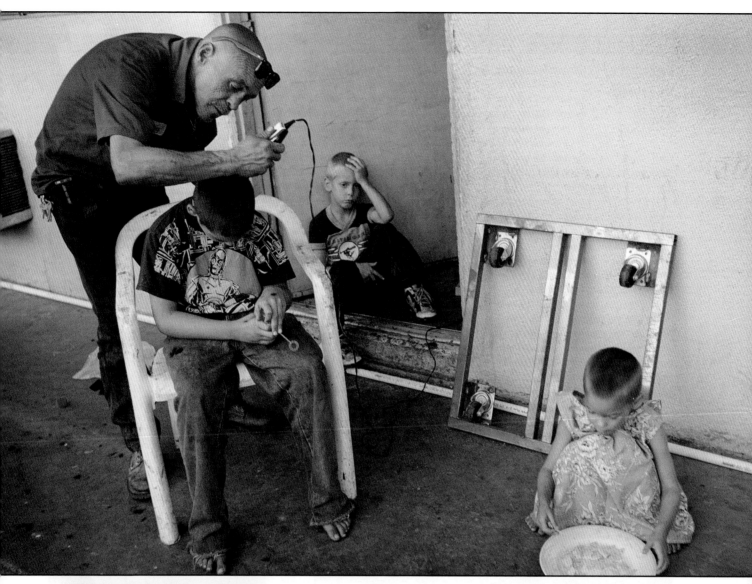

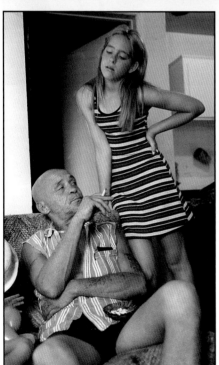

At 12, Cassie is a straight-A student but wants to wear a clingy dress with spaghetti straps that her aunt gave her for her birthday. Henry disapproves. He worries about his girls. "I don't want them to end up at 16, pregnant, like their mother, and relying on a man. If they stay in school, get a good education, they're not going to end up like that."

To save money, Henry cuts the children's hair as well as his own. Cailee wanted her head shaved, too.

FATHER IN MORE THAN NAME

Henry even organizes his motel neighbors to protest their living conditions and to take the owners to court. He buys an $11 pinstripe suit to go to court. Though the group loses the court case, Henry and his kids stay together as they move from that motel to another.

With his kids in school, Henry's next priority becomes finding a decent job. He joins a job program. He prepares a resumes, performs an Internet job search.

"God's gave me a second chance," he says. "He's gave me a second chance with a family. He taught me how to love and be loved."

With any great movie or book, the viewer or reader does not know the outcome at the beginning. The complication in Henry's story occurred when, alone, he faced whether or not to take responsibility for his family. In this type of saga, the photographer must keep shooting and wait and see what develops.

For the reader, the story lasts beyond the final picture. The story is gripping, its final outcome unknown. The story's theme is about taking advantage of a second chance in life.

As Hall says, "This is a story of somebody realizing what it means to be a father. It is a story of somebody finding a purpose in life and possible redemption through being needed."

Hall shot the story on her own time, after work, and on weekends, often sitting in a corner waiting and watching the lives of the family unfold. She processed more than 350 rolls of film and made 4"x6" prints at her local grocery store for editing. She paid for everything out of her own pocket.

Henry's story went on to win the Canon Photo Essay award in the Pictures of the Year Contest, as well as to appear on MSNBC.com, *www.msnbc.com/modules/ps/henry/splash.asp*. The *Los Angeles Times Magazine* also published it.

Following the publication of Henry's story on the Web and in the *Los Angeles Times Magazine*, estranged family members, including his brother, two of his older sons, and his first wife, contacted him. Strangers have donated money, gift certificates, mechanics' tools, clothes, and food. A reader paid Henry's driver's license fees. Credit bureaus cleared his record. Job offers rolled in.

"I now have a fresh start at life," he says. ∎

(BELOW, TOP) Henry decides to take on poor living conditions at the motel. He gathers other Ha' Penny residents to discuss their rights as outlined in sections in the *Landlord's and Tenant's Rights Book*. He also calls authorities to inspect the motel, which is cited with more than 300 infractions.

(BELOW, BOTTOM) The management responds with eviction notices, which spurs Henry to paint placards and lead a protest.

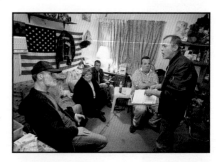

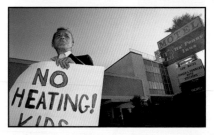

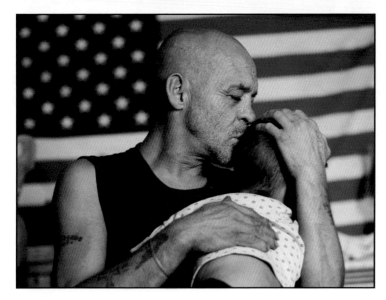

Seeing the misery of his four children when their mother left makes Henry realize how much his six others had suffered. "I seen the abandonment they felt. I've left my wives with the children, and I never got to see that part of it. . . .it's really nice to be able to feel your child cuddling up to you and know that they feel safe in your arms. And if my drinking and my rowdiness kept on or I would've blew my brains out, I never would've got to know these feelings or these emotions. I would never have got to hear a child saying, "I love you, Daddy." Here, he comforts Cailee, sick with a fever.

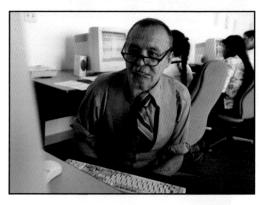

After years of only sporadic work as a part-time mechanic, Henry begins to search for employment that will adequately support his children. "If I don't find a job today, I'll find one tomorrow, but I will succeed. Because I've got four little ones depending on me."

Henry challenges the evictions in court, but loses the case when the management claims the evictions are necessary to renovate the building into a tourist motel. he and the children must leave the the Ha' Penny Inn, where they have lived for five years. Cailee tries to cheer up her dad by playing the saxophone when she catches him looking sad.

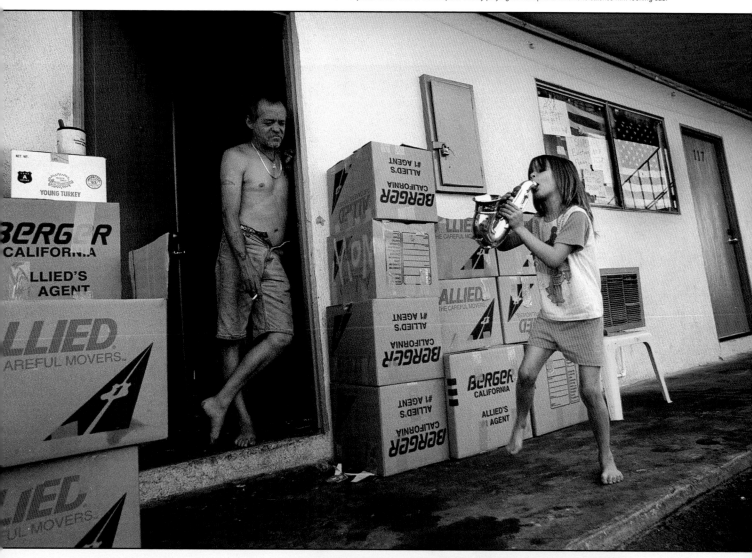

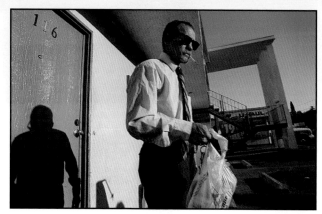

On the day Henry and the children must move, Henry puts on his suit and a clean white shirt, packs a change of clothes in a plastic bag, and heads out to search for a new home for his family. The move is a setback not a failure.

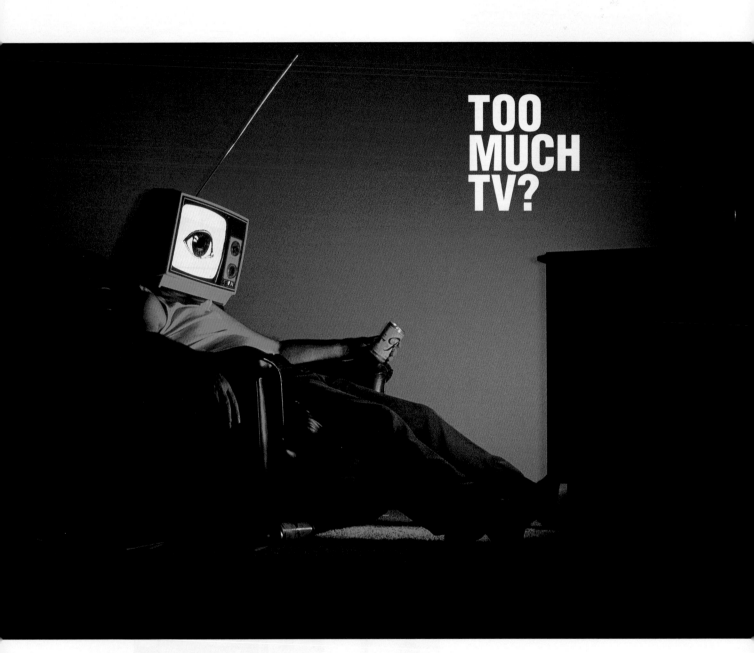

TOO
MUCH
TV?

In this photo illustration—visual metaphor—a TV set becomes the head (and brains) of a television addict. Peter Haley, *Tacoma* [Washington] *News Tribune*

Chapter 9

Illustration

ILLUSTRATE THE ABSTRACT

Today's photojournalists are borrowing the techniques of the advertising photographer to illustrate stories based on issues and abstract ideas. This blend of advertising technique and photojournalism—the editorial photo illustration—came about as newspapers and magazines shifted from the "simple account of what happened yesterday" to analysis of what happened over a period of time and to evaluations of what may happen in the future. This change in journalistic emphasis from immediate reaction to longer-term interpretation of the news has led to stories about more abstract—

A product illustration (below, top) is often an attractive still life that simply shows what an object looks like. An editorial illustration (below, bottom) depicts a concept. Here, the concept is how to protect yourself against the vapors of the odoriferous onion.
Joseph Rodriquez, *Greensboro* [North Carolina] *News & Record*

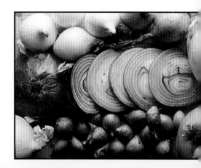

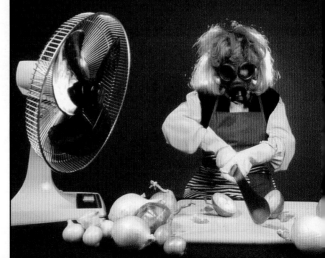

and nonvisual—issues, such as those dealing with economics, psychology, and science. Stories might include causes for a bull or bear stock market, cures for manic-depression, or potential results of gene splicing. To satisfy an increasingly visually literate readership, editors who understand photography's appeal often assign illustration photos rather than pen-and-ink drawings to accompany these difficult-to-visualize stories.

Photo illustrations work best when used to communicate concepts, feelings, and the intangibles for which a literal picture is not always possible, says Jay Koelzer, who specialized in photo illustrations for the *Rocky Mountain News*. "The photographer needs to take the reader somewhere outside the bounds of reality and the printed page," says Koelzer. "The photo illustration is the chance for the photographer to make people think."

According to a survey conducted by Betsy Brill for her master's thesis, more than three-fourths of the newspapers in the United States use photo illustrations. Almost every magazine, particularly *Time*, *Newsweek*, and *U.S. News & World Report*, uses editorial photo illustrations, especially on their covers. In fact, the rise of the issue-oriented photo illustration may be the most significant change in the history of photojournalism since the 35mm camera introduced the era of candid photography more than a half century ago.

Today's photojournalists are creating pictures from whole cloth. Subjects are actors, backgrounds are sets, lighting is artificial. Yet these pictures run on the same newsprint and often on the same page as documentary photographs, in which the photographer has traditionally remained only an observer, not a participant.

DIFFERENT KINDS OF PHOTO ILLUSTRATIONS
PRODUCT PHOTOS

The product photo is a photograph of a real object, usually involving food or fashion. For example, the food editor might assign a photo to accompany a story about the lowly onion. To show how onions differ, the photographer might artfully arrange a number of different onions, ranging from white to red (see preceding page).

Illustration fashion photos, too, are product photos that simply record what an outfit looks like. Some newspapers and magazines run fashion photographs of average people on the street—candids that accompany a story about new trends in hemlines or the new look in pleats. These types of photos are not illustrations. Instead, they are like other candid features a photographer might take. While the setting of a fashion show is staged, the photos document a real event.

A fashion shoot, on the other hand, might show off a new clothing line. Almost all pictures in fashion magazines result from photographers working with models to create idealized photographs of new clothing trends.

The setting might be a seamless background or an empty beach, but the pictures never look real. Stylists prop the photos so that the situations look better than real life. The photographer is not trying to illustrate an abstract editorial concept or imitate reality.

Whether the photograph is of an onion on a plate or a swimsuit on a woman, the

IMMEDIATE RIGHT: To illustrate an article about Andy Warhol, who turned ordinary objects—including soup cans—into art, Carl Fischer portrayed the artist as being consumed by his own icons.
© Photo illustration by Carl Fischer

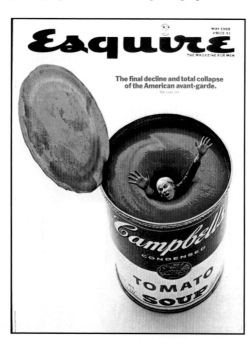

FAR RIGHT: This classic illustration of aging was created by photographing two women who strongly resembled one another, cutting their photos, combining them, and then having the resulting combination retouched by an artist. Today, the effect could have been achieved by combining the images with a computer.
© Photo illustration by Carl Fischer

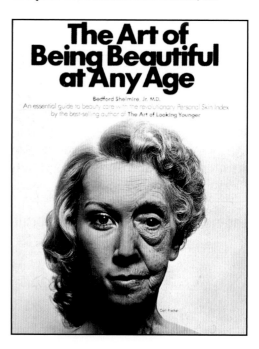

photographer tries to accurately and attractively record the object. The photographer is not trying to create a concept or dupe the reader into thinking the picture is really a candid.

EDITORIAL CONCEPT ILLUSTRATIONS

As the visualization of an idea, the editorial concept illustration may employ actors or models to create the photographic image, but the total effect is that the viewer instantly recognizes fantasy, not reality. By using subjects out of proportion with other props, backgrounds apparently reaching into infinity, and other trompe l'oeil, the concept photo (also called the issue photo illustration) lures the reader, like Alice, into a surreal Wonderland of ideas. No reader would mistake Wonderland for reality.

Carl Fischer's startling photo illustration of aging, for example, combines photographs to create an image of a woman's face—half-young, half-old. (See opposite page.) Through his covers for *Esquire*, Fischer pioneered the use of the modern photo illustration. He also used the concept approach for a story about Andy Warhol, the pop artist famous for transforming everyday objects into paintings. One of Warhol's most famous images showed row after row of Campbell's red-and-white soup cans. Fischer created a picture that gave the impression that Warhol was drowning in a huge can of tomato soup. (See opposite page.)

For a story about "latchkey children" (youngsters who come home to an empty house while their parents work), Jeff Breland created a collage for the *Columbia Missourian* that conveyed the concept of children—perhaps perilously—alone. In Breland's cut-and-paste image, a little boy dangles from a huge key ring in the lock to a gigantic door. (See page 189.)

On the day the article was set to run, John Burgess's editors at Santa Rosa's *Press Democrat* assigned him to illustrate the range of digital cameras available on the market. Faced with the daunting deadline, Burgess could have opted to put the cameras against a backdrop and take a product photo.

Instead he recalled a photo of Lily Tomlin taken by Annie Leibowitz in which the comedienne's face was hidden behind a TV set showing her own image. The television face of Tomlin seemed to float above her real body, suggesting the merger of reality and medium. This recollection gave Burgess an idea of his own: to photograph the new digital cameras with parts of faces on each model's LCD screen.

At a local camera store, Burgess took each point-and-shoot digital camera and recorded

part of a face. Then he activated the camera's LCD screens and had the store clerks hold the cameras in place. The engaging final illustration is certainly more interesting than a catalog shot of the equipment.

Faced with a different kind of potentially routine product shot—toothbrushes—Robert Hendricks imagined toothbrushes as trees in a fantasy forest. Letting his creativity fly, he conceived the idea that someone could be lost in this make-believe forest of toothbrush trees.

To execute the concept, Hendricks placed the brushes in a specially built, elaborate model made of floral foam and moss, shooting the setup in the studio. Hendrick looked up a beauty pageant contestant who had

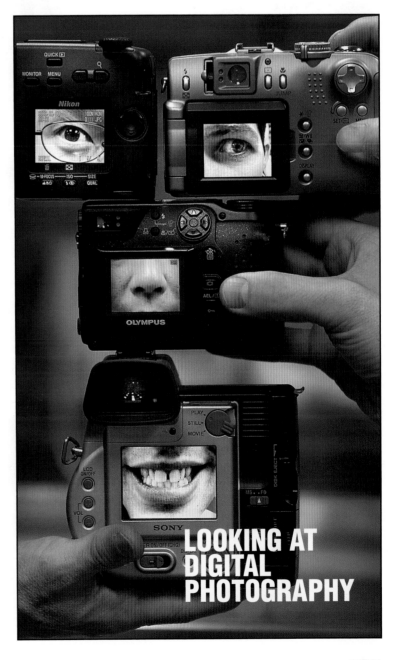

Rather than take a product picture of digital cameras, the photographer transformed them into a human face. At a local camera shop, he took pictures of several people's faces with different cameras and then arranged and photographed their LCD screens to form a single face. John Burgess, *Press Democrat* [Santa Rosa, California]

LOOKING AT DIGITAL PHOTOGRAPHY

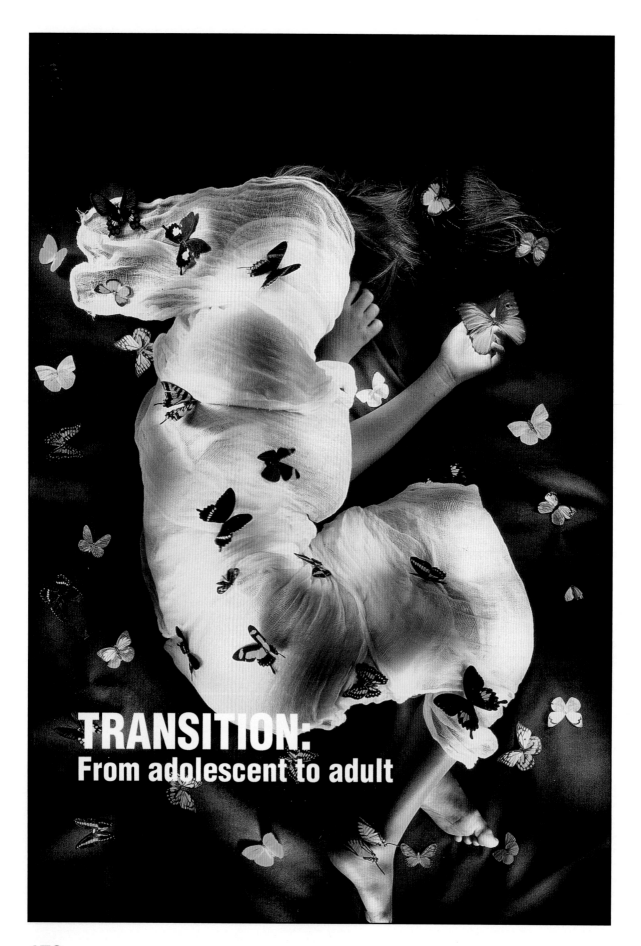

TRANSITION:
From adolescent to adult

dressed as a tooth fairy holding a large prop toothbrush. He photographed her in her costume against a seamless backdrop. A picture of a blue sky completed the original photography for the project. Then Hendricks combined the three images in PhotoShop® for his final picture.

Hendricks transformed what could have been a dull, routine product shot of household toothbrushes into a concept. The tooth fairy, lost in a forest of brushes, provides a more captivating image than a catalog shot of common teeth-cleaning instruments.

The subject of an editorial photo illustration may be about aging, latchkey children, or it might involve politics or food. But if you create a concept photo about onions, you won't produce a photo of the onion itself. Rather you may try to show how people defend themselves against the vegetable's vapors. A photo of a chef wearing a gas mask while cutting onions would illustrate the concept of protection against the odoriferous onion. (See page 173.)

DOCUDRAMA

The docudrama photo illustration, by contrast, actually appears to be real. Here, the photo looks just like a candid but is really a complete creation or recreation. Rather than abstracting or idealizing, like the product photo or the concept illustration, the docudrama photo imitates reality; intentionally or not, it fools the reader.

Avoid the docudrama at all costs.

The docudrama approach is a tempting one to photographers with little time to establish contacts for a story, or to conceive and prop a concept photo. To set up a real-looking photograph may not seem so far from what an artist does to "illustrate" a story, but such photographs threaten to undermine a publication's credibility.

Jeff Breland's picture of a latchkey child dangling from a key chain is clearly unreal. A docudrama photo illustration, on the other hand, depicts a lonely-looking child sitting on a doorstep. While this young model surely was not really alone or lonely, the reader's only clue to the deception was the tiny tag line "photo illustration." The reader has no way of knowing from the picture that the image was a purposely staged.

And, equally important, do latchkey children really look lonely? The one thing we know is that they do in the imagination of a docudrama photographer.

PRODUCING EDITORIAL ILLUSTRATIONS

After a photo illustration appears, you might overhear the following conversation in the newsroom.

The writer whines, "This headline doesn't go with the gist of my insightful story."

The copy editor replies, "When I wrote that head, the story wasn't ready, and I never saw the picture."

From the photo department: "The ugly headline type runs across the model's face.

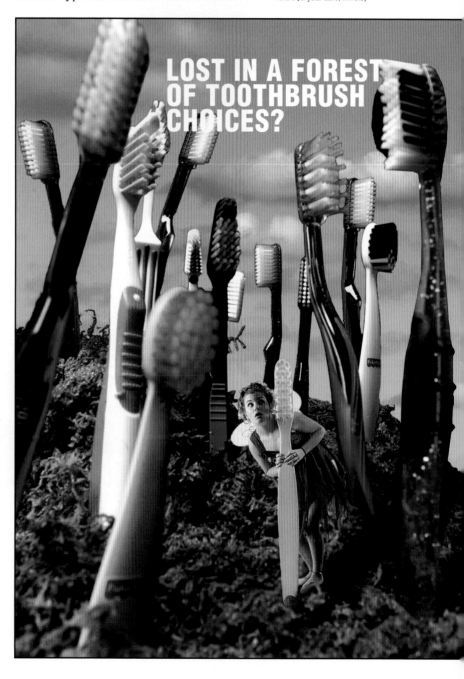

How can I create great art surrounded by insensitive people?"

And, from the page designer's corner of the room: "The inept photographer didn't leave room for type on the picture. And anyhow, the vertical picture didn't fit into the horizontal hole on the page left me by the copy desk." Avoid this scenario.

When producing an editorial photo illustration, get all the players together from the beginning. The advertising world calls a group like this a creative team. Businesses in Japan call it a quality circle. Regardless of what you call it, get everyone together who will participate in the creation and execution of the photo illustration. By communicating,

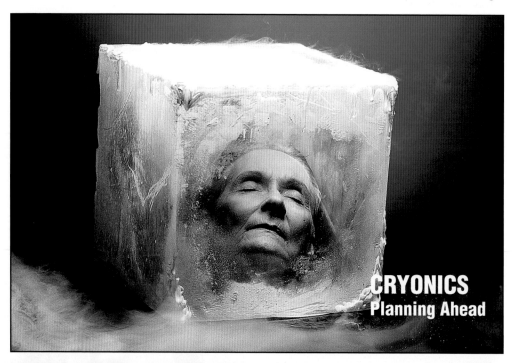

➤ This shocking photo illustrates cryonics, the practice of freezing people who have just died in hopes of reviving them with future medical advances.
Susan Gardner, *Fort Lauderdale Sun-Sentinel*

CRYONICS
Planning Ahead

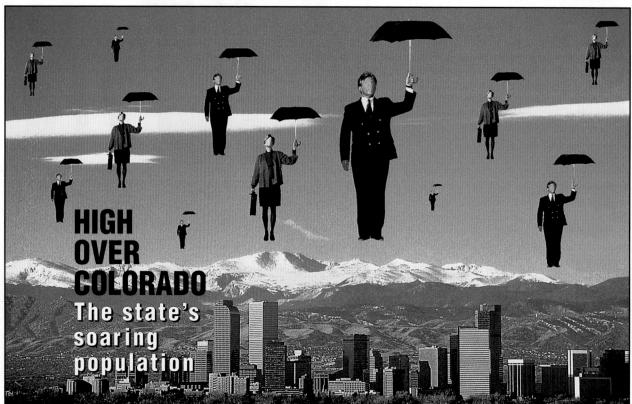

HIGH
OVER
COLORADO
The state's
soaring
population

178 ■ **Photojournalism: The Professionals' Approach**

not only will all team members perform their own creative tasks better, but knowing what others are doing will also help dissolve territorial battles.

BRAINSTORM THE CONCEPTS

Alex Osborn, a partner at Batten, Barton, Durstine, and Osborn (BBD&O), a large New York advertising firm, formulated the brainstorming method for bringing workable, productive ideas to the surface. He recommends getting a group of people in a small room where everyone can voice their ideas, no matter how foolish-sounding. Each suggestion stimulates and generates another suggestion. A brainstorming session can produce more than a thousand ideas, Osborn claims. Brainstorming works even if you just talk over your ideas with another person.

Philippe Halsman, who produced more than one hundred *Life* covers, explains why he uses the brainstorming technique in his book ***Halsman on the Creation of Photographic Ideas***. "You are not alone, you face someone who serves you as a sounding board, who prods you and who expects you to answer. . . . Your system is stimulated by the challenge of the discussion. There is more adrenaline in your blood, more blood flows through your brain and, like an engine that gets more gas, your brain becomes more productive."

One cardinal rule prevails when working in a brainstorming session: never put down anyone else's ideas. Like turning on the lights at a high school dance, a negative comment will be inhibiting. By the end of the brainstorming session, surprisingly good ideas will float to the surface and poor suggestions will sink out of sight from their own weight.

WRITE A HEADLINE

After each member of your group has read the story or heard a presentation of the central theme, everyone should try to write a headline. Compared with writing headlines for a news story and documentary picture, writing

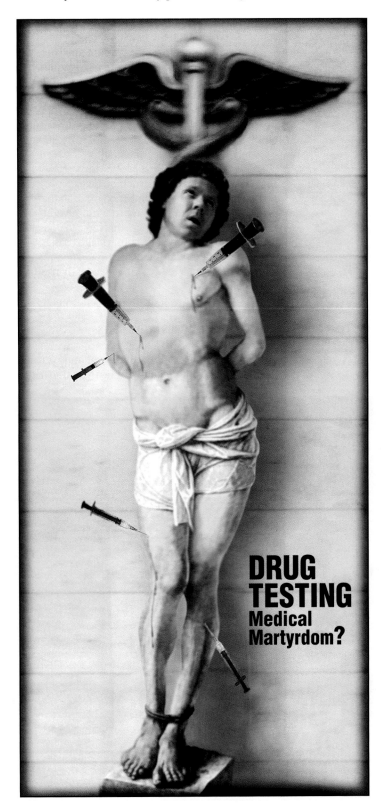

DRUG TESTING Medical Martyrdom?

◄ To illustrate the problem of population growth in Colorado, the photographer shot an overall of downtown Denver with the mountains in the background. In the studio, keeping the light from the same direction as the overall, he photographed two models holding umbrellas. With the computer, he cloned the models, obliterating their faces so that they would become generalized figures representing all newcomers. Finally, he melded all the elements together into one image. Jay Koelzer, for the *Rocky Mountain News* [Denver]

► Here, St. Sebastian, who was killed with arrows, symbolizes martyrdom. The photographer used the visual symbol to illustrate a story about college students who are paid to test new drugs. With the help of the computer and an out-of-copyright painting of the martyred saint, the photographer replaced the arrows with syringes and used the traditional symbol of the medical profession for a background above the figure. William Duke, for *Spy* magazine

headlines for a photo illustration requires the writer to take a different approach.

In a traditional news headline, the desk editor tries to summarize the story in a few words. The headline usually includes an active verb: "President proposes new legislation today."

A photo illustration headline might have no verb. In fact, the headline might consist of only a phrase or sentence fragment. The headline might play on words, like a pun, or it might work off a movie, play, or song title. Or the words might raise a question.

• "Is There a Hare in Your Soup?" for a story about rabbit stew.

• "M-M-M Mail Order" for a story about buying food through the mail.

• "Making the First Move" for a story about women asking men on dates.

Once all group members have read the story, the group must try to write several headlines. Don't stop to analyze each one. Never reject any idea at this stage of the process. Let your thoughts flow. Then read over each one to see if the idea lends itself to a photo.

Almost always, the best idea pops out.

TRANSLATE WORDS INTO IMAGES
Symbols
Once you have the headline you must translate words into pictures. When you translate to picture language, you speak with symbols, analogies, and metaphors. You are trying to find visual ways to express amorphous, sometimes theoretical ideas and concepts.

For photography, however, concepts must become something concrete.

For example, how do you say America or American without words? You might use a generally accepted visual representation of an idea—a symbol like the Stars and Stripes. You could use an actual flag or turn something else into a flag. You might decorate a cake in red, white, and blue to symbolize America's birthday. The Statue of Liberty also serves as a symbol of the United States, as does the "Uncle Sam Wants You" recruiting poster from World War I. Grant Woods's painting, "American Gothic," which shows a farmer and his wife staring stoically out at you, also has become a symbol of the United States.

Photographs themselves can become symbols. Joe Rosenthal's photograph of the flag raising at Iwo Jima has been reproduced and transformed so many times it has become a symbol of American patriotism.

The Eiffel Tower, a baguette, or a bottle of wine might symbolize France. Balanced scales suggest justice; a dove represents peace; a gun symbolizes war. A light bulb often stands in for abstract concepts like thinking or ideas.

Carl Fischer, who produced many famous *Esquire* magazine covers, says that some symbols come to exist in our subconscious, like those which the psychoanalyst Carl Jung described as archetypes. Some of these symbols, although they may originate in one culture, become cross-cultural icons that people instantly recognize. The multiarmed Hindu god, Shiva, appears over and over as a symbol for handling multiple tasks.

Literature, too, can provide visual symbols. The nose of Pinocchio, which grew longer with each lie he told, turns the act of lying into a concrete object. In an illustration for *Spy*, a humor magazine, William Duke played off the image of St. Sebastian, who has come to symbolize martyrdom. The story concerned college students who earn money by participating in tests for new compounds for drug companies (see page 179).

Symbols can be reinterpreted or newly invented. As pointed out by Steven Heller and Seymour Chwast in **The Sourcebook of Visual Ideas**, smokestacks were used at one time to symbolize progress. Today, they represent pollution. Still, the skull and crossbones, an ancient symbol for poison, continues to evoke the message "hazardous to your health."

The metaphor for danger—walking a frayed tightrope—helped illustrate a story about daytraders, who use the computer to bet on minute-by-minute swings in the stock market. William Duke for *Time* magazine

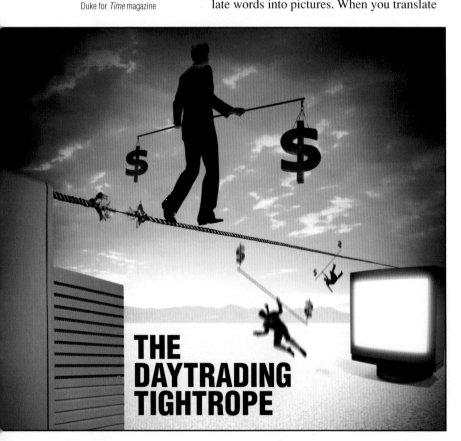

THE DAYTRADING TIGHTROPE

Will computers, which today convey the idea of technology, someday be associated with obsolescence?

Visual Metaphors

When you use a metaphor, you replace one image with another to suggest a likeness of some characteristic. For instance, you might substitute an hourglass for an old person to suggest aging. In this situation, the hourglass becomes the passing of time. The sand at the bottom of the hourglass represents age. Sand can also become power. Sand sifting through hands could become a metaphor for disappearing power.

In an illustration for *Time* magazine, William Duke used walking a tightrope as a metaphor for danger. His picture (opposite page) shows a man in a suit walking a fraying tightrope. The businessman balances with a pole on the ends of which hang dollar signs. The rope is attached between two computers. Other businessmen further down the rope have already fallen. The story is about day-traders, who use the computer to make quick trades betting the stock market will go up or down within a few seconds or minutes. While the practice can be lucrative, many traders have quickly gone broke with this approach to investing.

The metamorphosis from caterpillar to butterfly could represent the change from childhood to adolescence as in the photograph created by Jay Koelzer for the *Rocky Mountain News* (page 176). A TV screen becomes the head of a television addict (page 172).

SELECT THE MOST WORKABLE IDEA

Simplicity and practicality come into play when you are pondering a list of headlines to illustrate. Sometimes, the least number of props, models, backgrounds, and special effects give the best chance of producing a successful photo illustration. For instance, suppose you have selected the following headline: "The Nuclear Family Crumbles."

You could illustrate this idea by breaking apart clay figures in the form of a family. Great idea, but . . . You don't know how to work in clay, so you call a sculptor friend. She says, "Great idea, but . . . I'll need five days and $500." Your editor says, "Great idea, but . . . I need the illustration in three days, and we have a $20 prop limit."

It's time either to rethink the visual for the headline or to continue down the list to find a different headline that can be illustrated more easily. Remember, the nuclear family can unravel just as easily as it can crumble, and knitting a family portrait just might be easier than sculpting it.

PRODUCE THE PICTURE

Once you have a headline to accompany a visual and have drawn a sketch, you need to plan the location, props, and models. On a big-budget ad shoot, you might hire a stylist to find the props, call a casting director to locate models, and ask a location specialist to scout the best backgrounds. On a low-budget shoot, you probably will play all the roles yourself.

Props

Remember that precise propping can perfect the picture, whereas inappropriate props can destroy the desired illusion. For example, a photographer was assigned to illustrate a story about an English butler serving tea. The sketch called for the butler to wear a bowler hat. The photographer returned from the local theatrical prop shop with a hat that was black like a bowler but round on top like a hat worn by the Amish. No self-respecting English butler would be seen serving tea (or much else) in such a piece of headgear. While viewers of the picture might not spot the exact error, they would sense something was wrong about the high-tea scene.

On a low budget? Here are some ways to find props for a limited outlay of cash. You can find period props in antique and second-hand stores. High schools and colleges maintain costumes for their theater departments.

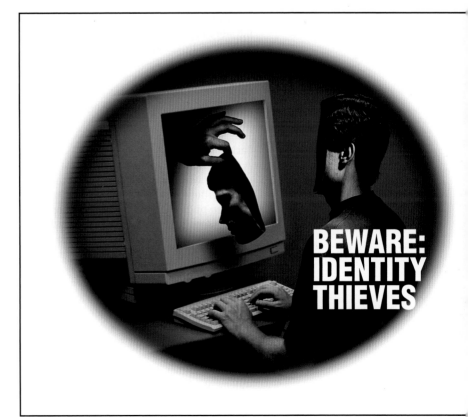

Via the Internet, thieves are stealing individuals' personal information to access financial accounts. To represent unique personal numbers and private codes like a social security number, driver's license, and birth date, the photographer selected a mask as a metaphor for individual identity.
William Duke, for *Newsweek* magazine

BEWARE: IDENTITY THIEVES

They, too, will often lend out period clothing for photo shoots.

For his daytrading illustration, William Duke needed to show a man on a tightrope. For one piece of the composite, he photographed a frayed rope against a white background. He then had a model stand on a stack of boxes in front of a white seamless and photographed him from a low angle. The desert in the picture came from a snapshot Duke had taken many years ago. The clouds were added from another scene Duke had previously photographed. Duke composited all the elements together in the computer to create the photo illustration, "The Daytrading Tightrope" (page 180).

John Burgess based his idea for "The Face of Today's Digital Camera" (page 175) on an Annie Leibovitz portrait of comedienne Lily Tomlin. Burgess found all the props he needed in a local camera shop.

Models

You don't need a trained Shakespearean actor to model in your photo illustration. Most illustrations don't depend on facial expressions or acting. They do, however, depend on stereotypes. You need a person who fits the part.

For an editorial photo illustration about runners hitting "the wall" at twenty-two miles, you may not need a world-class marathon runner, but don't pick a couch potato, either. Save your couch potato friend for the story on the dangers of being sedentary.

William Duke often uses himself as a low-cost model in his illustrations. For example, the photographer constructed his illustration of St. Sebastian from an out-of-copyright painting of the martyr's body topped with Duke's own face.

Backgrounds

A background is a photograph's most important layer when you are creating the mood of a photo illustration. To avoid the confusion between true and manufactured pictures, photographers have shot many successful photo illustrations against seamless paper backgrounds. The seamless paper adds an abstract quality to a photo since almost nothing in the natural world is ever seen against the purity of simple black or white.

Award-winning photographer Jay Koelzer, however, says that photographers can "look at the background not as something to make disappear but rather as something to add to the image so that it will carry a stronger statement." Koelzer frequently combines realistic backgrounds shot on location with subjects photographed in the studio to produce eye-catching, intellectually challenging images. For example, he photographed Denver's skyline for an illustration about population growth in Colorado (page 178).

In the studio, he photographed two models holding umbrellas. Using the computer to assemble the final image, he replicated the photos of his models, erased their faces, varied their sizes, and positioned them on the background. Like images from a René Magritte painting, the faceless characters appear to be gently rising and falling over Denver's cityscape with the Rocky Mountains in the background. Although the background is real, no one would mistake the final picture for a documentary photo.

The bottom line with all photo illustration, including use of the background, is that the reader should instantly know that the image is created, not recorded. Don't confuse the reader.

Time

Allow time—lots of time—to conceptualize, prop, and photograph an editorial photo illustration. Editors are accustomed to asking photographers to run down to Castro and 14th Streets to take a quick shot before the 5:00 p.m. deadline. Unfortunately, editors frequently maintain the same mindset when they request editorial photo illustrations.

Most photo illustrations, though, require much longer than two hours. Photo illustrations can take hours that stretch into days. Dreaming up concepts takes time. Rarely do the first headline and visual that come to mind result in the final photo. Propping takes shopping. Without the right props, the picture will look amateurish. Finding the perfect model can be as difficult as finding the perfect spouse. Then comes shooting. With the patience of Job, the meticulousness of a watchmaker, and the flair of a set designer, you will build the picture. The clock ticks as you move the props one inch to the left or right. Each change requires an adjustment of the lights.

After you've taken many test shots to check each detail, the time finally arrives to click the shutter release. The moment is almost anticlimactic.

When an editor at the *Fort Lauderdale Sun-Sentinel* in Florida assigned Susan Gardner to illustrate an article on cryonics—freezing corpses in the hopes of reviving them in the future—the photographer knew to allow time for the whole production. (See page 178.)

First, Gardner commissioned a fake block of ice from Plexiglas.

Then she sprayed this with fake snow, lit it with blue gels, and created a mist with dry ice. A hole in the bottom of a table allowed the model to slip her head inside the cube.

The first model, however, took one look at the set and backed out, saying it would be "detrimental" to her career. Her replacement, an elderly woman, was touched up with some white and blue makeup. One month elapsed from the original concept to the final exposed 21/4 chrome on Fujichrome 50D.

Melanie Rook D'Anna, shooting for the *Mesa* (Arizona) *Tribune*, wanted to illustrate the return of the movie "101 Dalmatians." She contacted the local Dalmatian kennel club and persuaded the members to bring their dogs to a movie theater—all at the same time. She positioned several highly trained dogs in the front row. These dogs followed the commands of their owners to stay.

The rest of the dogs were not so well-behaved, so their owners hid under the seats with their dogs resting comfortably above. The photographer filled the theater with more than eighty-one Dalmatians, all sitting in their seats at the same time.

The addition of popcorn, colas, and careful lighting gave this picture its striking look.

THINKING CREATIVELY: A STRUCTURE

John Newcomb's *The Book of Graphic Problem-Solving: How to Get Visual Ideas When You Need Them* is based on the premise that visual problem-solving starts with words. He suggests that the starting point is the editor's working title for the story.

Take a story about men who are losing their hair. The editor's working title: "Are You Worried about Balding?" Start by analyzing the nature of the subject.

LIST THE FACTS

What is balding? How would you describe balding to someone from another planet? What words might you use? Round, smooth, hairless. List some of the characteristics of the subject.

Source. What is the source of the problem or item you are illustrating? In this example, where does balding come from? What causes it? Balding in men is a hereditary trait that comes from their mothers, grandmothers, and great-grandmothers.

Theater distributors were bringing back the movie "101 Dalmatians." For an illustration, the photographer propped an entire movie theater with dogs from a local kennel club. The well-trained Dalmations in the front row sit unattended, but the less orderly animals in succeeding rows are firmly held in place by their owners, who are hiding under the seats.
Melanie Rook D'Anna, *Mesa [Arizona] Tribune*

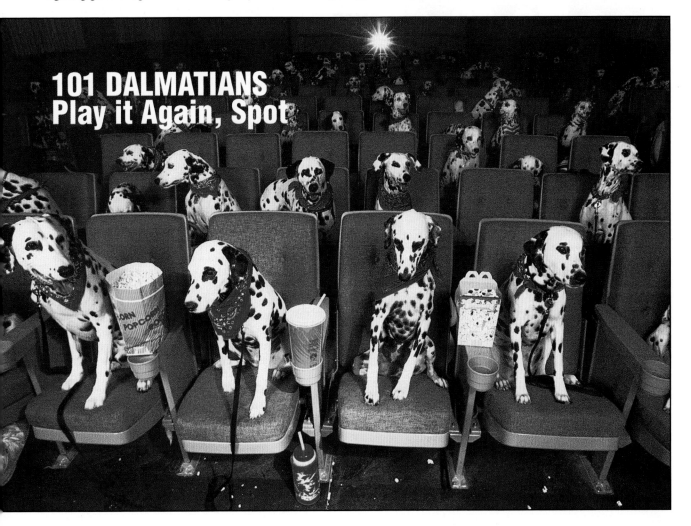

101 DALMATIANS
Play it Again, Spot

Delivery. If the topic is about a service or object, describe how it is delivered. If the story is about a new cure for balding, how would the patient get the cure? By pill, surgery, or diet?

Size. How large is the object or problem—both physically and emotionally? In the balding assignment, is the hair loss partial or complete? Does balding make men feel like jocks or like jackasses?

Weight. Is the subject of the assignment physically or emotionally heavy or light? Is it a crushing burden, or is it a minor irritant? Do those with only a few wisps of hair left on their heads feel dragged down or light-headed?

Winners or Losers. Who gains and who loses with balding? Most stories requiring illustration have a winner or loser, a survivor, or a

victim in the plot. At first, you might not think anyone gains from balding. But charlatans with patent cures gain, as do pharmaceutical companies that develop cures for baldness. Doctors who perform transplants gain. Wigmakers gain. Psychiatrists gain. Who loses? When hair falls out, men lose hair, and sometimes they lose their wives or girlfriends, too.

FACTS BECOME PHRASES

As you have just seen, Newcomb's method requires you to identify the facts about your topic. Write each answer down without worrying about being creative. Just start listing information.

Next, try sayings, phrases, proverbs, or any other bits of traditional wisdom. In the list of facts, we noted that the source of balding is genes inherited from the mother—not the father. Try the headline "Balding—Not Dad's Fault After All." To illustrate this idea, you could photograph a bald man holding a hairless baby.

In the fact list under weight, we noted that some bald men feel like jocks and others feel like jackasses. Think about twisting the emphasis. To suggest that bald men are not burdened by their hair loss, twist the line "Blondes Have More Fun" to "Balds Have More Fun." Now illustrate this line with a photo of a Telly Savalas-like character, bald and proud of it, surrounded by women.

Play Word Games

Now take the key words from each of the facts above and play word games with them. For instance, in describing the nature of a bald man's head, we listed the word "smooth." Smooth as a balloon, as a billiard ball, as a bowling ball. Imagine a bowling ball looking like a bald man's head. The phrase "Bowling, Anyone?" could evolve into a photo of a bald man with his head in a rack of bowling balls.

From the editor's original working title, "Are You Worried about Balding?" came first a set of facts about baldness. The facts led to plays on words and phrases. These sayings, puns, and double entendres produced visual ideas that could easily illustrate the story.

The final photograph, by the way, of the man's head lined up next to bowling balls, has since been shown to hundreds of editors, photographers, and others. The photo has never failed to bring the house down with appreciative laughter.

ELECTRONIC CUT AND PASTE

To create a surreal effect, you might want the picture's subjects to appear completely out of

First, write sample headlines for the story. Next, draw a rough sketch to go with each headline. Then select the best headline and sketch. Finally, locate the right props, costume, and background before taking the picture. Photo illustration by Marilyn Glaser; sketches by Ben Barbante

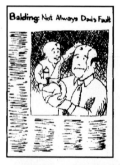
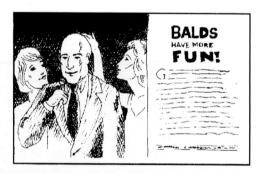
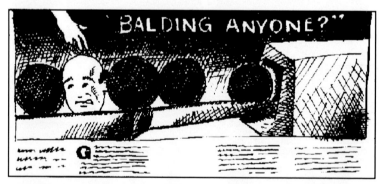
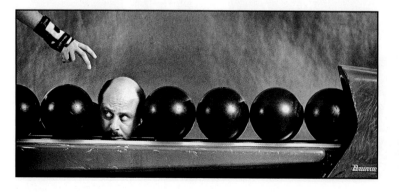

proportion. Perhaps you want the mayor of New York towering over the Empire State Building, or a sailor carrying the QE II under his arm.

To do so, you might need to photograph each element separately and then combine them. If you can't photograph all the subjects and props at the same time in the same location, remember to keep the light consistent for each image you plan on combining later.

For example, if the light appears to be diffused and coming from the upper left side of the scene, keep the same effect on all subsequent photos that you take in the studio. Then, when you put all the elements together, the final picture will have natural-looking light that appears to be coming from only one source.

Computers have come along to make life simpler for the photo illustration

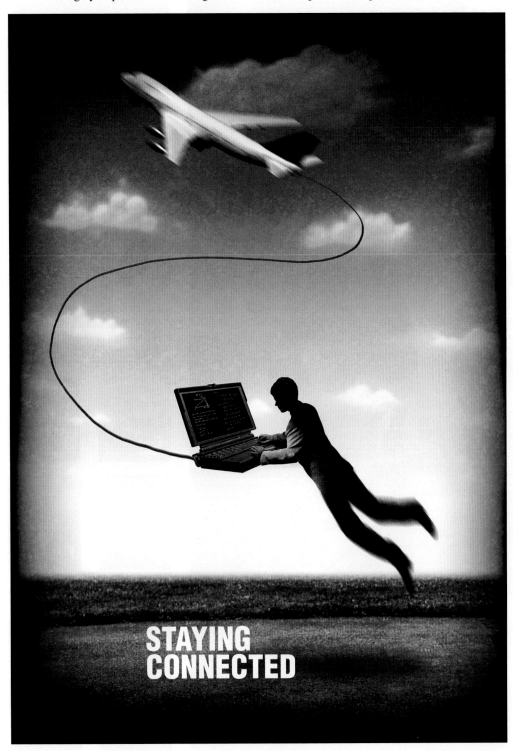

STAYING CONNECTED

Business travelers using their laptop computers on airplanes have become ubiquitous. To illustrate a story about the trend, the photographer combined three images to create a photo of a computer user tethered to an airplane. The photographer gave both the airplane and the man's legs the effect of movement by applying a computerized blur filter to that part of the image. William Duke, for *Fortune* magazine

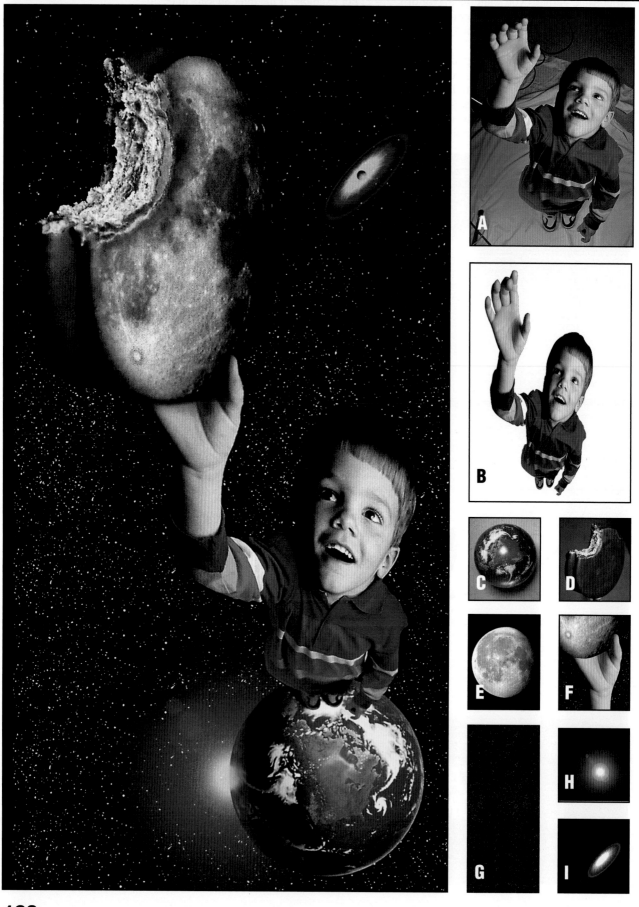

photographer. In today's high-tech age, you can scan in old images or new ones. Rather than physically cutting and pasting images, you can electronically alter them to your satisfaction.

Once you've scanned the pieces, you can easily change the size, color, and left-right orientation of each separate image.

You might place the subject into another setting (see pages 178, 180, 185, 186) or take the head off one subject and put it on another (see page 179). In fact, just about any effect you can imagine can be accomplished with the computer.

The computer usually speeds up the mechanics of creating a photo illustration. Having shot or gathered the individual pieces for the illustration and scanned them into the computer, you can manipulate and combine all the parts seamlessly.

Beware, however, that combining pictures with the computer can absorb much more time than originally planned. Even powerfully fast computers can take a long time to process complex images.

DON'T INFRINGE COPYRIGHTS

One word of caution. Copyright protection extends to "found" images in magazines, newspapers, and on the World Wide Web.

Unless the image is one you have shot or one that you have express permission to use, don't be tempted by the ease of scanning it into a computer to use someone else's photograph or work of art to enhance your photo illustration. Doing so is illegal—regardless of how much you change the original.

SOME WORK, SOME DON'T

Some editorial photo illustrations cause the reader to say, "Dear, you have to see this. It's just too funny." Others don't stop the reader at all, or, even worse, they cause the reader to ponder the strange picture, wondering why anyone would go to the trouble to publish it.

Why do some photo illustrations hit the reader like a sledgehammer and others leave no mark at all?

WEAK PHOTOS

Sometimes the photo is weak. Everyday, readers see slick ads produced by high-priced ad agencies. Consequently, readers are accustomed to illustrations that appear flawless.

Poorly planned editorial photo illustrations look unprofessional. If the models look like they were grabbed right out of the newsroom, if the set looks like it was a corner of the darkroom, and if the whole production looks like it was thrown together between assignments, then the final photo will look amateurish.

For an illustration titled "Sitters Can Be a Pet's Best Friend," the photographer had a subject pretend she was reading comics to two German shepherds. The scene, however, took place on a beat-up old couch. The rundown setting distracted from the concept.

One newspaper ran a photo illustration showing a man's handwriting on a chalkboard with the words "American education stumbles." The foreground contained a few books sitting vertically on a desk. The strong headline in this instance was not supported by an imaginative visual. The photographer failed to find a symbol for American education or to play off the idea of stumbling.

POOR HEADLINES

While editorial illustrations often fail because of poor photography, they also fail because of poor headlines. Rather than "leaving 'em laughing," an unclear headline leaves readers scratching their heads in confusion.

Sometimes, even a clear headline is not enough, if it is clear but dull. Beware of headlines that start out "Everything You Ever Wanted to Know about Pizza" or "The Entire History of Bicycles." These headlines do not suggest a theme but instead lend themselves to an encyclopedia entry on the topic.

Sometimes the writer has provided a label headline like "Potatoes." A headline like this probably came from a story that had no theme or focus. Suppose the story had focused on the role of the potato in the Irish

This headline and this picture leave the reader wondering just what the central theme of the story is. The headline, not the subhead, should tie the picture and the words together. A nicely executed photo loses its impact with a weak headline.

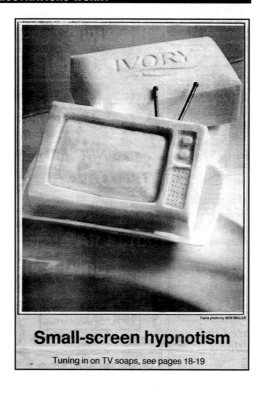

Facts photo by BEN BIGLER

Small-screen hypnotism

Tuning in on TV soaps, see pages 18-19

A good image in this example was matched with a weak headline. A better headline might read "Picture Perfect Pears."

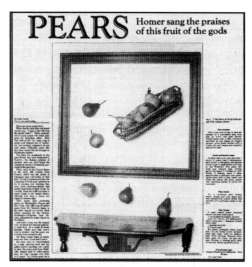

PEARS Homer sang the praises of this fruit of the gods

This illustration combines an unimaginative headline, "Super Bowl Snacks," with a picture that is too literal. Try thinking of some alternatives for both words and pictures.

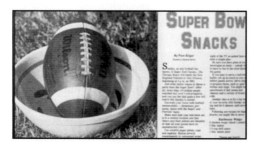

SUPER BOWL SNACKS

famine or had described the many ways to prepare potatoes. Either article would lend itself to a possible editorial photo illustration. If the story has no focus, however, the photographer is left to take a product photo of the potato itself, a vegetable all too familiar to most readers.

Sometimes headlines are too news-oriented. Photo illustrations work best with ideas, not events. Avoid headlines like "Stock Market Drops for Third Straight Day."

HEADLINE AND PICTURE DON'T MESH

Still, the headline might be great. The photo might be eye-popping. But if the two do not mesh, then the final package looks like an afterthought. Sometimes the reader gets the impression that the headline was written without the editor seeing the photo.

Or the page looks like the photographer never saw the headline or story before snapping the shutter.

One copy editor wrote this catchy headline: "When Marriage Seems Like War." The photographer produced a strong photo showing a couple having a highly stylized argument. The man's tie is blowing out behind him. Both models look like they are talking with their hands. The problem: they don't look like they are at war. The couple appears to be arguing in the wind, not battling. The words and pictures, like the married pair depicted in the photo, don't communicate.

WORDS OF CAUTION
DOCUDRAMA CONFUSION

Like editorial photo illustrations, docudramas are created situations. By mimicking reality, though, docudramas cause confusion in readers' minds. They are fake photographs that masquerade as authentic documentary images. Avoid these real-looking docudramas. Create photo illustrations that look unbelievable and cannot be confused with honest reportage.

Look at the images illustrating stories about "Latchkey Kids" on the opposite page. Isn't it conceivable that a photographer could have happened upon a child sitting on the front steps of his house, as depicted in the top image? The picture looks like a candid but in fact is a set-up docudrama. No reader, however, would mistake the bottom photo illustration, of a child dangling from a keychain, as real.

Even with the words "photo illustration" published beneath the picture, photographers should avoid docudramas. Docudramas detract from a paper's credibility. The reader should never have to ask, "Did that picture really happen that way?"

The job of the photojournalist is to show the world as it is, not as the photographer imagines it is. True editorial photo illustrations, by contrast, add to the reader's understanding and can even add a little fun. A picture should either be real or so outrageous that no reader is fooled. Don't leave the reader in the twilight zone of the docudrama.

PROBLEMS IN PLACEMENT AND IDENTIFICATION

Imagine for a moment a newspaper that sprinkles its editorials and analysis—unidentified—throughout its pages, including the front page. How would a reader, accustomed to the straight news on page one, know where fact ends and interpretation begins?

Failing to identify contrived photographs is every bit as serious as failing to properly identify written editorial comment—and playing editorial photo illustrations on the front page or alongside documentary photographs is as questionable as mingling editorials with unbiased news stories.

While newspapers prior to the Civil War did not hesitate to mix fact and opinion on the front page, most modern newspapers and magazines shy away from this practice and carefully limit opinions to a well-marked editorial page or clearly designated opinion column. The same stringent rules should be applied to editorial photo illustrations. Regardless of how unreal they may appear, they, too, should be labeled and segregated from straight photo reporting.

PRACTICAL AND ETHICAL GUIDELINES

The following are practical and ethical guidelines for using photo illustrations:
- Eliminate the docudrama. Never set up a photograph to mimic reality, even if it is labeled a photo illustration.
- Create only abstractions with photo illustration. Studio techniques, for example, can help to make situations abstract—the use of a seamless or abstract backdrop, photomontage, or exaggerated lighting. Contrast in size and content, juxtaposition of headline and photo—all can give the reader visual clues that what appears on the page is obviously not the real thing.
- Always clearly label photo illustrations as such—regardless of how obvious you may think they are.
- Never play photo illustrations on news pages. Restrict them to feature pages or to section fronts. Display them so that they are obviously distinct from news or feature pictures.
- If you haven't the time to do a photo illustration right, don't do it. Suggest another solution.

DOCUDRAMA VS. CONCEPT PHOTO

Avoid docudramas such as the top one, below. They fool the reader. Instead, create a concept photo like the one at the bottom, which is so abstract that no one will mistake it for real.

Photo illustration at bottom, by B. Jeff Breland

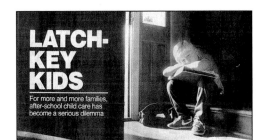

DOCUDRAMA

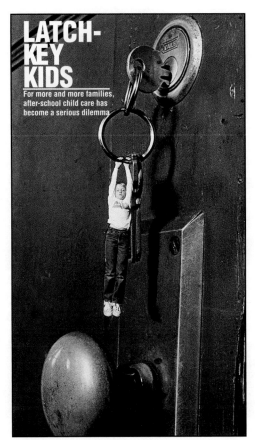

EDITORIAL PHOTO ILLUSTRATION

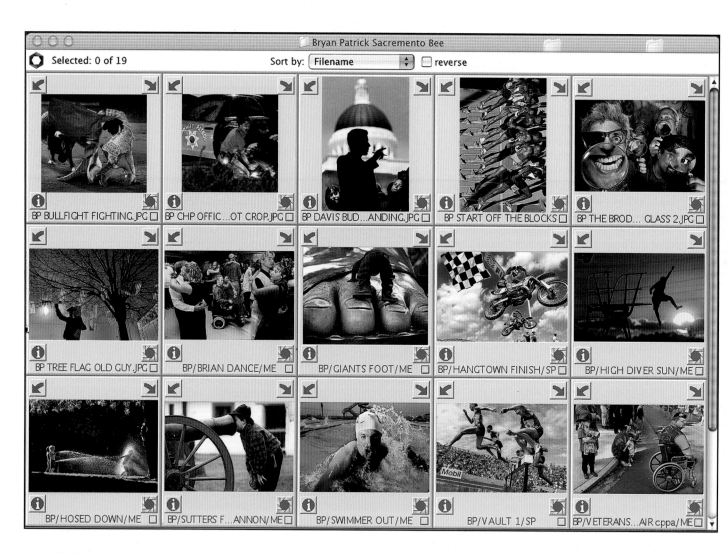

Choosing the right photo is an art. Surprisingly, some of the best photo editors were never photographers. All by Bryan Patrick, *Sacramento Bee*

Chapter 10

Photo Editing

THE ROLE OF THE PICTURE EDITOR

Are you ready for reality? You have less than three-quarters of a second to capture a reader's attention with a photograph. Using an innovative research tool, Sheree Josephson followed readers' eye movements as they looked at a variety of published pictures. The device she used consists of two tiny video cameras mounted on the subject's head that record where, how long, and in which order the person looks at photos in a newspaper, a magazine, or on a Web site. The startling result, revealed in her doctoral dissertation, was that readers spend less than three-quarters of a second looking at a photograph.

Eye-Trak research follows a person's eyes as they travel across a newspaper page or Web site. Recent studies suggest that in print, readers' eyes first go to photographs. On the Internet, however, they look at headlines and text before photos.

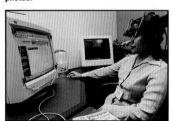

Now that is a challenge for any photo editor. How do you assign photographers and then select pictures that will communicate to the reader in less than a second?

Not surprisingly, photo editing takes strong eyes, a steady hand on the computer mouse, and the psychological strength to reject thousands of pictures while seeking the one frame or part of a frame that tells the story and has visual impact that will—literally—engage a viewer in an instant.

START WITH IMAGINATIVE ASSIGNMENTS
Striking pictures result from solid assignments. Daily, weekly, or monthly, picture editors at magazines, newspapers, agencies, or Web sites peruse lists of news stories to determine which lend themselves to pictorial reporting, which need an pen-and-ink illustration or computer graphic, and which need

no accompanying artwork at all. With limited staff and resources—and most newspapers, magazines, and Web sites fall into this category—editors must choose to cover articles or front-page stories with a certain amount of intrinsic visual interest.

When Bruce Baumann was assistant managing editor in graphics for the *Pittsburgh Press*, he warned that a photo department should not become a "service station." He pointed out that a photographer's job is not just to provide the service of illustrating a writer's story.

The enlightened photo editor, therefore, not only assigns the news stories of the day, but also generates pictorial story ideas.

For example, a news conference is called to announce a $4 million grant for nursing homes. Although a picture of the press conference may be necessary, it has little chance

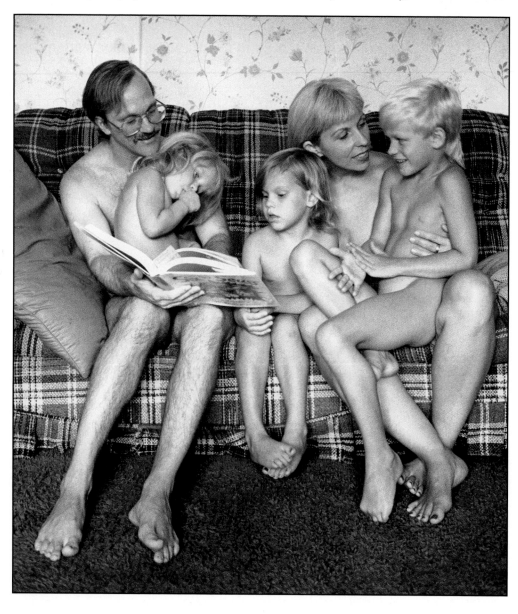

Good photos like this one start with good assignments. The members of this family, who wear no clothes at home, had been featured on "The Donahue Show." When the photographer's newspaper followed up the family's TV debut with a local story, he exposed carefully without revealing too much. Doug Kapustin, Patuxent [Maryland] Publishing Co.

of producing exciting photos and less opportunity for providing valuable information about aging or the crisis in care for the elderly. The story is about statistics—the percentage increase in care costs—and about the number of dollars spent on nursing home facilities.

A photo editor, on the other hand, might try to interpret these statistics visually by instructing the photographer to spend several days in a nursing home. These kinds of photos would help translate the dull, itemized costs into more human terms.

Readers would see the conditions of the facility and the regressive effects of aging on the home's clientele. Finally, photos showing an elderly patient slumped in a wheelchair in an empty hallway can bring the dollars-and-cents issue home to the reader (See Chapter 4, "Covering the Issues," page 62.)

SELECT THE PHOTOGRAPHER

A perceptive photo editor realizes the strengths and weaknesses of staff and free-lance photographers. Not all photographers like sports; only a few take funny pictures. Some photographers notice subtle shadings of light and shade, whereas others have an eye for action. Some photographers have a lot of experience traveling overseas, speak different languages, and can figure out how to transmit their pictures from any phone jack in the developing world. Matching the correct photographer with the appropriate assignment can be a complex task. Picture editors at magazines look at photographers' portfolios each week, searching for fresh work that represents new trends in photography. They also know the skills and talents of photographers associated with each picture agency, and they scan current magazines, as

Pairing the right photographer with the right assignment is a crucial job for the photo editor. In this case, the story required someone who could handle portable strobes. The photographer set up strobes with umbrellas on either side of an aquarium exhibit at the Alaska Department of Fish and Game.

The strobes froze the moment the large Pike opened it's mouth and swallowed the unsuspecting Rainbow fingerling.
Jim Lavrakas, *Anchorage Daily News*

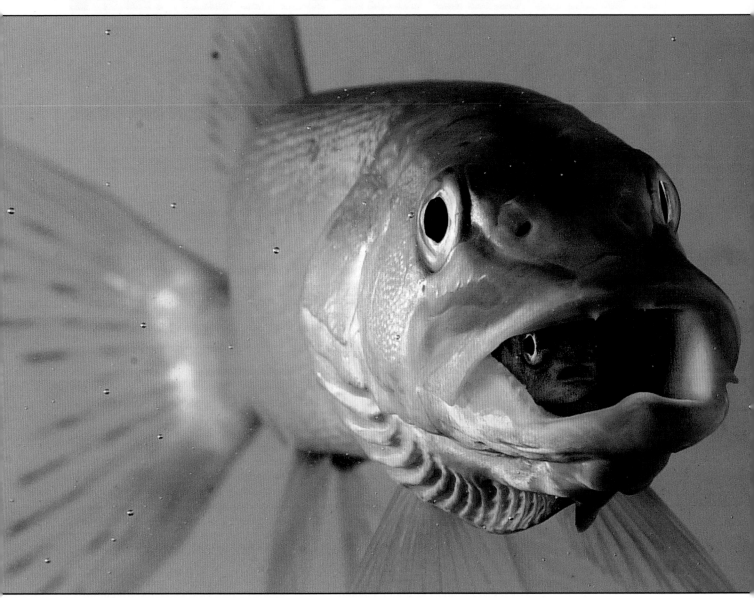

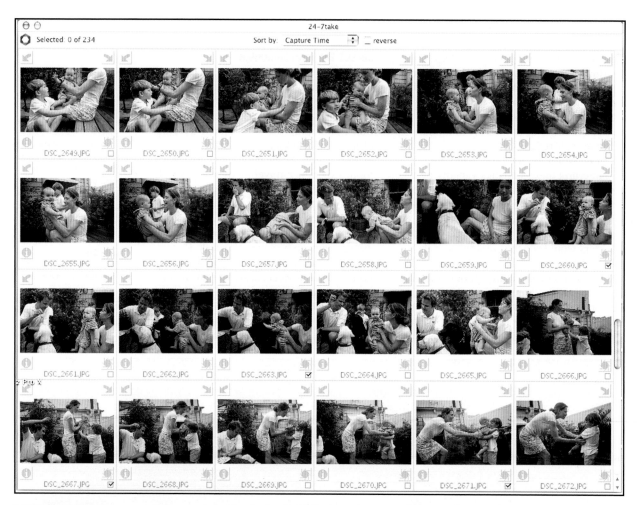

DSC_2649.JPG   DSC_2650.JPG   DSC_2651.JPG   DSC_2652.JPG   DSC_2653.JPG   DSC_2654.JPG

DSC_2655.JPG   DSC_2656.JPG   DSC_2657.JPG   DSC_2658.JPG   DSC_2659.JPG   DSC_2660.JPG

DSC_2661.JPG   DSC_2662.JPG   DSC_2663.JPG   DSC_2664.JPG   DSC_2665.JPG   DSC_2666.JPG

DSC_2667.JPG   DSC_2668.JPG   DSC_2669.JPG   DSC_2670.JPG   DSC_2671.JPG   DSC_2672.JPG

These images are part of a raw take on family life in the French Quarter of New Orleans. Notice how the photographer follows each situation as it unfolds. Which image would you select?

Jennifer Zdon, for *America 24/7*

well, to see the styles in the field. In fact, the primary way a magazine editor controls "the look" of the publication is through the selection of photographers with different styles, says Peter Howe. Howe has been photo editor of the *New York Times Magazine*, director of photography at *Life* magazine, and the director of photography and sourcing for Corbis/Bettman, an international picture agency and archive.

On the morning of Sept. 11, 2001, just after the first plane crashed into the World Trade Center, *Time* magazine picture editor Mary Ann Golon was still at home in New Jersey. On her ride into Manhattan that morning, she made several dozen calls to orchestrate coverage of the terrorist attacks of via cell phone. Eventually, she had about twenty-five photographers in the field. *Time*'s photo editors reviewed at least 15,000 pictures that day.

Knowing whom to call is Golon's special expertise, says *Time*'s director of photography, Michele Stephenson."This business is built on personal relationships," Stephenson told Caroline Howard for an article in *Columbia Journalism Review*. "Mary Ann Golon's success… comes from a reputation she has built through the years."

When making an assignment, a photo editor should provide the photographer with all the available information on an upcoming story. The more information about an assignment, the better photojournalist can cover it. Clips of previous and related stories help put the story in context; names and numbers of additional contacts may lead the photographer to further information.

And, of course, if the story is expected to run with a photo layout rather than a single picture, then the editor should forewarn the photographer about the number of pictures that will be needed.

RESEARCH, RESEARCH, RESEARCH

Sometimes a magazine or Web editor can't afford to send a photographer to China for a photo of the Forbidden City.

Other times, the publication needs a picture from the Civil War. In situations like these, photo editors sometimes turn to picture researchers. These specialists comb the publication's files or scour picture agencies' libraries to find the perfect images to accompany a story. Some royalty-free pictures are on the Internet, on CD-ROMs, from the public library, or the Library of Congress.

They can identify pictures to purchase by searching online databases maintained by agencies like Corbis, Getty, Magnum,

Black Star, as well as by wire services such as Wide World Photos, Reuters, and Agence France-Presse.

Today, many individual and groups of photographers also post pictures for sale on their own Web sites.

CAMERA SKILLS UNNECESSARY
Surprisingly, one skill that is not necessary to be an outstanding photo editor is the ability to take pictures. Many of the best-known photo editors never learned to use a camera; others, although they know the basic techniques, never practiced photojournalism.

The late John Durniak, who worked at various times for *Time*, *Look*, and the *New York Times*, and Tom Smith, who was *National Geographic*'s illustrations editor, both spent most of their lives handling pictures, not lenses. Roy Stryker of the Depression-era Farm Security Administration, which produced probably the most complete and lasting still-photo documentary of any era, never took pictures himself. The most famous example, however, is Wilson Hicks, an executive editor of *Life* magazine. He sent photographers to every point on the globe; he hired and fired the best photojournalists; and he set the direction of the field for years to come. Yet he never took a picture that was published in his own magazine.

THE HAZARDS AND SATISFACTION OF DO-IT-YOURSELF PICTURE EDITING
Should photographers edit their own work? Some editors say that photographers are too emotionally involved when taking pictures to evaluate their photographs objectively during the editing process. The photographer, who might have dangled from the top of a mountain in subzero weather to get a particularly evocative picture, might attach more significance to the image than would an impartial photo editor, who evaluates the picture's merits without considering the conditions under which the photo was taken.

Sometimes freelancers or staffers have no choice about who edits their pictures. On some magazines and newspapers, for example, photographers receive an assignment, cover the story, turn in the film, and wait until

Nancy Andrews, now director of photography at the *Detroit Free Press*, believes it is often easier to take great photographs of people undergoing trauma or working hard to triumph. But, she notes, "If we're constantly photographing communities in their extremes, we don't portray a complete picture. The story of Clyde Jackson isn't typical of the tons of stories in our database about African-American males.. . .Those stories aren't necessarily inaccurate. But they are incomplete because they represent extremes. Clyde Jackson isn't the Father of the Year. He's not struggling to overcome adversity. He's just trying to be the best father that he can be."
Nancy Andrews, for the *Washington Post* ©

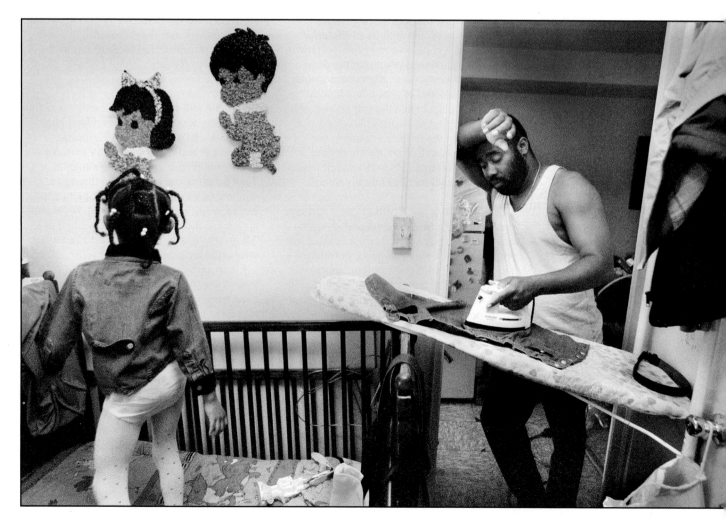

the story runs to see which of their pictures have been selected and how they have been played. These photographers have almost no control over stories after shooting them.

On the other hand, many photographers feel that since they were on the scene, they know the story best. Because they are journalists, they feel that they should decide which pictures best reflect the story. Rather than let an editor view the complete take, many photographers also edit their own film. On many small newspapers, magazines, and Web sites, the photojournalist gets the dual position by default—there is no one else to handle the job.

What the do-it-yourself picture editing system gains in efficiency, however, it loses in objectivity. While it isn't necessary for an editor to view the images, the photographer should find someone who wasn't present at the news scene to offer an impartial opinion on the take.

STRATEGIES FOR PHOTO SELECTION
THEORIES OF PICTURE SELECTION

Back in 1939, Laura Vitray, John Millis, Jr., and Roscoe Ellard tried to develop a mathematical formula for determining reader interest in pictures. As the authors of *Pictorial Journalism*, a book on news photography of the day, they assigned points for the degree of an event's news value, the subject's notoriety, and the amount of action in a picture. But few editors adopted the formula because it failed to define news, provide a yardstick for measuring the subject's notoriety, or establish a means to quantify the degree of action in the picture. Also, editors felt limited when judging all pictures on only three scales.

Stanley Kalish and Clifton Edom, in their classic book *Picture Editing*, added several new criteria. They advised editors to look for pictures that not only had news, notoriety, and action, but also eye-stopping appeal. By eye-stoppers, the authors meant pictures with interesting patterns, strong contrasts in tonal value, or those that could be uniquely cropped (like extra-wide horizontals or slim verticals). Then, once readers were engaged, the pictures should hold interest. What galvanized readers' attention, they said, depended on subject matter. A picture about love or war is more likely to maintain attention than a photograph about farming or economics. Some topics, the researchers concluded, are intrinsically more interesting than others, regardless of the quality of the photo.

THE *WASHINGTON POST'S* HIERARCHY OF PICTURES

Joe Elbert, assistant managing editor for photography at the *Washington Post*, and members of his photographic team have won practically every award the profession has to offer—from Newspaper Photographer of the Year to the Pulitzer Prize. Elbert himself has won the Pictures of the Year Contest's highest editing award. What is Elbert's secret?

Yes, the *Post* has an outstanding photo staff. But Elbert has a carefully considered and defined approach to editing pictures. He divides photographs into four hierarchical categories:
1) informational
2) graphically appealing
3) emotional
4) intimate

Purely informational pictures fall into Elbert's lowest category, while intimate pictures represent the ultimate photojournalistic challenge.

Informational

Informative pictures represent the "lowest common denominator" of photos, Elbert says. Like the standard five Ws (Who, What, Where, When, and Why) that lead in a written story, informational pictures report the facts without flavor.

Graphic

Better, but still not great in Elbert's eyes, are graphically appealing pictures. Good photojournalists, he says, will go to a routine assignment and try to find a way to make interesting pictures in a boring situation. They might frame by shooting through a window or a keyhole to give the picture a more interesting dark foreground, for example, or use the exaggerated perspective of a 24mm lens to add visual interest to an otherwise ordinary subject.

Elbert says that professional photographers tend to use the same techniques over and over, assignment after assignment, knowing that these pat approaches will bring back better-than-average, usable images from standard situations.

Emotional

Elbert tries to help photographers take and ultimately select emotionally appealing photos as often as possible. These photos cause the reader to feel something about the subject, not just intellectualize about the story. These photos add dimension to a story rather than repeat what is already written.

Some photos capture the subject's emotion. People crying, laughing, hitting, or

THE *WASHINGTON POST*'S HIERARCHY OF PICTURE SELECTION

1 INFORMATIONAL
White House aide Sidney Blumenthal follows attorney Jo Marsh from federal court in Washington, D.C.
Larry Morris, ©1998 *Washington Post*

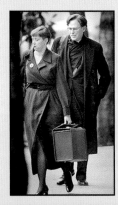

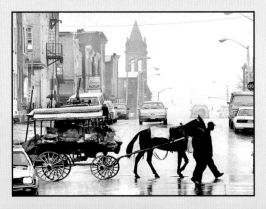

2 GRAPHICALLY APPEALING
A man selling his wares winds his horse and vegetable cart through the Sandtown neighborhood of West Baltimore.
Dudley M. Brooks, ©1997 *Washington Post*

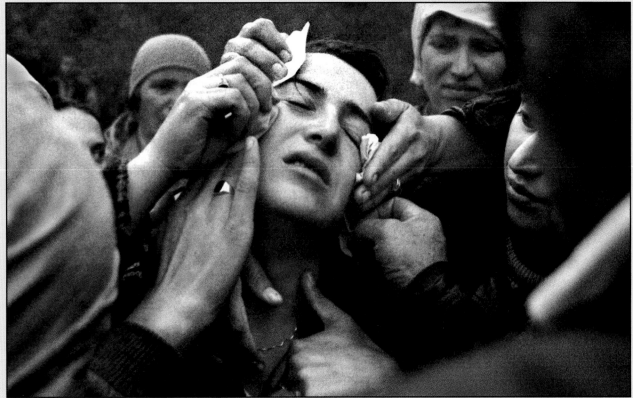

3 EMOTIONAL
A Kosovar woman is revived by friends and relatives at the funeral of her husband, a KLA soldier killed by Serbian police.
Dayna Smith, ©1998 *Washington Post*

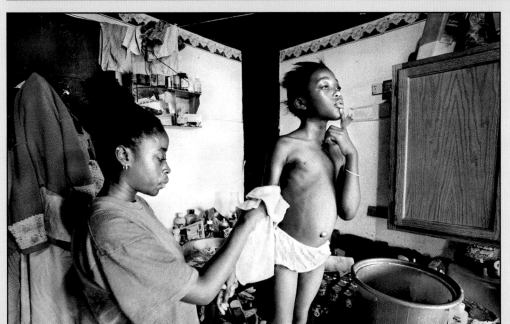

4 INTIMATE
Six-year-old Tiara gets two baths a day from water drawn from a nearby hand-pump well. Most of the homes in this area on Virginia's eastern shore do not have running water. Michael Williamson, ©1998 *Washington Post*

hugging each other result in emotionally appealing photos. But in the end, the test of the picture is with the viewer. Does the picture cause the viewer to laugh, cry, get mad, or come away curious or shocked?

To identify pictures in this category, Elbert says, editors must be open to their natural reactions toward the pictures. The reactions can't be anticipated, assigned, staged, required, defined, or prescribed. Sensitive editors must be in touch with their inner responses to pictures and, in the end, be willing to follow those instincts.

Intimate
Ultimately, Elbert looks for intimate pictures. Intimate pictures are the most private. This category, he says, is the hardest to define, but it includes pictures that make the reader feel close to the situation or in-tune with the subject. For just a moment, this kind of picture transforms the reader into a participant. Of course, as Elbert says, what is intimate for one reader might remain on the emotionally appealing level for another.

Photographers who don't care about their subjects bring back pictures with no feeling, Elbert maintains. He looks at the eyes of the subject in the picture to know if the photographer connected with that person.

BUILDING BLOCKS OF PICTURE SELECTION
Going beyond Elbert's four categories, consider an adaptation of the approach that looks for pictures combining at least two of the qualities. Emotional pictures that contain information about the story would be better than simply emotional pictures. Most readers would find informational pictures with graphic appeal better than purely graphic pictures that do not tell a story. Perhaps photographs that reach the highest rung of Elbert's hierarchy would combine information, graphics, emotional appeal, and intimacy.

While few images might achieve this level, the search for these combined qualities would guide first the shooter, then the photo editor, and finally the managing editor in deciding which images to play.

In the end, these categories help orient photographers for what to look for when shooting. They require the photographer to go beyond the routine or even the technique that has worked in the past. Simply making a factual picture is not good enough. Finding the right light or a clever angle is still insufficient. Discovering emotional pictures requires a photographer to look hard, to be thoughtful, and to have the patience to wait for a revealing moment.

A New Dialogue
If editors, photo editors, and photographers use Elbert's rankings, the conversation forces everyone to start looking at their own emotional reactions to the images. Rather than arguing about whether this or that element is in the picture, the discussion switches to how the pictures make the viewer respond. The picture editing decisions are instantly less cerebral and more heartfelt.

Putting informational pictures on the lowest rung of the picture ladder quickly puts these images aside. By devaluing graphic or pretty pictures, Elbert's system raises the bar and demands that pictures go beyond mere decoration. Elbert is saying that great pictures should hit you in the gut, not the head.

Once the conversation among decision makers focuses on which picture is most emotional or intimate, the battle for good photojournalism is won.

When everyone buys into this ranking scheme, the hard work for the photo editor is over. Strictly informational or solely graphic pictures have long since been left in the editing room. The task of finding the ultimate, intimate picture begins. Then, the only question left for the editing team is which picture approaches this prized status.

RESEARCH ON READERS' PREFERENCES
FIRES, DISASTER, AND HUMAN INTEREST
Researchers Malcolm S. MacLean and Anne Li-An Kao studied the responses of thirty-two people to a variety of photos and determined that test subjects generally liked "celebrities, children, happy old ladies, roses, and animals." They disliked pictures they were shown of "Mussolini and his mistress hanging by their feet, dead American soldiers, and dead bodies in general."

Yet liking photos and being interested in them are not the same. Because the respondents did not like what was in the pictures doesn't mean they weren't interested in the subject matter. Photographs at the extreme ends of the scale also tended to be those that respondents said aroused the most emotion.

In general, readers say they don't like to look at dead bodies. In a clever study conducted in the 1980s, James Roche altered captions to observe how readers would react if they thought the person in a photograph was dead vs. whether they thought the person was alive. Most respondents appeared more accepting of the "victim-lived" than of the "victim-died" photograph.

Controversial Images
More recently, Gretchen Farsai asked whether newspaper editors, as compared with

to that section.

CONCLUSIONS

With so few studies available, and the studies themselves conducted years apart and differing in sampling and survey techniques, generalizations have to be limited. Yet several conclusions seem justified. Human-interest pictures consistently receive high reader ratings. People like to look at pictures of people engaged in funny or unusual activities. Sports photos actually appeared at the bottom of all the surveys. In fact, one Lou Harris survey found that newspaper editors overestimated the general public's interest in sports stories.

CAN PROFESSIONAL EDITORS PREDICT READERS' PREFERENCES?

Who knows what kinds of pictures people like? Logically, you might assume that photo editors know their audiences, but another study by MacLean and Kao, published in *Journalism Quarterly*, suggested that editors are just guessing when they predict reader response to pictures. The researchers asked average newspaper readers to sort through pictures and to arrange them in order—from most favorite to least favorite photos.

Then the researchers gave a group of experienced photo editors and a group of untrained students statistical information about the readers. Armed with this knowledge, the group of editors and the group of students sorted through the same images and predicted how they thought the readers would have ordered their preferences.

MacLean and Kao hypothesized that the more information (such as age, gender, and occupation) the editors and students had, the more accurately they could predict the likes and dislikes of readers.

The researchers' hypothesis was wrong. Professional photo editors performed little better than even chance when given detailed information about their readers. Furthermore, photo editors did no better at their predictions than did the students.

However, once the professionals had seen how their readers sorted one set of photos, the editors could anticipate how the readers would sort a second set. These predictions were even better if the editors knew more about the reader, including the person's age, hobbies, and lifestyle.

Until the editors had seen the picture selections of the readers, however, they could not predict an individual's preferences.

Clearly, more editors should find out what pictures their readers are actually looking at, rather than make editorial decisions on their own biases.

The Bus Survey

Robert Gilka, former director of photography for *National Geographic*, tells a story about Charlie Haun, a newspaper picture editor in Detroit, who used to conduct his own surveys: "Every couple of days, Haun would ride the bus in Detroit and look over the shoulders of bus riders who were reading the paper. He would note which picture their eyes stopped at, how long they dwelt on each photo, and see if they read captions." Gilka points out that although Haun's method was primitive, "Charlie probably knows more about pictures than most of us today." Haun, from his bus rides, came to the same conclusion that MacLean and Kao did from their research. Identifying pictures people have picked in the past is the best determinant of what pictures they will choose in the future.

DO READERS AND EDITORS AGREE?

To discover if editors and readers agree on what constitutes interesting and newsworthy photos, the Associated Press Managing Editors photo survey mentioned earlier was designed to determine which kinds of pictures readers liked, as well as which type editors preferred, and whether readers and editors shared the same taste.

The results indicated a surprisingly close agreement between readers and editors.

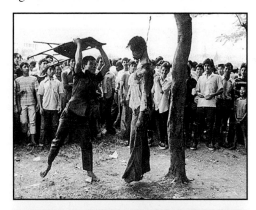

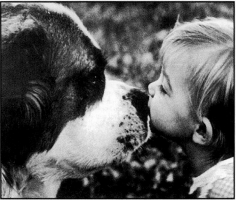

Which picture is your favorite? In an Associated Press survey, editors selected the hard news shot of a rightist striking the lifeless body of a hanged student in Bangkok, Thailand. Readers preferred the feature picture of a Saint Bernard and child.
© Wide World Photos

Both selected the same photos in the sports, general news, and feature categories.

Editors' and readers' opinions, however, differed radically on the use of dramatic news pictures. Editors were twice as likely as readers to choose action-packed, often violent, and sometimes gruesome news pictures. A majority of the readers not only disliked such pictures, but also thought that violent pictures should never be published.

As the pictures became successively more gruesome, fewer readers voted for photos in this category.

As MacLean and Kao discovered, editors cannot predict an individual's photo preferences. Yet, as the AP survey indicated, except for spot news, editors' and readers' tastes are generally similar.

When it came to picking a favorite picture, however, editors and readers diverged. Readers chose the Saint Bernard-kissing-child picture. Editors, by comparison, chose as most interesting the photo of the lifeless body of a hanged Bangkok student being beaten by a right-wing opponent.

The AP's Hal Buell tried to draw some conclusions from his picture survey. Newspapers and magazines have to be all things to a lot of different people, he said. Editors must print what people want and also what the editors think is significant.

In the end, a publication has to print some of both to present a complete picture of the world: pictures of dogs kissing kids as well as pictures of political violence.

NOVELTY

Many editors and certainly judges at contests complain that they have seen the same kind of picture over and over. Some even judge contests specifically looking for "novel" images. However, even these seasoned pros often have trouble defining what constitutes a novel news photograph. Like the Supreme Court judge who said he could not define pornography but that he knew it when he saw it, experienced photographers and editors claim they can recognize new styles and new content when they see it even if they can't define it.

Pulitzer Prize-winning photographer Kim Komenich describes his experience judging the 1993 Pictures of the Year Contest: "I was hypersensitive to clichés and to pictures that I had seen before and pictures I had made before…. The pictures I was looking to point out and offer support for were the ones that were the innovative photographs of photographers who are truly out there trying to define the next step in photojournalism."

Many of the judges felt that readers would not spend much time with newspaper or magazine photographs that show nothing "new."

Andrew Mendelson, now at Temple University, observed Komenich and the other judges that year and then carried out research for his dissertation to find out whether readers prefer news pictures with novel composition

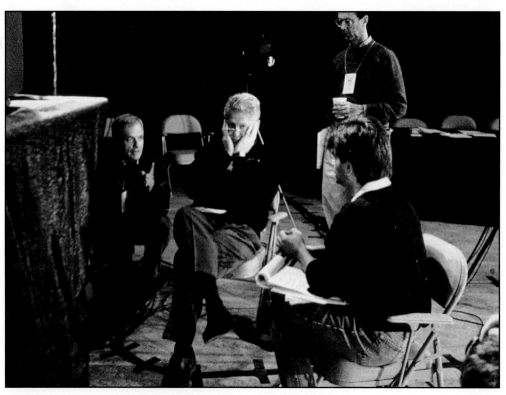

Researcher Andrew Mendelson asked whether the composition and subject matter of this and similar pictures were "novel." They asked judges to determine if the pictures, including this one of President Clinton during his reelection campaign, were active or calm; emotional or unemotional; simple or complex, etc.
Diana Walker, *Time*

and content to those that are more routine.

Not surprisingly, the researcher had great difficulty describing and then defining the concept of novelty in news photography, even in order to test his hypothesis.

In fact, his first group of research subjects—two different sets of journalism students—failed to consistently agree on which images in his study were novel and which were routine. Eventually, two professional designers went through the images and categorized eighteen of them, labeling each as either novel or routine.

In the next phase, a new group of subjects examined the photographs, without the labels, of course. In fact, pictures the designers identified as novel did attract attention and were better recalled than the routine images. However, once the photos were placed on a newspaper page and the experiments were conducted again, Mendelson

found no effective difference in preference between novel and routine pictures.

In the end, Mendelson remained unable to define the characteristics of novelty. However, his dissertation does raise provocative questions.

Does changing compositional elements like lighting, angle, or camera-to-subject distance cause the reader to look at or remember photos for a longer amount of time?

Just what effect does shooting style have on readers' attitude toward pictures? These elements had little impact on research participants and showed no influence when the study group saw the pictures in a newspaper.

Also, what are routine pictures? Do readers respond more to a subject they have never seen than they do to the routine subjects commonly covered in a paper or magazine? While almost every photographer, editor, and publisher is sure of the answers to these questions, very little research exists to guide

What effect does shooting style have on readers' attitude toward pictures? Do novel approaches to photography increase readership for a picture? Spectators venture inside a curiosity sideshow at a traveling carnival. Pat Tehan, *Mercury News* [San Jose, California]

the curious photojournalist who prefers facts to conventional wisdom.

WHAT READERS DON'T SEE

Pictures in the media should reflect our society. Sounds good.

Unfortunately, editors tend to ignore, on purpose or through benign neglect, whole population segments, including African Americans, gays and lesbians, Hispanics, Asians, and women of all races.

Researchers Paul Lester and Ron Smith found that only 1.1 percent of the pictures in *Life*, *Newsweek*, and *Time* in 1942 included African Americans.

Today, while these magazines run more images of African Americans (8.8 percent), this number does not match the 12.3 percent of the American population this group constitutes. Lester and Smith demonstrated that although coverage has increased, African-American content categories typically cluster around three primary topics—sports, entertainment, and crime. Such emphasis maintains the stereotypical assumptions of readers and viewers that the media often communicate. Researcher Michael Singletary came to the same general conclusions when he looked at how frequently African Americans are portrayed in newspapers.

In a 1974 study of the *Los Angeles Times* and the *Washington Post*, Susan Miller found that pictures of men outnumbered pictures of women in both papers. Roy Blackwood replicated Miller's study in 1980 and found that the imbalance had actually worsened over the intervening years. Men clearly dominated page one, inside news pages, business pages, and the sports section. Ratios of photos of men to women ranged from more than twenty to one for sports, to about two to one for entertainment. Overall, pictures of men outnumbered pictures of women nearly four to one in the *Post,* and nearly three to one in the *Times*.

Barbara Luebke came to the same conclusion when she studied four Connecticut newspapers in 1989. She found that men are shown not only more often, but also usually as professionals and sports figures, whereas women are portrayed as spouses—despite the fact that 23.8 percent of professional athletes in the United States at the time were female.

As well as African Americans and women, newspapers tend to ignore gays and lesbians. As recently as 1992, Joseph Bernt and Marilyn Greenwald found that 25 percent of the senior editors at daily newspapers would not run pictures of two people of the same sex kissing.

A series about teen gays titled "Growing Up Gay: A Crisis in Hiding," shot by Rita

Some newspaper editors overlook feature photo situations that include people who are physically challenged. Jason Clark, *Spokesman-Review* [Spokane, Washington]

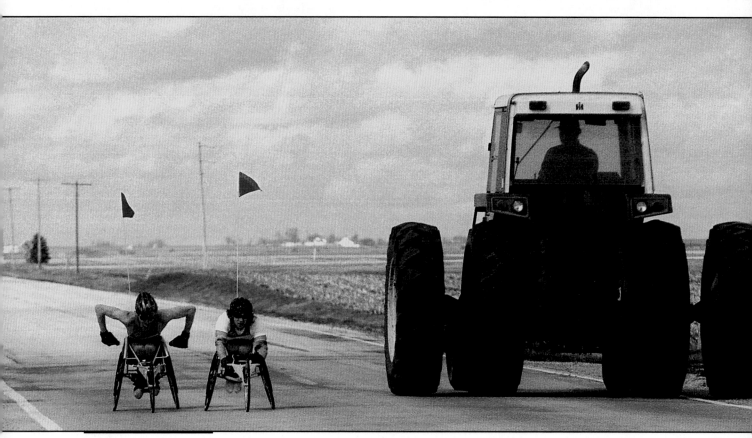

Reed and published in a fourteen-page, ad-free section of the *Minneapolis Star Tribune*, is a notable exception.

Readers rarely think about pictures they don't see. "Out of sight, out of mind." Editors, therefore, should be especially aware of the pictures they are not assigning or are omitting from their publications or Web sites. Readers depend on the news media for a balanced picture of the world. Leaving out whole segments of the population presents a notably biased view, even if editors believe readers might not like seeing certain pictures. (See pages 315–323, Chapter 14, "Ethics," for more on this issue.)

HOW READERS REACT TO COLOR

Although many photographers prefer to shoot in black and white, readers prefer color photos, according to different studies by J. W. Click and G.H. Stempel and by the Poynter Institute Color Project, conducted by Drs. Mario Garcia and Robert Bohle.

Readers think color photos are more realistic, an International Newspaper Advertising and Marketing Executives survey concluded. Not surprisingly, the researchers also discovered that readers dislike poor color reproduction. Readers remember color better, the Newspaper Advertising Bureau discovered in a test of recall as opposed to attention.

Color ads were recalled more frequently than were black-and-white ads. Readers, however, did remember black-and-white ads in greater detail and for a longer period of time.

In another Poynter Institute study, "Eyes on the News," Drs. Mario Garcia and Pegie Stark found that readers pay equal attention to single-color and black-and-white photos of feature subjects, but that color news and sports photos draw more attention than their black-and-white counterparts.

In research using an Eye-Trac device developed by the Gallup organization in Princeton, New Jersey, other researchers have found:

- Black-and-white news pictures received 77 percent attention, which rose to 88 percent when the same picture was shown in color. For sports pictures, the differences were even greater.
- A black-and-white sports picture grabbed readers' attention 64 percent of the time, whereas the same photo in color got 80 percent attention. Further analysis showed that this jump occurred because women pay attention to color but not black-and-white photos of athletes.
- Features nabbed readers' attention equally—about 78 percent of the time—whether in color or in black-and-white.

Some newspapers will not run pictures of two people of the same sex kissing. This photo was from a project about elderly gay people in long-term committed relationships. Pavlos Simeon, for master's thesis, "Elderly Gay Couples"

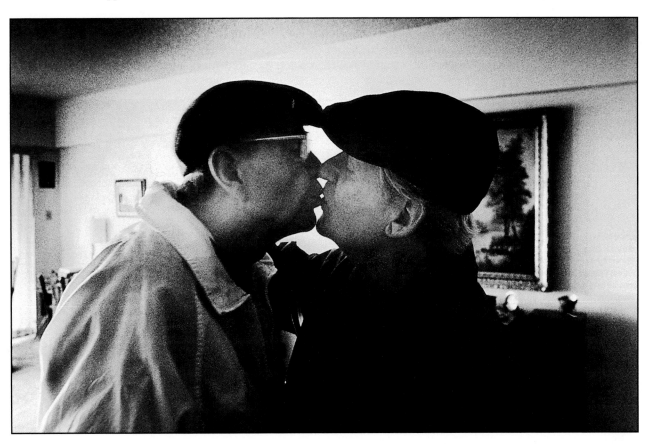

• Color does seem to stand out in photo packages. With a group of photos, the researchers found, subjects paid greater attention when the same pictures were reproduced in color.

In follow-up research, Sheree Josephson used similar technology in her study "Questioning the Power of Color." She found that in the first ten seconds of viewing a page, readers paid equal attention to color and black-and-white photos. However, if their only choices were a black-and-white photograph at the top of the page and a color image at the bottom, the readers went first to the bottom of the page and the color photo.

The number of times or the length of time readers looked at either black-and-white or color photos was about equal, according to Josephson's research.

During the first ten seconds, readers on average looked at photos two to three times for a surprising total of less than one second. In a post-test, the study found that readers could recall color photos they had seen previously in the newspaper more often than they could recall black-and-white pictures they also had viewed.

Josephson's research seems to conclude that when a person looks at the printed page for the first ten seconds, color images don't necessarily attract or hold attention more than black-and-white. Yet the color photographs are remembered longer.

Overall, readers prefer color photos and think they are more realistic. Black-and-white images grab attention as well as color,

except for sports pictures and picture packages. Readers seem to remember color photos color better than black-and-white.

COLOR VS. BLACK-AND-WHITE

Can you imagine Van Gogh painting sunflowers without knowing whether his yellows would be seen as shades of gray? Or Ansel Adams photographing "Moonrise over Hernandez" in color and black-and-white—just in case? Yet this is what editors ask of photographers, who must visualize the scene with and without color. They try to take pictures that work both ways.

While many news organizations today run all their photos in color, others have all assignments shot in color, which they convert to black-and-white if necessary. So photographers sometimes face the challenge of shooting pictures that might run in either color or black-and-white. Photographers faced with this problem usually choose to shoot for one medium or the other. They try to "think in color" or "think in black and white" and hope that editors in the office don't second-guess the decision.

Thinking in color requires photographers to develop a special eye. Color is a different language, points out Steve Raymer, the former *National Geographic* staffer. "I pass up pictures when the color gets in the way. It's a matter of learning to read color, light, and subject in a new way."

New photographers often make pictures filled with bold primary colors that can detract from a photograph's editorial content. Red, for example, is a color that produces

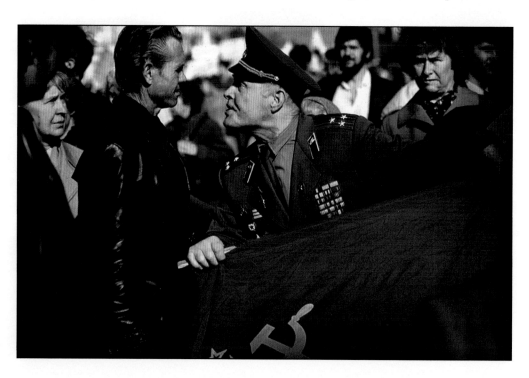

While on assignment for *National Geographic*, the photographer caught this retired Russian colonel arguing with anti-Communist demonstrators during the May Day celebration in Red Square. The picture captured the country's old and new attitudes and provided a visual synopsis for his story "Mother Russia on a New Course." The red flag adds to both the visual and story-telling power of the picture.

Steve Raymer, for *National Geographic*

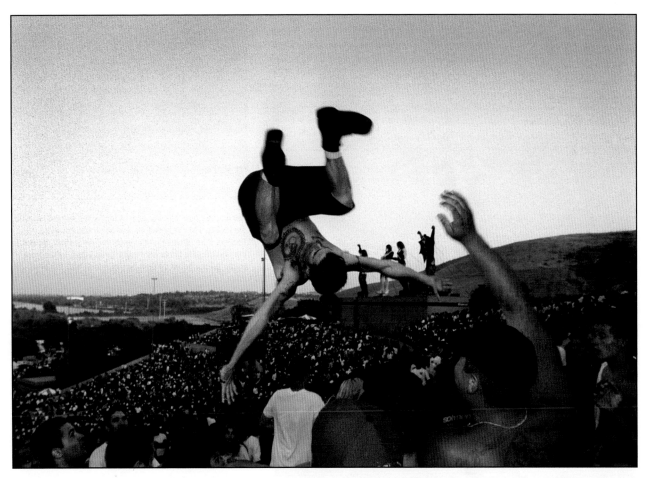

strong emotions. Like the bull attracted to the matador's red cape, photographers are equally drawn to bright red in the scene they are photographing. The color, unfortunately, tends to dominate a visual message so much that you must be extremely careful in how much red you include in a picture. If your assignment is an environmental portrait of a race-car driver, for example, be careful that the driver's red Ferrari doesn't take over the picture. On the other hand, if you're in Red Square, as Raymer was in Russia, including the country's red flag in a picture makes both visual and editorial sense.

Raymer recommends searching out colors that complement one another and create a mood. "Start with the concept of harmony," he says. "Before moving to dominant primary colors like red and blue, learn that when it comes to color less is usually more."

COLOR FOR COLOR'S SAKE?

When the *St. Petersburg* (Florida) *Times and Independent* began using color in the 1960s, editors often would send a photographer to the beach to photograph a pretty woman with a brightly colored beach ball for the Monday morning color project.

Barry Fitzsimmons, a San Diego *Union-Tribune* veteran, recalls the old days: "For many years, color pictures were picked for bright colors. If it wasn't bright, they wouldn't use it."

Back then, he says, photographers carried along red clothing, which they included in the pictures so that later the pressmen could match the reds when they adjusted the inks.

Today, Fitzsimmons says, "It's with news that editors and readers have a hard time with color. It shows the reality . . . while black-and-white covers it up. In black and white, blood can just blend in with the street. In color (the blood) jumps out, and the editors are left to deal with it more than ever before. Same goes for fires. In color they're unbelievable, but in black and white they're practically nonexistent."

BLACK AND WHITE BUT READ ALL OVER?

In a colorful world, black-and-white images sometimes stand out. Even though publications today can easily run color, some are choosing to publish black-and-white images instead. Black-and-white images convey an air of dignity and seriousness. Shades of gray connote the traditional, respected,

A radio station fan is catapulted by a friend into a "mosh" pit during an outdoor musical performance. This picture reads easily whether it's reproduced in color or black and white.
Al Schaben, © *Los Angeles Times*

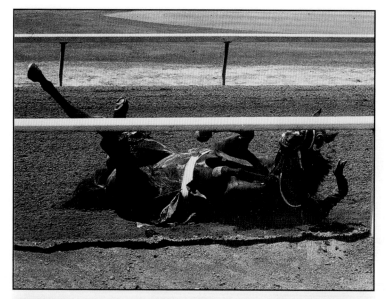

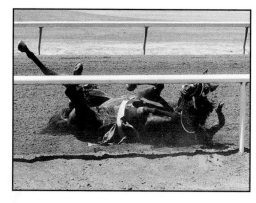

Missing the jump, the horse rammed into the rail and fell onto the jockey. The rider lived, but the horse was put away. Readers were furious that the paper ran the graphic picture, particularly with the horse's gushing red blood, on the front page. Jeff Vendsel, for the *Press Democrat* [Santa Rosa, California]

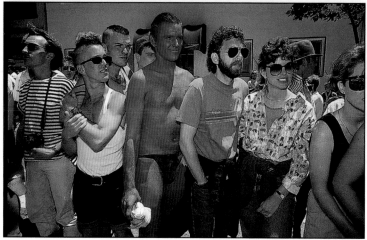

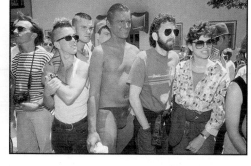

Color in this picture carries a layer of information unavailable in black-and-white. Color information is critical for some, but not all, photos. Ken Kobré, for Mercury Pictures

documentary style. Black-and-white journalistic photos stand out against competing, colorful advertisements.

Critic Susan Sontag writes in **On Photography** that monochrome, black-and-white pictures give an image a sense of age, historical distance, and aura.

While both *Time* and *Newsweek* magazines run mostly color photos, each publishes frequent behind-the-scenes political stories as black-and-white photo essays.

Time had dropped the traditional black-and-white photo essay when it went all-color, so bringing it back wasn't easy, recalls P.F. Bentley, a former *Time* contract shooter.

"The hardest part was to get the managing editor to understand the impact black-and-white can have," he says. "Once he looked at the first take and once they printed it, the essays got rave reviews. They have not questioned it at all since. Now it is being done not only by me but also by Diana Walker, Jim Nachtwey, Chris Morris, and others."

Diana Walker, who covers the White House for *Time*, shoots her behind-the-scenes exclusives on black-and-white film.

Black-and-white allows her to shoot in low light situations easily.

Time picture editor Michele Stephenson assigns black-and-white images to give a story a certain mood, to signal "documentary." In "*Time*'s Past in the Present: Nostalgia and the Black-and-White Image," she told researcher Paul Grainge that breaking news will almost certainly be shot in color, while black-and-white images are used to give a story qualities of introspection and poignancy.

(See black-and-white photos shot for *Time* by Diana Walker and P.F. Bentley in Chapter 3, "General News," pages 46, 48, and 49.)

Carol Guzy, a two-time Pulitzer Prize winner for the *Washington Post*, says, "I love black-and-white, and I've been with black-and-white all my life. Color can be distracting." She points out that her photograph of two nomad women carrying a baby between them (page 81) would not have worked in color because of the colors of the women's garments. "They were horrible colors that clashed really badly," she explains. "You lost the baby."

CONCLUSION

While editors should not use photos just because they are as multi-hued as Joseph's proverbial coat, neither should they forget that color carries a great deal of information that would be lost on black-and-white film. Journalists are in the information business. Giving readers more information usually adds to their understanding of a story. However, black-and-white can add authority to that story.

WORKING WITH IMAGES
CROPPING: CUTTING OUT THE FAT

Regardless of how good the original is, if a photo is butchered during editing or reduced to the size of a postage stamp on the Web, no one will see the picture. Newspapers do this every day. Says Roy Paul Nelson, author of **Publication Design**, "The typical daily or weekly newspaper is not designed, really; its parts are merely fitted together to fill all the available space, sort of like a jigsaw puzzle." To save their photographs, more and more camera journalists are getting involved in layout, at least on newspapers on online publications. These photographers want a say in how their pictures are cropped and sized.

Perfect Framing is Rare

When you take a picture, you must decide what to include in the viewfinder and what to leave out. The impact of a picture often depends on this decision. By including too much, you run the risk of distracting the viewer from the main subject. By framing too tightly, on the other hand, you might leave out important storytelling elements. Photographers carry a variety of lenses to enable them to zoom in or draw back to include only the important pictorial elements.

Even with tight in-camera framing, every subject does not fit neatly into a 35mm format. For that matter, all subjects do not fit naturally into a $2^1/_4$"x$2^1/_4$" square or a 4"x5" rectangle. Some subjects are low and wide, like the deck of an aircraft carrier (pages 210–211), whereas other subjects are tall and skinny, like the Washington Monument.

No matter how carefully you compose the picture in a camera's viewfinder, the image from the real world may not completely fill the frame. In these situations, all you can do is shoot and then crop the image later.

Reduced Quality: The Price of Cropping

A perceptive editor can improve a photo's impact using thoughtful cropping, but sometimes at a price. Enlarging only a very small portion of the original shot magnifies any defect in the image.

If the original photograph lacked perfect sharpness, then the published picture will look soft and indistinct. Even if the original is sharp, enlarging a portion of the image expands each grain of the film, thereby decreasing the photo's clarity. The more an image is enlarged, the more its grain is visible.

Enlarged grain can obscure a photo's detail to the point that the print becomes the visual equivalent of rough sandpaper.

Similarly, digital images enlarged beyond their ideal resolution are likely to appear pix-

The price of extreme enlargement is increased grain and decreased quality. Only for news as unusual as this airplane stowaway falling to his death should poor quality photos be enlarged to this extent. John Gilpin, Wide World Photos

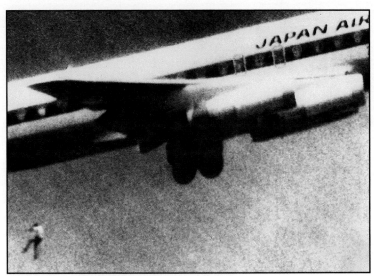

elated. (See page 248 for more about digital

resolution and picture quality.)

The photographer faces a dilemma, then. While the technical quality of a picture decreases when the image is drastically cropped and enlarged, its visual impact often is improved.

Cropping, therefore, involves a trade-off between possibly poorer quality and better composition. Taking a one-inch square segment of an eight-by-ten-inch photo and publishing it as a half-page spread in the newspaper or magazine might produce a perfectly composed picture that is too fuzzy or too pixelated to appreciate.

While few situations merit an extreme blow-up from such a tiny portion of a picture, a good photo editor generally will opt for a dramatic image at the expense of some sharpness and grain. The editor reasons that it is better to catch readers' attention with an exciting photo than lose them with a technically perfect but otherwise dull image.

Crop the Excess
Like a writer editing copy, the picture editor, designer, or photographer should emphasize significant elements in the picture by eliminating extraneous material that carries little meaning. If a person's expression gives the picture sparkle, zero in on the face and cut out the peripheral material.

Light, bright areas of the picture, like windows and lights, tend to attract the eye. If these windows and lights are extraneous to the main subject, they will pull the reader's attention away. Avoid a competing area that might distract a reader's interest from the photo's primary subject. Crop out these irritating sidelights from the picture. If the action occurs in one corner of the picture, focus on that area. There should be a good reason for leaving in each area of the picture. No corner of the picture should remain just because it happened to be in the original negative. The rule is save the meat of the photo by cutting out the fat.

Crop Ruthlessly
"Crop ruthlessly," advises Edmond Arnold, a pioneer of modern newspaper design. "Cut out anything that's not essential to the picture, so that the reader's attention won't be distracted or wasted. Ruthless cropping leads to stronger images."

Research supports the notion that eliminating extraneous details helps a picture's readability. Gallup's Sharon Polansky, recording eye movement as subjects perused printed material, found that the simpler a picture's background, the more attention the photograph received.

The USS Boxer, a multipurpose amphibious assault ship, sailed into San Francisco Bay for Fleet Week. Cropping this picture into a slim horizontal and running it across two pages gives it added impact. Ken James, *Examiner* [San Francisco]

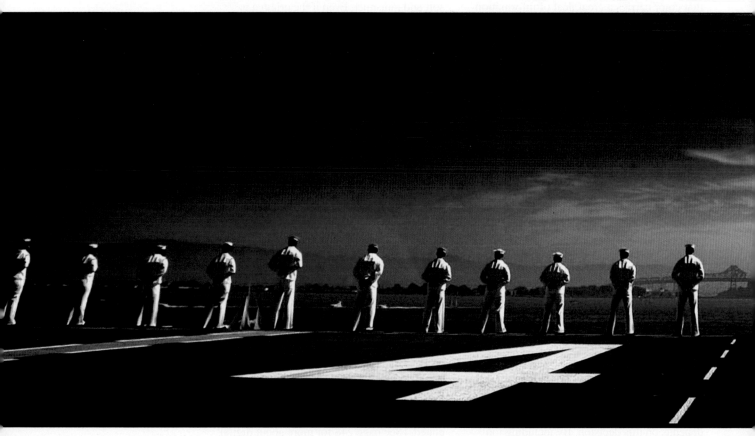

But Preserve the Mood

Cropping can improve a picture by eliminating irritating details. But mindless cropping can ruin a picture's intent by slicing off areas that give the image its mood. The sensitive slicer preserves the ingredients that give a photograph its arresting look by leaving the brooding gray sky in a scenic or including the cluttered bookshelves in a college professor's portrait.

Sometimes a blank area in the picture balances an active area. Leaving a little room on the print in front of a runner helps create the illusion that the athlete is moving across the picture. Similarly, some blank space in front of a profile portrait keeps the subject from looking as if he or she is peering off the edge of the print. Insensitive cropping can rip away parts of a picture that give it context. Sometimes it's important to know that a riot occurred in the ornate foyer of city hall or in a barren, dusty field. Overzealous cropping could eliminate these telling details.

SIZING UP FOR IMPACT

A battle between writers and photographers rages daily on many publications. Its outcome determines the size of the pictures in the next edition.

Space: The Final Frontier

Wordsmiths, backed up by the copy and managing editors, fight for small pictures to leave room for plenty of type. Reinforced by the photo editor, the photographer demands that the pictures be printed large enough so that readers will not miss them.

The camera contingent argues that the larger the picture, the more powerful its impact. And, in fact, ample evidence supports this claim. According to a study by Burt Woodburn, the average story is read by only 12 percent of a newspaper's subscribers. Yet Woodburn also found that an average one-column picture attracts 42 percent of the publication's readers.

Writing for *Journalism Quarterly,* Woodburn concluded in "Reader Interest in Newspaper Pictures" that as the size of a photo increases, so does the number of readers it attracts. The 42 percent drawn to the story, for example, grew to 55 percent when the photo ran two columns. A four-column-wide picture caught the attention of about 70 percent of the readers.

Both Seith Spaulding, in "Research on Pictorial Illustration," and Hyun-Joo Lee Huh, in "The Effect of Newspaper Picture Size on Readers' Attention, Recall and Comprehension of Stories," confirmed Woodburn's findings.

And when all other factors were equal, Gallup's Sharon Polansky came to the same

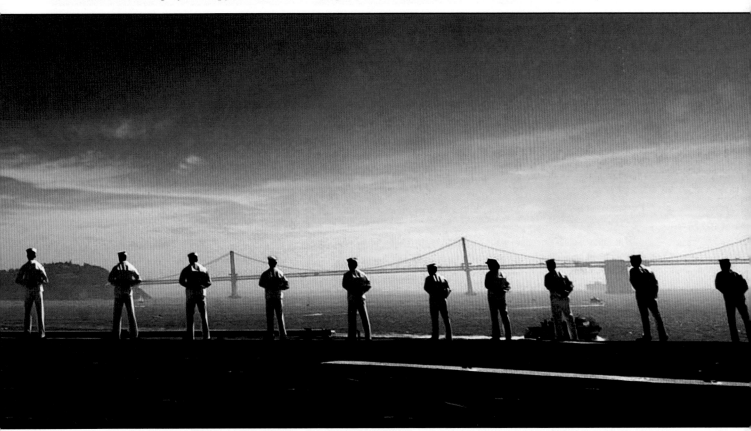

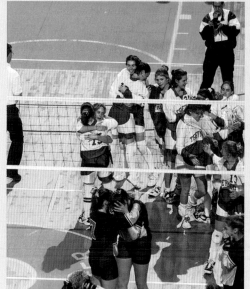

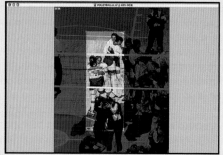

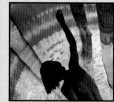

Careful cropping transformed this chaotic scene into a strong, easy-to-read image of victory and defeat. John Martin, *Cedar Rapids* [Iowa] *Gazette*

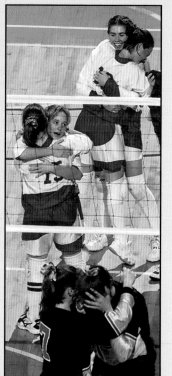

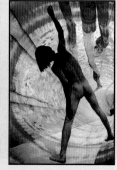

PLEASE, DON'T AMPUTATE AT THE JOINTS

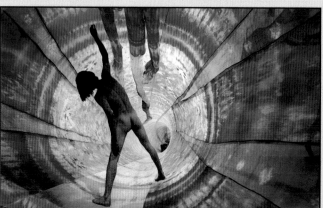

A man dances inside a giant windsock at Burning Man Festival, which takes place each year in California's Mojavi Desert. Julie Stupsker, *Examiner* [San Francisco]

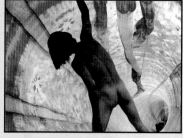

The editor's most perceptive skills come into play when cropping a picture containing a person. Parts of the body can be cropped, but usually the crop should not fall on a joint like an elbow or knee. If it's necessary to sever a head from a body in a photo, some of the shoulder should be left so that the head will have a platform on which to sit. It also can work to crop into the face of a person as long as the cut doesn't leave just half of an eye, for example, or just part of a mouth. Look at the pictures of the dancer here and decide which crops seem natural and which seem arbitrary or absurd.

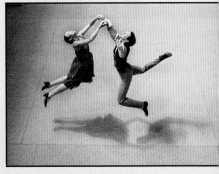

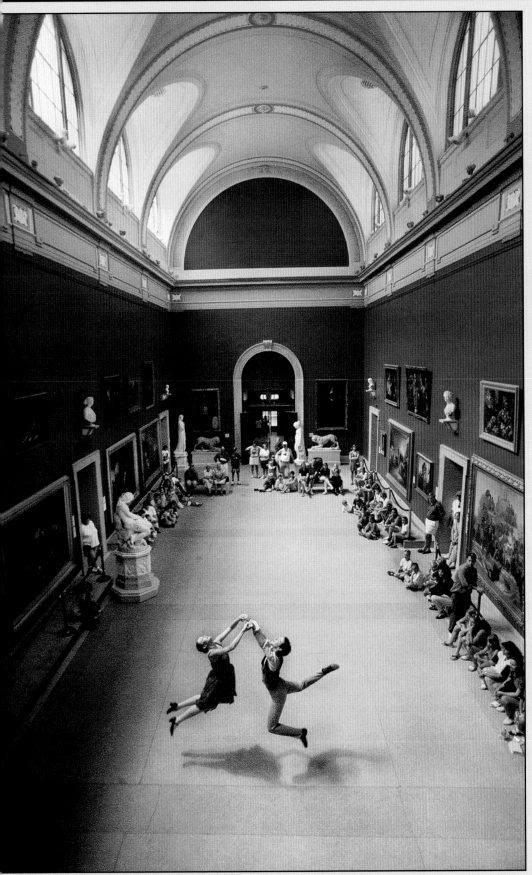

Be careful when you crop not to cut out story-telling, environmentally important elements that give the picture its impact. The beautiful hall would be lost with a tight crop that just included the ballet students giving their performance.
Cloe Poisson, *Hartford* [Connecticut] *Courant*

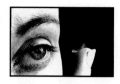

Pictures must be displayed large enough to see the detail in a close-up shot like this one of a woman replacing a contact lens.
Ken Kobré, for *Boston Phoenix*

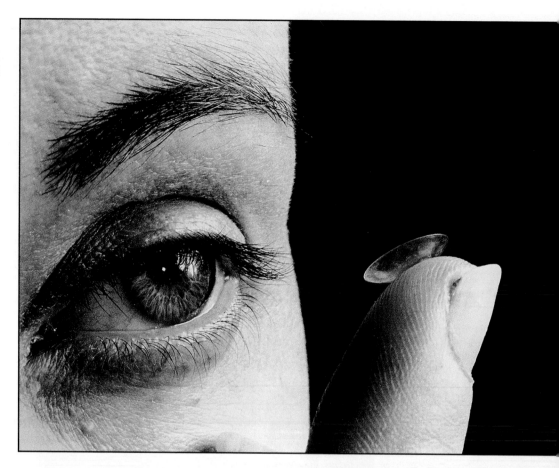

conclusion using Eye-Trac research.

Her research confirmed that increasing the size of an image also increases attention to it. Polansky found that one reason "mug shots" receive little attention is because editors play these portraits so small. The research demonstrated that 44 percent of the subjects looked at a one-column mug shot whereas the rate increased to 92 percent when readers viewed the same photo at three columns wide.

Even this axiom—bigger size gets more attention—has a corollary: if the subject matter is exceptionally galvanizing, even small pictures will be noticed.

Polansky noted during one of her studies that a tiny ad showing a female mud wrestler (with lots of torso showing)—played on the inside of a sports section—got much more attention than its size would have predicted.

When it comes to sex, at least, picture size is not the only determinant for reader attention.

Bigger pictures also draw readers into stories and aid them in recalling the material later. A study by William Baxter, Rebecca Quarles, and Hermann Kosak found that although a small, two-column picture accompanying an article does not help the reader remember the story's details, a large picture,

six columns wide, measurably improves readers' recall of details in the piece.

Hyun-Joo Lee Huh replicated those findings in a study at Syracuse University but went on to show that a larger photo also improves readers' comprehension of the story. When asked about the outcome of a story with no accompanying picture, only 13 percent of the readers gave a correct answer. However, comprehension increased with the addition of photographs, with well over 75 percent of those who read the same story accompanied by a large photograph understanding the text and explaining its significance. The picture's size induced readers to finish reading the article and helped them understand its implications.

According to the Syracuse researchers, the presence of a larger picture probably causes readers to read more of an accompanying story, which then results in greater recall and better comprehension. What's the message for reporters and editors? Reporters should be begging editors to run large pictures with their stories if they want readers to notice their writing, understand its implications, and recall the information later. Large pictures don't just decorate the page.

Reporters, editors, educators, and almost anyone else involved in communications constantly complain that the MTV generation does not read. Even for people more familiar with changing channels than with turning pages, editors have at their disposal a tool that influences reading. Like a magnet, big pictures draw in readers of all ages to the story associated with it.

Increasing a picture's size gives an editor more bang for the buck. True, editors will need to sacrifice the number and length of stories to handle larger pictures. However, subscribers will read, remember, and understand those that remain rather than overlook them altogether.

The never-ending battle between the word and visual camps continues, but the photographer can gain space if he or she is willing to sacrifice a few weaker pictures so that stronger ones can be printed larger.

Photographers should fight for space when their images are striking. Bad photos, of course, should not appear in the paper at all, but if they must be printed, play them small. Oversizing a technically poor photo calls attention to its deficiencies. On the other hand, underplaying an exciting, technically good photo does a disservice to photographer and reader alike.

WHEN SIZE IS IMPORTANT

Drama
Armed with research and Arnold's axioms, the photographer fights for larger photos so that the audience can easily see the textural detail of the original image. A one-column "head shot" is so small that it communicates almost nothing. The person is barely recognizable. With a four-column portrait, the reader can examine the two-day-old whiskers on the mayor's face, or the size of a contact lens on a woman's finger (above.)

Detail
A long shot, such as an overall of a church interior or an aerial shot from a plane, also demands space. Compressed into one column, all the details blend together and lose the bits of information that give the picture meaning.

"Exquisite," remarks the reader who sees a larger-than-life, oversized photo. A common object, like a pencil or pen, a contact lens, or even a media-worn face, becomes fresh and exciting when magnified beyond its natural size.

Pictures of large crowds also need considerable reproduction size, according to Tom Ang, author of *Picture Editing: An Introduction*. Ang notes that "the richness and intricacy of detail can make a fascinating

Good page layout usually involves playing pictures so that one image dominates. Dominance is achieved through size. The dominant picture seems large especially when it is played alongside considerably smaller images. If the dominant and subordinate images are too close in size, they compete for the reader's attention.
Yuki Saito, San Francisco

ACHIEVING CONTRAST WITH SIZE IN A LAYOUT

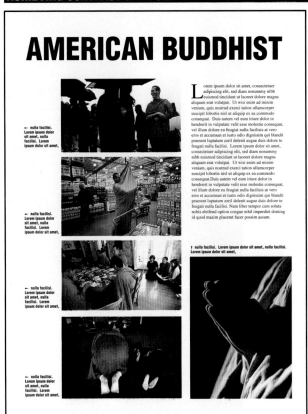

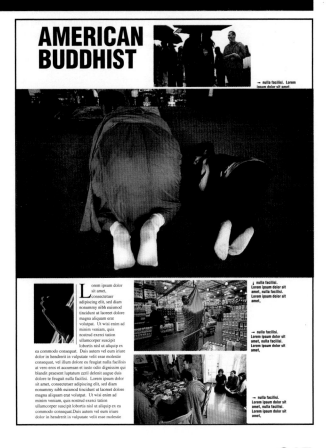

pattern when the picture is used small, but when used large, another layer of detail and meaning can be made out. A crowd scene that's an abstraction of color and pattern when seen small becomes full of individual human beings when enlarged."

Contrast in a layout

Publishing some pictures small and others big heightens contrast between them and adds interest to a page. Running them all in a 3"x5" size or shape produces a deadening effect. No photo dominates.

Just as a reporter or copy editor emphasizes certain points of an article by placing them in the lead, the photo editor or page designer spotlights certain pictures by playing them larger than others on a page.

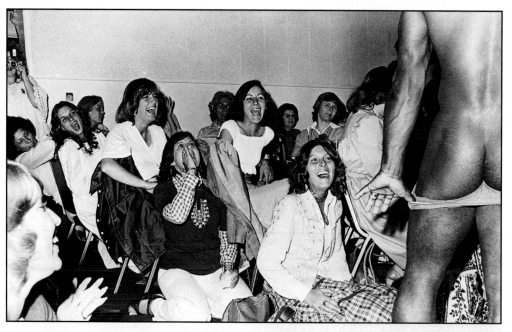

A risqué fashion show for women (ABOVE) is paired with a photo of a beauty contest (RIGHT). Played together, the pictures deliver a stronger editorial message about the sexes than either could alone. ABOVE: Curt Johnson, *Long Beach* [California] *Press-Telegram.* RIGHT: Mike Smith, for the *Dallas Times Herald*

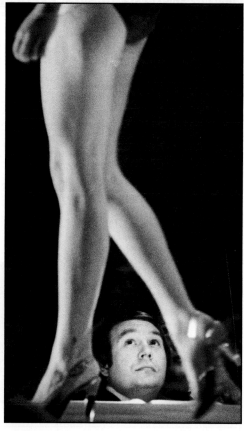

PHOTOGRAPHY AND THE INTERNET

A number of studies, such as "Eyes on the News" by Pegie Stark and Mario Garcia, have shown that a reader's first glance at the front page of a newspaper goes to photos and graphics. Only later does the reader turn to a story. Researchers call these graphic-and-photo elements entry points onto the page. The larger the photo, the more people look it. The photo also appears to motivate them to read the accompanying story.

Preliminary research by Marion Lewenstein, Andrew DeVigal, Greg Edwards and Deborah Tatat indicates that readers may respond differently to visuals on the Internet than they do to pictures in print. Conducted with Eye-Trac equipment, the Stanford-Poynter study, *www.poynterextra.org/et/i.htm,* found Web viewers to have a strong preference for text over graphics. Study subjects looked at 92 percent of all the articles on the screen but only 64 percent of the pictures. When the Web pages first came up, the subjects' attention was drawn to brief stories and captions, rather than to images.

To account for this strange reversal in behavior, researchers postulate that Web photos appear on the screen more slowly than the text and thus may lose their draw. Others suggest that photos on the Web are not large enough to attract viewers' attention.

If future research confirms these findings, photos in print may have a different magnetic hold on viewers than those on the Web. Even the study's authors, however, do not suggest that Web pages contain only text. The study does conclude that because Web users typically are busy and distracted, photos should be simple so as to encourage readers to spend more time looking before they start reading.

MULTIPLE IMAGES
PAIRING PICTURES FOR THE THIRD EFFECT

Sometimes one picture can sum up an event. The flag raising at Iwo Jima or the explosion of the Hindenburg needed only one photo to tell the story. Other situations require several. Pairing photos, according to Wilson Hicks in his landmark book ***Words and Pictures***, causes a third effect. The reader looks at the two pictures separately and then mentally combines them. The effect is different from what any picture alone can produce.

UNRELATED PICTURE PAIRING
Different Pictures—Similar Meanings

In written language, different words can have similar meanings. With pictures, different images can carry similar messages. Words with related meanings are called synonyms.

A thesaurus is filled with examples of synonyms. Pictures with similar messages could be called visual synonyms.

Pairing pictures taken at different times and places that carry the same editorial statement allows the reader to see the common elements in the different images and draw comparisons. Side-by-side pictures of a man judging a beauty contest and women watching husbands and boyfriends stage a risqué fashion show, though photographed at widely different times and places (one in Texas and the other in California) makes an editorial statement about the sexes even though the images were taken by different photographers. Similar in editorial content and point of view, the two pictures might be considered visual synonyms. They look different, but their underlying meaning is the same.

Visual Homonyms

On the other hand, some words—like "to," "two," and "too"—sound the same but carry completely different meanings. These are called homonyms. Likewise, some pictures look superficially similar but carry dissimilar information. For example, a picture of an Egyptian pyramid and a photo of a pile of oranges might look similar—both are triangle-shaped. Some pairs may be entertaining, but, because the pictures share no editorial relationship, a reader trying to find a common thread may be confused. The pictures share no real journalistic commonality.

Be careful, then, of visual homonyms, photos unrelated except by looks. Pairing such pictures can lead to editorial abuse, intended or not. Pairing pictures that are not intrinsically connected editorially can lead to silly or, in even worse situations, offensive results.

Consider a collection of unrelated pictures of overweight people—shot by different photographers for different purposes—published together on a page in an actual photo book. The editor may have thought it clever to assemble these editorially unrelated pictures because they shared a common visual element: overweight people. What was the message of this insensitive pairing?

Picture Sequences and Series

Sometimes a story takes place over time, even if only in minutes. One picture can't record this change. Two can make a comparison, but with three or more, the event unfolds. For example, the extent of Bo Jackson's fury at a strike-out is shown in a three-picture sequence in which he breaks his bat over his knee.

Packaging Pictures

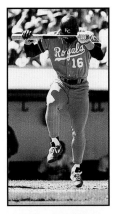

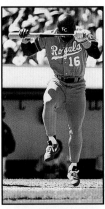

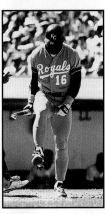

Running a three-picture sequence tells the story of Bo Jackson breaking a bat over his knee better than any single image in this set.
Brad Mangin, for *Sports Illustrated*

NOT JUST ANY ANIMAL SHELTER

John Burgess
Press Democrat
[Santa Rosa, California]

John Burgess's story about a holistic home shelter for infirm animals has a consistent theme. Every image shows an animal that has suffered some form of trauma. An injured dog whisks around in a special harness. A cat is administered an IV. A high-angle overall taken at feeding time that shows just some of the 68 cats living at Brighthaven gives the reader a sense of how many felines would be homeless without this retreat.

Each photograph adds another building block to the story—from a three-legged cat snuggling up to deaf and blind dog to an attendant bathing a raven.

The photos isolate the most visually interesting, distinctive aspects of the place while building a visual overview with the package.

This isn't a "how-to" story. The pictures don't try to tell how to run a hospital of this sort. They don't document every aspect of the place. The pictures don't show the owner buying the food or cleaning the floors, for instance.

Burgess did not shoot a "day in the life" of Brighthaven. The photographer felt no requirement to record the activities of the home from morning until night.

Nor did the photographer try to

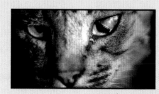

Eighteen-year-old Joey came to Brighthaven with ten BB pellets imbedded in his body. Later, a tumor was removed from his eye.

tell a narrative of one animal's course of recovery from the time of arrival until its eventual return to health. Nor did the photographer tell the hospital's story through the eyes or actions of one person such as the pet owner or hospice founder.

Instead, the project reveals the most interesting and exceptional aspects of this unusual animal clinic.

Since the story is not a narrative, the pictures do not have to be presented according to a time-line, starting with the first pictures and ending with the last. The layout relies on a dominant image with which to draw in the reader. This image must both captivate the reader's attention and summarize the exceptional aspects of the animal respite. Which picture would you have selected for this role?

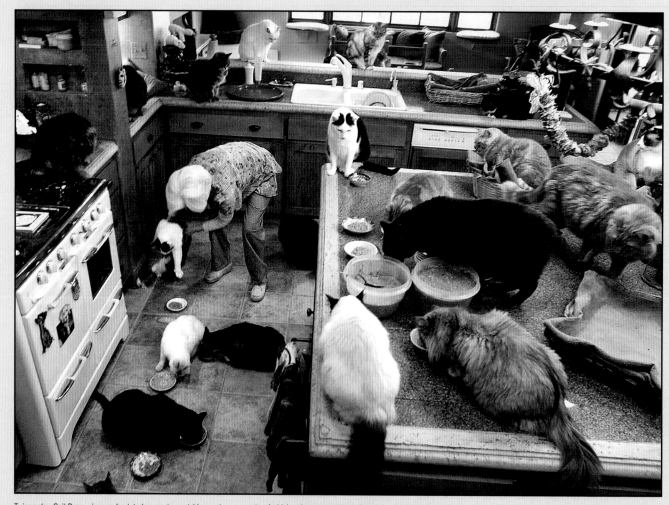

Twice a day, Gail Pope mixes up fresh turkey meat, vegetables, and supplements for the cats at Brighthaven. First she feeds the kitchen cats, of which only twenty-one are shown, then on to the living room and bedroom for the rest of the sixty-eight cats in their house.

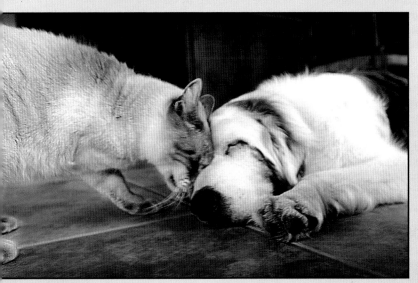

Oliver, the three-legged cat, left, snuggles up to his best friend, Sgt. Pepper, a deaf and blind dog who suffers from a brain disorder.

Ted the Toad arrived at Brighthaven with gangrenous back feet but now enjoys life with a female toad rescued after being crushed by a concrete slab. She was too shy to be photographed.

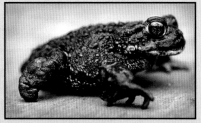

In a wheelchair following back surgery, Ollie the Dachshund navigates the steps on his way to the garden to bury his bone.

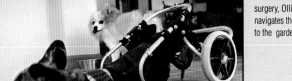

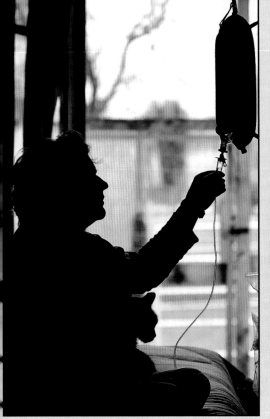

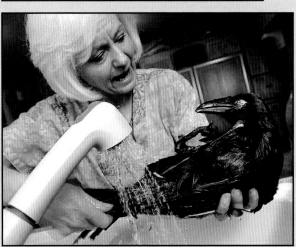

Susanna Anthony gives I.V. fluids to Yana the cat, who is in kidney failure.

Gail Pope gives Brighthaven's resident raven, Colin, his daily bath in the kitchen sink. Run over by a car, Colin was nursed back to health but was still eyeless, had deformed legs, and suffered from seizures. Pope was later forced to euthanize the bird.

Some situations are multifaceted. One or two photos just won't explain many elements.

John Burgess decided to document an unusual animal hospice called Brighthaven. Although the facilities are simple, the atmosphere is caring and family-like, to the point that animals' meals are prepared in the owners' kitchen.

A picture of one animal alone wouldn't tell Burgess's story. Nor would a single picture of one person helping an injured critter. Packaged together, though, pictures of twenty of sixty-eight cats being fed, a dog running about on wheels, and a three-legged cat nuzzling a deaf and blind dog all begin to show the range of care and after-care provided at Brighthaven. (See pages 218–219.)

THE CAPTION: STEPCHILD OF THE BUSINESS

Some pictures—such as Norman Rockwell's cover illustrations for the *Saturday Evening Post*—need no words. The idea portrayed is so simple or its emotional content so powerful that the illustration tells the story clearly and immediately without any captions.

But most photos do need words. An old proverb relates that "a picture is worth a thousand words," but the modern corollary to the proverb is that a picture without words is almost worth nothing.

A picture raises as many questions as answers. Look at the pictures on these two pages and ask yourself if, without captions, you would know who is in the pictures, what is happening, when the events took place, and why the action occurred. Pictures usually answer these questions only partially. A picture that can stand alone is rare. The point is not whether photographs can survive without words or words without photos, but whether pictures and words can perform better when combined.

WORDS INFLUENCE PICTURE MEANING

While assistant professor of journalism at the University of California, Berkeley, Jean Kerrick conducted research to determine the influence of captions on readers' interpretations of pictures. Captions, she found, can at least modify and sometimes change the meaning of a picture, especially when the picture itself is ambiguous. A caption can change the viewer's interpretation of the same picture from one extreme to another.

Kerrick presented a profile shot of a well-dressed man sitting on a park bench to two groups of subjects. She asked each group to rate the picture on several subjective scales. The scales ranged from "good to bad," "happy to sad," "pleasant to unpleasant,"

and so forth.

Then the first group was shown the same picture with this caption: "A quiet minute alone is grabbed by Governor-elect Star. After a landslide victory, there is much work to be done before taking office."

The second group was shown the same picture with a different caption: "Exiled communist recently deported by the U.S. broods in the Tuilleries Garden alone in Paris on his way back to Yugoslavia." Both groups were again asked to evaluate the picture.

After the first group read the positive caption, they rated the picture "happier," "better," and "more pleasant" than they had originally judged it.

The second group, who saw the caption about the brooding exiled communist, rated the photo "sad" and "unpleasant." In this instance, the caption completely reversed the impression initially given by the picture alone.

In a similar study, Fred Fedler, Tim Counts, and Paul Hightower used high-impact news photos and varied just one or two words in their captions. They did not find striking changes when they varied just a few words with this particular set of pictures.

Perhaps changing captions influences how viewers interpret neutral images but not how they read more clear, dramatic photographs like the ones in the news-oriented study.

Photographs appear to serve as a primitive means of communication that carry out their task instantly. Words function as a sophisticated means of communication, but lack the impact of the visual message. Pictures transmit the message immediately, but words shape and give focus to that message.

WRITING CLEAR CAPTIONS

The need for clear and concise caption-writing is obvious. Readers often determine whether they are going to read an entire article based on what they gleaned from a picture and caption. If you glance through some newspapers and magazines, however, you may get the impression that the first person to walk into the room wrote the captions in the paper or magazine that day. Writers polish their story leads, and photographers polish their lenses, but no one shines up the captions. Writers claim that caption-writing is beneath them, while photographers often seem to find an important blazing fire to cover when the time comes to compose captions. The caption—the stepchild of the media business—is the most read but least carefully written text in most publications.

Poor captions sometimes result when photographers fail to get adequate information at the time they take the pictures or forget to include the information when they write the captions. The late Howard Chapnick, who ran the Black Star picture agency for many years, once said, "One cannot err on the side of providing too much caption information. The editor who finds a photographer who understands the importance of detailed captioning will figuratively embrace him bodily and professionally."

One photographer even lost his job because of writing poor captions. After ten years of shooting for his paper, Victor Junco was released by the *St. Petersburg Times* because of caption errors.

Former *People* magazine photo editor John Dominis once told the story of holding up the magazine's production because a photographer did not send in one critical identification. Lights in the New York headquarters burned past midnight as the editors carried out a desperate search by telephone for the forgetful photographer. Editors, writers, layout artists, designers, and production staff all waited hour after hour for the missing caption, costing *People* magazine thousands of dollars in overtime.

PUTTING THE FIVE WS AND AN H IN A CAPTION

"A caption is a verbal finger pointing at the picture," wrote John Whiting in his book ***Photography is a Language***. Captions, like fingers, come in many sizes and shapes. The opening words of a caption must capture the reader's attention just as do the lead words of a news story or feature.

The caption writer starts off the sentence with the most newsworthy, interesting, or unusual facts. Copy desks have developed different kinds of captions, each emphasizing a different element of the story.

What?

The reader wants an explanation of what is happening in the picture; hence, the first words of the caption, also called a cutline in the newspaper business, should explain the action. Unless the situation in the picture is obvious, the cutline must describe what is going on. *After two years of drought, it rained yesterday in the southern part of the state. . . .* Further down in the cutline, the writer can fill in the other details of the story by giving the remaining four Ws.

Who?

The who may be emphasized in the caption when the person in the news is featured in the photo: *President Bush said yesterday that he will spend the weekend at Camp David.*

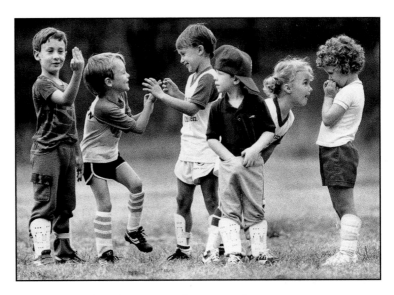

This fascinating but complicated vignette becomes more clear when the caption explains that these were bored kids entertaining themselves while waiting for their turns to kick the ball at soccer practice.
Scott Eklund, *Bellevue* [Washington] *Journal American*

In this situation, the newsworthy aspect of the picture is the person, President George Bush. The fact that the president was speaking outweighed what he had to say or where he said it.

A person's name should lead the caption only when that person is well-known to the readers of the magazine or newspaper. Do not start the caption, John Doe said yesterday that the budget should be slashed. No one knows John Doe, so placing his name prominently in the cutline neither adds to the picture's interest nor explains its news value.

However, if John Doe's face is recognizable in the photo, he should be mentioned somewhere in the caption. People's names are always included in the caption even if they are not famous. Someone—spouse, parents, friends—certainly will recognize them.

Also, readers can misidentify the person in the photo if the name is left out of the caption. Often you may hear, "That woman in the picture in the paper looks just like. . . ."

Many editors will not run a picture unless the caption includes the names of all recognizable people. The wire services, whose pictures go around the world, include the person's first and last name, as well as middle initial, regardless of the individual's prominence in the community or in the world.

The name and the age of any youngster in the picture are essential. This information often adds additional human interest: *The collie pup would have drowned if the Selleck girls (left to right) Debbie, 3, Heidi, 5, and Becky, 7, had not pulled their dog, Sam, from the stream in time.*

Note that the phrase "left to right" clearly identifies each girl. Sometimes the words "top row," "wearing the tie," or other identifying features will help readers match the faces in the photo with the names in the captions. Indicate to the copy editor that you are not sure about the spelling of unusual names.

When and Where?
Photos rarely tell readers exactly when or where a picture was taken. If this information helps readers understand the picture, supply the location and the time of the news event. Use the day of the week, not the calendar date: *Barry Bonds hit the home run yesterday that gave the A's their win over the Giants.* (Not "Bonds hit the home run July 6.")

The writer should begin the cutline with time or place only when that fact is significant or unusual: *At 3 a.m. Mayor Ted Stanton finally signed the zoning bill.*

Or: *Standing in the massive waterworks, Edna Lee, the water commissioner, explained the new drainage system.*

Why?
Some caption writers claim that explaining why the action occurred in a picture takes away the reason for reading the story and thus causes readers to skip the adjoining article. Other news photographers and editors argue that extensive captions pique reader interest for the main body of the story. *Because of the transit strike, highways leading into the city were jammed at the early morning rush hour today.* Without answering the "why," this photo and caption do not tell the full story.

FILLING OUT THE DETAIL
The caption is the place to tell readers if the

subject in the picture was posed. If the photographer took the picture with a special lens or manipulated the print in the computer, this should be noted. The caption should explain anything about the picture that differs significantly from the actual event and thus might distort the facts.

Small detail
Casually glancing at a photo, readers might miss an important but small detail. Cutlines can focus attention on various parts of the picture, emphasizing the elements the photographer thinks are important.

Cutlines can supply details about the four senses that the picture does not convey. How something tastes or feels might explain a subject's reaction in a picture. Without an explanatory phrase in the caption, the picture might not make sense: *David Krathwohl, 10, struggles to climb an oil-coated plastic pole.*

Quote
Sometimes this purpose can be accomplished by telling what the subject said with a catchy quote: *"Some days I wish I had never left Kansas," said rock star Dorothy Oz on the eve of her thirty-fourth record-breaking performance.*

Color
Even though black-and-white photos record the world in almost infinite detail, one visual element is omitted: color. When color is an important aspect of the scene, the caption must supply this missing dimension: *Members of the Franklin High football team, wearing their new bright pink and purple*

Special effects such as the close placement of the wide-angle lens (28mm) used in this picture should always be explained in a caption. Marshall Spurrier, *Chanute* [Kansas] *Tribune*

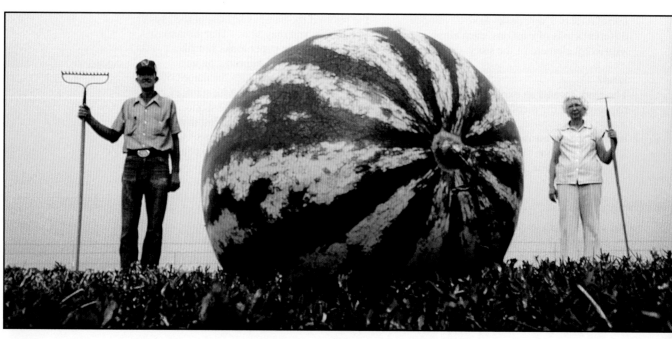

uniforms, yellow shoes, and lime-green helmets, performed practice drills yesterday before defending their fifteenth title in the state championships.

Before and After
A camera shutter, open for 1/500 sec., results in a photo that accurately describes what happens in that brief span of time. But the photo does not inform readers about what happened before or after that split second. The cause of the event and its effect are absent. Captions must supply the befores and afters.

Special Camera or Computer Effects
Whenever your picture's overall look is the result of a special photographic effect, your caption should let the reader know how you accomplished this.

When Marshall Spurrier was assigned to photograph the farmers who grew a large watermelon, he placed the vegetable on the ground, attached an ultra-wide lens to the camera and positioned the man and his wife on either side of the frame, several feet back. The resulting picture (opposite page) made the plant look as if it were almost as big as a house. Spurrier used the picture's caption to explain how he achieved the effect.

As well as the exaggerating effects of the wide-angle lens, you may also need to point out the compression effect of an extra-long telephoto, color shifts produced when shooting in mixed lighting, or elements changed with digital manipulation. (For a full discussion of ethical issues regarding computer-manipulated photos see Chapter 14, "Ethics.")

CAPTION-WRITING STYLES
Write short, declarative sentences with as few words as possible. Avoid complex sentences. Don't put unrelated facts in the same sentence. Keep facts separated with periods, not commas or other punctuation.

The AP's Hal Buell says, "Skip the adjectives and adverbs in a caption. Let the picture speak for itself."

Two schools of thought differ on the question of the tense of verbs in captions. The first group advises putting everything in the present tense, because the words in the caption are describing a photo immediately in front of the reader. The present tense also involves the reader more than does the past tense. Says Karen Cater of the *Seattle Times*, "Present-tense captions give a sense of action, immediacy, and life to a photo."

The opposing view advocates using the past tense because all the action in the picture has already taken place: *John Brown*

tags [tagged] the runner to make the last out in yesterday's game.

Be careful not to mix tenses. Writing coach Paula Larocque points out in *Quill* magazine that the most common problem with captions is pairing a present-tense verb with a past-tense time element. She points out that we would not say, *...a new mayor is (present tense) sworn in last (past tense) week.* Avoid the same problem with captions. Don't write: *Kelly holds her son Wednesday while he undergoes dialysis.* (The event has already taken place). Larocque calls this mistake a sequence-of-tense hash. Use the present tense or the past but not both in the same sentence.

Avoid the obvious. Phrases like *firefighter fighting blaze* or *basketball player going for hoop* are unnecessary because readers can see that, in the first picture, the people are firefighters, and, in the second, the athlete is a basketball player.

Phrases like "pictured above" also add no new information when accompanying a single image. Captions should avoid telling readers what they can find out for themselves by looking at the picture.

Avoid speculation about what a subject might be thinking. Such guessing can be inaccurate and give the wrong impression: *Claire Katz smiles with happiness as she receives a check from the president.* Perhaps she thinks the check is far too small for her efforts. You

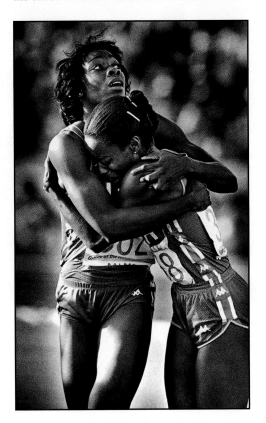

Sometimes pictures capture great emotion but, without a caption (which in this case the photographer supplied), readers may be unable to determine just what emotion they are seeing. Are these women happy or sad? Did they win or lose the competition? Paul Chinn, for *Herald Examiner* [Los Angeles, California]

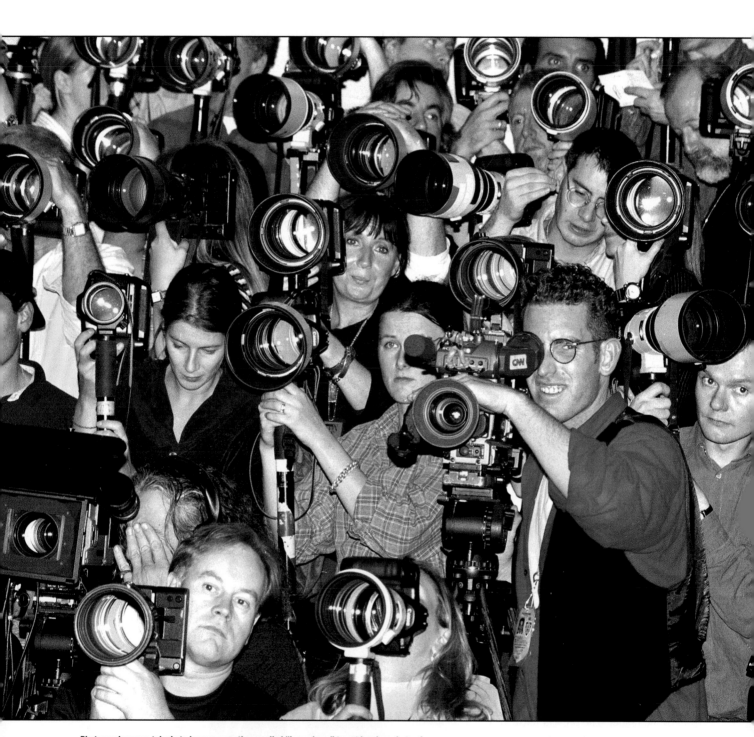

Photographers use telephoto lenses, sometimes called "long glass," to get head-on shots of models coming down the runway at a fashion show. Lucian Perkins, *Washington Post.* The picture appeared in his book ***Runway Madness***, Chronicle Books, 1998.

Chapter 11

Camera Bag

OUTFITTING THE PHOTOJOURNALIST

A photojournalist's bag is like a physician's—each contains the essentials for handling any emergency the professional might face. Like each doctor, each photographer carries different equipment, depending on professional needs and personal taste. Some photographers are partial to extra-long lenses, whereas others like wide-angle lenses. Yet all news photographers pack enough gear to handle any assignment, whether the event they cover takes place in the brilliant light of day or the pitch black of night. A news photographer must have a sturdy camera, a variety of lenses, a strobe, plenty of batteries, and, of course, lots of film or memory cards. The digital photojournalist often packs a laptop and cell phone, as well.

The most expensive purchase a photojournalist will make will be a camera system. Cameras and lenses can cost from hundreds to thousands of dollars, especially digital equipment. Working photojournalists want a camera sturdy enough to take the bashes of the business yet light enough so that the photographer can carry at least two bodies at the same time. Photojournalists need a camera that can be subjected to freezing weather one day and melting temperatures the next. Yet they want that camera to continue to function perfectly, frame after frame.

No perfect camera system exists. Each photographer weighs the trade-off of weight, ruggedness, and, of course, cost when outfitting a camera bag of photographic tricks.

CAMERA FEATURES
LIGHT METERS
Auto-Exposure

In-camera auto-exposure light meters are amazingly accurate. They measure the light reflected off a subject. Some can read the brightness of a tiny pinpoint in a scene while others can average the whole vista contained in the viewfinder. Some read primarily the center of the image and ignore the edges of the frame. These "center-weighted" meters are generally accurate except when the majority of the picture is either all white or all black. (See opposite page.)

Remember that a light meter sees the world as neutral gray, whether the scene is an igloo in a blizzard or a black cat in a coal bin. Joel Draut, who shot for the *Houston Post*, switched to manual when he shot a funny face carved in the snow (opposite). Knowing that his automatic light meter would read the snow as neutral gray, Draut opened the aperture about two stops above the reading to compensate.

Richard Koci Hernandez, who shoots for the *Mercury News* in San Jose, California, took a careful reading of Carolivia Herron (opposite), the author of the controversial children's book ***Nappy Hair***. The woman was wrapped in a dark cape in front of a dark, unlit wall. On automatic, the camera's light meter would have seen the dark scene as neutral gray and overexposed the picture. Backlit situations, such as a window or the sun behind the subject, also present a challenge to automatic center-weighted exposure meters.

Avoid incorrect exposures by taking a reflected-light reading of the subject's face or of your own hand in situations like this. (For light skin, open up half a stop; for dark skin, close down a stop.)

A camera's spot meter is particularly good for a light subject against a dark background, like a rocker spotlighted on a stage.

When setting up auto-exposure, some photographers prefer to select the aperture and let the camera select the appropriate shutter speed. This choice is good for the photographer who wants to have the minimum or maximum depth of field for a series of pictures. Determining the shutter speed, on the other hand, allows the camera to select the aperture. This approach allows the photographer to set a shutter speed that can freeze a subject's action, such as that of an athlete in motion, and avoids blurry surprises from routine camera movement.

ALERT: Using a hand-held incident light meter, which you must place in the same light that falls on the subject, will also provide accurate, unbiased light meter readings that won't be distorted by a scene with pure white snow or a person wearing a jet black coat.

The meter's sensor is covered by translucent plastic, usually a half dome that looks like half a ping pong ball. The photographer holds the light meter in front of the subject but aims the dome toward the camera. The meter measures the light falling on the subject. The main problem with incident readings is that the light meter has to be in the same light that is hitting the subject.

A photographer shooting from a dark place into an area of sunshine might find it difficult to take an incident light meter reading. Still, many photographers, including war photographer Jim Nachtwey, use an incident light meter for consistently correct, unbiased light meter readings.

● The Digital Camera's Unique Exposure Tool

Most digital cameras allow you to confirm a photograph's tonality while still in the field. Taking advantage of a histogram when it is available allows you to adjust your lighting set-up or make other exposure decisions so the highlights and shadows in the image aren't lost.

An in-camera "histogram" is a graph that displays the distribution of a photograph's tones, from highlights to shadows (see opposite). The graph shows how many times any of the 256 tones that make up a photograph occur. The height of the bars in the graph indicates the number of pixels, anywhere in the picture, at each brightness level.

A photograph with an average exposure, for example, will have tones distributed throughout the whole graph, with most bunched in the middle. An overexposed image will have most bars located on the right. You will need to adjust your exposure and take another shot if

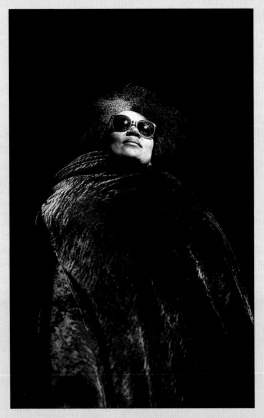

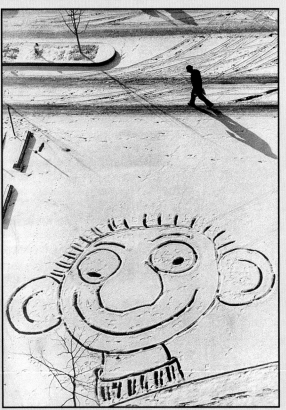

In a predominantly dark scene like this one, the camera's automatic light meter would be fooled into overexposing the final picture. In this situation, take a meter reading off the subject's face. Richard Koci Hernandez, *Mercury News* [San Jose, California]

A camera's automatic exposure meter would see this predominantly white scene as 18 percent neutral gray and underexpose the final picture. For proper exposure in similar situations, increase your exposure about two stops or take a reading off something in the same light that reflects a neutral gray. Joel Draut, *Houston Post*

DIGITAL EXPOSURE CONFIRMATION: THE HISTOGRAM

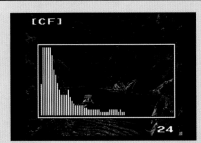

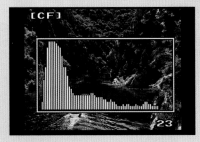

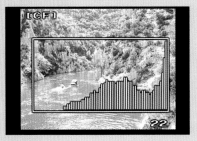

The graph of a dark-toned photo displays bars grouped to the left. Because the bars do not reach the right side of the graph, you can tell that the digital exposure will not capture the full range of possible tones. The darker tones represented by the bars at the extreme left will be pure black, with no available detail.

With the bars spread from one end of the graph almost to the other, the picture will capture a full tonal range and be correctly exposed.

Bars clustered on the right edge indicate that the photo is probably overexposed. The brightest tones represented by the bars on the extreme right will print as "paper white," with no detail at all.

that is possible. If all the pixels are skewed to the left, the photo has no detail in its shadows. You may need to adjust your next exposure to give it more light.

Typically, you can elect to view the histogram of an image you have just taken in the camera's LCD monitor.

The histogram is an ideal light meter. Without prayers or multiple light meter readings, you can determine with one test shot if your picture has detail in its highlights as well as its shadows. Then you can decide with confidence whether or not to adjust the exposure for the next snap.

AUTOFOCUS

Most photojournalists use autofocus cameras. Because autofocus cameras can adjust faster than the human eye-hand combination can twist the lens barrel, novice shooters using autofocus often can hold their own with pros.

The technique works well when you are tracking an isolated tight-end running down the sidelines. You'll get the highest number of sharp pictures in sports like track and field, where the focusing mechanism can lock onto a single runner and follow that person to the finish line. (See Chapter 7, "Sports.")

Using autofocus, the photographer selects an area of the viewfinder by pressing the shutter release halfway down. Provided the focus is then locked in, the picture should be sharp as long as the subject stays in the auto-focus "hot zone."

Yet autofocus is not a cure-all for producing sharp pictures under all circumstances on every frame. Because contrast is what guides the autofocus mechanism, the camera can be fooled, especially in low-light situations. Also, the bars of a cage, the wire in fence, or even a window's surface can cause focusing problems. The mechanism isn't smart enough

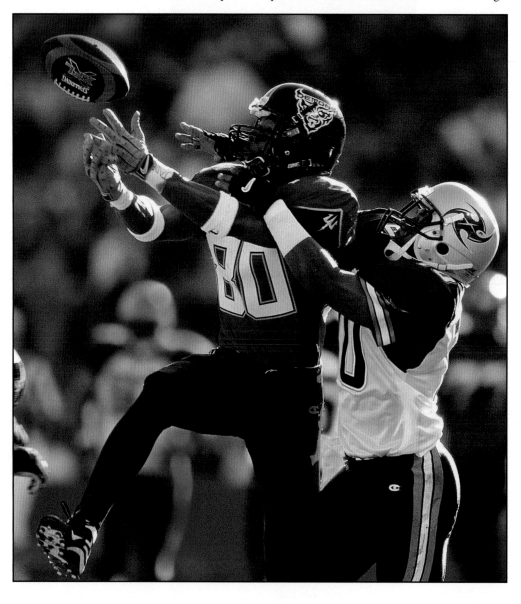

Most sports shooters use autofocus to follow the action. The lenses respond so quickly that the photographer can swing from a football quarterback to his receiver and still get a sharp picture of the play. Brad Mangin, for *Sports Illustrated*

to know to focus on the subject beyond the bars, the fence, or the window. Strong background light or a light source in the background also can throw off autofocus.

Personalizing Autofocus Controls

Autofocus shooting actually requires as much attention, concentration, and dexterity as manual focusing, but often results in a higher percentage of sharp images when following a moving target.

Not all the important action happens in the middle of the frame. Sometimes the primary subject should be sharp on the edge of the picture. Advanced autofocus cameras allow photographers to select the quadrant where they want to activate autofocus. A wheel on the back of some models allows selection from among five or more target areas in the viewfinder. When the target is framed in red, for instance, the autofocus feature will operate in the selected space (hot zone).

Some cameras allow customization of the autofocus setup. You can set autofocus to operate only when you press lightly on the shutter release, for example. Or you can have it go into action using an alternative button on the camera back. These options help you customize the camera to your shooting style.

With certain cameras you can still use autofocus to shoot—even in extremely low light or total darkness. These cameras use a dedicated strobe that emits near-infrared light. This technology allows the camera to focus the lens accurately and automatically in total darkness, within a certain distance. You can take pictures even in a pitch-black alley without focusing the camera. Just point, shoot, and get sharply focused photos as long as the subject is not too far away.

SHUTTER SPEED
● Digital Reaction Time

All cameras have a delay between the moment you press the shutter release and the shutter opens to take the picture. (See Chapter 7, "Sports," pages 131–132.) This delay is relatively short with film cameras but can be a problem with digital cameras.

Depending on the make and model of their cameras, digital photographers report slight delays between the instant they press the shutter release and when the camera actually records a picture. Less expensive as well as older professional cameras can have a marked delay time that hampers shooting candid photos. Consider this: a film camera has a lag time of one to two milliseconds. A digital camera might delay as much as 80 milliseconds. This digital hesitation can throw off your timing if you're shooting

sports, warns Deanne Fitzmaurice of the *San Francisco Chronicle*. The good news is that more sophisticated (but more expensive) digital cameras have virtually eliminated this drawback. Rapidly changing technology suggests further improvements with time.

● Faster Shutter Speeds with Digital

The shutter speed of a film camera is limited by how quickly the mechanical gears can open and close the focal plane shutter. A digital camera is not limited by these mechanical necessities. Some digital cameras no longer have a traditional shutter at all. Instead, the camera turns the chip (CCD) on and off during the exposure. No longer requiring a mechanical device, these cameras are boasting "shutter speeds" surpassing 1/16,000 sec.They also can sync with a strobe at speeds as high as 1/500 sec., a speed faster than their film-based cousins. (See pages 260, 262–263.)

ALERT: Turn off your digital camera when changing lenses, cautions Mike Phillips, technical representative for Nikon. When "on," the camera creates an electrical field that attracts dust to the CCD. When the inside of the camera is exposed during a lens change, dust particles can become attracted to the chip and result in unsightly white spots on future images. Turning off the camera when exchanging lenses can reduce this problem.

● Other Potential Digital Delays

Digital cameras can take a burst of pictures, but at some point must store the images—transferring them from temporary memory (a buffer) to the storage card. While sending the digital bits and bytes, some models require waiting for the buffer to empty before more

KEEPING YOUR CAMERA DRY

Marty Forscher, who spent more than 50 years in the camera-repair business, always warned photographers, "Keep your camera dry." His advice still holds true today, given film cameras' reliance on electronic circuitry and even more sensitive digital cameras. Electrical contacts can corrode on exposure to moisture, especially salty moisture at the beach. Forscher always told the story of how well-known war photographer David Douglas Duncan shot great pictures in Korea under the worst rain and mud conditions possible by using a simple underwater camera.

Today, various commercial "rain hoods" that fit over photographer and camera help keep both reasonably dry. Forscher suggests that if you're caught in the rain without a raincoat for your camera and have neither an underwater camera nor waterproof housing, wrap your regular lens and camera body in a plastic bag sealed with a rubber band. Cut one hole in the front of the bag to let the lens stick out, and another in the back of the bag to enable you to see through the viewfinder. Put the lens and eye-piece through the holes and secure them with rubber bands. Now you can operate the camera through the bag, but you can shoot and view through a clear area. Remember to keep the front element of the lens dry because drops of water here will distort the final image.

photos can be shot. This lag time can provide another frustration for photojournalists shooting in fast-moving situation. Naturally, more expensive cameras have buffers with higher capacities. A sufficiently large buffer is mandatory for a photojournalist, who can't ask the fleeing suspect to wait while the camera's memory buffer clears itself.

ALERT: When a digital camera is downloading pictures from its temporary buffer to a storage card, a small, usually green "access" light comes on. *Do not turn the camera off, remove the memory card, or remove or disconnect the power source until the light has gone out.* The picture that is downloading at the time could be lost, as may others waiting in the queue.

● LCD MONITOR: UNIQUE DIGITAL FEATURE
Most digital cameras have an LCD monitor on the back. One of the great advantages is being able to see a picture almost as soon as you have taken it. With some models, you can elect to view the images immediately. Or you can call up photos later, either one at a time or in a layout of thumbnails. These little thumbnails serve as a kind of electronic contact sheet. Note that even a single image at full display on the LCD monitor is small, less than two inches square. At this size you may still find it difficult to judge a person's expression or the overall sharpness of a scene.

ALERT: Viewing the camera's monitor quickly drains the battery. Some photojournalists call the act of looking at the screen "chimping," probably in reference to chimpanzees' fascination with their own image in a mirror or photograph. Don't "chimp" too much, photographers warn, unless you are packing lots of batteries or only plan to take a few pictures.

LENSES
Zoom Versatility
Today's camera engineers have developed an array of fast, sharp zoom lenses that cover the range of focal lengths most photographers regularly carry in their bags. These fast, wide-aperture zoom lenses also will snare a significant portion of your first paycheck—maybe your first few. Of course, using a single zoom lens does save the cost of owning two or three individual lenses.

Buyer beware, however.

First, some zoom lenses change apertures as you zoom through the focal-length range. For instance, an 80–210mm zoom lens might have a maximum aperture of f/4 at 80mm, but when at 210mm, the maximum aperture has decreased to f/5.6. In general, you will find variable-aperture zooms too slow for practical work when shooting indoors or in low light outside. For low-light photography, you usually need at least an f/2.8 zoom lens that maintains the same aperture at all focal lengths.

Second, zoom lenses are internally complicated and more prone to alignment errors when the lenses are knocked around at a football game or in a riot. Treat zoom lenses with care, and check their sharpness often.

Third, fast, wide-aperture zoom lenses are often very heavy. A number of professionals

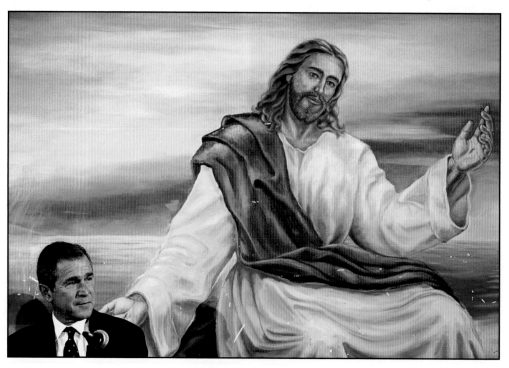

While on the road covering presidential candidates, the photographer could verify the quality of each image while shooting with a digital camera. Tom Gralish, *Philadelphia Inquirer*

report back and arm strain after using these lenses over long periods. Holding an f/2.8 80–200mm zoom lens to your eye for the entire length of a press conference can lead to hours at the chiropractor's office. Use a monopod in these situations lest you face the fate of photographers who have had to leave the field because of this workplace hazard.

Telephoto Lenses Bring Action Nearer

A telephoto lens can be a photojournalist's best friend when the shooter needs to hone in on a subject but can't get close enough. The obvious example is sports pictures where the key player scampers down the field but the photographer is restricted to the sidelines. Photographers also bayonet on their telephotos when they are forced behind a police barricade during a standoff between the cops and a criminal holding a hostage.

Besides filling a photograph's frame with the subject, telephoto lenses have another characteristic especially valuable to photojournalists when used at wide apertures. Suppose the photographer is taking feature pictures of young wrestlers at a meet, but the crowd behind the youngsters is distracting. Shooting with a telephoto lens, if the shooter focuses the lens on the little athletes and sets the aperture at f/2.8, the busy background will likely become blurry and indistinct. In the final image, an out-of-focus background will not distract the reader's eye from the expression on this referee's face, for example, as he tells the young contestants who won and who lost. Many photojournalists carry long lenses just to achieve this strong visual effect.

● And Even Nearer on Digital Cameras

In some digital cameras, the proportionate size of the CCD (charge-coupled device) sensor is smaller than traditional 35mm film.

This has led to a few differences that photographers must consider when using digital equipment. The smaller chip size on these models means that standard lenses used on them have a magnifying effect. On a digital camera with a small chip, for example, a 50mm lens provides the coverage of an 80mm; a 200mm effectively becomes a 320mm. To get the wide-angle effect of a 20mm lens requires shooting with a 14mm lens.

On the other hand, while the effective reach of the lens increases on the digital camera, the lens retains the same depth-of-field as when it was used on a film camera. The digital camera is not magnifying the image from the lens. Because of its relatively smaller chip size, the camera uses only the center segment of the image. The camera is cropping the

image from the lens, not magnifying it. For example, a 300mm lens provides the equivalent reach of a 480mm lens but with the same depth-of-field as the original 300mm lens.

Stabilization Telephoto Lenses

Generally, holding a 200mm lens requires a shutter speed of at least 1/250 sec. or faster to avoid "soft" (not sharp) pictures caused by routine camera movement. Stabilization lenses automatically counterbalance small movements that often occur when a photographer tries to keep a lens steady by hand.

With a Nikon 200mm stabilization lens, for example, you can shoot at 1/30 sec. or slower and still get crisp images. Because you can shoot at slower shutter speeds, these lenses tend to have smaller maximum apertures and so are therefore lighter in weight and easier to hand-hold.

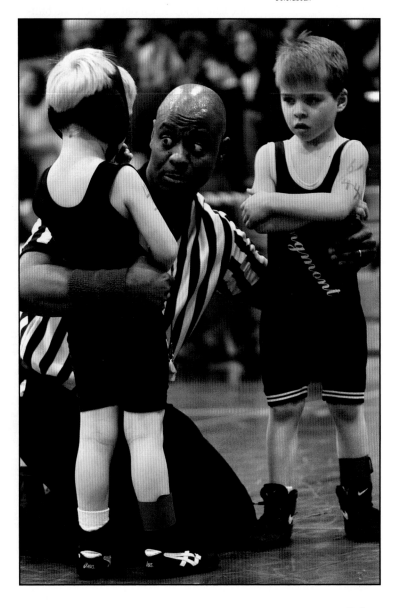

Used at a wide aperture like f/2.8, a telephoto lens helps blur the distracting background behind these 6-year-old wrestlers. The out-of-focus background keeps the readers' attention on the 44-pound grapplers and the referee between them.
Rich Abrahamson, [Fort Collins] *Coloradoan*

WIDE-ANGLE LENSES FOR INTIMACY

Most photojournalists who don't shoot sports exclusively take a large portion of their daily pictures with a wide-angle lens. Cartier Bresson, the French photographer famous for his candid images, used a 35mm lens for many of his classic photos. James Nachtwey, the outstanding war photographer, shoots primarily with wide-angle 17–35mm zoom lens. Other photographers prefer fixed-length wide angles that cover the same range. (See pages 16–17, Chapter 1, "Assignment.")

Wide-angle lenses allow photographers to work very near to their subjects, which provides an intimate feel to the pictures. Many times, a photographer's lens is only inches away from the subject's face or body. Shooting from almost ground level, Pat Tehan of San Jose's *Mercury News* was just inches away from a toreador dressing for the ring (below). The viewer looking at the picture can almost reach out and help the bullfighter adjust his sash.

For news photographers elbowing for a shot in a crowd, the wide-angle lens offers another advantage. Wide-angle lenses provide great depth of field. This feature allows shooting quickly without critically focusing the lens. Of course, the increased depth of field makes it more difficult to blur distracting backgrounds.

The 20mm or 24mm lens allows close focusing. By getting close to a subject like a candidate running for governor, photographers can avoid having their lenses blocked by the politician's handlers, competing members of the media, as well as well-wishers crowding the political hopeful, as he glad-hands his way through the crowd.

Wide-angle lenses also allow photographers to shoot in low light and still hand-hold the camera at relatively slow shutter speeds. Most photographers can comfortably shoot at 1/30 sec. with a 28mm lens and produce sharp pictures without blur from routine camera movement. Photographers report sharp images at 1/8 sec., sometimes even slower, when using 20mm lenses to photograph moving subjects.

Keep in mind that a camera held two feet away from the action might disrupt the spontaneity. On the other hand, sometimes subjects just ignore the close-in camera because their own activities are so compelling.

● **ALERT:** When using a digital camera with a CCD smaller than standard 35mm film, extremely wide lenses in the 14mm to 17 mm range are necessary to achieve the look and feel of images typically shot with wide-angle lenses. These lenses are expensive to manufacture and may prove to be too delicate for shooting in rough and tumble situations.

A wide-angle lens allows the photographer to work up close and personal with a toreador dressing for his upcoming confrontation with the bull. Pat Tehan, *Mercury News* [San Jose, California]

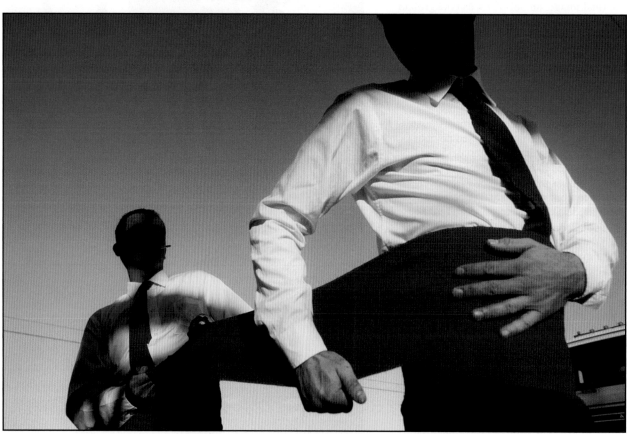

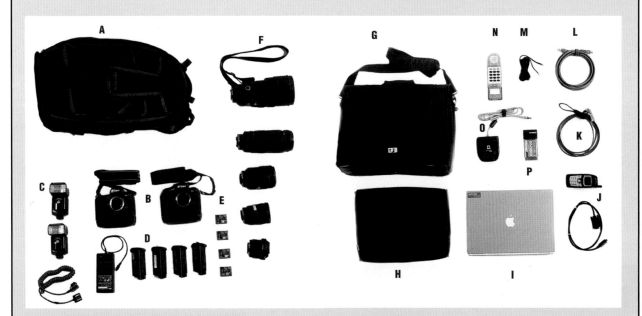

Dave Guralnick, a former Iowa Photographer of the Year, switched from shooting with film to using digital cameras when he went to the *Detroit News*. Guralnick shoots a lot of night sports assignments and is able to shoot more of the game without having to spend time processing film or driving back to the office. He uses his laptop and its internal modem to transmit pictures back to the office from the site of the match—right on deadline. Here Guralnick tells about essentials in his camera bag.

A. CAMERA BAG. Needs to be large enough to carry all your gear safely, but small enough to fit in the overhead compartment in a plane.

B. TWO BODIES. The Nikon D1x and D1h. One high-resolution camera for good quality images, and one high-speed camera for sports and low-light situations.

C. TWO STROBES AND AN OFF-CAMERA CORD FOR THEM.

D. AT LEAST ONE BATTERY CHARGER AND TWO BATTERIES PER CAMERA.

E. SEVERAL MEMORY CARDS FOR THE CAMERAS.

F. LENSES, from the bottom up:
Super-wide-angle (14mm)
Wide-angle (20–35mm f/2.8)
Medium zoom (28–80mm f/2.8)
Long zoom (80–200mm f/2.8)
300mm f/2.

G. COMPUTER BAG. It should be stiff enough to offer protection for the computer. Ideally, you should be able to drop the bag from waist height onto concrete and the computer should survive. Only the most expensive bags offer this kind of protection.

H. PROTECTIVE SLEEVE. This further cushions the computer and prevents scratches.

I. THE COMPUTER.

J. CELL PHONE CORD AND CELL PHONE. Subscribe to a cell phone service that allows connection to the computer and transmission from the phone.

K. LOCKDOWN CABLE FOR THE COMPUTER. Usually around $20–$30, this cord won't protect you from professional thieves but will keep your computer from being snatched easily.

L. ETHERNET CABLE. Internet access through Ethernet connection is becoming more common in hotels and public spaces, and provides an easy means to transmit back to the office.

M. REGULAR PHONE CORD. Handy in case regular phone service is necessary. Don't assume that a cord will be waiting for you.

N. SMALL HANDHELD PHONE. Good to call back to the office if cell phone service is unavailable where you are. Also good to check phone lines to make sure they work.

O. CARD READER. For downloading images from camera to computer.

P. WIRELESS CARD. A card that is 802.11b or 802.11g compatible is a good idea. Like Ethernet, wireless service in public spaces helps photojournalists who need to move images back to the newsroom without going there themselves.

Keys to Working Wide

A wide-angle lens is not a photographer's cure-all. The wider the angle of the lens, the greater the chance for apparent distortion caused by exaggerated perspective. This is because you can focus very close to a subject with a wide-angle lens. But the closer any part of a subject is to the lens, the bigger it will appear in the picture. This effect is particularly noticeable when the subject's face is at the edge of the frame.

Standing relatively close to and above a person and tilting the camera with its wide-angle lens down to include the subject's full length, head to feet, will cause the person's head to appear to be the size of a basketball and the feet small enough to fit into baby shoes. (See this effect used deliberately on page 186.)

The careful shooter can reduce these exaggerations by standing slightly farther back. Be careful not to make the mistake of many novice shooters, though. Standing too far away with the wide-angle lens can cause subjects to appear too small in the frame.

Pointing a wide-angle lens up to include a building's full height causes the structure to look as if it is falling over. This happens with any lens, but particularly so with a wide-angle lens. To avoid apparent distortion with the wide-angle lens, keep the back of the camera parallel to the subject. With a building, either get far enough away or high enough that the back of the camera is perpendicular to the ground and so parallel to the structure.

To use a wide-angle lens successfully, work in tight to your subject, keep the lens parallel to the subject if possible, but trade off some technical imperfections for the impact the lens can provide.

PACKING A LENS FOR EVERY OCCASION

While specific assignments often require specialized lenses—like 400mm "long glass" for sports action at a baseball game or a macro lens for shooting close-ups of insects at a science museum. News photographers typically try to be prepared to cover any event that pops up. Some newspaper photographers cover six or more different assignments a day. From a shootout in the morning to a playoff at night, a photojournalist's motto is "be prepared."

For that reason, most photojournalists carry an array of lenses in their camera bags. The choices usually include at least three fixed-length lenses or their zoom equivalents—a wide-angle, medium telephoto and telephoto. Depending on their preference for shooting with a wide-angle lens, photojournalists will tote a 20mm, 24mm, or 28mm. For the medium range, some select a lens in the 85mm to 135mm range. A number also carry a telephoto in the 180mm to 200mm category. Other photographers prefer two zoom lenses, one wide-angle-to-medium, and the other a medium-to-telephoto. Then there are those with exceptionally strong backs who, in addition to their standard kits, regularly haul lenses as wide as 14mm to as long as 400mm.

• Photographers using digital cameras with CCDs smaller than 35mm film usually carry an extreme wide-angle lens to compensate for the greater effective focal length caused by the smaller chip size.

BUYING A PHOTOJOURNALIST'S DIGITAL CAMERA

No company has yet built the perfect digital camera for journalists, one that will hold up to rain, sleet, hail, burning sun, flying sand, humidity, etc., and continue to perform. With that caveat in mind, here are a few pointers when buying a digital camera for shooting news, sports, features, and portraits.

1) Cost. Although prices are decreasing, digital cameras are still more expensive than traditional cameras with the same features.

2) Computer. You will need a computer, usually a laptop, to display, correct, and transmit your images.

3) Obsolescence. Digital cameras fall behind the technological curve much more quickly than film-based models.

4) Lens interchangeability. Cameras with fixed lenses lack the range from super-wide angle to extreme telephoto to macro.

5) Weight. Make sure the weight of the body won't wreck your shoulder when you haul the hardware.

6) Battery life. Your camera lives and dies on its batteries. Some models seem to devour batteries while others munch them daintily.

7) Continuous shooting. How fast and how many frames per second can the camera shoot before it must download the images to memory card? The more the better.

8) Shutter delay. Nothing is more frustrating than pressing the shutter release and having to wait for the camera to fire. Point-and-shoot digital cameras are notable for this hiccup.

9) Compatibility. Will the new digital camera work with your old lenses? Will you need a super wide-angle lens (17mm or greater) to compensate for the difference in format size between the CCD and film? Does the flash you use now work with a digital camera? Be sure to check out all your gear to confirm that it functions flawlessly before you head out for your first assignment.

10) File size. Many digital cameras do not have sufficient resolution (at least 5 megs) to produce a two-page spread in *Time* or *Newsweek*. Shoot full frame to avoid cropping, which reduces the file size further.

11) Handling ease. You want the camera to feel right in your hands, with controls at your fingertips. People's hands come in different sizes, but manufacturers build camera bodies for the average user, who may not be you.

Good luck, and remember: as soon as you buy your camera you will read an advertisement about a new one that is faster, lighter, and cheaper. Don't worry! Don't look back! You have to jump in sometime!

COMPARING FILM AND DIGITAL IMAGES

As more and more publications use computers to scan in and separate transparencies and negatives, there is little technical difference in how images shot on film or with digital cameras will reproduce. Still, many magazines and picture agencies prefer to receive slide film (transparency), also called color reversal or chrome. Some news magazines are assigning portraits and other non-deadline assignments to be shot on chrome but requiring digital images on deadline. Newspapers that have not switched to digital cameras use color negative film, which they can reproduce in either color or convert to black-and-white.

IMPACT OF CHOICES
Exposure Trade-offs
In terms of shooting, color negative actually has the greatest brightness latitude. The film can record detail over a wide range from dark to light in one photo. Negative film, then, has a wide tolerance for under- and overexposure. Some photographers say that they can expose one to two stops under and up to three stops over the meter reading, depending on the film speed, and still produce a usable image.

If an exposure on chrome film or an image taken with a digital camera is off by more than a third of a stop, the final image will be washed out or muddy. In fast-breaking situations where perfect exposures on every frame are not possible, the forgiving latitude of color negative film can save the once-in-a-lifetime shot.

• When shooting with digital cameras or chrome film, expose carefully for the highlights. A picture with deep shadows that lack details still looks better than an image with washed-out highlights. (See page 242.)

• Distance & Deadlines
Digital cameras, computers, and cell phones allow photojournalists with tight deadlines to stay at assignments longer, shoot more images, and transmit from the very site of the event. No more racing to the office or to a one-hour lab to process film. No more shipping film from the nearest airport to home offices in New York or London. The immediacy gained makes up for technical perfection that might be lost.

Color Balance
The colors of different light sources—outdoor noonday sun compared to indoor tungsten light, as one example—affect the overall hue of the final image. With transparency film, what you see is what you get. Even with the ability of computers to adjust color balance digitally, most correction for transparency film still must be done while shooting, whereas color negative film can be filtered in the enlarger or in the computer.

Photographers using transparency film must go to great lengths to match film to light sources, eliminate unwanted colors with filters or gels, or shoot aided by strobes to achieve attractive, color-balanced photos.

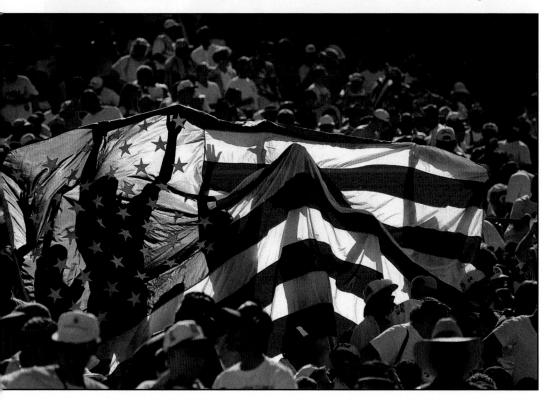

This photo at the World Cup soccer matches in Pasadena's Rose Bowl was shot on ISO 400 color negative film.
Paul E. Rodriguez, *Orange County Register*

Because a transparency has limited exposure tolerance, correcting after the original exposure can be difficult or impossible. This leaves little opportunity for color adjustment after the film has been shot.

 • While images shot digitally are subject to the same color balance issues, most digital cameras have a "white balance" feature that can compensate for different light sources (page 240) in each shooting situation without the hassle of special films, filters, or extravagant lighting setups.

Affect on Style

The photojournalist shooting fine-grain, low ISO transparency film cannot shoot quietly and unobserved from the corner of a room, using only available light and a few rolls of high-speed film. Today, the shooter with chrome in the camera often rolls into an

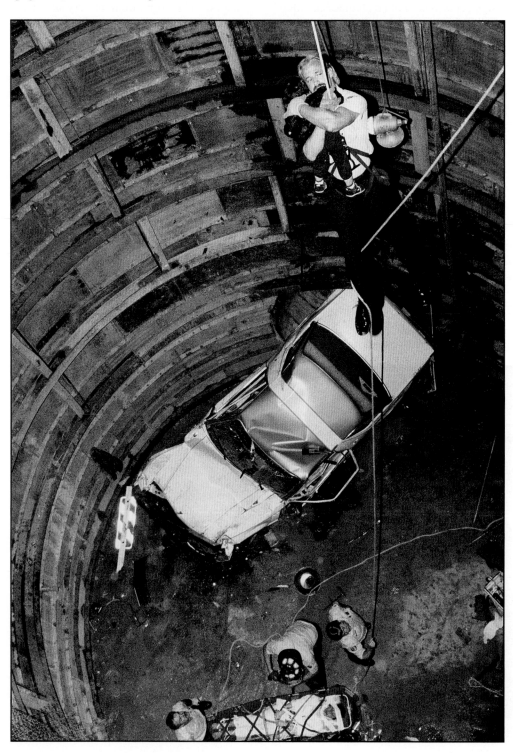

Color negative film, used for this rescue photo, has wide exposure latitude, which makes it ideal for spot news like this freak accident. Remarkably, no one was hurt.
Craig Hartley, for the *Houston Post*

assignment with 100 pounds of lighting gear on a cart.

After unpacking the lights, setting up the light stands, plugging in the power pack, putting together the soft box and umbrellas, test-firing the strobe, and exposing a Polaroid, the photographer turns to the subject and says, "Now let's have some candids."

In her survey "How the Use of Color Affects the Content of Newspaper Photographs," Cindy Brown found that several photographers said they create more "set-up photos" once they set up lights. The photographers observed that people's reactions are not as spontaneous when strobes are firing, and strobes limit the photographers' movements around a room.

These concerns were especially true from photographers using transparency film.

SHOOTING IN LOW LIGHT
Color Film
Film manufacturers offer both color negative and transparency films specifically designed for "push" processing. With certain films, manufacturers claim good results even when underexposing the film up to three-and-one-half stops and compensating with increased development.

Many photographers find that they get better results pushing a slower ISO 100 or 200 chrome film to a higher rating than they do using a high ISO film in the first place. With some specially designed chrome films, photographers find grain and contrast hold, despite the combination of underexposure and overdevelopment.

High-speed color negative films have less grain and more saturation than their chrome counterparts. High-speed color negative film like Kodak's PJ ISO 800 and Fuji's ISO 800 extend photojournalists' ability to shoot documentary-style images under the most severe lighting conditions.

Still aiming for the best of both worlds, some photographers will shoot chrome outdoors or in well-lit indoor situations but switch to color negative film in low light.

Black-and-White Film
Photojournalists working in black-and-white often use one type of relatively fast film, like Kodak's Tri-X to shoot most of their assignments. With high-speed film, they can handle everything from an outdoor rally at noon to an indoor press conference in a dingy city hall office without wasting time rewinding and changing to a different film.

Standardizing on one film minimizes mistakes when covering multiple assignments and meeting tight deadlines. Also, one film simplifies a camera bag. Photographers don't have to pack different emulsions for each event or change of the weather.

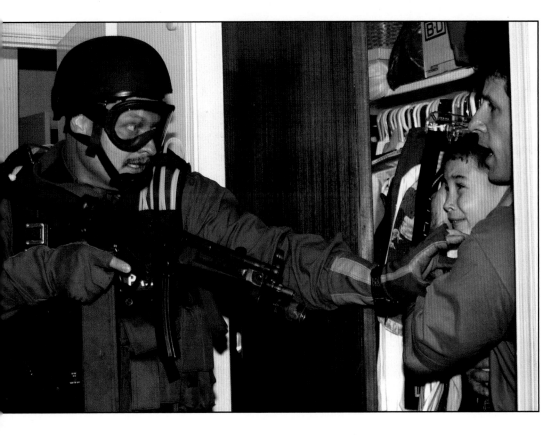

The fate of six-year-old Elian Gonzalez captivated the world for weeks. His mother had drowned while attempting to escape Cuba with the boy. Relatives in the United States demanded that the child stay with them, but his father wanted him back in Cuba. With U.S. authorities poised to return the child to his father, photographer Alan Diaz anticipated a showdown if the family refused to cooperate. After staking out the house for weeks, the photographer had come to know the family and was able to get inside the house when the raid by U.S. authorities occurred. Having previously set up access to a phone line, the photographer removed the memory card from his digital camera as soon as he took the pictures, inserted the card into his computer, and uploaded the pictures. The Associated Press immediately sent this image to the waiting world. Alan Diaz, Associated Press

Most film cameras today have shutter speeds above 1/1000 sec., and many can reach 1/8000 sec. This allows photographers to use even wider apertures outdoors—which, in turn, allows them to blur the background—while continuing to shoot with the same fast film.

For shooting in low light, black-and-white film can also be pushed.

Doubling a film's ISO rating combined with special processing can allow working at the higher shutter speeds necessary to stop the action of a basketball player in mid-jump.

However, pushing film can increase contrast and grain. Pushing film is effectively starving it of the light it normally needs for a correct exposure. You can starve film only so far before it becomes too weak to produce a well-exposed image.

"Magic" 3200 Film

When you need really high-speed black-and-white film, Kodak's P3200 T-MAX comes to the rescue. Originally dubbed "Magic" film by the photographers who tested it, the film

IS IT MAGIC?

IMMEDIATE RIGHT
Dizzy Gillespie, performing at the Monterey Jazz Festival, appears sharp as a tack with Kodak's "Magic" film rated at ISO 1600. Eric Risberg, Associated Press

FAR RIGHT
The photographer rated Kodak's T-Max 3200P film at ISO 3200 to get this candid photo of an adoptive father holding his new son for the first time.
Eric Slomanson, San Francisco

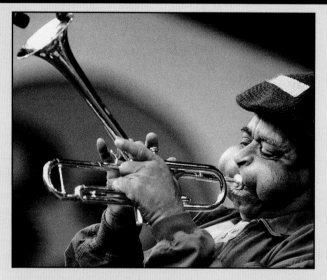

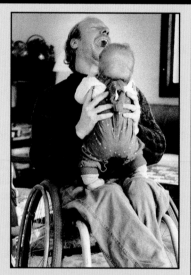

RIGHT
To photograph this homeless youth having fun at night by lying in the middle of a busy city street, the photographer used Kodak T-Max P3200 and rated it at ISO 6400.
Jennifer Cheek Pantaléon, Pacifica, California.

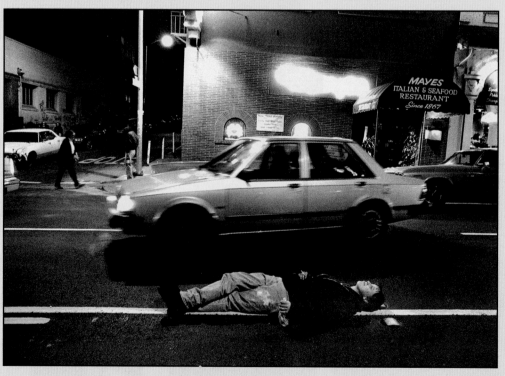

can be shot at ISO 1600, 3200, or even 6400 and beyond with excellent results. Ilford's fast black-and-white film, Delta 3200, has similar capabilities to Kodak's P3200 T-MAX.

Eric Slomanson rated Kodak's film at 3200 to capture the expression of a wheelchair-bound father holding his adopted son for the first time. Other photographers use the film under even more adverse conditions. (See examples on opposite page.)

● Digital "Grain"

With conventional cameras and film, you must change film if you need a film with a different ISO. Digital cameras, on the other hand, allow you to set each shot at a different ISO (film speed) for shooting under any lighting conditions. On some cameras, ISO ratings range between 200 and 1600 or even higher.

Just like the increased grain that occurs with film at higher speeds, though, increased "noise" appears in pictures shot at higher digital ISO ratings. Noticeable noise shows up at ISO 1600 or higher on some cameras. The noise looks like tiny brightly colored pixels in the darker areas of the picture. Photographers

often find noise more objectionable to the eye than old-fashioned grain. (See below.)

In low-light situations, some photographers recommend using on- or off-camera flash rather than increasing the ISO. Others shoot at 1600 with good results. Some people report better results by turning off "image-sharpening" mode in their cameras when shooting at a high ISO. This mode tends to exaggerate noise levels in some photographs.

Software programs, used when editing the picture in the computer, can help seek out and eliminate offending noisy pixels and thus improve the picture's overall appearance. Check out Rob Galbraith's website, *www.robgalbraith.com*, for information about noise reduction filters and other issues regarding digital photojournalism.

SHOOTING IN COLOR: FILM OR DIGITAL
TIME OF DAY IS CRITICAL

Editors often disregard the hour of the assignment when they set up a photographer's schedule. They ignore the angle and the color of the light.

For an indoor job, time of day might be less crucial, but for an outside assignment, timing is everything.

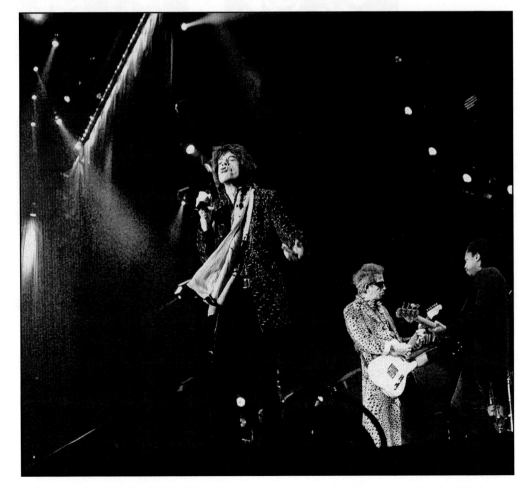

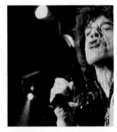

To cover a 9:00 p.m. Rolling Stones concert and still make a 9:15 deadline, the photographer shot the Stones's first three songs with his digital camera, raced to the parking lot, and transmitted the image to the newsroom from his laptop. Because of the low light in the concert hall, the dark areas in the picture displays "noise," a purplish pixelated appearance that can be reduced by using special software programs. See the effect here especially in the spotlights and in Mick's hair.
David Guralnick, *Detroit News*

DEALING WITH DIFFERENT LIGHT SOURCES

Ever notice that when you meet a friend for dinner by candlelight, the person seems to radiate a warm glow? Walk outdoors, and you'll see that your friend loses that radiant, reddish color. The color on your friend's face was caused not by the wine but by the candle-light's red wavelengths. The candle glowed red, with very little green or blue light waves mixed in.

Almost every light source—whether a candle in a nightclub, a fluorescent tube in an office ceiling, or the sun outdoors—casts a light that is not purely white but rather has a hint of color to it.

The color cast of most light sources is not as pronounced as that of a candle, so you rarely observe radical color shifts when you move from one light source to another. After

all, you know that a white shirt looks white, regardless of the kind of light illuminating it. Photographs, however, do pick up these color changes.

Scientists measure the color of light emitted by a light source on a Kelvin scale. Color films are balanced either for daylight (5500 Kelvin) or tungsten light (3200 or 3400 Kelvin).

TRANSPARENCY FILMS

DAYLIGHT FILM.

Noontime daylight contains relatively large amounts of blue wavelength light. Daylight-balanced color film is designed to filter out this excess blue. Generally, use daylight film when most of the light comes from the sun.

TUNGSTEN FILM.

Light from a common tungsten-filament light bulb (2900 Kelvin) or photo flood (3200 or 3400 Kelvin) contains an overabundance of wavelengths in the red portion of the color spectrum. Tungsten-balanced color film filters out this red cast. A few Type A color films are designed for use with 3400 Kelvin photo lamps. In general, use tungsten film for available-light shots indoors when most of the light comes from light bulbs. These situations include theaters and some sports arenas.

MISMATCHED FILM AND LIGHT SOURCE

Using a tungsten-balanced film out-doors results in a blue cast to the photo. Except when used at night, this effect rarely looks natural or pleasing.

Shooting with a daylight-balanced film in a room lit by tungsten bulbs will give an orange hue to everything in the picture. Sometimes this effect looks odd. Other times, the orange hue gives a picture a warm glow.

DAYLIGHT FILM

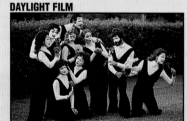

Daylight-balanced film used in daylight produces natural colors.

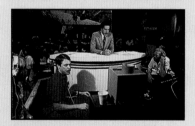

Daylight-balanced film used under tungsten light gives an orange cast to the picture. To shoot daylight film under tungsten light, use a #80 filter.

TUNGSTEN FILM

Tungsten film used in daylight produces a blue cast. Use a #83 amber filter to shoot tungsten film in daylight.

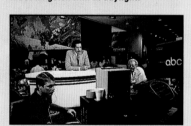

Tungsten film used with tungsten lights produces normal-looking color transparencies.

"WHITE BALANCE" WITH DIGITAL CAMERAS

Digital cameras provide internal controls for balancing color. When these controls are employed, a white object will look white in the final image regardless of the light source in the original situation. Once white is white, everything else, from faces to furniture, retains its appropriate color balance.

Most cameras provide several ways to work with what is called white balance. "Auto" white balance lets the camera make the decisions. When on auto, the camera reads the light source

and renders colors normally for that situation. This method tends to work most of the time.

For more precision, point the camera at a known white object, such as a piece of paper. Activating a white balance command adjusts the camera's sensitivity to the light source illuminating the white object. As long as you continue working in the same lighting conditions, your pictures will not have a color cast.

ALERT: Don't forget to reset the white balance command when the lighting changes.

Finally, many cameras provide a menu that usually includes symbols for incandescent, fluorescent, direct sunlight, flash, clouds and shade. Other cameras may provide choices in Kelvin degrees, a technical way of describing color.

Whichever method you use, test the camera and yourself by looking at the LCD monitor to see if images appear strangely blue or orange. A pronounced color cast usually indicates that you need to change the color balance setting.

SHOOTING UNDER FLUORESCENT LIGHTS WITH TRANSPARENCY FILM

Although most office buildings, hallways, classrooms, and other public spaces are lit with fluorescent tubes, no manufacturer makes a color transparency film specifically designed for use under fluorescent lights.

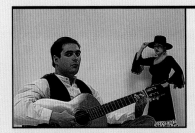

AVAILABLE LIGHT, NO FILTER ON LENS
This transparency was shot with only fluorescent light. Note the green overall hue.

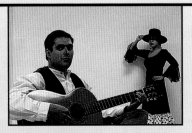

AVAILABLE LIGHT, LENS FILTERED
Adding a #30 magenta color correcting filter to the camera eliminates the picture's green cast.

AVAILABLE LIGHT

When shot under fluorescent lights with daylight-balanced color transparency film, pictures come out with a decidedly green cast.

Shooting under the same conditions with tungsten transparency film washes the pictures with a strong blue tint. To complicate things further, each type of fluorescent tube, whether warm white or cool white deluxe, emits a slightly different color. The name says white, but the resulting color on your transparency film won't be.

Because most photographers don't want to scale ladders to verify the make of each fluorescent tube before shooting, they use a standard filter or filter pack to subtract unwanted tints. The standard filter or pack adequately subdues the green of fluorescent lights in most locations. Some photographers use an FL-D filter with daylight film. Many, however, have found a #30 magenta color-correcting (CC) filter used with daylight film works well for handling most fluorescent-lit situations. When using tungsten film, an FL-B filter should do the trick.

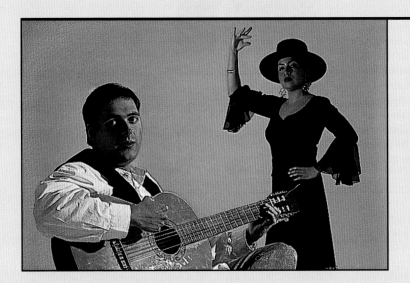

STROBE AND LENS, FILTERED
To use strobe and balance with available light fluorescent bulbs at the same time, put a #30 magenta filter on the lens and a "window-green" filter on the strobe.
Daryl Wong

BALANCING FOR FLASH PLUS FLUORESCENT

Sometimes photographers shooting with daylight film need to combine strobe and available fluorescent light. By placing a window-green gel over the strobe, both the light from the flash and the available light will have the same tint.

The addition of a #30 magenta CC filter in front of the camera's lens eliminates the green wavelengths from both the fluorescent lights and the green wavelengths from the filtered strobe, leaving only correctly balanced light to reach the film. The resulting transparency will look normally color-balanced.

shot of a building taken at noon becomes an *Architectural Digest* photo at 6 p.m. A common mug shot photographed at 10 a.m. becomes a gallery portrait taken at sunset. The selection of time to photograph is as important as the choice of lens or film.

A painter picks oils from a palette to create mauves and maroons. Likewise, a photographer picks the time of day to capture delicate morning pink or late afternoon red. The time of day determines the color of light striking your subject when shooting outdoors.

While working on a book about the Russian city of St. Petersburg, former *National Geographic* staffer Steve Raymer photographed Palace Square, scene of revolution and bloodshed during both the reigns of the Czars and Lenin's Bolsheviks. Searching for just the right combination of dramatic light and editorial content—in this case horses ambling across the square and suggesting a bygone era—he returned a dozen or more times until he found the perfect moment. "This picture took compulsive attention to light and color," Raymer says.

Raymer also photographed the broad and muddy Red River as it flowed across the mountainous border between China

---

HANDLING EXTREME BRIGHTNESS WITH TRANSPARENCIES & DIGITAL

Color transparency film and digital images have a low tolerance for contrasty situations in which important subjects are located both in bright light and in deep shadow. At a midday parade, for example, a group holds a rainbow of balloons that shadow some of the group's members (RIGHT). One person, however, is backlit by bright sunlight. The trees in the background are in deep shade. Shooting this scene on chrome or with a digital camera requires precise exposure. A half-stop over or under can wash out or dull down the final slide. The same applies to a digital image.

EXPOSE FOR THE HIGHLIGHTS
Still, some photographers, particularly those working for magazines, prefer slides that are a little richer and therefore regularly underexpose their film by a third of a stop. Other photographers stick with the film's ISO rating because they like their slides on the brighter side.

In general, when important parts of a scene are both in sun and shade and have extreme brightness differences, your transparencies will look better if you expose for the lightest area important to the picture. With transparency film, overexposed highlights look terrible (frames C and D) but underexposed shadows look acceptable (frame A). With transparencies, the general rule is to expose for the highlights. Exposing for the highlights will produce a transparency in which the content of the shadows will be dark but still recognizable, while the overall transparency will be color-rich. When shooting under a contrasty situation, consider using flash, even outdoors on a sunny day. "Fill flash" helps to fill in dark shadows on the subject's face and to reduce the brightness difference between the highlights and shadows.

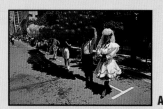

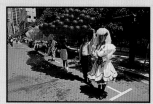

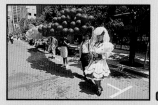

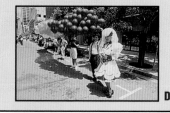

EXPOSURES VARIED BY ONE STOP FOR EACH PHOTOGRAPH

A

B

C

D

CONTRAST CONSIDERATIONS WHEN SHOOTING DIGITAL

Just as they do on transparency film, very bright areas in a scene shot with the digital camera tend to wash out. What does this limited brightness range mean in the field? Underexposing by a stop yields excellent results, but overexposing by more than a quarter-stop results in lost detail. Meter for the highlights when using the digital camera.

In his book *The Digital Photojournalist's Guide*, Rob Galbraith recommends using fill flash outdoors (see page 272)) even on bright sunny days. Set the basic camera exposure for skin tones in bright light and use flash to fill in the shadows, he advises. "I shoot everything I possibly can with fill flash because the printed results are dramatically improved by doing so," he says. This technique avoids bleached highlights, eliminates noise (page 239) in the underexposed areas, and produces better color requiring less correction in the computer.

and Vietnam. "I actually waited until after sunset . . . when the sky was filled with a reddish-pink afterglow," he explains.

In this situation, the reddish hues in the final image added to the message of tranquility he was trying to convey and also played off the river's name.

SHOOTING FROM DAWN 'TIL DUSK
While you can't control when a peace demonstration or a car wreck will occur, you often can select the time of day for shooting an outdoor portrait or a building exterior.

Dawn
For soft shadows and monochrome colors, shoot at dawn.

Midday
Some photographers try to avoid the harshness of the midday sun. Although colors might appear bright in transparencies or prints, people photographed on a sunny afternoon often have shadows running across their faces. These unflattering shadows can turn eye-sockets into billiard pockets.

If you must shoot portraits on a bright, clear afternoon, try (1) moving your subjects into the shade of a building or tree, or (2) turning your subjects so that their backs face the sun. Here is where you can use fill flash to your advantage. (See Chapter 12, "Strobe.")

Late afternoon
As the sun falls lower in the sky, its rays travel farther through the atmosphere. Molecules of water in the sky tend to scatter the short, blue wavelengths of light. The long, red wavelengths pass freely toward earth. This is why, as the sun sets, late afternoon light turns redder and redder. Also, as the sun drops, shadows stretch and lend a sculptured look to the landscape. This time of day is the choice of many photojournalists working in color.

Although the reddish light of late afternoon usually flatters a subject, you will occasionally need a more technically correct picture at this time of day.

As sunset approaches, the sky takes on its most flamboyant corals and oranges. You can silhouette subjects against this richly colored background. If you want to avoid a silhouette but still use the sky's palette, try balancing your strobe with the early evening sky. In this situation, your strobe would become the dominant light source for the subject. The ratio of strobe light to the skylight would be equal. Many photojournalists shoot portraits and fashion using this balanced-light technique. (See pages 258, 260, 261, and 278

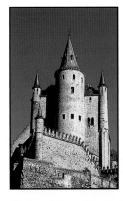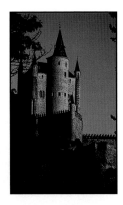

The time of day a subject is photographed—particularly a building—affects the mood of the final picture. The mood shifts from stark at noon (above left) to rich in late afternoon (above right). Ken Kobré

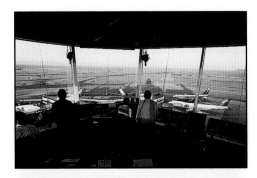

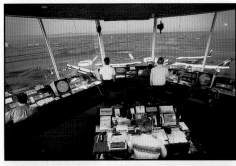

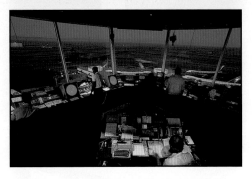

To show both the landing strip outside and the air controllers inside, the photographer waited until the waning afternoon light matched the exposure of the indoor light. Note also in this series of pictures how the color and quality of light changes as the time of day changes.

Ken Kobré, for *San Francisco Business*

for examples of this technique used in various circumstances.)

Evening

Lacking the warmth of the sun, evening light is cold and blue. Sometimes streets and buildings that look as bland as white bread during the day look haunting by night. Don't overlook the possibility of using flash to illuminate the foreground and a long shutter speed to pick up ambient light in the background. Also, tungsten film turns the nighttime sky a rich blue.

Saturation

Standard chrome film tends to reproduce the world as the eye sees it, but other transparency films can make the world look even brighter and more saturated than normal. These chrome films, like Fuji's Velvia or Kodak's Ektachrome E100VS, accentuate the reds or greens in a photograph to produce a highly intense slide. Landscape photographers

in particular like the visual bang from these highly saturated emulsions.

ALERT: Caucasian skin tones don't always come out looking natural with these films.

● GOING DIGITAL

At the *Detroit News*, bureau photographers no longer even come into the downtown office. Shooting exclusively with digital cameras, they send in all their pictures by telephone. Transmitting directly from the dugout, *San Francisco Chronicle* photographers can shoot six innings of a night baseball game and still meet their deadline. Two innings max was the norm in the past.

Photojournalists covering the second Iraq war downloaded pictures from their cameras into a device about the size of a cigarette pack called a Phojo. They used this tiny tool to crop, correct color, caption, and then send their images back to the newsroom using a satellite phone capable of transmitting from anywhere in the

STROBE LIGHT IS LIKE DAYLIGHT

An electronic flash emits a color approximating daylight. When using electronic flash with chrome, select daylight-balanced film. And because your electronic flash has a color balance similar to daylight, you can use your strobe as a fill light when taking pictures outdoors without affecting the final photo's overall color balance.

The early evening sky, just after sunset, offers a warm afterglow for a background. To capture both the mime and the view outside her luxury hotel, it was necessary to balance the exposure of the electronic flash with that of the outside available light. (See Chapter 12, "Strobe," for more on balancing strobe and available light.)

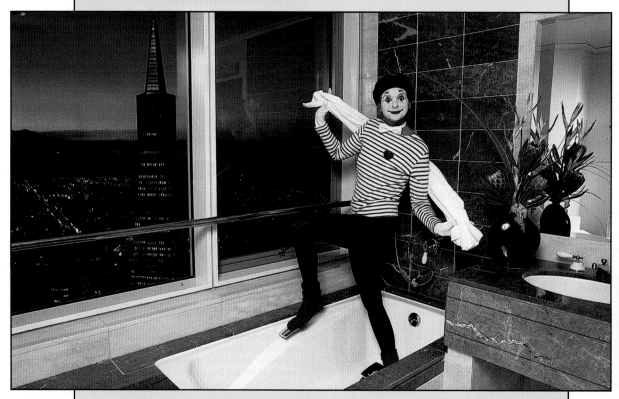

Ken Kobré, for *San Francisco Business*

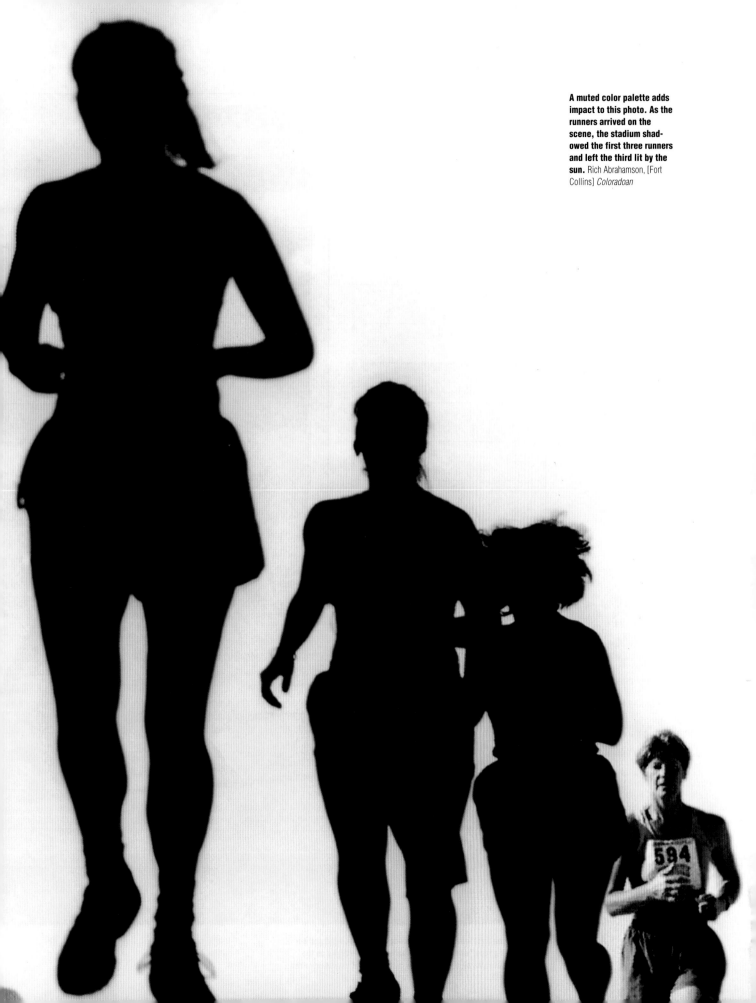

A muted color palette adds impact to this photo. As the runners arrived on the scene, the stadium shadowed the first three runners and left the third lit by the sun. Rich Abrahamson, [Fort Collins] *Coloradoan*

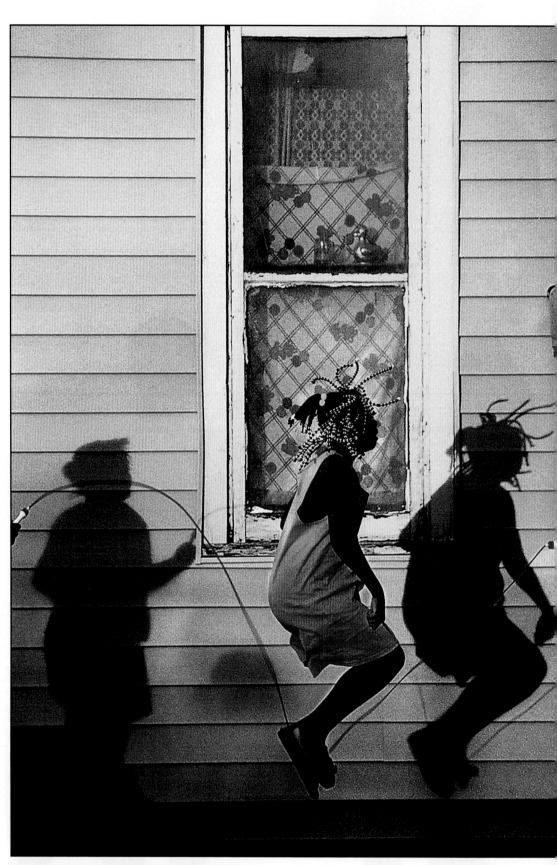

Late afternoon light leaves a crisp, distinct shadow of a girl and her friend jumping rope "double dutch." The warm glow results as the atmosphere absorbs blue wavelengths in the sky and leaves more red as the sun sets. Brian Plonka, for *Herald-News* [Joliet, Illinois]

world. The phone bounces its signal off a satellite, and from there it can connect to any publication with a receiver.

Of course, not all pros who are transmitting their assignments are doing so from war zones. Technology makes it possible for photographers to transmit from their favorite coffee shops or even from the backseats of their cars. (See a digital journalist at work in "Fire Photojournalist," on the DVD included with this book.)

● MEMORY CARDS

All digital cameras require a removable memory card, compact disk, or hard drive to store images before they are transferred to a computer or printer. They vary in the amount of data they can hold as well as in format.

The amount of memory you need depends on the resolution necessary for reproduction. Resolution is the number of pixels in an image, a key factor in determining quality. You will need at least three million pixels (three megapixels) to produce an 8"x10" image for a newspaper. An uncompressed three-megapixel image consumes 9.4 megabytes of memory.

You won't always need such a big file if a photo is intended for use on the Internet. But generally, the more pixels, the better the quality will be if the photograph is going to be printed or reproduced at a large size. (See page 248.)

CompactFlash® memory cards have no moving parts. They come in standard physical sizes but vary in how much information they hold. A 512-megabyte card holds twice as many pictures as a 256-megabyte card. Some memory cards can download information from the camera faster than others. (See *www.robgalbraith.com*) Greater memory with faster download time is the ideal choice when selecting a memory card. Bigger for storing more pictures, faster so that less time is required between shots as the photos actually travel from the camera to the card. Note that the various brands of memory cards aren't always interchangeable. Read your camera's manual to determine which memory cards are compatible with your model.

The portable Microdrive® is another storage choice. Since these drives have a miniscule whirling disk inside—like the one inside a computer—be particularly careful when handling them. Generally, they can store more pictures than CompactFlash cards.

HOW THE COMPUTER TRANSLATES PICTURES INTO NUMBERS

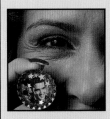

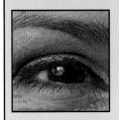

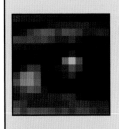

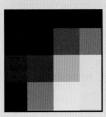

Do you remember paint-by-number canvases from your childhood? So that you could paint a picture of the Eiffel Tower, the canvas would indicate a specific number for each color of paint. When a segment of the picture needed a blue sky, the canvas would call for a number five (blue). When a section of the tower needed to be red, the canvas would call for a number three (red). On the original canvas, the area representing the sky was covered with number fives, and the Eiffel Tower itself was filled with number threes. All you had to do was match the paint color on the little jar with the number printed on the canvas. Even if you didn't know what the canvas was supposed to show, you would eventually produce a painting of the Eiffel Tower if you painted in all the numbers correctly.

Now, imagine a paint-by-number canvas in which sections are of equal size, like graph paper, but smaller than a pinpoint. These tiny squares are called picture cells—or pixels. Each pixel is assigned a number indicating its location and it brightness. Now imagine if, instead of a few jars in your paint set, your canvas called for 16.7 million jars, each a different shade, level of brightness, or saturation. Each square (pixel) on your canvas could be any one of these sixteen million plus colors. If the squares (pixels) are small enough and if you have enough paints, you can accurately represent in the computer any picture you might take. Now you can appreciate how many numbers the computer is crunching whenever it deals with a color image. Basically, a computer is selecting from millions of jars of colors to paint by number millions of tiny, evenly spaced squares.

Because the capacity of memory devices is increasing even as prices are going down, some pros recommend carrying several cards. This allows them to continue shooting while downloading a full card into a laptop or other storage device. Allocating shots to different cards also ensures that an entire assignment is not in one place if a card is damaged or lost.

Other shooters prefer one large-capacity memory card. The larger capacity permits fewer download sessions, an advantage when shooting in poor weather conditions or when covering a fast-breaking story.

● THE MEMORY/QUALITY TRADE-OFF

Digital photojournalists want great image quality, but they also must pack the maximum number of images possible per storage card. The size and quality of a digital image determine how much storage space (either in the camera or in your computer) the file for the photograph takes up.

High-quality images require high-quality

QUALITY AND FILE SIZE

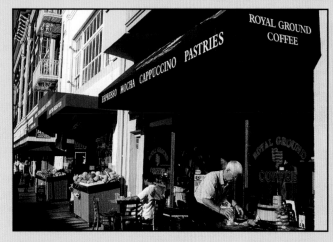

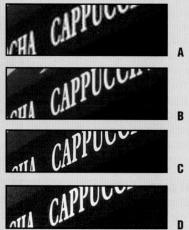

A

B

C

D

What is the final purpose for your image?

Intended use	Resolution
Internet	72 dpi
Newspaper	150 dpi
Photographic-quality print	
Inkjet or dye-sublimation printer	200 dpi
Glossy magazine, book	300 dpi

ABOVE. Compare compression vs. quality trade-offs. Each of the small images was shot at a different compression level, from lossless TIFF to lowest quality JPEG. The details from an 8x10 enlargement of each file were taken after the images had been decompressed.

A   Lowest-quality JPEG. File size: 66 kb. (900 kb when decompressed)
     Pixel dimensions: 640 X 480. Maximum dpi for an 8x10 image=64 dpi.
B   Medium-quality JPEG. File size: 188 kb (2.25 megabytes when decompressed).
     Pixel dimensions: 1024x768. Maximum dpi for an 8x10 image=102 dpi.
C   Highest-quality JPEG. File size: 2.9 megabytes (14.1 megabytes when decompressed).
     Pixel dimensions: 2560X1920. Maximum dpi for an 8x10 image=256 dpi
D   TIFF. File size: 14.1 megabytes.
     Pixel dimensions: 2560x1920. Maximum dpi available for an 8x10 image=256 dpi.

RESOLUTION AND FILE SIZE

Digital photos and digital images are often described by their resolution. Here is how resolution is calculated.

Final image size	Pixels per inch	WAYS TO DESCRIBE RESOLUTION			Final file size for color image
		Pixels x pixels	Millions of pixels	Megapixels	
8x10 inches	200 ppi	1600 x 2000 pixels	3.2 million pixels	3.2 megapixels	9.6 megabytes
5x7 inches	200 ppi	1000 x 1400 pixels	1.4 million pixels	1.4 megapixels	4.2 megabytes
4x6 inches	200 ppi	800 x 1200 pixels	.96 million pixels	.96 megapixels	2.9 megabytes

Multiply each dimension of your final image size by the number of dots per inch at which you will print it out. The examples above use 200 ppi, which provides a large enough file for reproduction with most desktop inkjet printers.

In the first row, for example, 8 inches times 200 equals 1600, 10 inches times 200 equals 2000. Pixel by Pixel dimension equals 1600 x 2000. This is one way to describe resolution. Now, multiply 1600 times 2000. The answer is 3.2 million pixels. Millions of pixels also describes resolution.

Divide 3.2 million pixels by one million to determine the number of megapixels, a shorthand way to state the total number of pixels—in this case, 3.2 megapixels (digital cameras are often described in terms of megapixels).

Now, because each pixel consists of three color values—red, green, and blue—multiply the number of megapixels times 3 to determine the final file size of the image.

An 8x10 color inkjet print requires a file size of at least 9.6 megabytes. A 4x6 snapshot needs only 2.9 megabytes.

FILE SIZE AND STORAGE CAPACITY

DIGITAL CAMERA MEMORY CARDS

Capacity	Number of 10 MB files (8x10, 200dpi inkjet prints)
32 MB	3
64 MB	6
128 MB	12
256 MB	25
1 GB	100

COMPUTER STORAGE

	Capacity	Number of 10 MB files (8x10, 200dpi inkjet prints)
200MB Zip Disk	196+ MB	19
Compact Disk	600+ MB	60
1GB Jazz cartridge	1 GB	100
3.9GB DVD	3.9 GB	380+
5.2GB DVD	5.2 GB	500+
100 GB hard drive	100 GB	10,000
200 GB hard drive	200 GB	20,000

digital files, which consume the most memory and storage space. If print quality is your goal, bigger is almost always better. A small file size is ideal when it comes to storage space, transmission over the Internet, or ease of working with an image.

A memory card may hold just a few pictures at top quality but many at low quality. If you are traveling without a laptop to which you can transfer the images, your memory cards will quickly run out of space if you shoot all your pictures at top quality.

● Resolution & Compression

To achieve smaller digital files, your camera uses either fewer pixels to take pictures, compresses the files, or does both. Low quality settings use the fewest pixels to take a picture in the first place and/or compress an image the most. High quality uses the most pixels and/or compresses the least.

Because of this trade-off between image quality and memory, most cameras provide a way to pre-select quality for each or all pictures. Some models record and save the images raw—uncompressed, exactly as they were taken, with all information saved—resulting in a very large file. You may find numerical settings for compression and resolution, choices such as high, medium, or low, or a system of stars or numbers. Your camera manual describes your choices.

How good is good enough? Your decision on which quality to choose will depend on how you want to use your photo. A low-quality image will look fine on the Web. But if you print out the same image at a large size, you probably won't like the results.

Photojournalists shot with digital cameras and transmitted their images around the world using laptop computers and satellite phones during the second Iraqi war.
Jon Mills, Associated Press

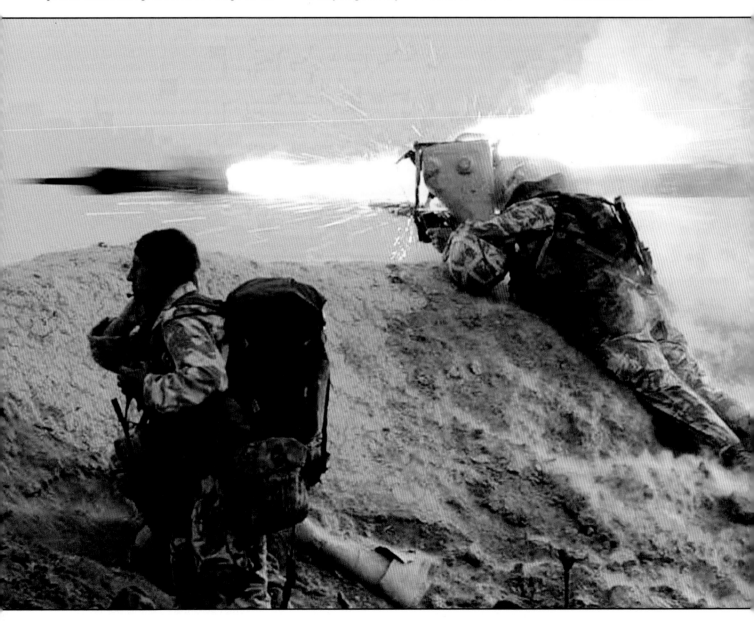

High quality is the choice for images intended for display or reproduction in books or magazines. Medium quality works well for some newspaper reproduction. Your publication will be able to tell you the optimum file size for the best reproduction on its presses.

ALERT: You can downsize a high-quality file for the Web, but you can't expand a low-quality file to create a double-page spread.

For the best quality—and thus the largest file size—select the highest resolution possible and do not compress the image at all. This choice makes sense for a photographer with lots of storage space on a CompactFlash or Microdrive who plans to use the pictures for a glossy magazine or book.

To create the smallest possible file, select the lowest resolution and highest compression ratio. This option is best for someone shooting only images for the Web.

ALERT: Manufacturers don't use the same terminology to describe resolution and compression. Review your camera's manual.

● Oops!

Have a favorite image shot at too low a resolution to be reproduced in a magazine or enlarged for the wall? There may be hope depending on the final size required. While upsampling in Photoshop and programs like

Genuine Fractals does not increase the detail in a picture, they do help avoid obvious pixelation. Many photographers report excellent results with software solutions like these.

● DIGITAL IMAGES USING A SCANNER

OK, you don't have thousands of dollars to spend on your first digital camera. You can still enter the digital revolution with your present camera and traditional film. You can take pictures with your trusty Nikon, Canon, Minolta, or any other camera using silver-based color or black-and-white films.

Once you have shot the pictures, you will need to develop the film as you have always done. Next, however, you will translate your negatives or slides into the digital information that the computer reads. A scanner does the translation for you.

The scanner acts just like a digital camera, although it doesn't photograph a scene. Instead, it takes a very precise picture of your negative, slide, or print, and passes the digital image, now in the form of ones and zeroes, into the computer. Once the image is in the computer, the picture can be sent across the world or by a direct cable to the presses in the back shop.

Many photographers today shoot with 35mm cameras and film, process their film (often in a mini-lab that develops the film dry-to-dry in twelve minutes), and then scan their negatives into the computer.

● Scanning Considerations

Scanners and software packages vary, so the publication where you work will provide specific technical directions on how to get the most out of scanned images.

However, there are a few things to keep in mind. The key to a good scan is that all the visual information on the original gets copied sharply, accurately, and completely. Some photographers recommend adjusting the image as much as possible based on a preview scan so that the final scanned file, imported into Adobe's Photoshop, will require the least amount of correction.

The final resolution at which you scan depends on how the image will be reproduced—in traditional printing terms, it will depend on the fineness of the halftone dot screen. Printed on coarse newsprint, newspapers have traditionally used an 80- or 85-dot-per-inch (dpi) screen. The paper quality is such that finer screens don't produce finer reproductions. Magazines and books, which use smoother, often coated paper, may use up to 150 or even 300 dpi to print fine reproductions. Publishing on the Web, on the other hand, needs only 72 dots per inch.

HOW DOES COMPRESSION WORK?

How do you squeeze a large picture file into a smaller space? By eliminating redundant information. Let's say you have a picture with a large blue sky. To represent the blue, the computer stores hundreds of individual identical numbers, each representing the color blue. To compress the information, software counts up the number of blue pixels that are the same and stores the total count rather than a number for each individual pixel.

If x stands for blue, the original file might be xxxxxxxxxxxxxxxxxxxxxxxxx xxxxxxxxxxxxxxxxxxxxxxxxx, while the new file would be (x50) and take up a much smaller space. When you decompress the image, the program lays out the original number of blue pixels representing the sky.

The method of compression called "lossless" throws away no data. The reconstituted picture is exactly the same as the original. The file size still remains relatively large, however.

The method known as "lossy" throws out some of those identical blue pixels, which can degrade quality. Depending on the degree of compression, though, the loss can be so slight that the degradation is not noticeable.

The commonly used JPEG format is a lossy method of compression. JPEG files can be saved in different quality modes—high, medium, low. You might also run across choices such as fine, normal, or low. High compresses a little but leaves the image looking almost perfect. Low, on the other hand, compresses a lot, and the loss will be obvious if the image is reproduced in a magazine but not when posted to a Web site. (Keep in mind that repeated editing and saving an image in JPEG format will eventually degrade its quality noticeably.)

TIP: After you have transferred an image to the computer and want to work with it, make a copy and work with that. This will preserve the original at its highest quality in case you need to start over again.

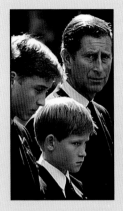

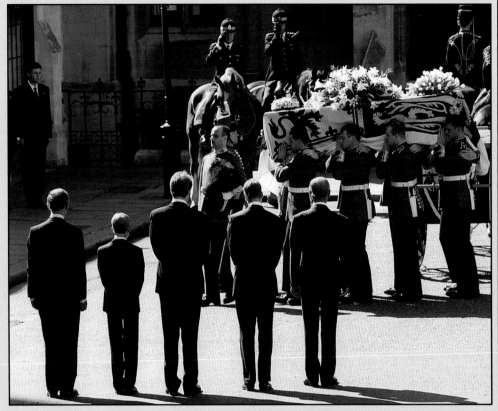

John Gaps III was one of the first photojournalists to go completely digital. Following the tragic death of England's Princess Diana, which captured headlines worldwide, Gaps used an electronic camera, portable computer, and cell phone to cover her funeral for the Associated Press, for whom he was working at the time. The AP had assigned several photographers along the funeral procession route that day but stationed only Gaps and one other staffer to the critical position in front of Westminster Abbey, where the services were to be held.

Gaps staked out his position at midnight before the services. "I thought there was one place to make the picture—perpendicular to the door of Westminster Abbey. My instinct was that I would be able to get the coffin, the four Princes, and Di's brother in one picture."

Gaps had to wait nearly eleven hours before the funeral began. He continued holding his position, and at 11:00 a.m., the pallbearers carried in the Princess's casket. He shot with a 200mm lens (effectively a 320mm on a digital camera) as the casket was carried inside.

"I shot my pictures and had my laptop computer ready under the tripod," recalls the photographer, whose computer was connected to a cell phone.

"I had thrown my coat over the tripod so that I could see the computer screen. The coat worked just like the hood on an old-time 4"x5" Graphflex."

By the time the casket came out of the Abbey, Gaps already had transmitted four pictures. With freshly shot film in his hand, a competing Reuters photographer looked over toward Gaps and moaned to his colleague, "He's f__ing me, Nigel. He's f__ing me." Gaps, with his electronic camera, computer, and cell phone, had already transmitted pictures around the world, while the Reuters photographer was still holding exposed, undeveloped film in his hand.

When the casket came out, Gaps focused tight with his 500mm lens (effectively an 800mm on the digital camera), and captured the despondence of Princess Diana's former husband, Prince Charles, and their two sons as her casket was carried by.

"You don't see the casket," says the AP photographer. "I just stayed on their faces. It was a big gamble. Nobody else really shot that tight."

Gaps's gamble paid off. His pictures ran on the cover of *People* magazine and in newspapers around the world. ∎

If the final image appears on newsprint or the Web, you are wasting time and computer storage space if you scan at too high a resolution. The image won't look any better, but it will take longer to scan and then to print—or in the case of the Web, to load. The finer the scan setting, the more memory is required.

The other important variable is the final size at which the image will appear. Scan the picture either to size or to a size slightly bigger than you anticipate it may appear. If it's scanned and saved at a size equivalent to a two-column picture, for example, but it's run at four columns wide, it will look jagged and unattractive. In "computer speak," there's not enough "information" for the image to be enlarged after the scan has been completed. If you've scanned it to run four columns wide, but it appears in three columns, you're okay. All the information is available to run it at a larger size, so there will be enough information to run it smaller, as well. Your best bet is to provide a scanned image at exactly the size at which it will run. But deadlines don't always allow the best of all worlds.

THE INTERNET: DELIVERING PHOTOS TO VIEWERS WORLDWIDE

While newspaper circulation per household has declined steadily since 1953, and most general-interest magazines have folded, the number of individuals owning computers has soared. "Home pages" on the World Wide Web developed by individuals and organizations provide a supplement or alternative to traditional print journalism.

Almost every newspaper, magazine, and television network in the country has a Web site. Some recycle material from their print or broadcast versions while others provide new content, including photos. Web sites that feature original reporting and photography are providing new jobs for photojournalists as editors and sometimes as shooters.

Some sites on the Web have no print counterpart. Anyone—from an individual with a computer and modem like freelance sports photographer Brad Mangin, *www.mangin photography.com*, to a large agency like Black Star, *www.blackstar.com*—can have a Web site.

Some photographers use their sites to display their portfolios. Others display their stock collections so that buyers from magazines or ad agencies can more easily shop. Still others just want people to see what they currently are shooting. By searching for the word "photojournalist" at *www.yahoo.com*, *www.google.com*, or other search engines, you will find a slew of personal and professional photographic sites.

Keith Philpott, *www.keithphilpott.com*, a magazine photographer who lives in Kansas, shoots regularly for *People*. He set up a web

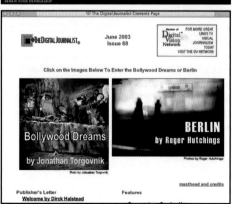

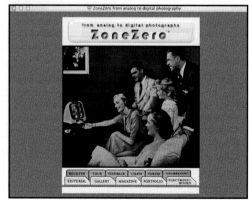

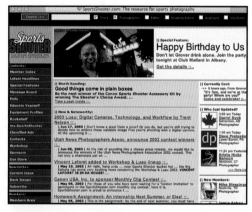

site to attract a wider range of magazine and commercial clients. Photo editors searching for a photographer in Kansas who specializes in people will easily find Philpott on the Web.

Philip Wartena had no commercial intentions when he set up The Photologist Collective, *www.ThePhotologist.com*. He just wanted to provide a showcase for photographers on the Web.

The Web is also a great tool for research. On practically any subject you can dream up, you will find interest groups, professional groups, chat groups, and commercial sites on the Web. Scientists and other researchers are publishing their findings on the Web. Using E-mail, you can easily contact experts around the country—and around the world.

The texts of most of the major magazines and newspapers are available in databases like Lexus/Nexus. You can check the card catalogues of libraries ranging from your local college to the Library of Congress without leaving the comfort of your chair. And, of course, you can send and receive photos via the Internet.

WHY THE WEB NEEDS PICTURES

Pictures have the same power on the Web as they do in print, according to researcher Sheree Josephson. In her paper "The Readability, Recall, and Reaction to On-Line Newspaper Pages with Visuals and Those Without," she found that subjects looking at Web pages with pictures spend 31 percent longer studying stories on those pages than they do on pages with the same content but no images.

People reading stories accompanied by pictures also could recall the articles 20 percent more often. (See Chapter 10, "Photo Editing," pages pages 211 and 214 for similar findings regarding pictures in print). And finally, all the subjects reported preferring the visual version to the nonvisual version of the Web page.

The Web is not only an ideal outlet for photojournalism, but it also needs images to hold readers' attention and improve what they remember about stories.For a comparison between the impact of photography on the Web and in print, see Chapter 10, "Photo Editing," pages 215–216.

Shooting Pictures for the Web

Many people viewing Web sites have relatively slow modems (56k or less) and look at the pictures on small monitors. Therefore, your pictures need to be high impact. Keep in mind that subtle details will get lost. Larry Dailey, who was a picture editor with MSNBC Online, says pictures he rejected for use on the site were those that would take too long to download. "A good picture for MSNBC is like an icon," Dailey adds.

PHOTOJOURNALISM WEB SITES TO EXPLORE

American Society of Media Photographers (ASMP)
Site for ASMP, a professional trade association promoting photographers' rights.
www.asmp.org

The Digital Journalist
Digital photojournalism site maintained by *Time* photographer and digital video pioneer Dirck Halstead. Interesting information and links to other photojournalism sites.
www.digitaljournalist.org

Editorial Photographers (EP)
An international discussion group for photographers who earn at least part of their income in the editorial market. Members share experiences and information related to the business of editorial photography.
www.editorialphoto.com

Focal Point
A photojournalism site featuring interactive photo essays.
www.f8.com

Musarium
Dirck Halstead calls it "one of the finest Web sites to feature multimedia photojournalism, period."
www.musarium.com/

MSNBC Photo Gallery
Top photojournalists cover everything from the birth of a nation to the birth of a child.
www.msnbc.com/news/173305.asp?cp1=1

LIFE's Virtual Gallery
Features classic photo exhibitions and provides links to similar sites, including photo archives and interactive museums.
www.pathfinder.com/Life/virtgal/virtgal.html

National Press Photographers Association
Online home of the NPPA, with lots of information of interest to photojournalists.
www.nppa.org

Reporter's Internet Resources
A massive resource for journalists maintained by the National Press Club. Links to most major news organizations, and a comprehensive list of information providers.
www.npc.press.org/library/reporter.cfm

The TIME LIFE Photo Sight
Drawing on its collection of more than 20 million photographs, the TIME LIFE Photo Sight features an extensive photo gallery, photo essays, and more.
www.pathfinder.com/photo/index.html

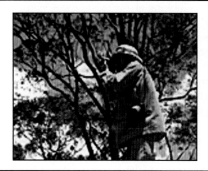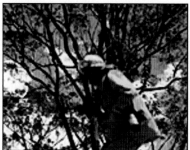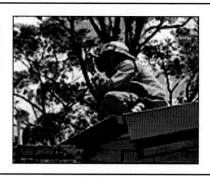

These frames were captured from a documentary digital video "Fire! Photojournalist" about a news photographer covering the largest wildfires to strike Australia. The documentary is included on the DVD in the back of this book. Because the quality of an individual frame from a digital video camera is still too low for an enlarged still picture, most photojournalists prefer to shoot with a still camera to produce pictures intended for the printed page.

"It makes you click through, but it is not necessarily a good piece of photojournalism."

Tom Kennedy knows intimately the differences between shooting for print and for the Web. He was the director of photography for *National Geographic* and now is director of design and photography for the *Washington Post/Newsweek* Web site. He says the *National Geographic* photographer will shoot thousands of frames to bring back one powerful image to sum up the whole experience. While such a summary can be accomplished, says Kennedy, in a certain sense it is always incomplete. "One single image misses the nuances and the complexities," he says.

Better than selecting one summary picture as he had to at *National Geographic*, Kennedy can now run an unlimited number of pictures on the Web site. This allows stories to be told on many different levels.

Photographers receive much more feedback from the reading public, Kennedy says. Web readers' responses are more immediate and more visceral, he says. People see a story on the Web and don't hesitate to immediately send an E-mail with praise, condemnation, or, more likely, a suggestion for the future.

In addition to pictures, many sites are incorporating sound and video. Photographers not only are shooting stories with still images, but also are recording natural sound and even collecting interviews. Many experts predict that the future of the Web resides in its multimedia capabilities. Photojournalists, in the future, will have to shoot compelling pictures as well as record high-quality sound and even shoot video for a complete Web package.

DIGITAL VIDEO

Many photojournalists today are telling stories with digital still cameras and also are using digital video cameras to shoot, write, and edit pieces for the Web and for television. Dirck Halstead, an early advocate of still photographers using video, calls this crossbreed photojournalist a "platypus," for the Australian creature that has characteristics of both bird and mammal. Like the platypus, the video journalist has traits of both a still photojournalist and a videographer.

Several intersecting factors have given rise to the photographer shooting both stills and video. From an economic point of view, magazines want to save money by cutting staff. Even magazines like *National Geographic*, which still runs lots of photo stories, primarily hire freelancers rather than maintain a photo staff. Only four staff photographers remain on *National Geographic*'s masthead.

News organizations like the *Orlando Sentinel* and the *Sarasota Herald Tribune* assign photographers to shoot both stills and video on the same assignment.

Another reason still photographers are taking up video is that the cost of video equipment has dropped dramatically. Digital video cameras selling for less than $3,000 now perform as well as those costing $50,000 just a few years ago.

Digital video cameras have excellent image quality and professional sound capabilities when used with high-end microphones. With a lightweight camera, a microphone, and a tripod to steady the camera, you can start shooting your first story on video.

The other technology shift is in editing, where it is now possible to now outfit a personal computer for editing video for less than $5,000, including software that combines many of the functions handled by separate experts in the past. Until recently, technology allowing the same functionality ran in excess of $100,000.

Finally, experts predict that the demand for independently produced video stories will grow in the future. The World Wide Web will need multimedia news, Halstead predicted in his definitive article for *Visual Communications Quarterly*. Visit Halstead's Web site at *www.digitaljournalist.org*.

Eventually, you will send and receive pictures and sound on your computer as easily as you tune your television set. Many Web sites already display still pictures, text, and short video clips.

As transmission speed increases, you will see more and more video packages, predicts Brian Storm, a former picture editor for MSNBC Online.

In fact, Storm predicts that all Web news sites will require multimedia elements like video and sound in addition to still images, articles, and captions.

MAKING THE TRANSITION

The skills of the photojournalist are ideally suited for this new dual role. A good photojournalist already conceives an idea, conducts research, makes contacts, shoots the story, edits the film, and suggests a layout for a coherent package to run in a newspaper or magazine. The new video journalist must serve as correspondent, photographer, sound person, and producer. The platypus journalist can also edit the piece, provide the voiceover, and, finally, upload the finished segment onto his or her own Web site or provide it to a local or national Web site or TV station.

Former *Newsweek* photographer Bill Gentile, for example, produced an Emmy Award-winning documentary on the Ebola virus for the Discovery Channel. P.F. Bentley, who shoots on contract for *Time*, used video to report on Haiti and Cuba for ABC's "Nightline."

Technically, shooting video is fun and an easy transition from stills. After all, still photographers are already shooting overalls, called establishing shots in the video world, as well as mediums and close-ups. Still photographers are accustomed to framing and following action.

DIFFERENCES EXIST

Still photographers will find some clear differences between shooting stills and video.

"The fact is that, in most cases, still and television moments exist in a separate time-space continuum," Halstead says.

The still photographer waits and watches for revealing candids. Henri Cartier-Bresson called that split second in which all the elements come together the "decisive moment."

The video photographer craves action that continues in time. Repetitive action, like a carpenter sawing a piece of wood, is the easiest to shoot on video, since it can be photographed from several angles, but the videographer must also track the movement of a subject through a crowd or follow unplanned breaking action. The last thing a videographer wants is just one, critical, split-second moment.

THE SOUND OF SUCCESS

To make the transition to video, the most important new technique the photojournalist must master is the use of sound. "If you close your eyes while watching '60 Minutes,'" says Halstead, "you will find that you can absorb the story with no problem. The images enhance the story, but it is the sound that is vital to understanding." The sound bites provide the narrative.

THINK AHEAD

To prepare for a cross-disciplinary career as a photojournalist who shoots stills and video, take courses using both media. Sometimes video courses are located in a university's journalism or mass communications department. At others, video is taught in the broadcast or film department. A number of good books and videos are available that will help you become a better switch-hitting shooter. ∎

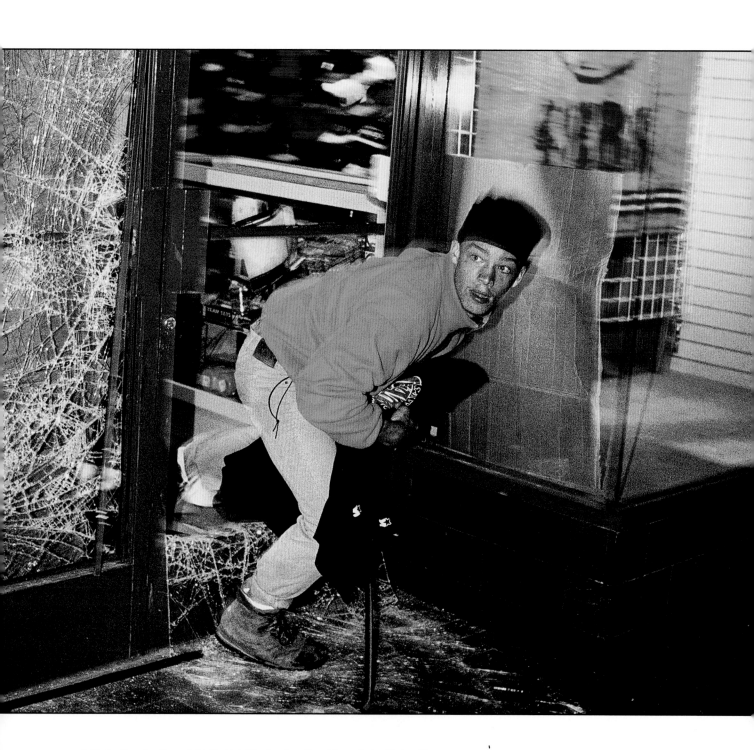

Following the not-guilty verdict in the trial of Los Angeles police officers who beat Rodney King, rioters in San Francisco broke into shops and hauled out stolen goods. The photographer used a relatively slow shutter speed (1/30 sec.) to balance the strobe's light with that coming from the store's interior. Ken Kobré, Mercury Pictures

Chapter 12

Strobe

SUNSHINE AT YOUR FINGERTIPS

Originally, photographers were limited to picture-taking only when the sun was out. Not all news, however, happens in the light of day. From flash powder through flash bulbs to electronic flash, photojournalists have searched for a convenient light source that would enable them to take pictures under any circumstances. Today, possessing a compact strobe is similar to having a pocketful of sunshine at your fingertips. In the 1970s, manufacturers brought out miniaturized, lightweight, high-powered strobes. With a thyristor (energy-saving) circuit, the strobes used only the power they needed for a correctly exposed picture. With the advent of strobes with automatic exposure control, the number of over- or underexposed negatives was reduced dramatically, and photographers no longer had to undertake complex calculations to determine the f-stop at which to shoot. The strobe's automatic eye, coupled with the unit's internal computer, releases just enough light to produce perfectly exposed pictures most of the time.

The next generation of electronic flashes was called "dedicated." The manufacturers designed each unit to work with—be dedicated to—one particular camera system. The strobe and camera work in tandem, relying on the same information about film speed, shutter speed, lens length, and aperture.

With some dedicated flashes, the camera measures both available and strobe light directly through the lens (TTL). With a through-the-lens dedicated flash system, the camera can read the available light of a scene and automatically set the strobe to dominate the available light, equal it, or just provide a fill light, according to how you set the controls.

Some camera systems employ what's called 3D matrix metering or A-TTL (advanced

through-the-lens). This technology lets the camera compare exposures reflected off the subject with distance information, and then combines the data for a correct flash exposure even if the subject is off center or wearing an all-black or all-white outfit. Camera-strobe combinations can even balance the light from the strobe with available light to produce a perfectly exposed photograph.

ELECTRONIC FLASH CONTROVERSY

Although designers have engineered a compact and convenient strobe, flash critics still point out that the strobe's light looks artificial in photos. These purists note that the strobe throws an unnatural black shadow behind the subject's body, producing pictures with the look of a police line-up. True, flash pictures can look stark. In the old days, with their flashguns mounted to the sides of their Speed Graphics, photographers churned out these unnatural, stylized pictures.

Today, the cause of harshly lit pictures does not lie with the flash but rather with the flash photographer. When photographers use techniques like bounce, multiple-flash, or fill flash, almost any lighting effect that occurs naturally can be created with the strobe.

To achieve this distinctive look, the photographer used the strobe off camera and set it to "telephoto" so it would emit a defined cone of light. He controlled the background light by using a fast shutter speed. Without the strobe, the subject would have been as dark as the person just behind and on the left. However, had the photographer used no flash and exposed for the subject, the background with its dramatic clouds would have washed out.
David Leeson, *Dallas Morning News*

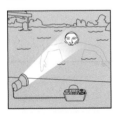

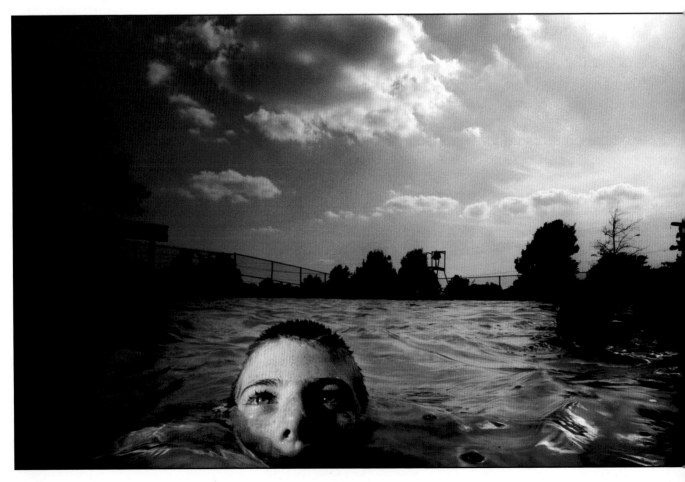

When used creatively, strobe light can provide the even feeling of fluorescent light, the dramatic effect of direct sunlight, or the moody flavor of window light. But when the flash photographer leaves the strobe on the camera and aims straight ahead, the harsh effect is unavoidable.

People who dislike flash argue one persuasive point, however. Initially, when a flash goes off, it does tend to draw attention to the photographer. The burst of light can throw cold water on a hot discussion. However, just as a mayor becomes accustomed to being followed by a photographer clicking off pictures, most subjects eventually will pay little attention to the firing of the strobe.

Strobe advocates point to the advantages of a portable light source for the photojournalist. A strobe can boost the overall quantity of light in a room, thereby enabling you to set a smaller aperture for greater depth of field. This is needed, for instance, when shooting an overall picture of a meeting in progress.

Also, the strobe light can last for only a brief instant, usually 1/1000 of a second or faster. This allows you to take a picture at an effective speed of 1/1000 of a second, freezing both subject and camera movement.

As a photojournalist, you must weigh the strobe's advantages against its disadvantages. In many circumstances, you would not be able to get any pictures without your strobe.

Without light from the strobe to expose the thief (page 256) and freeze the motion, the author could not have stopped the action of the criminal fleeing a store with goods in hand.

In other situations, you can produce a technically improved or visually more interesting picture with a portable light source. *Dallas Morning News*'s David Leeson, used an off-camera strobe at noon to add interest to his picture of a boy swimming. Without flash,the face of the swimmer would have been lost in shadow. The strobe added pop to the picture as well as light to the fellow's face (opposite).

Sometimes the strobe, especially in a sensitive situation such as a funeral, can be disruptive. Other times, natural light can add more visual variation to pictures.

However, few spot-news photographers would leave their offices without their electronic flash equipment in their camera bags.

SELECTING THE SHUTTER SPEED
STOPPING ACTION
The super-short flash duration of the strobe appears to freeze a subject's movement, no matter how fast the person is running or jumping. The strobe freezes a gymnast as he leaps in midair, a motorcyclist as she bends into a turn, or the skateboarder as he appears to hang, suspended in time and space.

In addition to stopping subject movement, because the flash is almost instantaneous,

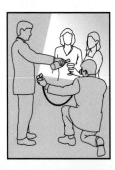

With the strobe in his left hand, the photographer reached under the arm of the person pouring the champagne and aimed the strobe so that light came from an unusual direction.
Tom Duncan, *Oakland Tribune*

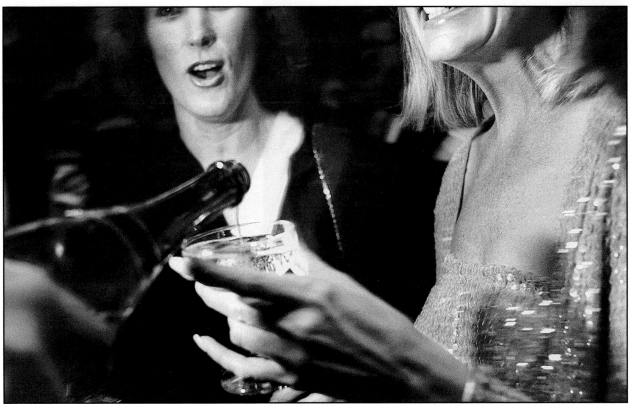

Jennifer Miller is director of the Circus Amok in New York. At mid-day, the photographer took the director/performer to the roof of her practice studio in Brooklyn and lit the portrait with a strobe aimed into a small umbrella. The strobe was attached to a light stand located to the right of the bearded lady and connected to the camera by a cord. The photographer exposed so that the light from the strobe was strong enough to overpower the background. This darkened the sky even at noon on a bright day. Kaia Means, Oslo, Norway

strobe light avoids blurry pictures caused by camera movement. Even if you are clicking pictures as you chase a city council member up the stairs of city hall, your pictures will come out sharp if you shoot with a strobe.

Sync speed

Note that if you are using a focal-plane shutter, found in single-lens reflex cameras, flash pictures will not come out correctly if your shutter speed is set too fast. On some cameras, the upper limit is only 1/60 sec. Other cameras synchronize with the flash up to 1/250 sec. Some even sync as high as 1/500 sec. If you use a shutter speed faster than sync, only part of the image receives the strobe's light. Some camera/strobe systems prevent a shutter speed above sync speed. Check your camera instructions. (See demonstrations on pages 262–263.)

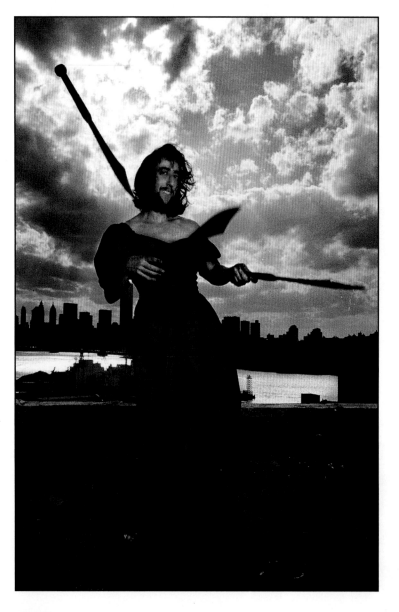

The digital camera brings a significant advantage to strobe photography by allowing relatively high sync speeds. Some newer model cameras will sync as high as 1/500 sec. Beware, though, that many standard strobes will not work with digital cameras in the metering mode known as TTL, through-the-lens.

COMBINING FLASH WITH AVAILABLE LIGHT

Each camera model does have an upper limit sync shutter speed. However, selecting a *slower* shutter speed often results in a more natural-looking flash photo. Indoors or outdoors at dusk, many photographers use slower shutter speeds to pick up ambient light from the environment and combine this with light from the flash. While the electronic flash captures a moving subject in midair, the available light from the longer shutter speed lightens the background.

In this approach, the shutter remains open longer than the duration of the flash. As the shutter speed slows to let in more and more available light, the background will appear brighter behind the subject (see pages 262–263). Once the amount of available light equals the strobe light in quantity, further slowing of the shutter speed will overexpose both the subject and the background.

Beware that some dedicated flash-camera combinations allow for limited or no variance in setting the shutter speed. Again, check your manual.

Many professional photographers also like the effect that the combination of strobe and a slower shutter speed has on moving subjects. Although the strobe freezes the subject's movement for one instant, the long exposure also captures the subject's continuing movement, adding a ghost-like blur. The result is a sharp image combined with the blur of motion (opposite).

While the author was photographing a riot, looters began breaking into stores and carting off armloads of leather coats and sporting goods through the broken windows. His strobe lit the looter and caught him in flight, but a slow shutter speed picked up light from inside the pillaged store. (See page 256.)

DETERMINING APERTURE

Strobe manufacturers build their strobes in different ways, so a brief check of your instruction book will indicate how to operate your unit. Some common principles apply.

MANUAL

To determine the aperture, measure the distance from the flash to your subject, and then check the distance scale on your strobe. Watch out. Some dials are marked in both meters and feet. Also, be careful to set the dial or read the scale for the particular film speed you are using.

AUTOMATIC EYE

The automatic strobe sensor always adjusts the strobe's light as if the subject were a neutral gray tone (18 percent gray). The automatic sensor works well as long as the subject is neither exceptionally dark nor exceptionally light.

The light meter in the camera and in the strobe function similarly. Both the strobe's sensor and the camera's light meter give correct readings most of the time because the average brightness of most scenes is equivalent to approximately 18 percent neutral gray.

For the exceptionally light or dark subject, however, most strobes with automatic sensors require adjusting the f-stop on the lens to compensate for extremes.

A strobe sensor considers a small, 5–10 percent angle of view in the center of the frame. What it sees in that frame is neutral gray. If a subject is wearing jet-black leotards while standing in front of a dark brick wall, the sensor eye will be fooled. To compensate, close down the lens's aperture one or two stops to avoid overexposing the picture.

For a subject wearing wedding white, perhaps standing in front of a chalk-white chapel, the sensor eye will be misled again. To compensate in this situation, open up one or two stops to avoid underexposed pictures. (See page 227 for examples where the camera's automatic light meter is fooled. Similar situations would fool the strobe's sensor.)

Through the Lens (TTL)

With some dedicated camera/strobe systems, the flash sensor is located in the body of the camera. With this setup, the flash is informed

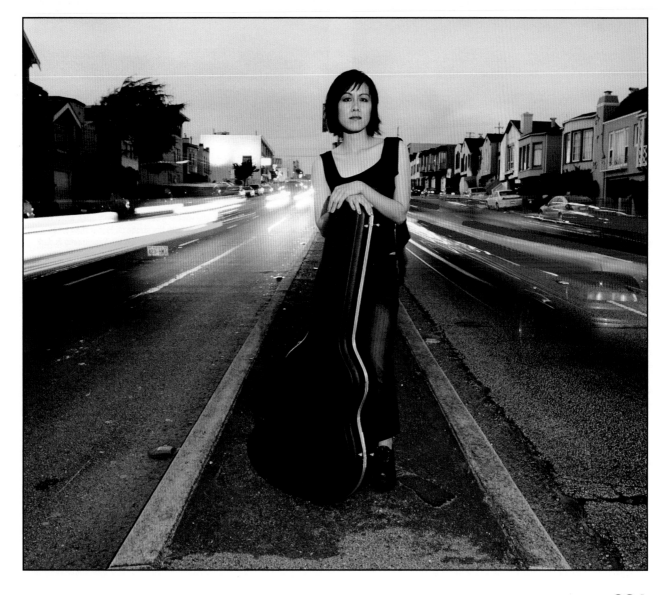

This portrait combined flash and available light. The longer the shutter remains open during an exposure, the brighter the background appears. As the shutter remains open longer—in this situation for 1/2 sec. at f/5.6 —the moving cars disappear and leave only trails of light from their head and tail lights. John Shearer, San Francisco

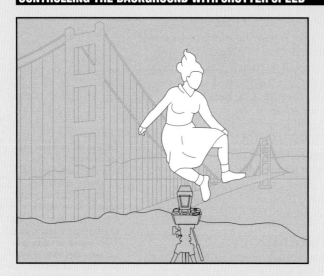

You can use the flash at any shutter speed at or below your camera's flash/sync speed. In these photos, the flash was set on manual, and its output remained constant.

For flash pictures, the f-stop is determined by the amount of light emitted by the flash that reaches the subject.

In this case, the photographer measured the amount of light with a strobe meter. The f-stop on the camera remained at f/5.6. With the camera on a tripod, the photographer simply varied the cam-era's shutter speed from 1/500 sec. to 1 sec.

To demonstrate the full range of shutter speeds, the photographer shot at dusk. He also had the subject jump in every frame.

Notice how changing the shutter speed influences the picture. The choice of shutter speed controls the amount of available light reaching the film.

As the shutter speed slows, the background gets progressively lighter in each picture.

Photos by John Burgess

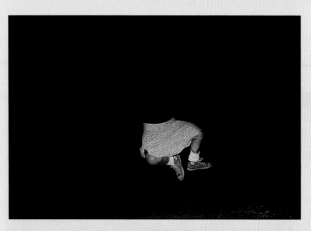

• **1/500 sec.** You can see that most of the subject is dark. The focal plane shutter on this camera drops from top to bottom like a guillotine. The curtain on the shutter was about half open when the strobe fired. F-STOP STAYS AT F/5.6.

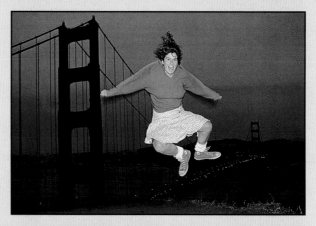

• **1/250 sec. (sync speed)** Here, the shutter's curtain was fully open when the flash fired. Some camera models sync with the strobe no higher than 1/125 sec. or 1/60 sec. The subject is correctly exposed, but the background is dark because at this exposure, the scene behind the subject is completely under-exposed. The flash froze the subject in mid-air. F-STOP STAYS AT F/5.6.

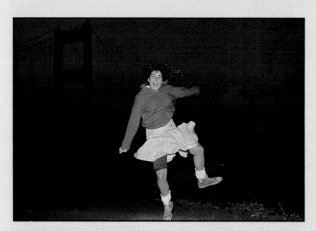

• **1/125 sec.** The background lightens as the shutter speed lengthens. The subject remains frozen. F-STOP STAYS AT F/5.6.

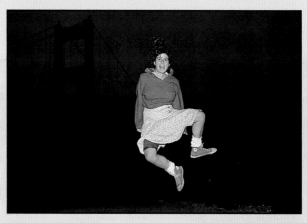

• **1/60 sec.** The subject remains correctly exposed while the background gets yet lighter. By keeping the exposure on the subject constant and varying the shutter speed, you can control the background's brightness. F-STOP STAYS AT F/5.6.

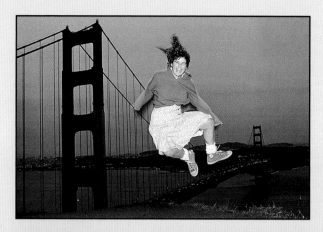

• 1/30 sec. Here, the subject "pops" out of the background, which is about two stops darker but still readable. F-STOP STAYS AT F/5.6.

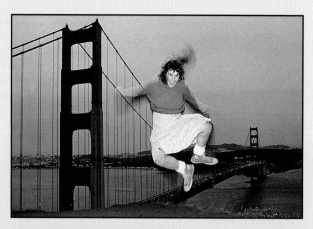

• 1/15 sec. The moving subject produces two images, the sharp one frozen by the electronic flash, the other blurring in the available light. The strobe's light lasts only a split second, thereby freezing the subject in mid-air, while the available light remains constant—lighting the subject's motion—throughout the entire exposure. The "ghosted" blur from the available light becomes noticeable only when the subject is moving. When the subject is stationary, the strobe and available light images exactly overlap. F-STOP STAYS AT F/5.6.

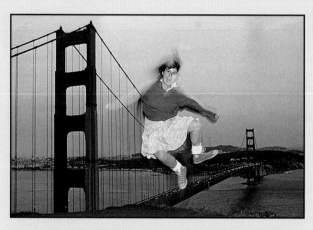

• 1/8 sec. Strobe/available light balance point for this lighting situation. As the shutter stays open longer, the available light image (the ghost) gets stronger. Here, the flash and ghost images become equal. At the point of equality, the picture is said to be balanced for flash and for available light. F-STOP STAYS AT F/5.6.

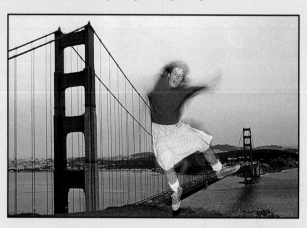

• 1/4 sec. As the shutter speed slows further, the available light begins to over-power both the background and the subject. The available light is washing out the flash picture. F-STOP STAYS AT F/5.6.

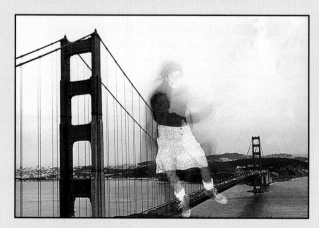

• 1/2 sec. At this exposure, the available light further overpowers the light from the strobe. The subject's face is starting to disappear. F-STOP STAYS AT F/5.6.

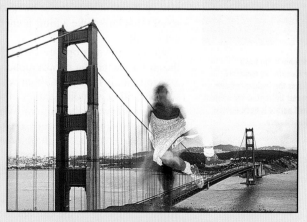

• 1 sec. The flash exposure leaves just the subject's legs and dress. The darker image is the subject's body after the jump. F-STOP STAYS AT F/5.6.

of the film's ISO automatically. You can select almost any lens aperture since the sensor is located behind the lens. When the flash fires, the light returns through the aperture and strikes the film or CCD. Regardless of where the flash is pointing, the internal sensor shuts off the strobe when it receives enough light.

A new generation of strobes, using 3D matrix metering, measures light reflected from the subject and compares this information with the subject's distance from the camera. If the through-the-lens (TTL) reading is wildly off the mark when compared with the distance to the subject, the camera will use its preprogrammed distance exposure instead. If, for example, the subject is only a few feet away but is wearing black, the auto sensor on a standard strobe would mistakenly direct the strobe to put out a lot of light, thereby overexposing the picture. With 3D matrix metering, the camera recognizes that, at this close distance, the light needed is much less than the reflected-light reading is reporting. The strobe, instead, would deliver the amount of light for a correct exposure at the close distance. The sensor won't be fooled by a subject wearing extremely light or dark clothes or standing out of the frame's center.

Other systems measure the available light and send out an infra-red beam that measures distance to the subject. Then the camera automatically selects the best aperture before making the final exposure.

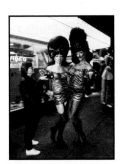

To check the flash exposure, an assistant holds the incident strobe meter in front of the subject and points it back toward the camera.

HAND-HELD STROBE METER
Unlike standard light meters, strobe meters can measure the fantastically short burst of light emitted by a strobe. Often the meters are accurate to within one-tenth of an f-stop. Most strobe meters measure incident light—the light falling on the subject. You'll recognize an incident light meter by its white sphere that looks like a ping-pong ball cut in half.

With the the appropriate ISO selected on the strobe meter, the photographer or an assistant holds the meter about where the subject will be standing and points the meter back toward the camera. When the strobe is fired, the meter measures the light falling on the sphere—light that would have struck the subject.

Note that the meter indicates the correct f-stop for that particular ISO. Now, leaving the strobe on manual, the photographer adjusts the f-stop on the camera to the setting indicated by the light meter.

Using a strobe meter works fine if the subject is a celebrity sitting for a portrait, but the measuring device proves more difficult to use if the subject is a crook running down the

courthouse steps. For fast-moving, slippery subjects, the internal sensor in the strobe or the through-the-lens sensor in the camera works best.

PROBLEMS TO AVOID WITH DIRECT STROBE
SHADOW ON THE WALL
The strobe mounted on the top or side of the camera produces a direct light aimed at the subject. At night, outside, or in a big gymnasium, direct strobe-on-camera works satisfactorily. However, direct strobe-on-camera

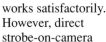

creates a harsh shadow behind a subject in a normal-sized, light-colored room.

To avoid the problem of the lurking black shadow, move the subject in front of a dark wall if possible. Now the black shadow created by the strobe will blend somewhat with the dark wall and be less prominent. Or move the subject away from the wall. If you and the subject move away from the wall, keeping the same distance between the two of you, the subject will receive the same amount of light, but the wall behind will get less. Again, the wall will darken and the obtrusive shadow will merge with the darkened wall and disappear.

Another way to eliminate unwanted shadows is to move the subject in front of a light source such as a window. The shadow will disappear into the light.

INCOMPLETE COVERAGE AREA
Some strobes have automatic zoom heads that allow you to adjust the area the light covers to match the lens on the camera. These units change the light pattern to coincide with the views of a range of lenses, usually from about 28mm to 85mm.

Most strobes, though, are designed to light only an area no wider than a 35mm lens. When you use a wider lens on your camera, you need to spread the light out farther.

For telephoto lenses, it helps to focus the light on a smaller area. Therefore, some strobes have attachments that will spread the light so the scene will be evenly illuminated (down to 20mm-lens coverage), or focus the light so that it will project farther.

REFLECTIONS
If you face someone wearing glasses to take a picture using strobe, often you will get an annoying bright reflection off the subject's

FRONT-LIGHTING

When the main light is placed close to the lens, few shadows are visible. Forms seem flattened and textures are less pronounced.

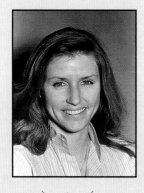

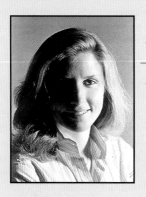

HIGH 45° LIGHTING

With the main light high and to the side of the camera, about 45°, shadows model the face, creating a more rounded shape. This is often the main light position used in commercial portrait studios.

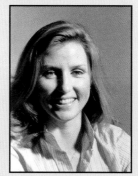

SIDE-LIGHTING

A main light that is at about a 90° angle to the camera will light the subject brightly on one side and cast long shadows across the other side.

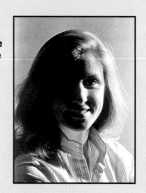

BACK-LIGHTING

Here the light is moved almost to the back of the subject. If the light were directly behind the person, her entire face would fall into shadow.

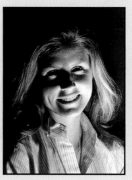

TOP-LIGHTING

The light is directly overhead and is casting dark shadows into the eye sockets and under the nose and chin. Few portrait subjects would pick this lighting arrangement.

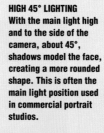

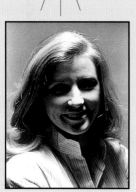

BOTTOM-LIGHTING

Lighting that comes from below looks distinctly odd in a portrait. This is because light on people outdoors or indoors almost never comes from below. This type of light casts unnatural shadows that often create a menacing effect.

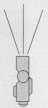

lenses. To avoid reflections of polished metal, glass, or eyeglasses, position the strobe at an angle to the reflective surface you are shooting.

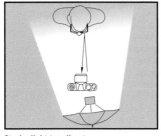
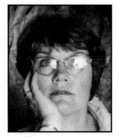

Strobe light too direct

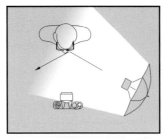
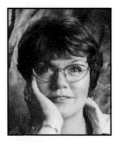

Strobe light angled farther to the right

UNEVEN LIGHTING

Sometimes you must photograph a group of people with direct strobe. A flash on the camera may overexpose group members nearest the light and underexpose those farthest from the light source. To avoid this problem, arrange the participants so they are approximately equidistant from the strobe light. When all the group's members are the same distance from the strobe, they will get the same amount of light and, therefore, be equally exposed.

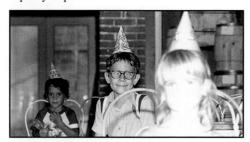

Subjects at different distances from strobe

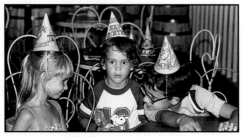

Subjects at same distance from strobe

CREATING DIFFERENT EFFECTS
OFF-CAMERA LIGHTING FOR BOLD EFFECT

Sometimes side lighting with direct strobe can add drama to a picture. To achieve this effect, remove the flash from the top of the camera. Attach the flash to the camera with a PC-extension cord or other remote-triggering device (see page 259). Aim the flash to the side so the light hits the side rather than the front of the subject. Moving the flash away from the camera will dramatically change the picture's light. (Also see pages 267 and 276 for pictures taken with strobe off-camera.)

BOUNCE STROBE FOR SOFTER LIGHT

To avoid the harsh effects of direct strobe, a photographer can bounce the strobe's light off a room's ceiling, walls, or any other light-colored surface.

The *Canton* (Ohio) *Repository's* Scott Heckel accompanied the girls' high school swim team to witness the first time their male counterparts shaved their legs for an upcoming swim meet. Because the locker room was too dark for shooting with available light, the photographer needed the extra light provided by a strobe. Heckel stayed outside the shower to watch for a girl's reaction. (See page 268).

Direct strobe on camera would have correctly lit the girl in the foreground but not the boys in the background. So Heckel bounced the light from his strobe off the ceiling, which provided even illumination so that the entire scene received the same amount of light.

When the light leaves the strobe, it comes out in a bundle of rays the size of the strobe face—about three inches in diameter, depending on the size of the flash.

The rays spread out as they head toward the ceiling. By the time they reach a typical ceiling, the rays cover an area about ten ten feet across. Because the surface of the ceiling is rough, the rays bounce off it in all directions, evenly lighting a much larger area below and leaving few shadows.

Bounce light has at least two advantages over direct strobe. Bounce light eliminates unattractive shadows, and it helps light a group of people evenly, removing the danger of burning out those in front or letting those in back go dark.

Not only can you bounce light off the ceiling, but you can also bounce light off a wall, partition, or any other large, opaque object. Light bounced off the ceiling results in a soft, relatively shadowless effect similar to that produced by fluorescent tubes found in most modern buildings. Light bounced off a wall or partition gives a more directional

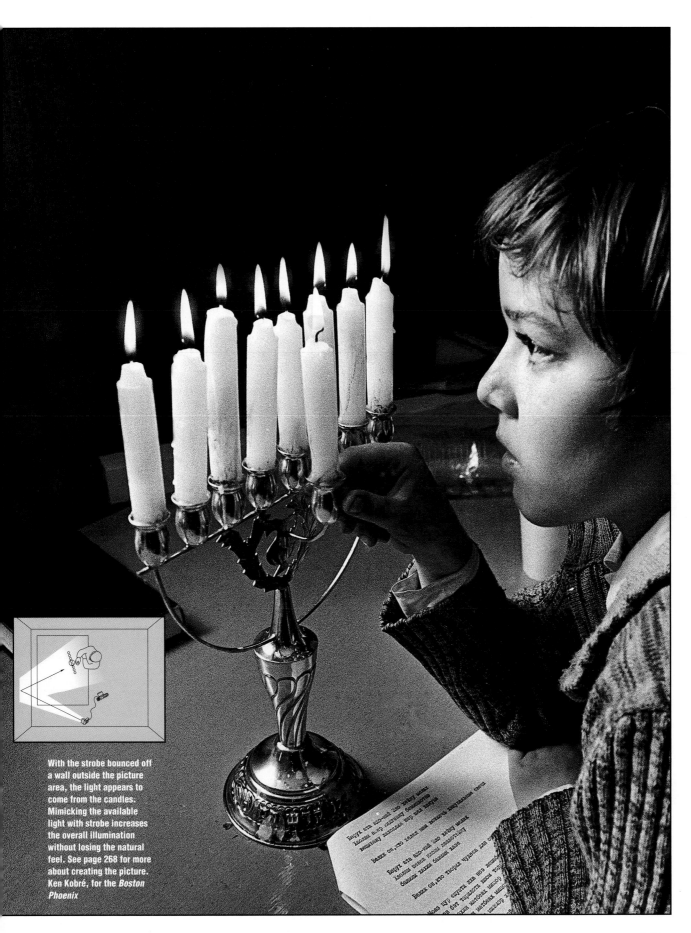

With the strobe bounced off a wall outside the picture area, the light appears to come from the candles. Mimicking the available light with strobe increases the overall illumination without losing the natural feel. See page 268 for more about creating the picture. Ken Kobré, for the *Boston Phoenix*

effect, such as light that comes from a window. The directional effect becomes more prominent the closer the subject and the flash are to the wall.

Many photographers attach a small white card behind and up about several inches from the top of the strobe head. The card picks up a little light when the strobe goes off and reflects the light into the subject's eye sockets. The reflected light avoids the raccoon look you can get with bounced light if you are standing near the subject.

When photographing a child lighting candles for Hanukkah, the author could have taken the picture by the available light from the candles. He knew, however, that in the final image the candles in relation to the boy's face were so bright that they would wash out. The rest of the picture would fall into deep shadow. Bouncing a strobe's light off a nearby wall gave the impression that the light was coming from the candles. The effect leaves both the candles and the young boy in sharp relief. (See page 267.)

Rather than bouncing the strobe off a wall, photographers find it more convenient to bounce the light off the inside of a white or silver-lined umbrella. A large umbrella on a light stand is easy to move around and position. The light bouncing out of an umbrella emulates the soft light from a north window. The demarcation between shadow and highlight on the subject is gradual rather than the abrupt line produced from a direct strobe. The shadow on the background becomes indistinct (pages 271 and 275).

For a soft effect with even more control photographers use a "soft box." The box consists of nylon fabric held together with tension rods. The box contains several layers of diffusion material inside and a translucent window. The strobe is mounted inside the box facing the window. The setup is mounted on a sturdy stand. The soft box gives a light effect similar to the umbrella, but the photographer can control fall-off at the edges of the light source more precisely (pages 270 and 275).

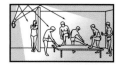

A female swimmer reacts after entering the boys' locker room to see the team shaving their bodies in preparation for the district meet. The photographer bounced the strobe off the ceiling to increase the overall illumination in the locker room and freeze movements by the subjects. Notice how the light from the bounce strobe falls off toward the back of the shower. There, the subjects are lit only by the available ceiling light.
Scott Heckel, *Canton* [Ohio] *Repository*

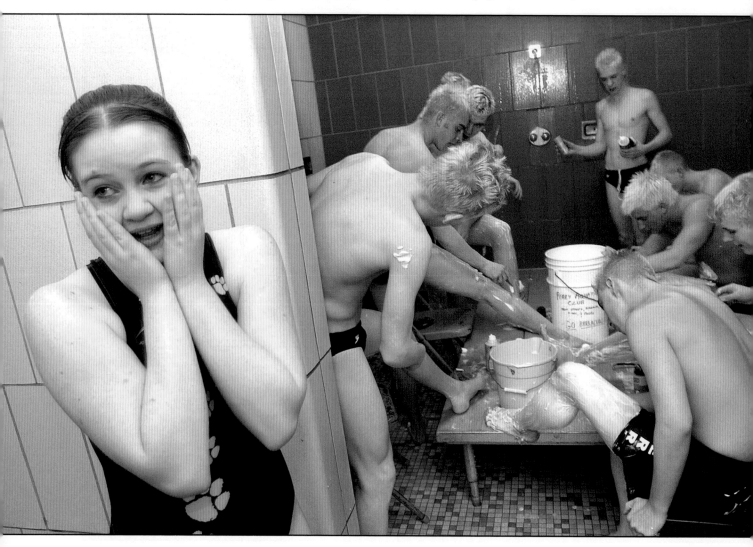

CAUTION WITH BOUNCE FLASH

The light leaving the face of a strobe is spread over a wide area when it reaches the bounce surface. When it strikes a ceiling, wall, or umbrella, the light is partly absorbed by the surface. Once reflected off that surface, the light scatters in many directions. With bounce strobe, then, much less light reaches the subject than when you are using direct strobe. With bounce strobe, use caution:

- Save the bounce-flash technique for medium to small rooms.
- In an auditorium or gymnasium, the ceilings are usually so far away that not enough light will return from the ceiling to light up your subject adequately.
- Bounce your strobe off a light-toned surface. A dark wall, for example, will absorb the light rather than reflect it back toward your subject.

- Small, cigarette-pack-sized strobes don't put out enough power to produce an efficient bounce light in most rooms.
- With color film, don't bounce your strobe light off a pink, blue, or any other colored surface. The tint will color the strobe's light, giving the whole picture a color-cast that you may not like.

- When you bounce a strobe that has a sensor eye, make sure the eye remains pointed toward the subject. Don't try to bounce with a unit that has a sensor that points only at the bounce surface.
- When bouncing, always set the strobe for its widest automatic aperture. Bounce works perfectly with a medium-to-large portable strobe, in a normal room, with eight-to-ten-foot-high white ceilings and a subject standing within three to twenty feet of the photographer.

Aim Correctly . . .

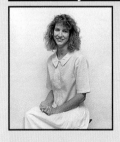

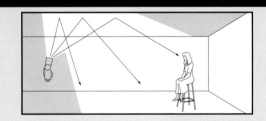

◄ When bouncing, aim the strobe carefully so that all the light bounces off the ceiling.

. . . or Pay the Price

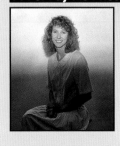

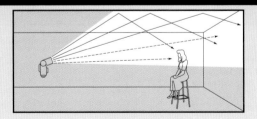

◄ Do not aim the strobe too low, or direct light from the strobe's head will hit the subject, producing an undesirable uneven lighting effect.

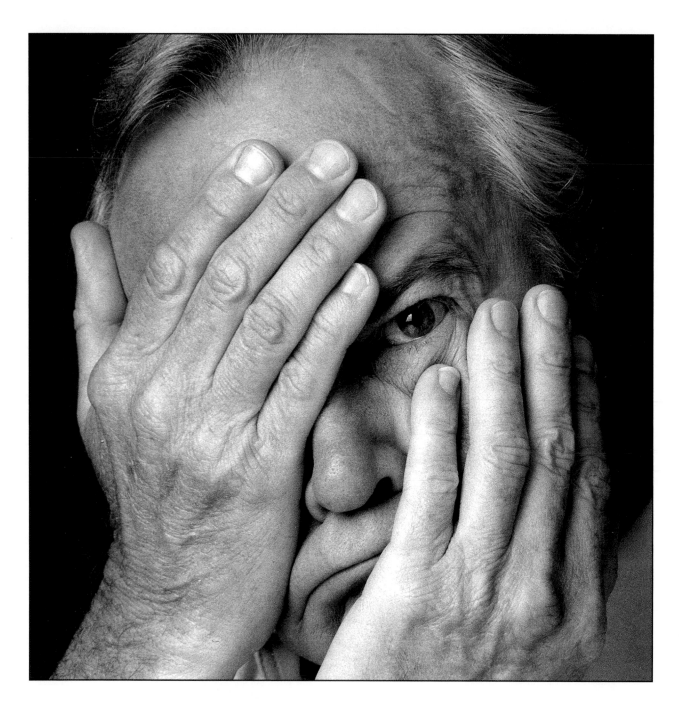

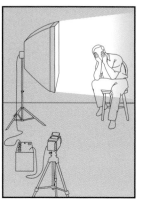

To achieve a broad, relatively soft, lighting effect for this photograph of Jack Lemmon, the photographer used a single, large soft box in front and slightly to the left of the actor.
Michael Grecco, Inc., for Jack Lemmon

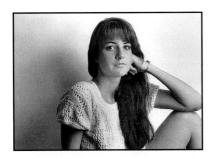

Two and a half feet from subject

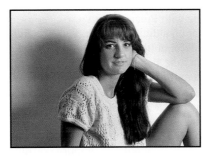

Six and a half feet from subject

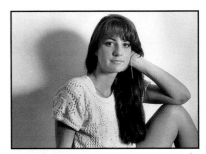

Eleven feet from subject

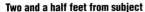

Whether the light is from an umbrella (like these examples) or from a soft box (see opposite and page 273), the shadows it produces will be softer and less distinct when the source is near the subject, and sharper and more defined as the light source is moved away. Ron Bingham, *Edging West* magazine

FILL-FLASH HANDLES HEAVY SHADOWS

At noon on a sunny day, the sun's harsh light can leave some subjects buried in shadow while others scorch in the sunlight. Shadowed eye sockets on faces turn into raccoon-like masks. Fill-flash to the rescue.

The light from the strobe opens the shadow areas of subjects who are within ten or fifteen feet of the strobe. With fill-flash, light from the strobe fills in the shadows without overpowering the highlights. You will find fill-flash particularly useful when you shoot color transparencies, which can record hue and texture in either brightly lit areas or deeply shadowed ones, but not both at the same time.

If important shadow areas meter more than one or two stops darker than highlight areas, adding fill light will probably improve your picture. (See page 272.)

Many portable strobes today have a fill-flash setting that automatically balances the available and strobe light. In fact, some strobes allow you to dial in just the amount of fill-flash you might want to use. You can let the strobe balance the fill or adjust it yourself to put out one to three stops less than the available light.

POWERING THE STROBE
SHOE-MOUNT STROBES

Most shoe-mount strobes are powered by AA batteries. Lithium batteries last the longest but are the most expensive choice.

Alkaline and NiCad batteries are easily available, but rechargeable batteries are cheaper over the long haul.

Rechargeable nickel-cadmium batteries (NiCads), which store the least amount of juice, do provide a consistent recycle time before they completely and suddenly lose their charges. Lithium and Alkaline batteries, on the other hand, run down gradually,

resulting in excessively long recycle times as they wear out.

ALERT: Always carry backup batteries. Nothing is more frustrating than waiting eons for dying batteries to recycle the strobe.

While Lithium, Alkaline, and NiCad batteries designed for shoe-mounted strobes are convenient, none provide enough power for more than a few rolls of 36-exposure film when the flash is used at full power.

As Jon Falk says in his book, ***Adventures in Location Lighting***, "Throw away all wimpy AA and NiCad battery clusters." Many photojournalists who need power continuously over an extended time turn to external rechargeable batteries. It is possible to recharge these external low- or high-voltage batteries repeatedly.

Some of these batteries attach to a belt, screw onto the bottom of the camera, attach with Velcro onto the strobe back, or hang from a shoulder strap. What they all have in common is the ability to provide 100 to 350 flashes at full power—some with less than a two-second delay between complete strobe recharge. These external batteries have become a mandatory part of most working pros' flash kits.

MEDIUM-POWERED STROBES

The typical battery-powered strobe most photographers use has a maximum output of 50 watt-seconds of light. When working with slow transparency film, many photographers have turned to more powerful portable strobes that can generate anywhere from 200 to 1,200 watt-seconds.

Although heavier and more costly, these strobes provide the needed light power for using umbrellas or soft boxes with slow films. With some of these medium-powered portable strobes, you can add on batteries for more power.

AC-POWERED STROBES

Unless you're testing with Polaroids or viewing the LCD monitor on a digital camera, you can't see lighting effects until you have developed your film—after the shoot has ended. With most AC-powered strobes, a modeling light is built into the strobe head. This allows you to see where the light will fall without anxiety, or even a lot of test shots.

Manufacturers have built AC-powered strobes with tremendous light output—important when working with slow color films.

Also, large-format cameras like the 4"x5" or 8"x10" view camera need this quantity of light for maximum depth of field. Much of the photography shot in studios requires high-output power supplies. You can buy an AC-powered strobe with 500, 1,000, 2,400, 4,800 or more watt-seconds of light. These AC-powered units can drive two or more strobe heads at the same time.

Many photographers regularly haul medium-sized AC units on assignment. These allow shooting color film at small apertures—

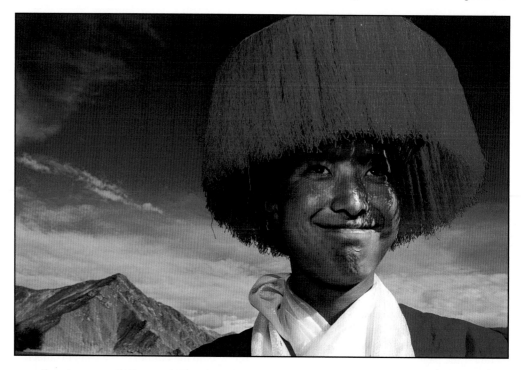

Without fill-flash adding light to the Tibetan horseman's face, the subject would be lost in a shadow from his hat. John Kaplan, Gainesville, Florida

FILL-FLASH

You can use strobe outdoors on a bright day to help fill in deep shadows on a subject if the person is within ten or fifteen feet from the camera. Some of the dedicated camera/strobe combinations will allow you to select the ratio of fill-flash to available light. The camera and strobe do the rest automatically.

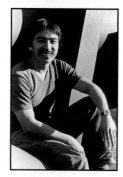

AVAILABLE LIGHT left the subject's face obscured in shadow.

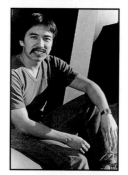

FILL-FLASH ONE STOP LESS bright than the available light from the sun leaves open but delineated shadows as well as catch-lights in each eye. The subject looks well-lit but natural.

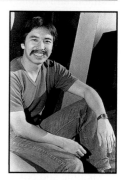

FILL-FLASH BALANCED with the available light from the sun eliminates almost all shadows but looks overly lit in this situation.

and they also provide fast, dependable recycling. High-wattage strobes with modeling lights allow photographers to light a room and see where all the shadows will fall. While these strobes usually have more power than a portable unit, they also require AC power and are consequently less convenient than their smaller counterparts. AC units always operate on manual, so a handheld strobe meter is necessary to determine exposure.

When shooting outdoors, remember to bring along either a long extension cord or a portable generator. The strobes' fast recycling, practically limitless number of flashes, and powerful light output make them ideal for multiple-light photography.

PHOTOJOURNALISM GOES HOLLYWOOD

With the increasing use of color, photographers often are lighting scenes with several strobes. Fine-grain transparency film requires lots of light. Neither transparency film nor digital images can handle great brightness differences within a scene. Suppose you are taking pictures that include the corporate president inside his fifty-second floor office and the sun-drenched, spectacular view outside his window.

The eye has no trouble seeing both the wrinkles on the president's face and the sparkling bay outside. But this brightness range is beyond the capability of transparency film or the digital camera. You may need to

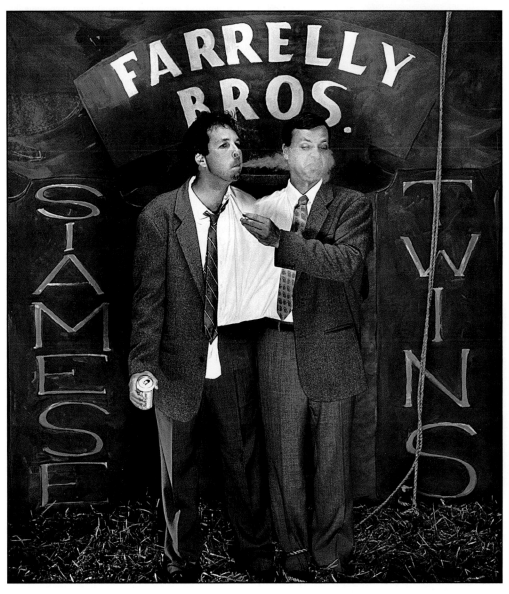

To produce this edgy picture of the Farrelly brothers, who wrote and directed the comedy films "Dumb and Dumber" and "Something About Mary," the photographer hired a set builder to paint a circus scene on a backdrop. He rented the props from a costume shop to create this carnival sideshow atmosphere. To light the set, he used a soft box near the camera as well as a small soft box, low and to the left of the subjects.
Michael Grecco, Inc., for *Entertainment Weekly*

When a wall or ceiling is not available for bouncing the strobe light, photographers use a number of other techniques and devices to attempt to soften the light and reduce shadows. Umbrellas and softboxes take the concentrated bundle of light coming from the strobe's face and broaden it before the light heads toward the subject. The broader the light source, the softer the effect. (See demos on opposite page.)

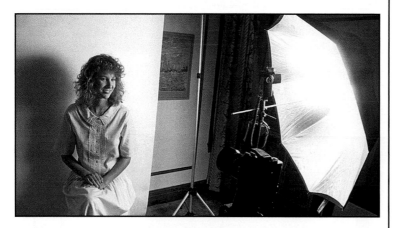

UMBRELLA

Because direct strobe light comes from a small light source, it produces a harsh effect on the subject. Light bounced off the ceiling is soft but produces somewhat featureless pictures. Many photographers use photographic umbrellas as alternatives.

The photographic umbrella is similar to a standard rain umbrella, only the inside is covered with a white or silver material, and the handle can easily be attached to a light stand. When the photographer aims the strobe into the center of the umbrella, out comes a soft white blanket of light that wraps around the subject. Because the umbrella is on a light stand, the photographer can move it easily from side to side or up and down—allowing for total control of the light's direction. The nearer the light to the subject, the more the rays will encircle the person.

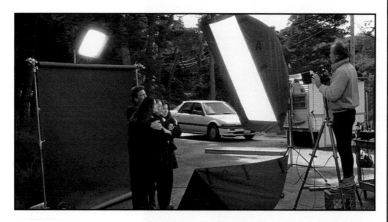

SOFT BOX

The strobe is attached inside a lightweight nylon box that contains diffusion panels to evenly spread the light. The result is a window-like light that is portable. Compared to reflecting light off an umbrella, the soft box gives more even light with a defined edge.

In the setup above, A is the main light, B is the fill light, and C is the hair light.
Deborah Whitney Prince

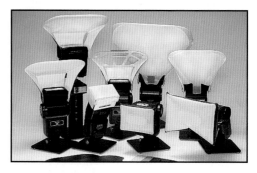

LITTLE EFFECT FROM SMALL DIFFUSERS

Small devices placed over the strobe increase the effective light area somewhat. Some attempt to combine the characteristics of direct and bounce light. The indirect light bouncing off the ceilings and walls is supposed to help soften the direct light coming straight from the strobe. Others are supposed to enlarge the effective light source by reflecting light off an angled hood to scatter the rays so that they will bounce off nearby surfaces and further soften the light on the subject.

However, if you look at the tests on the opposite page, you will see that small diffusers are not effective at all outdoors. Indoors, the diffuser actually is not as effective as bouncing the light off a ceiling or wall.

Generally, diffusers work best not in softening light but in broadening it. When using direct strobe aimed at the subject, the light might not spread evenly across a wide area.

This problem occurs when you are shooting with a wide-angle lens. The diffusers help spread the light so that when you take a picture with a wide-angle lens the light will be even from corner to corner. The small diffusers will give satisfactory results when the ceiling is low, but keep in mind that in the same circumstances, you could just as easily bounce the light off the with no accessory at all.

Indoors   Indoors   Outdoors
no reflective surfaces

The harshest light comes from a camera-mounted strobe aimed at the subject. So photographers use different accessories to soften the light and reduce dark shadows behind the subject.

Generally, the larger the effective light source, the softer the light will be. The light from a 3'x4' soft box will produce softer light than the light from a 2"x3" direct strobe. When you bounce light off a ceiling, the effective light source becomes the wide spot on that ceiling. Photographic umbrellas, whether you are shooting through them or reflecting off them, also provide a relatively large light source, depending on their size.

Although smaller devices such as the Omnidome and Lumiquest Pocket Bouncer are not as effective as the larger light sources, many of the smaller items work well indoors. In a light-colored room, some light rays bounce off the ceiling, walls, and floor. This extra scattered light helps soften the shadows when the devices are used within a small room.

Outdoors or in a large ballroom or gymnasium, all the accessories work less well at softening shadows. The scattered light rays coming from the accessories have few surfaces to bounce off. Notice, in the outdoor series, that the shadow behind the model is darker in almost each situation. For these tests, the strobe was located nine feet from the subject.

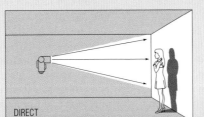
DIRECT

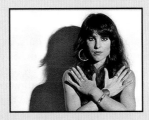

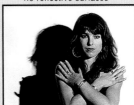

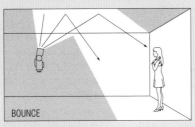
BOUNCE

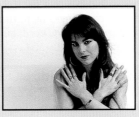

NO CEILING
OUTDOORS

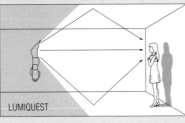
LUMIQUEST

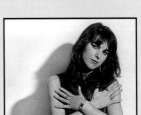

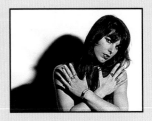

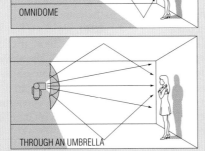
OMNIDOME

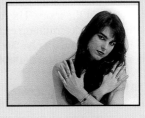

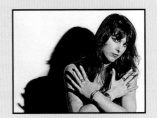

THROUGH AN UMBRELLA

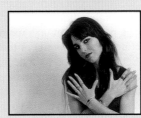

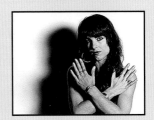

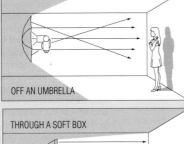
OFF AN UMBRELLA

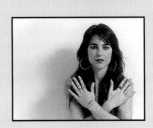

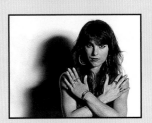

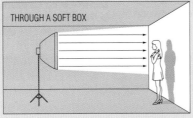
THROUGH A SOFT BOX

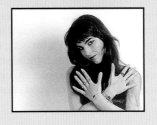

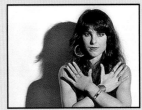

Photos by John Burgess

set up several lights to bring the two worlds into brightness balance.

Sometimes you may simply want more control of a scene than the light from one strobe can produce. You want to produce a special effect. Perhaps you seek to add a highlight to someone's hair, or you want to feature one member of a group more than the rest, or you want to use a light on either side of a dancer to emphasize the person's form.

For another approach, use an AC-power supply with cords running to each strobe head. You can trigger them from your camera with a hard-wired PC cord, an infrared trigger, or a radio slave.

WHERE TO PLACE THE LIGHTS
LIGHTING A WHOLE ROOM

To light an entire room, you can set up several strobes around the room and bounce all of them off the ceiling or off umbrellas. Even if the room is not perfectly evenly lit—a common problem in this circumstance—you can still shoot freely by taking a reading with your handheld strobe meter at different parts of the room ahead of time. Knowing the predetermined exposure readings, you can leave the lights in one place, and as you move from one area to another, adjust the aperture for each section of the room. This technique of lighting and predetermining exposure allows you to shoot in a relatively candid manner, even with slow film and multiple lights.

MULTILIGHT SET-UP

While you will find no two lighting situations identical, you often can use a basic lighting combination (see page 274) for shooting portraits: set up a main light and reflect it into an umbrella or through a soft box. Set the light about 45 degrees to one side of the camera. Bring the light as near as possible to the subject while still evenly lighting the person. This is your main light. Next, use a large reflector card to bounce light into the shadow side of the subject's face. Attach a second strobe to a boom, a weighted arm that extends over the subject's head. Locate the strobe above and behind the subject to provide a hair light. Direct a third light toward the background.

Setting up multiple lights can result in time delays as well as accidents caused by the cords running from the camera to the strobes. To eliminate the need for long cords between your camera and strobes, you can use a "photo slave," which is an optical sensor that will fire a strobe. Attach the slave to your strobe with a hot shoe or a PC connection. Put a second strobe on your camera. Now the light from the camera's strobe will activate the photo slave and fire the remote strobe.

You can replace the strobe on your camera with an infrared trigger that emits infrared light instead of strobe light. High-sensitivity photo slaves such as those made by Wein will pick up the infrared light and fire remote strobes from distances as great as 500 feet.

As long as a slave is attached to each flash unit, you can fire as many as you like. You also can fire multiple strobes without cords by using a radio transmitter attached to the camera and receivers on the strobes.

Several strobe manufacturers sell units with built-in slave sensors. These permit firing two or more flashes simultaneously, allowing you to control the light to produce a perfectly exposed picture.

CONTROLLING MULTIPLE STROBES FROM THE CAMERA

Some camera manufacturers, including Nikon and Canon, have developed systems from which it is possible to control the flash output of multiple strobes individually and simultaneously—from the camera itself. The systems employ a built-in wireless transmitter that controls multiple remote strobes set-up as slave units. The photographer can adjust the output of each unit separately in order to achieve any lighting ratio. The camera's through-the-lens (TTL) system will then correctly expose the image even though the light is coming from two or more strobe units, with no cords connecting them to the camera.

ALERT: Unless it has a special frequency, the slave-eye can be tricked. If any other flash in the area fires, the slave-eye can accidentally trip your remote units. The setup works best when other pros are not firing their strobes and, even more irritating, when amateurs are not around with their instant cameras. ■

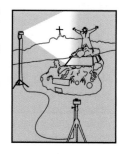

The photographer shot "The Buick of Unconditional Love" for a story about art cars. The image was made just after sunset while there was still enough light to illuminate the monument behind the car. The photographer stationed a portable flash on a stand to the left, and fired it directly at the subject. The strobe light was adjusted so that it was slightly brighter than the available light on the monument. The exposure was f/8 at 1/8 sec. Paolo Vescia, for SF Weekly, San Francisco

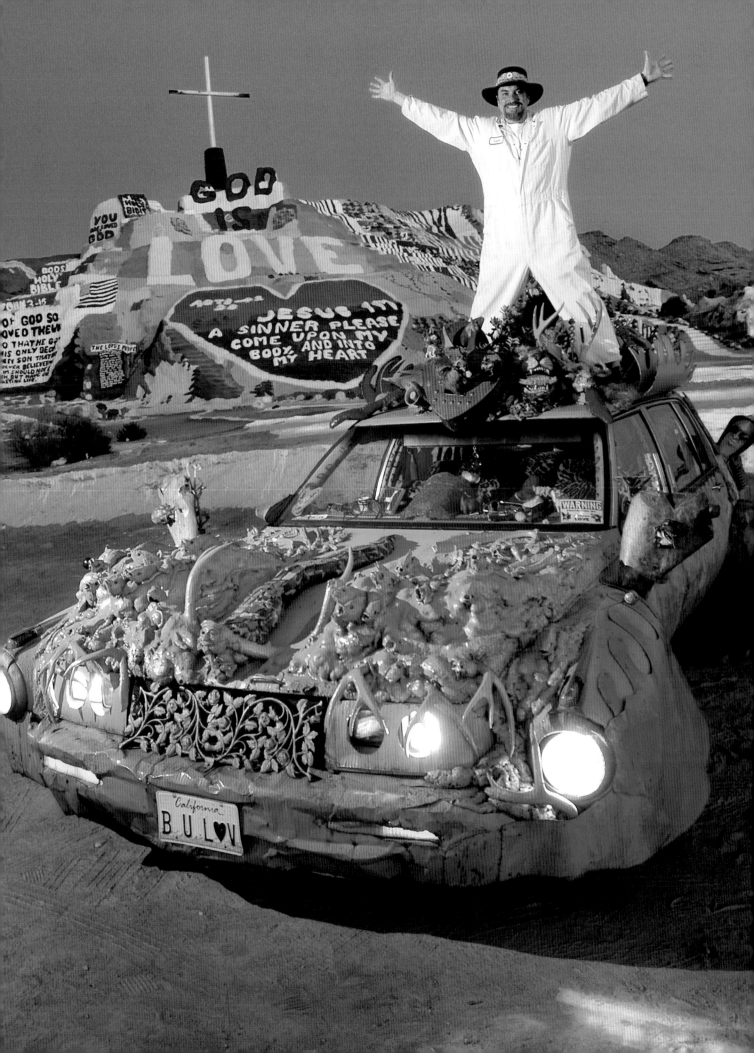

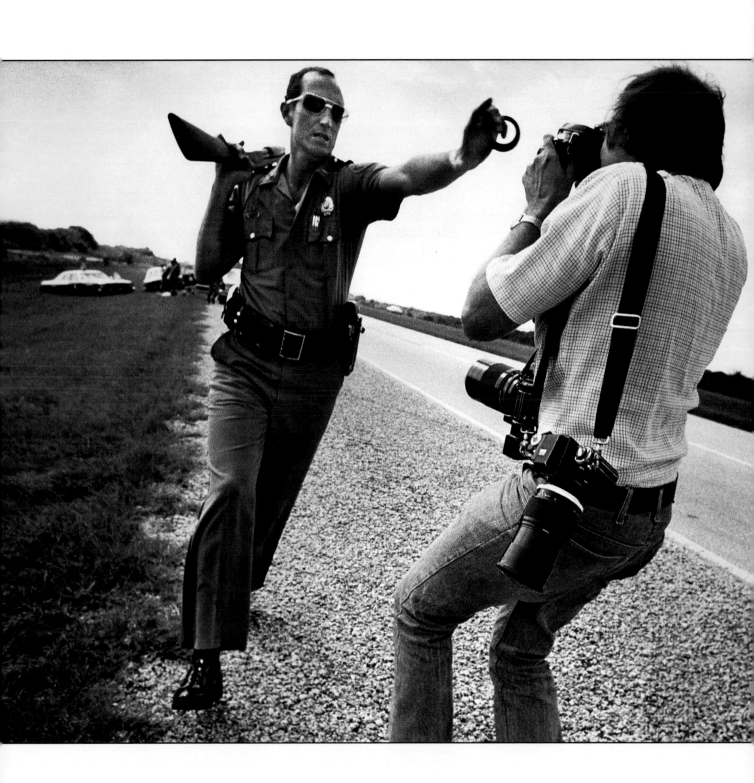

Chapter 13

Law

WHERE CAN PHOTOJOURNALISTS TAKE PICTURES?

You may photograph in most public places and in a wide variety of publicly owned property. You can take pictures on main street, on the sidewalk next

to main street, in Golden Gate Park, as well as at a city-owned zoo.

This chapter was revised with the help of Dr. Michael Sherer, Department of Communication, University of Nebraska at Omaha

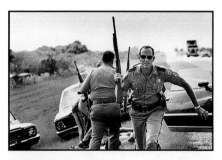

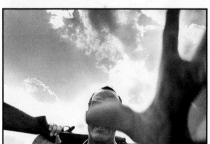

You can photograph in a city-owned airport like Logan in Boston or O'Hare in Chicago. Some restrictions, such as not going onto an airplane runway, do apply. You can photograph on the campus of a

A state trooper illegally tried to block the cameras of two photographers from the Palm Beach Post who were covering the arrest of an armed robber.
Opposite page, C.J. Walker. Near left top and bottom photos, Ken Steinhoff, *Palm Beach Post*

publicly owned higher education institution like Florida State University or the University of Michigan. The law does not forbid taking pictures in a lab, a classroom, or a gym. However, without the teacher's permission, you can't take pictures of Mr. Weintraub's physics class or Miss Herbrich's English class while they are in session.

TAKING PICTURES IN PUBLIC PLACES

Although a public grade school or high school is publicly owned, it falls under its principal's jurisdiction. While there is no law against photographing inside public schools, the principal has the authority to determine who comes and goes on school grounds, effectively granting or denying access to photojournalists. Typically, you can gain access to these buildings with permission from someone in authority that works in the principal's office.

You may take pictures of elected officials or private citizens in public places, such as on the street or in the park. They may be the center of interest in your photo, or just part of the crowd. If a news event occurs on public property, then you may cover that event as long as you do not interfere with police or the flow of traffic.

There are times when bystanders try to physically prevent photographers from taking pictures. In such instances, the courts have generally protected photographers when they shoot in public places, according to George Chernoff and Hershel Sarbin in their book *Photography and the Law*. They note that, some years ago, the state of New York even made it unlawful to damage the equipment of news photographers engaged in the pursuit of their occupation in public places.

Difficulties arise when police authorities try to stop photographers from shooting on public property. In many situations, an overeager police officer may block a photographer's lens.

In Iowa, photographers were once prevented by highway patrol officers and the National Guard from taking close-ups at the scene of a civilian airline crash. When airline officials arrived, photographers were given a free hand. In Philadelphia, police forcibly prevented photographers from taking pictures as officials bounced a heckler from a political rally. Philadelphia's city solicitor issued a formal opinion in which he told the police commissioner, "Meaningful freedom of the press includes the right to photograph and disseminate pictures of public events occurring in public places."

Police and fire officials have the right to restrict any activity of a photographer that might interfere with the officials' actions. But taking pictures and asking questions do not constitute interference.

Unfortunately, if an insistent police officer stops you at the scene of a breaking-news

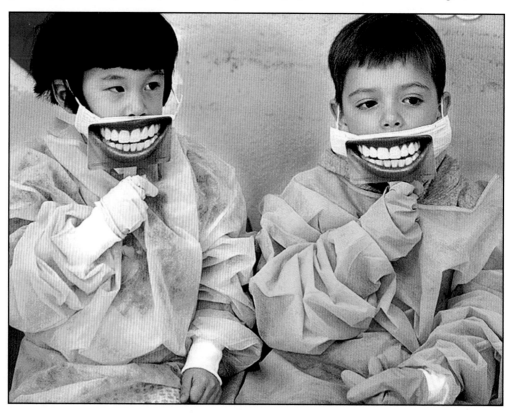

You can take pictures of children in public places, such as at the community center where these children were photographed. At a school, you would need permission of the principal to enter the school grounds.
Chris Riley, *Gilroy* [California] *Dispatch*

event, you might find it hard to argue a fine point of law. Photographers who disregard police directives—even if they have the right to be where they are—can be arrested for disorderly conduct or for interfering within the performance of a police officer's duty. Continuing to take pictures or failing to move after a policeman gives you a direct order could constitute a possible felony. The National Press Photographers Association (NPPA) and some of its chapters have for years worked with fire and police academies to improve the graduates' understanding of the role of the news media in society. NPPA members have written police/press guidelines designed to reduce the conflict between working photojournalists and law enforcement officers. The result has been improved cooperation between photographers and fire and police personnel.

GOVERNMENT BUILDINGS:
PUBLIC BUT UNDER SPECIAL RULES

Although facilities may be publicly owned, a photographer does not have unlimited access to government buildings, such as the U.S. Senate and House of Representatives, the state legislature, or the chambers of the city council. The mayor's office and city hospital also fall under the special-rules category. Military bases and jails also are strictly controlled, especially in the aftermath of the 2001 terrorist attacks in the United States.

Hospitals, even if they are publicly owned, publicly supported, and publicly operated, occupy a special place under the law. It's true that the admission list to hospitals is public information, but that's about all. You might be allowed to photograph scenes in a hospital for, say, a feature story. But check your pictures. Are there people in the pictures? Yes. Are some of them patients? Yes. Are they identifiable? Yes. Do you have a release? No. You say the people in the photo are "incidental"? For instance, a picture taken of a corridor or waiting room shows several people sitting and reading magazines. Don't even think about it. You must either (a) get a release; (b) not run the picture.

The halls of the U.S. Congress are certainly public places, as are meeting rooms of state legislatures and city councils. But such places are generally run by their own unique rules. Even though the House of Representatives does allow television cameras limited access to debates, this legislative body will not allow photographers to take still pictures at a regular session of Congress. Senators and congressmen are afraid that the uncensored film of the still photographer will catch one of the members of this august body

WHERE AND WHEN A PHOTOJOURNALIST CAN SHOOT				
	ANYTIME	IF NO ONE OBJECTS	WITH RESTRICTIONS	ONLY WITH PERMISSION
PUBLIC AREA				
Street	X			
Sidewalk	X			
Airport			X	
Beach	X			
Park	X			
Zoo	X			
Train Station	X			
Bus Station	X			
IN PUBLIC SCHOOL				
Preschool			X	
Grade School			X	
High School			X	
University Campus	X			
Class in Session				X
IN PUBLIC AREA— WITH RESTRICTIONS				
Police Headquarters			X	
Government Buildings			X	
Courtroom				X
Prisons				X
Military Bases				X
Legislative Chambers				X
IN MEDICAL FACILITIES				
Hospital				X
Rehab Center				X
Emergency Van				X
Mental Health Center				X
Doctor's Office				X
Clinic				X
PRIVATE BUT OPEN TO THE PUBLIC				
Movie Theater Lobby		X		
Business Office		X		
Hotel Lobby		X		
Restaurant		X		
Casino				X
Museum			X	
Shopping Mall				X
Store in Mall				X
PRIVATE AREAS VISIBLE TO THE PUBLIC				
Window of Home	X			
Porch	X			
Lawn	X			
IN PRIVATE				
Home		X		
Porch		X		
Lawn		X		
Apartment		X		
Hotel Room		X		
Car		X		

taking a nap, reading the newspaper, or, as is more often the situation, absent from his or her seat. Photographers are usually allowed in the U.S. House or Senate chambers only during ceremonial sessions, such as the opening day of Congress.

Photographers can snap legislators in committee meetings, elected officials in the halls of Congress, or legislators in their offices. Certain buildings—the Capitol and its grounds, all House and Senate office buildings, the Library of Congress, and the General Accounting Office—are controlled entirely by rules passed by Congress. The Constitution grants Congress the right to formulate the rules for operating these buildings. These rules are not subject to judicial review.

THE COURTROOM: ANOTHER SPECIAL SITUATION

The U.S. Supreme Court does forbid the presence of photographers in federal but not in state courtrooms.

The effort of photojournalists to obtain access rights to both federal and state courtrooms has had a turbulent history. A low-water mark in photographing in the courtroom occurred during the trial of Bruno

Richard Hauptmann for the kidnapping and murder of Charles Lindbergh's infant child. Lindbergh had captured the world's imagination and admiration for his nonstop, solo, trans-Atlantic flight. The kidnapping and murder of his child attracted international interest, and an estimated 700 reporters, including 129 photographers, came to the old courthouse in Flemington, New Jersey, to cover the trial. Photographers were allowed to take pictures in the courtroom only three times each day: before court convened, at noon recess, and after court adjourned. Early in the trial, however, a photographer took unauthorized pictures of Lindbergh on the stand. The photographer claimed that he was "new on the job, having been sent as a relief man, and he did not know the rulings."

Another illegal picture was taken at the end of the trial. Dick Sarno of the *New York Mirror* concealed a 35mm Contax camera when he entered the courtroom on February 13, 1935, the day the verdict and sentence were announced.

At the key moment of the proceedings, Sarno, who had wrapped his Contax in a muffler to conceal the noise, took a

During Bruno Richard Hauptmann's trial for kidnapping and killing Charles Lindbergh's baby, the judge prohibited photographers from taking pictures while court was in session. On January 3, 1935, Lindbergh himself took the stand. Despite the judge's orders, a photographer snapped this picture during the trial. Following this incident, with only a few exceptions, trial cameras were barred from the courtrooms until the 1970s.

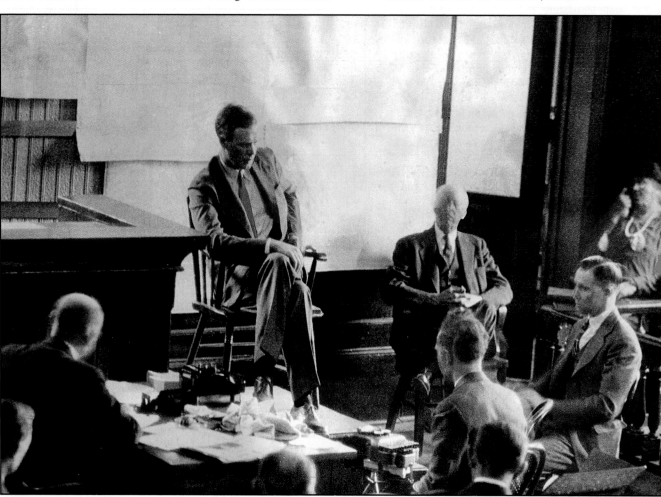

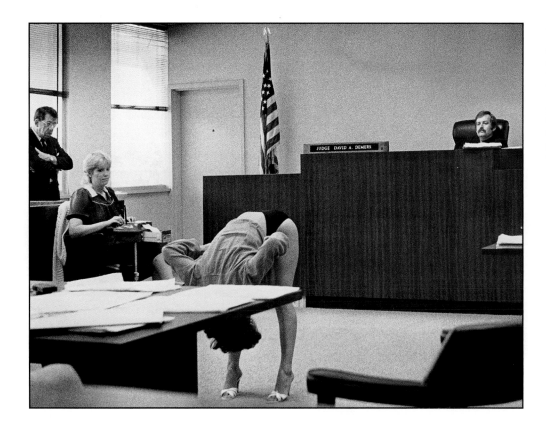

one-second exposure of the courtroom. Sarno later related, "As Hauptmann stood up and faced the jury, you could hear a pin drop. I tilted the camera, which I had braced on the balcony rail. The judge was directly in front and below me. If he looked up, I was sure he could see me."

As the foreman of the jury stood to recite the verdict, Sarno recorded the instant.

Prejudicial press reports, contemptuous statements by trial attorneys and police, the rowdy behavior of the 150 spectators and numerous reporters added to the holiday atmosphere of the proceeding, according to extensive research by Sherry Alexander in her report, "Curious History: The ABA Code of Judicial Ethics Canon 35." The raucous atmosphere created by journalists covering the trial outside the courtroom as they mobbed each witness, as well as indiscretions by still and newsreel cameramen inside the courtroom, shocked a committee of the American Bar Association (ABA) that reviewed the legal proceedings in 1936.

Nevertheless, Alexander found, the original ABA Committee did not recommend a total exclusion of photography and broadcasting in the courtroom.

Instead, it was the 1937 convention of the group that adopted a flat ban on cameras in court as the 35th Canon of Professional and Judicial Ethics. Many states, but not all, adopted these canons, effectively slamming the courtroom door shut on photojournalists for forty years.

Courtroom restrictions easing

Florida's judicial system and legal code are viewed as the model to follow by many states. In the late 1970s, when the Florida Supreme Court opened the courtroom to photographers and television equipment on a limited basis for a one-year period, the event was significant. The Florida test allowed nationwide broadcast of the trial of 15-year-old Ronnie Zamora, who was charged with killing his 82-year-old neighbor.

Zamora's attorneys tried to blame television for the murder committed by their client. Noting that he avidly watched Kojak, a popular detective program, defense attorneys claimed the boy was under "involuntary subliminal television intoxication."

While the defense proved unsuccessful, the experiment allowing photographers to cover the trial worked well. With modern fast films and compact electronic television cameras, photographers did not require excessive lighting, and their behavior did not interfere with the trial's progress. Florida permanently opened its courts to the camera.

In 1980, the Supreme Court upheld the constitutionality of Florida's open courts law.

In *Chandler v Florida*, two police officers convicted of burglarizing a restaurant claimed that the presence of TV cameras

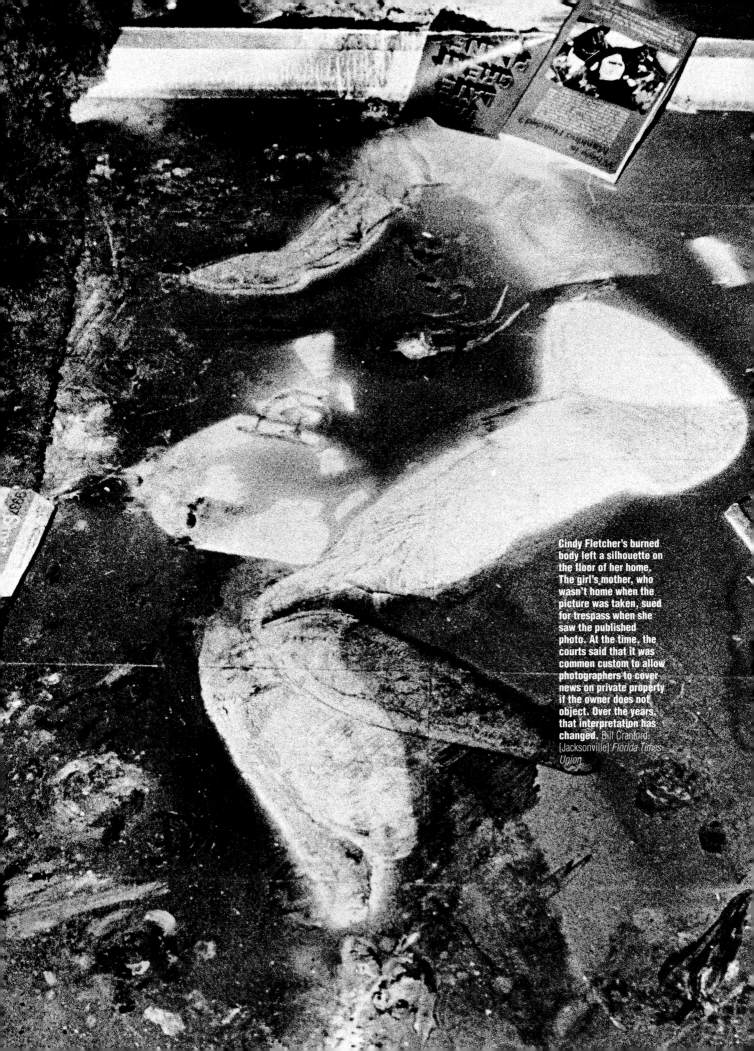

Cindy Fletcher's burned body left a silhouette on the floor of her home. The girl's mother, who wasn't home when the picture was taken, sued for trespass when she saw the published photo. At the time, the courts said that it was common custom to allow photographers to cover news on private property if the owner does not object. Over the years, that interpretation has changed. Bill Cranford, [Jacksonville] *Florida Times-Union*

denied them a right to a fair trial because local stations broadcast only highlights of the prosecution's case.

But when the Supreme Court considered the officers' appeal, the justices ruled unanimously that states are not prohibited from allowing still and television cameras in their courts. The decision was a major victory for photojournalists' First Amendment rights.

In spite of research indicating that most state Supreme Court justices dislike cameras in the courtroom, all states have opened their trials to camera coverage. There is even a cable television channel devoted to covering trials. Each state, however, continues to have unique and individual restrictions. Some states permit only coverage of criminal trials and then only with the defendant's permission. Other states prohibit coverage of sex-crime trials or divorce proceedings. Some states allow coverage of first trials but not appeals. Verify your state's regulations before shooting. Also check with the presiding judge before taking pictures in a courtroom.

Cameras are still banned in federal trial courts and in the U.S. Supreme Court.

TAKING JOURNALISTIC PICTURES IN PRIVATELY OWNED PLACES

Without going onto a person's property, you may, from the street, photograph someone in her yard, on her porch, or even inside her house if you can see the person. You don't need the subject's permission. For instance, the courts consider people sitting on their verandas, mowing their lawns, or standing behind a picture window in their living rooms to be in "public view" and therefore legitimate subjects for photography.

The photographer still should be somewhat cautious when shooting onto private property, however, and should not step onto the grounds to get the picture. Nor should the photographer use an extremely long telephoto lens, which would capture more than the naked eye could see.

In fact, the court says you shouldn't go to any extra trouble to get this porch-sitting, lawn-mowing, or window-standing shot. You shouldn't even climb a tree to gain a better view. Although not all photographers follow these guidelines, all are limited essentially to the view of an average passerby, according to the courts.

PHOTOGRAPHING NEWS ON PRIVATE PROPERTY
Access vs. Trespass

Cindy Fletcher, 14 years old, died in a house fire in Jacksonville, Florida. Her mother, away at the time, learned about the tragedy in the next day's edition of the *Times-Union*.

Alongside the story appeared a picture that showed where her daughter's burned body had left a silhouette scorched on the floor. Newspaper photographer Bill Cranford had entered the Fletcher home to take the photo. Mrs. Fletcher sued the Florida Publishing Company, owner of the *Times-Union*, on grounds that the photographer had invaded her home, hence her privacy.

This actual court case serves to illustrate the problem of access for the working photographer. Did the photographer, as a representative of the news media, have the right to enter the house? Which right comes first: the right of Mrs. Fletcher not to have someone trespass in her house, or the right of the public to know what happened in that house? Would you have entered Fletcher's home if you were the photographer?

In *Florida Publishing Co. (Times-Union) v Fletcher*, the court found in favor of the photographer. He had the right to enter the house and take the pictures. Yet, in other cases, the courts have recognized the right of private ownership over newsworthiness.

Trespass generally means entering someone's home, apartment, hotel, motel, or car without permission. This right of private ownership prohibits someone from walking in and taking pictures inside a house, without the permission of the resident.

Why, then, did the court find that the *Times-Union* photographer had the right to enter the Fletcher house and take pictures of the silhouette left from Cindy Fletcher's burned body?

Why was this not a case of trespass?

In the Fletcher case, the police and the fire marshal had invited the news photographer into the home. No one objected to the cameraman's presence. In fact, the authorities had asked the photographer to take pictures because they needed photos for their investigation, and the fire marshal's camera was out of film.

Mrs. Fletcher's suit was dismissed because it was "common custom" for the fire department or police department to permit the press onto private premises for the purposes of covering such newsworthy events.

Also, in the Fletcher case, no one had objected to the photographer's presence. Immediately, one asks, "How could Mrs. Fletcher object when she wasn't there?" That's the "Catch-22"—a legal dilemma. Had she been there and had she said "no," the photographer, despite official invitation, would have been trespassing. But Mrs. Fletcher did not say "no," and the fact that she couldn't say "no" wasn't relevant, according to the courts. . . at the time.

Judge: CBS' Street Stories "like rogue police"

More recent court findings, however, call into question the "common custom" of the Fletcher case (*Tawa Ayeni v CBS Inc.*, and *United States of America v Anthony Sanusi, et al.*). The facts: a CBS camera crew was shooting an episode for "Street Stories," a real-life cop show, when police invited the news team to participate in a raid on a suspect's home. The police were looking for evidence of credit-card fraud.

However, the suspect was not at home when the raid occurred. Only his wife, Tawa Ayeni, and her small child were there when the police officers pushed their way into the apartment—with the CBS video crew right behind them. The woman, clad only in her nightgown, implored the all-male crew, "Please don't take my picture."

She cowered, covered her face with a magazine, and directed her preschool-aged son not to look at the camera. "Why do you want to take a picture?" she asked. When the raid was over, law enforcement officials found nothing they had sought, but the CBS crew had footage of the raid, including shots of personal letters and paycheck stubs.

Tawa Ayeni sued CBS and won at both the trial level and in the U.S. Court of Appeals. Judge Jack Weinstein wrote, "Allowing a camera crew into a private home to film a search-and-seizure operation is the equivalent of a rogue policeman using his official position to break into a home in order to steal objects for his own profit or that of another."

Although law enforcement officials generally have a right to enter private property to conduct a reasonable search, Judge Weinstein maintained that this privilege does not extend to photojournalists invited along for the affair.

Judge Weinstein wrote that inviting a camera crew into a private home is a violation of the Fourth Amendment, which protects citizens against "unreasonable searches and seizures."

Note that this finding runs counter to the "common custom and practice" concept that was established in the Fletcher case, where fire officials had invited the photojournalist into a private home to shoot the aftermath of a fatal fire. In the ruling against CBS, Judge Weinstein's views are more in line with contemporary court opinions that generally find little support for a police officer's right to invite photojournalists and reporters onto private property.

Supreme Court: Ride-alongs Violate Fourth Amendment with Illegal Search and Seizure

The question of ride-alongs finally reached the Supreme Court. In the early morning hours of April 16, 1992, a special team of U.S. Marshals called the "Gunsmoke Team" had invited a reporter and photographer from the *Washington Post* to accompany them as part of a Marshals Service ride-along policy.

At around 6:45 a.m., with media representatives in tow, the officers broke into Charles and Geraldine Wilson's home while the couple were still in bed. The Marshals were looking for Charles Wilson's son, who was not at home. The father, dressed only in a pair of briefs, ran into his living room to

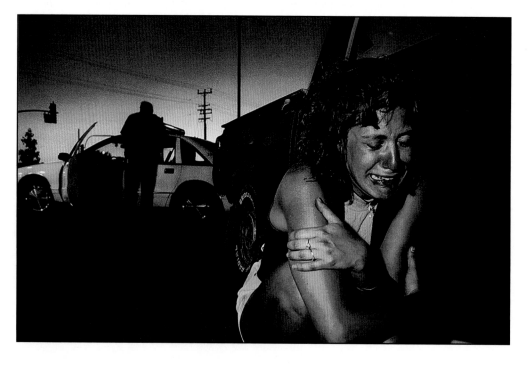

A photographer has the legal right to take this picture because the accident occurred on a public street.
Carolyn Cole for the *Sacramento Bee*

investigate the noise. Discovering at least five men in street clothes with guns in his living room, he angrily demanded that they state their business and repeatedly cursed the officers. Believing him to be the subject of the warrant, the officers quickly subdued Wilson on the floor. Geraldine Wilson next entered the living room to investigate, wearing only a nightgown.

When the protective sweep was completed, the officers learned that Dominic Wilson, the couple's son, was not in the house. They left. During the time that the officers were in the home, the *Washington Post* photographer took pictures, although the newspaper never published the photographs of the incident.

Mr. and Mrs. Wilson sued the law enforcement officials (*Wilson v Layne*). They contended that the officers' actions in bringing members of the media to observe and record the attempted execution of the arrest warrant violated their Fourth Amendment rights.

The case wound its way to the Supreme Court, which came to unanimous agreement. "While executing an arrest warrant in a private home, police officers invited representatives of the media to accompany them," wrote Chief Justice William Rhenquist. "We hold that such a 'media ride-along' does violate the Fourth Amendment."

In all probability, this Supreme Court finding will have a discouraging effect on opportunities for photographers to accompany police when they enter a house to execute a search warrant.

Most police will not want to violate the Fourth Amendment, or have their cases thrown out of court in the future, because they invited or allowed photographers to go along on a drug bust or police raid inside someone's home. However, the ruling does not stop the police from allowing photographers to cover their activities on public property such as streets or sidewalks.

Challenging Custom

Can you photograph a newsworthy event in a person's home if the owners do not object and the police have not yet arrived? If you were riding down the street and heard a gunshot followed by a scream coming from a house, you could park your car, enter the house, and begin photographing the victim and the assailant.

If the homeowner realized what you were doing and didn't like it, the owner could ask you to leave. You would have to obey or be arrested for trespassing. Even if the police were there, you would have to leave if the homeowner objected to your presence.

The Florida Highway Patrol, after a strong protest from the *Palm Beach Post Times* about the harassment of two staff photographers (see pages 278–279), issued a policy statement regarding "Journalists' Right of Access to Crime, Arrest, or Disaster Scenes." The statement said, in part, "It is the long-standing custom of law-enforcement agencies to invite representatives of the news media to enter upon private property where an event of public interest has occurred . . . " *Wilson v Layne* (see above) certainly challenges that long-standing custom.

"Invite," in this case, means to allow the photographer to enter. The common custom had existed for photographers to cover news events and not be harassed or otherwise blocked by the police. Still, photographers should not wait for an engraved invitation from the cop at the scene before beginning to photograph. Nor should photographers expect an invitation to follow police into people's homes during searches or arrests, especially following the Supreme Court's decision.

The Florida Highway Patrol's policy statement goes on to say, "the presence of a photographer at an accident, crime, or disaster scene and the taking of photographs at the scene does not constitute unlawful interference and should not be restricted."

TIPS FOR AVOIDING JAIL

The following suggestions come from Lucy A. Dalglish, executive director of the Reporters Committee, a nonprofit organization dedicated to protecting journalists' First Amendment rights.

- Carry your credentials at all times.
- Do not trespass onto property that is clearly private or marked with a police line.
- Do not take anything from the crime scene—you'll be charged with theft.
- Do whatever a police officer orders you to do, even it seems unreasonable or ridiculous or interferes with your job, unless you're willing to live with the consequences of being arrested.
- Do not call the arresting officer names or get into a shoving match.
- If covering a demonstration or other event likely to result in arrests, keep $50–$100 cash in your pocket to purchase a bail bond.
- Give your film or memory card, if possible, to another journalist who can get it to your newsroom promptly.
- Keep a government-issued photo ID (in addition to a press pass) in your pocket at all times. It may speed up your release from custody.
- Know the name and phone number of a criminal lawyer, bail bondsman, and the police department spokesperson.

Unfortunately, this position is a policy statement of the Florida Highway Patrol, not a national or even a state law; therefore, police and firefighters in the rest of the states do not necessarily follow it. In fact, only California has a specific law that states "accident and disaster areas shall not be closed to a duly authorized representative of any news service, newspaper or radio or television station or network." Even this law, however, does not protect the photojournalist if the police claim that the photographers will interfere with emergency operations.

PRIVATE PROPERTY OPEN TO THE PUBLIC

Do you have the right to take pictures on private property that is open to the public, such as a restaurant or grocery store? This area of the law is murky. Some authorities hold that you can take pictures unless the management has posted signs prohibiting photography or unless the owners object and ask you to stop.

However, CBS was sued when its photographer entered the Le Mistral restaurant in New York, with cameras rolling, to illustrate a story about the sanitation violations of the establishment. The management objected, but CBS kept filming.

Although no signs prohibiting photography were posted, CBS lost the suit on the ground that the photographer had entered without the intention of purchasing food and was therefore trespassing. Although CBS was covering a legitimate news story in a private establishment open to the public, the network was found guilty of trespassing.

In a 1972 case (*Lloyd Corp., Ltd. v Tanner*) the court ruled that "the public's license to enter a private business establishment is limited to engaging in activities directly related to that business and does not normally extend to the pursuit of unrelated business, e.g., news gathering."

Camera journalists have no right to enter the property, even in a spot-news situation, if the owners of the establishment prohibit them from doing so. Photographers must take their pictures from the public street, or they can be arrested for trespass.

This means that even if a fire is raging inside a business the management can exclude photographers. If the management asks you to leave, you must comply with the request or risk arrest for trespass.

You can still publish any pictures you have already taken. The proprietor can stop you from taking more pictures but can't prevent publication of the ones you already have.

Retired California Appeals Court Justice John Racanelli points out that penalties for trespass are usually "nominal" if there is no intent to "do actual harm or injury."

Sometimes the owner or manager of a store will demand your film or the memory card with images you have taken inside a shop. On this point the law is clear. You do not have to give up either. The owner or manager can ask you to stop taking pictures but can't take away your film or memory card. These are your personal property, and you have every right to keep them. Touching you or your camera to take your property may constitute battery against you.

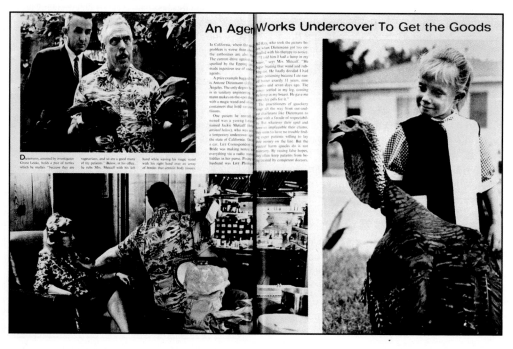

A *Life* photographer took pictures of Antone Dietemann in his house without his knowledge. Dietemann sued the magazine and won.
Courtesy, *Life* magazine

PRIVACY: WHEN DOES A JOURNALIST'S CAMERA ILLEGALLY INFRINGE?

When people talk about "privacy," they usually mean the "right to be left alone." But privacy is simply not a broad constitutional right basic to American citizens. The U.S. Constitution does not explicitly grant us this general right to be left alone. In fact, most analysts believe that there never will be an explicit, expressed constitutional right of privacy similar to the rights outlined in the First Amendment that protects and guarantees free speech and a free press

Over the years, however, some commonly recognized legal principles of privacy have evolved, based on federal and state laws and court cases. As applied to photography, these principles protect individuals from anyone:

- intruding by taking pictures where privacy could be reasonably expected
- using a picture to sell a product or service without consent;
- unfairly causing someone to look bad; and
- taking truthful but embarrassing photos.

At first glance, this list might appear somewhat intimidating. You may ask yourself, "May I ever take a picture of anyone, anywhere?" In practice, though, the courts have severely limited the meaning of each of the four principles of privacy.

INTRUDING WHERE PRIVACY COULD BE EXPECTED
Shooting Surreptitiously Inside Someone's Home
Do you need an invitation into someone's home to take pictures? Take the case of Antone Dietemann, a West Coast herbalist who had achieved a considerable amount of public recognition and was newsworthy, but who declined to be photographed in his home-laboratory garden.

Life photographer Bill Ray posed as the husband of a patient and visited the herbalist along with Ray's wife-for-a-day, also a *Life* staffer. She complained of a lump in her breast and asked to be examined. With a hidden camera, the photographer snapped pictures of the herbalist as he became engrossed in his therapy. Dietemann placed his hand on the patient's breast. He claimed that he could cure people by simply laying hands upon them. Bill Ray discreetly and quietly clicked off several frames. *Life* editors published the photos without Dietemann's permission. He sued the magazine because he claimed his privacy was invaded. He won on the grounds that the photographer took the pictures surreptitiously. Dietemann had not given his permission for the pictures to be taken. Individuals do have privacy rights in their own homes.

Outside the House
In general, you can take pictures of anyone including politicians and celebrities when they are in public. The case of Ron Galella, self-styled paparazzo and pursuer of Jacqueline Kennedy Onassis for most of her public life, indicates how far the courts have

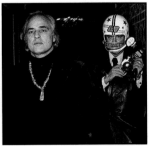

After Marlon Brando broke photographer Ron Galella's jaw, Galella began wearing a football helmet to protect himself whenever he snapped pictures of the actor. Paul Schmulbach

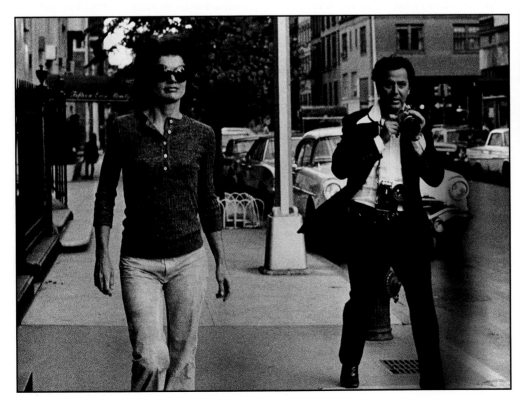

◄ The late Jackie Kennedy Onassis sued Ron Galella, self-styled paparazzo photographer, for harassment, and she won. The court eventually restricted Galella from taking pictures within twenty-five feet of Onassis. Joy Smith

extended this right. The case exemplifies the problem of intruding into someone's privacy outside the home. The former First Lady was newsworthy. Almost anything she did appeared in newspaper gossip columns. Like Princess Diana a generation later, any photo of Jackie a photographer could grab soon appeared on the cover of a national magazine.

Ron Galella was a full-fledged, full-time paparazzo who specialized in photos of Jackie. The word paparazzo in Italian means an insect similar to a mosquito. Director Federico Fellini, in his movie "La Dolce Vita," named the freelance photographers who covered the movie stars and other celebrities paparazzi "because they buzzed like mosquitoes."

Galella, who made his living buzzing after the stars, started tracking Jackie Kennedy Onassis in 1967. Galella hung around her New York City apartment and waited for her to step outside the door. When she bicycled in Central Park, he and his camera were tucked into the bushes. As she peddled by, he would shoot her picture. When she shopped at Bonwit Teller's, he ducked behind a counter and snapped away. When she ate at a restaurant in New York's Chinatown, he hid behind a coat rack to get the first photographs of the former First Lady eating with chopsticks. He even dated her maid for a few weeks in an attempt to learn Jackie's schedule.

Onassis sued Galella, charging him with inflicting emotional distress. The court had to balance Onassis's right of privacy against Galella's right to take pictures.

The court found in Onassis's favor.

Galella was restricted from coming closer than 100 yards of her home and within 50 yards of her personally. The ruling was later modified to prohibit him from approaching her within 25 feet.

Note that the court did not stop Galella from taking and selling pictures of the former First Lady, as long as the pictures were used for news coverage and not advertising. Few cases of this kind have arisen since the Galella-Onassis proceeding.

While U.S. law is still generally tolerant of photographers taking pictures of people on the street, French law has outlawed any published images "that would infringe the dignity of the individual." In other words, anyone can sue a French publication for printing his or her photo no matter how innocuous it is and regardless of where the photo was taken.

This bizarre rule holds true even if the subject is involved in a crime. French magazines resort to blocking out recognizable faces in a candid photo even if the picture was taken during a news event. Luckily, U.S. law has not become so severe.

USING SOMEONE'S IMAGE TO SELL A PRODUCT OR SERVICE

The law holds that you cannot publish a photo of a person for commercial purposes without obtaining consent from that individual. A company can't sell a product or service by identifying that product or service with someone without getting permission first.

Publishing someone's picture on the cover of a magazine or the front page of a newspaper is permissible if it is newsworthy.

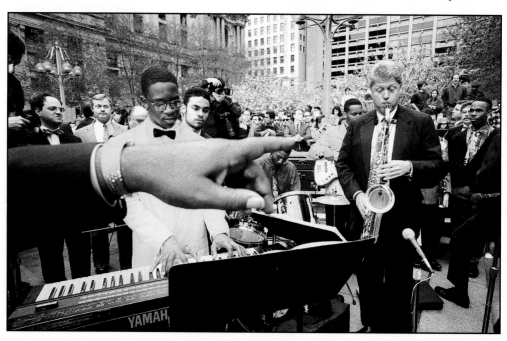

There are no problems publishing this picture of former President Bill Clinton in a newspaper or magazine story. But without Clinton's written permission, the photo could not appear in an ad selling saxophones.

P.F. Bentley, for *Time*

The court does not consider the newspaper or magazine itself a product. However, printing the same picture as part of an advertisement, without the subject's prior consent, is a violation of the person's right of privacy.

Say that famous movie personality John Starstruck is driving down the street in a new Ford Thunderbird. Thinking your editor at the *Daily Sunshine* might want to use the photo because no one knew Starstruck was in town, you snap a picture of the movie star. You were right. Your editor runs the picture of Starstruck in his new car on page one. No problem. You've done nothing wrong, nor has your editor done anything illegal.

Ford Motor Company, however, seeing the picture, recognizes its advertising value because the photo shows a famous movie star driving in a Thunderbird. The company, after legally obtaining a copy of the photograph from your newspaper, uses the picture in an advertisement. If Starstruck is recognizable in the Ford advertisement, then the movie star's privacy—in the sense of commercial appropriation—is violated Ford is using Starstruck's image to sell its cars. Starstruck

may sue the Ford Motor Company, and unless Ford can produce a consent form—called a model release—in court, the movie star will win. The model release, signed by the subject, gives the photographer or publication the right to use the photo in an ad.

The right to control the commercial use of one's image is not limited to the famous. All individuals have the right to protect themselves from this form of commercial exploitation.

When you take a picture for the newspaper, you do not need a model release from the subject, famous or unknown. But when you take a picture that you want to sell to a company for use in an advertisement, brochure, fundraiser, and the like, then you must get a model release signed, even if the subject is unknown.

UNFAIRLY CAUSING SOMEONE TO LOOK BAD

The law holds that people have the right of privacy not to be placed in a "false light." In other words, photos can't make a person look bad without cause. For example, a photographer photographed a child who had been

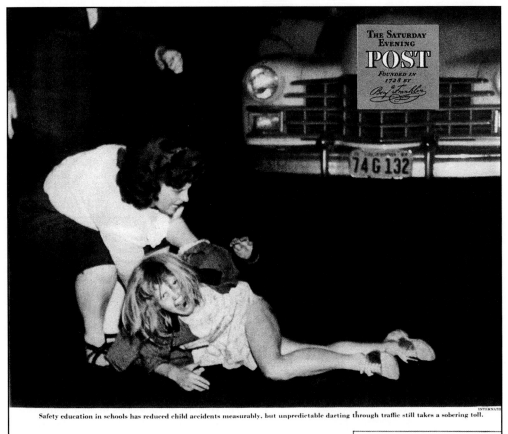

Safety education in schools has reduced child accidents measurably, but unpredictable darting through traffic still takes a sobering toll.

They Ask to Be Killed

By DAVID G. WITTELS

Do you invite massacre by your own carelessness? Here's how thousands have committed suicide by scorning laws that were passed to keep them alive.

The parents of this child claimed that the combination of words and pictures implied that they were careless, thus placing them in a false light. When they sued the *Saturday Evening Post,* the court decided in their favor. Reprinted from the *Saturday Evening Post,* © 1949, The Curtis Publishing Co.

struck by a car, and the picture appeared in a newspaper. No problem so far. Two years later, the *Saturday Evening Post* ran the same picture under the title, "They Ask To Be Killed," with a story about child safety. The original use of the picture was a legitimate publication of a newsworthy event. But when the *Saturday Evening Post* used the headline with the picture and placed the subhead "Do You Invite Massacre with Your Own Carelessness?" next to the photo, the parents

claimed that the words and photo implied carelessness on their part. The words and photo gave the impression that the child had willingly run out in front of the car. The court decreed that the photo/headline combination placed the parents in a "false light." The parents won the lawsuit.

Saturday Evening Post editors used a picture from their old photo file to accompany this new story. They used the old picture as an illustration of a general, ongoing problem. Often, this use of file photos provides the grounds for later lawsuits.

In another such incident, John Raible even signed a model release allowing *Newsweek* magazine to publish his picture with a story about "Middle Americans." The editors, however, chose the headline "Troubled American—A Special Report on the Silent Majority," and printed Raible's picture below the headline. Raible felt that the headline, associated with his picture, implied he was troubled, thus putting him in a false light. He sued and collected damages.

Both the *Saturday Evening Post* and the *Newsweek* cases show a picture's meaning can be affected drastically by the words associated with it. Although the picture itself might have been legal when it was taken, after captioning or headlining, the photo-plus-word combination when published can be considered illegal. Robert Cavallo and Stuart Kahan, in their book ***Photography: What's the Law?***, say that "Pictures, standing alone, without captions or stories with them, generally pose little danger of defamation. However, an illustration is usually accompanied by text, and it is almost always that combination of pictures and prose which carries the damaging impact."

The *Newsweek* case points up a second legal danger for the photographer to watch for. The model release signed by Raible did not protect the photographer. The model release is not a carte blanche; it is a limited authorization given by the subject to the photographer, warning the photographer to use the picture in an understood and agreed-on manner. A model release does not give photographers or picture editors the right to use a picture in any way they see fit.

TAKING TRUTHFUL BUT PRIVATE OR EMBARRASSING PHOTOS

The right of privacy does include some restrictions on printing truthful but private or embarrassing information about a subject. Generally, if the information is newsworthy and in the public interest, the press can photograph and publish the facts. The courts have liberally interpreted "public interest" to

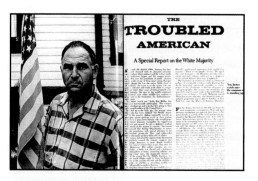

Even though John Raible had signed a consent form, he sued *Newsweek* and won because he felt the headline and this picture put him in a "false light." Reprinted from *Newsweek*

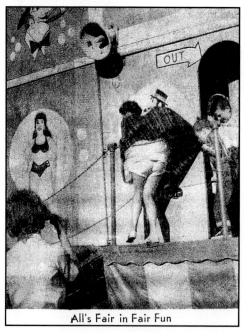

Ms. Graham was in a public place and her face wasn't even visible when she was photographed at the Cullman County Fair. She said her children were recognizable, and the courts agreed with her that this picture, though truthful, was embarrassing, and therefore, she could collect damages. Reprinted from the [Alabama] *Daily Times Democrat*

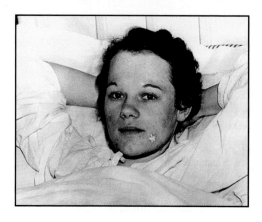

Without Dorothy Barber's permission, a photographer took her picture in her hospital room. When the photo ran in *Time* magazine, Barber sued for invasion of privacy and won. International News Pictures

mean anything interesting to the public—and there are few things that won't interest at least some people.

Public But Embarrassing

The courts, however, have put certain limitations on the right of the public to know and see true but confidential facts about a person. Photographs, even if taken in a public place, should not ridicule or embarrass a private person unless the situation is patently newsworthy. The photos should not be highly offensive to a reasonable person and must be of legitimate concern to the public.

A Ms. Graham went to the Cullman, Alabama, county fair. After several rides, she entered a sideshow fun house. In the fun house, she walked across a grate that blew up her dress. At that unlucky moment, a photographer from the *Daily Times Democrat*, Bill McClure, was on his first photo assignment for the paper—looking for "typical" features at the fair. With his Speed Graphic, he snapped Graham's picture just as her skirt blew up around her hips, exposing her underwear. After the picture was published, Graham called and complained. Getting no satisfaction from the photographer with an apology or retraction, Graham hired an out-of-town lawyer and successfully sued the *Democrat* for damages. The picture was truthful, but the jury found that the photo was embarrassing and contained no information of legitimate concern to the public.

Special Children

You may take pictures of children; however, if they are in a special education class, and you take a picture, their parents may consider that photo truthful but embarrassing. They could sue you and your newspaper. Getting the teacher's permission is not sufficient.

To run the picture of a mentally or physically disabled child, you must have the consent of the parent or legal guardian.

You can take and publish pictures of children in schools and public parks. You are open to suit only if the photo might be considered embarrassing or derogatory. Because of concern over kidnapping and sexual molestation, however, be cautious when photographing children you do not know. Always try to explain what you are doing to a parent or other responsible adult at the scene. While you might have the legal right to take and publish the picture, dealing with an irate parent can deter you from your original assignment.

Hospitals

In 1942, an International News Photo photographer entered the hospital room of Dorothy Barber, who was in the hospital for a problem with an eating disorder.

Without Barber's consent, the photographer took a picture of her, which *Time* magazine bought and ran under the headline "Starving Glutton." Barber sued the magazine, and *Time* lost the case. A Missouri court said, "Certainly if there is any right of privacy at all, it should include the right to obtain medical treatment at home or in a hospital without personal publicity."

Dorothy Barber had what the court considers a "private medical condition." Therefore, a photographer could not take her picture without her permission.

Accidents

If someone is injured in an automobile accident or plane crash, falls out of a tree, nearly drowns, or is struck by lightning, that person would have a "public medical condition." Or, if a person has been shot by someone committing a crime, the victim's condition would be considered "public." People who are victims of a crime, accident, or an "act of God" are considered newsworthy, and they can be photographed outside the hospital.

If an accident happens at the corner of Pacific and Hyde Streets, the photographer can begin taking pictures of the victim upon arriving at the scene, because the victim has a public medical condition and is not in the hospital. As the rescue team places the victim on the stretcher and slides the injured person

It is legal to take pictures at accident scenes in public places because accident victims have what is called a "public medical condition." Below, once the woman on the stretcher was moved into an ambulance, her medical condition became private. The photographer would have needed her permission to continue taking photos.
Dan Poush, *Statesman-Journal* [Salem, Oregon]

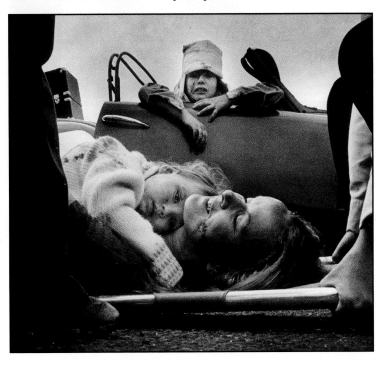

into the ambulance, the photographer is still within legal rights to continue to photograph.

Once the victim enters the emergency van, however, the person is covered by the right of privacy and is off limits to photographers. The same off-limits rule inhibits photographers once the victim enters the hospital.

If a person's condition is newsworthy, interesting, and historic, but was not caused by crime, accident, or an act of God, the person's medical condition is considered private. Barber's treatment was private. The first heart and kidney transplants and the first test-tube baby were both private medical conditions, even though they were newsworthy. Photographers could take pictures inside the hospital only if the patients involved granted permission.

LIBEL AND THE PHOTOGRAPHER

Libel is a printed, written, or pictorial statement that is defamatory, meaning harmful to somebody's good name, character, or reputation. The image must have been published or shown to another individual due to negligence on the part of the photojournalist or due to a willful disregard for the truth.

Since truth is a defense in libel cases, and since photos represent actual scenes and are

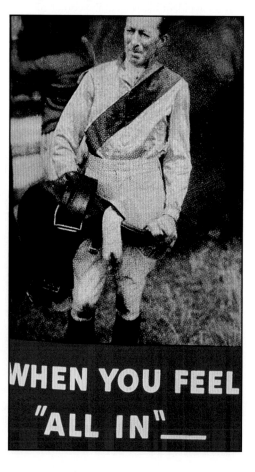

Although truth is an absolute defense for libel, and this picture was "true," Mr. Burton sued when he saw what he looked like in this portion of a Camel cigarette ad. Burton had given permission for the ad, yet the court found publishing the picture was libelous.

WHEN YOU FEEL "ALL IN"___

truthful, it might seem that a person should not be able to win a libel suit against a photographer. However, a number of successful libel suits have been based on photographs, which can subject someone to ridicule, contempt, or hatred just as effectively as words can. Photographs can lie, or at least appear to lie, and photos in conjunction with print may form the basis for a libel suit.

Usually, a photo alone is not libelous, although such cases have occurred. The most famous involved a Mr. Burton, who was paid for a cigarette endorsement (below). For the advertisement, Mr. Burton was photographed holding a saddle. In the photograph, quite by accident, the saddle's wide girth strap appeared to be attached to the man, giving, in the court's words, a "grotesque, monstrous, and obscene" effect. The photo was deemed libelous.

In some situations, when words have been added to photos via headlines, captions, or stories, the combination has resulted in libel. The photograph itself may be harmless, but the accompanying words may add the damaging element.

For example, the *New York American* once printed a photograph of a wrestler, a Mr. Sbyszko, next to that of a gorilla, with the caption: "Not fundamentally different in physique." The photo-plus-word combination was libelous. As in cases involving privacy, photographers must be particularly careful how their pictures are associated with words.

Many photographic libel suits have involved individuals arrested as suspects, according to Michael Sherer of the University of Nebraska at Omaha. In his report, "No pictures please: It's the law," Sherer notes that individuals allegedly involved in murder, illegal drugs, smuggling, police corruption, financial misdealing, illegal gambling, organized theft rings, and organized crime have sued for libel when their pictures appeared in print. In addition, he notes, people have sued because they felt photos of them implied sexual promiscuity or abnormal or illegal sexual activity.

To prove that a photo is libelous, the defendant must show that the photojournalist acted with willful disregard for the truth or was unprofessional and/or negligent. By using proper reporting procedures in gathering and publishing the photos, several media defendants have successfully survived libel cases.

Sherer notes that problems arise when courts discover that proper reporting techniques were not used to obtain the photos. For instance, photographers failed to verify that individuals who were photographed during arrests were indeed suspects in the robberies or suspects accused of prostitution.

Finally, Sherer cautions that, if you have any doubt that the subjects pictured are not the same people as those mentioned in the accompanying caption or news story, find another way of illustrating the story.

BREAKING A PROMISE OF ANONYMITY TO A SUBJECT

Cornell Anderson was a patient of Dr. William Valenti, an AIDS specialist who was being profiled in the Rochester *Democrat and Chronicle*. Promising a photo for the story would not reveal the patient's identity, the photographer nonetheless allowed a picture in which the patient was recognizable to be published.

Upon seeing Anderson's photograph in the paper, his family recognized him. Anderson sued and won the case. The court found that the photographer had made a verbal contract with his subject and there was no value in the public knowing the man's identity.

In a review of cases like this, "Negative Identification: Photographer's Consequences for Breaking Promises of Confidentiality to News Subjects," Laurence Alexander found few involving still photographers.

Still, he recommends sidestepping the problem by not making confidentiality promises whenever possible. Once you agree, you have made a legal binding contract not to show the subject's face.

PRESS CREDENTIALS USEFUL BUT LIMITED

Press credentials issued by the newspaper or magazine for which you work are a means of identification and nothing more. Press passes entitle you to nothing.

Authorities use press credentials to determine if you are an official media representative and then may invite you to the scene of a crime or disaster.

Essentially, your press pass gives you no more rights than those enjoyed by the public. The press credential does not give you a right to break the law, even if you are in hot pursuit of a big news story. Sergeant Carl Yates of the Louisville, Kentucky, Police Department works regularly with the media. He characterizes the situation this way: "You have no more right of access than the general public. What you do have, and what you hope the police will recognize, is that you have more of a reason to be there than the general public."

Credentials issued by the highway patrol or the state police carry no legal weight other than providing proof you work for a newspaper or magazine. Official credentials can be ignored or recalled at any time by the law enforcement agencies that issued them.

On the other hand, authorities cannot discriminate against you or your newspaper at the scene of a crime or disaster. All reporters, photographers, and TV camera operators must have an equal opportunity to cover the story.

The police cannot select one newspaper photographer and reject another. Nor can police choose to let in television camera crews and keep out still photographers. If the crime scene is crowded, however, they can ask photographers to cooperate and form a pool. One pool representative will photograph in the restricted area, and then share the pictures with the other photographers.

SUBPOENAS FOR NEGATIVES

A reporter for the *Louisville* (Kentucky) *Courier-Journal* wrote a story about making hashish from marijuana. The article included a photograph of a pair of hands working over a laboratory table with the caption identifying the substance in the photo as hashish. After the article and photograph were published, the reporter was subpoenaed to appear before a grand jury and ordered to testify about whose hands had appeared in the photograph. The reporter claimed that both the First Amendment of the U.S. Constitution and a state law protected his confidential source of information. The U.S. Supreme Court said the reporter had witnessed a crime and that the sources did not deserve special protection (*Branzburg v Hayes*).

While a number of states have laws that, to some extent, shield reporters and photographers from courts subpoenaing negatives and notes, each state's laws are different. Unfortunately, the federal government has no shield statute that protects journalist-source confidentiality. And existing state laws provide only limited protection, especially when the photojournalist witnesses a crime. As the Supreme Court ruled in the marijuana and hashish case, "The crimes of news sources are no less reprehensible and threatening to the public interest when witnessed by a reporter than when they are not."

While 30 states have shield laws that protect journalists when they gather information, including photographs, many of these laws do not cover freelancers or student journalists even if they are reporting on a major news event. A subpoena for negatives and prints, surprisingly, is the number one legal problem faced by news photographers, according to a survey of NPPA members by Michael Sherer.

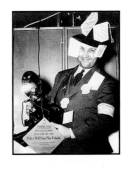

Press credentials provide identification but do not supply any special legal rights. © Wide World Photos

He found that 25 percent of the survey respondents had been subpoenaed for photographic materials in street riots and other law-breaking incidents. Sherer recommends not complying with a subpoena without first consulting with a lawyer and your editor. Finally, he cautions against destroying photographs sought by a subpoena. This can result in a contempt-of-court citation.

To avoid becoming an investigative arm of the police, who otherwise might rummage through all a newspapers' negatives from such events, some publications destroy all images except the one that was published and perhaps the frames immediately adjacent to it. If asked, these newspapers need only turn over the published picture.

COPYRIGHT: WHO OWNS THE PICTURE?
WHEN AN EMPLOYER OWNS PHOTOS

When you are an employee, your employer owns the copyright to your photos. The employer holds the rights to the pictures and can reprint or resell them. Protecting those rights is the employer's concern. Usually an entire newspaper or magazine is copyrighted, including all material contained in each issue. For your company to own your work, you must be a full-time employee, and your employer must pay benefits as well as give you specific assignments. If you fit this definition, you have a "work-for-hire" arrangement with your employer.

You may form other specific contractual arrangements with your employer. For example, when a company hires you for a staff position, you can agree to take the job on the condition that you own your images, along with the rights to sell the photos after the company has published the originals. In fact, you can negotiate any contract you like with your employer as long as you arrange the details before you sign on the dotted line.

Your right to sell pictures you originally took for your employer differs among companies. Some organizations keep the images permanently. When some outlets sell a picture, they retain the profits but often give the photographer a credit line. Others give the photographer a percentage of the profits from any sales. Some give the images to the photographer after a fixed period of time; others let the photographer retain the images immediately after publishing the photos the first time.

As a freelancer, though, remember that if you agree in writing to a "work-for-hire" contract, your client can reuse or resell the photos without your permission. You no longer own the images. Without a written contract, the images remain yours.

WHEN YOU RETAIN THE COPYRIGHT

If you are not a full-time employee, however, and have not signed a "work-for-hire" agreement, the company does not own the copyright to your photos. Unless you make a special agreement, you keep the copyright.

When you accept an assignment from a newspaper, magazine, Web site, CD-ROM manufacturer, or any kind of company, you are not an employee of that organization. When you turn over your photos to the assigning editor or art director, you are granting one-time rights. The pictures can be published or used only once. Any other use the company wants to make of the photos is up to you—and all slides, negatives, and prints should be returned to you.

If you take pictures on your own time without an assignment, even if you are a full-time employee, you own the negatives and the copyright.

When you sell a picture that was shot on your own time with your own film, you can form several arrangements with the organization buying the picture—as long as you form the agreement at the time of the sale.

If you sell one-time rights, you can resell the image elsewhere after it has run.

In a second type of arrangement, you can sell the picture along with exclusive rights to it for a specified period of time. In a third type of agreement—for a lot more money, one hopes—you can sell your copyright. This means that only the agency or publication has the right to distribute and sell the photo. You no longer have that right.

Remember, if you formed no specific agreements when you sold the picture, you automatically retain your copyright. The agency or publication has first rights, but you can resell the photo to other outlets later.

COPYRIGHTING YOUR OWN PHOTOS

If you don't work full-time for a news organization, how do you protect yourself from someone reprinting your photos and not giving you credit or paying you? How do you prove the printed photo is yours if it does not carry your credit line?

If you are a freelance photographer you have copyright protection of your work as soon as you take a picture and develop the film or save it to a digital file.

To protect your rights, put your copyright notice on the back of each print with either of the following notations: © or the word "Copyright," with your name and the year you shot it. Although not required, it is a common practice to include a statement that reflects the concept of "all rights reserved" or "permission required for use."

After you've placed the copyright notice, you can register the image with the U.S. Copyright Office in Washington, D.C., *www.loc.gov/copyright*. Do this by completing a form you will find online, sending two copies of the photo, and paying a fee. Or, after the photo has been published, send the form, two tearsheets, and the fee. You can register your work in bulk—a body of work, tearsheets, videotapes of your slides, contact sheets, etc. Copyright attorney Jeff Berchenko suggests doing this every quarter for all your published work.

You do not have to register the image with the Copyright Office immediately, though. In fact, you never have to register the photo with the Copyright Office at all unless someone prints your picture without paying you, and you want to sue. Registration of the copyright is not necessary to maintain your rights, only to defend against infringement of them. If you do register your images after you take them, you will simply have an easier time winning your case if you must sue.

If someone publishes your image without permission, you are likely to win the fee you would have charged for the picture as well as compensatory damages. For instance, if *Train Lovers* magazine published your photo of a train wreck without your permission, you may have lost sales from other magazines that would have purchased the image.

With the image registered, you can sue for the money the publication should have paid you as well as the money you lost from possible future sales.

You can also sue to stop *Train Lovers* magazine from using the picture again or featuring it in their upcoming calendar. If you register your copyrighted train picture in Washington within three months before or after *Train Lovers* magazine publishes your photo, you can collect up to $150,000 if you prove the magazine willfully published the image without your consent. You can also possibly recover legal fees. Fore more information, see the Nolo Press web site, *www.nolo.com.*

RESPECTING THE COPYRIGHTS OF OTHERS

The ease of scanning images and incorporating them into photo illustrations makes it easy to forget that other photographers or artists enjoy the same copyright protection you do. Remember not to employ "found" images from newspapers, magazines, or the Web without express permission to do so. Just as no one can legally make a painting or sculpture from your photograph, you can't photograph someone else's painting or sculpture. Your photo becomes a derivative work, which only the copyright owner—usually the creator of the work—can create or license to be created. ∎

LAW REFERENCES

Barber v. Time, 1 Med. L. Rep. 1779 or 159 S.W. 2d 291 (Mo. 1942).

Branzburg v. Hayes, 408 U.S. 665 (1972).

Burton v. Crowell Publishing Co., 81 Fed. 154 (2d Cir. 1936).

Chandler v. Florida, 449 U.S. 560 (1981).

Daily Times Democrat v. Graham, 276 Ala. 380 162S. 2d 474 (1964).

Dietemann v. Time, 449 F. 2d 245.

Estes v. Texas, 381 U.S. 532, 536.

Florida Publishing Co. v. Fletcher, 340 So. 2d 914.

Galella v. Onassis, 487 F. 2d 986.

Le Mistral v. Columbia Broadcasting System, N.Y. Sup. Ct., N.Y. L.J. (1976).

Leverton v. Curtis Publishing Co., 192 F. 2d 974 (3d Cir. 1951).

Lloyd Corp. Ltd. v. Tanner, 407 U.S. 551, 92 S. Ct. 2219, 33 L. Ed. 2d 131 (1972).

People v. Berliner, 3 Med. L. Rep. 1942.

People v. Zamora, 361 So. 2d 776.

Raible v. Newsweek, Inc., 341 F. Supp. 804 (1972).

Sbyszko v. New York American, 1930: 239 NYS, 411.

Tawa Ayeni v. CBS Inc., 848 F. Supp. 362 (E.D. N.Y. 1994).

United States of America v. Anthony Sanusi, et al., 813 F. Supp. 149 (E.D. N.Y. 1992).

Wilson v. Layne, 27 M.L.R. 1705 (1999).

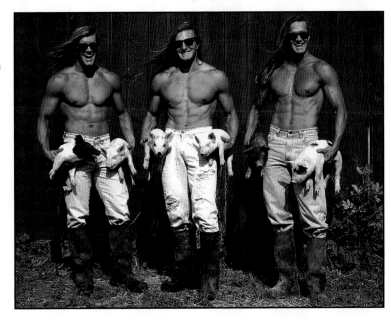

On assignment for *People*, the photographer took this picture of buff brothers who made the career transition from hog farming in Nebraska to modeling for a New York talent agency. The magazine has the right to use the picture one time but the photographer retains the copyright. Three months after the picture first appeared, the photographer could sell the picture to other publications.
Keith Philpott, for *People*

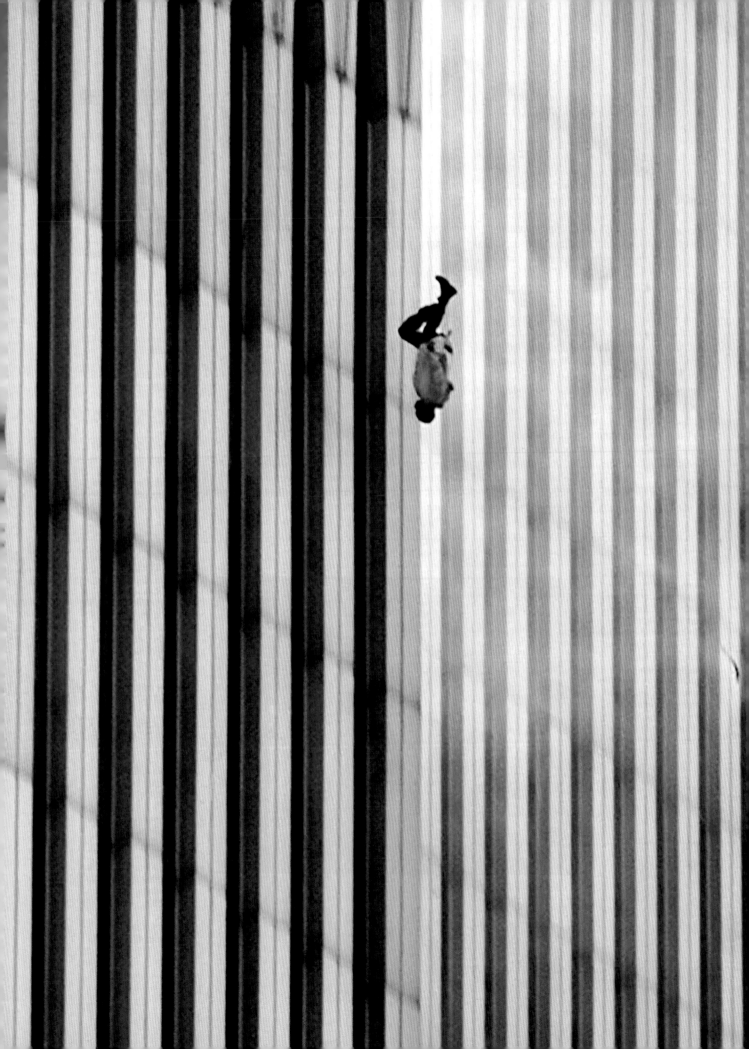

Chapter 14

Ethics

DOING THE RIGHT THING

Photojournalism as a profession imposes a set of responsibilities. Some are fairly routine and fall neatly into the "daily duties" category: get to the scene, frame and focus the shot, collect the caption info, and so forth.

Beneath these functional tasks lie broader ethical considerations.

Confronting these issues is often more challenging than the assignment itself. At times, these ethical issues pit the photographer's professional duties against his or her own conscience, that internal barometer that guides behavior and ultimately maintains social order.

Without other routes of escape, people jumped to their deaths from the World Trade Center towers before the buildings collapsed following terrorist attacks on September 11, 2001. Many publications declined to run this picture. Were they right? Richard Drew, Associated Press

Photographers may, in the course of completing their assignments, be forced to choose between how they might act as individual citizens and how they feel they should act as visual journalists.

This dilemma—personal choice versus professional responsibility—is certainly not unique to photojournalism. Consider, for example, the plight of the public defender charged to represent a rapist who he knows is guilty; the doctor who has the resources and training to prolong artificially the life of a suffering patient. In these examples, the U.S. Constitution and the Hippocratic oath, respectively, are compelling codes, but what about the individual rights of the attorney, the private conscience of the physician?

Now consider the less dire but still clouded situation of a photographer shooting a story about suburban high schools. While scanning a clattering lunchroom scene, the photographer spots a trio of students exchanging twenty-dollar bills for bags of white powder.

Does the photographer, acting as a genuinely concerned citizen, try to stop or at least to disrupt the deal? Report the incident to the principal and offer a description of the players? Or, does the photographer take the picture and publish it?

Almost every day, photojournalists face decisions of morality—ranging from removing a distracting item from a photograph to taking a gruesome picture at a murder site.

But a looming deadline or the logistical challenge of a six-site assignment sheet can pressure the photographer into making snap judgments about even the most morally delicate situations.

Thus, thinking about issues ahead of time may allow the photojournalist to avoid a crisis on the scene or regret after a picture has been published.

Photojournalists use several arguments to explain their decisions to shoot or print controversial pictures. One argument, which sometimes fails to distinguish between practices and standards, relies on the familiar "other guy" argument: "I did it because that's the way other photojournalists do it."

These photographers are comparing their actions with a perceived industry standard. Whether the action is inherently right or wrong is irrelevant to their argument.

"This is the way everyone does it." While such a decision-making strategy might reflect professional practices, it does not create a standard grounded in the norms of ethical decision making.

FOUNDATIONS OF ETHICAL DECISION MAKING

Many photographers, whether they realize it or not, turn to an established ethical framework to try to guide their decisions.

UTILITARIAN

That framework includes the "utilitarian" principle as defined by ethicists. Here the overriding consideration is "the greatest good for the greatest number of people."

The utilitarian position recognizes that photojournalism provides information critical to a democratic society. Photography can show the horrors of war, the tragedy of an accident, or the hardship of poverty. Therefore, it is right to take and publish pictures. Without information, in general, and pictures, specifically, voters cannot make informed decisions.

ABSOLUTIST

However, the utilitarian principle of "the greatest good . . ." bumps up against a competing ethical principle that says, "Individuals have certain rights . . . ," among them, the right to privacy. These rights are absolute and inviolable regardless of the benefits to society, says this principle.

Taking a picture of the distraught family of a drowned child and then publishing it might cause others to be more cautious, but invading the privacy of their grief—regardless of the benefits—is not acceptable, according to the absolute rights argument.

THE GOLDEN RULE

Another of the ethical cornerstones is the Judeo-Christian precept, "Do unto others as you would have them do unto you." This rule, too, sometimes conflicts both with professional standards and with actions that might benefit a democratic society in need of information.

In the last example, if you put yourself in the place of the grieving parent, you might not want your picture taken. On the other hand, if you are trying to save children from drowning in the future and think that running the picture might caution parents or affect funding for extra lifeguards, you might run the photo anyway.

Without providing a behavioral prescription for photographers, this chapter lays out some of the ethical dilemmas faced by professional photojournalists and picture editors.

The young boy in the body bag had just drowned. His family was grief-stricken. Might running the picture in the paper help prevent future drownings? For a discussion about the photo, see page 320.
John Harte, Bakersfield, California

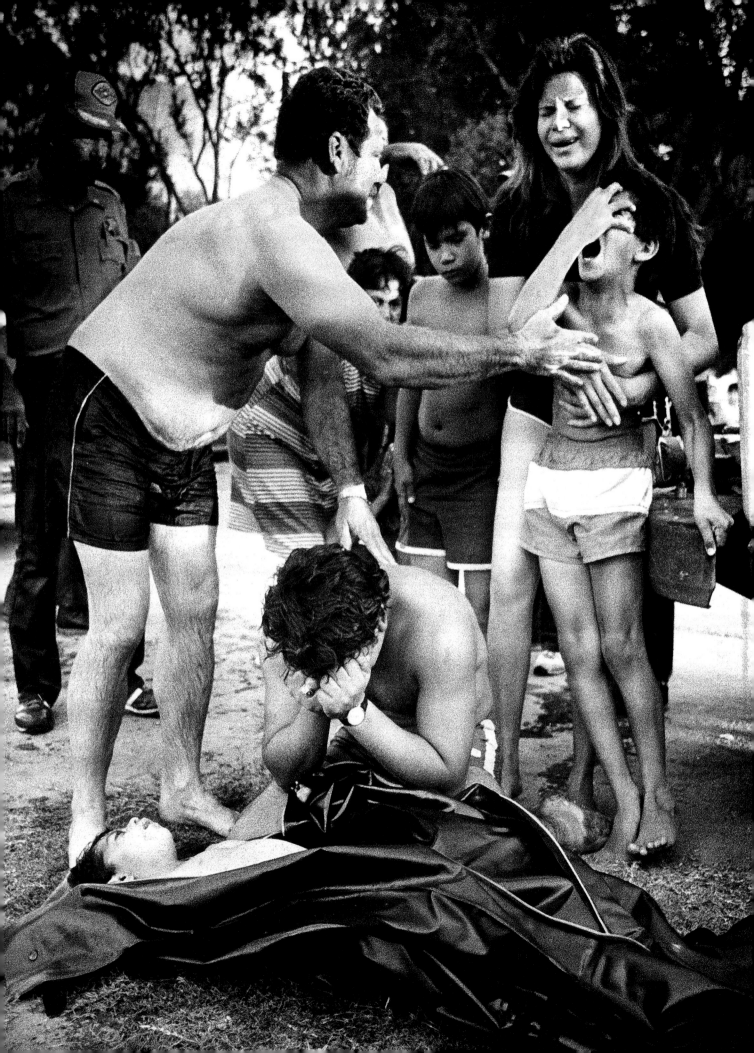

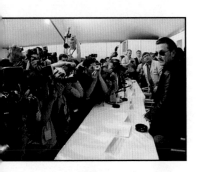

Would it be wrong to stage-manage a publicity event like this press conference? Do readers care? Larry Laszlo

Rather than deal with cases of obvious fraud, fakery, and patent sensationalism, the chapter tackles the gray area between right and wrong—the zone that troubles photographers on an almost daily basis.

SET UP OR JUST CLEAN UP?

The author once saw the well-known photo editor of a national magazine—and one of the most respected elders in the business—remove a Coke® bottle to improve the scene before he took a picture. While removing a pop bottle is a fairly trivial act, the incident does illustrate a basic ethical question: when can the photographer alter the scene without altering the message and creating an untruth? When does a comment become a stage direction? And, if some set-up is permissible, when does "some" become too much?

WHEN DO PROFESSIONALS POSE PICTURES?

In a precedent-setting study in 1961, Walter Wilcox, then-chairman of the Department of Journalism at the University of California, Los Angeles, designed a study to determine the attitudes of readers, photographers, and editors toward staging news pictures. He sent questionnaires to three groups of subjects: general readers, working photographers, and managing editors.

On a three-level scale, each group evaluated sample situations that a photographer might face as "definitely unethical," "doubtful," or "not unethical." Here are three sample situations from Wilcox's study:

Murder trial: a photographer attempts to get a shot of a defendant, but she consistently evades him by shielding her face or ducking behind her escorting warden. The photographer spots another woman who looks like the defendant and by diffusing the light and adjusting the focus, he gets a striking picture, which no one will challenge as being fake.

Ground-breakers: a photographer covers a ground-breaking ceremony for a new church. Local dignitaries have already turned the first bit of earth before the photographer arrives. He asks that the ceremony be repeated. The dignitaries cooperate, and he gets his picture.

Cricket plague: a plague of crickets is devastating the hinterland. A photographer goes out to cover the story, but he finds the crickets are too far apart and too small to be recognizable in a photograph. He thinks he could get a better picture if the crickets were shown in a mass, and, to that end, he builds a device that brings crickets through the narrow neck of a chute. He gets his shot of closely massed crickets on the march.

Wilcox found that the general public, managing editors, and working photographers agreed to a remarkable extent on what was ethical and what was not. In the survey, 92 percent of the public, 93 percent of the photographers, and 99 percent of the editors said the court photographer was wrong to photograph one person and claim it is another, even if the two look similar.

By comparison, 83 percent of the public, 88 percent of the photographers, and 94 percent of the managing editors said it was not unethical to re-enact the groundbreaking ceremony.

Thus, it seems that these three groups operate within the same ethical framework that allows "set-up" pictures but rules out clearly faked photos.

The third scenario, however, in which the photographer collected and choreographed the crickets, sparked disagreement within each of the three groups. The general readers were almost evenly divided along the three-point ethics scale: 29 percent considered the photographer's actions "definitely unethical," 39 percent considered them "doubtful," and the remaining 32 percent considered them "not unethical." Managing editors were similarly split between definitely unethical (23 percent), doubtful (34 percent), and not unethical (44 percent).

Photographers, however, who probably have faced similar problems, were much more likely to consider amassing the crickets part of a photojournalist's routine job. Only 7 percent of the photographers polled felt the photographer in the example was definitely unethical; 30 percent considered his behavior doubtful; but a whopping 63 percent said that the cricket photographer was not wrong. One could assume that two-thirds of the photographers polled would have rigged the shot if faced with the same situation.

In a 1987 study for the National Press Photographers Association (NPPA), Ben Brink found that re-creating a situation was acceptable to more than a third of the professional photographers he surveyed. However, staging a scene from scratch was acceptable to only 2 percent of the working pros.

The staging-from-scratch vignette: a hypothetical photographer is assigned to cover the aftermath of a big storm. She notices a phone booth turned over in about two feet of water. She asks a child riding a bike in the water next to the phone booth to pick up the phone and pretend to make a call. The photographer hands in the photo without telling the editor it was a set-up photo.

Only 2 percent of the photojournalists responded that this situation was acceptable. On the other hand, 91 percent said they would definitely not stage this picture without telling their editors.

A second scenario in the NPPA study produced a different result, however. For this one, a hypothetical photographer is doing a picture page on a visiting nurse in a rural farming community. The one element she lacks to tell the story is a shot of the nurse walking across the field to the farmhouse.

The photographer has seen her walk across the field before, but she's never been at the right place at the right time to get the shot, so she asks the nurse to meet her at the house and walk across the field just as she normally would do. She has the nurse repeat the scene a couple of times to make sure she gets just the right shot.

The survey results, based on the responses of 116 professional photographers, indicated that 38 percent would re-create the scene.

On the other hand, 28 percent of the respondents were not sure how they would handle the situation. Another 34 percent indicated that they definitely would not have the visiting nurse walk across the field just for the camera.

CHANGING VALUES
In fact, photojournalists' ethics are changing. In 1961, Wilcox found that none of the pros he surveyed thought twice about repeating a groundbreaking ceremony for the camera.

Twenty-six years later, a third of the photographers in Brink's NPPA survey would not repeat or re-create a picture. While the two vignettes, the repeated ceremony and the nurse crossing the field for the camera, are not identical, the radical difference in photographers' responses over time does suggest a shift in photojournalistic ethics.

Re-creations of picture situations that were acceptable to every pro in the 1960s were anathema to a large segment of the professional community by the 1980s.

GROUNDS FOR DISMISSAL?
Staging or manipulating pictures can be highly damaging to careers. Take the case of Edward Keating, a Pulitzer Prize-winning photographer for the *New York Times*. Keating photographed a young boy pointing a toy gun outside an Arabian grocery store near the town where the FBI raided an alleged al Qaeda cell. Other photographers at the scene claimed Keating posed the boy. Shawn Dowd of the *Rochester Democrat and Chronicle* reported seeing Keating point with his arm to show the boy which way to look and aim the gun. After *Columbia Journalism Review* reported the incident, Keating was forced to leave the *Times*. He joins other photographers including Mike Meadows (above), formerly of the *Los Angeles Times*, and Norm

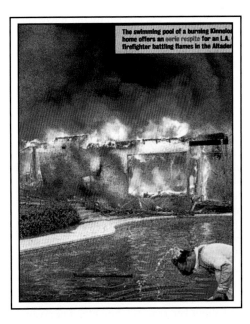

The swimming pool of a burning Kinneloa home offers an eerie respite for an L.A. firefighter battling flames in the Altadena

Zeisloft of the *St. Petersburg Times* (pages 304–305) who were found to overstep the ethical boundaries that divide acceptable practices from journalistic manipulation.

On the other hand, what is not acceptable in the United States may well be permitted in other countries. In his book ***Picture Editing: An Introduction***, Britisher Tom Ang observes, "In press photography, one can ask demonstrators to face their placards towards the camera but encouraging them to make threatening gestures at a policeman would be widely regarded as going too far." In the United States, most photojournalists would consider asking demonstrators to face the camera an ethical breach.

WHOSE RESPONSIBILITY?
Surprisingly, many photographers in the Brink study felt that telling their editors absolved them of ethical responsibility.

In a follow-up question to the staging vignette, the study showed that 33 percent of the photographers no longer found staging the picture unethical if they explained the facts to their editors. Telling a higher authority seemed to eliminate feelings of responsibility on the part of these pros.

Can photographers avoid ethical decisions this easily?

DO READERS BELIEVE THEIR EYES?
Below a headline in the *New York Post* that read NUKE LEAK AT INDIAN POINT, a picture ran showing a woman holding a child covered by a blanket. The mother appeared to be trying to protect her child from radiation from the atomic energy plant. The picture was published by the *Post* as well as by

Mike Meadows of the *Los Angles Timess* was covering a major wild fire sweeping southern California. His pictureof a fireman cooling himself off from the water in a pool ran not only in the *Times* but also nationally.

Prior to submitting the photograph for a contest, however, the newspaper's editors contacted the fireman, who said he had been asked by the photographer to go over by the pool and splash water on his head. The photographer responded that "I may have been guilty of saying 'this would make a nice shot,' but I did not directly ask him to do that."

What Meadows did not understand was that even a suggestion to a subject in a news situation is a form of interference—and thus out of place on the continuum of control. The unfortunate photographer's picture was withdrawn from competition, and he left the paper.

Reproduced from *Newsweek*

Time, and also was carried by the Associated Press and United Press International.

When several newspapers in the Northwest printed the photograph, the editor and publisher of the *Centralia* (Washington) *Chronicle*, Jack Britten, attacked the picture's integrity in an editorial.

"Come on," the editorial demanded.

"Who do they think they're conning? Any discerning reader could quickly see that the photo is very likely staged . . . the photo is an obvious put-on, a misrepresentation of the actual situation, and the editors should have known it. If they didn't know it, they shouldn't be editors."

In fact, photographer Martha Cooper and *Post* reporter Deborah Orin came across the woman as she was leaving her house, her baby covered with a blanket. Orin interviewed the woman, who had been worried about her year-old daughter's exposure to radiation. She had been ready to climb into her car and leave the area when the *Post* team found her. Cooper took the pictures during the interview.

In a follow-up story in the *Washington Star*, columnist Mary McGrory confirmed the photo's authenticity.

If a seasoned newspaper editor questioned the photo's truthfulness, how often do readers wonder whether what they see in newspapers, magazines, and computer screens really took place? After all, people watch professional photographers pose pictures at class reunions, bar mitzvahs, and weddings. While such photographers are not photojournalists, how many readers make the distinction?

WHEN FACTS CONFLICT WITH PHOTOGRAPHS

Just how widespread is disbelief in photojournalism? No one knows for sure, but the disbelief extends at least to Waterville, Maine.

"Kids for sale," shouted the July 20, 1986, cover of *Parade* magazine. "It can happen anywhere." Three small color photos of unidentified and unidentifiable, sultry adolescent "girls of the street" dotted the text-dominated black cover, which announced a "special report" on child prostitution.

Anywhere, the article purported, included New York City, Van Nuys, California, and "placid little towns like Waterville, Maine."

A local Maine newspaper challenged the story. Reporters discovered that the Attorney

ONE PHOTOGRAPHER WHO DIDN'T CHANGE WITH THE TIMES

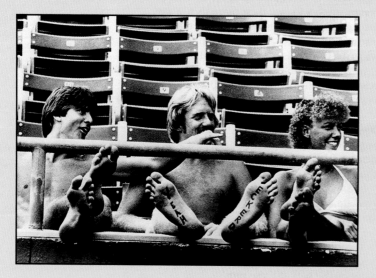

Not long after the Janet Cooke affair (see page 308), one *St. Petersburg* (Florida) *Times* staff photographer selected a spot on the continuum that proved out of sync with changing times. The results were disastrous for him.

The incident began with a routine assignment for 61-year-old Norman Zeisloft, a veteran photographer and past president of his regional NPPA chapter. He had been shooting for the *St. Petersburg Times* and *Evening Independent* for more than seventeen years.

HELPING ALONG A FEATURE

Zeisloft had been assigned to cover a baseball game between Eckerd and Florida Southern Colleges. "It was quite a nothing event," he recalled for Jim Gordon, who later wrote a comprehensive story about the incident for *News Photographer* magazine.

Spotting three bare-soled fans with their feet up, Zeisloft approached them and said it would be "cute if you had 'Yeah Eckerd' written on the bottom of your feet."

They agreed, and Zeisloft pulled out a felt-tip pen and began writing on the soles of one man's feet. Zeisloft found that his pen was dry and the spectator's feet were too dirty to accept writing. Meanwhile, one fan left the stands, washed his feet and reappeared with "Yeah Eckerd" on his soles. Zeisloft took the photo, and it ran two days later in the *Evening Independent*.

"It was just a whimsical thing, just for a little joke," Zeisloft recounted. "It was just a little picture to make people smile rather than an old accident scene."

But nearby was Phil Sheffield, a *Tampa* (Florida) *Tribune* photographer since 1974 and a photographer for Miami's Associated Press bureau before that. Almost instinctively, Sheffield said, he snapped one frame as Zeisloft originally applied pen to sole.

Posted as a joke on the bulletin board of the *Tampa Tribune*, Sheffield's photo eventually found its way to the president and editor of the *St. Petersburg Times*—Norm Zeisloft's boss, a judge on the Pulitzer committee

General's office in the Maine jurisdiction had prosecuted only two cases of prostitution in Waterville, none involving teenagers—and that the young Waterville "prostitute" in the photo was actually a model.

When freelance photographer Dean Abramson was unable to find an actual streetwalking teen in Waterville, his *Parade* magazine editors told him to hire a model. Abramson complied and eventually snapped the posed picture.

Although *Parade* editors initially denied the subterfuge, later they recanted, saying that an explanatory line of type had been omitted. In a follow-up article for *News Photographer* magazine, they further rationalized the situation by telling writer Betsy Brill that they routinely used models for stories involving minors.

In interviews with other photographers on the project, however, Brill discovered that, despite editors' claims, only two of the three pictures had been set up with models for the *Parade* cover. A third photographer captured an actual candid moment.

Camera 5 freelancer Neal Preston verified that his assignment from *Parade* had been to find and photograph actual teenaged prosti-

tutes (not models). He had done so in Van Nuys, California.

"I could have saved a lot of time and film if I had hired a model," he told Brill, when he learned the other photos had been set up. "I'm proud my picture was the one that was real."

Award-winning photojournalist Eddie Adams, who photographed the New York City set-up, told Brill that concern over the staged photos was "a lot of bullshit." He said that the hiring of models for stories involving children is done "all the time"—not just by him, he said, and not just by *Parade*, but by all magazines, especially for cover stories.

"There's a difference," Adams said, "between an illustration and a straight picture." (See Chapter 9, "Illustrations.") Yet, he acknowledged, the reader has no way of knowing the difference without words.

Adams, however, begged the ethical question and relied on the familiar "everybody does it" argument. The question is not: "do photographers hire models regularly when taking pictures of children?" The real question is: "should photographers use models—and pose them so that they look as though they're in real situations?"

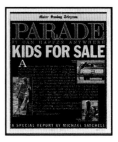

On this cover, two of the girls are models. One is not. How would the reader know which is candid and which is set up? Would a reader have known what "photo illustration" means had the disclaimer been included? © *Parade.*

that had been caught in the web of Janet Cooke's dishonesty.

STANDARD PROCEDURE OR GROUNDS FOR DISMISSAL?

Zeisloft was fired on his first day back from vacation. Later, in an administrative appeal hearing over denied unemployment benefits, Zeisloft explained that news photographers often set up pictures about society and club news, recipe contest winners, ribbon-cutting and ground-breaking ceremonies, awards and enterprise features.

He took to the hearing pictures that had won professional contests, some from the old *Life* "Speaking of Pictures" department. Others, he explained, had gone "nationwide via AP and UPI wire services. The pictures had won awards plus applause from editors.

"These pictures were not intended to bamboozle the public or to 'distort' the news. They were shot with good humor and were merely designed to give the reading public a good chuckle. They were harmless and entertaining. That and nothing more," Zeisloft said.

"To me," Zeisloft said, "it seemed like cruel and unusual punishment to be fired after seventeen and a half years of faithful service on the basis of one photo that was designed merely to bring a chuckle to our readers. There was not one phone call or letter from our reading public in regards to the picture.

"If a cop shot a person he'd get a suspension. Doesn't seventeen and a half years count for anything?" he asked.

A CONTINUUM TEMPERED BY TIME

Unfortunately, Norm Zeisloft had selected a spot on the control continuum that was not professionally acceptable for the time and place he was working. Ten years earlier or at another newspaper or magazine, the set-up feature might have been perfectly accepted by the profession and even by the public. Zeisloft found himself out of register with the current dividing line between acceptable and unacceptable practice on the continuum of control.

Because the place acceptable to fellow professionals and the public on the continuum shifts with time and events, all photojournalists should reevaluate their own set points. Do theirs coincide with other members of the profession, with editors, and with the public?

Finally, even if a practice is acceptable in the field, the photographer must answer a more difficult question: is the behavior ethically right? Should I do this even if all my peers are doing it? While photographers should be aware of standards in the field, they should also deal with the more basic question of right and wrong. ■

Whether you're a magazine reader in Waterville or a newspaper reader in New York City, your belief in all pictures drops when you discover that some of the images you are seeing are figments in the imaginations of photo editors.

CONCLUSION

For photojournalists, the issue of posing often centers on a photographer's role as reporter versus his or her role as an artist with a camera, says Shiela Reaves in her article "Re-examining the Ethics of Photographic Posing: Insights from the Rank-and-File Members of ASMP (American Society of Media Photographers)." Editors in particular and the profession in general convey a double message, she observes. The message reads "produce both a truthful picture and one that demonstrates artistic merit." Observe an event—and be inventive and creative.

Sometimes those two distinct roles come into conflict.

The key to making an ethical decision is to know which professional role is required in a given situation. If the assignment from the food editor requests a photo illustrating hot dogs as the quintessential American food for the Fourth of July, the photographer's creative juices need to flow. With the studio's seamless backdrop as a canvas, the photographer becomes an artist bringing together hot dogs, American flags, and sparklers into a pleasing and storytelling composition.

On the other hand, if the scanner radio announces that a murder/suicide in a college dorm has just occurred, the photographer's purely observational skills need to kick in. No invention should be needed as the police bring out the stretcher and dorm-mates cry. No studio. No props. No direction.

Reality will suffice. The photographer's role is to record, not to influence. Of course, the problem lies with assignments that fall between these two extremes.

As they go from assignment to assignment, most working pros find themselves at different points on the continuum of photographic control. Generally, photojournalists find decisions about how to handle the ends of the continuum fairly easy. How the photojournalist approaches a sports event or five-alarm fire is quite different from how that person handles a fashion or portrait assignment. Photojournalists set up some pictures but not others. The questions each photographer must ask is, "Where should I be on the continuum of control? At any given time, what part of the continuum should I choose? Which spot along the continuum is appropriate for this

A CONTINUUM OF CONTROL

Between moving an obstructing cola bottle and hiring a model to impersonate a teenage hooker lies a large, gray ethical chasm. This gray zone, with its myriad shadows and shadings, can challenge even the most clear-sighted photographer. Are all situations alike?

Do the same rules apply to features, portraits, and illustrations, as well as to hard news? Far from being a fixed commodity, the photographer's level of control is variable, logistically and ethically. A photojournalist's weekly assignment sheet is likely to represent a continuum of control—from strictly hands-off to complete manipulation.

Photojournalists cover subjects ranging from a war in the Middle East to a fashion shoot in midtown. Like the fashion shoot, some pictures require complete control. Other situations, like accidents or arrests downtown, require the hands-off, fly-on-the-wall approach.

Any time you take pictures, you are affecting the scene to some degree. According to noted physicist Werner Heisenberg, observation itself alters the object being observed. This principle applies to photography as surely as it does to the subatomic world.

For instance, whether a subject consciously thinks about the photographer or not, that person's behavior changes in the presence of a camera. Some subjects exaggerate their behavior; others shy away from the camera. Even thinking a camera might be present can alter some people's behavior.

Even though photographers and their cameras have some influence on the scene they are photographing, the question the working pro must ask is, "When should the photojournalist remain an observer, removed as much as possible from the scene? When should the photographer intervene?"

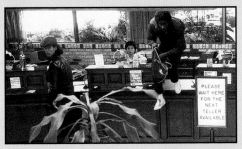
Photo courtesy Bank Security

• Hidden cameras represent one extreme of the continuum. The security camera at First Local Bank automatically snaps a picture at regular intervals, regardless of who is standing at the teller window. The bank camera, which exercises no control over the subject, exerts no control at all. Despite its passivity, however, even the bank camera alters the scene being observed: most criminals would take different precautions if robbing a bank under constant photographic surveillance.

• Sports photography is near this end of the continuum. A hurdler races down the track. Even if she wanted to, the sports photographer could have little influence on the athlete. She would not tell the runner to run to the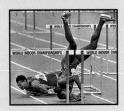
Michael Meinhardt, UPI

right for a better picture. The sports photographer has virtually no control over the subject but does select the moment to release the camera's shutter.

• Hard news. Elsewhere along the continuum you will find the news photographer covering a riot. Most photographers would hesitate to direct a demonstrator or tell a policeman to stand aside to improve a pho-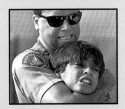
Charlie Fellenbaum, the *Hemet* [California] *News*

tograph's composition. The photographer could initiate control but refrains in a true hard-news situation.

• Features. This is where the continuum becomes slippery. Here, photographers disagree about when to intervene and when to merely observe. The action is touching, but the light is not great. Is it okay to ask the subject to move over a few feet so you could get perfect backlighting?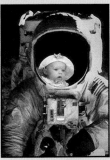
Juanito Holandez, *Long Beach* [California] *Press-Telegram*

Different photographers have determined different points where they will draw the control line when faced with a feature assignment. Some photojournalists would not hesitate to ask the subject to move. Other shooters would never consider disturbing the moment, even if leaving the situation untouched meant that they would not get a superb picture.

• Portraits usually require some direction on the part of the photographer. If the assignment is to take pictures of the president of the local university, the photographer usually must tell her where to sit and what to do with her hands. The photographer might ask the president to look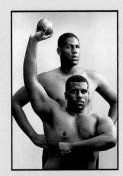
Pat Crowe, *Wilmington* [Delaware] *News Journal*

directly at the camera. This way the reader knows that the administrator was aware of the photographer and won't think the picture is a candid photo. An unwritten but probably accurate rule holds that, if the subject is looking at the photographer (i.e., the reader), the subject is aware of the camera.

• Photo illustrations represent the the other extreme, the full-control end of the continuum. Photojournalists manufacture every aspect of an illustration— including editorial concept photos, food photos, and studio and location fashion shoots. The photojournalist arranges the props, perhaps builds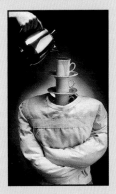
Bob Farley, *Birmingham* [Alabama] *Post-Herald*

the set, and hires and even dresses the models. The viewer has no illusions about the photo or the photographer's role. If the photographer has been careful, the created photo cannot be mistaken for real. Through the use of exaggerated size, seamless backgrounds, and other visual devices, the photojournalist can assure the reader that the picture is constructed and not a slice of real life. (See Chapter 9, "Illustrations.") With photo illustrations, the photographer exercises complete control. ∎

assignment?"

KEEPING UP WITH SHIFTING STANDARDS

The decision regarding control is a choice often based more on a photographer's time in history than on any established guidelines (see pages 304–305).

Photojournalism has no Bible, no rabbinical college, no Pope to define correct choices. And although surveys like those by Wilcox and Brink help establish current practices in the field, professional values do not remain fixed in time. Professional standards are changing, and so are readers' expectations. Staying abreast of professional standards and evaluating decisions with an eye to the ethical foundations described at the beginning of this chapter should be helpful when faced with difficult moments.

Keep in mind that setting up feature pictures was at one time perfectly acceptable to most newspaper photojournalists. *New York Post* photographer Barney Stein wrote his book, *Spot News Photography,* in the early 1950s. Stein proudly described as a routine photojournalistic activity how he went about setting up feature pictures of a cowboy performing for crippled kids or of a Dalmatian firedog wearing the fire chief's hat.

John Faber, historian for the National Press Photographers Association (NPPA), told of traveling around the country as Kodak's professional representative, teaching newspaper photographers how to create imaginative feature pictures.

In his 1961 survey, Wilcox found that no photojournalist objected to restaging a ceremony for a photo. Yet, today, according to the Brink survey, at least a third of the photographers who are NPPA members would object to restaging a situation.

W. Eugene Smith, the famous *Life* magazine photographer, wrote in 1948, "The majority of photographic stories require a certain amount of setting up, rearranging and stage direction to bring pictorial and editorial coherency to the pictures." Smith noted, however, that if the changes become a perversion of the actuality for the sole purpose of making a "more dramatic" or "salable picture," the photographer has indulged in "poetic license."

In his book *Truth Needs No Ally*, Howard Chapnick, long-time head of Black Star Picture Agency, observed that in the 1990s the "changes in camera and film technology have made it a truism that anything we can see we can photograph." He argued that now there is no excuse for the photojournalist to manipulate people in real-life situations.

JANET COOKE

What has caused this change in standards for the profession?

Many observers point to one incident as the pivot-point for journalists.

In 1981, Janet Cooke, a reporter for the *Washington Post*, won a Pulitzer Prize based on a story she wrote about a 6-year-old drug addict. After the prize was awarded, investigators discovered that the child had never existed. The young addict was a figment of Cooke's imagination—a "composite" of characters and incidents she had come upon in her research. Cooke lost the prize and gained a place of dishonor in journalism history. The journalism profession threw up its arms in outrage and began a hard, soul-searching reexamination of its ethical practices. Professional groups sponsored seminars, authors wrote books, and universities initiated classes in journalism ethics. The public's opinion of the press, its practices, and its prizes dropped to a new low.

The outgrowth of this examination was an increased sensitivity, even vigilance, to how the profession performs its work. The profession began to question some of its accepted standards. The spotlight on the Cooke case also heightened sensitivity toward ethical standards within the photojournalism community.

MONITORING ETHICAL STANDARDS

For the neophyte photographer or the seasoned pro, the profession does not provide a fixed yardstick, a definitive set of guidelines, or a regular measure of what other photojournalists in the trade are thinking and doing.

In fact, photojournalists disagree among themselves about the correctness of many choices. Craig Hartley, in a national survey of professionals for his thesis on photojournalistic ethics, found that of nineteen hypothetical problems presented to working pros, almost half the questions resulted in a wide split among respondents.

On nine questions, at least a third of the photojournalists did not agree with their other responding colleagues. Clearly photojournalists do not think as a monolithic block when the topic turns to ethics.

Read about the Profession
Interested photographers can use the trade media and other resources to monitor the thoughts of their fellow journalists and shape their own ethical touchstones. *News Photographer* magazine, the trade publication of the National Press Photographers Association, reports on controversial issues. Read, in particular, the magazine's "Letters to the Editor" column to check the pulse of the working pro. *Visual Communication*

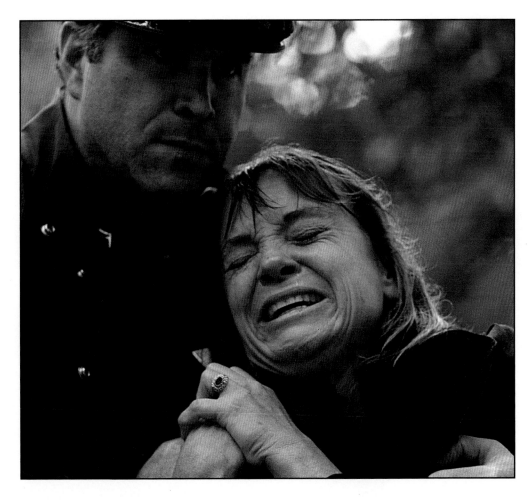

A mother is close to hysteria as she watches rescuers try to save her daughter from drowning. (See the rescue photo on page i.) Even in emotional times like this, photographers must take pictures. Photojournalists should get their photos as unobtrusively as possible, preferably using a telephoto lens. If a wide-angle lens is necessary, try not to linger in the subject's face.
Annie Wells, for the *Press Democrat* [Santa Rosa, California]

Quarterly, inserted in the magazine four times a year, showcases research in the field.

In addition, magazines like *Columbia Journalism Review, American Journalism Review*, and *Photo District News* report on changing professional standards. *Journalism Quarterly* also publishes research on ethics.

In addition to magazines, workshops such as NPPA's Flying Short Course and the organization's online discussion list, NPPA-L, provide valid insights into photojournalism's shifting standards. Websites where professionals discuss ethical issues are *www.digitaljournalist.com, www.poynter.org,* and *www.SportsShooter.com.*

Let Your Subjects Guide You

Besides looking to other professionals, photographers should also monitor the reaction of their subjects to gauge shifting values in photojournalism.

In her study "Listening to the Subjects of Routine News Photographs: A Grounded Moral Inquiry," researcher Cindy Brown surveyed individuals whose photographs had appeared in a number of Midwestern newspapers. She asked them about their experiences with the photographer when the original pictures were taken and how they felt about the published images. Happily, Brown reports that the people she questioned generally liked the photojournalists who took their photographs and found the experience positive. Even when the news situations were anything but upbeat, the subjects felt good about the published photos and understood why their pictures were in the paper.

Considering a subject's responses and ethical concerns can help sensitize you to your news outlet's constituency.

A GENERAL RULE

What if you're not abreast of current standards, and you find yourself in a touchy situation on assignment? You might use this test of your own honesty, originally suggested by Elisabeth Biondi. Biondi has been a photo editor for *Geo, Vanity Fair*, and *Stern* magazines. She suggests that photographers test their ethical decisions by considering whether they would feel comfortable writing a note to the reader explaining how the picture was taken. For example, would the photographer mind explaining, "I brought these clothes for the subject to wear, and then I told him to make that crazy face?" If the

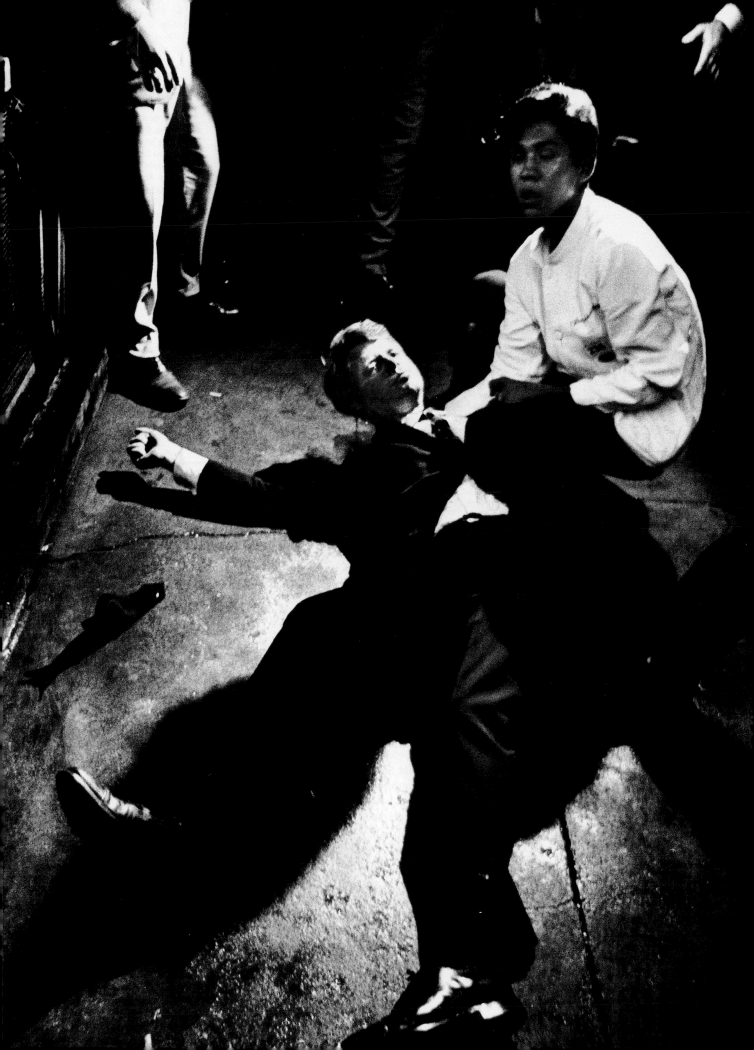

photographer is willing for the reader to know how the picture was constructed, what props were added, and what direction was given, then, Biondi says, the photo is probably ethically acceptable. However, if the photographer would feel uncomfortable revealing to the reader his or her methods, then the picture likely falls on the unethical side of the line.

COVERING TRAGEDY AND GRIEF

When injuries occur at a car crash, a hotel fire, or a natural disaster, bystanders and relatives often block a camera reporter from taking pictures. Understandably these people are upset. In his book *The Messenger's Motives*, John L. Hulteng writes, "Photographers have acquired the reputation of being indifferent to the human suffering they frame in their viewfinders."

While the law gives the photographer the right to take a picture, the law is an institution, not a human being who has just lost a son or daughter.

Using the utilitarian principle of ethical decision making, on the other hand, photographers have a moral responsibility to their readers to picture the world accurately, showing both its triumphs and its tragedies. A democracy in which citizens must be informed to vote intelligently depends on information. Photos provide information. In the long run, individuals cannot make informed decisions without a balanced and accurate picture of the world. Utilitarianism argues that people will benefit from seeing both the good and bad, the happy and sad, and the joyful and tragic elements that comprise our world.

However, does this case for the "common good" supersede the rights of the grief-stricken individual? Do photographers have the right—or the obligation—to record moments of individual loss? These issues are complex, but there is one clear tenet to guide photographers' behavior in traumatic situations: photographers have a responsibility not to inflict greater suffering than necessary on survivors of a tragedy. "Than necessary" is obviously a troublesome phrase here, one defining that difficult gray zone. There is no clear measure of necessity. In the end, photographers must balance the harm to an individual caught in the jaws of tragedy with the long-range needs of society to see an unvarnished picture of the world.

When Robert Kennedy was assassinated, a bystander blocked Boris Yaro's camera. He said to the woman, "Goddammit, lady, this is history!" and took this unforgettable picture. See pages 313 for a discussion about the situation. Boris Yaro, © *Los Angeles Times*

GUIDELINES FOR PHOTOGRAPHING TRAGIC MOMENTS

For an article in *News Photographer* magazine, Michael D. Sherer collected comments from photographers who had covered tragic events. Here are some of their guidelines:

ON CONDUCT
Be early, stay out of the way, and don't disrupt what's going on. Be sensitive to your subjects and the situation. Be compassionate. Do not badger or chase subjects to the point of annoyance. "How would I feel if I were the person being photographed?"
Jim Gehrz, *Worthington* [Minnesota] *Daily Globe*

ON EQUIPMENT
In sensitive situations, carry as little gear as possible, leave the motor drive behind, and use the longest lens possible. Don't become a spectacle.

ON SELECTIVITY
Pick your shots carefully—look for angles and subjects that will not offend subjects' and readers' sensitivities.

ON DRESS
Wear "appropriate" clothing. "Dress is an important part of the way the public perceives us and in their acceptance of us in times of stress. I think many of us can dress better day-to-day without having to wear a three-piece suit."
Mark Hertzberg, *Racine* [Wisconsin] *Journal Times*

ON FOLLOW-UP
"Consider contacting the subjects sometime after publication to discuss the reason for, and reaction to, publishing the image."
Dave Nuss, *Salem* [Oregon] *Statesman-Journal*

Pictures of grief personalize the news. Statistics about car accidents, spousal violence, murders, and accidental drownings distance the reader from the event. Seeing a picture of a particular person who was hit by a drunk driver gives the issue a face. No matter how large the numbers, issues remain abstract.

From "Thousands die on the road every year" to "Katy Smith was struck by hit-and-run driver in a Honda yesterday and here is what she looked like," photographs transform an otherwise abstract issue into a personal event. The reader is more likely to care about Katy than all the thousands of other people who died last year.

Pictures can actually help victims and families. Some families understand that running the picture of a tragedy may prevent the same thing from happening to others. A published pictures can give a family some rationale for a terrible calamity. Dave LaBelle observes in his book *Lessons in Death and Life*, "Although many cry foul when photographs of grieving subjects are published, often the subjects themselves are helped to deal with their grief." He notes this story: "Two days after the *Albuquerque* (New Mexico) *Tribune* published graphic pictures of a burn victim, Sage Volkman, it ran a letter from the girl's parents explaining why they thought the public needed to see the photos. 'We would like you to be aware of her struggle from when she was first burned and almost through

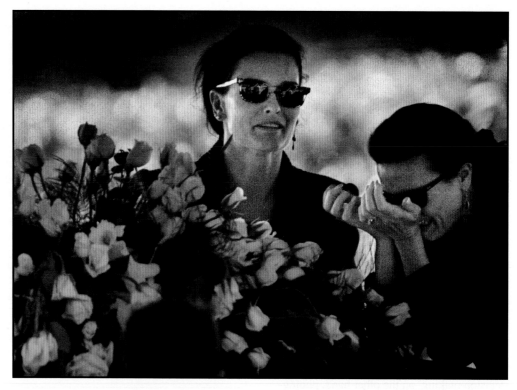

These women are crying over the coffin of their recently murdered sister, Nicole Brown. Brown was the former wife of football legend O.J. Simpson, accused but found innocent of her murder. When photographing a funeral, call ahead to express your sympathy and to let the family or friends know you are coming. At the graveside, wear appropriate clothing.
Al Schaben, *Los Angeles Times*

death's door to her return to us as a 6-year-old girl with feelings who sees life in terms of Barbie dolls and her Brownie troop. When you come upon her unexpectedly in a store or restaurant, your first reaction may be one of sadness. But if you do run into her, we hope you will see her as we do—as a brave little girl.'" Publication of the photos helped raise more than $50,000 to aid with Sage's medical bills.

DO ALL TRAGEDIES NEED PHOTO COVERAGE?

If you are familiar with your equipment, you can usually take a few quick, available-light candid shots nearly unnoticed at any accident scene. Beyond these photos, you must weigh the short-range pain of your presence versus the long-range value of your potential photos—a difficult judgment each photographer must make. Neither photographers at the scene nor editors back at the office are clairvoyant. Neither can look into a crystal ball and predict a picture's effect.

Photojournalists must maintain a belief in the overriding long-range importance of photos and the specific contribution of their particular image. Emotion-laden events lead to a cautious, continuous balancing act.

Eddie Adams, who won the Pulitzer Prize for his photograph of a Viet Cong suspect being executed in the streets of Saigon (see page 326), told the author about a photo he didn't take while covering that war:

"On a hilltop in Vietnam, I was pinned down with a Marine company. Machine guns were going off. Dead bodies were lying on either side of me. Rocket fire seemed to be coming from everywhere. I was lying on the ground five feet away from an 18-year-old Marine. I saw fear on that kid's face like I had never seen before. I slid my Leica, with its preset 35mm lens, in front of me. I tried to push the shutter, but I couldn't. I tried twice more, but my finger just would not push the button. Later, I realized that I was just as scared to die as that kid was. I knew my face looked exactly like his, and I would not have wanted my picture seen around the world. I think his and my face said WAR, but I still think I did the right thing by not taking that picture."

Adams chose to invoke the "do unto others . . ." Golden Rule. However, the photographer might also have considered the possible value to society from seeing the censored image. Adams's Pulitzer Prize-winning picture of the Vietnamese colonel executing a suspected Viet Cong did help to change the course of the Vietnam War. In the execution situation, society's greater good was served by photographing the scene.

Adams's hesitation at taking pictures on the hilltop in Vietnam was rare. Most professional photographers don't hesitate to take pictures when faced with a gut-wrenching accident or tragic murder.

In fact, many photographers say that because the critical moment is fleeting they shoot instinctively. They point out that you can always decide not to use the picture, but you can't revisit the moment. The consequences of taking someone's picture, the momentary disturbance or embarrassment, is relatively minor. Publishing the picture, which will be seen by friends, colleagues, and strangers, has a different and perhaps longer-lasting impact on the subject.

Finally, hesitating to take pictures can conflict with the professional role of the photojournalist. In most circumstances, professional standards would support the "shoot now—edit later" approach.

Boris Yaro, a *Los Angeles Times* photographer, had no trouble making the decision to take pictures when he photographed Senator Robert Kennedy's assassination at the Ambassador Hotel. Later he told the story to John Faber, author of **Great News Photos**.

"I was trying to focus in the dark when I heard a loud Bang! Bang! I watched in absolute horror. I thought, 'Oh my God it's happening again! To another Kennedy!' I turned toward the Senator. He was slipping to the floor. I aimed my camera, starting to focus, when someone grabbed my suit coat arm. I looked into the dim light, seeing a woman with a camera around her neck screaming at me. 'Don't take pictures! Don't take pictures! I'm a photographer and I'm not taking pictures!' she said." For a brief instant, Yaro was dumbfounded. Then he told her to let go of him. "I said, 'Goddammit, lady, this is history!'"

He took the photographs. (See page 310.)

RESPECTING PRIVACY AT FUNERALS

Funerals are sad, stressful, and emotionally draining. They provide a context for grief and a forum for sharing sorrow among family and friends—not photographers. But sometimes they are newsworthy.

The decision to cover a funeral generally rests with an editor, but once that decision is made, it's the photographer's responsibility to complete the assignment. And it is the photographer, not the editor in the office, whom mourners notice, resent, and berate.

Photographers and the public have widely differing views about professional ethical conduct at these ceremonies. Craig Hartley surveyed NPPA members and citizens of Austin, Texas. He wanted to compare each group's reactions to a number of ethical situations, including one that involved the funeral of a slain police officer, an event that an uninvited photographer attends and photographs even after being asked to leave.

Hartley found that although 63 percent of the news photographers he surveyed found the photojournalist's behavior at the funeral "ethical," 85 percent of the public found the

behavior "unethical." Readers, who vehemently denounced the actions of the photojournalist at the funeral, did not perceive the picture's value as meriting this intrusion into the private ceremony.

PROFESSIONAL VERSUS GOOD SAMARITAN

When should the photographer act as a professional photojournalist, and when should the cameraperson act as a responsible citizen? What happens when the roles conflict? Consider these scenarios:

You are driving along the street and see a man running out of a pawnshop carrying a television set under his arm with the proprietor in hot pursuit. Do you try to stop the thief with the intent of holding him for the police, or do you take a picture of the scene as the criminal escapes around the corner?

Later in the day, you see an accident by the side of the road. A child, stuck behind the car's dashboard, cries inconsolably. Do you take the little girl's picture, or sit and comfort her?

A terrorist group has agreed to let you photograph their activities. They take you on a secret mission to plant a bomb. Do you take their pictures or try to stop them from activating the explosive? How would you handle the situation if you were photographing a similar raid, only this time the group was a unit of the U.S. army, not a terrorist cell?

The argument for professionalism often parallels the utilitarian principle of ethics. The photojournalist has a role in society just as a doctor or lawyer has. That role is to inform the public. Information allows citizens to make intelligent decisions. By actually seeing what is going on—a thief in the act of stealing a television set; terrorists planting a bomb; a person committing suicide; or even the agony of a child in a car wreck—citizens can perhaps learn enough or be moved enough to create public debate. Information can lead to changes in public policy, laws, funding, or perhaps just improved behavior.

A photographer's job is to record the news, not to prevent it or to change it. Like an anthropologist observing a foreign culture, the photojournalist should look, record, but not disturb what is going on.

The Good Samaritan argument, on the other hand, is absolutist: a photojournalist is, first and foremost, a human being. A photojournalist's primary responsibility is to the person needing immediate help. Journalism comes second. No one can measure the good a photo will do later, but you can see the immediate needs of the present.

Joe Fudge, of the *Newport News* (Virginia)

Daily Press Times Herald, had no problem making the ethical choice between being a Good Samaritan and a professional photojournalist when he saw smoke pouring from the third floor of a house.

First asking the newspaper office via two-way radio to notify the fire department, Fudge charged into the burning house and alerted residents that their attic was ablaze. "I went into the house and found three people sitting around eating. They didn't know that a fire was burning off the top of their house. The woman said, 'Oh, my God, my husband is asleep in the third-floor bedroom.' By this time, the flames were coming through the ceiling of the third floor. We went up and woke him up. Then all of us escaped."

When Fudge jumped out of his car after spotting the fire, he did not take in his cameras. Rather than photograph the burning house, Fudge decided to save lives first. Later, he returned for his equipment and photographed the father saving the family dog.

A group of photographers faced ethical decisions when presidential candidate Bob Dole fell through a platform railing during an appearance in Chico, California. In the split second when Dole tumbled through the weak stage banister, Agence France-Presse (AFP) photographer J. David Ake prevented Dole's head from hitting the ground in the four-foot fall. Ake didn't get the picture, but he saved Dole from a potentially disastrous head injury. Reuters photographer Rick Wilking, too far away to help, recorded the accident.

Said Ake, "If someone is falling toward you, the human thing to do is to try to help him, not stand back and let him crash." Wilking, on the other hand, was not in a position to assist Dole, so he did not have to choose between aiding the candidate and shooting pictures.

Wilking did cover the sequence photographically. The photograph of Dole grimac-

ing in pain after the fall from the campaign stage became a visual icon of Dole's slipping campaign.

SUICIDE: A SPECIAL CASE?
Photographer William T. Murphy, Jr., when he worked for the *Oregon Journal*, faced the dilemma of taking pictures or trying to help a woman stop her husband from killing himself. He tried to do both—by taking five shots as he attempted to talk the man out of jumping one hundred feet into the Columbia River and as he yelled at another motorist on the bridge to go for help. But the man soon struggled free from his wife's desperate grip and jumped to his death in the swirling river.

Few readers sympathized with Murphy's ethical dilemma. According to "Ethics of Compassion," an article by Gene Goodwin in *Quill* magazine, many readers complained about Murphy's photo of the suicide, which went out over the UPI (United Press International) wires.

"Don't the ethics of journalism insist that preservation of human life comes first, news second?" asked a reader from Philadelphia. A New York reader wrote, "He let a man die for the sake of a good photograph."

Murphy replied to the criticism, "I don't know what I could have done differently. I am a photographer, and I did what I have been trained to do. I did all I could."

SUICIDE AS A FORM OF PROTEST
No one attempted to stop a Buddhist monk who set himself afire protesting the 1963 Diem government in South Vietnam. The shocking picture showed readers dramatically and convincingly how serious the country's problems were. The monk used his death as the ultimate form of political protest (page 199). The AP's Peter Arnett, who reported the event, said that he could have prevented that immolation by rushing at the monk and kicking the gasoline away. "As a human being I wanted to; as a reporter I couldn't."

One person's private turmoil resulted in a national issue when Pennsylvania State Treasurer R. Budd Dwyer called a press conference just hours before he was to be sentenced for his conviction in a $300,000 kickback scandal. Dwyer, forty-seven, was facing up to fifty-five years in prison. After thirty minutes of proclaiming his innocence to reporters and photographers, Dwyer picked up a large manila envelope and pulled out a long-barrel, blue-black handgun. He placed the gun in his mouth and pulled the trigger.

Could photographers, reporters, or TV camera crews have stopped Dwyer? The consensus was no. Once the gun was out of the envelope, only fifteen seconds elapsed before

At a press conference called by R. Budd Dwyer, Pennsylvania's state treasurer, he proclaimed himself innocent of a kickback scandal and then killed himself. No photographer could have stopped him.

Should these pictures have been published?
Gary Miller (BELOW LEFT)
Paul Vathis (BOTH, RIGHT)
Associated Press

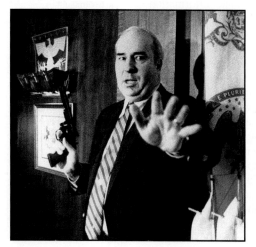
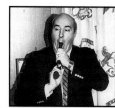
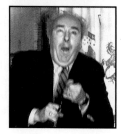

Dwyer shot himself. Also, Dwyer had built a barricade of chairs and tables between himself and the press.

Should photographers have stopped Budd Dwyer if they had the opportunity? Was Dwyer making a political statement? In any case, are the pictures so upsetting to the public that they cause the reader to look away rather than consider the underlying issues?

At least on the front page, according to one study, almost every editor surveyed (95 percent) thought that the photo of Dwyer's body slumping after he fired the shot was too shocking for their readers.

Robert Kochersberger surveyed newspapers in three states to see how they used the photos. He found that most newspapers (66 percent) used the photo of Dwyer holding out his hand, but exercised restraint by not publishing either the photo of the pistol in Dwyer's mouth or the one of his body slumping to the floor.

SUICIDE AS MENTAL ILLNESS

Beyond the political question of suicide as a form of expression, photographing suicide raises the issue of documenting severe mental problems.

In Wichita Falls, Texas, a former mental patient committed suicide with a twelve-gauge shotgun. In this situation, the photographer had no chance to stop the man. Don James, the executive editor of the normally conservative *Record News*, explained the picture to readers by saying, "We felt the story leading up to the suicide illustrated a shocking failure on the part of our system."

In the United States, mental illness remains hidden behind closed doors. Yet half the deaths by gunshot are a result of suicide. Rarely does the problem of mental illness become apparent enough to be photographed. The relatively rare pictures of someone in the act of suicide might help to call attention to the failure of mental health policies in the United States.

MORAL DILEMMAS OF A PICTURE EDITOR
GRUESOME PICTURES: SEEN OR SUPPRESSED?

Editors who deal with pictures are also on the ethical firing line. A photographer at the scene of an accident or disaster does not have the time to determine if a particular picture is too gruesome or horrible to appear on the paper's front page. Only when the film has been processed can the photographer and the editor study the images with an impartial eye toward deciding if the photos are too indecent, obscene, or repulsive for publication.

The reader, with the morning edition of the *Republican-Democrat* neatly folded between

his coffee and his oat bran, might gag on a gory front-page accident photo (ultimately tossing both the paper and his cereal). Editors sometimes refer to this as the "breakfast test" for hard-to-digest pictures.

Yet editors must not whitewash the world. Murders, accidents, wars, and suicides happen. Eliminating violence presents readers with a false view of their community and the world. (See Chapter 10, "Photo Editing.")

In fact, totalitarian dictators always try to muzzle the press in order to suppress information and hide truth.

Despite the best of intentions, the press also self-censors with written or unwritten guidelines. Newspapers at the beginning of World War II, for example, never showed dead American soldiers, because editors wanted to keep morale high on the home front. Until *Life* magazine ran a photo showing dead American soldiers strewn on a beach, the public was sheltered visually from some of the war's impact. Is it right or even responsible for the press to protect the public in this way? Is it possible that, by withholding these scenes, the press actually prevented Americans from developing a healthy outrage about events in Europe, a fury that perhaps could have fueled the war effort? (See "War Censorship," pages 364–365, in Chapter 16, "History.")

The corpseless photos were not inaccurate per se. They were merely incomplete. Arbitrarily editing out death—or any other sign of violence or tragedy—gives readers a false sense of their own security and a skewed view of their world.

Sebastian Balic, an Associated Press stringer, shot a grisly set of pictures of youths stoning, then stabbing, and finally setting a man on fire in Soweto, South

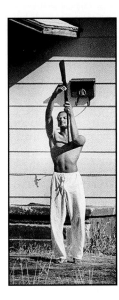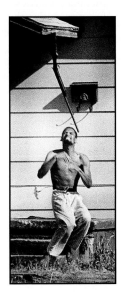

A former mental patient shot himself with a 12-gauge shotgun. Do the pictures help call attention to the problems of the mentally ill? Peter Bradt, *Wichita Falls* [Texas] *Time Record News*

Africa. The *New York Daily News* ran the photograph of the stoning. Referring to the pictures in an article by Sue O'Brien, Jeff Jarvis, the newspaper's Sunday editor, said, "I don't think the breakfast test works for the 90s."

Mike Zerby, photo editor at the *Minneapolis Star Tribune*, agreed. "The standard line," he said, "is 'we don't bleed on your eggs,' but I think at this particular newspaper we've grown past that."

Curtis MacDougall, author of ***News Pictures Fit to Print . . . Or Are They?***, recalled that, when he was a reporter on the old *St. Louis Star Times*, the managing editor once spent a full hour soliciting the opinions of everyone in the newsroom regarding the propriety of using a picture of a lynching. The photograph showed a corpse slumped at the base of the hanging tree.

MacDougall recalled the photo and the incident: "No facial expression was visible; nevertheless the decision was made to black out the body and substitute an artist's drawn 'X' to mark the spot."

This conservatism was typical of American editors through a century of brutal torture and murder of African Americans. According to MacDougall, plenty of photographs were available to document this inhuman treatment; however, when those photographs reached newsrooms, they were relegated to files rather than to news pages.

Of another lynching picture described as "shocking and unnecessary," Ernest Meyer wrote in the *Madison* (Wisconsin) *Capital Times*, "So was the crime. The grim butchery deserved a grim record. And those photographs were more eloquent than any word picture of the event."

At the time, newspaper editors argued that lynching pictures were too grisly to print. However, during that same era, editors did play up pictures of blood-soaked, maimed car-accident victims.

Editors rationalized that accident pictures served as a warning to careless drivers and thus improved highway safety. Sadly, no one thought to add that lynching pictures might also have had a positive benefit by stirring up moral outrage against racism and mob rule.

Today, the number of accident photos has decreased. Because accidents have become so common, they are less newsworthy. Accident photos, too, are often more difficult to get because the police remove bodies promptly. But the underlying moral question remains. Does the sight of mutilated victims in a mangled car frighten readers into caution when they drive their cars? And should this type of picture be published?

The *Akron* (Ohio) *Beacon Journal* said in an editorial about accident coverage: "The suddenness and finality of death, the tremendous force of impact, are vividly depicted in crushed, twisted bodies, and smashed vehicles. The picture implants in the minds of all who see it a safety lesson that could not be equally well conveyed in words alone. How long the shock value of such a picture persists, varies. But one can be sure that a majority of those who see photographs of traffic accidents are more concerned with their safety than they had been before seeing the picture. 'This can happen to you!' is the unwritten message of every picture of an accident."

WEIGHING IMPACT

Do powerful photographs drive home a social message, shock readers to distraction or have no effect at all?

Susan Sontag, critic and author of ***On Photography***, doubts that strong, graphic pictures continue to have an impact in our super-saturated media environment. She argues that photographs of human suffering no longer actually move the public. Further, she claims that little good comes of seeing photographic horrors when viewers have no power to relieve them.

She concedes that a few photographs retain their power to shock—like that of a napalm-burned Vietnamese girl fleeing a bomb attack. Images like these, she says, become moral reference points. But in general, Sontag maintains, repeated exposure to photographed atrocities habituates us to horror, leading us to view even the most grotesque images as "just pictures." Could she be right?

Would Sontag have published a picture of the journalist Daniel Pearl's severed head after his murder by Pakistani extremists?

The Ethics Committee of the Society of Professional Journalists wrote of the *Boston Phoenix*'s decision to publish the image, "Granted, there is a certain awful truth that the photo represents. The hatred his murderers have for Jews and Americans is crystallized in the image, but that truth does not outweigh the harmful shock to readers and to Pearl's family."

Stephen Mindich, the *Phoenix*'s publisher, told the Ethics Committee it would have been unethical not to bring the information to the attention of the American public—which had not felt the full weight of the event nor fully understood that Pearl was killed because he was Jewish.

The photo published by the *Phoenix* came from a video taken of the execution and titled

"The slaughter of the Spy-Journalist, the Jew Daniel Pearl."

SEPTEMBER 11, 2001

When people fell to their deaths from the burning World Trade Center after terrorists crashed two planes into the towers on September 11, 2001, editors were faced with perhaps their most difficult ethical task. Several photographers, including Susan Watts of the *New York Daily News* and Richard Drew of the Associated Press,

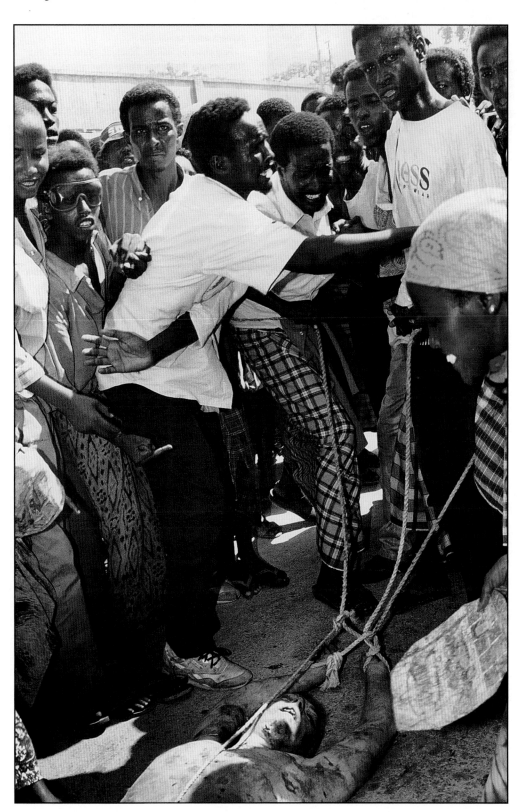

On a mission in Africa to provide food for starving Somalians, an American soldier was killed and then dragged through the streets of the city of Mogadishu. The picture was so powerful that it helped to change U.S. policy toward involvement in Somalia. Paul Watson, *Toronto Star*

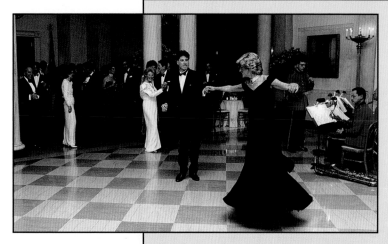

Diana, Princess of Wales, danced at the White House with actor John Travolta. The White House photographer was allowed to take this picture. Paparazzi, on the other hand, shot thousands of pictures of the princess during public as well as private moments without her permission.

Pete Souza, Reagan Library Collection

What is the difference between paparazzi, who photograph celebrities, and photojournalists, who cover the news?

Both kinds of photographers use the same cameras, film, and strobes. They look alike, and sometimes their work is even printed in the same publications. However, the purposes of the two breeds of photographers are quite different. Photojournalists hope to inform the public. Paparazzi take pictures to entertain or titillate. (For more on paparazzi, see page 289–290, Chapter 13, "The Law.")

Unfortunately, the general public often lumps paparazzi and photojournalists in the same category. That is what happened following the death of Britain's Princess Diana. She died in a horrific car crash during a high-speed chase in which her car's driver was attempting to outrun seven or more photographers. The public was outraged at the paparazzi.

After the tragic accident, photographers who had nothing to do with the accident and, in fact, had never staked out a celebrity in their lives, faced a barrage of insults on their regular assignments. Covering a routine news event, bystanders yelled "Photographers killed Princess Diana" at Scott LaClair of the *Herald-Standard* in Pennsylvania. One man even started swinging at LaClair with his fists. During the incident, the photographer's glasses were scratched, but he wasn't injured. When Susan Watts photographed the memorial for Princess Diana outside the British Embassy in Manhattan, a passing motorist shouted "Murderer . . . paparazzo assassin . . . You killed Diana."

Photographers killing people? What is this all about?

Diana's death pushed the public's patience over the edge. Even before the tragedy, surveys indicated that the public feels the news media are too invasive. A 1996 poll by the Center for Media and Public Affairs found that 80 percent of those surveyed thought the media ignored people's privacy. After Diana's death, more than 95 percent of respondents to an informal

USA Today online survey thought the Princess had been unfairly hounded by the news media.

Perhaps the public has a right to confuse the paparazzi and the photojournalist. Aside from the use of the same cameras and film, other similarities do exist between them. Sometimes both kinds of photographers cover celebrities.

Few photojournalists, however, spend their lives staking out a Hollywood star or international glamour figure in the hopes of catching a private or risqué moment.

The distinction between the two types of photographers grew narrower during the coverage of Monica Lewinsky, the intern whose affair with President Clinton nearly ended his presidency. When independent counsel Kenneth Starr focused his five-year $47 million investigation into alleged presidential misconduct on Clinton's relationship with the young woman, photographers of all stripes staked out her apartment and tried to get any image they could of the former intern.

Although the behavior of photojournalists in the Lewinsky situation mimicked that of paparazzi, from an ethical standpoint their purpose was different. Lewinsky was an accidental celebrity for the moment. Though she had not thrust herself into the public eye, her relationship with the President did culminate in an impeachment trial that could have changed the course of history.

The lives of Hollywood stars and glamour figures, the standard subject matter for paparazzi lenses, on the other hand, rarely have an effect on the nation or the world.

Of course, even when photojournalists cover a legitimate news story like alleged presidential misconduct, they should not resort to using ladders to peer over fences into the private homes or engage in high-speed car chases to grab a snap of a reclusive subject, points out David Lutman, past president of the National Press Photographers Association.

Because photojournalists look like paparazzi, and sometimes even act like them, the public naturally confuses legitimate news gatherers with shooters who survive by selling pictures of celebrities. The key difference, however, between these two distinct forms of photography is their intended purpose. Photojournalists take pictures to show readers events that they could not see for themselves. Paparazzi shoot pictures to satisfy the public's insatiable curiosity about the lives and love affairs of the famous. Hopefully, the behavior of the paparazzi will not lead to such a backlash from the public that the work of authentic photojournalists will be further impeded. ∎

photographed the tragic sight of people falling, sometimes headfirst, from the buildings. Of all the images taken on that horrific day—and there were thousands—those of people falling to their deaths caused by far the most consternation and controversy for editors and readers.

James Kenney, professor at Western Kentucky University, reported for *American Editor* that most newspapers decided against front-page use of the most graphic images of people jumping to their deaths. Kenney points out that intense pictures like these can "shift readers' attention away from the event and redirect their outrage to demanding why a newspaper would run such a picture? " But, he notes, "…predicting reader reaction is tricky."

Eric Meskauskas, picture editor of the *New York Daily News*, argued that a photo of victims jumping to their deaths…" was part of the story and we shouldn't shield our readers from it." Brian Storm, who was multimedia director at MSNBC.com at the time, made his decision under the extreme deadline pressure that faces an Internet site editor. He reasoned that the picture was an "essential part of the story" but presented the material in a way that allowed readers to choose whether to view the image or not.

READER COMPLAINTS

In Craig Hartley's survey comparing photojournalists' and general readers' reactions to ethical situations, he found that the two groups differed widely in their reactions to shooting and transmitting gruesome pictures.

Fifty-eight percent of the professionals he surveyed considered ethical the actions of a hypothetical photojournalist who photographed the removal of a famous actress's body from an automobile crash and the editors' subsequent decision to send the pictures over the wires. However, nearly three-fourths (71 percent) of the public disapproved of the journalists' actions.

Interestingly, the public's approval does not always coincide with its curiosity. Regardless of their opinion on news coverage, drivers routinely slow down to "rubberneck" a highway accident.

When editors select and publish strong, compelling, but perhaps hard-to-look-at pictures that include mangled bodies, blood, or victims' or bystanders' tearful reactions, readers often complain. From an economic point of view, editors certainly care what readers do and don't want to see on page one.

However, most readers today subscribe to their newspaper rather than buy a copy on the street. Single-copy sales and, therefore, individual front-page pictures do not control circulation sales as they did in the days when competing tabloids ran shocking pictures for the sole purpose of attracting readers. Editors are looking for a sustained readership, not a one-day circulation boost.

From the ethical perspective, however, should editors make decisions based on reader preferences? Do editors have a responsibility that supersedes the likes and dislikes of their audience?

THE "DISTANCE" RULE

For stories involving tragedy, journalists sometimes make conflicting decisions regarding the play of written stories compared to photos. For written stories, geographic proximity is one of the determining criteria in assessing news value. The closer the event, the more importance and, therefore, more prominent play it is given. Yet, because readers are more likely to complain about gruesome local pictures than images from far away, editors often will play down or suppress strong pictures that involve hometown residents but run revealing pictures of atrocities in other parts of the world.

In fact, some newspapers, like the *Tampa* (Florida) *Tribune*, even have policies mandating this practice. Denise Costa of the *Tribune* says that she wants to "protect the people involved more than she would want to run the photo." This attitude toward photography is counter to traditional news criteria for written stories—top among them, proximity—coverage of events that take place near or in a newspaper's community. Editors apprently don't like fielding calls from irate readers.

Jessica Fishman confirmed in her doctoral dissertation, "Photojournalism and Spectacles of the Morbid in the Tabloid and Elite Newspaper," U.S. newspapers' reluctance to show American bodies in most all circumstances. However, she also found that respected broadsheets like the *New York Times* or *Los Angeles Times* are more likely to publish graphic images of corpses (of non-Americans in foreign countries) than the oft-maligned tabloids. Despite their reputations for outrageous coverage, the tabloids tend to publish pictures of bombed buildings, destroyed busses or airplanes, closed caskets, or other discrete references to death.

HIDING DEAD BODIES

When to run and when to hold a photo often comes up when editors must deal with a picture containing a dead body. A front-page photograph of a firefighter carrying a dead child from a house shocked readers of the

Detroit Free Press. Locked inside, alone, seven brothers and sisters had died in a tragic blaze (below). Doors and windows that had been barricaded or barred to keep out burglars trapped the children inside.

Initially, readers complained about the picture, shot by stringer Bill Eisner. But within a few days, calls and letters supporting the paper's decision started coming in. The response was about 50 percent positive, then-director of photography Mike Smith reported, and about 50 percent negative.

Detroit Free Press columnist Susan Watson wrote: "Callers—some callers, not all—found the picture disgusting. Sickening. Inappropriate. The paper was accused of overstepping the bounds of good taste.

"Well, it's a good thing that I don't make the final call—or any call, for that matter—on what runs on page one.

"If I did, I would have spread that picture across the entire page. Heck, I wouldn't have stopped there. I would have made a huge poster out of it and hung the poster from the top of this building and city hall and even the Capitol in Lansing. I would have done it as a

chilling reminder of the ungodly price we pay when we take risks with our children. . . . It screamed, loudly and rudely, that we have to stop endangering our loved ones to protect our belongings."

Joan Byrd, a *Washington Post* ombudsman, summarized the counter-argument: "The family should not have to see news photos of someone killed in an accident or a crime. Families of victims have said that years later something haunts them every single day: The picture of the body at the scene, the description of the person in the newspaper. Images on TV are here and gone. Still photos in the newspaper last."

The two columnists eloquently summarize conflicting ethical points of view. Running the picture, the *Free Press* columnist argues, helps the most people and hurts the fewest. The *Washington Post* ombudsman, on the other hand, takes an absolutist position by pointing out that if the picture hurts just a few relatives and friends, it is wrong to run the picture because the media must protect those few from more pain.

Similar reactions and arguments apply to pictures of drowned children, like John Harte's photo in the *Bakersfield Californian* (page 301). Harte's photograph of lifeless five-year-old Edward Romero, lying partially exposed in a plastic body bag and surrounded by grieving family members, is a powerful image. After running it, the paper received 400 phone calls, 500 letters, and a bomb threat. The editor subsequently ran an apology to the readers for publishing the photo.

The number of drownings in the Bakersfield area, however, dropped from fourteen in the month previous to the picture's publication to just two in the month after the paper printed the photo.

In a fascinating case study called "Choice Processes in a Newspaper Ethics Case," Sandra Borden followed the decision-making path of one newspaper as its editors and photographers wrestled with the choice of running a fatal accident photo.

In this situation, the social worker and rabbi of the family involved called the paper and asked the editor not to run the picture. The staff held extensive discussion reviewing the newspaper's inconsistent policies regarding running fatal accident pictures. The editors noted that the paper regularly covered these kinds of accidents in its news columns. The editors also considered the relative news value of this fatal accident picture. Though routine, the photo of the accident could have provided a warning to young people tempted to speed. Ultimately the top editor decided to spike the picture. During the process, Borden

Initially, readers objected to this picture of a fireman carrying the lifeless child who had been trapped in a building with locked burglar bars on the windows. Many papers will not run any picture that shows a dead body. For more about the photo, see ■ page 321. Bill Eisner, for the *Detroit Free Press*

observed, no one from the newspaper ever contacted the family. A polite and sympathetic phone call could have determined just how distressed the family was about the photo, what it was about the image that disturbed them, and how adamant they were about keeping it out of print.

Based on the principle "do unto others as you would have them do unto you," editors often act as they presume families would want them to. Sometimes, however, relatives or friends of a victim recognize that publishing a picture may be one of the few beneficial outcomes of a tragic situation.

When a child fell through the ice and drowned in a pond in Columbia, Missouri, the *Columbia Missourian*, after much discussion regarding the family's feelings, ran a picture showing rescuers recovering the child's body. The next day, the child's mother came to the office, where she picked up extra copies of the newspaper after thanking the editors for running the photograph. She said she hoped that the front-page picture of her child would help deter others from playing on the thin pond ice.

Perhaps news outlets should routinely call victims' families to warn them that an emotional photograph will run. This procedure would diminish a family's shock at seeing the image but still allow the wider public to be informed in the strongest way possible about the news event. (For more on censorship, see pages 364–365, Chapter 16, "History.")

Kenneth Jarecke's photo from the end of the 1991 Gulf War (below) provides a revealing case study of how the media handle a tough but thought-provoking image. Jarecke was on assignment for *Time* magazine when he photographed the blackened corpse of an Iraqi soldier incinerated at the wheel of his vehicle. American pilots had relentlessly attacked the retreating convoy of a thousand vehicles. Some of the pilots referred to the attack as a "turkey shoot," reports Colin Jacobson in his book, **Underexposed**. Estimates of this "turkey shoot" put the number of dead between 400 and 2000.

Although Jarecke was shooting for *Time*, the magazine hesitated to publish the picture. The Associated Press (AP) received the photograph in its New York office but did not transmit the image under the assumption that "Newspapers will tell us 'We cannot present pictures like that for people to look at over breakfast.'"

Life magazine laid out a two-page spread

To the reading public, the 1991 Iraqi war was almost surgical in its precision and presumed lack of bloodshed. Most Americans never saw this horrific image of a dead Iraqi soldier, incinerated while retreating in his tank at the close of that earlier conflict. Might exposure to the war's brutal realities have influenced U.S. opinion about waging the 2003 war in that country?
Kenneth Jarecke, Contact Press Images

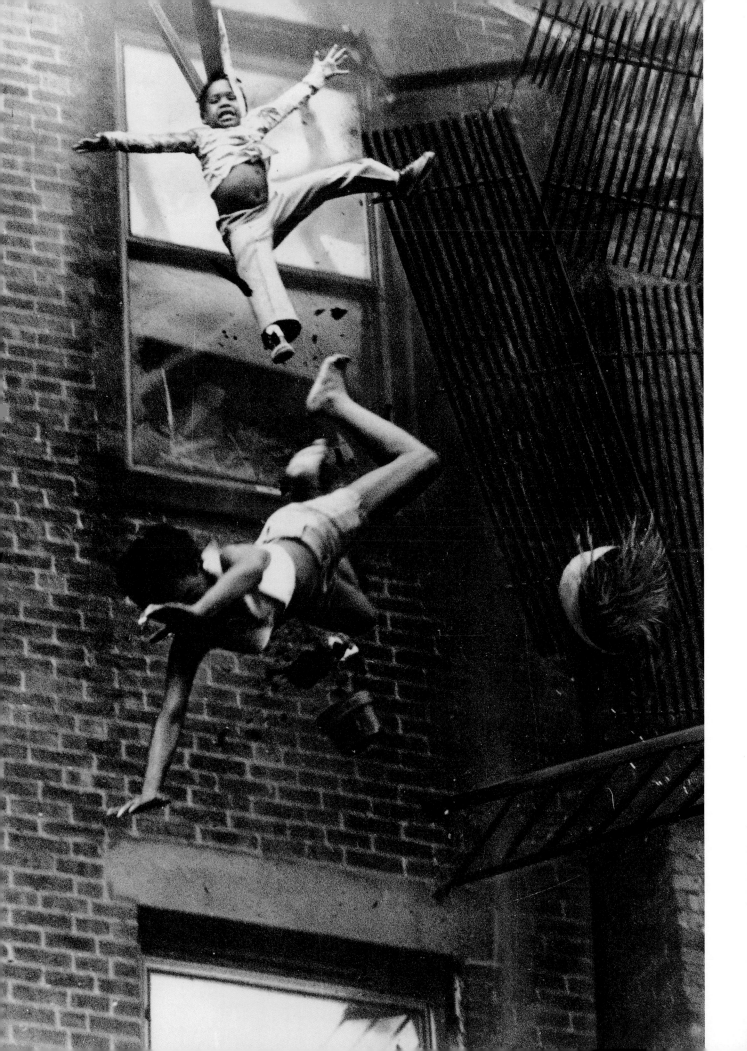

This fire escape collapsed during a fire, plunging a woman to her death; the child miraculously survived. After the picture ran on hundreds of front pages around the country, telephone calls and letters deluged newspapers, charging sensationalism, invasion of privacy, insensitivity, and tasteless display of human tragedy— all to sell newspapers. Would you have printed this picture? Stanley Forman, Boston

with the photo but pulled it before publication. The managing editor cited the effect it would have on children as his reason for rejecting it. Eventually the image appeared in *Time*'s end-of-year special and ran the size of a postage stamp.

In *Underexposed*, former picture editor Jacobson writes, "The Gulf War was presented to the world as a squeaky-clean technological masterpiece and the public were not encouraged to associate computer-controlled, laser-directed weapons with subsequent human carnage."

Photographer Jarecke, in a TV interview, said, "If the U.S. is tough enough to go to war, it should be tough enough to look at the consequences."

PHOTOGRAPHY CAN MAKE A DIFFERENCE

Stanley Forman's photo of a collapsing fire escape during a blaze in Boston—a woman plunging to her death along with a falling child who miraculously survived—was printed on more than one hundred front pages across the country. Later, telephone calls and letters to newspapers charged sensationalism, invasion of privacy, insensitivity, and tasteless display of human tragedy for the purpose of selling newspapers.

Hal Buell, who was AP's assistant general manager for news photos at the time, said he received more reaction to the Forman picture than to any other news photo. Buell wagered that if the woman had survived, there would have been very little reaction.

"The pictures would not have changed, but the fact of death reached into the minds and feelings of the readers," he said.

Most of the nation's editors published Forman's picture on their front pages. Yet in a survey taken by the *Orange County Daily Pilot* in Costa Mesa, California, 40 percent of its readers did not approve of publishing the photo. Wilson Sims, editor of the *Battle Creek* (Michigan) *Enquirer and News*, defended publishing the picture: "The essential purpose is not to make the reader feel pain or to bring the reader happiness. It is to help the reader understand what is happening in the world. Therefore, we ran the picture."

Forman's photograph of the falling woman and child not only won a Pulitzer Prize, but it

is also a classic example of how photography can bring about change. That shocking image contributed to a change in fire-safety laws in Boston. Forman's editor, Sam Bornstein, said, "Without the picture, the word-story would have been 'page 16.' Only pictures of this magnitude would have resulted in something being done by the safety agencies."

Sometimes pictures not only can change a state's laws but can influence a country's foreign policy. In response to the starvation of Somalians in Africa, the United States sent its troops to help United Nations peace keepers to quell fighting and distribute food in that country. Despite the presence of U.S. troops, warlords continued to pillage. At one point a U.S. soldier was killed by the followers of one of the warlords. At great personal danger, the *Toronto Star*'s Paul Watson photographed the screaming crowd as they dragged the almost nude body of the soldier through the city streets. The horrifying picture of the body of an American soldier being desecrated in the streets of a country halfway around the world was so shocking to the U.S. public that the administration quickly reversed policy and pulled U.S. troops out of Somalia. (See page 317.)

While a single picture alone did not change American foreign policy, this image, which generated immediate reaction from the public, commentators, and legislators, certainly played a significant role in hastening the withdrawal of U.S. troops.

MATTERS OF TASTE

Nudity in pictures generates more disagreement among editors than even the most gruesome picture. An editor's judgment about nudity in pictures generally reflects his or her understanding of readers' attitudes and of

---

SHOCKING-PICTURE WARNING SIGNS

If five or more of the following conditions apply to a shocking picture, editors should prepare for reader reactions before the firestorm hits:

- images that show subjects overcome with grief
- pictures containing dead bodies
- pictures portraying mutilated bodies
- pictures run in color
- photos containing nudity
- photos taken for a local story
- photos taken by a staff photographer
- images printed in a morning paper
- images printed on the front page
- images with no accompanying story

Paul Lester, *Photojournalism: An Ethical Approach*

mores in the host community. In most cases, the standards for pictorial nudity are more a matter of taste than a question of ethics. With the advent of Hustler and other "skin" magazines, almost no part of the human anatomy is reserved for the imagination.

Yet most American newspapers and magazines refrain from printing nudity on their pages. AP's Hal Buell says that the wire service won't carry frontal views of nude men or women, except in extreme cases. "Such a story has yet to occur," he observes.

Professionals and the public again dis-

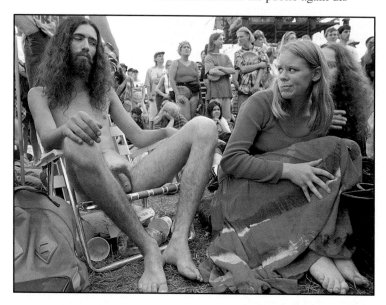

Taken by their staffer at the 25th anniversary of the Woodstock music festival, this photo was too risqué for *Washington Times* editors, who refused to run it. Trade magazines *News Photographer* and *Editor & Publisher* did publish it, uncensored, with stories about the controversy it generated as a contest winner. *E&P*'s headline: "No Nudes is Good Nudes." Kenneth Lambert, *Washington Times.* (For publication in this book, the following special credit note was required by the editor-in-chief of the *Washington Times*: "This photograph did not run in the *Washington Times* due to reasons of taste.")

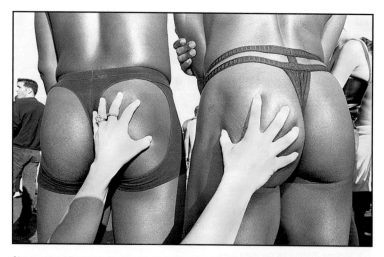

At a gay street festival in San Francisco, bystanders check out the local talent. While thousands of people from around the country attend this festival each year, local newspapers downplay the event by running few if any photos. (For more on coverage of the gay community, see pages 201 and 202, Chapter 10, "Photo Editing," and page 326 in this chapter.) Alain McLaughlin, Impact Visuals

agreed in Hartley's ethics survey when he turned to the question of nudity. Here is the hypothetical situation: two women athletes collide in a volleyball game, with one falling in such a way that her shorts are pulled down and her bare buttocks are exposed.

While a majority of the professionals surveyed endorsed sending out a photo of the athlete's derriere, a whopping 75 percent of the public turned thumbs-down on the bottoms-up picture.

Robert Wahls, who was a photo editor for the *New York Daily News*, avoided running nudes except under unusual circumstances. Despite the *Daily News*'s reputation as a genuine tabloid, Wahls felt that, although nudity is acceptable in film and theater, "it is inappropriate when you can sit and study it." The photo editor made an exception when there was an overriding news value to a picture. The photos from the original Woodstock, a massive outdoor rock concert in 1969, showed members of the audience frolicking in the muddy field without their clothes on. The sheer size of the audience—300,000— gave the activities news value.

Wahls, however, pointed out that, even if nude pictures help push up the circulation of a newspaper, the gain might be useless if advertisers start to consider the paper pornographic. "A newspaper's job is to inform, not to titillate," Wahls said.

Twenty-five years later, the *Washington Times*'s Ken Lambert photographed Woodstock's silver anniversary, which, like the original, gave kids an excuse to party, wear tie-dye, and "get naked." Although only a few got naked this time around, Lambert took a picture of a young woman glancing disapprovingly at a long-haired "hippie" wearing only his birthday suit—a true testament to the difference between the eras. The picture was too dicey for the *Washington Times*, whose editor, Josette Shiner, called the *Times* "a family newspaper."

The photo, however, was not too spicy for judges of the White House News Photographers Association (WHNPA) photo contest, who awarded it a first place for features.

Judges for the Best of Photojournalism competition, conducted by the National Press Photographers Association (NPPA), faced a moral/ethical decision about a sexually explicit news picture. The judges awarded a first place for domestic news to an unpublished picture that showed a half-naked woman being sexually assaulted while attempting to struggle free from a crowd of out-of-control men at a Mardi Gras event in Seattle. Her face, as were those of her attackers, was clearly visible. The judges decided that the photo, taken by Mike Urban of the *Seattle Post-Intelligencer*, should be published in the contest's book and on the web site. But the image was so disturbing that even the organization that represents photojournalists, the NPPA, censored the photo by putting a digital mask over the woman's face.

Resulting after a highly unusual and hotly contested debate, the judges' decision was certainly not unanimous. They weighed the woman's privacy and potential embarrassment against the need for readers to fully comprehend the violence and brutality that erupted during this public event. Urban had not obtained the victim's name, so no one could solicit her opinion.

Neither Urban's own newspaper, the *Post-Intelligencer*, nor The Poynter Institute for Media Studies Web site, which published other winning pictures from the contest, ran the photo at all—with or without the digitized face.

Maria Mann, director of photography for Agence France Presse and one of the contest judges, wrote, "The commission of any act of hate is not easy to take—whether in the form of crimes against humanity in war, or in every day life. But the truth cannot be a convenience; it needs to be a constant. We have a mission—to document the truth. If this mission has given way to politics or queasy stomachs then we have yet another important mission—to defend the very essence of our profession."

In an instance that enraged many readers, editors in the San Francisco Bay Area published John Burgess's picture of convicted murderer Richard Allen Davis gesturing with upraised middle fingers following the jury's guilty verdict in his trial. Davis's abduction and murder of 12-year-old Polly Klaas had horrified Bay Area citizens.

Burgess, who shoots for Santa Rosa's *Press Democrat*, was the pool photographer in the emotionally charged case. Bay Area papers all ran the photo on their front pages. Executive editor Jerry Ceppos, of the *Mercury News* in San Jose said his newspaper logged 1,284 messages from readers, overwhelming voice mail, E-mail, fax, and online systems. Ceppos said 817 readers agreed with publishing the photo, while 481 did not.

At the *San Francisco Chronicle*, said editorial-page editor John Diaz, "the overwhelming majority" of callers and writers objected to the picture's page-one play. Diaz defended running the picture. "The moment captured by Burgess's Nikon added new dimension to the story. It may well have an impact on jurors as they decide whether to sentence the defendant to death or life in prison. It certainly says something about the murderer. . . . The Davis verdict story would have been incomplete without the photo."

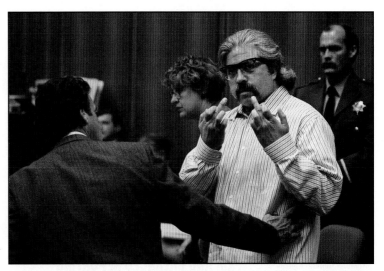

Publication of the photo of this defiant act by convicted child-murderer Richard Allen Davis upon hearing the jury's guilty verdict generated a firestorm of negative response for newspaper editors in the San Francisco Bay Area. The shocking picture, however, provided a revealing insight into the man's character. Previously, he had remained quiet and subdued. John Burgess, *Press Democrat* [Santa Rosa, California]

TOO DISTURBING TO SEE?

The *Seattle Post-Intelligencer* did not publish a picture that showed a half-naked woman being sexually assaulted while attempting to struggle free from a crowd of out-of-control men during Seattle's Mardi Gras. Her face, as were those of her attackers, was clearly visible. Shot by Mike Urban, the picture was entered and won first prize in its division in the Best of Photojournalism contest sponsored by the National Press Photographers Association. On the organization's Web site (right) and in its book, the picture appeared with the women's face digitally obscured.

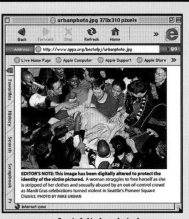

EDITOR'S NOTE: This image has been digitally altered to protect the identity of the victim pictured. A woman struggles to save herself as she is stripped of her clothes and sexually abused by an out-of-control crowd as Mardi Gras celebrations turned violent in Seattle's Pioneer Square District. PHOTO BY MIKE URBAN

www.nppa.org/bestofpj/urbanphoto.jpg

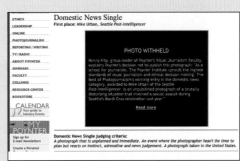

The Poynter Institute for Media Studies, a sponsor of the contest, refused to run the picture in any form because the woman's face was visible (left).

www.poynterextra.org/centerpiece/photo/DomNews.htm

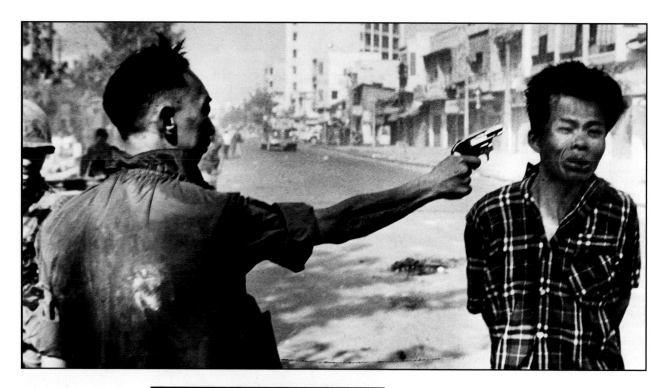

FAIR AND BALANCED REPORTING

The experienced professional reporter continues to dig up the facts of a news story until he or she feels prepared to write an unbiased, balanced report of the event. News reporters take several paragraphs to explain the position of each conflicting party.

Many stories have no clear heroes or villains; hence, the reporter simply extends copy to explain the complexities of the situation. The writer has not only the advantage of several paragraphs, but the subtlety and precision of the English language, with its great store of adjectives and adverbs. These modifiers enable the writer to emphasize an idea or soften a phrase.

Think of the difference between the words "the suspect stared at me" and "the criminal glared at me."

The photographer has no adjectives or adverbs, no pictorial thesaurus to refine an image. A single picture captures only one moment in time, one set of circumstances, one expression or action. If the newspaper's managing editor has allotted space for just one picture to illustrate a complex story, then the photo editor is faced with a task as difficult as if the writer had to tell a multifaceted tale in one sentence. Of the two hundred or so exposed frames shot on an assignment, which single image tells the whole story?

The Vietnam War presented a constant challenge for photo editors. Each day they had to sum up a complicated, tragic event in a few pictures. Eddie Adams won a Pulitzer Prize for a shocking photo of a South Vietnamese colonel executing a suspected Viet Cong on a Saigon street (above). During this war, the South Vietnamese were our allies. The overwhelming message of the picture, however, spoke of the cruelty of the South Vietnamese officer.

To balance this view of the war, many editors chose to run, on the same day, another picture portraying the terrorism of our enemies, the Viet Cong. Although not as dramatic as Adams's picture, the photo showed a soldier leaving a civilian house recently bombed by the Viet Cong.

Do the two photos really explain both sides of the conflict? Can any two pictures be balanced?

The question of balance also arises in local stories. Many groups point out they receive scant if any media coverage, and when they do, they see stereotypes of themselves. Nancy Andrews, director of photography at the *Detroit Free Press*, has won numerous awards, including Photographer of the Year. "I believe a lot of stereotypes are visual stereotypes," she says. "In my own community, as a gay person, [I see how] photographers have often looked for the most arresting pictures. The most arresting are valid—it's valid to show people dying [of AIDS] or dressed in drag at a gay pride parade—but if these are the only pictures used to represent the gay community, then it's an inaccurate picture of the whole community.

"Being aware of how visual images are used to show my own community," she says, "has made me aware of how important it is to show the average people in other communities." (See one image from Andrews's picture story about an African-American single father on page 195.)

SELF-CENSORSHIP

Censorship often occurs before the shutter is ever released or a print ever made. For a variety of reasons, photographers decide not to take or publish photographs.

A photographer might not photograph two men holding hands, for fear that the community "is not ready to deal with homosexuality" or that "my paper won't run that." A photographer might not want to "embarrass the men."

In addition to gays and lesbians, newspapers traditionally have ignored various ethnic groups over the years. Through neglect or, perhaps, in deference to a predominantly white readership, mainstream newspapers have overlooked large segments of the population—African Americans, Hispanic Americans, Asian Americans, and others.

Through self-censorship on a conscious or subconscious level, photojournalists can create an artificial reality for their readers. Each journalist must look at his or her biases.

- Who is being protected by not taking or running a picture?
- Are you sure your editor won't publish a picture?
- Are the regulations about acceptable subjects and topics written down or just unofficially passed on to new members of the staff?
- Are you responding to your own fears and prejudices when you hesitate to release the camera's trigger or turn in an image?
- Have you challenged your publication's written or unwritten policy?

The message is this: examine your own motives. Scrutinize your actions for patterns that may reveal your own prejudices. Are elements or groups from your community consistently absent from your shots? Is it coincidence—or choice—that your pictures display these patterns? Then apply the same vigilance to your editor and your organization. A responsible journalist must remain alert to even subtle signs of prejudice, at all levels. If you discover that prejudice is part of the "corporate culture" at your paper, you have three options: accept it, change it, or quit. Each carries a price.

REMEMBER THE READER

Photojournalists don't take pictures for contests, editors, or other members of the profession. They take pictures for readers—pictures that provide information about sad moments as well as happy ones. Without complete and well-rounded reporting, including both written and visual facts, a democratic society cannot function.

When faced with a tough ethical question, try phrasing the problem in this way:

First, what do other professionals in the field do when in a similar situation? What is the professional standard for this action?

Next, are the actions of other professionals right or wrong? To borrow a reminder from mothers everywhere, "Just because everyone else does it doesn't mean you have to."

Then ask yourself, "Will taking or running a photo serve the greatest good for the greatest number of people?" Although you will find it hard to predict a photo's effect, can you hypothesize a positive outcome from readers seeing the photo? What is the negative impact if readers don't see the picture?

If you decide the photo has potential social significance, you should next ask, "Who will be hurt by taking or running the picture? Is this a situation in which an individual's rights supersede those of society?" You might ask, "How would I feel if I were the person in the photo?" Can you soften the pain with a phone call informing relatives about what they will see in the next day's paper?

Finally, though some individual rights are absolute, others are not. Keep in mind that you must weigh an individual's rights against society's need for accurate, complete information.

LOOKING FOR A YARDSTICK

Not all pictures showing dying and death help readers or society. A picture of a man dying at home of natural causes does not provide information that society can use to change anything. No laws can prevent this death. No public policy issues are at stake. Pictures of a death that could not have been prevented are not necessarily news or newsworthy. On the other hand, pictures of a drowned child or one falling from a poorly maintained fire escape graphically highlight either behavior that individuals could prevent or laws that should be enacted.

In his book *News Pictures Fit to Print . . . Or Are They?* Curtis MacDougall struggled to find a common rule to help editors decide when to splash a controversial picture on the front page or when to file the picture in the bottom desk drawer. "My yardstick is the public interest," said MacDougall. "I would run any picture calculated to increase the public's understanding of an issue about which the public is able to act."

MacDougall's yardstick, however, does not take into account competing claims like privacy, which in certain circumstances must also be considered.

Each editor will use a personal yardstick of

public versus private interest, but photographers should not rely on editors to shoulder the ethics burden. Photographers must determine for themselves what they find valuable about taking and then publishing photos. The photographer provides the first line of ethical defense. In the end, the photographer's name runs under the photo. The photographer must take responsibility for the final image that appears.

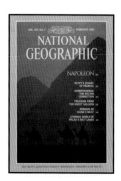

COMPOSING PHOTOS ON THE ELECTRONIC LAYOUT TABLE

In a now-famous incident at the *National Geographic*, editors puzzled over what could have been a terrific cover shot of the great pyramids of Giza. Unfortunately, the foreground's camels and the background's pyramids were not lined up to fit correctly on the vertical cover. The answer: send the picture to the scanner and computer. Through the magic of computer manipulation, the computer operator actually moved the pyramids in the photos. The final picture left no trails.

Rich Clarkson, who became director of photography at the *Geographic* after the incident, defended the magazine's digital alteration of the picture.

"It's exactly the same as if the photographer had moved the camera's position," he tells Shiela Reaves in the NPPA special report, "Ethics of Photojournalism."

Clarkson's argument, however, made no distinction between acceptable and unacceptable methods to obtain a photo. Is fudging a photograph electronically really the same as moving the photographer—even if both methods result in photos that look the same?

As if moving pyramids was not enough, Collins Publishing Company, which published *A Day in the Life of America*, found moving the moon a necessity.

Reviewing their take from a shoot, editors decided that an evocative picture of a cowboy, tree, and crescent moon would make a perfect cover. Like the *Geographic*'s uncooperative photo, however, the horizontal shot would not fit on the full-bleed vertical cover—so a computer technician moved the cowboy and moon nearer to the tree and then finished composing the picture by adding branches and a bit of extra sky.

So, although more than one hundred photographers submitted thousands of frames of film, editors determined that only the picture of a cowboy who was too far away from a tree would succeed as a cover. And instead of redesigning the cover to accommodate the photo, they redesigned the photo.

ADDING OR SUBTRACTING ELEMENTS

Editors don't have to stop at moving the moon or just limit themselves to rearranging pyramids. They even can add or subtract elements from the original picture.

Some newspapers have used the computer to remove small distracting items from a picture, others to change the background color of the picture. The *St. Louis Post-Dispatch* removed a Coca-Cola® can from a portrait of its Pulitzer Prize-winning photographer. The *Louisville* (Kentucky) *Courier-Journal* extended a stripper's sweatshirt when her high kick proved a little too exciting.

The *Orange County* (California) *Register* increased the saturation of the blue sky in some of their prize-winning Olympics pictures. On another day, employees in the back shop of the same newspaper changed the color of a swimming pool to blue not realizing that the point of the picture was that someone had dumped red dye into the pool. On a more mundane level, the *San Francisco Examiner* once changed the color of a wall behind the mayor to enhance the appeal of a front-page picture. The list goes on and on.

Did these newspapers cross the ethical boundary between normal picture handling and doctoring photos?

Long Island's *Newsday* featured a picture of ice-skating rivals Nancy Kerrigan and Tonya Harding practicing together for the Olympics. The two athletes, however, did not skate in practice together until the day after the paper ran the photograph on its front page. The computer-combined montage was a fake.

Newsday had one photo of Harding going through her routine and a separate picture of Kerrigan practicing. Fueled by public interest in the rivalry, in which Harding had been accused of engineering an attack against Kerrigan, editors used the computer to seamlessly meld the pictures of the two separate practices into one—and presented the result as if the two rivals were skating simultaneously. The decision was made against the protests of the photography department, and had editors waited another day, the newspaper could have published a real picture of the two skaters on the rink together rather than printing a day-early-but-fake photo.

Texas Monthly went even further when it depicted then-governor of Texas Ann Richards in a white, leather-fringed outfit atop a Harley Davidson motorcycle. Although Richards does ride a motorcycle, the picture actually showed Richards's face melded onto a professional model's body. (Richards retorted that she was happy the model had good thighs.)

Redbook took Julia Roberts's face from a

paparazzi photo and put it on her body taken from a movie premiere four years before. The magazine apologized for this incident, but was not embarrassed at all by when it changed Jennifer Aniston's hairstyle and color of her shirt for another cover photo.

The computer provided instant weight loss for actress Kate Winslet, photographed for the cover of *GQ* in Britain. Inside the magazine, the actress says, "Women think in order to be adored they have to be thin. Very thin. I just don't understand that way of thinking." Winslet said later that she never saw the cover photo, which trimmed 30 pounds off her.

Perhaps one of the most shocking instances of computer manipulation was when the *National Enquirer* used the computer to add bruises and a black eye to a photograph of Nicole Brown Simpson, O. J. Simpson's murdered ex-wife. With the former athlete on trial for his ex-wife's murder, the *Enquirer* doctored the photo to "illustrate" how the victim would have appeared following an earlier instance of alleged abuse by her ex-husband. Labeled as a computer manipulation, the image nonetheless stunned shoppers in grocery stores everywhere. How many people, do you suppose, knew what the *Enquirer* meant by computer manipulation?

HOW FAR WILL MAGAZINE EDITORS GO?

Curiously, some magazine editors show little hesitation in altering cover photographs. "Magazines, I think, can get away with a little more," said Rocco Alberico of *Sports Illustrated for Kids*. "I mean, they can fool around a little bit more than newspapers."

"The practice of airbrushing cellulite and stretch marks or tweaking an errant nipple is standard procedure at most magazines that count on their flawless cover shots to woo readers," according to Lia Haberman in *E! Online* (www.eonline.com).

In her study "Digital Alteration of Photographs in Magazines: An Examination of the Ethics," Shiela Reaves found that all thirteen magazine editors and art directors she interviewed said emphatically they would never digitally manipulate a news photo. However, most had no problem in "cleaning up" an image by removing indistinguishable blobs or extending the sky or a background tone so a news photo could fit the layout.

Michele Stephenson, *Time* picture editor, noted that it was like cropping people out of a picture. "You crop a picture, there's a corner of an elbow, and somebody says 'We'd better take that out. It looks funny.' We do that sort of thing . . . everybody does that."

Newsweek went a bit further when it became the digital dentist for Bobbi

CAN YOU BELIEVE YOUR EYES?

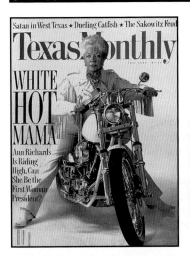

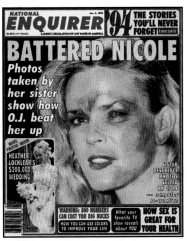

The head on the woman in the picture is the former governor of Texas, Ann Richards. The body belongs to a model.

The picture of Nicole Simpson is real, but in this published image, it was the *National Enquirer* that battered her.

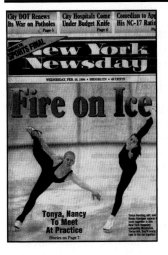

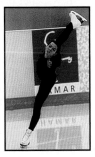

Reuters

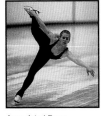

Associated Press

The competing ice skaters had not practiced together, so *Newsday* editors used the computer to combine two separate images for the page-one picture. Had the editors waited one more day, they could have had a picture of the real thing.

McCaughey, the new mother of septuplets. The smiling mom on *Newsweek*'s cover enjoyed straighter and whiter teeth thanks to careful computer manipulation.

Surprisingly, readers approved of this digital dental work, according to a survey by researcher Edgar Huang. Sixty-seven percent of surveyed readers approved the editor's digital dentistry in a feature photo or as a photographic illustration because they liked the new mother and did not want her to be presented with crooked teeth.

As part of her survey, Shiela Reaves asked Bob Furstenau, director of magazine production for Meredith Corporation (publisher of *Better Homes and Gardens* and other magazines) what kinds of things he would change in a picture.

"Anything," he replied, "that interferes with the ultimate aesthetic of the picture—

spots, telephone wires, people, whatever." He estimated that forty-five of the forty-eight covers he had worked on at the time had been digitally manipulated.

Sports Illustrated for Kids featured one of the NBA's shortest basketball players dribbling through the legs of a large player.

"We do a lot of that, especially on covers, but it's pretty obvious that they're basically fantasies," said the magazine's art director. "That's such an obvious fake; kids know people that size really don't exist."

Do they?

Reaves found that newspaper picture editors were significantly less tolerant of digital manipulation. She also discovered that only 22 percent of the magazine editors had a photojournalism background, whereas 85 percent of those at newspapers had previous professional photojournalism experience. Perhaps this difference in professional background accounts for the stricter standards regarding digital manipulation held by daily newspaper photo editors.

HISTORY OF ALTERING PICTURES

In the 1920s, manipulation of photos was not only a standard procedure but was considered a high art. (See pages 348–349 for more on the topic.) In a fascinating paper, "Altered Plates: Photo Manipulation and the Search for News Value in the Early and Late Twentieth Century," Wilson Lowrey showed how conditions that encouraged photo faking in the 1920s have reappeared with the advent of the digital darkroom.

In the early days of photojournalism, art departments controlled photography. Artists didn't (and still don't) hesitate to rearrange a sketch or creatively interpret events with a painting or drawing. This thinking overlapped into their use of photographs, which they saw as just another artistic medium.

The *Evening Graphic*'s staged hanging nearly cost the life of the art department assistant when he accidentally kicked over the stool on which he was posing for a "composograph." Combining images did not start with the invention of the computer. Editors created composographs by cutting and pasting posed photographs to create staged scenes. (For more about the *Evening Graphic* and composographs, see pages 348–349.) Harry Grogin, *New York Evening Graphic*

As the profession of photojournalism matured, photojournalists began controlling the use of photography, and higher standards for the treatment of journalistic photographs evolved. Unfortunately, Lowrey reports, photo departments at many publications today have again reverted to the control of art directors and designers, who often have little regard for the integrity of the photojournalistic approach to photography.

Also, Lowrey observes, photography in the 1920s was still a novel addition to newspapers. Publications had no set policies about when and how to use photographs.

In the 1990s, he says, magazines and newspapers had established no industry standards when they began digitally manipulating pictures. As with any novel technique, editors and art directors experimented. Always on the search for a new way to lure in readers and tickle their curiosity, these editors turned to photo manipulation much like their counterparts enthusiastically cut and pasted photographs some eighty years ago.

LOSING CREDIBILITY?

What will happen as the public discovers that news outlets alter images electronically? Will the profession lose credibility? Will people believe photographs if they know that editors can easily alter images?

In part, the credibility of the photograph depends on the reputation of the photographer and the publication that produces it, observes Paula Habas in her thesis, "The Ethics of Photojournalistic Alteration: An Integrated Schema of Determinants."

In another study, James Kelly and Diona Nace compared how much subjects believe a photograph before and after being shown a video demonstrating the techniques of computer manipulation. After watching the video, the subjects, perhaps surprisingly, maintained their trust in photos. Seeing the computer's wizardry does not automatically destroy the believability of a photographic image.

Based on a survey of 350 college students, Tom Wheeler found that respondents held newspapers to a higher standard than general interest magazines like *Cosmopolitan*, *Esquire*, *MacWorld*, and *National Geographic*.

They found digital manipulation by newspapers more unacceptable than manipulation by general interest magazines. The researcher also discovered that while some types of manipulation—like removing a distracting tree from the background—were not offensive to the majority of subjects, more extensive photo manipulation like retouching a model's facial blemishes, increasing her cleavage, or enhancing her nipples, was unacceptable. Finally, Wheeler discovered, women were consistently more critical of photo manipulation than were men.

In a follow-up study, Jennifer Greer and Joseph Gosen found women continued to be less tolerant than men of major technical manipulation. Women were found to be more tolerant than men of minor technical alterations like dodging and burning.

Researcher Edgar Huang found that 57 percent of surveyed residents of Bloomington, Indiana, thought that digital retouching of cover photos on *Time* magazine and the **Day in the Life of America** was acceptable. Only 31 percent objected. Huang reported that readers found that removing a cola can from a picture was fine if journalists erased it for editorial purposes. Not surprisingly, study participants found digital alteration of photos like photo illustration more acceptable than for hard news photos.

After showing an audience a video of computer manipulation, researcher Mara Vernon discovered no significant effect on the group's faith in photojournalism. Other researchers have not found the public to be overly upset by minor digital manipulations to some types of journalistic pictures. So far, the public still generally trusts photojournalistic pictures.

THEORY IN PRACTICE
When readers saw a real-life comparison of altered and unaltered photos on newsstands, however, they reacted strongly and loudly. *Time* magazine electronically altered a police mug shot of O.J. Simpson, who had been arrested for the alleged murder of his former wife. Labeling the image a "Photo Illustration," *Time* ran it on the cover the same week that *Newsweek* published the untainted original. The American public joined a loud debate about the use and misuse of digital alteration.

On every newsstand across the country, the two covers sat side-by-side—each with the same police mug shot. Yet the covers were different. *Time* hired an illustrator who darkened the image and reduced the police identification numbers. *Time* editors thought they had covered themselves by using the label "Photo-Illustration for *Time*" in the table of contents.

Shocked at public outrage—including 70,000 messages on America Online as well as articles in the *New York Times* and Associated Press—a *Time* editor pondered, "but we do illustrations all the time. Why is this different?"

While Kelly and Nace demonstrated that just knowing about digital manipulation does not cause readers to disbelieve photos, Wheeler has shown that readers object to certain kinds of manipulation. The reaction to the *Time* cover confirms that when people care about the event or the person, and when they can see both the altered and unaltered photos, they will respond—loudly.

In almost all cases, viewers do not realize photographers or, more likely, editors have manipulated some of the photos they see in magazines and newspapers. The studies mentioned above show that when told, some viewers find certain kinds of manipulation of pictures objectionable. However, that does not mean that viewers doubt pictures they see in publications. Photography critic Andy Grundberg once predicted, "In the future, readers of newspapers and magazines will probably view news pictures more as illustrations than as reportage, since they can no longer distinguish between a genuine image and one that has been manipulated." No evidence to date demonstrates that this depressing forecast is coming true.

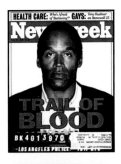

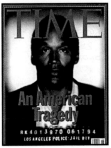

GOING TOO FAR?
While few photographers object to dodging and burning a negative in the darkroom, most are outraged at digitally retouching a person into or out of a news picture. How far should electronic retouching go? Should it:
- remove a distracting branch behind a person's head?
- tone the sky to a deeper blue?
- smooth out wrinkles from a star's face?
- alter a news picture if the manipulation will produce a more telling picture?
- change a feature photo?
- electronically sharpen an image?

Digital manipulation has not been around long enough for the photojournalism community to form agreed-upon standards. In coffee shops, at national meetings, and in newsrooms, the topic has been hotly debated since *National Geographic* moved the pyramids for its 1982 cover.

Photojournalists who take the absolutist's position argue that editors should not digitally retouch or manipulate photos at all. They say that the final picture should look as near as possible to the original slide or negative. They maintain that the original is "truth" and any change from that is categorically wrong. Bob Gilka, who was the director of photography at *National Geographic* when the pyramids were moved, later decided that "limited electronic manipulation is like a limited nuclear war. There isn't any such thing."

Others hold that editors should only make global changes—changes made to the entire photo similar to the way photographers in the field switch filters on a camera. This group says that shooters and editors should not electronically manipulate parts of the photo after it's been taken because photographers cannot do that in the field.

A less stringent position holds that editors should restrict manipulation to the same techniques practiced in the traditional dark-room—dodging, burning, lightening, darkening, and changing contrast. In an extensive survey of 511 picture editors, Shiela Reaves found they were intolerant of computer alterations or manipulations, with the overwhelming majority disapproving of any computer alterations other than burning and dodging.

One respondent summarized the feelings of most other editors: "The philosophy at our newspaper is not to publish any image which we cannot produce in negative form. Thus, the only manipulation is lightening and darkening, boosting the colors, dodging/burning, and spotting scratches and dust spots. No cloning pixels. No moving elements. No combining different negatives. No sanitizing images after the shutter has clicked."

John Long, a past president of National Press Photographers Association and a photographer for the *Hartford* (Connecticut) *Courant*, falls into this category. He says there is nothing wrong with fixing flaws using the computer. "These are merely technical in nature and have nothing to do with the actual content or meaning of the photo." Dodging and burning, he says, are integral to the medium of photography—part of the "grammar" of how we communicate. "The public understands this (at least unconsciously), so it is not wrong."

But Long argues that photographers should not try to improve a photo by eliminating even minor elements like distracting phone lines. Long uses this test, "Does the electronic change in the photo deceive the reader?"

Some editors, though, hold that the computer should be used to "clean up" a photo—to remove a distracting wire or a protruding telephone post from behind a subject, or close an open, embarrassing pants zipper.

Finally, some photographers argue that if the photographer could have taken the picture with a different lens or from a different angle, then manipulating the electronic image to get the same result passes muster. (See Rich Clarkson's comments, page 328.)

In a paper titled "Photography or Photofiction," Tom Wheeler and Tim Gleason define the latter as photography that is "manipulated enough during processing to change readers' perceptions of its meaning—whether material elements are altered, added, removed within the frame or rearranged and regardless of the method employed."

WHO BENEFITS?

How should the profession resolve this dilemma? Perhaps photojournalists should consider who benefits by altering photos. The photographer? The editor? The reader?

Consider this. In the situations where *National Geographic* moved the pyramids and Collins Publishing Company moved the cowboy and the moon, editors and designers sought to fit a horizontal picture onto a vertical cover format. Could another picture have sufficed? Could the cover design have been changed to fit the shape of the image? Who benefited? Editors and designers. Was the reader any better off? Not really.

Removing a cola can from a picture cleaned up the image for an editor. But did the reader gain anything from this move?

In all of these instances, electronic manipulation eased the jobs of editors, designers, or publishers. Not one was carried out to benefit readers.

Digitally "imagining" a victim's injuries or electronically bringing people together in one image goes beyond making jobs easy to simply fooling the reader because there's technology available that makes it easy to do so. Here, the reader not only fails to benefit but becomes the butt of a joke, as well.

FACILITATE, DON'T FOOL THE READER

On the other hand, when a photographer burns or dodges a print in the darkroom or similarly darkens or lightens the print in the computer, the reader benefits by seeing more clearly items in the picture that might have been missed with an unaltered picture. In the same way, the computer's ability to sharpen pictures or blur backgrounds to make the subject stand out more distinctly and legibly also benefits the reader.

Perhaps an ethical guidepost might read: "Electronically alter pictures only when doing so clearly benefits the reader. Avoid

L.A. TIMES PHOTOGRAPHER FIRED OVER ALTERED IMAGE

To see the altered image and comments by the *Los Angeles Times* and the Tribune company, visit *www.poynteronline.org/content/ content_view.asp?id=28082&sid=29*

Reprinted with permission of The Poynter Institute For Media Studies

by Kenny F. Irby
Contributor: Larry Larsen

April 1 [2003] may forever haunt Colin Crawford, *Los Angeles Times* director of photography, and Brian Walski, a staff photographer covering the war in Iraq for the paper.

That was the day Walski was fired, after it was revealed that a photo he submitted on Sunday was actually a composite of two images he had captured.

The photo was shared primarily with other Tribune properties including the *Hartford Courant*.

Thom McGuire, the *Courant*'s assistant managing editor for photography & graphics, had edited about 500 pictures from various services when he saw the picture from Walski. He liked the image so much that he called the *Times* for additional caption information, then published the image across six columns on the front page.

"It was a great image," McGuire says, "and I missed the manipulation, and I feel bad for everyone involved."

Others did not miss it. A *Courant* employee was looking through images for a friend and noticed what appeared to be duplication in the picture. The employee brought it to the attention of the copy desk, which then immediately alerted McGuire.

"After about a 600 percent magnification in Photoshop, I called Colin to ask for an investigation," McGuire says.

Across the country, the director of photography at the *LA Times*'s immediate reaction was one of "shock and disbelief."

"I said out loud, 'No way! There must be a technical, digital... satellite glitch explanation.'"

"He sent us 13 very good images Sunday," recalls Crawford, "We had to get information and give him the benefit of the doubt. And it took a day to raise him."

Walski, by telephone in southern Iraq, acknowledged that he had used his computer to combine elements of two photographs, taken moments apart, in order to improve the composition.

In an E-mail to the entire photography staff of the *Times*, Walski admitted his lapse in judgment and accepted responsibility for it. In his 214-word apology, he writes, in part:

"This was after an extremely long, hot and stressful day but I offer no excuses here. I deeply regret that I have tarnished the reputation of the *Los Angeles Times*, a newspaper with the highest standards of journalism, the Tribune Company, all the people at the *Times* and especially the very talented and extremely dedicated photographers and picture editors and friends that have made my four and a half years at the *Times* a true quality experience."

Interviewed by Poynter Online via sat phone from Kuwait City, *LA Times* staff photographer Don Bartletti recounts seeing his colleague and former co-worker Wednesday afternoon, after Walski returned from the desert.

"He is my friend and I respect the heroic images that he made and the tremendous effort that he has contributed," Bartletti said.

"When I saw him, I really did not recognize him. He was sunburned, had not eaten in days, nor slept in 36 hours, his clothes were filthy, his beard—all over the place. And he smelled like a goat."

Bartletti recalls asking him, "How could you do this?"

Walski said: "I f—-ed up, and now no one will touch me. I went from the front line for the greatest newspaper in the world, and now I have nothing. No cameras, no car, nothing."

Bartletti thinks he understands what happened. "He got into a zone. He was on a head roll, making fantastic images, and it got out of hand. He told me that he did not plan to send the image and was just messing around. He sent it

anyway... didn't know what he was doing, but he did it. With all that he was facing, how did he have the presence of mind? It just got out of hand."

Fatigue and horrific conditions are only part of why crazy things can happen in war zones, and Crawford admits that he "really worried about him [Walski], but was confident that he was stable after several conversations (via sat phone)." He contends the firing was "the right thing."

"What Brian did is totally unacceptable and he violated our trust with our readers," Crawford says. "We do not for a moment underestimate what he has witnessed and experienced. We don't feel good about doing this, but the integrity of our organization is essential. If our readers can't count on honesty from us, I don't know what we have left."

Chicago Tribune associate managing editor for photography Bill Parker agrees, adding that he is "profoundly saddened by this incident."

The *Tribune* planned to publish a correction in Thursday's paper.

On Tuesday at 8:30 p.m. Pacific Time, the *Los Angeles Times* posted an editor's note on its website notifying readers about the breach of its photographic ethics policy, the investigation and the subsequent firing of Walski for altering the photo of a British soldier and a group of Iraqi civilians. All three photos—the two originals and the altered composite—were published by the *Times* and the *Courant* on Wednesday.

"Unfortunately the stain of this photograph will harm journalists collectively," said Betty Udesen, a *Seattle Times* staff photographer. ■

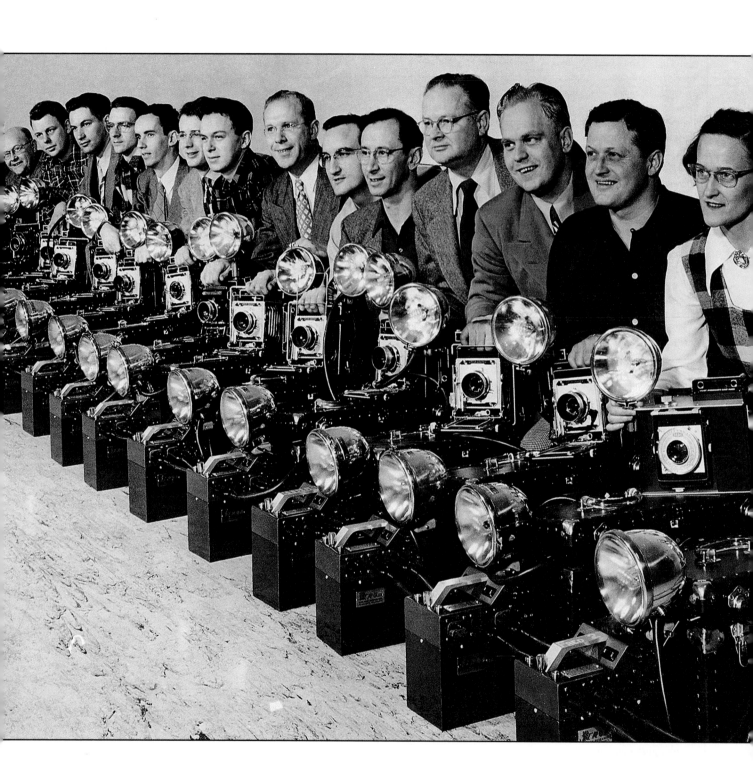

Chapter 15

History

THE GOOD OLD DAYS

O n a balmy April day in 1877 the staff of the *Daily Graphic*, the first illustrated daily newspaper in the United States, conducts business as usual.

Written with Julie Levinson, assistant professor, Babson College.

Reporters labor to complete their copy in time for the morning deadline. Artists put the finishing touches to their drawings, which will comprise three and a half of the tabloid's eight pages. In a makeshift darkroom, where a janitor stores mops and brooms, a lone photographer places 5"x7" precoated, dry-glass plates into light-tight holders. The photographer is so engrossed in the delicate operation that he barely

The first "portable" strobe for the news photographer was perfected and manufactured by Edward A. Farber for members of the *Milwaukee Journal* photo staff. *Milwaukee Journal*

hears the sudden commotion in the news-room over a passing fire engine. For the *Daily Graphic*'s staff, whose every sense is attuned to such signals, the fire engine's clanging bell tolls news.

Several reporters drop what they're doing, grab pencil and paper, and dash out to cover the late-breaking story. Someone remembers to inform the photographer about the fire alarm. He, too, puts aside his work and carefully balances his cumbersome view camera and tripod on one arm and a case containing twelve previously prepared glass plates on the other arm. The *Daily Graphic* camera-man sets off with his unwieldy load.

By the time he reaches the blaze, it is raging full force. He sets up his tripod and camera as quickly as possible, points his lens at the action, and takes his first exposure. Normally he would take only one exposure, or perhaps two, of a given event. Because this is such a huge fire, however, he decides to expose several of his glass plates. He has only one lens, so if he is to get different per-spectives on the action, he must change his position, pick up his bulky equipment, lug it to the new spot, and take the time to set up again. He then covers his head and the back of the camera with a black focusing cloth. Next he opens, focuses, closes, and sets the lens. Following this he loads the plate holder into the rear of the camera body and removes the dark slide. Finally, he takes the picture.

Before he can make the next photo, he must replace the dark slide and carefully put the holder back into his case. If he acciden-tally knocks the holder too hard, the glass plates will shatter. Unfortunately, the crowd jostles him as he works.

He attracts much attention because a news photographer is still a curiosity. But the Graphic photographer doesn't mind; he is particularly excited about the challenge posed by this event. Usually his assignments limit him to photographing portraits of famous people or carefully posed tableaux. Because of the technical limitations of his slow film (equivalent to ISO 24 by today's standards), he can photograph only under optimum conditions, with bright light and minimal subject movement. On this day, he gets some action shots by carefully panning his camera with the movement of a late arriv-ing horse-drawn fire engine.

After several hours, the *Daily Graphic* photographer finishes making his twelve exposures, and by the time he packs his case, camera, and tripod, the firemen finally have the blaze under control. But as the photogra-pher heads back to the newspaper office, weary from his physical exertion, his own

ordeal has just begun. Now he must develop his pictures in chemicals he mixes from a formula he found in a copy of the *Philadelphia Photographer*, one of the country's first photo magazines.

Enlargers are not commonly used. The 5"x7" negative is large enough for reproduc-tion when it is simply contact-printed on photographic paper. More than an hour after returning from the fire, the photographer has his first picture. After all that work, however, there is no way to reproduce the photograph in the newspaper.

The photographer now hands his pictures over to an artist, who draws replicas of them. Unfortunately, the artist often changes details from the original if he thinks the new varia-tions improve the picture. The artist, in turn, gives his drawings to an engraver, who repro-duces them onto a zinc plate. The plate is then printed on a Hoe rotary press.

Sometimes several days pass between the hour of the fire and the moment when these line-drawn renderings of the photographs appear in the newspaper. Yet the drawings receive front-page play.

EVOLUTION OF THE CAMERA REPORTER
How did the photographer of 1877 evolve into the modern photojournalist? Two major factors contributed to this development. First, the technical innovations: the invention of roll film, smaller cameras, faster lenses, and the introduction of portable light sources enabled the photographer to shoot pictures more easily and get better results. The inven-tion of the halftone process for reproducing photos and the improvement of printing presses led to better reproduction.

Meanwhile, with the creation and expan-sion of the wire services and the development of picture transmission devices, photogra-phers could send photos across the nation and around the world almost instantaneously.

The technological leaps made in photogra-phy since 1877 enable today's resourceful photographer to reach virtually any action anywhere and send home a photograph. Because of these scientific and engineering innovations, photographers can capture events previously impossible to capture with cameras: night pictures, fast action, and suc-cessive motion now can all be recorded with the camera.

But technological strides are only half the answer to this evolutionary question. Photographers broadened the scope of news pictures by introducing feature and sports pictures to newspapers. Photographers sought candid photos that revealed natural moments rather than the posed, frozen

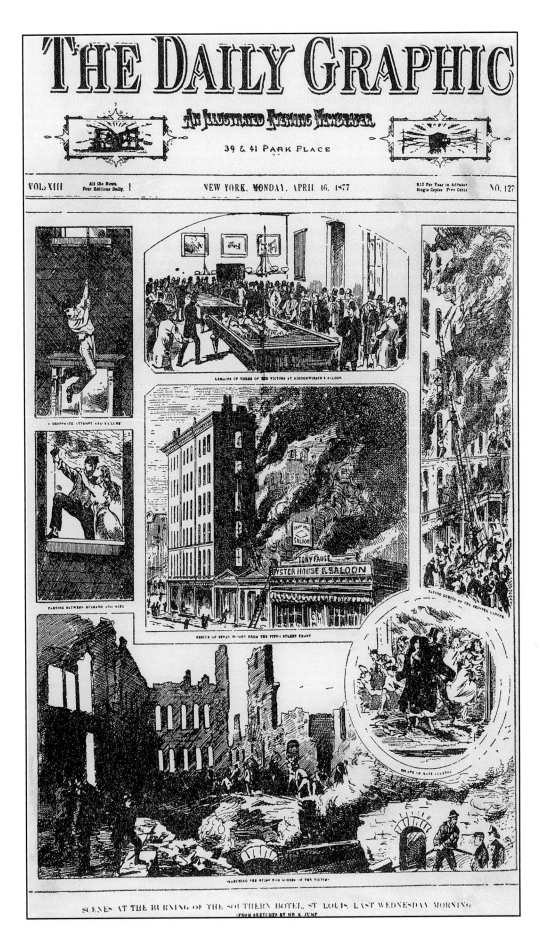

In 1877, the *Daily Graphic*, the first U.S. illustrated daily newspaper, devoted an entire front page to seven fire pictures. The *Daily Graphic*'s hand-drawn sketches were often based on photographs taken at the news scene.

New York Public Library

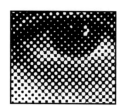

This is an enlargement of a halftone dot pattern showing an eye.

images typical of early photo reportage. Photographers today do more than just record the news. They have become visual interpreters by using their cameras and lenses, sensitivity to light, and keen observational skills to bring readers a feeling of what an event was really like.

The ingenuity of individual photographers in taking photos also laid the foundations of modern photojournalism. From the days of the *Daily Graphic* to the present, photographers first have had to figure out a way to get to the news event no matter where it is located—skyscraper or coal mine. They often must work around obstacles, both physical and human. Once photographers have the picture, they face the pressure of the deadline. Whether they transmit electronic images or develop film in a darkroom, they still must deliver the picture in time for the next edition. The daring and cleverness of the early photojournalists are the kinds of traits successful photographers have exhibited throughout the history of photojournalism.

Thus, technical advances and the imagination and resourcefulness of the photographer have gone hand-in-hand. The two have had complementary developments, each contributing to the gradual evolution of reportorial photography.

HALFTONE SCREEN REPRODUCES PHOTOS
SCREENS FIRST USED IN 1880

In 1877, our *Daily Graphic* photographer had little way of knowing that he stood on the threshold of a new age in photography. The next twenty years would see several rapid technological advances that would revolutionize the field of pictorial journalism: light,

handheld cameras, faster lenses, improved shutter mechanisms, and roll films.

But perhaps the most momentous technological occurrence in the history of photojournalism was the development of the halftone printing process.

Before the introduction of the halftone process, there was no practical way to transfer the photograph directly onto the printed page. An ordinary press could print only blacks and whites—full tones—and was incapable of rendering the intermediate shades of gray, the halftones. As such, newspaper illustrations, based on artists' original sketches or photographs, consisted of black-and-white line drawings, hand-carved on wood blocks or etched on zinc plates.

After years of trying, inventors found a method that could reproduce the full tonal range of photographic images. This process involved the use of a screen with an ordered dot pattern. This screen is held rigidly against a sensitized film in the engraver's camera. The engraver's camera copied the original photo through the screen, which broke up the photo's continuous tones into a series of tiny dots of varying sizes. The darkest areas of the original photo translated into a series of large dots. As the tones in the picture changed from black to gradations of gray and white, the dots became progressively smaller.

The engraver developed the film and contact printed it onto a metal plate. The pattern of dots was chemically transferred onto this printing plate. On the press, the dots transferred the ink onto the paper. Where they were largest and closest together, the image was darkest, and where they were smallest and farthest apart, the image was lightest.

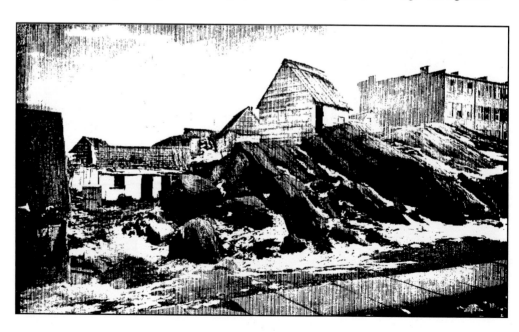

The first photograph reproduced on a printing press using the halftone process: on March 4, 1880, this photograph of Shantytown dwellings appeared in a special section of the *Daily Graphic* in New York. Notice that this first halftone used different sized lines to create shades of gray rather than the varying-sized dots of modern halftones. Henry J. Newton, New York *Daily Graphic*, courtesy of the New York Historical Society, New York City

Thus, the resulting printed image duplicated the shadings of the original photograph.

How much detail could be reproduced depended upon the fineness of the screen and the quality of the paper. By holding a magnifying glass up to any newspaper or magazine picture, you can easily see the tiny dot pattern of the halftone screen. A newspaper generally uses an 85-dots-per-inch (dpi) screen. This book uses 133 dots per inch.

Today, the computer has taken over much of what the engraver used to do. Computer software now translates a continuous-tone photo into a pattern of large and small dots (still referred to as "dpi") that are either burned into a plate or, in some circumstances, sent directly to the press.

THE FIRST HALFTONE

In Canada, the *Canadian Illustrated News* has the distinction of printing the first halftone in a magazine. Using glass plates ruled with a diamond point, engraver William Leggo produced a series of halftone pictures for the magazine.

The first halftone image published directly from a photograph was of His Royal Highness Prince Arthur. The *American Newspaper Reporter* in November 1871 described the accomplishment. "The photographic lens was employed in each instance, and not a square inch of boxwood, or one stroke of the graver, was needed."

Leggo later moved to New York, where he helped to start the *Daily Graphic*, which published the first halftone in an American daily newspaper on March 4, 1880: a picture of Shantytown, a squatter's camp in New York City. Stephen H. Horgan, the photographer in charge of the *Daily Graphic*'s engraving equipment, produced the halftone. Although Horgan had been perfecting this process for several years, his successful experiment in 1880 did not immediately affect the look of the newspaper. His halftone invention, however, did encourage further experimentation.

Georg Meisenbach, a copperplate engraver from Nuremberg, Germany, patented the autotype in 1882. This innovation introduced varying-sized round dots on a copper plate to translate a continuous-tone photograph into a halftone image. For the next 100 years, magazines and newspapers reproduced black-and-white as well as color photos with processes similar to this one.

By the beginning of the 1880s, magazines in both Europe and America adopted the halftone process to publish marvelously reproduced photographs. Readers saw everything from the World's Fair to immigrants on New York's East Side. *Harper's Weekly*

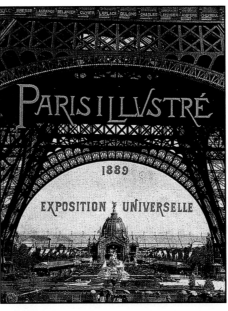

Paris Illustré published a full color photo of the recently built Eiffel Tower in 1889.

visually reported exotic scenes from far-away India. *Leslie's Weekly* horrified its readers with photographs of dead bodies during the war in the Philippines, covered by more than 500 reporters and photographers

By the turn of the century, *Leslie's Weekly* printed full-bleed (edge-to-edge) photographs on its cover—and even provided bylines for its photographers. Early illustrated magazines developed the entire repertoire of photojournalism—from complete coverage of catastrophic rail accidents and coal mine explosions to photographic reports on leisure activities and sports. Editors particularly liked to show off panoramic views of city life. Following the invention of Autochrome color film, magazines began publishing colorful, beautifully reproduced, fully chromatic pictures. The photos ran the gamut from stage actresses to scenics from Mongolia to participants at a costume ball.

OPPOSITION TO PHOTOS

In 1893, four years after the demise of the *Daily Graphic*, Horgan, who helped introduce the halftone to New York, was working as art editor for the *New York Herald* when he recommended the use of halftones to James Gordon Bennett, the paper's owner. After a brief consultation with his pressmen, Bennett pronounced the idea unfeasible.

Similarly, Joseph Pulitzer, who had been publisher of the *New York World* since 1883, initially expressed reluctance to print halftones. In fact, Pulitzer feared that widespread use of any pictures, including line drawings, would lower the paper's dignity, so he tried to cut down on the extensive use of woodcuts, which already had made his paper famous. When circulation fell as a result,

Pulitzer reconsidered his decision and reinstated the drawings.

As Pulitzer recognized the paper-selling potential of such illustrations, he began to increase their size from the original one-column to four- and five-column spreads. When the halftone was finally perfected, the *World* was one of the first newspapers to make liberal use of the new process. The daily's circulation rose rapidly. Other publishers and editors soon jumped onto the pictorial bandwagon. One such newsman, Melville Stone, investigated the potential of newspaper illustrations for the *Chicago Daily News*. He ultimately concluded, "Newspaper pictures are just a temporary fad, but we're going to get the benefit of the fad while it lasts."

Today we know that newspaper pictures were neither temporary nor faddish, but, in the closing years of the nineteenth century, the halftone continued to struggle for legitimacy in newspapers despite its outstanding showcase in magazines of the period.

By the late 1890s, the process had yet to achieve daily use, although the *New York Times* did print halftones in its illustrated Sunday magazine, begun in 1896. Skeptical newspaper publishers still feared that their

readers would lament the substitution of mechanically produced photographs for the artistry of hand-drawn pictures; also, artists and engravers were well-established members of the newspaper staff.

Thus, long after the halftone was perfected, carefully drawn copies of photos continued to appear in many papers. Gradually, however, papers joined magazines and adopted the halftone process. By 1910, hand engraving was becoming obsolete and the halftone, in turn, had became a staple of the newspaper's front page.

THE MAINE BLEW UP, AND JIMMY HARE BLEW IN

While these technological strides were taking place in the latter part of the nineteenth century, several photographers were setting photojournalistic precedents. Jimmy Hare, one of the most colorful of the pioneer photojournalists, wrote the handbook for future photographer-reporters.

During his career, Hare covered nearly every major world event, from the wreckage of the U.S. battleship Maine in Havana harbor during the Spanish-American War in 1898 to the closing days of World War I

Jimmy Hare (below left), with his two folding cameras carried in their leather cases, covered the globe for Collier's Weekly. He photographed everything from the Spanish-American War (right) to the closing days of World War I in Europe.
Jimmy Hare Collection, Humanities Research Center, University of Texas at Austin

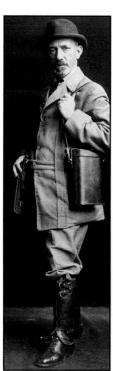

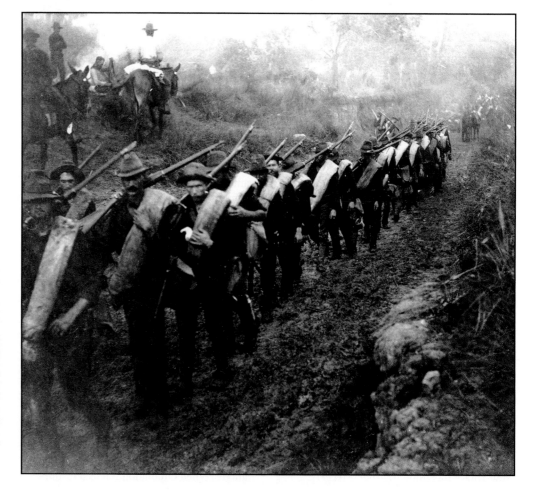

in Europe. His ingenuity and his no-holds-barred attitude when it came to getting the picture set a standard for the new profession of photojournalism.

London-born Hare, whose father crafted handmade cameras for a living, came to the United States in 1889. One magazine, the *Illustrated American*, committed itself to using halftone photographs. From 1896 to 1898, Hare worked as a freelance photographer, supplying the magazine with photos of events ranging from presidential inaugurations to sporting matches. A month after he left the *Illustrated American*, the battleship Maine exploded, thus signaling the start of the Spanish-American War. The ever-enterprising photographer promptly presented himself to the editors of *Collier's Weekly*, and offered to take pictures of the wreckage. Twenty years after the Maine episode, then-editor Robert J. Collier was to recall, "The Maine blew up and Jimmy blew in! Both were major explosions!" Jimmy continued "blowing in" to important world events for the next several decades.

So successful were his pictures of the Maine and of Cuba, where American soldiers were fighting the Spanish in the Spanish-American War, that the publisher named Hare special photographer for *Collier's*, thus beginning a long and productive association.

Whether trekking over the Cuban countryside, touring battlefields with Stephen Crane, author of **Red Badge of Courage**, or following Teddy Roosevelt's Rough Riders, Hare remained intrepid and resourceful in his coverage of the Spanish-American War. Hare made use of the new folding cameras (with lenses as fast as f/6.8) and of roll film (with twelve exposures per roll). His lightweight equipment gave him more mobility than his competitors, who were shooting with fragile glass plates and awkward 5"x7" Graflexes, the popular news cameras of the day.

Regardless of his folding camera's light weight, Hare still had to get to the middle of the action to take a picture. In one battle during the Spanish-American conflict, a soldier spotted Hare snapping away as wounded bodies dropped all around him. "You must be a congenital damn fool to be up here! I wouldn't be unless I had to!" the soldier shouted. Hare's even-handed reply: "Neither would I, but you can't get real pictures unless you take some risks."

In addition to his exploits in the Spanish-American War, Hare's photographic escapades brought him to the combat lines of the Russo-Japanese War, the Mexican Revolution, the First Balkan War, and World War I. Hare described these experiences as

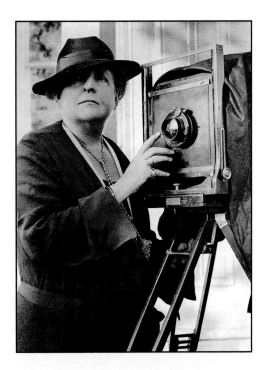

Frances Benjamin Johnston, an early photojournalist around 1900, represented the Bain News Service in Washington, D.C.
Library of Congress.

"one-sided adventures in which it was always my privilege to be shot at but never to shoot." But shoot he did—with his camera, that is—and his pictures contributed greatly to *Collier's* rapidly rising circulation and national prominence.

HARE COVERS FIRST FLIGHT

Not all of Hare's exploits took place on the battlefield. The story of how Hare managed to record on film the experiments of the Wright brothers in 1908 is indicative of his tenacity and his skill. The Wrights' first successful flight had taken place in 1903, but, five years later, the public remained unconvinced that men had actually flown. Rumors abounded but no one had documented proof of any flight. The brothers refused to allow reporters to witness their experiments at Kitty Hawk.

Hare was determined to check out the rumor for Collier's, however, and, along with four reporters from various newspapers, he secretly went to the Wright brothers' testing area. The five intrepid men spent two days hiking over the sands of Kitty Hawk, North Carolina. Approaching the site of the rumored flights, the newsmen took cover in a clump of bushes and anxiously waited for something to happen. Covered with mosquito bites and tired of lugging his camera, Hare was tempted to dismiss the rumors as false and head back home. But suddenly an engine noise was heard, and, as the reporters watched in disbelief, an odd-looking machine glided across the sand and gradually rose into the air. Hare ran out of the bushes

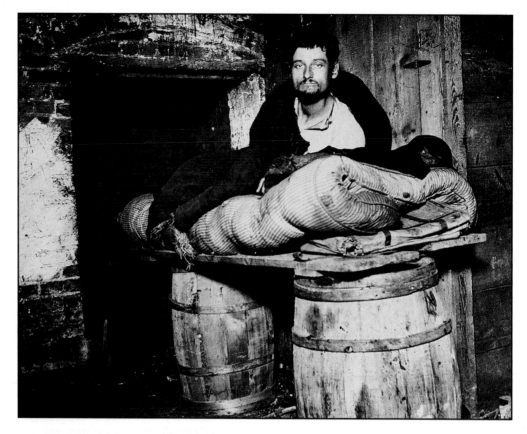

With flash powder lighting the way, Jacob Riis exposed New York's slum conditions endured by recent immigrants. This man slept in a cellar for four years.

Jacob Riis Collection, Museum of the City of New York

and managed to snap two photographs of the airborne machine. The party of reporters then sneaked back to their base and prepared to reveal their booty to the world.

Because Hare was far away from the plane, the image in his photo was small and indistinct. But *Collier's* was proud to publish the picture in its May 30, 1908, issue. The photo proved at last that man could indeed fly. Hare had the distinction of taking the first news photograph of a plane in flight.

Hare began chronicling his world during photojournalism's infancy. When *Collier's* first published his photos, editors considered pictures mere embellishments of the text. But through his dogged efforts to capture with his camera a sense of immediacy and excitement, Hare served as a catalyst in the evolution of the photographer into a full-fledged "reporter with a camera."

WOMEN ENTER THE FIELD

Since 1900, female photojournalists have made their mark in the newsroom. Frances Benjamin Johnston, an indomitably spirited photographer, managed to transcend the constraints usually imposed on Victorian women. She documented early educational methods in black, white, and Indian schools. She shot a series of photographs on the activities in the White House and on the visits of foreign dignitaries. Then Johnston sold her

pictures to the newly formed Bain News Service (see pages 358–359) and became its photo representative in Washington. Johnston was considered the unofficial White House photographer, according to C. Zoe Smith's article "Great Women in Photojournalism." D.C. Bain, the agency's owner, suggested that Johnston photograph Admiral George Dewey aboard his battleship after his successful takeover of the Philippines. With great ingenuity she made her way to Italy, where Dewey's ship first docked. She managed to endear herself to the crew and, when it came time to fill out an enlistment record, she earned five out of five possible points for everything from seamanship to marksmanship, but only a "4.9" for sobriety.

Jessie Tarbox Beals was another photojournalistic pioneer. She started out as a schoolteacher but soon discovered the lure of photography. In 1902 the *Buffalo* (New York) *Inquirer and Courier* hired her as a press photographer. Early on, she exhibited an important skill of the photojournalist—the "ability to hustle," as she once put it. Before her career ended, Beals sneaked photographs through a transom at a murder trial, rode the gondola of a balloon above the St. Louis World's Fair for a photo, and photographed Mark Twain.

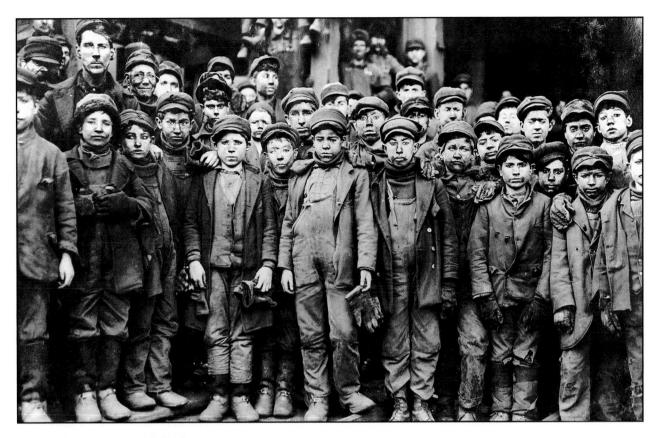

THE CAMERA AS A REFORMER'S TOOL

Social-documentary photographers, notably Jacob Riis and Lewis Hine, demonstrated that the camera could not only provide a record of events but could also serve as a potent tool for social change. Hine once summarized his goals as a concerned photographer: "There were two things I wanted to do. I wanted to show the things that had to be corrected. I wanted to show the things that had to be appreciated." As America moved into the new century, crusading photographers chose to concentrate on Hine's goal to correct social injustice. Riis and Hine were among the first to press the camera into service as an agent for social awareness.

Their photographic pleas for reform placed them in the ranks of such late 19th-century and early 20th-century social muckrakers as Upton Sinclair, Lincoln Steffens, and Ida Tarbell. Together with these writer-reformers, the camera journalists probed the underside of city life, exposed the unimaginable, and brought into the open what had previously been shielded from view.

The tradition established by Riis and Hine carried through to the 1930s with Farm Security Administration (FSA) photographers such as Dorothea Lange, Walker Evans, Marion Post Wolcott, Gordon Parks, and Arthur Rothstein, who used their cameras to record Depression-ridden America. Under the direction of Roy Stryker, the FSA photographers recorded not only the devastating effects of a prolonged drought on farmers but also the Roosevelt administration's New Deal programs that were helping farmers and workers get back on their feet. The agency gave the photographs to newspapers and magazines to publicize the problems of the farm worker and to show how government money was helping. The pictures also were used to persuade congressional representatives to allocate more money for the Farm Security Administration programs. The FSA photo project not only helped at the time but has left us with one of the greatest photographic records of any period of our past.

Riis Exposes Slum Conditions

Neither Riis nor Hine, in fact, began as a photographer. The Danish-born Riis started out in the 1870s as a carpenter and then got a job as a reporter for the *New York Sun*. He wrote firsthand accounts of the indignities and inequities of immigrant life. When he was accused of exaggerating his written descriptions of life in the city slums, he turned to photographs as a means of documenting the human suffering he saw.

For Riis, the photograph had only one purpose: to aid in the implementation of

Lewis Hine photographed the soot-blackened children who worked in the coal mines. In part because of Hine's photos, Congress passed protective child-labor laws. Lewis Hine, Library of Congress

social reform. Pictures were weapons of persuasion that surpassed the power of words and the absolute veracity of the photographic image made it an indispensable tool. As Riis stated, "The power of fact is the mightiest lever of this or any other day."

But Riis was up against many obstacles as a photographer. The crowded tenements were shrouded in darkness and shadows. To show the perpetual nighttime existence in the slums, Riis pioneered the use of German Blitzlichtpulver—flashlight powder—which, although dangerous and uncontrollable, did sufficiently illuminate the scene. Lugging a 4"x5" wooden box camera, tripod, glass plate holders, and a flash pan, Riis ventured into the New York slums with evangelical zeal. With a blinding flash and a torrent of smoke, he got his pictures. The scenes he recorded of immigrant poverty shocked and goaded the public into action for reform.

The Riis pictures are remarkably poignant glimpses of ghetto life. Grim-faced families stare at the camera with empty eyes. Shabbily clothed children sleep amid the garbage of a tenement stoop. A grown man stands in the middle of the street and begs for someone to buy one of his pencils. An immigrant sits on his bed of straw. In a coal bin, a newly arrived American citizen prepares for the Sabbath.

Unfortunately, when Riis was photographing, the halftone had yet to achieve widespread use. Consequently, his actual pictures were not directly reproduced in printed sources and so were seen by only limited numbers of people, such as those attending his lantern-slide shows. At these talks, he used his pictures to buttress his plea for attention and reform.

When Riis' first book, **How the Other Half Lives**, was finally published in 1890, it consisted of seventeen halftones and nineteen drawings modeled on his photographs. The halftones were technically poor—somewhat fuzzy and indistinct—but the pictures exerted a powerful influence that drew attention to slum conditions. They remain moving documents of human suffering.

HINE'S PHOTOS HELP INSTITUTE CHILD LABOR LAWS

Lewis Hine began as an educator and, like Riis, turned to photography as a means of exposing "the things that had to be corrected." In turn-of-the-century urban America, many conditions begged to be noticed and changed. The influx of immigrants into the cities and the simultaneous growth of industrialism were important characteristics of the new century. With the reformer's commitment, Hine set out to catalogue how people survived in this new way of life.

HAPPY ACCIDENT AT THE *NATIONAL GEOGRAPHIC*

IMMEDIATE RIGHT
On deadline at *National Geographic* and faced with eleven open pages, editor Gilbert Grosvenor used free pictures from Lhasa, Tibet, to fill the space for the magazine's first extensive photo layout. Courtesy of *National Geographic*

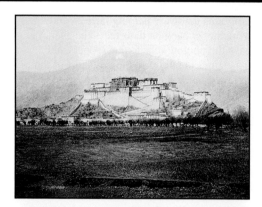

IMMEDIATE RIGHT
George Shiras III took the first night nature photos for *National Geographic*.

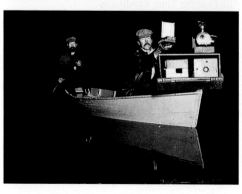

FAR RIGHT
Readers were so delighted with the magazine's first picture layout that editor Grosvenor ran 32 pages of pictures about the Philippines in the next issue.

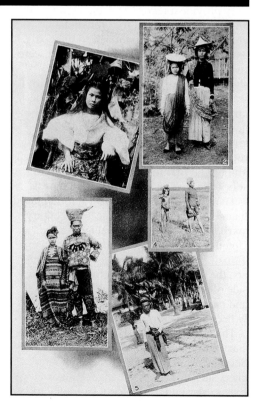

In 1908, the magazine *Charities and the Commons* published a series of his pictures of immigrant life. The series included some of Hine's most famous pictures: portraits of newly arrived immigrants at Ellis Island. The power and eloquence of these pictures attracted much attention. With the further refinement of the halftone, Hine published his work in books and magazines and gained a good deal of public exposure for his social issues.

That same year, Hine began to work as an investigator and reporter for the National Child Labor Committee. His work took him everywhere, from St. Louis slums to California canneries. To get through the doors of offending factories and mines, Hine posed as every type of worker, from a fire inspector to a Bible salesman. One time he packed his camera in a lunch pail, filed with the workers into a clothing factory, and surreptitiously snapped pictures of sweatshop conditions. Hine juxtaposed diminutive children against huge machines. The weary stares of young knitting mill operators and seamstresses spoke more eloquently than words. The impact his photos, including those of soot-blackened faces of child coalminers, helped facilitate the passage of Child Labor Laws restricting exploitation of youth.

PHOTOS FILL MAGAZINES AND "ROTO" SECTIONS
PICTURES COME IN HANDY AT *NATIONAL GEOGRAPHIC*

National Geographic did not start out as a picture magazine. In fact, its first issue in 1888 contained no photos. It wasn't until 1903 that the magazine ran its first halftone, a photo of a Filipina at work in the rice fields.

Not until 1905 did the magazine try a photo spread unbroken by text. As it happened, the photo display was unintended.

On the day the magazine was scheduled to go to the printer, the editor, Gilbert Grosvenor, was faced with eleven open pages and no material whatsoever to fill the space. By coincidence, he had received that same day a package of photographs from the Imperial Russian Geographic Society.

These pictures of the previously unphotographed Tibetan city of Lhasa had been taken by two Russian explorers and were being offered to the *Geographic* for publication. Grosvenor, fascinated by the photographs, decided to take a risk. He laid them out as an eleven-page spread—all pictures and almost no text—and sent them to the printer.

Grosvenor was sure he would be fired for having made this unprecedented and expensive editorial decision. Instead, readers stopped him in the street to congratulate him.

Although Grosvenor had run the Lhasa pictures primarily to fill up empty pages, he repeated the experiment after seeing the stir they created. In April 1905, he ran thirty-two consecutive pages of 138 photographs of the Philippines—a turning point in the magazine's history.

National Geographic contributed many photographic firsts, including the first night-time nature pictures ever published, shot by George Shiras III, in 1906.

The magazine's first color photos, in 1910, were not color photos at all. In fact, they were hand-painted black-and-white pictures from Korea and China by William C. Chapin. Coloring black-and-white pictures continued until 1916, when Autochromes Lumieres, real color photos, made their debut in the magazine's pages.

The first series of Autochromes had no particular theme other than that they were all natural-color photographs. In fact, the magazine invited amateurs to submit photos and ran them alongside pictures made by scientists, writers, and professional photographers. Since those early Autochromes, the magazine has published color photos from every part of the world as well as from the bottom of the sea and from outer space.

ROTOGRAVURE AND THE PICTURE PAGE APPEAR

In 1914, the *New York Times* began publishing the first Sunday rotogravure section. Several other newspapers followed. The rotogravure process, which usually used a dark sepia ink, offered a cheap printing process that could print sixteen pages simultaneously—and an unlimited number of screened photos.

That same year, the *Times* also started the *Mid-Week Pictorial War Extra* to absorb the flow of World War I pictures pouring in from Europe. Printed on a superior grade of paper that yielded reproductions of higher quality, the supplement was sold separately at newsstands. Despite severe U.S. censorship, picture agencies managed to obtain photos of trench warfare, the effects of poison gas, and the wholesale destruction of small towns taking place in Europe.

Die Hamburger Woche, a German newspaper, devoted its entire cover to a photo of the incident that actually triggered World War I. The photo shows Gavrillo Princip as he was arrested in Sarajevo on June 28, 1914, just after he had assassinated the heir to the Austria-Hungarian throne.

Once the war started, photographers were explicitly forbidden to visit the battlefield. In fact, censorship was so severe that the Allied command assigned an officer to each correspondent to control what the journalist saw and what scenes were photographed.

Photographers covering the war had to be ingenious to circumvent the censors. Many of the photographs that finally appeared were taken by soldiers who happened to be amateur photographers. By 1916, the *New York Times* expanded the coverage of the *Mid-Week Pictorial*, sold it for ten cents, and dropped the words "War Extra."

A photographic highlight occurred in 1924 when the magazine reproduced Autochrome photographs of Tutankhamen's treasure. Color reproduction in newspapers and magazines was rare for that time, although color roto had appeared as "tintogravure" in Joseph Pulitzer's *Sunday World* in 1923.

Mid-Week Pictorial took pride in its exclusive photographs, touting "the first photography" whenever possible. Tremendous coverage was given to Charles A. Lindbergh's solo nonstop trans-Atlantic flight in 1927.

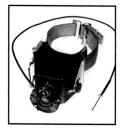

The New York *Daily News*, a tabloid, hired Thomas Howard to get a picture of murderess Ruth Snyder's electrocution in 1928. He strapped a miniature glass-plate camera (above) to his ankle and released the cable as he hiked his trouser leg. He exposed the plate three times, once for each electric shock administered to Snyder.
ABOVE: Smithsonian Institution; RIGHT: Thomas Howard, New York *Daily News*

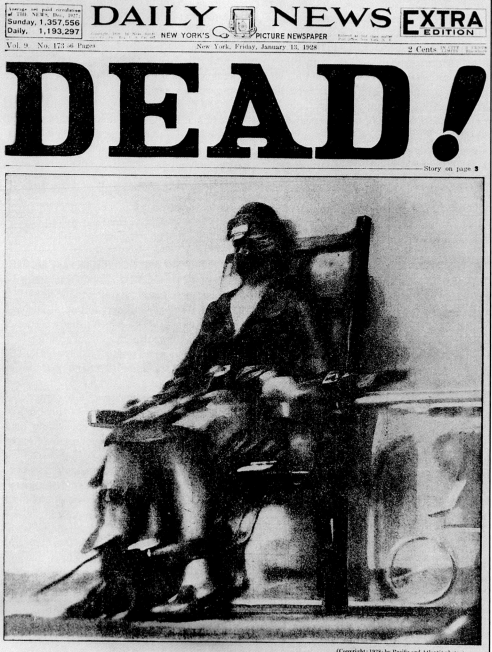

Average net paid circulation of THE NEWS, Dec., 1927. Sunday, 1,357,556 Daily, 1,193,297

DAILY ◼ NEWS EXTRA EDITION
NEW YORK'S ⬤ PICTURE NEWSPAPER

Vol. 9. No. 173 36 Pages   New York, Friday, January 13, 1928   2 Cents IN CITY 3 CENTS ELSEWHERE

DEAD!

—Story on page **3**

(Copyright: 1928; by Pacific and Atlantic photos)

RUTH SNYDER'S DEATH PICTURED!—This is perhaps the most remarkable exclusive picture in the history of criminology. It shows the actual scene in the Sing Sing death house as the lethal current surged through Ruth Snyder's body at 11:06 last night. Her helmeted head is stiffened in death, her face masked and an electrode strapped to her bare right leg. The autopsy table on which her body was removed is beside her. Judd Gray, mumbling a prayer, followed her down the narrow corridor at 11:14. "Father, forgive them, for they don't know what they are doing?" were Ruth's last words. The picture is the first Sing Sing execution picture and the first of a woman's electrocution.—*Story p. 3; other pics. p. 28 and back page.*

To show readers the magazine's concern with timely news coverage, one photographic caption read, "A Radio Photograph . . . This picture was taken, was then carried to London by airplane and flashed across the ocean to New York by Radiograph."

Mid-Week Pictorial, however, ran far more features than news. Through the 1920s, pictures of movie and theater stars, fashion, sports, and high school beauty queens regularly filled its pages. One had to look below or alongside the oval, circular, and odd-shaped photographs to find minimal caption information. Overall, according to Keith R. Kenney and Brent W. Unger's study titled "The *Mid-Week Pictorial*: Forerunner of American News-Picture Magazines," the 1920s began a period of slow decline for the Mid-Week. With faster and faster picture transmission and higher quality newspaper reproduction, the best photographs had begun appearing in daily newspapers. Circulation for *Mid-Week Pictorial* fell every year until 1937, when America's first modern picture magazine folded.

Picture Pages

Presses of the period were technically incapable of interspersing pictures with print and still achieving good halftone reproduction throughout the paper. Therefore, almost all the photos were grouped together on one single page. Printers achieved this improved reproduction by putting a specially designed ink blanket on the press cylinder that carried the halftone engravings. Thus, a page-one story would have its corresponding picture printed inside on this special picture page.

THE TABLOIDS: THRILLS AT TWO CENTS A COPY
IMMIGRANTS UNDERSTAND PICTURES

The immigrants photographed by Hine and Riis couldn't read English very well, but they could understand pictures. At a time when the country was bustling with non-English-speaking immigrants, photographs became a universal language and, along with movies, a visual handle on the new world. Also, because of the new industrialism, people had more leisure time to spend reading newspapers and magazines. With the wiring of cities for electricity, families could study published pictures long after dark.

The public went picture crazy. To meet this appetite for photos, photographers, encumbered with their large cameras and slow film, usually posed pictures, often in novel ways.

Researcher Wilson Lowrey studied early newspaper coverage in "Alter Plates: Photo Manipulation and the Search for News Value in the Early and Late Twentieth Century." He found a wide variety of novel photographic poses: tall people posed next to very short people, or very fat people juxtapositioned with very thin people. Photographers encouraged subjects to mimic their professions: A comic would grimace humorously; an actor would take a dramatic stance; singers would open mouths wide as if singing a high note.

Harry Coleman of the *New York Journal* didn't stop at posing his subjects, which, after all, was a bit difficult when some of them turned up dead. As he recounted in his autobiography, **Give Us A Little Smile, Baby**, Coleman would locate a body in the morgue, dress it in a shirt and tie, prop it up, and shoot it as a "life-like" portrait.

Altering photos to please subjects was common, as well. Underwood & Underwood, one of the early picture agencies, capitalized on the fact that elderly women didn't like the way they looked in pictures. The agency's art department removed their wrinkles during retouching. Artists continued the cosmetic artistry by altering facial expressions, rearranging and removing elements, and cutting photos into odd shapes.

In the late 1910s, another journalistic phenomenon caught the public's fancy: the tabloid, a half-size newspaper filled with pictures and brief stories. The tabloid was ideal for the less-educated masses and newly arrived immigrants. And the commuter could easily read the small publication on the trolley or subway.

The first twentieth-century tabloid in the United States was *New York's Illustrated Daily News*, launched in 1919. Circulation of the heavily illustrated *Daily News* soared rapidly, and it became one of the most remarkable success stories in journalism. The name of the paper was changed to the *Daily News: New York's Picture Newspaper*, and survives to this day.

In its early days the *News*'s stock and trade was titillation—crime and sex scandals, vicarious thrills for only two cents a copy. One of the most famous stories, illustrating the lengths to which the *Daily News* would go to get a provocative picture, involved the electrocution of Ruth Snyder in January 1928. In what was dubbed "the crime of the decade," a jury found Snyder guilty of murdering her wealthy husband with the aid of her lover. The *Daily News*'s editor felt the public was entitled to see Snyder's execution, but photographers were barred. The editor devised a plan to sneak a cameraman into the room. Thomas Howard, a news photographer from the *Chicago Tribune*, sister paper of the *Daily News*, was brought in for the occasion.

He strapped to his ankle a prefocused miniature glass-plate camera. The camera had a long cable release running up Howard's leg into his pants pocket. Howard aimed his camera simply by pointing his shoe and hiking his trouser leg. To get sufficient light to the film, Howard, when the time came, exposed the plate several times—one for each shock administered to the body of Ruth Snyder. The following day, Friday the thirteenth, the picture ran full page with a single-word headline: DEAD!

The Composograph

If the *News* was "a daily erotica for the masses," as it was sometimes called, it still paled in comparison to its fellow scandal monger, the *Evening Graphic*, commonly known at the time as the "Porno Graphic."

In the *Evening Graphic*, the composograph, the first staged and faked news photo, was born. The occasion was the Kip Rhinelander divorce trial. Alice Jones, an African American, was sued for annulment by Rhinelander, a Caucasian.

The husband maintained he had married her without knowing her race. The wife's defense attorney had her strip to the waist as if this would prove the husband should have known. Barred from the proceedings, newspaper photographers assigned to the case brought back no pictures of the sensational event.

The *Graphic*'s assistant art director, Harry Grogin, wasn't deterred. "Hell with photographers," he is reported to have muttered. "What we need 'em for?" He found morgue pictures of Alice, of the judge, of opposing counsel, of Rhinelander, of Alice's mother, of Rhinelander's father.

Meanwhile, Harry sent for Agnes McLaughlin, a showgirl, and got her to pose, wearing as little as possible, as he imagined Alice Rhinelander had stood before the lawyers and the judge. Grogin tinted Agnes McLaughlin's skin, faintly, to give the effect of being lightly colored. He used twenty separate photos to arrive at the one famous shot, but for the *Graphic*, it was well worth the effort. The picture was believable. With Alice humble in the foreground, one of the lawyers points at her husband accusingly.

Emile Gauvreau, the managing editor, and the city desk loved it. But what headline? One suggestion: ALICE UN-DRESSES. They decided on ALICE DISROBES IN COURT TO KEEP HER HUSBAND.

So the *Graphic* composograph was born. The Graphic's circulation rose from 60,000 to several hundred thousand after that issue. The composograph was a *Graphic* depiction, posed in the art department, of a sensational real-life scene that, for one reason or another, could not be photographed. It was officially called a "composograph" in the paper and identified as having been made in the art department.

Editor and Publisher, a newspaper trade publication, called the trial picture "the most shocking news-picture ever produced by New York journalism." The "shocking" aspect presumably had to do with putting an almost-nude woman on the front page but not for its cut-and-paste technique, observes Bob Stepno in his paper "Staged, Faked and

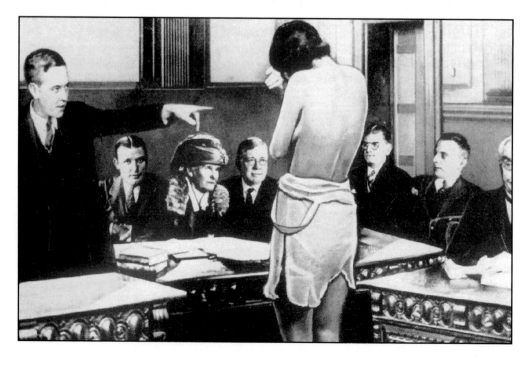

Because they couldn't take a picture inside the courtroom during the sensational Rhinelander divorce trial, the *Evening Graphic* staged the courtroom scene at the newspaper office with actors playing the parts of real individuals. Faces of actual participants were pasted on later. The new technique was dubbed a "composograph"—and repeated many times.

Harry Grogin, *Evening Graphic*

Mostly Naked: Photographic Innovations at the *Evening Graphic* (1924–1932)."

As might be expected, the *Graphic* continued to exploit the popularity of the composite picture, while admitting in tiny print at the bottom of the composograph that the pictures were faked. Later, while staging a phony hanging of thief Gerald Chapman, Grogin called on one of his assistants to pose with a noose around his neck, bound hands and feet, and a mask over his head. The man stood on an empty box that later would be blocked out of the picture. (See page 330.) Just as the picture was to be snapped, the stand-in victim accidentally kicked the box away. Luckily, Grogin acted with lightning reflexes and caught the suspended man seconds before the fake hanging became a real one.

Of course, not all of the tabloid pictures were composographs. If a real-life picture was gruesome and lurid enough to satisfy the thrill-hungry public, the *Graphic*, the *Daily News*, and other tabloids were more than happy to run the photo.

At one point, the New York Society of the Suppression of Vice persuaded the police to arrest Gauvreau and several other *Graphic* staff members for violating the obscenity provisions of the city's penal code. Constant legal hassles and the threat of a citywide

boycott organized by religious leaders took a toll on the *Graphic*. Although the *Graphic*'s circulation averaged nearly 300,000 from 1926 to mid-1931, businesses were wary of advertising in the scandalous publication. Department stores like Macy's and Gimbels would not buy ad space. The paper was a losing proposition in the otherwise profitable empire, according to Michael Carlebach's book *American Photojournalism Comes of Age*. In 1932, Macfadden pulled the plug on the *Graphic*.

WEEGEE: KING OF CRIME PHOTOGRAPHERS

The most famous photographer to capitalize on the tabloid mentality and concentrate his energies on the seamier side of city life was Arthur Fellig, universally and simply known as "Weegee." Weegee acquired his name because, like the Ouija board, he supposedly had an uncanny ability to predict what would happen when and where, and he would miraculously be there—often ahead of the police. However, because he was a poor speller he wrote his new name phonetically, "Weegee." His news sense, of course, was a helpful quality for a photojournalist and, with the advantages of his police radio and strategically located living quarters near the police station,

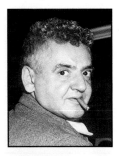

Weegee (Arthur Fellig) (PICTURED BELOW TOP) intuitively understood people's fascination for crime, which attracted the attention of both the bystander at the scene and the reader at home. Weegee was the first photographer to use a police radio to get early tips about gangland shootings. BOTTOM: Photo by Arthur Fellig

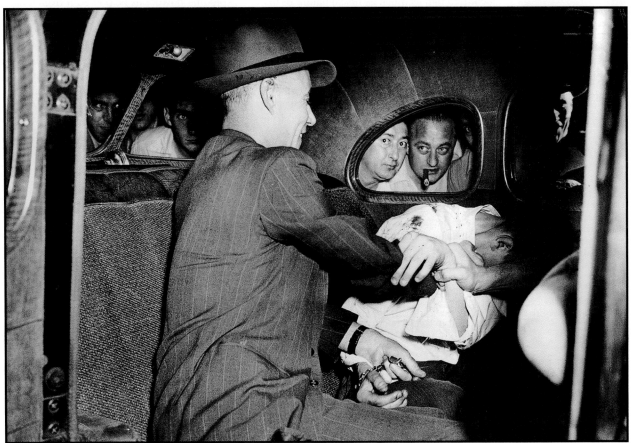

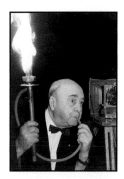

Flash powder fired in a pan left the room filled with smoke, unfortunately delaying the possibility of taking a second photo. Here, Harry Rhodes demonstrates his flash technique. Rhodes, we hope, never inhaled.

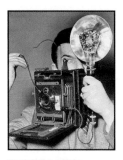

Flash bulbs, which replaced flash powder, were smokeless and safe but cumbersome and awkward.

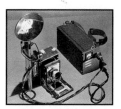

Edward Farber of the *Milwaukee Journal* modified the electronic flash, making it portable and convenient for news photographers.

Photos above from the files of the National Press Photographers Association, courtesy of John Faber

Weegee managed to keep on the scent of the city's assorted crimes, auto crashes, and fires. The city was his working space, the night was his time, and violence was his specialty. Too independent to be tied to any one publication, Weegee remained a freelancer and a free spirit for most of his career. He cruised the city streets nightly in his car, always ready to cover the happenings of urban nightlife.

Weegee poked his inquisitive camera into every dark corner of the city, photographing life as he saw it—stark and uncensored. His book, *Naked City*, was later made into a movie and then a television show. Its title is an apt summation of his style and his subject. In his pictures, the city was indeed naked, unadorned, and exposed.

Weegee knew not only how to get a picture but how to sell it as well. He explained his technique, "If I had a picture of two hand-cuffed criminals being booked, I would cut the picture in half and get five bucks for each." For a photo of a bullet-ridden corpse, he had an entrepreneur's price scale. Weegee's going rate: $5 per bullet! Never one for modesty, he would stamp the back of his pictures, "Credit Weegee the Famous." The stamp was hardly necessary, though, as his direct, unflinching style of photography identified him as much as his signature or his omnipresent cigar.

Weegee reveled in his role as a special character, and he played it to the hilt. With his chewed-up cigar, crushed-felt hat, and bulging eyes, he sometimes looked like the popular stereotype of a crime photographer. He gloried in beating the cops to the scene of the action. Rushing from his car he would point his camera at the subject without bothering to focus or adjust the f-stop—ten feet at f/11 with flash covered most situations.

Besides covering violent scenes, Weegee also shot ordinary life—people relaxing at Coney Island, fans at Frank Sinatra concerts, children sleeping on a fire escape. Later in his career he photographed Hollywood stars.

In Weegee's work, the flashbulb's explosion intruded on the night's protective darkness, violating its cover and exposing the startling scenes that he witnessed. In all of his photos, the flashbulb is a real presence. It is evident in the strong tonal contrasts from the harsh light of a flash used on the camera. Somehow, in Weegee's world, everyone looks like a victim, caught unaware by the insistent light of the camera's flash.

Weegee, however, was not above setting up pictures, according to Louie Liotta, also a New York street photographer of Weegee's generation. In an article for *People* magazine,

Liotta recalled how one famous Weegee picture came to be. Weegee dressed an old woman from the Bowery in a ragged fur coat and had her stand in front of Metropolitan Opera. He waited for two well-dressed attendees wearing expensive minks to walk by as he shot the picture of the old woman scrutinizing the wealthy patrons. "They were authentic, he just helped them a little bit," recalled Liotta. Weegee sold the picture to *Life* magazine, and it has become a classic. (For more on early set-up pictures, see Chapter 14, "Ethics," page 330.)

SEARCH FOR A CONVENIENT LIGHT SOURCE
DANGERS OF FLASH POWDER

Although Weegee had to replace the flash-bulb after each exposure, flashbulbs proved infinitely more convenient than the flash powder used in Jacob Riis's day. Horror stories about flash powder are legion. Flash photographers in the old days wore special cuffs so the powder wouldn't roll down and burn their arms when the chemical was ignited. Eddie McGill, a *Chicago Tribune* photographer, suffered a skull fracture when a big flash pan bent as it fired. Another Chicago photographer, Nick McDonald, of the *Chicago Herald-Examiner*, lost a hand from exploding powder as he poured it from a bottle onto a hot flash pan.

When several photographers were on the scene, they had to decide which one would set off the flash powder. Once the substance was lit, smoke filled the room, eliminating the possibility of anyone taking a second picture. An additional problem, of course, was the subjects gasping for air, sometimes between curses. Needless to say, photographers and their flash pans were not exactly welcome in most places.

Three kinds of flash lamps were available for the photographer: the Caywood, the Imp, and the Victor. The Caywood flash was used for indoor portraits and group pictures. The Imp lamp, manufactured by the Imperial Brass Company, worked well for large groups indoors. Outdoors, at night, when lots of light was needed, the news photographer used a long Victor flash pan.

A photojournalist could choose between three types of flash powder manufactured by the Excel Fire Works Company. The powder in the red-labeled can burned the fastest ($1/25$ sec.) so it was selected for sports. Yellow-labeled powder fired slower but brighter. Blue-labeled powder, used for portraits, burned the slowest but gave off the most light.

Photographers always filled the flash pan with four times as much powder as needed to make sure they would have enough light, as Frank Scherschel, a news photographer in those days, once recalled. Besides packing a camera and plates, a news photographer always carried a tube of ointment to treat burned hands. With the lens set at f/16, the photographer fired the flash lamp and prayed.

FLASHBULBS: SAFE BUT INCONVENIENT

Although smokeless flash powders were developed over the years, it was not until 1925 that a superior method of lighting was found. In this year Paul Vierkotter patented the flashbulb—a glass bulb containing an inflammable mixture that was set off by a weak electric current.

Four years later, the flashbulb appeared in an improved form, with aluminum foil inside. Although these bulbs were infinitely preferable to the smoky, noisy, and dangerous flash pans, flashbulbs still were inconvenient for press photographers. Some of the biggest bulbs were close in size to a football. Static electricity or electromagnetic energy could cause them to fire. In addition, the bulbs had to be replaced after each shot, a delay that could cause the photographer to miss important pictures.

In her book *Eyes of Time*, Marianne Fulton points out that the flashbulb gives an artificial quality to photographs. The light coming from the on-camera flash is always bright and tends to flatten the subject in the foreground, separating it from the rest of the scene, which becomes a separate, darker background. All flash pictures, regardless of content, tend to take on the same look.

EDGERTON DEVELOPS THE ELECTRONIC FLASH

Although it did not change the character of the light, the electronic flash was far more convenient than the flashbulb. The forerunner to the modern electronic flash was designed in the early 1930s by Harold Edgerton (see opposite page) of the Massachusetts Institute of Technology (MIT). While investigating motors, Edgerton developed an electronic stroboscope that flashed at repeated fixed intervals, synchronizing with the moving parts of the machine. Edgerton later used his stroboscope to take single and multiple-image photos, not only of moving machine parts but also of tennis players, golfers, and divers, as well as hummingbirds in flight.

Basically, his electronic flash worked by discharging high voltage from a capacitor through a gas-filled tube, producing an extremely brief burst of light. The light was powerful enough for photography despite the relatively insensitive films available at the time. The light from the electronic flash exceeded the combined output of 40,000 50-watt bulbs.

Edgerton designed his electronic flashes for research. George Woodruff, a photographer with International News Photos (INP), heard about the scientist's invention and dropped by Edgerton's MIT lab. Woodruff

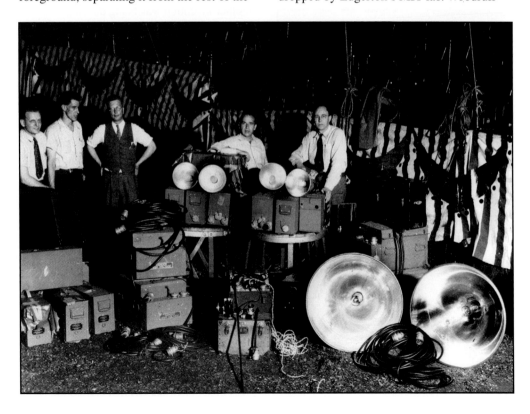

Harold Edgerton (NEAR RIGHT), inventor of the electronic flash, took pictures with local photojournalists at the circus to demonstrate how his equipment could be used to cover events outside the lab. Courtesy of MIT Museum.

asked if the electronic flash had any use in news photography. Edgerton answered by helping Woodruff lug three flash units to the circus playing in town that night.

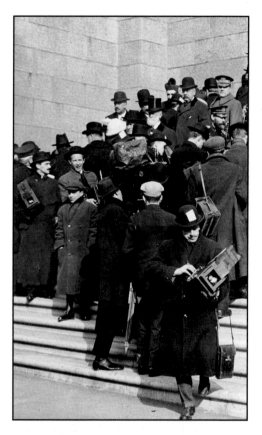

To view through the Graflex camera, the photographer looked down into the hood on top of the box. The bulky camera used glass plates.
(Files of the National Press Photographers Association, courtesy of John Faber.)

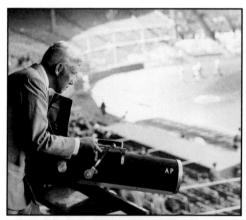

The Graflex camera in the foreground, nicknamed "Big Bertha" when fitted with a telephoto lens, was used by many papers to cover sports until the mid-1950s.
Courtesy of the Associated Press

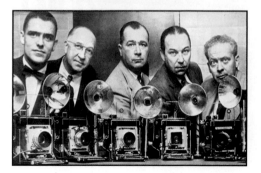

The 4" x 5" Speed Graphic was the standard news camera of the business from the 1920s to the 1950s. Experienced photographers didn't focus: they just guessed the distance. Old Speed Graphic users claimed the camera had only three distance settings: here, there, and yonder.

Each strobe had a large capacitor, which stores electricity, that put out 4,000 volts (9,600 watt-seconds). The flash duration lasted less than 1/50,000 of a second. On successive nights, the pair tried their strobe setup at a variety of sporting events. With Woodruff on camera and Edgerton on strobe, the team of photographer and scientist stopped the action of runners, boxers, and swimmers in their natural environments.

While working for the *Milwaukee Journal*, photojournalist Edward Farber designed an electronic flash that could be synchronized with the common shutter found on most press cameras. Farber's first working electronic flash weighed ninety pounds and had oil capacitors and an AC power supply. The Journal sent Farber back to the lab to design a more portable model.

By October 1940, Farber had the flash's weight down to twenty-five pounds. Powered by a motorcycle battery, it also had a plug for household current. In fall 1941, Farber found a lighter battery, and around it built a "dream" portable flash weighing only 13$^{1}/_{2}$ pounds. In the 1950s, the electronic flash design was sold to Graflex Inc., in Rochester, New York, and remained for many years a standard piece of equipment for the news photographer.

CAMERAS LOSE WEIGHT AND GAIN VERSATILITY

About the time the flashbulb was perfected, another invention was being developed that allowed pictures to be taken in dim indoor light without any artificial illumination at all. The candid camera, as it came to be known, was to change the course of news photography and redefine the role, as well as the potential, of the photojournalist.

GRAFLEX USED UNTIL 1955

At the beginning of the century, the most widely used press camera was the Graflex and its German counterpart, the Ica. These cameras were portable, although still heavy; they used either a 4"x5", 4"x6", or 5"x7" glass plate. Because of the large size of the negative, the resulting print was of high quality and had adequate detail for reproduction.

The Graflex looked like a large rectangular box with a hood on top. To view through this oversized single-lens reflex camera, the photographer would look down the hood at an angled mirror that would reflect what the lens saw—except that the image was reversed left to right.

The photographer could attach a forty-inch telephoto lens for shooting sports from the press box. When the Graflex carried the telephoto, the seventy-pound combination was affectionately known as Big Bertha. The large negative produced by the Graflex meant that photographers did not have to frame perfectly on every play—they were secure in the knowledge that if they captured the action on at least part of the film they could make a usable blow up. James Frezzolini, a news photographer, modified the Big Bertha with a notched lever for rapid focusing between first, second, and third bases at a baseball game. John Faber, a former historian for the National Press Photographers Association, found that some photographers continued to shoot with the Graflex at sports events until as late as 1955.

SPEED GRAPHIC:
A NEWS PHOTOGRAPHER'S BADGE
For general news, the Speed Graphic, introduced in 1912 by Folmer and Schwing (a division of Eastman Kodak), replaced the Graflex by the 1920s. The front of the Speed Graphic folded down to form a bed with tracks. The lens slid out on these tracks. A bellows connected the lens to the box of the Graphic and expanded or contracted as the photographer focused.

The film was carried in holders, two shots to a holder. Whereas a range finder came attached to the side of the camera, a seasoned pro often removed this device and just guess-focused. While the camera could be used with a tripod, it was more conveniently hand-held. The 9¹/₂-pound camera could take intensive pounding, and even after the development of the small 35mm camera, many news photographers continued to shoot with Speed Graphics.

Bob Gilka, who later became director of photography for the *National Geographic*, was picture editor of the *Milwaukee Journal* in 1955 when he issued a memo that read in part, "This 35mm stuff may be okay for magazines . . . but we might as well face the facts. We are wasting our time shooting the average news assignment on 35mm."

Robert Boyd, a past president of the National Press Photographers Association, was once asked what the press camera could do that the 35mm couldn't. Boyd put the big camera on the ground and sat on it.

Since editors rarely ran more than one or two images anyway, most newspaper photographers in the 1920s and 1930s saw no need to take additional pictures.

Dickey Chapelle told how photographers shot with the Speed Graphic. "It is so big that snap-shooting, or making a picture casually, can't be done." Instead, the photographer must carefully "plan the picture . . . and move

to the vantage point from which to shoot before raising the camera."

The days of the Speed Graphic, however, were numbered.

LEICA LIGHTENS THE LOAD
The earliest miniaturized camera was the Ermanox, a German-designed small camera that took single glass plates and had an extra-fast lens. The lens, at f/1.8, had an almost incredible light-gathering capability for the period. The manufacturer of the Ermanox lens proudly claimed, "This extremely fast lens opens a new era in photography and makes accessible hitherto unknown fields with instantaneous or brief time exposures without flash-light."

He was right that the lens opened a new era in photography. Unfortunately, one major drawback aimed the Ermanox for extinction. The camera used only individually loaded 4.56cm glass plates—an obvious inconvenience for news photographers. Still, the Ermanox was important in that it was the forerunner to the camera that would revolutionize photojournalism.

Oskar Barnack, a technician at the E. Leitz factory in Germany, invented the Leica. Like the Ermanox, the Leica had an extremely fast lens but, rather than glass plates, the Leica used a strip of 35mm motion-picture film with as many as forty frames per roll possible in the original models. Barnack continually worked on his design and, in 1924, the first Leicas were put on the market. By 1932, Leitz mass-produced the camera in fully refined form with extremely fast, removable lenses and a built-in range finder.

The implications of this handy, small-format camera were wide-ranging. Now, with existing light, the photographer could take pictures without bothering with flashbulbs. The Leica's lightness, ease of handling, and fast lens allowed photographers to move freely, unencumbered by heavy accessories, flash attachments, tripods, or glass plates.

Because the film could be rapidly advanced, photographers could make exposures one after another, thus enabling them to capture an unfolding event without stopping between pictures.

The Leica gave news photographers unprecedented mobility and the ability to take pictures unobtrusively. Photographers no longer had to stop life in its tracks to snap a picture; people no longer posed for the camera's lens.

Now, subjects could be more relaxed and natural, leaving photographers free to concentrate on atmosphere and composition rather than on technical matters.

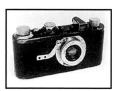

The early Leica camera

These new capabilities did nothing less than change the relationship between photographers and the world. Because they could use available light and remain unobtrusive, news photographers could imbue their pictures with a new sense of realism, of life in the making.

ERICH SALOMON: FATHER OF CANDID PHOTOGRAPHY

The man who first exploited this photographic impression of life was Erich Salomon. Often called "the father of candid photography," he is credited with coining the term photojournalism to describe what he was doing. Salomon began his photography career in 1928 with the new Ermanox camera. Salomon's arenas of action were diplomatic gatherings and government functions; his subjects were the foremost statesmen and political personalities of Europe. When he initially tried to penetrate these carefully guarded events, the officials refused to let him in, claiming that flash powder and large cameras would disrupt the orderly proceedings. But when Salomon demonstrated his unobtrusive camera, he was not only given entry into these private quarters, but he also became a habitué of diplomatic circles. French Prime Minister Aristide Briand at one time remarked, "There are just three things necessary for a conference: a few Foreign Secretaries, a table, and Salomon."

Even the ingenious Salomon, however, could not charm his way into all top-level, top-secret meetings. When barred from an important conference, the dapper photographer would don his top hat, white gloves, and tails and set to work concocting a scheme to allow him entry into this private world.

Salomon's ruses are legendary. He once managed to take pictures in a courtroom that was off-limits to photographers. He shot his film by cutting a hole in the crown of his hat and hiding his camera there.

Following the success of this technique, he used a similar ploy to photograph a roulette game in Monte Carlo. He hollowed out several thick books and hid his camera inside. While he appeared absorbed in the game, he was actually busy clicking away with his concealed camera.

The man pointing had just learned that press photographers were not being allowed in. The politician said he doubted that and wagered that at least one would be there. Slowly, he peered around the room until he discovered Erich Salomon just as the photographer was taking a picture of him. Salomon was the first photographer to use extensively the Ermanox miniature camera to catch candid photos. Salomon specialized in diplomatic gatherings and governmental functions. If Salomon couldn't get in openly, he hid his camera in the crown of his hat, in a temporary sling around his arm, or in a hollowed-out book.
Erich Salomon

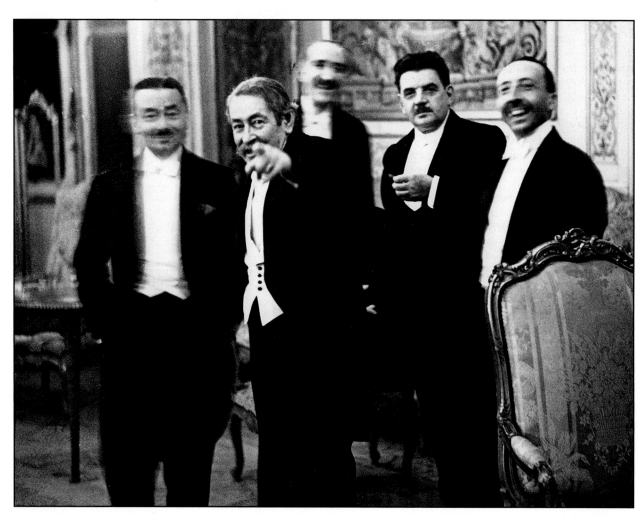

The urbane, multilingual Salomon moved with ease among dignitaries and heads of state, capturing with his camera the personalities of the people who shaped history and the atmosphere of their inner sanctums. With the Ermanox, and later with the Leica, he penetrated the masks of public personae to reveal the very human characteristics that lay underneath—dozing diplomats, bored-looking royalty, down-to-earth movie stars.

There is a remarkably intimate quality to Salomon's work. Because his camera enabled him to catch prominent people off guard, his pictures give the impression that the camera, rather than being an intruder, is simply a watchful observer who happens to be present at the scene. Salomon's candid photography attracted a good deal of attention, and he numbered among his subjects such luminaries as Albert Einstein, Herbert Hoover, and Marlene Dietrich.

Salomon's fame at one point caught the attention of William Randolph Hearst, who brought Salomon to New York to demonstrate his candid technique. The publisher was so impressed that he ordered nearly fifty Ermanox cameras for his staff photographers.

Salomon later died in one of Hitler's concentration camps. As one of the first to demonstrate the possibility of recording events with the candid camera, Salomon truly deserves the title of "father of candid photography."

THE GERMAN PHOTO ESSAY
EUROPEAN MAGAZINES DEVELOP THE PHOTO ESSAY

Salomon's candid style proved that current events could be captured pictorially and naturally. The impact of this discovery was felt strongly in Germany, in such picture magazines as the *Müncher Illustrierte Presse* (MIP) and *Berliner Illustrirte Zeitung* (BIZ), and in England, in the *Illustrated London News*, where the photo essay first appeared in embryonic form. At the end of the 1920s, Stefan Lorant, editor of the *Müncher Illustrierte Presse*, developed the notion that there could be a photographic equivalent of the literary essay.

Magazines in both America and Europe already had run extensive picture packages from the late 1880s on. In 1891, *Leslie's Illustrated Newspaper* published multiple pictures of Chicago street scenes for a layout on the windy city.

Only a few years later, *Harper's Weekly* published Frank Jay Haynes's photos of Yellowstone National Park.

Previously, however, when several pictures appeared together on an inside spread, they were arranged either arbitrarily or sequentially, with little regard for the conceptual logic of the layout, captions, cropping, or picture size. Lorant and his colleagues began experimenting with a new photographic story-telling form, in which several pictures appeared not in isolation, but as a cohesive whole. The editor laid out the multiple photos more like a movie than a collection of still pictures in an album.

The photo essay developed in German picture magazines was built on multiple images that showed different aspects or visual points of view. German magazine photographers using the small 35mm cameras shot overalls (also called establishing shots) of a scene, middle range shots of the action, and close-ups of the participants—shooting from high and low camera angles rather than eye level. In laying out pages, editors varied the sizes of images and used a dominant photo supported by smaller images. The editors created visual flow by making the photograph's dominant lines lead the viewer's eye from one image to another, observes historian C. Zoe Smith (see selected bibliography), who has analyzed early German and American picture magazines.

German and later American magazines did cut pictures into cookie cutter shapes, overlap pictures, and remove picture backgrounds to try to increase impact and interest. Wilson Hicks, long-time executive editor of *Life* magazine, labeled these techniques a "holdover from the past," that amounted to physical abuse of photographs. This kind of manipulation later disappeared from *Life* as the editors came to respect the integrity of each photograph.

Illustrated magazines were not a new

The *Müncher Illustrierte Presse* experimented with creative picture layouts such as this issue in 1929 that featured candid portraits of politicians taken by René Kraus. Stefan Lorant, a pioneer in integrating photography with publication design, was editor.

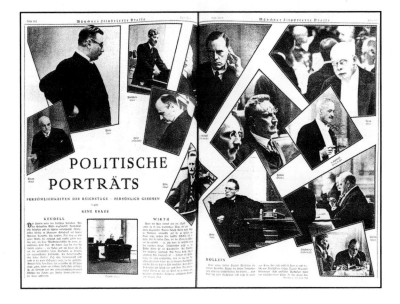

phenomenon in the United States. In the nineteenth century, *Harper's Weekly* and *Leslie's Illustrated Newspaper* relied on drawings to elucidate their articles. After the invention of the halftone, those publications as well as *McClure's*, *Cosmopolitan*, and *Collier's* continued the tradition of adding pictures to supplement their stories.

The difference between these early American magazines, the German picture publications, and the great American glossy magazines that followed lay not only in the number of pictures used but also in the way they were used. In the new magazines, several pictures were grouped together with an overall theme and design. Picture editors discovered truth in the old adage, "The whole is worth more than the sum of the parts." Accordingly, the role of the picture editor became all-important. Along with the photographer, the picture editor shaped the story and, with the aid of shooting scripts, mapped out the photographer's plan of attack. Single photographers would work on stories to give them visual cohesion.

AMERICAN MAGAZINES ADOPT PHOTOGRAPHY
NEWS-WEEK SPURS *TIME*'S USE OF PHOTOGRAPHY

Although Europeans were developing imaginative new uses for photography on the printed page, these developments had not effected American news magazines like *Time*. *Time* primarily published poorly reproduced conservative head-and-shoulders portraits. Robert Benchley, a wit of the era, said that the pictures inside *Time* were reproduced so poorly that they appeared to

The first cover of *LIFE* magazine (RIGHT) was taken by Margaret Bourke-White (BELOW). Bourke-White photographed a massive WPA dam in New Deal, Montana, for the cover story. Her essay inside focused on the residents of New Deal. © 1936 Time Inc., courtesy of Time Incorporated

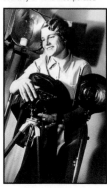

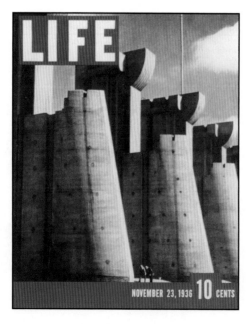

have been "engraved on slices of bread." *News-Week*, as it was first known, started in 1933. By splashing dramatic spot news photos on its covers, it quickly drained circulation from *Time*.

FORTUNE REVOLUTIONIZES PICTURE USE

Surprisingly, Henry Luce, who founded *Time*, launched the business magazine *Fortune* in 1930, in the heart of the Great Depression.

While *Time* magazine had used pictures almost as an afterthought, *Fortune* hired photographers such as the legendary Margaret Bourke-White, who, to make her pictures dramatic, did not hesitate to bring in multiple flashbulbs to light whole steel mills. She used her large-format camera to glamorize American industrial might from dynamos to skyscrapers.

In *Fortune*, pictures held equal status with words. The respectful treatment of pictures worked so well that by the middle of the decade, though the country was still in a severe depression, *Fortune* had amassed 100,000 readers.

THE BIRTH OF *LIFE*

Life was the brainchild of Henry Luce, the publisher of *Time* and *Fortune* magazines, and his general manager, Ralph Ingersoll. Spurred by the success of similar European ventures like *BIZ* and *MIP*, and the development of slick-coated, quick-drying paper, Luce and his colleagues felt the time was ripe in the United States for a new, large-format picture magazine. Kurt Korff, former editor of the *Berliner Illustrirte Zeitung*, consulted with Luce (1935–36) on the prototype of *Life* magazine.

Life was born in the 1930s. In its manifesto, the new magazine stated its credo:

To see life, to see the world; to eyewitness great events; to watch the faces of the poor and the gestures of the proud; to see strange things—machines, armies, multitudes, shadows in the jungle and on the moon; to see man's work—his paintings, towers and discoveries; to see things a thousand miles away, things hidden behind walls and within rooms, things dangerous to come to; the women that men love and many children; to see and to take pleasure in seeing; to see and be amazed; to see and be instructed.

For the first issue, November 23, 1936, *Life*'s editors dispatched Margaret Bourke-White to photograph the construction of a WPA dam—the Peck Dam—in New Deal, Montana. In the 1920s Bourke-White had made a name for herself as a freelancer and later as a top-notch industrial photographer on the staff of *Fortune* magazine. Her pictures celebrated the burgeoning machine aesthetic of the time, and her expertise in capturing on film structural and engineering details made her the perfect candidate for the assignment.

When she returned with her pictures, however, the editors of *Life* were in for a surprise. Not only had she captured the industrial drama of the dam under construction, but she took it upon herself to document the personal drama of the town's inhabitants as well. Bourke-White turned her camera on the details of frontier life—the hastily erected shanty settlements, the weather-beaten faces of the townspeople, the Saturday night ritual at the local bar—and enhanced her story by adding the human dimension.

On the cover of the first issue of *Life* is a picture of the huge dam in all its geometrical splendor. And inside is Bourke-White's photo essay: nine pages of carefully laid-out, strategically chosen pictures of New Deal's residents. The first issue was a sellout. The editorial offices of *Life* in New York were besieged by phone calls and telegrams asking for more copies. The presses were restarted to meet the demand. "During the first year you had to hurry to the news stands on publication day to grab up a copy before they were all gobbled up," recalled Arthur Goldsmith in an article about the magazine. Within a year the magazine's circulation had grown to five million copies.

The Peck Dam essay became the prototype for a form that flourished in the pages of *Life*, a form that expanded the scope of photojournalism and redefined the way we see.

Aside from Margaret Bourke-White, the other three photographers who appeared on the magazine's masthead were Peter Stackpole, known for his photographs of the construction of the Golden Gate Bridge; Thomas McAvoy, an expert on the use of the 35mm for political candids; and Alfred Eisenstaedt, a specialist in the new German style of candid photography.

During its first few years, *Life* had the reputation of a magazine that ran sensational pictures. The magazine's first real shocker was titled "How to undress in front of your husband." The story, tame by today's standards, was supposed to be sophisticated satire, but many readers let it be known they thought it indecent.

Several issues later, *Life* ran an article titled "Birth of a Baby." The feature ran four pages and showed in drawings how the unborn child grows in the womb and the progress of the baby from the mother's body. In the actual birth pictures, the only things visible in the frame were the baby's head, the doctor, and

masses of sterile dressing. After publication, a furor broke out. The magazine was banned in thirty-three U.S. cities and in Canada, and publisher Roy Larsen was arrested for selling indecent literature.

As Dolores Flamiano showed in her paper "The Naked Truth: Gender, Race, and Nudity in Life, 1937," the magazine was not above using sex to attract readers and drive up circulation—even in the 1930s. In general, the editors at *Life* tried to create an image of a unified and classless nation where middle-class values and capitalism were celebrated.

COMPETING WITH LIFE
LOOK BASED ON SURVEY

The astounding success of *Life* was matched by that of its fellow picture magazine, *Look*. *Look* was founded by the Cowles brothers, a newspaper publishing family who commissioned George Gallup to discover what part of the newspaper was most widely read. When Gallup's poll revealed that the picture page was most popular, the brothers founded *Look*, which first appeared in January 1937, a few months after *Life* began. *Look* quickly developed a reputation for sensational stories. One description at the time claimed that Look was a combination of "gall and honey." Gardner Cowles answered, "*Look* has been criticized as sensationally thrilling. My only reply is that life itself is thrilling."

Look toned down its sex-and-violence image to concentrate on feature stories. Known for its writer/photographer team approach, *Look* hired many outstanding shooters, including Arthur Rothstein, Paul Fusco, and Stanley Tretich.

SEE, PEEK, CLICK, SCOOP

The rapid rise in *Life*'s and *Look*'s circulations persuaded other publishers to start picture magazines. Within two years of *Life*'s first issue, the picture magazine field was crowded with thirteen periodicals sporting one-word, punchy names like *See, Click, Peek, Pix, Picture*, and *Scoop*, and boasting a combined circulation of 16 million per issue. The magazines' content ranged from "girlie" pinups to the social ills of drinking. Stories included the "Truth about Cremation" and "How You Should Tell your Child about Sex." Most stories in these *Life* and *Look* imitators were highly scripted with few candids. Each represented a little melodrama, and sometimes actors even played parts in the photos. The proliferation of picture magazines, starting in 1936 and continuing through the 1940s and 1950s, has caused historians to call the period before television's dominance the "golden age of photojournalism."

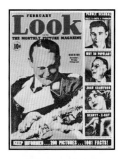

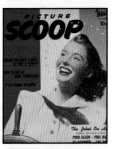

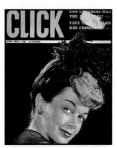

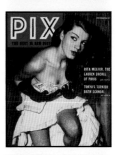

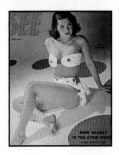

The success of *Life* and then *Look* spawned many picture magazines in the days before television.

PICTURE AGENCIES SUPPLY

BLACK STAR AGENCY: HOME TO GERMAN ÉMIGRÉS

Life had a tiny staff of only four photographers when it began publishing. The editors needed photos, lots of them, so they turned to Black Star, a recently formed picture agency that represented many newly emigrated German photojournalists. Three German Jews, who had worked in Germany's publishing industry before immigrating to the States, started the agency.

A large file of photographs brought from Europe by Ernest Mayer helped get the firm off the ground. Kurt Safranski, the idea man, stayed in the office, and Kurt Kornfeld, described by historian C. Zoe Smith as a gentle salesman, handled the *Life* account. Smith's book ***Black Star Picture Agency: Life's European Connection*** details the agency's history.

Life needed the agency because it used 200 pictures per issue but had just four staff shooters. Of course, the agency also needed this popular picture magazine. *Life* accounted for a quarter of the agency's business.

German photographic émigrés who spoke little English turned to Black Star, where the principle owners were bilingual. The agency helped them get assignments and handled the business aspects of freelancing in the United States. Black Star took a 30 to 40 percent commission but paid photographers a weekly retainer against their annual sales.

Many of the agency's émigré photographers, including Fritz Goro, Andreas Feininger, Hebert Gehr, Walter Sanders, and Werner Wolff, became *Life* staffers. Others, like Philippe Halsman, were under contract to the magazine for decades. According to Wilson Hicks of *Life*, by 1952 more than a quarter of the photographers working for *Life* had emigrated to the United States from Europe in the late 1930s and early 1940s. At least half of those European photographers were at one time associated with Black Star.

MAGNUM: THE LEGENDARY PHOTO AGENCY

Magnum, like Black Star, was another picture agency formed by European émigrés.

Black Star was owned by three former photo editors who secured assignments for photographers and kept a percentage of their fees. Magnum, by contrast, was formed in 1947 as a cooperative that shared its profits among its photographer-members.

Magnum was founded by Henri Cartier-Bresson, a wealthy French photojournalist; George Rodger, an English photographer who worked for *Life* magazine; David Seymour, known to everyone as Chim; and

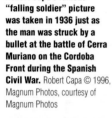

Robert Capa's famous "falling soldier" picture was taken in 1936 just as the man was struck by a bullet at the battle of Cerra Muriano on the Cordoba Front during the Spanish Civil War. Robert Capa © 1996, Magnum Photos, courtesy of Magnum Photos

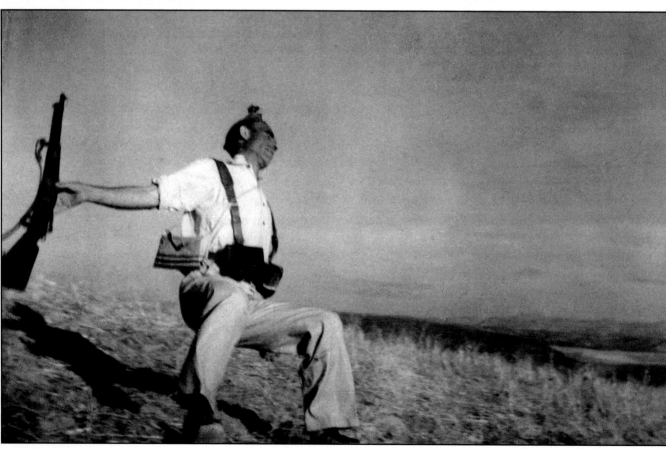

André Friedmann, a Polish photographer who immigrated to the States and changed his name to Robert Capa. (Friedmann supposedly took the American name so editors would think of him as a successful American photographer rather than a struggling young émigré.)

The agency actually was born as a way for its founders to have a political impact. Cartier-Bresson, Rodger, and Chim spent many hours at the Café du Dome discussing liberal politics rather than photography. They were interested in how they could use their cameras to examine the social and political problems of the day. For a long time Capa had been toying with the idea of a cooperative picture agency, so that photographers could hold on to more of their earnings and retain rights to their images. During World War II, Capa met Rodger in Naples when both were taking pictures for *Life*.

Capa: The Greatest War Photographer

By the time he and his friends founded Magnum, Capa was already a legendary war photographer who had covered both the Spanish Civil War and World War II. He took perhaps the most famous war photograph of all time—a Spanish Republican militiaman, arms flung wide, dropping back-

ward at the instant he was killed by a bullet (opposite page).

During World War II, Capa photographed the landing at Normandy on D-Day and produced classic photographs that people still associate with that battle. Two thousand men lost their lives that day. Capa landed with the first wave of soldiers.

"The water was very cold and the beach was still more than a hundred yards away. The bullets tore holes in the water around me, and I made for the nearest steel obstacle," Capa later wrote.

Using two cameras, he took 106 pictures of the bloody battle on the beach before rushing back through the surf to clamber onto a landing craft returning to the invasion fleet offshore. A messenger delivered the undeveloped film to *Life*'s London office, where the deadline to send the pictures to New York was rapidly approaching. John Morris, picture editor for *Life*, took the four rolls of 35mm film and gave it to an assistant to develop. In his book *Get the Picture*, Morris recounts the story of when his darkroom assistant ran into the office, sobbing, "They're ruined! Capa's films are all ruined!"

Recalls Morris, "Incredulous, I rushed down to the darkroom with him, where he explained that he had hung the films, as

Working with an unobtrusive Leica camera, Henri Cartier-Bresson roamed the streets of Seville looking for the combination of the perfect instant within the ideal composition. He called the combination the "decisive moment." Besides shooting for himself, Cartier-Bresson took on many magazine assignments around the world. Henri Cartier-Bresson © 1933, Magnum Photos, courtesy of Magnum Photos

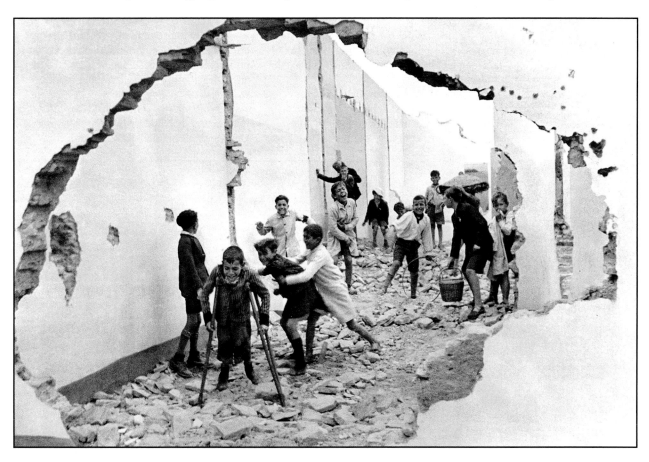

usual, in the wooden locker that served as a drying cabinet, heated by a coil on the floor. Because of my order to rush, he had closed the doors. Without ventilation the emulsion had melted.

"I held up the four rolls, one at a time. Three were hopeless: nothing to see. But on the fourth roll there were eleven frames with distinct images . . . their grainy imperfection—perhaps enhanced by the lab accident—contributed to making them among the most dramatic battlefield photos ever taken. D-Day would forever be known by these pictures."

Capa went on to cover the liberation of Paris, the Battle of the Bulge, and the war between Israel and the Arabs. Later he photographed the war in Vietnam, always taking his own advice, recorded by his biographer, Richard Whelan: "If your pictures aren't good enough, you're not close enough."

Henri Cartier-Bresson: Photojournalist of the Decisive Moment

After joining Magnum, Henri Cartier-Bresson, who during his career shot more than 500 pictures and stories for magazines, sailed for Bombay in the summer of 1947 to cover the partition of India. The political and religious animosities there had turned into a bitter and violent struggle. At least ten million Hindus, Muslims, and Sikhs were abandoning their homes and fleeing in both directions across the new border between India and Pakistan. At least one million Indians were slain, and hundreds of thousands were made refugees during the exodus.

In January 1948, Cartier-Bresson photographed the Indian independence leader Mohandas Karamchand Gandhi on the day he broke his fifteenth fast. Margaret Bourke-White was also in India to cover Gandhi and the breakup of India for *Life* magazine.

The same day that Cartier-Bresson photographed Gandhi, the world leader was shot and killed by a Hindu opposed to Gandhi's defense of Muslims. When Margaret Bourke-White took a flash picture of the slain Gandhi lying in state, Gandhi's entourage felt that the flash was disrespectful and took the film from Bourke-White. She tried to slip in again but was blocked. She left empty-handed, reports historian Claude Cookman in his dissertation, "The Photographic Reportage of Henri Cartier-Bresson."

Hearing that Gandhi had been shot, Cartier-Bresson, meanwhile, returned to the compound on his bicycle. With his Leica and available light, he succeeded in taking and keeping several photographs of the deathbed scene. "All night the crowds rushed into the garden of Birla House and pressed forward to try and see him," Cartier-Bresson recalled in his book ***The Decisive Moment***. "I managed to reach one window, greasy from the pressure of many foreheads, and polished with my elbow a place big enough for the lens of my camera." *Life* magazine eventually paid Magnum a handsome price for the exclusive photos of an event that Bourke-White, their own staffer, had been unable to photograph.

Agency Adds New Recruits

Magnum, which eventually had offices in both Paris and New York, added several more photographers to its stable. Werner Bishof, an abstract still-life photographer associated with Black Star, joined the agency.

Austrian photographer Ernst Haas left *Life* magazine to become a Magnum photographer. Despite the limitations of slow color films of

Magnum's founders, pictured in the two photos below, created a picture agency in which earnings were shared among all the photographers.

(BELOW LEFT) Hungarian-American Robert Capa, perhaps the world's greatest war photographer (left), and Englishman George Rodger both covered World War II in Europe.
Henri Cartier-Bresson © 1943, Magnum Photos Inc., courtesy of Magnum Photos

(BELOW RIGHT) David "Chim" Seymour (left) greets Henri Cartier-Bresson.
Magnum Photos, Inc. © 1938, courtesy of Magnum Photos

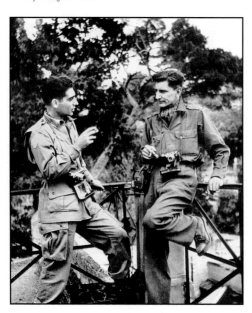

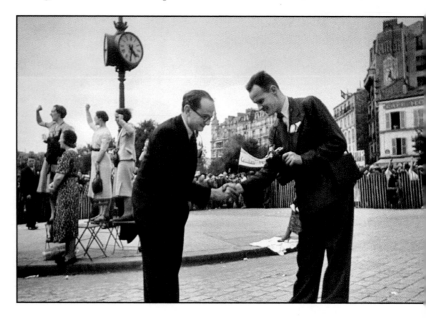

the day, Haas was a color specialist. "I am not interested in shooting new things," he later wrote. "I am interested to see things new. In this way I am a photographer with the problems of a painter; the desire to find the limitations of a camera so I can overcome them."

Aspiring photographers found joining Magnum in the early days a casual, nonbureaucratic experience. Marc Riboud showed his pictures to Robert Capa while the famed war photographer was playing pinball in the café below Magnum's Paris office. Without a vote, without consulting anyone, Capa took one look at Riboud's portfolio and said, "OK, come with us. Allez!"

Eve Arnold showed up at the New York office with a portfolio containing just two stories—a fashion show in Harlem and an opening night at the Met. She was immediately invited to become a stringer—a freelance contributor. After Dennis Stock won a *Life* competition for young photographers, Capa invited him to join the agency.

Today applicants undergo a lengthy process that includes a trial period and a vote by all the member photographers.

Agency Survives Deaths in the "Family"

Magnum suffered a tremendous setback in 1954 when, within days of one another, Capa was killed by a land mine in Vietnam and Werner Bishof died in an accident in Peru. Two years later, Chim was killed while covering the aftermath of the Suez crisis between Egypt and Israel. After the death of two of its original founders and one of its members, Magnum lost direction, observes Russell Miller in *Magnum: Fifty Years at the Front Line of History*. Robert's brother Cornell then joined the agency and, according to Miller, helped steer it back on course. Magnum went on to attract some of the most outstanding photojournalists in the world.

Burt Glinn covered Fidel Castro's triumphant entrance into Havana after the overthrow of the Batista regime in Cuba. Philip Jones Griffiths produced a soul-searching book from his coverage of Vietnam that shattered many American myths about the country. He showed that everything happening in Vietnam was being done against the will of the people. Magnum's Marc Riboud was one of the few outsiders to get into North Vietnam during the war.

In 1968 Magnum produced the book *America in Crisis*, which included its photographers' coverage of the assassinations of Martin Luther King and Bobby Kennedy, the rise of black power, and riots at the Democratic Convention in Chicago.

As big picture magazines like *Look*, *The Saturday Evening Post*, and, eventually, even *Life* folded, Magnum photographers survived by shooting corporate annual reports and advertisements in addition to editorial work.

THE COMPLICATED CAREER OF W. EUGENE SMITH

Perhaps the most influential, controversial, and well-remembered photographer ever to work for *Life* was W. Eugene Smith, who also was associated at different times with both Black Star and Magnum. He signed a contract with *Life* magazine in 1939, and subsequently shot many photos and photo essays for the magazine. He quit the magazine not once but twice. Smith resigned first in 1941 because he felt he was in an assignment rut at *Life*.

He referred to his pictures at this time as having "a lot of depth-of-field but not much depth-of-meaning." He covered World War II at first for Ziff-Davis Publishing Company and then was rehired by *Life*.

Obsessed with the gap between the reality of war and the comfortable headlines about war seen by the people back home, the 24-year-old correspondent hurled himself into the front lines, trying to catch on film the horror of killing. Smith followed thirteen invasions, taking memorable pictures of the war—a tiny, fly-covered, half-dead baby held up by a soldier after being rescued from a cave in Saipan; a wounded soldier, bandaged, stretched out in Leyte Cathedral; a decaying Japanese body on an Iwo Jima beach.

Then, while shooting a story on a day in the life of a soldier, Smith was hit by a shell fragment that ripped through his left hand, his face, and his mouth—critically wounding him. Two years of painful convalescence followed.

In 1947, Smith resumed his work for *Life* magazine. During the next seven years, he produced his best-known set of photo essays: the exhausting dedication of a country doctor; the poverty and faith in a Spanish village; the pain of birth, life, and death being eased by a nurse midwife, Smith's own favorite essay. "In many ways, shooting these photos was the most rewarding experience photography has allowed me," said Smith of the midwife essay.

According to Jim Hughes's extensive biography, *Shadow and Substance*, Smith himself was not an easy photographer to work with. While most *Life* staffers shot their assignments and shipped the film back to New York, Smith developed his own negatives and then held on to them. With control of his negatives, Smith could threaten to withdraw a story if he felt the editors were not going to play the photos accurately.

In 1954 Smith photographed the essay "Man of Mercy," about Dr. Albert Schweitzer and his leper colony in Africa. After carrying the Schweitzer essay back to America, Smith quarreled with *Life*'s editors about it. In a futile attempt to affect the use of pictures and captions, and to expand the Schweitzer layout, Smith resigned from *Life* for the second time.

With the help of his wife, Eileen, Smith later photographed a moving story about mercury poisoning in Minamata, Japan, which was published first in Life and eventually appeared as a book, **Minamata**.

PHOTOGRAPHERS COMPETE
RIVALRY AMONG NEWSPAPER PHOTOGRAPHERS

The success and style of the picture magazines had some important effects on newspaper photojournalism. The photo essay layout influenced many newspapers to adopt a similarly simple and direct arrangement of pictures about one subject. Likewise, newspapers began running more feature stories and using larger pictures.

Philadelphia boasted twenty daily newspapers during the 1920s and more than 200 press photographers. Their photos, however, ran without by-line credit. During the Depression, however, many papers died. While newspapers competed for readers, press photographers competed for scoops. Photographers were not above sabotaging one another. Joe Costa, who worked for the New York *Morning World* and later the *Daily News*, recalled that photographers never let

their camera bags out of their sight. He called it a "dog-eat-dog" business. A competitor might expose the film in a fellow photographer's holders or simply switch holders: the exclusive picture would be in the opposition's newspaper the next day!

On the other hand, photographers sometimes helped each other. A B-25 bomber, lost in the fog, crashed into the seventy-ninth floor of the Empire State Building. Glenn Lowry describes staffer Ernie Sisto's photographic heroics on behalf of the *Times* as well as his competitors in **Pictures of the Times: A Century of Photography from The New York Times**.

Sisto asked his competitors to hold him by the belt as he leaned perilously from the eighty-first floor to photograph the disaster. In return for the favor, he continued to dangle there while making an exposure for each of them.

Using the basic 4"x5" Speed Graphic, photographers of this period covered gangland slayings and bootlegged booze all without the aid of an exposure meter. Photographers determined most exposures by "guesstimations." The effective film index at this time was around ISO 25.

Guessing lighting exposures was just one of the shooting techniques photographers learned from one another, because few went to school to learn photojournalism. In fact, almost no universities prior to the 1940s offered photojournalism as a major. News photographers often got started as copyboys or copygirls on newspapers. If they expressed a leaning toward pictures, they could start an

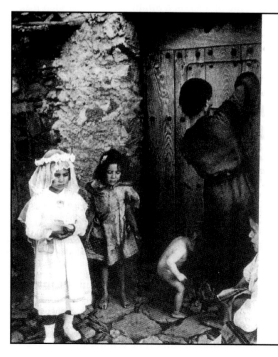 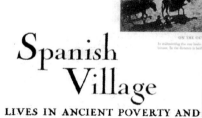

W. Eugene Smith's landmark essay "Spanish Village," for *LIFE* magazine, opens with a young girl preparing for confirmation and closes with a wake for a dead villager.
LIFE, April 9, 1951

apprentice program in which they mixed chemicals and loaded film holders in the darkroom—progressing then to developing film and printing. They also carried equipment for photographers in the field. Moving from printing in the lab to covering news in the street was a major hurdle that took some photographers five years or more to leap, according to Sam Psoras, who started with International News Photos (INP) before joining the *Philadelphia Daily News*.

Photographers were held in low regard on some newspapers. Frank Gannett opined that "with the proper technology anyone could take pictures, even 'girls.'" The emphasis on some papers in the Gannett chain was on saving money, not taking great images.

One newspaper that maintained a large photographic staff was the *Milwaukee Journal*. Historically, the *Journal* staff worked under a unique setup. They were a part of the engraving department rather than the editorial department. Because they were part of the production team, managers were not shocked by large capital outlay expenses for equipment. As a result, the photo department instigated many technological advances, including the early use of the 35mm camera. Staff photographer Brownie Rowland brought back a Leica from Germany, and Frank Scherschel was interested enough to borrow the little camera and try it out. History books credit Bob Dumke with inventing a synchronizing switch for his Speed Graphic that allowed him to shoot flash pictures in daylight. Ed Farber developed the portable electronic strobe for covering news events. The *Journal* continued to experiment with color pictures throughout the paper during the Depression.

The *Des Moines Register and Tribune* was also noted for outstanding use of pictures. In 1928, the paper bought an airplane and hired a pilot to transport film from rural areas of Iowa. In the latter half of the 1930s, the trade journal *Quill and Scroll* ranked this paper first in the number of pictures published.

The *New York Times* began hiring a staff of full-time photographers to cover local events in the early 1920s, and by 1927 sent photographers to cover Lindbergh's arrival in Paris following his solo flight across the Atlantic. It took more than a week for the pictures to return to New York by boat from Europe. Luckily for the *Times*, someone had taken a head shot of Lindbergh before he launched his historic flight.

A PROGRESSIVE VISUAL NEWSPAPER

PM, a short-lived, liberal tabloid, exhibited the most progressive and modern use of

pictures by a newspaper. Founded in 1940 by Ralph Ingersoll, who previously had helped edit Time and Life, the paper combined the textual approach of the newsweekly with the visual approach of the picture magazine in a daily, tabloid newspaper. The tabloid hired the best photographers of the day, including Weegee (Arthur Fellig) and Margaret Bourke-White. The paper was beautifully printed with special ink and stapled so that the pages would not fly apart. Its sections, with eight consecutive pages of full-page pictures, constituted an approach that was unheard of in its day and, in fact, rarely if ever seen since. The crusading paper used photographs to document its exposés, including one series on the unsanitary conditions in the New York poultry market.

Researcher Cindy M. Brown, in "*PM*: Just Another Picture Paper?" reports that *PM* not only ran more pictures than its New York rivals—including the *Post*, *Sun*, and *Mirror*—but that it ran them larger and grouped them in a more storytelling way. In fact, the paper approached a fifty-fifty picture-text split, unheard of in today's newspapers. Brown wrote that *PM* not only ran more visually interesting pictures, but the pictures had stronger compositional elements than did its rivals. *PM's Weekly*, the paper's Sunday edition, featured a gallery of full-page photographs. The paper crusaded against racism and the excesses of big business. Unfortunately, relying on newsstand sales and subscriptions alone, *PM* eventually died, because it contained no advertising and thus lacked sufficient revenues to survive.

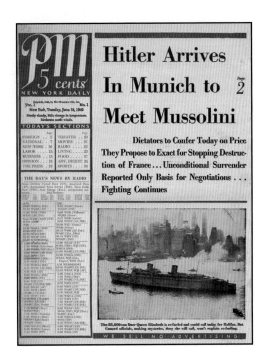

PM combined a news-magazine's approach to writing and a picture magazine's approach to photos into a strikingly different daily newspaper. Collection of Sidney Kobre

WAR CENSORSHIP

World War II produced corpses in abundance. Nonetheless, during the war, American citizens saw few dead soldiers. When they did, it was thanks to the U.S. government's attempt to influence public opinion. This censorship was not new. During the entire nineteen months of American involvement in World War I, the government prohibited publication of any photographs of dead American soldiers. A similar prohibition lasted for the first twenty-one months of American involvement in World War II.

However, unlike World War I, in which the government tried to completely restrict photographers' access to the front lines, photojournalists during World War II could move freely on battlefields and accompany naval assaults. Photographers could shoot where, when, and what they wanted, but all exposed film was screened by two layers of censors—one in the field and another in Washington. Early in the war, censors placed all photographs of dead and badly wounded Americans in a secret Pentagon file known to officials as the "Chamber of Horrors."

Initially, censors were worried that if the population saw pictures of dead American soldiers they would press for a compromise settlement with Germany and Japan. Later, as government leaders became concerned about public complacency brought on by Allied victories, they released some of these photographs of war's brutality. For instance, *Life* published George Strock's photograph of three American soldiers lying dead on Buna Beach in New Guinea. After almost two years of American involvement in the war, this photo was the first released to show dead American soldiers. The *Washington Post* said it was time that the government treated Americans as adults, and that photographs "can help us to understand something of what has been sacrificed for the victories we have won." Yet even the *Post* went on to say "an overdose of such photographs would be unhealthy."

But until the war's end and after, the government continued to censor photographs of mutilated or emotionally distressed American soldiers, even though more than a million soldiers suffered psychiatric symptoms serious enough to debilitate them for some period. The censors held back any pictures showing racial conflicts at American bases, and other visual evidence of disunity or disorder. In *The Censored War*, George Roeder tells how American opinions about World

This World War II photo of a frozen American soldier with a stake driven through his body was censored by the U.S. government for fear of discouraging citizens on the home front.
Courtesy of the National Archives

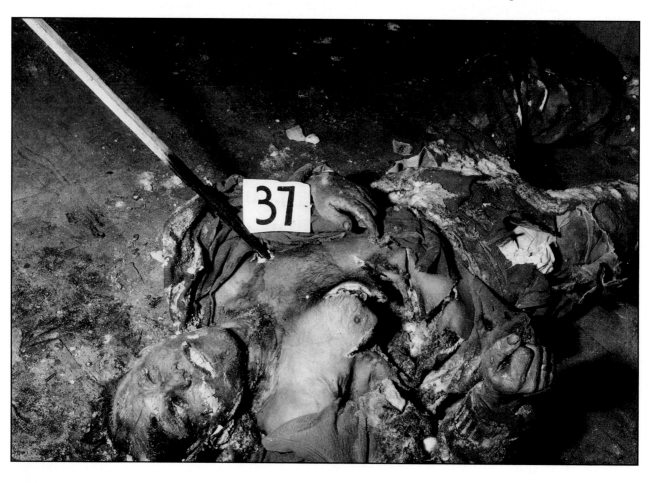

War II were manipulated both by wartime images that citizens were allowed to see and by the images that were suppressed.

Until the Normandy invasion of Europe, photographs had to be passed through the long chain of official headquarters and censors. The photographs taken by W.Eugene Smith on Guam appeared in Life some three or four months after the event. It was only with the invasion of Europe that pictures were processed on the spot and made immediately available for publication. By then, the Allies were winning, observes Jorge Lewinski in his book, *The Camera at War*.

At the beginning of the Korean War, photographers were under a system of voluntary censorship. However, on November 2, 1950, American troops came into direct contact with Chinese forces as the Chinese Communist army entered the war in full strength.

What followed was a long and difficult retreat covered by the media. Embarrassed personally, General Douglas MacArthur ended the voluntary censorship system and imposed full military censorship on news media. Before the general clamped down, photographers had covered all aspects of the Korean War. Despite relatively free access, and limited only by self-censorship, fewer than 5 percent of the photos published by *Life*, *Newsweek*, and *Time* were actual combat photos.

The same reticence about showing soldiers under fire did not hold true for America's next war. During at least part of the Vietnam War, 40 percent of the published pictures run by *Life*, *Newsweek*, and *Time* portrayed soldiers in the heat of battle, according to a study by Michael Sherer. The American public saw more of the brutal side of combat during the Tet offensive in Vietnam than during major battles in Korea.

During the Vietnam War, images of dead and wounded, plus photographs of people in immediate, life-threatening situations, were offered to the public on a regular basis.

THE RISE OF PROFESSIONALISM
PHOTOGRAPHERS ORGANIZE

As the public began to recognize such names as Margaret Bourke-White and Alfred Eisenstaedt, photographers began to achieve parity with writers.

Originally, the photographer was a second-class citizen in the newsroom.

According to one common story, when a news photographer's job opened up, the editor would find the nearest janitor and hand him a camera, telling him to set the lens at f/8 and shoot.

Frank Luther Mott, former dean of journalism at the University of Missouri, wrote that news photographers had long been "looked upon as queer fellows—half artist and more than half roughneck, and his product was referred to as 'embellishment of a story or a feature.'"

In a *Library Journal* book review, Michael Rogers describes photographers of the period as "whiskey-breathed news hacks and cigar-chomping shutterbugs leering out from behind weathered and monstrous 4"x5" Speed Graphics."

Attached to their Speed Graphics were light saber flashes and no. 2 press bulbs. They carried PRESS cards tucked into the bands of sweat-stained fedoras. News photographers were thought of as the people who chased fires and took cheesecake pictures. Taking cheesecake pictures involved meeting incoming passenger ships to take snaps of pretty women with "lots of leg showing."

Along with steamships, cheesecake pictures slowly went out of vogue. Editors began acknowledging the contribution of pictures as a means of reporting the news. The photographer's status gradually rose.

In 1945, Burt Williams, a photographer with the *Pittsburgh Sun-Telegraph*, started organizing a professional association for photographers, The National Press Photographers Association.

According to Claude Cookman's history of the organization, *A Voice Is Born*, Williams obtained financial backing for the organization from the Cigar Institute of America and began the groundwork with a ten-city coast-to-coast telephone conference in which leaders in press photography took part. (Perhaps photographers' "cigar-chomping shutterbug" reputation had some truth in it?)

At a meeting in New York City on February 23 and 24, 1946, the group adopted a constitution and elected officers: Joseph Costa, *New York Daily News*, president; Burt Williams, *Pittsburgh Sun-Telegraph*, secretary; and Charles Mack, *Hearst Metrotone News*, treasurer.

Today the organization holds an annual conference, runs educational seminars, publishes an attractive, well-written magazine, *News Photographer*, maintains an informative Web site, and hosts a lively electronic discussion list on the Internet. With more than 10,000 members, including pros and students, the association also administers a photo contest and sponsors professional workshops in photojournalism and electronics.

FORMAL EDUCATION SPREADS

The first college grad to work on the picture side of a newspaper was Paul Thompson, who graduated from Yale in 1902.

In 1943, the University of Missouri hired Cliff Edom to teach news photography. Edom had never been a newspaper or magazine photographer and had never taught journalism. At the time the school had no major in the subject. In fact, the word photojournalism had yet to be coined.

Despite his inexperience, Edom had a vision. Along with his teaching duties, Edom sought a way to bring to the isolated midwestern college town the work of the finest professionals. He created a contest, which came to be known as the Pictures of the Year Contest. Thus, his students had the opportunity to view the contest entries and then to meet the professionals who came to collect their awards. The contest served to further professionalize the field by recognizing the work of America's best image-makers. Edom also created the week-long Missouri Photo Workshop, to which he recruited well-known picture editors to coach young or mid-career photojournalists seeking more hands-on training in the field.

Today many schools offer courses and even degrees in photojournalism. More than ninety colleges and universities offer at least one class in news photography. Some universities even grant a Ph.D. in journalism or communications with an emphasis in photojournalism.

DISTRIBUTING PICTURES ACROSS THE LAND
BAIN CREATES A PICTURE SERVICE

In 1895, a newspaper writer and photographer, George Grantham Bain, started the Bain News Photographic Service in New York City. As manager of the Washington, D.C., United Press office in the 1890s, Bain realized that he could accumulate pictures on his own and sell them to subscribers.

After leaving United Press, he began his own photo service. He catalogued and cross-indexed photographs he had bought from correspondents or newspapers that subscribed to his service. From newspapers throughout the country, he received pictures, copied them, and sent the copies to his list of subscribing newspapers. Bain's business expanded rapidly and, by 1905, he had acquired a million news photographs. Many of his pictures were the first of their kind, including the first federal courtroom pictures, the first photos of the Senate in session, and the first automobile race. Although a massive fire in 1908 completely destroyed Bain's archives, he immediately set about rebuilding his collection.

Other picture services developed, including Underwood and Underwood (1896), which started out making stereoscopic pictures. Newspaper editors would call on the Underwoods for pictures to illustrate stories about remote countries where the Underwoods had operators. The Brown brothers, too, saw the possibilities of selling news pictures from their experience as circulation managers on *Harper's Weekly*.

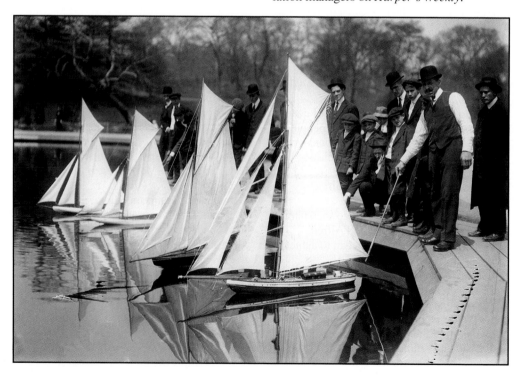

Bain News Photographic Service provided a steady supply of photos, including light feature pictures like this one, to member papers around the country. Bain Collection, Library of Congress

Soon the Underwood, Brown, and Bain photographers were all competing for scoops.

In 1907 United Press (UP) was founded. By 1919 the Hearst organization formed International News Photos (INP). Wide World Photos, which was started by the *New York Times*, followed. In 1923 Acme News Pictures appeared. The Associated Press News Photo service began in 1927. By 1933, some fifty photographic news services were operating in New York.

These services sent their pictures by train, giving a tip to the porter to hand-deliver the package of photos for extra-quick service. Local event photos were no longer limited to the immediate area. If the picture had enough sensational interest or sex appeal, it would be sent around the world. Acme and INP later combined into United Press International (UPI), and Wide World Photos became part of the Associated Press (AP).

INSTANT PICTURE TRANSMISSION

Ever since newspapers began publishing pictures, the search was on for a way to transport the images quickly over long distances. As early as 1907, Professor Alfred Korn of the University of Munich, Germany, had demonstrated an electrical system using a photocell, which would transmit and receive a picture over a telegraph wire.

In the same year, *L'Illustration* of Paris and the *London Daily Mirror* inaugurated a cross-channel service that later included other capitals of Europe.

Not until 1925 was there a permanent transmission line set up in the United States. In that year the American Telephone and Telegraph Co. (AT&T) opened a commercial wire linking New York, Chicago, and San Francisco. It was first come, first served, and cost $60 to send a picture coast-to-coast.

On May 1, 1926, the first commercial radio photograph transmitted from London appeared on page one of the *New York Times*. The picture of the Viceroy of India had been made three days earlier. Because of bad weather, the transmission took two hours.

AT&T sold its wire transmission service to the Associated Press in 1934. Many AP subscriber newspapers tried to block the sale because of the $5 million cost, a major expense during the Depression. Besides the steep cost, Frank Knox of the *Chicago Daily News* claimed that there would only be two pictures a day worth sending by wire. In the end, though, the AP bought the Bell Lab equipment, leased AT&T wire, and set up twenty-five stations. On January 1, 1935, the AP transmitted an aerial picture of a plane wreck in the Adirondack Mountains, and the

age of rapid photo transmission began in the United States. Soon other picture services, including International News Photos and Acme, started their own wire photo transmission networks. For a long time, such uncontrollable factors as poor weather would wreck the quality of pictures sent on long-distance transmission lines. Even worse, pictures sent across the Atlantic by radiophoto were often fuzzy and indistinct. Newspapers and magazines used pictures sent by land lines or by radio even though they were of poor quality because they could accompany the immediate story rather than appear days after the news had broken, according to Jonathan Coopersmith in his paper "From Lemons to Lemonade: The Development of AP Wirephoto."

In 1960 a picture of President Eisenhower was sent from Cedar Rapids, Iowa, to Dallas, Texas. The clear, crisp image was the first to be relayed by satellite, which eliminated quality interference from bad weather or the poor condition of long-distance land lines. With today's digital technologies, individual photographers as well as wire services can send photos instantaneously all over the world, with the quality of the final product looking as good as that of the original. The improvement in fast lenses, introduction of digital cameras, cellular and even portable satellite phones and high-speed modems, have all freed the photojournalist from many earlier technical limitations.

Instead of cheesecake and composograph photos taken with flash-on-camera, today's photojournalist can produce creative and expressive photographs. These in-depth pictures, taken with available light or light from portable strobes can capture candid moments that were impossible in those days of New York's *Daily Graphic*. ∎

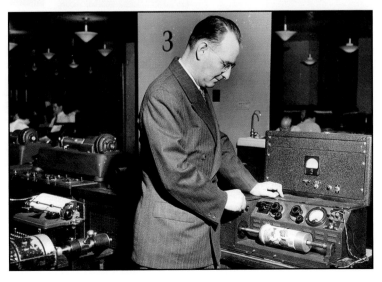

Transmitters like this Associated Press machine did for photographers in the 1930s what the telegraph had done for writers prior to the Civil War. The device allowed photographers to send pictures by wire across the country and eventually around the world. Courtesy of the Associated Press

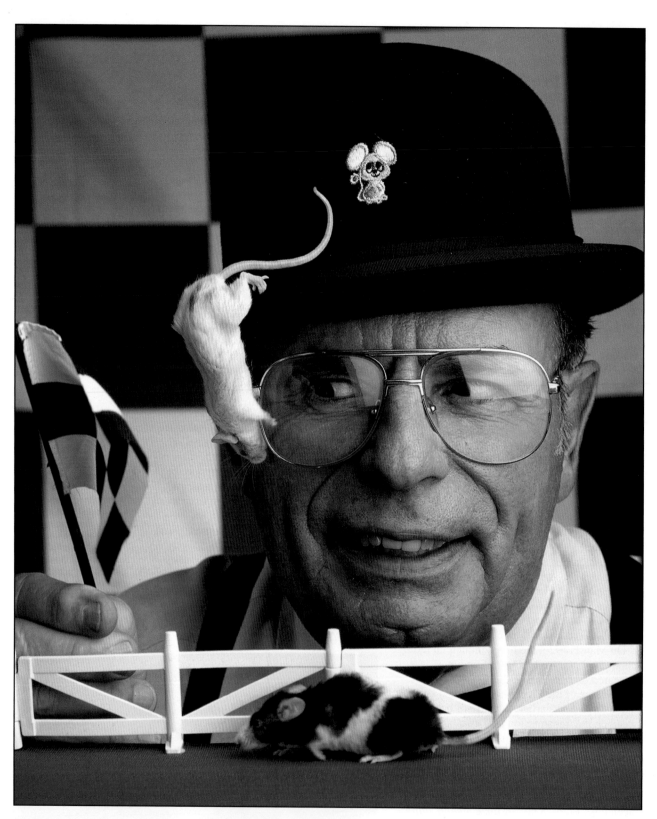

The photographer received an assignment from *People* magazine to take a picture of this retired aerospace engineer, who began racing mice after he stopped designing fighter jets. The magazine paid a day rate for the assignment but would have upped the fee had the picture run on the cover. The copyright belongs to the photographer, not to the magazine. Keith Philpott for *People* magazine

Chapter 16

Turning Pro

MAKING A LIVING IN PHOTOJOURNALISM

B reaking into photojournalism is hard to do, says Jim

McNay, a professor of photojournalism at Brooks

Institute of Photography, and a contributor to this

chapter. The chapter contains advice from three professionals who

have "been there" and beyond. David Weintraub, a longtime freelance

photographer and book author, spells out the how-to's of the business

of freelance photojournalism. McNay, a former newspaper photo edi-

tor and photographer, takes on internships, workshops, and contests.

Pulitzer Prize-winner John Kaplan, now professor at the University of

Florida, outlines the essentials of a journalistic portfolio.

SO YOU WANT TO FREELANCE

by David Weintraub

Can you make a living in photojournalism? Most photographers who do follow one of two routes: staff or freelance. There are about 1500 daily newspapers in the United States, and most of these use staff photographers. There are also many weekly and alternative newspapers that use staffers. Some large magazines employ staff photographers, but these positions are few and hard to get; most magazines rely on freelancers. If you are a staff photographer, you are usually an employee of the publication. This means you are paid a salary, have taxes withheld from your paycheck, and are generally provided with equipment, supplies, and benefits such as health insurance and a pension plan. In return, you give up your copyright to the photographs made under the terms of your employment—the publication owns the pictures you create for it. (Depending on the terms of your employment, you may or may not receive a share of any income the publi-

cation receives from reselling your work.)

If you choose the freelance route, you will join the ranks of the self-employed. Being self-employed is a dream many people share: You strike out on your own, set your own schedule, and earn your living by your wits and talent. But there are some hard realities to consider.

First, you have to be a damn good photographer, because you probably will be competing for each and every job, at least until you build up a steady clientele.

Second, you need to have substantial savings, or be gainfully employed, to finance your venture. And third, you have to be skilled in all aspects of running a business, including marketing, self-promotion, negotiating, sales, bookkeeping, financial planning, and time management. Of course, as your business grows, you may be able to outsource some or all of these tasks. But initially, they all will rest on your shoulders. Ask yourself if this sounds like a challenge you look forward to meeting, and answer

PORTFOLIO: CONTENT FIRST

By John Kaplan, University of Florida

A strong photojournalism portfolio needs to demonstrate versatility. For newspaper work, this means a command of news, sports, features, and picture stories. A portfolio does not have to include every category, but to work at better publications and compete in portfolio competitions, picture stories are absolutely essential. Magazine photojournalism portfolios may instead be highly specialized, but those first breaking into the business almost always get their start at a paper.

The best portfolios are intimate and filled with emotion. They have a point of view and a fresh vision that goes beyond a merely literal interpretation of a scene. However, to fall back on a cliché, "Do not put the cart before the horse." Look first to tell any story well through photography, with technically solid pictures that can be understood and appreciated by any reader. Quit trying so hard to be deep or

subtle, or to impart secondary meaning in your work. Be sure that your pictures communicate on a primary, visceral level. Let your style and strengths evolve naturally rather than forcing yourself into a formula.

Consistently ranked as one of the finest small newspapers in the nation, the *Concord* (New Hampshire) *Monitor* is able to hire many of the brightest young photojournalists. It does not pay as well as some larger papers, but photographers clamor to work or intern there because it uses pictures superbly and can be a stepping-stone to other opportunities. Its director of photography, Dan Habib, started at a newspaper and later became an award-winning freelancer doing assignments for *People*, *Time*, and *Fortune*. Habib returned to newspapers because "I missed having some control over my work and how it gets published. I also like having a close connection with a community."

Known for his thoughtful feedback, Habib sends a letter to each job or intern candidate that gets at the crux of what most editors want to see. Here's an excerpt:

"Those who reached the final round had a few things in common. They had at least one strong photo story, which showed an ability to obtain access to intimate and difficult situations. Original ideas are a big bonus. Stories are often the best forum for a photographer to convey a sensibility for subtle moments and strong journalistic instincts.

"Stories were complemented by diverse singles, a range of sports, spot news, general news and features. They demonstrated technical proficiency, ideally in color and black-and-white, as well as the use of flash. The top contenders had unusual, complex compositions as well as tight, high-impact moments. All of the photographs were thoughtfully composed and cropped, and led

the viewer's eye through the frame."

In terms of editing and packaging, Habib likes to see one picture story and eight to twelve singles for an internship application. From an experienced photographer seeking a job, he expects two strong stories and ten to fifteen single images. What hurts the package are badly duped or poorly printed images, he says. "Most editors agree that if photographers can't make excellent dupes (or have them made) they may not make technically excellent photos every day."

Habib receives stacks of portfolios in many forms. Whatever the packaging, he says, "what really sets a portfolio apart is good emotion with socially relevant subject matter.

Photographers get so caught up in their vision they forget that editors want to see sports, too, particularly shot with long lenses." ∎

Excerpted from *Photo Portfolio Success*, Writers Digest Books, 2003.

honestly. The best time to find out you are not suited for self-employment is before you dive in.

Peter Howe, who served as director of photography at *Life* and as picture editor for the *New York Times Magazine*, spent 13 years as a freelance photojournalist. He says a newspaper staff job, an internship with a publication (pages 372–373), stringing for a wire service, or assisting an established photographer are all great training for a career as a freelance photojournalist. When you are ready to freelance, having a great portfolio (opposite) and lots of persistence is essential. Howe also advises finding a project to work on, something that will create a solid body of work. He cites the example of Lauren Greenfield, whose books **Fast Forward** and **Girl Culture** have established her as a leading editorial photographer. (See page 375.)

Greenfield initially began photographing young girls growing up in Los Angeles, a world she understood and that was literally in her backyard. "Coming of age" has interest and relevance, says Howe, and Greenfield made a valuable contribution by documenting its many aspects in her books. The power of those personal projects has established her as a leading editorial photographer.

Be prepared to live on a tight budget, Howe cautions, because very few photojournalists get rich. In fact, he compares the profession to teaching or acting, which rely on passion rather than on financial rewards to attract practitioners. (According to the Bureau of Labor Statistics, in 2001 only the top 10 percent of photographers earned more than about $48,000, and the median income for photographers was around $23,000.)

AGENCIES

Are there other alternatives besides running the whole show yourself? Many leading photojournalists are members of agencies that handle many, if not all, of the business aspects, leaving the photographer to do what he or she does best—shoot pictures. Some agencies work with photographers with different shooting styles to appeal to a wide range of potential clients.

These agencies—Corbis, Getty Images, Magnum, Black Star, Contact, and VII are among the best known—circulate portfolios, pitch story ideas (either proposed by a photographer or by someone within the agency), get assignments, negotiate rates and rights, maintain picture files, and explore resale possibilities for their photographers.

In return, an agency takes a percentage of the assignment and resale fees and, in some cases, control the copyrights to their photographers' images. With international sales, both the rep in the other country and the agency take a cut of the proceeds.

In addition to copyright ownership, agency contracts may address questions of duration—how many years a photographer is signing up for—and exclusivity. Some photographers find the larger agencies to be impersonal and imperial, with a "take it or leave it" approach to percentages and rights. New technologies have influenced the way agencies do business. Corbis and Getty in particular have imposing Web presences and are committed to making shopping for pictures a completely online affair. The large agencies can and do undercut the price charged by smaller boutique agencies. Smaller agencies have gone out of business. Others, like Network Photographers, which is in the process of digitizing its collection, are trying to compete with the two giants of the photography business.

ALERT: If you have a unique picture of an important news event, you can approach an agency to handle the sale of that image even if you are not a member.

Jason Grow has looked at photography from all sides—as a newspaper staffer, an agency photographer, and a freelancer. He says agencies perform many valuable functions, especially for two groups of photographers. Up-and-coming photographers benefit from the stamp of approval and instant credibility that agency affiliation can bring. Established photographers who need help running their business affairs benefit from the agency's organizational and managerial skills. In return, Grow says, agencies take from 30 to 50 percent of assignment and reuse fees. Agencies may also help with production, such as making travel arrangements and getting assistants in far-flung locations. Sometimes an agency will help pay for travel and materials so a photographer can shoot a story on his or her own. In that case, the agency will pursue publication outlets for the story to recoup its investment. For many photographers, whether or not to sign with an agency is a purely economic decision. A photographer billing several hundred thousand dollars a year in fees might find an agency relationship worthwhile, whereas a photographer making $50,000 per year might prefer to continue solo, Grow says.

CONTRACT PHOTOGRAPHERS

Another option is to become a contract photographer for a magazine. Contract photographers are not staffers, but like staffers they enjoy some measure of financial stability. How does this work? Only elite publications

By Jim McNay, Brooks Institute
of Photography

Professional editors like to know a new hire can meet a deadline—regularly. They like to know a new staffer can produce pictures at an acceptable level—regularly. They like to see if someone has the inventiveness and passion to go beyond the ordinary picture or project—regularly.

And this is true whether the publication is in Scapoose, Oregon; Scooba, Mississippi; or Sacramento, California. Student who demonstrate these skills while in school—probably through internships—have the edge when it comes to landing a job.

Spending ten to twelve weeks shooting two to five assignments a day lets you show you can come to grips with a new town, a new part of the country, perhaps a new regional culture, and still deliver solid storytelling pictures made in an unfamiliar landscape. Your resourcefulness to learn an unfamiliar town and get to know people in the community will be tested.

The resulting glowing reports from your bosses or supervisors will circulate among other editors with lightening speed. Other pros will be lining up to look at your portfolio, waiting for the chance to offer bigger challenges with the next internship or even your first job. Nothing beats a "win" at a publication. Any editor who happily nurtured a hard-working intern is going to be in that photographer's corner for a long time.

INTERNSHIP SEASON
Summer break is the traditional internship window. This is when publications across the nation expect to have interns and the budget to pay them. The traditional time to apply for summer internships is in

January after the holiday break. Sometimes the internship hunt continues right up until June 1, when the only option left may be that night manager's job at Pup and Taco.

Many students start with internships at small publications and move up to larger ones in succeeding years.

Part of the good news is that an increasing number of excellent internships are offered year around.

RÉSUMÉ
Résumés should be standard. Include your contact information at the top: name, address, telephone, e-mail address, cell phone if you have one, perhaps a Web site address. Address the following:

- Educational background, such as any degrees you've earned, your current educational path. You need not review your high school career. Start with your your current school first, the one immediately before that, and so forth.
- Employment history, including your current job, followed by one or two before.
- Special skills, interests, or certifications. Part of the aim of a résumé is to say something about yourself that separates you from the pack of other aspiring photographers out there. This is the place for scuba and water-safety certification and pilot's licenses. Foreign languages or overseas study experience are important to point out.

While no one wants to stifle creativity, your résumé is not where to get cutesy. Day-glow paper, angels flying across the page, glitter sprinkled on the paper will irritate, not endear you to, potential employers.

The creative challenge is to fit all this information on one page. For students just completing a degree (any degree, first or fourth) the bias is toward a one-page résumé, unless, perhaps, you have had a distinguished career in some other field.

This should leave room for about three references on the page. Listing references—with telephone numbers and email addresses—accelerates the process.

COVER LETTERS
The challenge is to write in an interesting way without slipping into silliness or bragging. A cover letter should briefly introduce you and explain why you are writing.

Touch on a couple of your college career highlights, such as work on the student or local newspaper, or a previous internship. Even if in the résumé, these are worth repeating since a potential employer may miss them at first glance. Explain what you did and what you learned from these different experiences.

Why do you want to intern for that news organization in that town? It helps to have looked at the publication or researched what happens in that part of the country. Avoid saying you "like people" and your goal is to become "a photojournalist." These points are obvious and won't differentiate you from other applicants. Do, however, include aspects of your life that make you stand out such as experiences in which you have taken a leadership role, handled dangerous situations, or worked under pressure.

Wrap up the letter with a thank you. That's it. Oh, yes. As you address the letter ask yourself,

how does the editor spell her name? Sarah or Sara? Or is his name John Smith or Jon Smyth?

Ya wanna know.

AFTER THE INTERNSHIP
No, it's not time to send flowers. But do maintain regular contact with your old editor. The best place to start is with a thank-you note. Make this a hand-written project on good paper found at a local stationary store. Like your portfolio, the stationary should be simple, clean, and professional. Thank the pro for his or her time. Say something about what you learned. Be brief, polite, and appreciative.

Follow up every couple of months with some examples of recent work. Editors like to see what you have done lately. A simple note with three or four clips will keep you on an editor's radar screen. Class assignments printed on a desktop printer are another fine opportunity for sharing work.

E-mailed images may work, too, but only if you have asked if your editor is willing to accept them. Professionals are so flooded with excessive E-mail that they may just hit delete before ever opening your file.

The idea is to keep your name in front of someone for whom you'd like to work—either in the next internship, the one after, or perhaps for a job opening—without being an obnoxious pest. Most editors will appreciate your effort to stay in touch. Bottom line: follow up. Few students make the effort, so yours will make you easier to remember. ■

Jim McNay writes a regular column for young photojournalists at *www.SportsShooter.com*.

LETTER HOME
FROM AN INTERN
by Krista Niles

Krista Niles had recently begun a photojournalism internship at the *New York Times* when terrorists attacked the World Trade Center on Sept. 11, 2001. Her friends' first news of her safety was when they saw a photo she had taken, right, in the *Times*. Her photos, including the top two on this page, were part of the coverage that won the *New York Times* a Pulitzer Prize in news photography.

Part of Krista's first E-mail to her friends after the attack is reproduced below with her permission. All photos by Krista Niles, © *New York Times*.

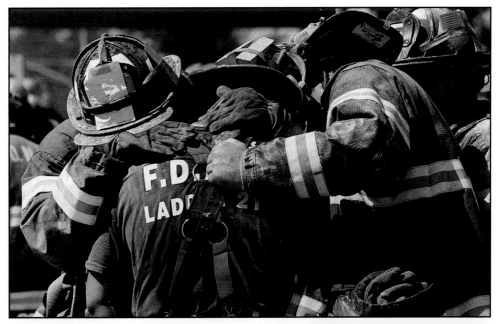

Subject:
    i cannot even comprehend
Date:
    Thu, 13 Sep 2001 19:26:07

hey gang. i am indeed alive, but not all that well.

i wish i could describe what i've seen these last three days, but my mind isn't functioning all that well... from physical and mental/ emotional exhaustion.

i got on scene about 20 minutes after the towers fell... the last photos i shot as i was heading into the subway from brooklyn was of people watching the towers burning. when i finally got out from underground after train delays, i kept searching for the towers to orient myself...no towers to be found...thinking they were just blocked from view by the buildings in front of me it took a good while for me to realize that they had collapsed. i could see how the first may be fallen, but surely not both. and as i ran past thousands of people running the opposite way i wondered what the hell i was getting myself into. the thing i keep grappling with is this...in any accident, fire, disaster scene there are injured people running, being carried and being helped.

THERE WERE NO INJURED PEOPLE. NONE. not one person bleeding. not one person limping. not one person crying for help. nothing. it was quiet, except for explosions and shifting debris and shouting from police and firefighters trying to figure out how to rescue people.

i did not see a single injured civilian in the six hours i was at "ground zero"...and i was literally at the base less than 100 yards to my right and portions of the top about 200 yards to my left. i only saw one firefighter pulled from the debris.

the debris was amazing. a fine dust, inches thick, coated the entire area. breathing was impossible. thankfully i ran into co-nyt photographer angel franco who gave me a mask. my eyes are still recovering from all the dust.

angel and i were talking today about what we saw...and about the fine dust. as troubling as this is for me to put into words... that dust is the ash of people...mixed with cement and everything imaginable.

that thought kept running through my head as i kept walking. i just wanted to see one person...all i saw were helpless firefighters who were in such a state of shock they didn't know what to do, or how to start.

having been to the WTC observation deck (86/7th floor of tower 2) one month ago with my mother and sister at that same time of day, this was even more bizarre. i knew there had to be thousands of people in those buildings.

i'm still in shell-shock, especially after the last two days. yesterday and today i was photographing people looking for missing people. i cried today standing in front of a wall that was plastered with pictures of missing people. seeing their faces and names made it so real to me... especially since i know most of these people will never be found. i cried again when i had to ask people for caption information. some photos i have to force myself to take... the one that you all have seen is one of them. that firefighter in the center couldn't locate his brother, who was also a firefighter at the base of WTC1 when it collapsed. i keep telling myself that i have to document this horrible event. i just can't make much sense of it all.

i apologize for my stream of consciousness. thanks to all of you for your emails and concern. i send my best and i'll send some photos soon... krista

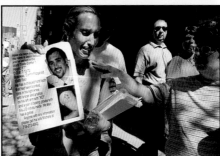

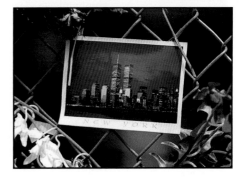

like *National Geographic*, *Sports Illustrated*, and *Time* use contract photographers, and these plum positions are awarded to only a select few. A contract photographer agrees to be available—in other words, to drop everything and run—for a certain number of days each year to work for a particular publication. In return, the publication guarantees to pay the photographer an annual fee, which is determined by the number of days multiplied by the magazine's day rate. Both parties benefit, because the photographer receives a stable income and the publication gets the services of a top photographer. At the end of the year, the contract can be renewed, altered, or cancelled. Unlike staffers, contract photographers generally own the rights to their photographs. Some publications may demand ownership of published images, and there may also be restrictions when and where contract photographers can resell work originally made for their publications.

FREELANCE

In order to be a successful freelancer, you have to answer these three questions: What do I do? Who buys what I do? How do I reach them and get work? If you answered "I'm a photographer; I make pictures" to the first questions, take a deep breath and find a pad and pencil. Now write down all the things that photographers and photographs do: record events, capture decisive moments, communicate ideas, illustrate a story, grab the viewer's attention, and solve a client's visual-communication problems. Now get up close and personal. What do you love to photograph? What do you bring to the party? Every photographer has a set of life experiences, interests, and skills that inform his or her images. Successful photographers use these to develop a personal style—a way of seeing the world and expressing it visually. Ultimately, your personal style is what will help you develop a career.

On to question number two: Who buys what I do? Here's where your research skills come to the fore. Get that pad and pencil. Spend a couple of hours browsing the newspaper and magazine rack at your local library or bookstore. After a while, you should begin to get a sense of the types of pictures that get published, day after day, week after week. See any that look like yours? See any that look better? Be honest. Or worse? Make a list of the publications you could shoot for today based on your skill level and expertise. Be brutally honest. Make another list of "dream" publications, ones you would love to work for someday, when your talents develop. Magazines are particularly easy to

research, because most have a masthead that shows the address and phone number of the editorial office, and the name of the art director, photo editor, or director of photography. Write these down. Repeat this process whenever you find yourself near a collection of publications—this is a productive way to use the hour or so waiting at an airport for your flight.

Now you've got a basic list of newsstand, or consumer, publications, but this is just the tip of the iceberg. And it's the same list most photojournalists have. But there are many more publications out there besides *National Geographic*, *Time*, and *Newsweek*. These are the specialty, or trade, magazines that cater to a specific audience, group, profession, or industry. We're talking here about publications like *Construction Site News*, *Diagnostic Imaging*, *Information Week*, *Motorcycle Product News*, and *Poultry International*. You won't find trade publications on most newsstands, but many are listed in books such as **Photographer's Market**, and they also can be found on the Web at *www.tradepub.com*. Researching trade publications involves making lots of phone calls to find out who assigns photography. This is boring, frustrating work, but it does pay off.

ALERT: Don't just concentrate on publications located where you live. Newspapers and magazines that rely on freelancers need them to be where the stories are.

Also, don't forget the lucrative international market, with magazines such as *Paris Match* (France); *Airone*, *Focus*, and *Oggi* (Italy); and *Stern* and *German Geo* (Germany). Some of these have offices in the United States, usually in New York. As in the United States, many Sunday newspapers overseas have photography-rich magazines.

According to Peter Menzel, whose pictures routinely appear in publications around the world, there are three ways to work with overseas clients. The first is to deal with the publication directly and be assigned to cover a story. The second is to have agencies in various countries representing your stock photography. And the third is to resell stories that have appeared in U.S. publications. If you are interested in pursuing resale options, Menzel says, it is important not to sign away your rights when you take a magazine assignment. Menzel keeps in touch with editors via e-mail, and supplies his eleven overseas agents with pictures and brief story descriptions.

REACH YOUR PROSPECTIVE CLIENTS

Now you're ready to answer question three: how to reach your prospective clients and get

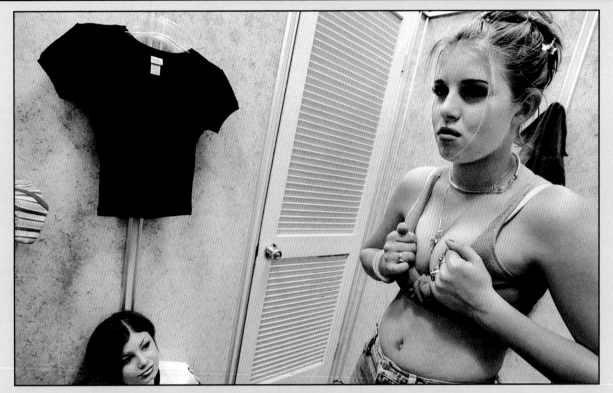

Sheena tries on clothes with her friend Amber, 14, in a department store dressing room in San Jose, California.

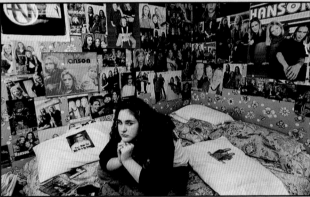

Lisa, 13, in her room, Edina, Minnesota.

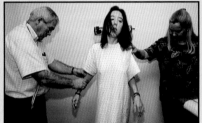

Erin, 24, is blind-weighed at an eating disorder clinic in Coconut Creek, Florida. She has asked to mount the scale backward so as not to see her weight gain.

by Lauren Greenfield

Girl Culture has been my journey as a photographer, as an observer of culture, as part of the media, as a media critic, as a woman, as a girl.

These photographs are both very personal and very public. ...They are about the girls I photographed. They are also about me. I was enmeshed in girl culture before I was a photographer, and I was photographing girl culture before I realized I was working on *Girl Culture*.

In this work, I have been drawn to the pathological in the everyday. I am interested in the tyranny of the popular and thin girls over the ones who don't fit that mold. I am interested in the competition suffered by the popular girls, and their sense that being popular is not as satisfying as it appears. I am interested in the costly and time-consuming beauty rituals that are an integral part of daily life. I am interested in the fact that to fall outside the ideal body type is to be a modern-day pariah...

These interests, my own memories, and a genuine love for girls, gossip, female bonding, and the idiosyncratic rituals of girl culture, have motivated this five-year photographic journey.

... The body has become the primary canvas on which girls express their identities, insecurities, ambitions, and struggles. It has become a palimpsest on which many of our culture's conflicting messages about femininity are written and rewritten.

Photography is an ideal medium with which to explore the role of image in our culture. The camera renders an illusion of objective representation, just like a mirror. But as every woman knows, a mirror provides data that, filtered through a mind and moods, is subject to wildly differing interpretations. This project has been my mirror and my attempt to deconstruct the illusions that make up our reality.

© Lauren Greenfield/VII. From the book *Girl Culture*, Chronicle Books, 2002

assignments. Do you have a killer portfolio? What about eye-grabbing mailers? These are essential if you are going to break into the competitive world of freelance photojournalism. A portfolio should represent your best work. (See page 370.) Each photograph should stand on its own merits, but the entire portfolio should have a rhythm and a flow that leads the viewer from beginning to end. Your portfolio should contain from twelve to twenty pages presented in a visually pleasing way. Each portfolio page should consist of one or more photographs and your name printed in a simple font. This repeated conjunction of name and photographs helps create your visual identity, or brand, in the viewer's mind. Remember: You often ship or drop off your portfolio, so it represents you in your absence. It gets only one chance to make a great first impression.

PORTFOLIO

As a collection of your best work, your portfolio represents the past—what you have done. But many photographers create images for their portfolios that look to the future—what they want to do. Photographers often refer to this as personal work, as opposed to assigned work. Some create a separate portfolio for their personal work, and it is often these images that propel their careers forward. You also want to consider whether you see yourself as a generalist or a specialist. Generalists shoot everything—spot news, environmental portraits, sports, food, and fashion. Specialists carve out a niche—such as underwater photography or wildlife—and become well known for that type of work. Do you want to compete with all the other generalists for a wide range of assignments? Or do you want to focus on the subjects (and therefore the markets) that you feel passionate about? Only you can decide. Clients are sometimes frustratingly literal: if the assignment is to shoot red lawnmowers, you'd better have red (not green) lawnmowers in your portfolio. Yet art directors and photo editors are often artists too, and they will appreciate the artistic, adventurous images that push the envelope of your creativity.

As for practical matters, you need to pay attention to your portfolio's size and weight: It must be large enough to display your images properly, yet easy to carry and to ship. Never send original transparencies—these may get lost or damaged. Make several identical portfolios, so you always have one to show if the other is with a client. Get help editing your work and be ruthless. A picture that needs explaining doesn't belong (you often aren't there to explain). Just because a

picture was tough to get doesn't make it portfolio material. Make sure the subject matter is appropriate for the client; avoid pictures that may offend. If you are not well versed in typography and layout, seek professional assistance. Although once quite costly, portfolios are now more affordable thanks to computers. Many photographers are turning to scanners and ink-jet printers to create their own portfolios and mailers.

ALERT: Although most newspapers accept digital portfolios, it's important to do your research in other industries to see if editors and art directors are willing to review CDs or other electronic portfolios. See opposite page for information on preparing electronic portfolios. Resist the temptation to show tear sheets—samples of your published work—unless the printing, layout, and design are all first rate. Most of the people you are showing your portfolio to will immediately recognize flaws in these areas, and the value of your photographs, by association, will be diminished. Also resist the urge to show 35mm slides (too small).

SHOWING YOUR WORK TO MAGAZINES

Many magazines are based in New York City, so photographers often find it productive to visit there at least once a year. Before you book your flight, do some planning. First, have a clear goal in mind, such as a dozen portfolio showings and four personal visits. Then draw up a list of target publications that use the type of pictures you shoot. Call each in advance to find out its policy regarding portfolios. Most publications accept only drop-offs, meaning that you leave your portfolio for a few hours or overnight (this is a good reason to have multiple portfolios).

In some cases, you may be able to schedule personal meetings, but these may also happen on the spur of the moment, for example when you come to pick up your portfolio. If you are lucky enough to meet face to face with an art director or photo editor, use your (limited) time wisely. Make sure you are intimately familiar with the publication. Ask questions: What are the current and future needs for photography? What problems does the publication face in getting consistently great pictures? Which topics or geographic regions are particularly tough to cover? If the editor or art director could change just one thing about the photographs submitted each week or month, what would it be?

The most important part of a personal visit comes when you are ready to say goodbye. Take this opportunity to agree on the next step—remember, you are trying to build a relationship, not just entertain someone for a

STUDENT PORTFOLIOS: A WORD ON PRESENTATION

By Jim McNay, Brooks
Institute of Photography

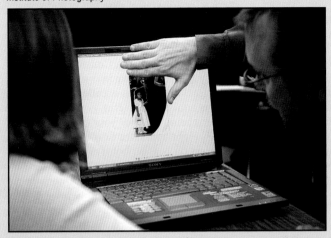

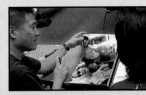

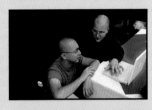

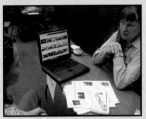

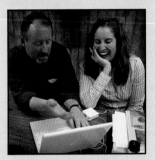

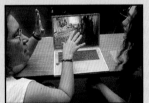

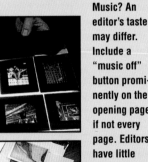

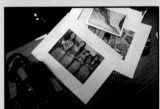

Most newspapers are set up to review digital portfolios. Call or E-mail first to see if the people you will see prefer to look at CDs, Zip disks, or perhaps even a Web site. It also helps to know if their computers are Macintosh® or Windows®-based. Just in case, configure the portfolio for both Macintosh and Windows-based computers. You'd hate to have the perfect portfolio incapable of being seen!

Test your digital portfolio on a couple of computers—other than your own—before visiting a pro in the newsroom. It's embarrassing to make a long journey only to watch an editor trying unsuccessfully to open a disk.

For slide-show programs that run when the disk is opened, include buttons on each screen that allow reviewers to either hold an image to view for longer reflection or to click through the slides one at a time. These options allow editors to move through portfolios at their own pace. A stop or hold feature also allows them to call someone over to the screen to see a particularly interesting image.

Music? An editor's taste may differ. Include a "music off" button prominently on the opening page, if not every page. Editors have little time to devote to student work. For digital portfolios, always use JPEGs. They open quickly. Don't give busy professionals an excuse to bail out early.

If you're not ready for high-tech yet, prints, slides, and clips are usually fine in student portfolios as long as the presentation looks professional. Pictures shown in print form need not be larger than 8"x10", since most editors rarely use pictures on the page larger than that.

Include spell-checked and grammar-checked captions on the front or back of each image.

This last bit of advice applies to all material you send to an editor. ∎

few minutes with your pictures. Did you discuss ideas for stories? Then you should agree to send a list of ten story ideas within the next few weeks (and do it). Ask your contact how you should stay in touch: through regular mailers, monthly phone calls, E-mail? Try to use questions—how, what—that cannot be answered with a simple yes or no. These are called open questions, and are very helpful at continuing the dialogue and getting the information you need. In most cases, the editor or art director won't have an immediate need for your services, so don't be disappointed if you leave without an assignment. Remember, most publications depend on having a network of freelancers they can call on to provide pictures for each issue, rain or shine. You perform a valuable service by staying in touch and coming up with leads and story ideas. Eventually, your persistence will be rewarded.

ALERT: You can also pitch your story ideas and proposals to someone on the publication's editorial side (as opposed to the art or photography side). Look on the masthead to find the names of various editors. Look for someone several rungs down from the top, such as an associate editor. If the editors have specific beats, such as travel or technology, find the appropriate one.

THE INTERNET
Don't forget the Internet as a marketing tool. With a well-designed site and appropriately selected keywords, picture editors and researchers can more easily find the photographer who has a specialized collection of images, say, of rickshaws in Bangladesh, or women working in Asian countries. When a researcher turns to the Web to find sites on a topic like rickshaws or women working, the photographer's page appears. Then the researcher can write or call for a high-quality image. At this point, the buyer and seller would determine a price and rights for using the image. For more on copyright, see Chapter 13, "The Law."

SELLING A BREAKING NEWS PICTURE
If a story has significant national or international appeal, a news magazine like *Time*, *Newsweek*, or *U.S. News & World Report* might buy a freelancer's photo, especially if it's in color. These magazines maintain very small full-time photo staffs, so they also buy outside photos. Good editors don't mind a quick telephone call on a spot-news story because they can't afford to ignore you and possibly miss the chance of publishing a Pulitzer Prize-winning picture.

RATES
As a freelancer you don't get paid a salary, the way staff photographers do. Instead, you earn a fee for your photography and you get reimbursed for your expenses.

The fee-plus-expenses model is one of the keys to understanding the economics of freelance photojournalism. Consider fees first. Newspapers and magazines generally pay their freelancers what is called a "day rate." This is a misleading term, because it implies you are being paid for your time—a "day" equals eight hours, for example—rather than for your skills as a photographer. Your assignment might take two hours or ten, it might be simple or complex, it might draw on all your creativity or simply involve recording an event such as a press conference—no matter, the pay is fixed. (But it never hurts to negotiate for a higher fee.)

In fact, the day rate is just part of the equation. Magazines and newspapers also have what is called a space rate—how much they pay for pictures based on the size and placement of the image. In other words, a quarter-page photo run inside may be worth $150, whereas a cover may command $800 or even $1200. The day rate is meant to be a guarantee against the space rate. In other words, you are guaranteed the day rate, let's say $450, no matter how your picture is used. Even if it is used as a quarter-page photo, you still get $450. But if it runs on the cover, you get paid the cover rate, which could be twice or even three times the day rate, depending on the publication.

FEE PLUS EXPENSES
What about your expenses, such as film and processing, mileage, an assistant, meals, etc? These are called billable expenses. This means they are billed to the publication and itemized separately from your fee. When you talk to a potential client about price, make sure you understand whether or not the amount quoted includes expenses. For example, a magazine photo editor calls and says she has an assignment, and her magazine usually pays $450 per day. Your first question should be: Does that include my expenses, or is that my fee? It is not uncommon to have at least half the total cost of an assignment be for expenses, especially when an assistant and travel are involved. In the case of our hypothetical assignment, if the $450 includes your expenses, your fee will probably work out to be around $200, or less than half the going rate. If the $450 is just your fee, you will probably end up billing the magazine about $700 to $800 for the assignment. Check with Editorial Photographers,

www.editorialphotographers.com, a Web site devoted to helping independent photojournalists gain fair pricing.

RIGHTS

What exactly is the publication getting for its money? First of all, photojournalists rarely sell photographs. Instead, they license the use of their images for specific uses.

Licensing photographs is based on the copyright law, which says that ownership in a freelance situation belongs to the creator, NOT to the party commissioning the work. This means that you, as a freelance photographer, own all your photographs from the moment they are made. You (and only you) have the right to license their use however you see fit.

CONTESTS CAN OPEN DOORS

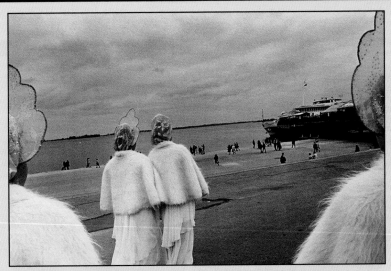

Andrea Hoyer was an unknown young photographer when she submitted twelve images to be considered for Leica's Oskar Barnack Prize. The photographs were from her self-funded, five-year effort to document the vestiges of the former Soviet Union in Russia. She joined the ranks of well-established photographers like Sebastião Salgado and Magnum photographer Larry Towell to win the prestigious international award.   photo by Andrea Hoyer

Are you ready to compete with the pros? If you can say yes honestly, you may want to make the effort and investment to enter other contests aimed for professionals. The same caveats apply. Use contests as away to review the power of your work and then to put it out there if you feel it may meet the challenge.

Atlanta Photojournalism Seminar
www.photojournalism.org

Best of Photojournalism
www.nppa.org/bestofpj

Leica's Oskar Barnack Prize
www.leica-camera.com/kultur/events/ wettbewerbe/obp/index_e.html

Pictures of the Year International
www.poy.org

World Press Photo
www.worldpressphoto.nl

By Jim McNay, Brooks Institute of Photography

A frequent question from young talent is, "How do I get recognized, get noticed?" One way—though not the only way—is to participate in photojournalism competitions, especially those available to students. One of those, the prestigious College Photographer of the Year (CPOY) competition, has a fall deadline, usually early October.

You can do well in this competition either by excelling in the overall portfolio category or by earning recognition in one of the individual picture categories. Such a performance signals potential employers that coming out of school you are ready to produce advanced work. Names of portfolio finalists spread quickly among editors and photographers throughout the country.

One of the beauties of the competition is that entries need not have been published, just created within the last year. This allows you to enter pictures you think will represent your best work.

There also are many individual picture categories—sports, features, portraits, stories—if you are not yet ready to take on the full portfolio competition. There is room to participate in the CPOY competition for students at all levels.

And compete you should. Review your work for the past year and enter at least one picture in one category. Being a part of the competition is a sign of being "engaged" in the process of serious journalism, of striving to improve, to get in the game, to grow, and to be recognized.

At the same time, keep a clear head about contests. Yes, they are useful. Recognition is important in the job search. But contest results are unpredictable. Excellent work is often overlooked. And, sometimes, good journalism may be lost in the flurry of images that speed by judges' weary eyes. Contests should not be what a photographer is about or why one takes pictures. Your pictures should be about your audience, about your community.

Let contests provide you the opportunity to review your year's work—a crucial endeavor for pushing yourself toward improvement. And if you win? Winning can bring recognition that ignites the afterburners of a young career. ∎

College Photographer of the Year
www.cpoy.org

OTHER CONTESTS FOR STUDENTS

Student members of the National Press Photographers Association (NPPA) may enter published as well as unpublished work in the Quarterly Student Clip Contest. *www.nppa.org/contests/stuclip/default.htm*

The Society of Photographic Educators (SPE) gives the $5000 Crystal Apple Award to a student member of that organization who is majoring in photography at a college or university. This prize won't put your name in front of photo editors, but it may help pay for some equipment. *www.spenational.org*

Historically, magazines and newspapers asked for one-time rights for assignment pictures generated by freelancers. Subsequent reuse and/or use in another edition (foreign language, for example) were negotiated and paid for separately. This was true, despite the fact that the publication paid the photographer to create the image and paid for the expenses.

With the consolidation of the publishing industry and the advent of the Internet, however, this is changing. Photography contracts now routinely ask for electronic rights (for a publication's Web site), or even outright ownership, forever. In return, the photographer may get an increased day rate (best case) or perhaps be told to "take it or leave it" (worst case). Before working for a publication, ask to see a copy of its contract. Pay particular attention to the words "work made for hire." If you sign a work-for-hire contract, you lose your copyright and ownership of all photographs made under that contract. Avoid at all costs signing Work for Hire contracts or

WORKSHOPS ARE A WAY TO NETWORK AS WELL AS TO LEARN

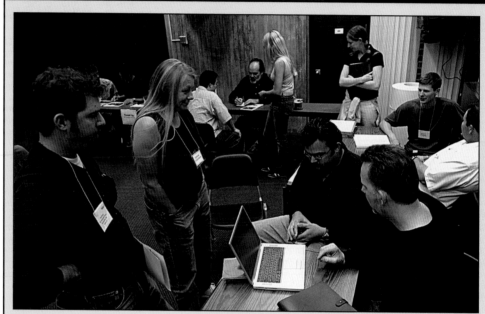

by Jim McNay,
Brooks Institute of Photography

Workshops are terrific for hands-on portfolio critiques and for getting to know editors and other shooters. Many of the best in photojournalism are sponsored by NPPA (National Press Photographers Association).

These include one-day seminars like the Flying Short Course, shown above, and weekend workshops including the Northern Short Course, Southern Short Course, and Atlanta Seminar.

The Mountain Workshop, sponsored by Western Kentucky University, or the Missouri Workshop, sponsored by the University of Missouri, are both excellent for learning to shoot photo stories.

Neither students nor professional attendees must be affiliated with the schools that sponsor the workshops.

Young professionals and students interested in freelancing learn from top shooters and New York picture editors at the Eddie Adams Workshop.

To make the jump to international photojournalism and editorial freelance photography, Visa Pour L'Image, held each September in Perpignan, France, is perhaps the most influential in the world. (See the documentary video "Visa Pour L'Image" on the DVD included in this book.)

Good technical workshops abound, including the Maine Photographic Workshops and the Palm Beach Photographic Workshops. The Sports

Photography Workshop is a great place to learn from *Sports Illustrated* shooters and Allsport photo agency editors. ∎

NPPA Workshops
www.nppa.org
The Mountain Workshop
www.mountainworkshop.com
Missouri Workshop
www.mophotoworkshop.org
Eddie Adams Workshop
www.eddieadams.com
Visa Pour L'Image
www.visapourlimage.com
Maine Photographic Workshops
www.theworkshops.com
Palm Beach Photographic Workshops
www.workshop.org
Sports Photography Workshop
www.richclarkson.com

any other agreement in which you sign over the copyright to your images. Remember, all contracts can be negotiated; that's what lawyers are for. (For more on copyright see Chapter 13, "Law," pages 296–297.)

MORE ON WHY "WORK FOR HIRE" IS A BAD DEAL FOR PHOTOGRAPHERS

"Work for hire" (or "work made for hire" of "WFH") is a contract term meaning that all work being done under the contract becomes the property of the person paying for it, not of the photographer. Under a contract like this the photographer becomes an "employee-for-a-day." But as Editorial Photographers points out, this relationship "almost always fails to adequately compensate freelancers for the usual expenses of being self-employed: employment taxes, liability coverage, equipment and automobile depreciation and insurance, office overhead, computers and software, health and disability insurance, retirement plans, non-billable time such as marketing, accounting, and image management, etc., as well as for all the potential lost revenue from secondary licensing."

Many contracts simply state the job is a "work for hire" without offering additional compensation at all. Editorial Photographers recommends avoiding work for hire contracts in editorial work in all but the most rare circumstances and for the most extraordinary compensation.

ALERT: Check the sources under More Information on this page and talk to other photographers to get the scoop on standard business practices—particularly on their experiences with bad contracts.

FIXED COSTS

Billable expenses are the expenses you can bill to your client. But there are other expenses that are part of the cost of doing business, such as camera and computer equipment, office supplies, telephone, and utilities. These are called fixed costs. You pay them day in and day out, whether you are busy shooting assignments or waiting for clients to call.

Who pays for these costs? You do—they come out of your fee. The only way to know if a fee is reasonable or not is to figure out your fixed costs. Find out how much you spend each month to be in business. Let's say it is $1000.

Now let's go back to our hypothetical assignment.

In the first example, your fee was $200, so you must have five similarly priced assignments just to break even.

In the second example, your fee was $450,

so you would break even (and even show a little profit) after your third such assignment.

PROFIT

Did you notice that word profit? It is not a dirty word. In fact, you need to make a profit if you are going to survive as a freelancer. Profit is what enables you to pay yourself a salary and thus pay the rent, put food on the table, pay your taxes and insurance, and contribute to a retirement fund. Profit also enables you to put money back into your business to make it grow.

Where does profit come from? It is what's left over after you've paid your fixed costs and the cost of your billable expenses such as film, processing, assistants, and travel expenses. There are only a few ways to increase profit: do more assignments, charge higher fees, charge more for billable expenses (called a "markup"), reduce fixed costs, and/or reduce the cost of billable items. If you pay close attention to these details, you just may flourish in today's tough freelance market. ■

MORE INFORMATION

BOOKS AND MAGAZINES
ASMP Professional Business Practices in Photography
Photography: Focus on Profit
    by Tom Zimberoff
Business and Legal Forms for Photographers
    by Tad Crawford
Pricing Photography
    by Michal Heron and David MacTavish
The Photographer's Guide to Marketing and Self-Promotion
    by Maria Piscopo
The Photojournalist's Guide to Making Money
    by Michael Sedge and Ron Engh
Photo District News (PDN), www.pdn-pix.com

ORGANIZATIONS AND WEB SITES
American Society of Media Photographers (ASMP)
    www.asmp.org
National Press Photographers Association (NPPA)
    www.nppa.org
Editorial Photographers (EP)
    www.editorialphotographers.com
The Digital Journalist
    www.digitaljournalist.com
Sports Shooter
    www.SportsShooter.com

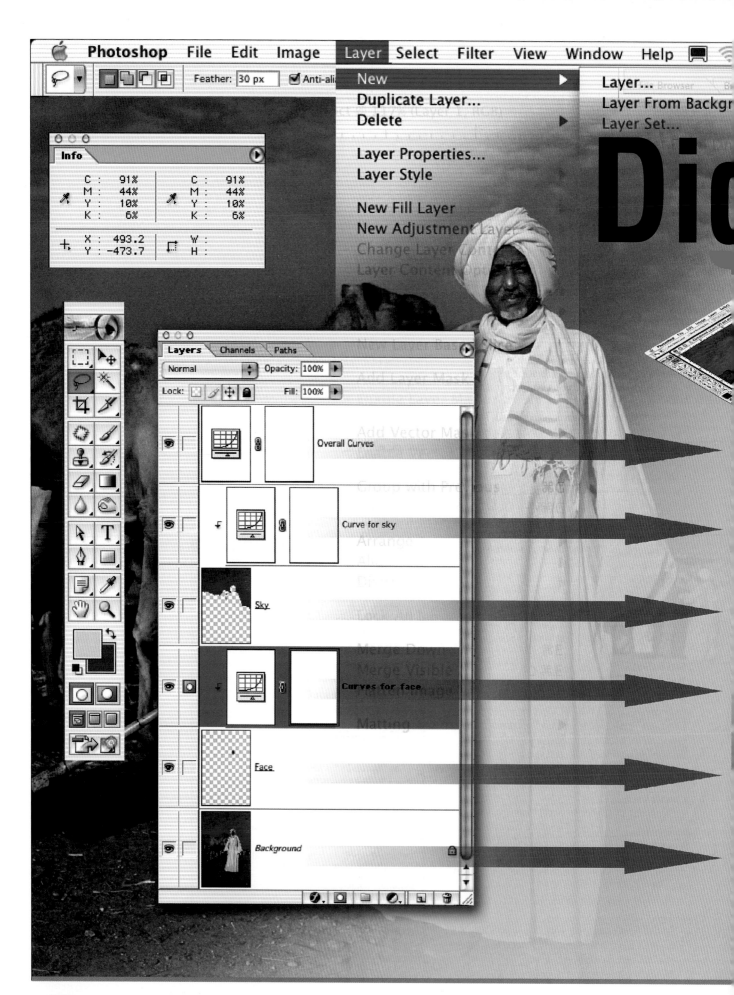

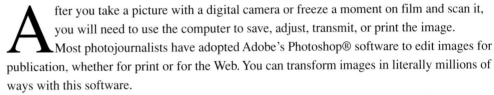

tal Darkroom

After you take a picture with a digital camera or freeze a moment on film and scan it, you will need to use the computer to save, adjust, transmit, or print the image. Most photojournalists have adopted Adobe's Photoshop® software to edit images for publication, whether for print or for the Web. You can transform images in literally millions of ways with this software.

However, photojournalists typically follow a restricted set of operations for assignments other than photo illustrations. These basic darkroom adjustments include correcting contrast, brightness, and color balance, as well as cropping, digitally sharpening, and setting the appropriate size and resolution for an image's ultimate use. Photographers have devised seemingly limitless ways to accomplish these tasks. Photoshop itself is so robust and multifaceted that you can attack each problem with a choice of solutions. Some approaches take more time. Others might degrade an image if not carried out properly. The choices can be dizzying.

This special section features one straight-forward method to handle the majority of your images in Photoshop. The method uses numbers to establish blacks and whites with details as well as to neutralize color casts. The "Curve" command recommended in this section is only one place where you can establish numerical tonal values, but working in Curves offers the most flexibility as you become more proficient in Photoshop. You also will learn a simple technique to select one part of a picture in order to darken or lighten it without obvious "burning" or "dodging" effects. Finally, you will learn to work in "Layers," a technique that will provide ultimate flexibility without permanently altering the original image.

Use the method shown in the following step-by-step procedure, and feel free to modify the steps as you become more comfortable with Photoshop. Keep in mind the ethical limitations placed on all photojournalistic pictures except photo illustrations. See Chapter 14, "Ethics."

With film-based photography, a few numbers were important: film ISO, shutter speed, and lens f/stops. The photographic vocabulary of digital photography requires a few more relevant numbers. In fact, a digital image is nothing but numbers, thousands of them, even for the smallest photograph. Those numbers, from bits to bytes to pixels and beyond, make up the foundation of the digital photograph.

As with traditional photography, the aim with digital technology is to produce the highest quality image possible for any of the lives a photograph may have—whether on the Web or in a newspaper or magazine. Manipulating the numbers that make up a digital image allows precise quality control—from tonal scale to color balance to sharpness. Whether you are scanning negatives or slides or importing files from a digital camera, preparing photographs by the numbers will almost always yield the best results.

Numbers are particularly useful for color adjustments. Color gamut, the range of colors you can see or that can be printed, varies drastically from digital cameras and scanners to computer monitors to the printing press. Without sophisticated color management equipment and software it can be difficult to know if what you see while editing will be what appears in print.

The adaptive nature of the human eye and our own expectations affect how we perceive color. Even your eyes can't be trusted. Someone standing in a room lit by fluorescent light looks fine to the eye, but an uncorrected photo will probably have a decided green cast.

Luckily, while equipment may mislead you, and your eyes may deceive you, numbers don't lie. Neutral tones—black, white, or any shade of gray—are not subjective. A neutral tone in a digital color image has equal amounts of Red, Green, and Blue (RGB). The three colors cancel out one another and produce neutrality, whether it's black,

white, or any shade of gray in between. Pure black (0) has no Red, Green, or Blue. A black with no colors prints as black with no detail. Pure white has the maximum tonal level of each color (255). At the maximum value of 255, the three colors cancel out one another to create a white that uses NO ink and thus has no detail. Middle Gray is 128 of each color—halfway between 0 and 255. Any other tone without a color cast has equal amounts of each primary color. As long as the three colors are in balance, an RGB tone is neutral, so the photograph will be cast-free.

Do note that there are some pictures where the color of the light itself may be important. You may not want to fully neutralize, for example, photos of situations where the flamboyant shades cast by a setting sun are important.

Set up a Workspace

Open the toolbox

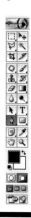

Open the layers palette

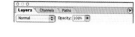

Open the info palette

Before adjustment/After adjustment

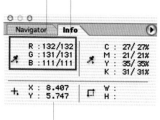

When the cursor or an eyedropper tool is positioned over a point in a photograph, the numbers that appear in the Info palette indicate the different color values on that exact point (notice the X-Y coordinates below the numbers outlined in red).

You can tell that the numbers here are for an unedited image because those to the left of the slash are the same as those on the right. After editing, the numbers on the right side will reflect their adjusted values.

Exact coordinates of where you have placed the eyedropper.

Black, White, and Neutral

1. Open Photoshop. Open any picture.

2. With the Toolbox open (Window>Tools), open the Toolbox Options Bar (Window>Options).

3. Highlight the Eyedropper Tool, select an eyedropper, and in the option bar at the top of the screen, define the sample size as 3x3 average (3 pixels x 3 pixels). 1x1 selects just one pixel. Selecting only one pixel may throw off the average.

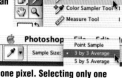

5. Open the Curves dialog box by choosing Image>Adjust>Curves.

6. Locate the three eyedroppers.

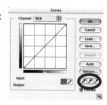

7. Click twice on the black eyedropper to open the Color Picker box (below). Look for the RGB settings (circled).

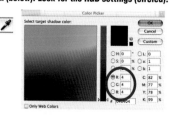

ALERT: The publication where you are working will have numbers that produce the best file for its press. Ask before you prepare images for reproduction.

8. Set the Red, Green, and Blue values at 4 to define the darkest black with some detail. (Zero in each color would produce a pure black with no detail at all.) Click OK.

9. Click twice on the white eyedropper to reopen the Color Picker box. Set Red, Green, and Blue values at 244 each for the brightest white with detail. (The number 255 in each color would produce a white without any ink at all, with no detail. This is sometimes called paper white because the paper shows without any dots of ink.) Click OK.

10. When prompted, allow these settings to become the new default. Quit Photoshop to save the settings.

ALERT: The middle eyedropper represents neutral gray. Clicking on a nearly neutral point in a photograph will bring the RGB settings into neutrality and help eliminate remaining color casts. Do not set any numbers here.

Curves Overview

The Curves command is the ideal tonal and color correction tool for photojournalists. Here, you can use eyedropper tools to quickly establish whites and blacks with detail. You also can precisely adjust as many as sixteen points on the Curve to change specific highlight or shadow areas, for example, or just the mid-tones. See the following two pages for how to change the curve. **ALERT:** Although the Curves command is available at Image>Adjust> Curves, go instead to Layers>New Adjustment Layer>Curves. See pages 388–391 for a full exploration of Layers.

The diagonal line in the Curves dialog box represents the potential tonal values of ANY image—from 0 (pure black) to 255 (paper white). Every "curve" starts as a straight line, regardless of what the image looks like! Black is at the bottom left, white is at the top right. The middle point, 128, is middle gray. Changes to the line become the curve.

Click and hold the mouse at a point on the line to pull the curve. To delete a point, select it, drag it off the curve, and release.

Black-point eyedropper

Neutral-point eyedropper, for color adjustments, not B/W. This tool establishes a neutral gray and removes color casts from areas in an image that should be neutral in tone.

White-point eyedropper

Preview button. Leave it checked to see changes as you make them. Unclick to compare your adjustments to your last unsaved version.

☐ **Preview**

Pure Black
0

Middle gray
128

Paper White
255

ALERT!
Clicking on the bar reverses the direction of the curve. Blacks become whites and whites become blacks!

ALERT: If the publication you work for requires you to prepare files in CYMK, you will receive specifications on how to best to prepare them for your press.
The basic concepts are the same. Equal numbers create neutrality.

SCANNING?

If you are scanning negatives or slides, always set the black and white points and use the neutral-point tool on a PREVIEW scan. This neutralizes extreme tones in a color photo and shifts all the others accordingly. This initial shift resolves most basic problems with color cast. An adjusted preview scan will produce a final file in which a bridal dress is white regardless of whether the bride was lit by fluorescent or tungsten bulbs or daylight.

Color Balance by the Numbers

With the Info palette available (Menu>Window>Info), open an Adjustment Layer Curve. At this stage, you will only use the eyedroppers.

First, set a clean white in the highlights and a good black with detail in the shadows. This will go a long way toward cleaning up color casts.

The neutral-point eyedropper is a powerful color correction tool. Make sure the Info palette is open. Identify a neutral area in the image. Without a gray card in your photo, pinpointing an area that "should" be neutral is always subjective. Because equal amounts of color neutralize one another, a point at which the color values are very near is probably an area that should be neutral.

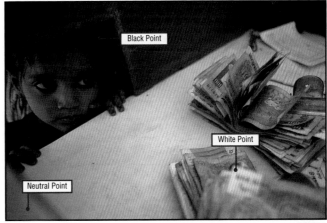

BEFORE

 Set the white point. With the info box open, move the white-point eyedropper over the image to find the brightest area in which you want detail. Clicking with the eyedropper creates a white with detail and no color cast.

 Set the black point. With the info box open, move the black-point eyedropper over the image to find the blackest area in which you want detail. Clicking with the eyedropper creates a black with detail and no color cast.

 Set the neutral point. With the info box open, move the neutral-point eyedropper over the image to find an area you know or expect to be neutral. A spot where the color values are near one another is a likely choice if you don't know for sure. Clicking with the eyedropper brings the color values into balance and thereby removes any color cast for the whole image.

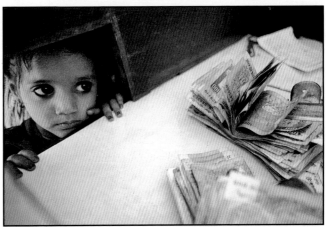

AFTER

How Curves Work

The Curve dialog box for every image opens with a diagonal line. Clicking on the midpoint of the line identifies 128 as middle gray. 0, at the bottom left, is pure black; 255, at the top right, is pure white. Pure white prints with no ink at all.

➕ Cursor is first a crosshair ✛ and becomes a grab tool once a point is selected.

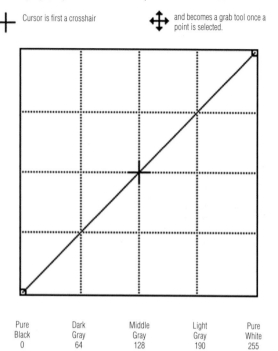

Pure Black 0	Dark Gray 64	Middle Gray 128	Light Gray 190	Pure White 255

The terms to the left are among those used to describe darkness and lightness values in an image.

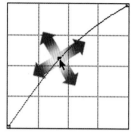

Click and hold the mouse at a point on the line to pull the curve.

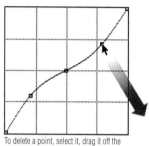

To delete a point, select it, drag it off the curve, and release.

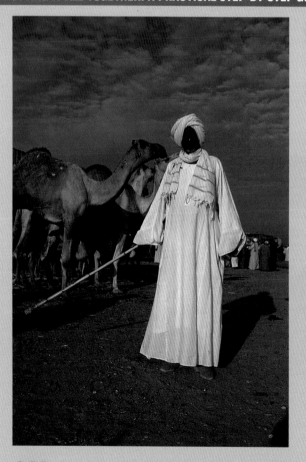

THE UNCORRECTED IMAGE.

1. **Make a New Adjustment Layer.**
Make an Adjustment Curve Layer (Layers>Make New Adjustment Layer>Curve). This is the layer on which to set the white point, black point, neutral point and make basic lighten or darken decisions.

2. **Name the layer.**

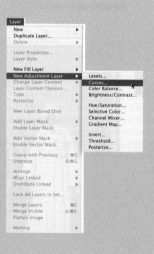

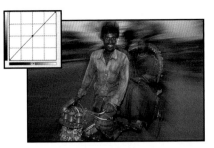

Original photo.

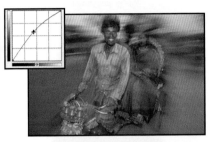

Click on the middle of the line and drag the curve up to lighten the image overall. See how all the points on the line except black and white have changed?

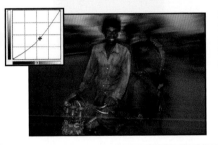

Moving the mid-point down darkens the image overall. Again, all the points on the line have changed, yet the black and white points remain intact.

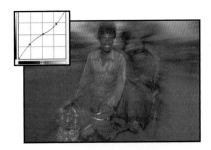

A downward pull in the highlights and an upward pull in the shadows flattens contrast. Here, the mid-point happens to be locked at middle gray, but it can be moved, too.

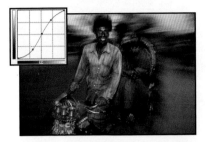

Pulling the shadows down and the highlights up increases contrast. Again, the mid-point happens to be locked here but does not have to be.

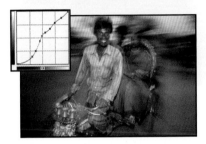

You can lock down many points on a curve to make fine adjustments between the points.

3. Select the white-point eyedropper.

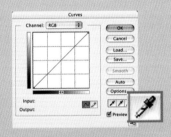

4. Click on the part of the image that should be the whitest with detail.

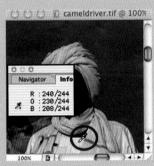

5. Select the black-point eyedropper.

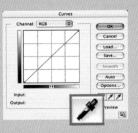

6. Click on the part of the image that should be the blackest with detail.

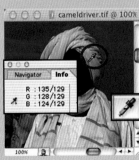

7. Select the middle, neutral-point eyedropper, and click on an area that should be neutral yet still has a color cast.

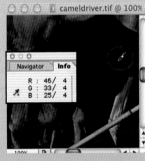

8. If the image is still too light or too dark, bend the curve accordingly. Dragging the curve downward lightens the entire image.

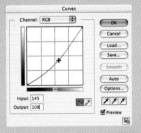

CLICK-DRAG LASSO TOOLS TO OUTLINE ITEMS AND DRAW SHAPES

FREEHAND. Once the regular Lasso has been clicked on a starting point, continue to hold it until you have returned to that point. The area inside will be selected. The Polygonal Lasso lets you click on multiple points before returning to the start. This provides more precision when outlining irregular shapes. The Magnetic Lasso snaps to the edges of an area being outlined. A Lasso set to feather edges at a minimum of 30 pixels creates an inconspicuous blend between the adjusted and unadjusted edges. For the purposes of "burning" and "dodging," which is essentially what is happening here, a loose selection with the regular lasso, set to feather at 30 pixels or more, will give excellent results even without the precision offered by the other lassos.

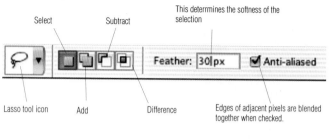

Select   Subtract   This determrines the softness of the selection

Feather: 30 px   ☑ Anti-aliased

Lasso tool icon   Add   Difference   Edges of adjacent pixels are blended together when checked.

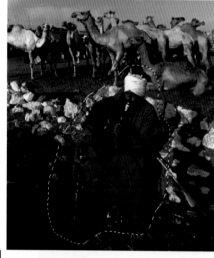

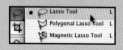

Use the Lasso tool to click-drag around the area that you want to select.

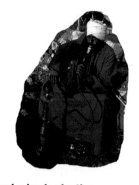

Hard-edged selection
This selection was made with Feather set to 0 pixels.

Feathered selection
A soft transtion is created by setting Feather to a minimum of 30 pixels.

PUTTING IT ALL TOGETHER: A PRACTICAL STEP-BY-STEP GUIDE (CONTINUED)

9. Lasso Tools.

To adjust part of an image, do the following.

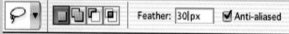

Feather: 30 px   ☑ Anti-aliased

Set the lasso to feather edges at 30 or more pixels to create an inconspicuous blend between the adjusted and unadjusted edges.

10. Select the face with the Lasso Tool.

With the background layer highlighted, use a selection tool to outline the part of the image to be adjusted.

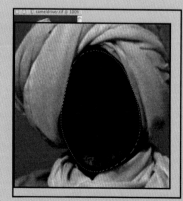

NOTE: It is possible to make tonal adjustments directly on a selection (for example, this face). However, doing so permanently alters the pixels in the file. If you find it necessary to make another change to the face later—to compensate for a different printing press, for example—you will be further altering the pixels. Working in layers protects the integrity of the original image and allows limitless changes as long as you always save the merged file with a new name.

11. Copy the selection.

Keyboard command Command-J (PC, use Control-J) copies the selection and creates a new layer for it simultaneously. This layer contains only the pixels selected from the background layer.

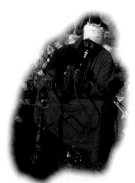

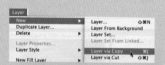

12. Apply a Curve adjustment to the new layer.

Create a new adjustment layer curve. Important: when the naming box appears, check "Group with Previous Layer" to confine the changes to the selected area below it.

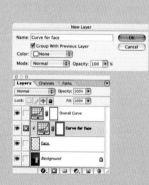

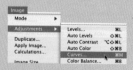

13. Raise or lower the curve to adjust just the selection on the linked layer. Here, lowering the curve lightens the face.

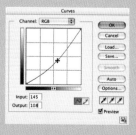

LAYERS (MENU>LAYERS) ARE THE ULTIMATE "OOPS" COMMAND.
The concept underlying all types of layers is the same. Layers protect the original photograph and its pixels during editing and compositing tasks. This results in ultimate flexibility for working with the image today and into the future.

What is a layer? Think of it as a glass plate that sits on top of your photograph. The glass plate is where you darken, lighten, or otherwise edit the image without ever actually touching it. Because the glass is clear, you can see the effects of the changes, but the original photo (A) remains unaltered. It is possible to have many pieces of glass stacked above a photograph, each with different effects. The cumulative changes are applied from the top plate to the bottom, with each plate changeable and interchangeable.

Here, for example, the first adjustments on the top layer (B), Overall, apply to everything below that layer.

You also can copy part of the original photo onto a different glass plate (C). Here, the pipe-smoking man was too dark after the overall adjustment that made the rest of the image just right. He was selected with a lasso tool feathered at 30 pixels, copied from the original layer (A) and pasted onto a new, separate layer (C). Another adjustment layer (D) was added and linked to (C) the man. [Note: Layers (C) and (D) are linked to restrict the adjustments only to the man. These changes don't penetrate to the rest of the image or to any other layers that might come later.]

Regardless of how many plates are in use, you can save the file with all its layers and corrections preserved, and return later if you change your mind. You can eliminate a plate and its changes altogether or return to a plate to fine-tune the corrections made there.

Adjustment Layers (Menu>Layers>Adjustment Layers) are ideal for making even basic changes to photographs. Because each correction is performed and saved on a separate layer, you can easily try out different approaches and then compare results by clicking on

or off the eyeball to the left of each layer.

Most experienced photographers work in layers when applying Curves or other adjustment commands.

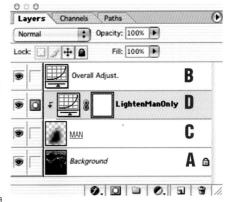

Photo illustrators have long used Layers for complex image combinations like many in Chapter 9, "Illustration." To make composites, you can open a completely new picture, adjust its size to equal the one currently open, and, using the Move tool, simply slide the new photo into the current file. Photoshop automatically creates a layer for the second photo. This new layer can be manipulated and eventually merged with the others in the file. (See pages 174–181 for examples of illustrations composited in Photoshop.)

Once you are satisfied, flatten the layers into a single image (Menu>Layers>Flatten Image OR access the command from the Layers Palette). At this point, all the changes are applied and cannot be undone. **ALERT:** Before merging, give the file a new name so you don't mistakenly save over the layered file, which would prevent returning later to alter the layers for other purposes.

---

14. **Select the sky with the Lasso tool.**
With the background layer highlighted, use a selection tool to outline the part of the image to be adjusted. For this picture, the sky was still flat.

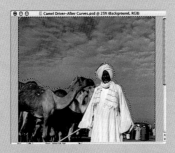

15. **Copy the selection.**
Keyboard command Command-J (PC, use Control-J) copies the selection and creates a new layer for it simultaneously. This layer contains only the pixels selected from the background layer.

16. **Apply a Curve adjustment layer to the new layer.**
Create a new adjustment layer curve. Don't forget: when the naming box appears, check "Group with Previous Layer" to confine the changes to the selected area below it.

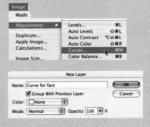

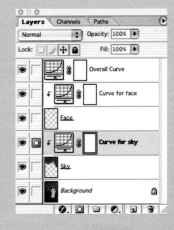

17. **With the curve for sky layer selected, adjust the curve as necessary.**

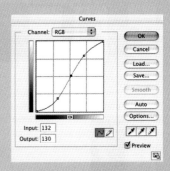

LAYERS: THE POWER TOOL

Blend mode: "Normal" Is the default. Leave here initially; explore other effects later.

Preserve transparency & lock pixels. Use this default while learning.

The eye is an icon indicating that changes made on that layer are visible on the monitor. Click the eye off to see how the photo looks without the changes applied. Here, the cumulative effects are visible.

The arrow pointing down indicates that adjustments on this layer apply only to the layer directly beneath it, here the pixels that make up the man smoking his pipe.

A symbol appears in these boxes when the layer is active. A paintbrush indicates that a layer contains pixels and that changes impact those pixels.

Just pixels selected and copied from the Background Layer are visible. Adjustments to a layer like this affect these specific pixels. It is not possible to make changes to other areas in the photo from this layer.

Shortcuts to choices also available under the Menu>Layers Command.

An icon, here a curve, identifies the type of adjustment layer.

The white box is the "glass plate" (in reality a mask) where the adjustment to the left is being applied. The icon is white —or blank—because it contains no pixels.

The opacity of each layer can be controlled. When working with more than one image, decreasing the opacity of the active layer makes the layer below it visible. For basic adjustments, leave at 100%.

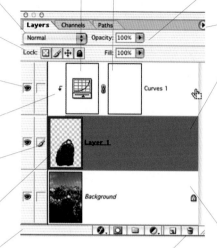

Shortcuts to choices available under the Menu>Layers Command.

A highlighted layer is the ONLY active layer. Only one layer can be active at a time.

ALERT: Except when the Background layer is invisible (eye off), you will always see the entire image along with changes made on other visible layers (eye on). If it seems no changes are occurring where you are altering the picture, you have not highlighted the layer where you want to make changes.

For example, it is impossible to adjust anything else in this photo except what is on the active layer —here, the man and his pipe. What you would see on the monitor is the entire image with the changes being applied to the selection

Confusion might arise if you decide to select, copy, and adjust the sky, for example, while on the active layer holding just the man. No sky pixels are on the active layer. Those pixels are on the original Background Layer.

"Background" is the layer with the original image and where all its pixels reside. You should never change this layer.

Because the Background layer is where the pixels are, it must be active (highlighted) when copying the photo or selecting and copying part of it onto another layer. For example, the Background layer above was highlighted when the lasso tool selected the man in order to copy and paste him onto a new layer.

Deletes the active (highlighted) layer.

ALERT: Deleting a layer eliminates only the changes made on it. The original (background) image and all the changes on other layers remain untouched.

PUTTING IT ALL TOGETHER: A PRACTICAL STEP-BY-STEP GUIDE (CONTINUED)

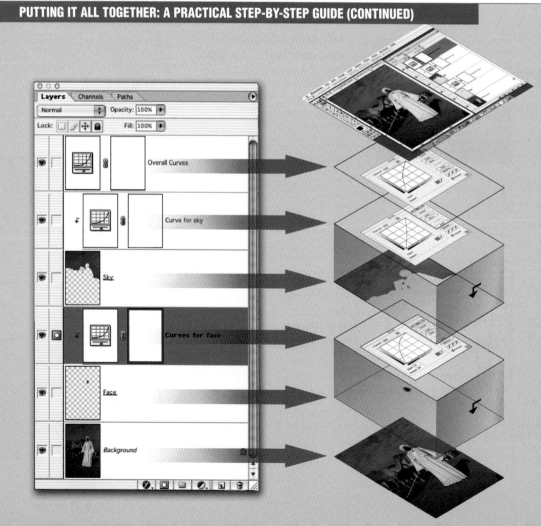

What You See on the Screen
A composite image showing the cumulative adjustments is visible in the Photoshop window, along with the Photoshop tools and palettes on your desktop.

What is Actually Happening
Steps 1–8. An Adjustment Layer/Curve was applied to the image. It affects overall contrast and lightness. Even with a good overall exposure, parts of an image may need lightening or darkening.

Steps 14–17. For example, the sky remained too flat, so it was selected with the Lasso tool and copied to a new layer.

An Adjustment Curve applied only to the sky brightened it while leaving the rest of the image intact.

Steps 9–13. Just the man's face was selected with the Lasso tool and copied to a new layer. An Adjustment Curve restricted to the layer with the face left the rest of the image intact.

The original image remains the same until the layers are compressed. The compression (see opposite) will apply all the changes at the same time.

SHARPENING AN IMAGE

Don't be confused by the name. Unsharp Mask sharpens a digital image. By emphasizing the edges between different tones, the mask corrects softening of detail that occurs in images captured by digital cameras as well as scanned or resampled images (pages 394–395). You may need to experiment with the settings to determine the best results for your images. Remember, sharpening cannot correct a technically blurry or out-of-focus photo.

Choose Filter>Sharpen>Unsharp Mask.

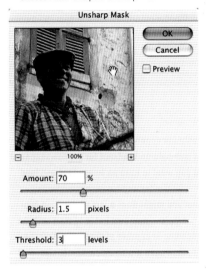

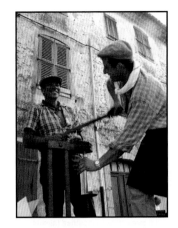

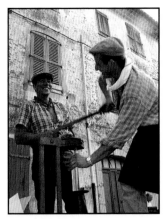

Before sharpening   **After sharpening**

Photographers have different preferences for sharpening. You are likely to hear a different "recipe" from every other professional you meet. Also, different images will require different amounts of sharpening. To start, try setting the amount to 70 percent. Use the radius and threshold figures here. One to 1.5 pixels usually works. A threshold of 0 affects all pixels; a higher threshold minimizes noise because it affects only those edges with a high tonal difference. Compare effects by placing the hand pointer on the preview image and then releasing it. Some photographers apply Unsharp Mask more than once in smaller percentages.

18. Finished? Save the file with a new name, flatten the image to a single layer. Save it in the appropriate format (page 395).

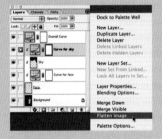

19. Use the Unsharp Mask filter to sharpen the flattened file.

Note that is possible to select certain areas, paste them into a layer, and sharpen them there. For example, you might want to sharpen everything BUT the sky. You will want to experiment for the best results with your images.

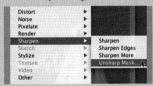

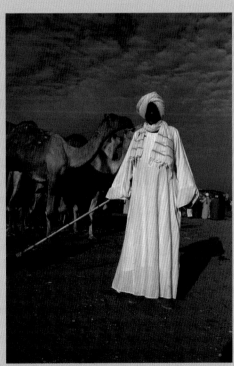

Original Image

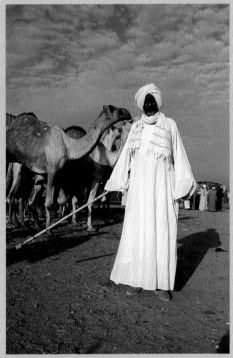

Image after Adjustments

Whether you plan to work on a photograph taken with a digital camera or on a traditional print or negative scanned into digital form, you will find it valuable to think about the size of your final image before you ever begin. Understanding the impact of file size and resolution on your final image is crucial when technical quality is important.

Think of a digital image file as a set of virtual tiles with all the colors necessary to create a realistic scene in a mosaic. The more tiles in the mosaic, the more detail in the scene. Each pixel in a file is one tile in the mosaic. The total number of tiles is the image file size.

Image size (the physical size of a photograph, or the document size in Photoshop's dialog box, right) is like the surface where the mosaic is being installed—a 3'x5' bathroom, for example.

Resolution is the number of tiles per foot you have to work with in your bathroom—the number of pixels per inch in a photo. You can see the problem if there are enough tiles to create a image on a 3'x5' bathroom floor, but you decide to install the same image in an 8'x10' kitchen instead. When you spread the same number of tiles meant for a small bathroom over a large area like the kitchen floor, the image will break up.

You can actually view the interrelationships among image size, file size and resolution using Photoshop's Image Size command. In Photoshop, open File>Image Size to see the dialog box to the right.

Do not check "Resample." Observe what happens as you change the dimensions in "Document Size" (final print size) box. Notice that the resolution changes. Now vary the number in the "Resolution" box. The document size changes. The file size (the number of tiles) never changes. Resolution and image size work in tandem. Changing the picture size changes the resolution; changing the resolution changes the picture size.

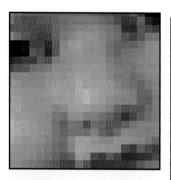

Until they are viewed on a monitor or as a print, pixels are just a set of ones and zeros indicating color, position, and brightness. When magnified (above) each can be seen as a tiny square.

The Image Size command can't add new tiles, but it can "stretch" them to cover the kitchen floor. The larger the floor, the more coarse the image will appear as the tiles grow larger. The command can also shrink the tiles should you prefer a mosaic for a small panel on the wall instead of a large one on the bathroom floor. The total number of tiles remains constant.

Now, check Resample. It appears possible to change the number of tiles along with the resolution and image size! This isn't the same as going out and buying the correct number, color, and size of tiles necessary for the mosaic to be as pleasing to view in the kitchen as it would have been in the bathroom. Resampling, also called interpolation, evaluates existing tiles and makes duplicates next to them of approximately the same color, brightness, etc. The detail possible with the correct number of original tiles is missing, but a fair rendition is possible. To create a little wall panel instead of a bathroom floor, for example, the software discards unnecessary tiles for a reduced version that keeps its detail.

To open the Image Size dialog box in Photoshop, first open an image file (File>Open). Then open the dialog box (Image>Image Size).

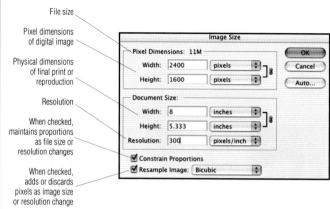

Decisions about file size and resolution depend on the intended use for the photograph. Are you preparing a one-column headshot for the newspaper or an 8.5"x11" magazine cover? Do you want to have an image that will load quickly on a website?

If there is ever a possibility that you might want a large image—a two-page spread in a magazine, for example—your best bet is to start with the largest file size your camera or scanner is capable of producing. Edit the largest size possible, save it, and then save it with a new name, size, and resolution as appropriate for the Web, a newspaper, or magazine. (In other words, buy enough tile now because you won't be able to buy more later!)

INTENDED USE	RESOLUTION
Internet	72 dpi
Newspaper	150–200 dpi
Photographic-quality print	
Inkjet or dye-sublimation printer	200 dpi
Glossy magazine, book	300 dpi

Resampling discards or adds pixels to decrease or increase file size and resolution. Discarding pixels isn't a problem. Adding them results in less-than-ideal quality. Recapturing them is impossible.

Why throw away pixels? A small file for viewing on the Web does not require all the tiles necessary for the kitchen floor—or for a magazine cover. The software analyzes the pixels and discards unnecessary ones. The file will upload faster but still have enough resolution (tiles per square foot) for a good image on a monitor. A smaller file size is almost always best for transmitting images or viewing them online.

What about going larger? To add pixels when a file is too small—or to create tiles for a larger floor—the software analyzes the color and brightness of each pixel and tries to create similar new ones to surround it. Like making do with tiles of approximate color and brightness, resampling to make a picture that ran two columns in a newspaper for a glorious new life as magazine cover can smooth out the differences but cannot supply missing detail (see opposite page).

ALERT: Photoshop and software like Genuine Fractals® resample digital files with increasingly good results. However, for the best technical quality, it's better to shoot large files or to rescan a photo or negative to the correct size and resolution than to resample. Knowing the maximum final size and use for your digital image will protect against disappointment later.

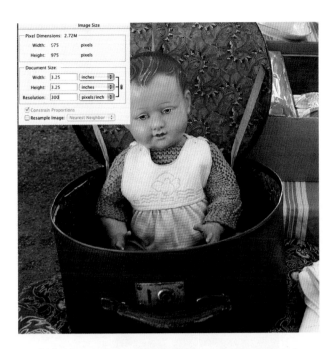

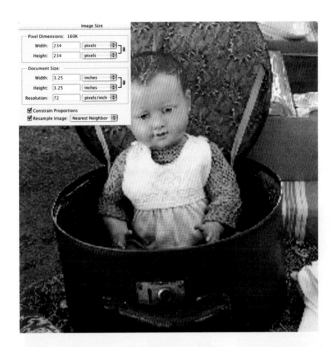

IMAGE #1, above, was digitized at 300 ppi at 3.25 inches by 3.25 inches. A resolution of 300 ppi is ideal for book and magazine reproduction and for subtly detailed inkjet and dye-sublimation prints. Compare this quality to that of the resampled image below, #3. Note that the image above would look good on a website, but it would take a long time to download on the viewer's screen because of its large file size.

IMAGE #2 would look as fine on a computer monitor as #1, left! A monitor cannot display more than 72 pixels per inch—regardless of how much resolution an image has. This image's small file size allows it to transmit easily over the Internet and load quickly on a website. But its quality as a printed image is poor. It also would print poorly on an inkjet or dye-sublimation printer.

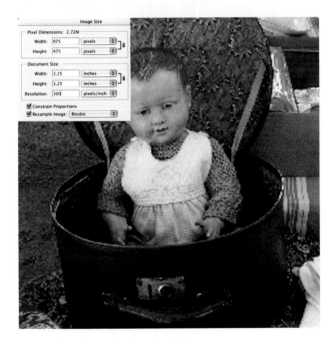

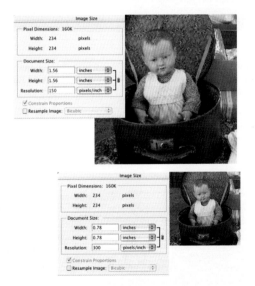

IMAGE #3, directly above, began life as the 72 ppi Image #2 (above, right), but has been artificially pumped up (resampled) to the same resolution and file size as #1. It's smoother-looking than #2, but can't compare to #1.

Three sizes and resolutions from the same file.

Note that the number of pixels in each of these images is the same, but that the resolution increases as the physical size of the images diminishes. The quality of each image also improves as its physical size decreases. Why? Because the same number of pixels has less surface to cover, more detail becomes visible in the image as it grows smaller.

ALERT: The quality of these images would have appeared identical when viewed at 100 percent on a computer monitor.

You can crop any digital image, whether it was scanned or imported from a digital camera.

 The Cropping Tool is available whenever Photoshop is open, so you can always crop later. These and the examples on upcoming pages assume you are working on an image that is open in Photoshop.

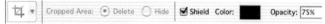

Setting the Tool Option Bar to display a semi-opaque screen (Opacity 75%) will darken the part of the image that is being deleted, as below.

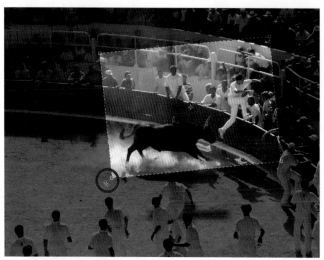

Select the Crop tool.

Click at one corner of the picture, and then drag the tool diagonally across the image until you have selected the area you want. Releasing the tool outlines the selection.

Prepare the angle change. With the Crop tool still highlighted, move the cursor slightly away from the edge of the photo until a bent arrow (circled above) appears. This tool lets you change the angle of the cropped area to match that of the scan.

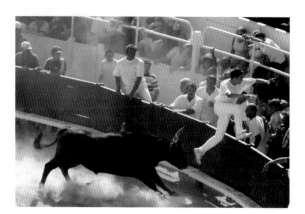

Saving images for Web display is another exercise in trade-offs among resolution, file size, and quality. Typically, you need to keep file sizes small (no more than 30 kilobytes per picture). The larger the file, the longer it takes to appear on a Web site, and viewers may not be willing to wait several minutes for a photograph to download.

Photoshop (File>Save for Web) allows you to preview quality and resolution choices before making a final decision.

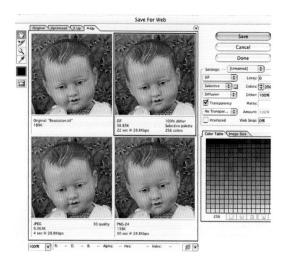

Take advantage of Photoshop's File Info to include your name and caption information for each picture. Some archiving software calls on information you enter here. So do some image browsers and Web browsers. A little up-front preparation can save lots more work later.

Shooting session strategy: download the images into a folder, then open one photo, enter the general data, enter the session name in "job name." Save, then move through the other menus and save. For every subsequent photo from that session, you can load the saved information and, if necessary, add or edit caption information individually. **ALERT:** Learn about Batch Actions in Photoshop and how to fully automate this process. (Set it in motion and then go do the laundry.)

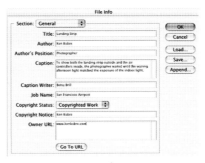

General: Lets you enter the caption, your name and copyright information, etc. To display a copyright symbol in the title bar of the image window, choose Copyrighted Work in the Copyright Status menu.

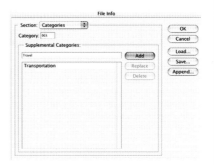

Categories: Defaults are 3-digit Associated Press codes.

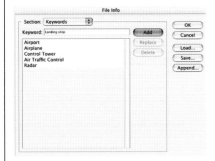

Keywords: Provide a way for some image browsers and archiving software to categorize and search for an image.

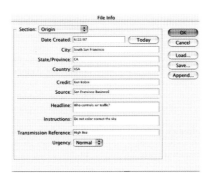

Origin: Enter date taken, location, etc.

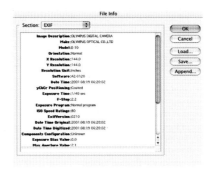

EXIF: Displays information imported from a digital camera, such as the date and time a picture was taken, resolution, ISO rating, f/stop, compression, and exposure time. For more about EXIF annotations, see the manual for your digital camera.

When you save a file from a digital camera or scanner, or after working on it in Photoshop, you can save it in a variety of formats. Some options are more versatile, allowing the image to be used in different applications or across computer platforms, in print or on the Web. Some will work only with the program in which they were created. Following are common options for photographers.

JPEG (.jpg)	compresses photos by discarding those pixels the software determines to be redundant. JPEG was designed for compressing full-color or grayscale images like photographs. A 24-bit image saved as a JPEG file can be reduced to about one-twentieth its original size. JPEGs, with their smaller file sizes and faster transmission time, are the preferred means of displaying continuous-tone photos on the Internet. Digital cameras offer this format as a file option. It's possible to save JPEGs at various quality levels. See pages 393–394 to compare the quality and size trade-offs when making this choice.
	ALERT: Opening and closing a JPEG image without manipulating it will not change its quality but multiple changes to and resaves of a JPEG file will degrade its look. After you have opened an image from a digital camera and changed it, save it as a TIFF file (see below). With TIFF, you can open, change, and close a picture without losing quality. You can always save the picture later in JPEG if you need to save space or transmit the image on the Internet.
GIF (.gif)	produces small Web files and is best for flat-color images with type or line drawings, not the for photos.
TIFF (.tif)	is a common format for bringing an image into a page-layout program and for exchanging files between computer platforms. Almost all desktop scanners can produce TIFF images.
EPS (.eps)	is also commonly used for bringing images into page-layout programs but is less flexible between PCs and Macintosh.

PNG (.png)	is a format used for Web-based photos. It is a lossless compression format, can interlace images, is displayable in browser windows and uses up to 256 colors. PNG might replace .gif format Web display, but not all browsers can use the new format.
PICT (.pct)	is useful when images are designed for presentations, screen displays, and video work.
PSD (.psd)	can only be opened and edited in Photoshop. However, you can still re-save the file in a variety of other formats that are readable on both Macintosh and PCs without affecting image quality.
	ALERT: A layered photo saved as a PSD file is a truly multi-purpose file because you can activate or deactivate the layers for different uses. Saving in most other formats means having to permanently combine the layers.
	For example, you might want to include your copyright information on a text layer for an image to be displayed on the Internet, but then deactivate the text layer to make a file for a magazine. For the Internet file, you would compress the necessary layers, save the file as a JPEG, and send the picture on its way. For the magazine, you could deactivate the text layer, compress the layers, save the file as a TIFF, and send it to the art director. There would be no need in either case to keep copies of the JPEG or the TIFF file because all your work remains stored in layers and preserved in the PSD format.

In addition to listings from previous editions of *Photojournalism: The Professionals' Approach*, this bibliography includes articles and books derived from searches of a number of different electronic databases.

A

"A Public Suicide: Papers Differ on Editing Graphic Images." Associated Press Managing Editors (APME) *Report: Photo and Graphics*. New York, 1987.

"A Question of Ethics." *News Photographer* (July 1983). (multiple-article anthology).

"Eyewitness. A Century of Great Photojournalism." *Life* 22, no. 11 (Oct. 2001): 16.

"Future Stock: Predictions on the Fate of Photojournalism." *American Photo* (Sept./Oct. 1996): 78–80.

"Life's Work: The Photojournalism of Earl Dotter." *Columbia Journalism Review* 35, no. 5 (1997): 40.

"News Views: Edward Farber, Portable Strobe Inventor, Dead." *News Photographer* (Apr. 1982): 3.

"News Views: Milwaukee Sentinel Photographer Helps Firemen in Rescue." *News Photographer* (Mar. 1988): 4.

"Photo Essays." *Nieman Reports* 52(2) (Summer 1998): 8–27.

"Photojournalism—Journalists Learn How to Protect Themselves in War a Panel of Instructors." *Nieman Reports* 54, no. 3 (2000): 59.

"Photojournalism. A Touching Moment from the Heart of the Jungle." *American Photo* 11, no. 6 (Nov. 2001): 82.

"Photojournalism." *Nieman Reports* 54, no. 3 (2000): 45.

"Suicide." (multiple-article anthology). *News Photographer* (May 1987): 20–32, 34–43, 62.

"The Golden Age of the Picture Magazine." *Photographic Journal* 126 (Mar. 1986): 104–8.

"The Process of Recording Conflict" *Aperture* 97 (Winter 1984): 6–77. (five-article anthology).

"To Publish? Pro and Con." *News Photographer* (May 1993): 12–17.

"U.S. Supreme Court to Review Two 'Ride-Along' Cases." *News Photographer* (Dec. 1998): 32.

"Why Do They React? Readers Assail Publication of Funeral, Accident Photos." *News Photographer* (Mar. 1981): 20, 22–23.

"Women in Photojournalism." *News Photographer* (Dec. 1984): 16–17; (Feb. 1985): 25–29; (Apr. 1985): 22, 24.

20 Years with AP Wirephoto. New York: Associated Press, 1955.

Abramson, Howard S. *National Geographic*: Behind America's Lens on the World. New York: Crown Publishers, 1987.

Adams, Jonathan. " . . . They Should Have Published It." *4Sight* (Nov./Dec. 1993): 17.

Adams, R. C., Copeland, Gary A., Fish, Marjorie J., and Hughes, Melissa. "Effect of Framing on Selection of Photographs of Men and Women." *Journalism Quarterly* 57 (1980): 463–67.

Agence France-Presse. *Facing the World: Great Moments in Photojournalism*. New York: Harry N. Abrams, 2001.

Alabiso, Vincent J. "Prospects for Photojournalism at a Time When Readers Are Bombarded by Information," *Media Studies Journal* 13, no. 2 (Spring 1999): 58.

Alabiso, Vincent, Tunney, Kelly Smith and Zoeller, Chuck, eds. *Flash! The Associated Press Covers the World*. New York: Associated Press in association with Harry N. Abrams, 1998.

Alabiso, Vincent. "Changing with the Times." *Nieman Reports* 52 (Summer 1998): 5–7.

Alexander, S. L. "Curious History: The ABA Code of Judicial Ethics Canon 35." Paper presented at the Annual Meeting of the Association for Education in Journalism and Mass Communication, Portland, Oregon, 1988. ERIC, ED296422.

Alland, Alexander. *Jacob A. Riis*. Millerton, New York: *Aperture*, 1974.

American Photo. May/June 1994. Special issue on the future of photojournalism.

Ang, Tom. *Picture Editing: An Introduction*. Oxford, Boston: Focal Press, 1996.

Anonymous. "Ethics committee criticizes Pearl photos publications." *Quill* 90, no. 7: S2.

The Art of Seeing: The Best of Reuters Photography. Ulli, Michel, editor. London, New York: Pearson Education, 2000.

Artusa, Marina. "Did You Run This Photo?" *Columbia Journalism Review* 41, no. 2 (July/Aug. 2002): 47–Back Cover.

ASMP: 1944–1994 50th Anniversary Bulletin 13 (Dec. 1994). Princeton: The American Society of Media Photographers, 1994.

Associated Press News and Photo Staff, eds. *One Day in Our World*. New York: Avon Books, 1986.

Auer, Michel. *The Illustrated History of the Camera: From 1839 to the Present*. Translated & adapted by D.B. Tubbs. Boston: New York Graphic Society, 1975.

B

Baker, Robert L. "Portraits of a Public Suicide: Photo Treatment by Selected Pennsylvania Dailies." *Newspaper Research Journal* 9 (Summer 1988): 13–23.

Barney, Ralph D., and Black, Jay. "Toward Professional Ethical Journalism." *Mass Communications Review* 17 (1/2) (1990): 2–13.

Barnhurst, Kevin G. *Seeing the Newspaper. New York*: St. Martin's Press, 1994.

Barnhurst, Kevin, and John Nerone. "Civic Picturing Vs. Realist Photojournalism. The Regime of Illustrated News, 1856–1901." *Design Issues* 16, no 1 (2000): 59–79.

Barrett, Wayne M. "Margaret Bourke-White: New Vistas in Photojournalism." *USA Today* 118 (Sept. 1989): 55–63.

Barry, Ann Marie. "Digital Manipulation of Public Images: Local Issues and Global Consequences." Paper presented at the Annual Meeting of the International Communication Association. Montreal, May 1997.

Baxter, William S., Quarles, Rebecca, and Kosak, Herman. "The Effects of Photographs and Their Size on Reading and Recall of News Stories." Paper presented at the Annual Meeting of the Association for Education in Journalism. Seattle, Washington, 1978. ERIC, ED159722.

Baynes, Ken. *Scoop, Scandal and Strife*. New York: Hastings House, 1971.

Benson, Harry. Harry Benson: *Fifty Years in Pictures*. New York: Harry N. Abrams, 2001.

Benson, Harry. *Harry Benson on Photojournalism*. New York: Harmony Books, 1982.

Bentley, P.F. "It's All in the Eyes." *Columbia Journalism Review* (May/June 1996): 45–47.

Bergeman, Rich. "Photo Editing: A Neglected Art." *Community College Journalist* 15 (Winter 1987): 18–20.

Bergin, David P. *Photojournalism Manual: How to Plan, Shoot, Edit and Sell*. New York: Morgan & Morgan, 1967.

Bernt, Joseph P. and Greenwald, Marilyn S. "Senior Newspaper Editors and Daily Newspaper Coverage of the Gay and Lesbian Community: A Summary of Past Findings and Discussion of New Findings on Reporting Sexual Orientation." Paper presented at the National Conference of Lesbians and Gays in Mainstream Media. San Francisco, California, June 25–27, 1992. ERIC, ED347599.

Bessie, Simon Michael. *Jazz Journalism: The Story of the Tabloid Newspapers*. New York: E.P. Dutton, 1938.

Best of Photojournalism. Annual, 1977–present. Publisher varies.

Bethune, Beverly, ed. *Women in Photojournalism*. Durham, NC: National Press Photographers Association, 1986.

Bethune, Beverly. "Under the Microscope: A Nationwide Survey Looks at the Professional Concerns and Job Satisfaction of the Daily Newspaper Photographer." *News Photographer* (Nov. 1983): R1–R8.

Bezner, Lili Corbus, and F. Jack Hurley. "Photography and Politics in America: From the New Deal into the Cold War." *Journal of American History* 87, no. 4 (2000): 1546–1547.

Bissland, James H. "The News Photographer's Career Ladder." An NPPA Special Report (also appears in the Oct. 1984 issue of *News Photographer*).

Bissland, James H. and Kielmeyer, David. "Bypassed by the Revolution? Photojournalism in a Decade of Change." Paper presented at the Annual Meeting of the Association for Education in Journalism and Mass Communication. Montreal, Aug. 5–8, 1992. ERIC, ED349623.

Blackman, Victor. *Naff off! Confessions of a Fleet Street Photographer*. London: BFP, 1987.

Blackwood, Roy E. "International News Photos in U.S. and Canadian Papers." *Journalism Quarterly* 64 (1987): 195–99.

Blackwood, Roy E. "The Content of News Photos: Roles Portrayed by Men and Women." *Journalism Quarterly* 60 (1983): 710–14.

Borden, Sandra L. "Choice Processes in a Newspaper Ethics Case." *Communication Monographs* 64, no. 1 (Mar 1997): 65–81.

Bourke-White, Margaret, and Sean Callahan. *Margaret Bourke-White: Photographer*. 1st ed. Boston: Little Brown, 1998.

Bourke-White, Margaret. *Portrait of Myself*. New York: Simon & Schuster, 1963.

Bowden, Charles, and Eugene Richards. *Eugene Richards*. London; New York: Phaidon, 2001.

Bowden, Robert. *Get That Picture*. Garden City, New York: Amphoto, 1978.

Bowers, Matthew. "Following the Yellow Brick Road or how this newspaper in Norfolk won the McDougall." *News Photographer* (May 1997): 14–20.

Bowie, Jennifer. "Out of Their Hands: Framing and its Impact on Newsmagazine Coverage of Indians and Indian Activism, 1968–79." Paper presented at the Proceedings of the Annual Meeting of the Association for Education in Journalism and Mass Communication, New Orleans, Louisiana, Aug. 3–8, 1999 1999.

Boylan, James. "Underexposed." *Columbia Journalism Review* 38, no. 6: 71.

Brauchli, Marcus. "Prize Under Glass . . . Chance, Ingenuity, Violence Often Cited as Key Factors in Pulitzer Winners." *News Photographer* (June–July 1981): 20–23.

Brecheen-Kirkton, Kent. "Visual Silences: What Photography Chooses Not to Show Us." *American Journalism* 8 (Winter 1991): 27–34.

Brecher, Ellie. "Reporter-Photographer Relationships and How to Improve Them." *4Sight* (Nov./Dec. 1993): 12–13.

Brennen, Bonnie, and Hanno Hardt. *Picturing the Past: Media, History, and Photography, The History of Communication*. Urbana: University of Illinois Press, 1999.

Brennen, Bonnie. "Strategic Competition and the Value of Photographers' Work: Photojournalism in Gannett Newspapers, 1937–1947." *American Journalism* 15, no. 2 (1998): 59–77.

Brill, Betsy. "Pictures Don't Lie . . . or Do They?" Master's thesis, University of Missouri, 1988.

Brill, Betsy. "Town Protests Staged Photo, Hooker Image." *News Photographer* (Sept. 1986): 4–8.

Brill, Charles. "The Early History of the Associated Press Wire Photo: 1926–1935." Paper presented at the Annual Meeting of the Association for Education in Journalism. Madison, Wisconsin, 1977.

Brink, Ben. "Question of Ethics: Where Does Honesty in Photojournalism Begin? 'The Foundation Is Basic, Simple Honesty,' an Editor Says." *News Photographer* (June 1988): 21–22, 23–33.

Brock, Oliver Eugene. "Digital Imaging in Photojournalism: Technological and Ethical Impact." Master's thesis, University of Mississippi, 1993.

Brower, Kenneth. "Photography in the Age of Falsification." *Atlantic Monthly* (May 1998): 92–111.

Brown, Cindy M. "How the Use of Color Affects the Content of Newspaper Photographs." Paper presented at the Annual Meeting of the Association for Education in Journalism and Mass Communication, Washington, DC, 1989. ERIC, ED308525.

Brown, Cindy M. "Listening to Subjects' Concerns about News Photographs: A Grounded Ethical Inquiry." Ph.D. diss., Indiana University, 1998.

Brown, Cindy M. "PM: Just Another Picture Paper?" Paper presented at the Annual Meeting of the Association for Education in Journalism and Mass Communication, Visual Communication Division, Aug. 12, 1994.

Brown, Cindy M. "The Use of Search Warrants in Canada and the United States to Obtain Photographic Evidence from Journalists." Paper presented at the Annual Meeting of the Association for Education in Journalism and Mass Communication. Kansas City, Missouri, Aug. 11–14, 1993. ERIC, ED362918.

Brown, Jennifer E. "*News Photographer* and the Pornography of Grief." *Journal of Mass Media Ethics* 2 (Spring/Summer 1987): 75–81.

Brown, Theodore M. Margaret Bourke-White, Photojournalist. Ithaca, New York: Andrew Dickson White Museum of Art, Cornell University, 1972.

Brumbaugh, L. P. "Shadow catchers or shadow snatchers? Ethical issues for photographers of contemporary Native Americans." *American Indian Culture and Research Journal* 20, no. 3 (1996): 33–49.

Brust, James S. "Photojournalism, 1877: John H. Fouch, Fort Keogh's First Post Photographer." *Montana* 50, no. 4 (2000): 32–39.

Bryant, Michael. "The Problem with Illustrations." *News Photographer* (July 1987): 36.

Buckland, Gail. *Shots in the Dark: True Crime Pictures*. Boston, Mass. London: Bulfinch, 2001.

Buell, Hal, and Pett, Saul. *The Instant It Happened*. New York: Associated Press, 1975.

C

Callahan, Sean, and Astor, Gerald. *Photographing Sports: John Zimmerman, Mark Kauffman and Neil Leifer*. Los Angeles: Alskog, 1975.

Callahan, Sean, ed. *The Photographs of Margaret Bourke-White*. Boston: New York Graphic Society, 1972.

Callahan, Sean. "The Last Days of a Legend (Margaret Bourke-White)." *American Photo* 9 (Sept./Oct. 1998): 33–4, 95, 97.

Campbell, Gregory D. "A Study of Photo Editing Duties at the Small American Daily Newspaper 1994." Master's thesis, Memphis State University, 1994.

Campbell, W. Joseph. "Not likely sent: The Remington-Hearst 'telegrams.'" Paper presented at the Annual Meeting of the Association for Education in Journalism and Mass Communication. New Orleans, Louisiana, Aug. 4–7, 1999.

Cannon, Brian Douglas. "Photographs as Icons: Toward a Theory of Iconicity of Still Images in Photojournalism." *DAI* 61, no. 12A (2001): 345.

Cannon, Brian. "Discourse on Philosophical Methods for Determining Ethics in Photojournalism: Analysis of a Pulitzer Prize Winning Photograph." Paper presented to the Association for Education in Journalism and Mass Communication, Washington, DC, Aug., 1995.

Cannon, Brian. "Icon of the Oklahoma City Bombing: Revealing Connotative Meaning in a News Photograph of Tragedy and Heroism." Paper presented at the Annual Meeting of the Association for Education in Journalism and Mass Communication, Visual Communication Division, Anaheim, California, Aug.,1996.

Capa, Cornell. *The Concerned Photographer*. New York: Grossman Publishers, 1968.

Capa, Robert, and Richard Whelan. *Robert Capa: The Definitive Collection*. London: Phaidon, 2001.

Capa, Robert. *Robert Capa, Photographs*. New York: *Aperture*, 1996.

Capa, Robert. Slightly Out of Focus. New York: Modern Library, 1999.

Capture the Moment: the Pulitzer Prize Photographs. Cyma Rubin and Eric Newton, editors. New York: Norton, 2001.

Caputo, Philip. "Photojournalism—Do Images of War Need Justification?" *Nieman Reports* 54, no. 3 (2000): 51.

Carlebach, Michael L. *American Photojournalism Comes of Age*. Washington, DC: Smithsonian Institution Press, 1997.

Carlebach, Michael Lloyd. "The Origins of Photojournalism in America, 1839–1880." Ph.D. diss., Brown University, 1988.

Carnes, Cecil. *Jimmy Hare News Photographer: Half a Century with a Camera*. New York: Macmillan, 1940.

Carrigan, Michael Andrew. "The Media Print Pool and Censorship as a Department of Defense Public Relations Tool during the Persian Gulf War." Master's thesis, University of Nevada Reno, 1997.

Carroll, Darren, Cox, Stephanie, Dwyer, Jonathan J., Kenig, Nick, Layton, John and Wind, Andrew. "Sports Photography: Getting Pictures of Action." *Communication: Journalism Education Today* 31 (Summer 1998): 2–7.

Cartier-Bresson, Henri. *Europeans*. London: Thames & Hudson, 1998.

Cartier-Bresson, Henri. *The Decisive Moment*. New York: Simon & Schuster, 1952.

Cartier-Bresson, Henri. *The World of Henri Cartier-Bresson*. New York: Viking Press, 1968.

Case, Tony. "Photo Illustration on Page One Story." *Editor & Publisher* (Aug. 31, 1996): 3.

Cavallo, Robert M., and Kahan, Stuart. *Photography: What's the Law?* 2nd ed. New York: Crown Publishers, 1979.

Cavouras, Krissa Corbett. "See It Now: Photojournalism, Not Art, at the Perpignan Festival in France." *American Photo* 13, no. 5 (Sept./Oct. 2002): 10.

Chapnick, Howard. "Looking for Bang Bang: Photojournalists are Flocking to Trouble Spots Like El Salvador, and Too Many Are Not Returning Alive. Are the Results of War Photography Today Really Worth the Risks?" *Popular Photography* (July 1982): 65–67, 99, 101–102.

Chapnick, Howard. "Markets and Careers: American vs. European Picture Editing." *Popular Photography* (Dec. 1986): 38–39.

Chapnick, Howard. "Markets and Careers: Changing Views on Picture Editing." *Popular Photography* (Dec. 1986): 38–39.

Chapnick, Howard. "Markets and Careers: Getting the Pictures is Only the First Worry for Photojournalists; How it Affects Subjects is the Other." *Popular Photography* (Aug. 1983): 40, 93.

Chapnick, Howard. "Markets and Careers: Keeping News Pictures Meaningful." *Popular Photography* (Mar. 1983): 18, 130.

Chapnick, Howard. "Markets and Careers: Photographic Captions." *Popular Photography* (Feb. 1979): 42, 64, 127, 143.

Chapnick, Howard. "Markets and Careers: Words Tell the Reader What Pictures Can't: They Make a Photographer a Photojournalist." *Popular Photography* (Feb. 1979): 40, 64, 127, 143.

Chapnick, Howard. "Photojournalism Should Work On More Than One Level—and Its Images Should Be Clear, Simple, and Spontaneous." *Popular Photography* (Sept. 1984): 36–37.

Chapnick, Howard. ***Truth Needs No Ally: Inside Photojournalism***. Columbia, Missouri: University of Columbia Press, 1994.

Chernoff, George, and Sarbin, Hershel B. ***Photography and the Law***. 5th ed. Garden City, New York: Amphoto, 1975.

Cichy, Rose M. "Seeing America: Women Photographers Between the Wars." *Library Journal* 124, no. 19: 81.

Clarke, Lois E. "Features—Community Service—Another Aspect of Photojournalism." *PSA Journal* 66, no. 6 (2000): 26.

Cockerham, Michael. "Colin Jacobson's Belief in Reportage. Interview." *RPS Journal* 139, no. 9 (Nov. 1999): 404–7.

Cohen, Lester. ***The New York Graphic. The World's Zaniest Newspaper.*** Philadelphia: Chilton, 1964.

Cohen, Stuart. "Focusing on Humanity: The Life of W. Eugene Smith." *Boston Phoenix* (Oct. 31, 1978).

Coleman, A. D. "Documentary, Photojournalism, and Press Photography Now: Notes and Questions." In Coleman, A. D. (Allan D.). Depth of Field University of N.M. Press, 35–52, 1998.

Coleman, A. D. "New York exposed: Photographs from the *Daily News*." *Artnews* 101, no. 2 (2002): 94–+.

Coleman, Renita. "Civic Journalism on the Right Side of the Brain: How Photographers and Graphic Designers Visually Communicate the Principles of Civic Journalism." Paper presented at the Proceedings of the Annual Meeting of the Association for Education in Journalism and Mass Communication (83rd, Phoenix, Arizona, Aug. 9–12, 2000). Civic Journalism Interest Group, Phoenix, Arizona, Aug. 9–12, 2000

Coleman, Renita. "Design Characteristics of Public Journalism: Integrating Visual and Verbal Meaning." Paper presented at the Annual Meeting of the Association for Education in Journalism and Mass Communication. Baltimore, Maryland, Aug. 5–8, 1998. ERIC, ED423576.

Coles, Robert. "A place for words and images to call home." *Nieman Reports* 55, no. 3: 37.

Collins, K. "Get the picture: A personal history of photojournalism." *Library Journal* 123, no. 16 (1998): 84–84.

Converse, Gordon N. ***All Mankind: Photographs***. Boston: Christian Science Publ. Society, 1983.

Converse, Gordon N. ***Reflections in Light: The Work of a Photojournalist***. Boston: Christian Science Monitor, 1989.

Cookman, Claude. "Compelled to Witness: The Social Realism of Henri Cartier-Bresson." *Communication Abstracts* 21, no. 6 (1998).

Cookman, Claude. "The Photographic Reportage of Henri Cartier-Bresson, 1993–1973, Volume I." Ph.D. diss., Princeton University, 1994.

Cookman, Claude. A Voice is Born: The Founding and Early Years of the National Press Photographers Association Under the Leadership of Joseph Costa. Durham, NC: National Press Photographers Association, 1985.

Coontz, S., and M. Parson. "*Life's* America: Family and nation in postwar photojournalism" *Signs* 22, no. 2 (1997): 440–452.

Cooper, Guy. "Stock Photography: A Biased View from the Trenches." *News Photographer* (Aug. 1998): mgr 3, 5.

Coopersmith, Jonathan. "From Lemons to Lemonade: The Development of AP Wirephoto." *American Journalism* 17, no. 4 (2000): 55–72.

Corrigan, Don. "Future of newspapers belongs to visual artists." *St. Louis Journalism Review* 28, no. 206 (1998): 1+.

Costa, Joseph, ed. ***The Complete Book of Press Photography***. New York: National Press Photographers Association, 1950.

Costa, Joseph. "Does press freedom include photography?" *Nieman Reports* 53/54, no. 4/1: 174.

Costa, Joseph. "Cameras in Court: A Position Paper." Muncie, Indiana: Journalism/Public Relations Research Center, Ball State University, 1980.

Costa, Joseph. Collected Papers. George Arents Research Library. Syracuse University: Syracuse, New York.

Coupland, K. "A focus on the Web: @tlas, a showcase for serious photojournalism and multimedia." *Graphis* 53, no. 307 (1997): 32–32.

Covert, D. C. "American photojournalism comes of age." *Journalism & Mass Communication Quarterly* 75, no. 2 (1998): 429–431.

Covert, Douglas C. "Color Preference Conflicts in Visual Compositions." *Newspaper Research Journal* 9 (Fall 1987): 49–59.

Crager, Jack. "See It Now: Photojournalism Thrives at Perpignan." *American Photo* 12, no. 5 (Sept./Oct. 2001): 9.

Craig, R. Stephen. "Cameras in Courtrooms in Florida." *Journalism Quarterly* 56 (1979): 703–10.

Culver, Kathleen B. "An Open Door with a Big Spring: Cameras in Federal Courts." *VCQ* (Spring 1994): 17–18.

Cunningham, Brent. "David Pierini: Stopping time." *Columbia Journalism Review* 41, no. 2: 57.

Cunningham, Brent. "The Photographer: 'to Come up with a Different Image No Matter What It Takes'." *Columbia Journalism Review* 38, no. 5 (Jan./Feb. 2000): 40–1+.

Cunningham, Brent. "What's wrong with this picture?" *Columbia Journalism Review* 41, no. 4:11.

D

Daniel, Pete, and Smock, Raymond. ***A Talent for Detail: Frances Benjamin Johnston***. New York: Harmony Books, 1974.

David, Prabu. "News Concreteness and Visual-Verbal Association: Do News Pictures Narrow the Recall Gap between Concrete and Abstract News?" *Human Communication Research* 25, no. 2 (Dec 1998): 180–201.

Davis, M. "Lee Miller—Bathing with the Enemy (World War II Photojournalism, Hitler)." *History of Photography* 21, no. 4 (1997): 314–318.

Davis, S. E. "Digital Photo Illustration." *Graphis*, no. 296 (1995): 20.

Denton, Craig L. "Supercharged Color: Its Arresting Place in Visual Communication." Paper presented at the Annual Meeting of the Association for Education in Journalism and Mass Communication, Gainesville, Florida, 1984. ERIC, ED244292.

Desbarats, Peter. ***Canadian Illustrated News 1869–1883***. Toronto: McClelland and Stewart Limited, 1970.

Deschin, Jacob. "W. Eugene Smith Recalls Brutal Beating While Documenting a Poison Scandal." *Popular Photography* (Oct. 1973): 14, 20, 212.

Devine, Heather Catherine. "Controlling Digital Manipulation in Photojournalism: An Aggressive Solution to a Contentious Problem." Master's thesis, Carleton University (Canada), 1996.

Dewitz, Bobo von, and Robert ed Lebeck. ***Kiosk: A History of Photojournalism 1839–1973***. Boston: Dap, 2002.

Dick, David B. "'What Did Mr. Dwyer Do, Daddy?' 'Well, As You Could See, He Committed Suicide, Darling.'" *Quill* (Mar. 1987): 18–20.

Domke, David, David D. Perlmutter, and Meg Spratt. "The Primes of Our Times? An Examination of the 'Power' of Visual Images." *Journalism* 3, no. 2 (2002): 131–59.

Dorfman, John. "Digital Dangers." *Columbia Journalism Review* 41, no. 2 (July/Aug. 2002): 60–3.

Dorfman, John. "Photojournalism on the Web: Three Models." *Columbia Journalism Review* 41, no. 2 (July/Aug. 2002): 62–3.

Drapkin, Arnold. "Journalism's idea man, John Durniak, transformed news, picture magazines." *News Photographer* (Jan. 1998): 28, 32.

duCille, Michel. "The Use of Front-Page Photography in the *Washington Post*." Master's thesis, Ohio University, 1994.

Duggan, Dennis. "Louis Liotta: He was one from the 'glory days.'" *News Photographer* (Aug. 1997): 19–20.

Duncan, David Douglas. ***Self Portrait: U.S.A.*** New York: Abrams, 1969.

Dunn, Philip. ***Press Photography***. Sparkford, UK: Oxford Illustrated, 1988.

Durham, Michael S. ***Powerful Days: The Civil Rights Photography of Charles Moore***. New York: Stewart, Tabori & Chang, 1991.

Durniak, John. "10 Stories Around You." *Popular Photography* (June 1959): 72.

Durniak, John. "Focus on Wilson Hicks." *Popular Photography* (Apr. 1965): 59.

Dykhouse, Caroline Dow. "Prior Restraint on Photojournalists." *Journalism Quarterly* 64 (1987): 88–93, 118.

Dykhouse, Caroline Dow. "Privacy Law and Print Photojournalism." Paper presented at the Annual Meeting of the Association for Education in Journalism, Seattle, Washington, 1978. ERIC, ED1655144.

Dykhouse, Caroline Dow. "Privacy Law as It Affected Journalism, 1890–1978: Privacy Is a Visual Tort." Paper presented at the Annual Meeting of the Association for Education in Journalism and Mass Communication, Memphis, Tennessee, 1985. ERIC, ED262399.

Dykhouse, Caroline Dow. "Public Policy's Differential Effects on *News Photographers*." Paper presented at the meeting of the Association for Education in Journalism, Photojournalism Division, Seattle, Washington, 1978.

Dykhouse, Caroline Dow. "Shuttered Shutters: The Photographic Statutes and Their Faithful Companion, 18 USC 1382—An Examination of Photographic Access to Military Areas." Paper presented at the Annual Meeting of the Association for Education in Journalism, Athens, Ohio, 1982. ERIC, ED218678.

Dykhouse, Caroline Dow. "The Detroit Workshop, 1949–1951: Robert Drew and the *Life* Photojournalism Essay Formula." Master's thesis, Michigan State University, 1980.

Dykhouse, Caroline Dow. "The Response of the Law to Visual Journalism, 1839–1978." Ph.D. diss., Michigan State University, 1985.

E

Edey, Maitland. *Great Photographic Essays From Life*. Boston: New York Graphic Society, 1978.

Edgerton, Harold E. *Electronic Flash/Strobe*. 3rd ed. Cambridge, Massachusetts: M.I.T. Press, 1987.

Edgerton, Harold E., and Killian, James R., Jr. *Moments of Vision: The Stroboscopic Revolution in Photography*. Cambridge. Massachusetts: M.I.T. Press, 1979.

Edom, Clifton Cedric. *Photojournalism: Principles and Practices*. 2nd ed. Dubuque, Iowa: W. C. Brown Co., 1980.

Edwards, Owen. "A Mover Among the Shakers: Arnold Newman's Photographs Are a Tribute to the Staying Power of a Good Idea." *American Photo*grapher (Nov. 1985): 68–73.

Eisenstaedt, Alfred. *Eisenstaedt on Eisenstaedt: A Self-Portrait*. New York: Abbeville Press, 1985.

Eisenstaedt, Alfred. *Eisenstaedt: Remembrances*. Expanded rev. ed. Boston: Little, Brown, 1999.

Eisenstaedt, Alfred. *Eisenstaedt— Germany*. Edited by Gregory A. Vitiello. New York: Abrams, 1981.

Eisenstaedt. Alfred. *People*. New York: Viking Press, 1973.

Eisenstaedt. Alfred. *The Age of Eisenstaedt*. New York: Viking Press, 1969.

Eisenstaedt. Alfred. *Witness to Our Time*. New York: Viking Press, 1966.

Elbies, Jeffrey. "The Eyewitness." *American Photo* 12, no. 5 (Sept./Oct. 2001): 20–2, 88.

Eskin, Blake. "Features—Getting the Big Picture—the Power of Photojournalism Is Increasingly Resonating in the Mainstream Press as Well as in the Art World, with Images Finding a Prominent Place in Museum Holdings and Private Collections." *Artnews* 101, no. 2 (2002): 100.

Evans, Harold, and Edwin Taylor. *Pictures on a Page: Photo-Journalism, Graphics and Picture Editing*. rev. ed. London: PIMLI-CO, 1997.

Evans, Harold. *Front Page History: Events of Our Century that Shook the World*. London: Quiller Press in association with Photo Source, 1984.

Evans, Harold. *Eyewitness 2: 3 Decades through World Press Photos*. Updated ed. London: Quiller Press, 1985.

Evans, Harold. *Eyewitness: 25 Years through World Press Photos*. London: Quiller Press, 1981.

F

Faas, Horst and Page, Tim, eds. *Requiem, by the Photographers Who Died in Vietnam and Indochina*. New York: Random House, 1997.

Faber, John. "On the Record: Birth of *Life* Magazine." *National Press Photographer* (Aug. 1958).

Faber, John. "On the Record: Development of the Electronic Flash." *National Press Photographer* (Mar. 1959).

Faber, John. "On the Record: Development of the Halftone." *National Press Photographer* (Feb. 1957).

Faber, John. "On the Record: History of the Photo Syndicates." *National Press Photographer* (Dec. 1958).

Faber, John. "On the Record: Sacrificial Protest of Quang Duck." *News Photographer* (July 1983): 10.

Faber, John. "On the Record: The Atomic Bomb, Hiroshima." *News Photographer* (July 1980): 30.

Faber, John. "On the Record: Wire Transmission of Photos." *National Press Photographer* (Apr. 1958).

Faber, John. "This is How NPPA Came into Being." *National Press Photographer* (June 1960).

Faber, John. *Great News Photos and the Stories Behind Them*. 2nd ed. New York: Dover Publications, 1978.

Faber, John. Telephone interview with author. Sept., 1988.

Falk, Jon. *Jon Falk Presents Adventures in Location Lighting*. Rochester, New York: Eastman Kodak, 1988.

Farsai, Gretchen Jeanette. "A Review of Moral Standards Used to Select News Photographs." Master's thesis, California State University, Long Beach, 1985.

Fears, Lillie M. "Colorism of Black Women in News Editorial Photos." *Western Journal of Black Studies* 22 (Spring 1998): 30–36.

Fedler, Fred, Counts, Tim, and Hightower, Paul. "Changes in Wording of Cutlines Fail to Reduce Photographs' Offensiveness." *Journalism Quarterly* 59 (1982): 633–37.

Feinberg, Milton. *Techniques of Photojournalism*. New York: John Wiley & Sons, 1970.

Ferrato, Donna. "The eye behind the lens: photojournalists discuss their art." *WHY* magazine, no. 30 (1998): 26–30.

Fesperman, Dan. "'You're writing with light'." *Columbia Journalism Review* 38, no. 4: 44.

Finberg, Howard I., and Itule, Bruce D. *Visual Editing: A Graphic Guide for Journalists*. Belmont, California: Wadsworth Publishing Co., 1990.

Finberg, Howard I., ed. *Through Our Eyes: The 20th Century as Seen by the San Francisco Chronicle*. San Francisco: Chronicle Publishing Co., 1987.

Fincher, Terry. *Creative Techniques in Photo-journalism*. London: Batsford, 1980.

Fishman, Jessica Morgan. "Documenting Death: Photojournalism and Spectacles of the Morbid in the Tabloid and Elite Newspaper." *DAI* 62, no. 02A (2001): 345.

Fitzgerald, Mark. "Final exposure: Should newspapers publish graphic execution photos?" *Editor & Publisher* 133, no. 17: 26.

Flamiano, Dolores Louise. "Larger than Life: Collective Memory and Gender in *Life* Magazine's Photographic Essay, Photographic Pin-up, and Commemorative Photojournalism." *DAI* 61, no. 4 (2000): 1208.

Flamiano, Dolores. "The Naked Truth: Gender, Race, and Nudity in Life, 1937." Paper presented at the Annual Meeting of the Association for Education in Journalism and Mass Communication, New Orleans, Louisiana, Aug. 4–7, 1999.

Flash, The Associated Press Covers the World. Introduction by Peter Arnett. New York: Abrams, 1998.

Floren, Leola. "The Camera Comes to Court." Columbia, Missouri: Freedom of Information Center, 1978. ERIC, ED163559.

Flowers, Jackie Walker. "'Life' in Vietnam: The Presentation of the Vietnam War in 'Life' Magazine, 1962–1972." Ph.D. diss., University of South Carolina, 1996.

Fosdick, James A., and Shoemaker, Pamela J. "How Varying Reproduction Methods Affect Response to Photographs." *Journalism Quarterly* (Spring 1982): 13–20.

Fosdick, James A., and Tannenbaum, Percy H. "The Encoder's Intent and Use of Stylistic Elements in Photographs." *Journalism Quarterly* 41 (1964): 175–182.

Fosdick. James A. "Stylistic Correlates of Prescribed Intent in a Photographic Encoding Task." Ph.D. diss., University of Wisconsin, 1962.

Foster, D.Z. "Photos of Horror in Cambodia: Fake or Real?" *Columbia Journalism Review* (Mar. 1978): 46–47.

Fox, Rodney, and Kerns, Robert. *Creative News Photography*. Ames, Iowa: Iowa State University Press, 1961.

Foy, Mary Lou. "Feminine Touch." *Nieman Reports* 52 (Summer 1998): 42–3.

Foy, Mary Lou. "Photojournalism: Covering the Worst and Best." *News Photographer* (May 1993): 14–15.

Franklin, Tom. "The After-Life of a Photo That Touched a Nation." *Columbia Journalism Review* 40, no. 6 (Mar./Apr. 2002): 64–5.

Frascella, Larry. "The Searchers: Four of Today's Most Committed Picture Editors Talk about How They Hunt Out the Best Photographs, Where Visual Style Is Headed, and Why Photographers Need to be More Original." *American Photographer* (Dec. 1989): 48–51.

Freeman, John. "Are Journalism Schools Teaching the Right Skills?" *News Photographer* (Mar. 1994): 23–24.

Freeman, John. "Job Satisfaction among Photojournalists Past 40: A National Survey Looks at 'The Lifers.'" Paper presented at the Annual Meeting of the Association for Education in Journalism and Mass Communication, Washington, DC, Aug. 9–12 1995. ERIC, ED392085.

Friend, David. "The world of photojournalism." *Columbia Journalism Review* 41, no. 2: 40.

Fulton, Marianne, ed. *Eyes of Time: Photojournalism in America.* Boston: Little, Brown, 1988.

G

Galella, Ron. *Jacqueline.* New York: Sheed and Ward, 1974.

Gans, Herbert J. *Deciding What's News: A Study of CBS Evening News, NBC Nightly News, Newsweek and Time.* New York: Pantheon, 1979.

Garcia, Mario R., and Fry, Don. *Color in American Newspapers.* St. Petersburg, Florida: The Poynter Institute for Media Studies, 1986.

Garcia, Mario R., and Stark, Pegie. *Eyes on the News.* St. Petersburg, Florida: The Poynter Institute for Media Studies, 1991.

Garrett, W. E., ed. *Photojournalism '76.* Boston: Godine, 1977.

Gatewood, Worth. *Fifty Years in Pictures: The New York Daily News.* Garden City, New York: Doubleday, 1979.

Geraci, Philip C. *Photojournalism: Making Pictures for Publication.* Dubuque, Iowa: Kendall/Hunt, 1976.

Geraci, Phillip C. *Photojournalism: New Images in Visual Communication.* 3rd ed. Dubuque, Iowa: Kendall/Hunt, 1984.

Gibson, Rhonda, and Zillman, Dolf. "Reading Between the Photographs: The Influence of Incidental Pictorial Information on Issue Perception." Paper presented to the Association for Education in Journalism and Mass Communication. New Orleans, Louisiana, Aug. 4–9, 1999.

Gidal, Tim N. *Modern Photojournalism: Origin and Evolution, 1910–1933.* New York: Macmillan, 1973.

Gilbert, Kathy, and Schleuder, Joan. "Effects of Color Complexity in Still Photographs on Mental Effort and Memory." Paper presented at the Annual Meeting of the Association for Education in Journalism and Mass Communication. Portland, Oregon, 1988. ERIC, ED298579.

Gleason, Timothy Roy. "The Development of a Photojournalism Historiography: An Analysis of Journalism History Approaches." DAI 61, no. 07A (2000): 181.

Gleason, Timothy Roy. "The Development of Standard and Alternative Forms of Photojournalism." Paper presented at the Annual Meeting of the Association for Education in Journalism and Mass Communication. Baltimore, Maryland, Aug. 5–8 1998. ERIC, ED423576.

Goldberg, Vicki and Silberman, Robert Bruce. *American Photography: A Century of Images.* San Francisco, California: Chronicle Books, 1999.

Goldberg, Vicki. *Margaret Bourke-White: A Biography.* New York: Harper & Row, 1986.

Goldberg, Vicki. *The Power of Photography: How Photographs Changed Our Lives.* New York: Abbeville Press, 1991.

Golden, Anthony R. "The Effect of Quality and Clarity on the Recall of Photographic Illustrations." Paper presented at the Annual Meeting of the Association for Education in Journalism and Mass Communication, San Antonio, Texas, 1987. ERIC, ED287162.

Goldsmith, Arthur. "A Lesson in Portraiture from a Master: A Look Over Arnold Newman's Shoulder as He Photographs Dr. Francis Crick for His Notable 'Great British Series.'" *Popular Photography* (Dec. 1979): 100–107, 123–25.

Goodwin, James. "There It Is: New Journalism, Photojournalism, and the American War in Vietnam." *Genre* 31 (Summer 1998): 159.

Gordon, Jim. "Death of a Photograph: Assaults on Credibility or Much Ado about Nothing?" *News Photographer* (Apr. 1994): 4.

Gordon, Jim. "Here we go—again. A little photo manipulation goes a far piece." *News Photographer* (Feb. 1998): 4–5.

Gordon, Jim. "Judgement Days for Words and Pictures: To Print or Not to Print." *News Photographer* (July 1980): 25–29.

Gordon, Jim. "Nothing But the Real Thing: No Playing with Pixels—Including the Front Cover." *News Photographer* (Mar. 1994): 4.

Gordon, Jim. "Zeisloft Incident: Foot Artwork Ends Career." *News Photographer* (Nov. 1981): 32–36.

Gosen, Joseph Dorcy. "Digitally Altered News Photographs: How Much Manipulation Will the Public Tolerate before Credibility Is Lost?" *MAI* 38, no. 06 (2000): 76.

Gould, Lewis L., and Greffe, Richard. *Photojournalist: The Career of Jimmy Hare.* Austin: University of Texas Press, 1977.

Grace, Arthur. *Choose Me: Portraits of a Presidential Race.* Waltham, Massachusetts: University Press of New England/ Brandeis, 1989.

Gramling, Oliver. *AP, the Story of News.* New York: Farrar and Rinehart, 1940.

Greenwald, Marilyn, and Bernt, Joseph. "Newspaper Coverage of Gays and Lesbians: Editors' Views of its Longterm Effects." Paper presented at the Annual Meeting of the Association for Education in Journalism and Mass Communication. Montreal: Aug. 5–8 1992. ERIC, ED349621.

Grevstad-Nordbrock, Anne. "A Stolen Kiss: Robert Doisneau's Photographic Icon." *Visual Resources* 13, no. 2 ('97): 189–97.

Griffin, Michael, and Lee, Jongsoo. "Picturing the Gulf War: Constructing an Image of War in *Time, Newsweek,* and *U.S. News & World Report.*" *Journalism and Mass Communication Quarterly* 72 (Winter 1995): 813–25.

Griffiths, Philip Jones. "The Book That Lost a War, Interview with Colin Jacobson." *Creative Review* 22, no. 2 (Feb. 2002): 68–9.

Grigsby, Bryan. "Can't stand stand-alone art? For and against discussed." *News Photographer* (Feb. 1996): 10–11.

Grigsby, Bryan. "Diana's death and public perception." *News Photographer* (Nov. 1997): 16, 18.

Grigsby, Bryan. "Disappointment at funeral dress." *News Photographer* (Oct. 1995): 16–17.

Grigsby, Bryan. "Is it dying or just a bit sick? Photojournalism special issue sparks string of 'net postings." *News Photographer* (Nov. 1996) 10–12.

Grigsby, Bryan. "The wider, the better." *News Photographer* (Dec. 1998): 14–15.

Grigsby, Bryan. "Damned if you do—and if you don't. Reflections upon relationships between photographers and editors." *News Photographer.* (Aug. 1998): 10–11.

Grigsby, Bryan. "Helping Police or a Blind Eye?" *News Photographer* (Feb. 1999): 16–17.

Grigsby, Bryan. "It's Posed?" *News Photographer* (June 1999): 12–13.

Grigsby, Bryan. "Just Photographers or Photojournalists?" *News Photographer* (Nov. 1998): 10–12.

Grigsby, Bryan. "People Photos Require Trust, Responsibility." *News Photographer* (July 1996): 10.

Gross, Deborah M. "Visual Design for the World Wide Web: What Does the User Want?" Paper presented at the Annual Meeting of the Association for Education in Journalism and Mass Communication, Baltimore, Maryland, Aug. 5–8, 1998. ERIC, ED423576.

Grossfeld, Stan. *The Whisper of Stars: A Siberian Journey.* Chester, Connecticut: Globe Pequot Press, 1988.

Grossfeld, Stan. "Restricting a photojournalist's access." *Nieman Reports* 53, no. 3: 45.

Grossfeld, Stan. "Photo Opportunities: Local Photographers Go Global." *Washington Journalism Review* (May 1986): 39–41.

Grossfeld, Stan. "Trials with Editors." *Nieman Reports* 52 (Summer 1998): 30–31.

Grossfeld, Stan. *The Eyes of the Globe: Twenty-Five Years of Photography from the Boston Globe.* Chester, Connecticut: Globe Pequot Press, 1985.

Gutman, Judith Mare. *Lewis W. Hine: Two Perspectives.* New York: Viking Press, 1974.

Guzy, C. "First-person shooter." *Media Studies Journal* 14, no. 3 (2000): 94.

H

Habas, Paula J. "The Ethics of Photojournalistic Alteration: An Integrated Schema of Determinants." Master's thesis, University Of Windsor (Canada), 1996.

Haberman, Irving. *Eyes on an Era: Four Decades of Photojournalism.* New York: Rizzoli, 1995.

Hagaman, Dianne. *How I Learned Not to Be a Photojournalist.* Lexington, KY: University Press of Kentucky, 1996.

Hagaman, Dianne. "'The Joy of Victory, The Agony of Defeat:' Stereotypes in Newspaper Sports Feature Photographs," *Visual Sociology* 8 (1993): 48–66.

Hagen, Charles. "Robert Doisneau Dies at 81; Photos Captured Gallic Spirit." *New York Times* (2 Apr. 1994): 9.

Hale, Donna, and Church, Janet. "Helping hands. News photographer's save of Dole in continuing tradition." *News Photographer* (Dec. 1996): 22–23.

Hale, Donna. "Anatomy lesson: Louisville's cover-up caper; much ado about nothing?" *News Photographer* (Dec. 1996): 16, 18.

Hale, Donna. "Photo Editor Reprimands Photographer for Helping Firefighter at Barn Fire." *News Photographer* (Jan. 1999): 29, 32.

Hale, Donna. "Trapped by riptide, swimmer saved by news photographer." *News Photographer*. (Jan. 1998): 26.

Hale, F. Dennis. "Cameras in Courtrooms: Dimensions of Attitude of State Supreme Court Justices." Paper presented at the Annual Meeting of the Association for Education in Journalism and Mass Communication. Chicago, Illinois, 1997. ERIC, ED415547.

Halliday-Levy, Tereza. "The Connotation Dimension of News Photographs." Paper presented at the Annual Meeting of the Association for Education in Journalism, Athens, Ohio, 1982. ERIC, ED217475.

Halsman, Phillipe. *Halsman on the Creation of Photographic Ideas*. New York: Ziff-Davis, 1961.

Halstead, Dirck. "One Year Later." *American Photo* 13, no. 5 (Sept./Oct. 2002): 25–6.

Halstead, Dirck. "The Platypus Papers Part One." *The Digital Journalist,* www.digitaljournalist. org/platypus/platypus2.html.

Halter, Peter. "Werner Bischof: A Portrait of the Artist as Photo-Journalist." *History of Photography* 22, no. 3 (Autumn 1998): 237–46.

Hamblin, Dora Jane. *That Was the Life*. New York: W.W. Norton, 1977.

Hamilton, John Maxwell, David D Perlmutter, and Emily Arnette Vines. "Graphics and journalism." *Nieman Reports* 56, no. 3: 47.

Hamilton, Peter, and Marc Riboud. "Witness of Our Time, Witness of Reality." The *Photographic Journal* 138, no. 10 (Dec. 1998): 465–70.

Hanka, Harold. *Positive Images: Photographs*. Willimantic, Connecticut: Chronicle Print, 1982.

Hannigan, William. *New York Noir: Crime Photos from the Daily News Archive*. New York, N.Y.: Rizzoli, 1999.

Hansen, Mark Alan. "Fundamental Philosophy of Photojournalism Ethics: An Exploration of the Philosophical Underpinnings of Ethical Behavior in Photojournalism." Master's thesis, University of Nebraska, Lincoln, 1996.

Hanson, Art. "A Comparison of Documentary Approaches: Margaret Bourke-White and Erskine Caldwell, Authors of You Have Seen Their Faces" and Dorothea Lange and Paul S. Taylor, Authors of An American Exodus. Paper presented at the Annual Meeting of the Association for Education in Journalism. Boston, Massachusetts, Aug. 9–13, 1980. ERIC, ED191075.

Harris, C., and Lester, P. *Visual Journalism*. Boston: Allyn and Bacon, 2002.

Harris, John. *A Century of New England in News Photos*. Chester, Connecticut: Globe Pequot Press, 1979.

Harry Benson: Fifty Years in Pictures. New York: Harry N. Abrams, 2001.

Hart, Russell, and Zwingle, Erla. William Albert Allard: *The Photographic Essay*. Boston: Little, Brown, 1989.

Hart, Russell. "9/11 in Detail." *American Photo* 13, no. 3 (May/June 2002): 18–19, 73.

Hart, Russell. "The Digital Photojournalist." *American Photo* 9 (Sept./Oct. 1998): 30–1.

Hartley, Craig H. "Ethical Newsgathering Values of the Public and Press Photographers." *Journalism Quarterly* 60 (1983): 301–4.

Hartley, Craig, and Hillard, B.J. "The Reactions of Photojournalists and the Public to Hypothetical Ethical Dilemmas Confronting Press Photographers." Master's thesis, University of Texas, Austin, 1981.

Harwood, Philip J., and Lain, Lawrence B. "Mug Shots and Reader Attitudes toward People in the News." *Journalism Quarterly* 69 (Summer 1992): 293–300.

Haworth-Booth, Mark. *Donald McCullin*. London: Collins, 1983.

Hazard, William R. "Responses to News Pictures: A Study in Perceptual Unity." *Journalism Quarterly* 37 (1960): 515–524.

Heartfield, John. *Photomontages of the Nazi Period*. New York: Universe Books, 1977.

Heller, Robert. "Photojournalism Education: Contradictions for the Nineties." *Journalism Educator* 46 (Spring 1991): 29–31.

Heller, Steven, and Chwast, Seymour, eds. *Sourcebook of Visual Ideas*. New York: Van Nostrand Reinhold, 1989.

Heller, Steven. "Photojournalism's Golden Age (Through the Great Picture Magazines of the '20s and '30s)." *Print* 38 (Sept./Oct. 1984): 68–79, 116, 118.

Herde, Tom. "Editorial Illustration." *News Photographer* (July 1979): 28–29.

Heyman, Ken, and Durniak, John. *The Right Picture: A Photographer and a Picture Editor Demonstrate How to Choose*. New York: Amphoto, 1986.

Hickey, Neil. "Magnum at 50." *Columbia Journalism Review* 39, no. 2 (July/Aug. 2000): 43.

Hicks, Wilson. *Words and Pictures: An Introduction to Photo-Journalism*. 1952. Reprint. New York: Arno Press, 1973.

Hightower, Paul Dudley. "The Influence of Training on Taking and Judging Photos." *Journalism Quarterly* 61 (1984): 682–86.

Hine, Lewis. *America and Lewis Hine: Photographs 1904–1940*. Millerton, New York: *Aperture*, 1977.

Hobsbawm, Eric, and Weitzmann, Marc, Eds. *1968: Magnum Throughout the World*. Paris: Editions Hazan, dist. by D.A.P., 1998.

Hockman-Wert, Cathleen. "Images of African Famine in U.S. Newsmagazines, 1968–1993: A Content Analysis and Exploration of Ethics." Master's thesis, University of Oregon, 1997.

Hope, Terry. *Photo-Journalism: Developing Style in Creative Photography*. Hove: RotoVision SA, 2001.

Horenstein, Henry. *Color Photography: A Working Manual*. Boston: Little, Brown, 1995.

Horton, Brian. *Associated Press Guide to Photojournalism*. 2nd ed, The Associated Press Series. New York: McGraw-Hill, 2001.

Horton, Brian. *The Associated Press Photo-Journalism Stylebook*. Reading, Massachusetts: Addison-Wesley, 1990.

Horton, Brian. *The Picture: An Associated Press Guide to Good News Photography*. New York: Associated Press, 1989.

Hovde, Ellen, Muffie Meyer, Ronald Blumer, Harris Yulin, Vicki Goldberg, Robert Bruce Silberman, KTCA-TV (Television station: Saint Paul Minn.), MiddleMar. Films, and PBS Home Video. "American Photography a Century of Images." Alexandria, Va.: PBS Home Video, 1999. Videorecording.

Howard, Caroline. "Picking Shots." *Columbia Journalism Review* 41, no. 2 (July/Aug. 2002): 45–6.

Howe, Peter. "A Passion in Search of a Market." *Columbia Journalism Review* 41, no. 2 (July/ 2002): 23–6.

Howe, Peter. "Exposure to light." *Columbia Journalism Review* 41, no. 2: 22.

Howe, Peter. "Photojournalism at a crossroads." *Nieman Reports* 55, no. 3: 25.

Howe, Peter. "The Documentary and Journalism—Photography and the Written Word— Photojournalism at a Crossroads." *Nieman Reports* 55, no. 3 (2001): 25.

Howe, Peter. "Wake Me After the Revolution." *The Digital Journalist,* www.digitaljournalist.org.

Howe, Peter. *Shooting Under Fire: The World of the War Photographer.* Artisan (a division of Workman Publishing Inc.) New York New York, 2002.

Hoy, Frank P. *Photojournalism: The Visual Approach*. Englewood Cliffs, New Jersey: Prentice-Hall, 1986.

Hoyt, James L. "Cameras in the Courtroom: From Hauptmann to Wisconsin." Paper presented at the Annual Meeting of the Association for Education in Journalism, Seattle, Washington, 1978. ERIC, ED158307.

Huang, Edgar Shaohua. "Readers' Perception of Digital Alteration and Truth-Value in Documentary Photographs." Ph.D. diss., Indiana University, 1999.

Huang, Edgar Shaohua. "Afterthoughts on the Representational Strategies of the FSA Documentary." Paper presented at the Annual Meeting of the Association for Education in Journalism and Mass Communication. Baltimore, Maryland, Aug. 5–8, 1998. ERIC, ED423576.

Hughes, Jim. "The Nine Lives of W. Eugene Smith." *Popular Photography* (Apr. 1979): 116–117, 135–141.

Hughes, Jim. W. Eugene Smith, *Shadow & Substance: The Life and Work of an American Photographer*. New York: McGraw-Hill, 1989.

Huh, Hyun-Joo Lee. "The Effect of Newspaper Picture Size on Readers' Attention, Recall and Comprehension of Stories." Paper presented at the Annual Meeting of the Association for Education in Journalism and Mass Communication. Kansas City, Missouri, Aug. 11–14, 1993. ERIC, ED361672.

Hulteng, John L. *The Messenger's Motives: Ethical Problems of the News Media*. 2nd ed. Englewood Cliffs, New Jersey: Prentice-Hall, 1985.

Hurley, Forrest Jack. *Portrait of a Decade: Roy Stryker and the Development of Documentary Photography in the Thirties*. 1972. Reprint. New York: Da Capo, 1977.

Hurley, Gerald D., and McDougall, Angus. *Visual Impact in Print: How to Make Pictures Communicate; A Guide for the Photographer, the Editor, the Designer*. Chicago: American Publishers Press, 1971.

L

Israel: 50 Years, As Seen by Magnum Photographers. New York: *Aperture*, 1998.

Ianzito, Christina. "Photojournalism: A Life's Work—Earl Dotter." *Columbia Journalism Review* (Jan./Feb. 1997): 40–43.

Ianzito, Christina. "Photojournalism: Tobacco Road—Rob Amberg." *Columbia Journalism Review* (Nov./Dec. 1996): 39–41.

Images of Our Times: Sixty Years of Photography from the Los Angeles Times. New York: Abrams, 1987.

Irby, Kenny. "Preserving the old while adapting to what's new." *Nieman Reports* 54, no. 4: 23.

Irby, Kenny. "L.A. Times Photographer Fired Over Altered Image" *PoynterOnline.org*. (April 2, 2003) www.poynteronline.org/content/content_view.asp?id=28082.

J

Jacobs, Rita D. "James Nachtwey." *Graphis* 50 (Nov. 1994): 48.

Jacobson, Colin. "Class Action." *British Journal of Photography*, no. 7150 (Nov. 1997): 22–3.

Jacobson, Colin. "The Last Picture Show: The State of Photojournalism and Its Publication." *Creative Review* 15 (Apr. 1995): 39–40.

Jacobson, Colin, ed.. *Underexposed: Censored Pictures and Hidden History*. Vision On Publishing, London: 2002.

James, Simon. "Vietnam: The Truth Was as We See It." *RPS Journal* 141, no. 8 (Oct. 2001): 344–7.

Jaubert, Alain. *Making People Disappear: An Amazing Chronicle of Photographic Deception*. Washington: Pergamon-Brassey's International Defense Publishers, 1989.

Jett, Anne. "Diversity and a Local Newspaper: When Photojournalism Becomes Public Relations." Paper presented at the Annual Conference of the Association for Education in Journalism and Mass Communication. Atlanta, Georgia, Aug. 10–13, 1994. ERIC, ED376531.

Jobey, Liz. "In the Age of Celebrity Journalism, Newspapers No Longer Want Pictures of Disaster and Starvation; but Some People Will Buy Them for the Living Room Reissue of Book *Pictures on a Page*." *New Statesman* (London, England: 1996) 126 (May 1997): 42–3.

John, Alun. *Newspaper Photography: A Professional View of Photojournalism Today*. Marlborough: Crowood, 1988.

Johns, David. "All about Boo-Boos: Is It Ethical to Photograph Embarrassing Moments? Is Prominence Enough Justification?" *News Photographer* (July 1984): 8.

Jones, Barbara Sue Hemby. "The Photojournalism of Mary Ellen Mark." Master's thesis, East Texas State University, 1994.

Josephson, Sheree. "The Readability, Recall, and Reaction to Online Newspaper Pages with Visuals and Those Without." Paper Presented at SCA. San Diego, California, Nov. 24, 1996.

Josephson, Sheree. "Questioning the Power of Color." *News Photographer* (Jan. 1996): *VCQ* 4–7, 12.

Juergens, George. *Joseph Pulitzer and the New York World*. Princeton, New Jersey: Princeton University Press, 1966.

Junas, Lil. "Ethics and Photojournalism: Photographer Qualities and Picture Selection." *News Photographer* (June 1984): 24.

Junas, Lil. "Ethics and Photojournalism: Posed, Set Up, Faked, Controlled or Candid?" *News Photographer* (Mar. 1982): 19–20.

Junas, Lil. "Ethics and Photojournalism: Techniques and 'Bring Back Something.'" *News Photographer* (June 1982): 26–27.

K

Kahan, Robert Sidney. "The Antecedents of American Photojournalism." Ph.D. diss., The University of Wisconsin, Madison, 1969.

Kalish, Stanley E., and Edom, Clifton C. *Picture Editing*. New York: Rinehart, 1951.

Kaplan, Daile. *Lewis Hine in Europe: The Lost Photographs*. New York: Abbeville Press, 1988.

Kaplan, John. "The *Life* Magazine Civil Rights Photography of Charles Moore (1958–1965). *Journalism History* 1999–2000 25(4): 126–139.

Kaplan, John. *Photo Portfolio Success*. Cincinnati: Writers Digest Books, 2003.

Karsh, Yousuf. *Portraits of Greatness*. New York: Thomas Nelson & Sons, 1959.

Keaton, Diane. *Local News: Tabloid Pictures from the Los Angeles Herald Express, 1936–1961*. New York, N.Y.: DAP, 1999.

Keene, Martin. *Practical Photojournalism: A Professional Guide*. 2nd ed. Oxford, Boston: Focal Press, 1995.

Keim, Denise. "Exploring the relationship between photographer and subject." *Nieman Reports* 55, no. 3: 22.

Kelly, James D. "Going Digital at College Newspapers: The Impact of Photo Credibility and Work Routines." Paper presented at the Annual Meeting of the Association for Education in Journalism and Mass Communication. Anaheim, California, Aug. 10–13, 1996. ERIC, ED401533.

Kelly, James D. "The Adoption of Digital Imaging Technology at Daily College Student Newspapers and the Credibility of News Photos." Paper presented at the Annual Meeting of the Association for Education in Journalism and Mass Communication, Atlanta, Georgia, Aug. 10–13, 1994. ERIC, ED374494.

Kelly, James D., and Nace, Diona. "Digital Imaging and Believing Photos." *VCQ* (Winter 1994): 4–5, 18.

Kelly, James D., and Nace, Diona. "The Effects of Specific Knowledge of Digital Image Manipulation Capabilities and Newspaper Context on the Believability of News Photographs." Paper presented at the Annual Conference of the Association for Education in Journalism and Mass Communication. Kansas City, Missouri, Aug. 11–14, 1993. ERIC, ED362917.

Kendall, Robert. "Photo 1978: Some Provisions of the 1976 Copyright Act for the Photojournalist." Paper presented at the meeting of the Photojournalism Division, Association for Education in Journalism, Madison, Wisconsin, 1977.

Kendall, Russ. "Photographers' personal pages." *News Photographer* (Mar. 1997): 15–16.

Kennedy, Thomas. "Content and Style: How Do Limited Expectations Affect the Creative Process?" MGR (insert in *News Photographer*) (Jan. 1989): 1–3.

Kennerly, David Hume. *Photo Du Jour: A Picture-a-Day Journey through the First Year of the New Millennium*. 1st ed, Focus on American History Series. Austin: University of Texas Press, 2002.

Kennerly, David. *PhotoOp: A Pulitzer Prize-Winning Photographer Covers Events That Shaped our Times*. Austin, Texas: University of Texas Press, 1995.

Kenney, Keith R., and Unger, Brent W. "The *Mid-Week Pictorial*: Forerunner of American News-Picture Magazines." *American Journalism* 11 (Summer 1994): 201–216.

Kenney, Keith Raymond. "Newspaper Photography in China." Ph.D. diss., Michigan State University, 1991.

Kenney, Keith. "Building Alliances: PhotoJournalism Educators and Members of NPPA." Paper presented at the Annual Meeting of the Association for Education in Journalism and Mass Communication, Washington, DC, Aug. 9–12, 1995. ERIC, ED388974.

Kenney, Keith. "Effects of Still Photographs." *News Photographer* (May 1992): 41–42.

Kenney, Keith. "Ethical Attitudes." *News Photographer* (Nov. 1991): 12–14.

Kenney, Keith. "Follow-Up: Ombudsmen under Glass." *News Photographer* (Oct. 1993): 40–41.

Kenney, Keith. "Forces Affecting Selection of Photos and TV Stories." *News Photographer* (Feb. 1992): 51–52.

Kenney, Keith. "Fund-Raising Pictures: Do 'Starving Baby' Photos Really Work?" *News Photographer* (Apr. 1993): 46–47.

Kenney, Keith. "How Groups of People are Portrayed." *News Photographer* (Jan. 1992): 43–46.

Kenney, Keith. "Memory and Comprehension of TV News Visuals." *News Photographer* (Aug. 1992): 52–53.

Kenney, Keith. "Mid-Week Pictorial: Pioneer American Photojournalism Magazine." Paper presented at the Annual Meeting of the Association for Education in Journalism and Mass Communication, Norman, OK, 1986. ERIC, ED271767.

Kenney, Keith. "Photojournalism Research: Computer-Altered Photos: Do Readers Know Them When They See Them?" *News Photographer* (Jan. 1993): 26–27.

Kerns, Robert. *Photojournalism: Photography with a Purpose*. Englewood Cliffs, New Jersey: Prentice-Hall, 1980.

Kerrick, Jean S. "Influence of Captions on Picture Interpretation." *Journalism Quarterly* 32 (1955): 177–184.

Kerrick, Jean S. "News Pictures, Captions and the Point of Resolution." *Journalism Quarterly* 36 (1959): 183–188.

Kessel, Dmitri. *On Assignment: Dmitri Kessel, LIFE Photographer*. New York: Abrams, 1985.

Kielbowiez, Richard B. "The Making of Canon 35: A Blow to Press-Bar Cooperation." Paper presented at the Annual Meeting of the Association for Education in Journalism, Photojournalism Division, Houston, Texas, 1979.

Kifner, John. "Pictures from Hell: James Nachtwey's Photojournalism." *Columbia Journalism Review* 39, no. 2 (July/Aug. 2000): 44–5.

Kim, Connie. "A Single Day, a Thousand Images." *The Quill* (Chicago, Ill.) 89, no. 9 (Nov. 2001): 22–3.

King, John Mark. "Political Endorsements in Daily Newspapers and Photographic Coverage of Candidates in the 1995 Louisiana Gubernatorial Campaign." Paper presented at the Annual Meeting of the Association for Education in Journalism and Mass Communication, Chicago, Illinois, July 30–Aug. 2, 1997. ERIC, ED415547.

King, John Mark. "Visual Communication and Newspaper Reader Satisfaction." Ph.D. diss., The University of Tennessee, 1995.

King, John Mark. "Who Gets Named?: Nationality, Race and Gender in *New York Times'* Photograph Cutlines." Paper presented at the Annual Meeting of the Association for Education in Journalism and Mass Communication, Baltimore, Maryland, Aug. 5–8, 1998. ERIC, ED423576.

Kobré, Ken. "Last Interview with W. Eugene Smith on the Photo Essay." Paper presented at the Annual Meeting of the Association for Education in Journalism, Houston, Texas, 1979. ERIC, ED178948.

Kobré, Ken. "Something Different for the News Photographer: Illustrations Solve Problems." *News Photographer* (July 1979): 28–30.

Kobré, Ken. "Critiques." *News Photographer* (January 1994): *VCQ* 18.

Kobré, Ken. "Picturing Assisted Suicide." *News Photographer* (April 1994): *VCQ* 20–21.

Kobré, Ken. "Unearthing Outtakes." *News Photographer* (July 1994): *VCQ* 13–16.

Kobré, Ken. "Rwanda: Witnessing a Holocaust." *News Photographer* (October 1994): *VCQ* 12–16.

Kobré, Ken. " 'The *New York Times'* is Not What She Used to Be." *News Photographer* (January 1995): *VCQ* 15.

Kobré, Ken. "The Long Tradition of Doctoring Photos." *News Photographer* (April 1995): *VCQ* 14–16.

Kobré, Ken. "Good Things Do Come in Small Packages." *News Photographer* (July 1995): *VCQ* 20–23.

Kobré, Ken. "Where Have All the Great Portraits Gone?" *News Photographer* (October 1995): *VCQ* 13–17.

Kobré, Ken. "Slicing Into the World of Photo Non-Realism." *News Photographer* (January 1996): *VCQ* 14.

Kobré, Ken. "Comparison Photos— There's No Comparison." *News Photographer* (April 1996): *VCQ* 21–22.

Kobré, Ken. "Progress In Style Does Not Always Accompany Improvement in Substance." *News Photographer* (July 1996): *VCQ* 13–16.

Kobré, Ken. "Is the Feature Disappearing?" *News Photographer* (October 1996): *VCQ* 13.

Kobré, Ken. " 'The London Independent' Breaks Rules for Refreshing Change." *News Photographer* (January 1997): *VCQ* 13.

Kobré, Ken. "Nudity and News: How Would You Play It?" *News Photographer* (April 1997): *VCQ* 13–14.

Kobré, Ken. "Help Now or Possibly Change the World Later?" *News Photographer* (July 1997): *VCQ* 20–23.

Kobré, Ken. "The Sex Industry From A Woman's Point of View." *News Photographer* (October 1997): *VCQ* 8-12.

Kobré, Ken. "Changing the Market for a Princess' Image." *News Photographer* (January 1998): *VCQ* 14.

Kobré, Ken. "What Can We Learn From the British Press?" *News Photographer* (April 1998): *VCQ* 13–15.

Kobré, Ken. "Should Still Photographers Fear New Video Technology?" *News Photographer* (October 1998): *VCQ* 11–15.

Kobré, Ken. "When Words and Pictures Complement Each Other." *News Photographer* (January 1999): *VCQ* 16.

Kobré, Ken. "Editing for Intimacy." *News Photographer* (April 1999): *VCQ* 18–20.

Kobré, Ken. "Shedding Light on Posed Portraits." *News Photographer* (July 1999): *VCQ* 12–15.

Kobré, Ken. "Looking for Candid Moments in Posed Portraits." *News Photographer* (October 1999): *VCQ* 12–16.

Kobré, Ken. "Narrative Storytelling." *News Photographer* (January 2000): *VCQ* 12.

Kobré, Ken. "Covering Politicians In and Out of Office." *News Photographer* (April 2000): *VCQ* 14–16.

Kobré, Ken. "Finding Fun Features." *News Photographer* (July 2000): *VCQ* 14–17.

Kobré, Ken. "Discovering Pictures That Can Effect Change." *News Photographer* (October 2000): *VCQ* 14–18

Kobré, Ken. "Weegee Lives." *News Photographer* (January 2001): *VCQ* 14.

Kobré, Ken. "Freelancing Your Work." *News Photographer* (April 2001): *VCQ* 13–14

Kobré, Ken. "The Picture Story Finds a Friendly Home." *News Photographer* (July 2001): *VCQ* 14–17.

Kobré, Ken. "Visa: An International Festival and Marketplace for Photojournalism." *News Photographer* (October 2001): *VCQ* 12.

Kobré, Ken. "What's Up Down Under: Australian Photojournalism." *News Photographer* (January 2002): *VCQ* 14.

Kobré, Ken. "Ready for a Job (Ex)Change;" "Talented…AND a Nice Guy." *News Photographer* (April 2002): *VCQ* 12–13.

Kobré, Ken. "Survival on the French Riviera OR Shooting Stars at Cannes." *News Photographer* (July 2002): *VCQ* 14–17.

Kobré, Ken. " '*Life*' May Be Dead, but Photojournalism Isn't." *News Photographer* (October 2002): *VCQ* 16–20.

Kobré, Ken. "Photojournalism Thrives On-Line." *News Photographer* (January 2003): *VCQ* 14.

Kobré, Ken. "How PR Pros Became a Photographer's Best Friends." *News Photographer* (April 2003): *VCQ* 12–13.

Kobré, Ken. "How to Invent a Photo Illustration." *News Photographer* (July 2003): *VCQ* 18–21.

Kobré, Kenneth. *Photojournalism: The Professionals' Approach*. 4th ed. Boston: Focal Press, 2000.

Kobre, Sidney. *Behind Shocking Crime Headlines*. Tallahassee, Florida: Florida State University, 1957.

Kobre, Sidney. *Development of American Journalism*. Dubuque, Iowa: Wm. C. Brown, 1969.

Kobre, Sidney. *Modern American Journalism*. Tallahassee, Florida: Florida State University, 1959.

Kobre, Sidney. *News Behind the Headlines: Background Reporting of Significant Social Problems*. Tallahassee, Florida: Florida State University, 1955.

Kobre, Sidney. *Press and Contemporary Affairs*. Tallahassee, Florida: Florida State University, 1957.

Kobre, Sidney. *The Yellow Press and Gilded Age Journalism*. Tallahassee, Florida: Florida State University, 1964.

Kochersberger, Robert C. "Survey of Suicide Photos Use in Newspapers in Three States." *Newspaper Research Journal* 9 (Summer 1988): 1–12.

Kodak Milestones: 1880–1980. Rochester, New York: Eastman Kodak, 1980.

Koenig, T. "Taro Gerta— Photojournalist During the Spanish Civil War: A Biography." *History of Photography* 19, no. 4 (1995): 375–376.

Kostyu, Paul E. "Picturing the Past, Media, History & Photography." *Journalism and Mass Communication Quarterly* 77, no. 2: 434.

Kostyu, Paul E. "The Burden of Visual Truth: The Role of Photojournalism in Mediating Reality." *Journalism and Mass Communication Quarterly* 78, no. 1: 195.

Kowalski, Shelley Kara. "A Poor Picture: The Failure of Concerned Photography to Arouse Social Change." Paper presented at the Society for the Study of Social Problems (SSSP), 1997.

Kozol, Wendy. "Documenting the Public and Private in '*Life*': Cultural Politics in Postwar Photojournalism." Ph.D. diss., University of Minnesota, 1990.

Kratochvil, Antonin, and Michael Persson. "The Documentary and Journalism—Photography and the Written Word—Photojournalism and Documentary Photography." *Nieman Reports* 55, no. 3 (2001): 27.

Kunhardt, Phillip B., Jr. *The Joy of Life*. Boston: Little, Brown, 1989.

Kuykendall, Bill. "Inner Eye." *Nieman Reports* 52 (Summer 1998): 46–49.

L

LaBelle, David. *Lessons in Life and Death*. Durham, NC: NPPA Bookshelf, 1993.

LaBelle, David. *The Great Picture Hunt*. Bowling Green Kentucky: Western Kentucky University, 1989.

Lacayo, Richard. *Eyewitness: 150 Years of Photojournalism*. 2nd ed. New York: Time Books, 1995.

LaClair, Scott. "Attacks, gibes, jeers after Diana." *News Photographer* (Nov. 1997): 14.

Lain, Laurence B. "How Readers View Mug Shots." *Newspaper Research Journal* 8 (Spring 1987): 43–52.

Lange, George. "Feature: Riding Shotgun with Annie (Leibovitz)." *American Photographer* (Jan. 1984): 56, 59.

Lasica, J. D. "Photographs That Lie: The Ethical Dilemma of Digital Retouching." *Washington Journalism Review* (June 1989): 22–25.

Lauterer, Jock. "Wrestling with the bear, Photojournalism ethics in your face." *News Photographer* (Apr. 1998): 46–47.

Lee, T. "Body horror: Photojournalism, catastrophe, and war." *Harvard International Journal of Press-Politics* 4, no. 2 (1999): 113–113.

Leekley, Sheryle, and Leekley, John. ***Moments: The Pulitzer Prize Photographs.*** Updated ed. 1942–1982. New York: Crown, 1982.

Leggett, Dawn, and Wanta, Wayne. "Gender Stereotypes in Wire Service Sports." *Newspaper Research Journal* 10 (Spring 1989): 105–114.

Leibovitz, Annie. ***Annie Leibovitz: Photographs.*** New York: Rolling Stone Press, 1983.

Leifer, Neil. ***Sports!*** Text by George Plimpton. New York: Abrams, 1983.

Leslie, L. Z. "Newspaper Photo Coverage of Censure of McCarthy." *Journalism Quarterly* 63 (1986): 850–53.

Lester, Paul Martin and Miller, Randy. "African American Pictorial Coverage in Four U.S. Newspapers." Paper presented at the Annual Meeting of the Association for Education in Journalism and Mass Communication. Anaheim, California, Aug. 10–13, 1996. ERIC, ED401571.

Lester, Paul Martin. "Front Page Mug Shots: A Content Analysis of Five U.S. Newspapers in 1986. *Newspaper Research Journal* 9 (Spring 1988): 1–9.

Lester, Paul Martin, ed. ***Images that Injure: Pictorial Stereotypes in the Media.*** Westport, Connecticut: Praeger, 1996.

Lester, Paul Martin. "Pedagogical Discussion on Pictorial Stereotypes." *Journalism and Mass Communication Educator* 52 (2) (1997): 49–54.

Lester, Paul Martin. "Pictorial Stereotypes in the Media: A Pedagogical Discussion." Paper presented at the Annual Meeting of the Association for Education in Journalism and Mass Communication, Anaheim, California, Aug. 10–13, 1996. ERIC, ED401571.

Lester, Paul Martin. "The Ethics of Photojournalism: Toward a Professional Philosophy for Photographers, Editors and Educators." Ph.D. diss., Indiana University, 1989.

Lester, Paul, and Smith, Ron. "African-American Picture Coverage in Life, Newsweek, and Time, 1937–1988." Paper presented at the Annual Meeting of the Association for Education in Journalism and Mass Communication, Washington, DC, 1989. ERIC, ED310460.

Lester, Paul. "African-*American Photo* Coverage in Four U.S. Newspapers, 1937–1990." *Journalism Quarterly* 72 (Summer 1994): 380–394.

Lester, Paul. "Computer Aids Instruction in Photojournalism Ethics." *Journalism Educator* 44 (Summer 1989): 13–17.

Lester, Paul. "Use of Visual Elements on Newspaper Front Pages." *Journalism Quarterly* 65 (1988): 760–63.

Lester, Paul. ***Photojournalism: an Ethical Approach***. Hillsdale, New Jersey: Lawrence Erlbaum Associates, 1991.

Lewinski, Jorge, comp. ***The Camera at War: A History of War Photography from 1848 to the Present Day.*** London: W.H. Allen, 1978.

Lewis, Charles W. "From Brady to Bourke-White: An Examination of the Foundations of American Picture Magazine Photojournalism, 1860–1940." Master's thesis, Mankato State University, MN, 1986.

Lewis, David M. "Electronic Cameras and Photojournalism: Impact and Implications." MS study, Ohio University, Athens, 1983.

Lewis, Greg. "A Tribute to W. Eugene Smith." *The Rangefinder* (Dec. 1978): 35.

Lewis, Greg. ***Photojournalism: Content and Technique***. 2nd ed. Boston: McGraw Hill, 1995.

Lewis, Vickie. "The Impact of Technology on Ethical Decision-Making in Photojournalism." Master's thesis, Ohio University, 1997.

Li, Xigen. "Web Page Design and Graphic Use of Three U.S. Newspapers." *Journalism and Mass Communication Quarterly* 75(2) (1998): 353–365.

Li-An. "Picture Selection: An Editorial Game." *Journalism Quarterly* 40 (1963): 230–232.

Li-An. ***Editorial Predictions of Magazine Picture Appeals.*** Iowa City, Iowa: School of Journalism, University of Iowa, 1965.

Life 50, 1936–1986: The First Fifty Years. Boston: Little, Brown, 1986.

Life, the First Decade, 1936–1945. London: Thames & Hudson, 1979.

Life, the Second Decade, 1946–1955. Boston: Little, Brown, 1984.

Life, Through the Sixties: An Exhibition and Catalogue. New York: Time, Inc. 1989.

Life Sixty Years: A 60th anniversary celebration, 1936-1996. Editors of Life. New York: Life Books, Time, Inc. Brown, 1996.

Light, Ken. ***Witness in Our Time: Working Lives of Documentary Photographers.*** Washington D.C.: Smithsonian Institution Press, 2000.

Linderman, Eric. "Kiosk: A History of Photojournalism 1839–1973." *Library Journal* 127, no. 10: 142.

Liotta, Louie, and Wadler, Joyce. "Candid Cameraman: After 50 Years of Shooting for the Front Page, *News Photographer* Louie Liotta Spills." *Time* (11 Dec. 1989): 171.

Lipton, Joshua. "A visual record of a violent year." *Columbia Journalism Review* 40, no. 4: 65.

Lipton, Joshua. "Ron Haviv: Shooting War." *Columbia Journalism Review* 41, no. 2: 48.

Livingston, Jane. Odyssey: ***The Art of Photography at National Geographic.*** Charlottesville, Virginia: Thomasson-Grant, 1988.

Loengard, John. "The Role of the Picture Editor." *Nieman Reports* 52 (Summer 1998): 44–45.

Loengard, John. ***Life Classic Photographs: A Personal Interpretation.*** Boston: New York Graphic Society Books, 1988.

Loengard, John. ***Life Photographers What They Saw.*** Boston: Little Brown, 1998.

Loengard, John. ***Pictures Under Discussion.*** New York: Amphoto, 1987.

Logan, Richard, III. Elements of Photo Reporting. Garden City, New York: Amphoto, 1971.

Li, Xigen.

Lowrey, Wilson. "Altered Plates: Photo Manipulation and the Search for News Value in the Early and Late Twentieth Century." Paper presented at the Annual Meeting of the Association for Education in Journalism and Mass Communication, Baltimore, Maryland, Aug. 5–8, 1998. ERIC, ED423576.

Lowrey, Wilson. "Routine News: The Power of the Organization in Visual Journalism." *News Photographer* (Apr. 1999): *VCQ* 10–15.

Luebke, Barbara F. "Out of Focus: Images of Women and Men in Newspaper Photographs." *Sex Roles* 20 (1989): 121–33.

Lukas, Anthony J. "The White House Press 'Club.'" *New York Times Magazine* (15 May 1977): 22, 64–68, 70–72.

Lutman, David R. "An invasion of privacy?" *News Photographer* (Mar. 1998) 8.

M

MacAdam, B. A. "Focus on Capa (War photographer Robert Capa)." *Artnews* 99, no. 7 (2000): 36–36.

MacDougall, Curtis D. ***News Pictures Fit to Print . . . Or Are They?*** Stillwater, OK: Journalistic Services, 1971.

MacDougall, Kent A. "*Geographic*: From Upbeat to Realism." *Los Angeles Times* (Aug. 5, 1977): 1, 8–10.

MacLean, Malcolm S., Jr. "Communication Strategy, Editing Games and Q." In Science, Psychology and Communication. Edited by Steven R. Brown and Donald J. Brenner, 327–44. New York: Teachers College Press, 1972.

MacLean, Malcolm S., Jr., and Hazard, William R. "Women's Interest in Pictures; The Badger Village Study." *Journalism Quarterly* 30 (1953): 139–162.

Maddow, Ben. ***Let Truth Be the Prejudice: W. Eugene Smith, His Life and Photographs***. Millerton, New York: *Aperture*, 1985.

Magistad, Mary Kay. "Photojournalism—Dying to Get the Story." *Nieman Reports* 54, no. 3 (2000): 58.

Magmer, James, and Falconer, David. ***Photograph + Printed Word***. Birmingham, MI: Midwest Publications, 1969.

Magna Brava: Magnum's Women Photographers — Eve Arnold, Martine Franck, Susan Meisalas, Inge Morath, Marilyn Silverstone. Munich, London: Prestel, 1999.

Malcolm, Janet. "The View from Plato's Cave." *Aperture*, 67–76, 1997.

Mallen, Frank. *Sauce for the Gander. [The New York Evening Graphic.]* White Plains, New York: Baldwin Books, 1954.

Mallette, Malcolm F. "Ethics in News Pictures: Where Judgement Counts." Paper presented at Rochester Photo Conference, George Eastman House, Rochester, New York, 1975.

Mallette, Malcolm F. "Should These News Pictures Have Been Printed? Ethical Decisions Are Often Hard but Seldom Right." *Popular Photography* (Mar. 1976): 73–75, 118–120.

Manchester, William Raymond. *In Our Time: The World as Seen by Magnum Photographers.* New York: American Federation of the Arts with Norton, 1989.

Manion, B.C. "Faking It! Omaha Daily Fabricates Photo." *News Photographer* (June/July 1981): 30–31.

Marable, Darwin. "Carl Mydans: An Interview." *History of Photography* 26, no. 1 (Spring 2002): 47–52.

Marckx, Hilary F., and Graduate Theological Union. "Reformer/Photographer Jacob A. Riis within the Context of U.S. Religious History." Ph.D. diss., Graduate Theological Union 1999.

Marcus, Adrianne. *The Photojournalist: Mary Ellen Mark and Annie Leibovitz*. Los Angeles: Seskog with Crowell, 1974.

Margolick, David. "*PM*'s Impossible Dream." *Vanity Fair* (Jan. 1999): 116–132.

Mark, Mary Ellen. "An Interview with Mary Ellen Mark." Rockport, ME: Maine Photographic Workshops, 1989. (Recording).

Mark, Mary Ellen. *The Photo Essay*. Washington, DC: Smithsonian Institution, 1990.

Martin, Peter. "Gene Smith as 'The Kid Who Lived Photography.'" *Popular Photography* (Apr. 1979): 130,149–150.

Martin, Rupert, ed. *Floods of Light: Flash Photography, 1851–1981*. London: Photographers Gallery, 1982.

Marwil, Jonathan. "Photography at War." *History Today* 50, no. 6 (2000): 30–37.

Matthews, Mary L., and Reuss, Carol. "The Minimal Image of Women in *Time* and *Newsweek*, 1940–1980." Paper presented at the Annual Meeting of the Association for Education in Journalism and Mass Communication, Memphis, Tennessee, 1985. ERIC, ED260405.

Mauro, Tony. "Paparazzi and the Press." *Quill* (Chicago, Ill.) 86, no. 6 (July/Aug. 1998): 26–8.

Mauro, Tony. "The Camera-Shy Federal Courts: Why are Cameras Accepted in State Courts but Dreaded in Federal Courts?" *Media Studies Journal* 12(1) (1998): 60–5.

Mayes, Stephen. *This Critical Mirror: 40 Years of World Press Photo*. London: Thames & Hudson, 1996.

McCullin, Don, Harold Evans, and Susan Sontag. *Don McCullin*. London: Jonathan Cape, 2001.

McCullin, Don. *Hearts of Darkness*. London: Secker & Warburg, 1980.

McCullin, Don. *Sleeping with Ghosts: A Life's Work in Photography*. London: Vintage, 1995.

McCullin, Don. *Unreasonable Behaviour: An Autobiography*. New York: Knopf, 1990.

McDonald, Michele. "Photojournalism —the Unbearable Weight of Witness." *Nieman Reports* 54, no. 3 (2000): 48.

McMasters, Paul. "Public's Rights Must Be Protected Excerpt from Testimony before the House Judiciary Committee." *The Quill* (Chicago, Ill.) 86, no. 6 (July/Aug. 1998): 30–1.

McNay, Jim. "The Importance of Content, Content, Content." *VCQ* 2 (Fall 1995): 3.

Mellon, Steve. "Carefully choosing the images of poverty." *Nieman Reports* 55, no. 1: 33.

Meltzer, Milton. *Dorothea Lange: A Photographer's Life*. New York: Farrar, Strauss, Giroux, 1978.

Mendelson, A. "Effects of novelty in news photographs on attention and memory." *Media Psychology* 3, no. 2 (2001): 119–157.

Meredith, Roy. *Mr. Lincoln's Camera Man Mathew B. Brady*. 2nd rev. ed. New York: Dover, 1974.

Metz, Holly. "Interview: Susan Meiselas." *The Progressive* 62 (Apr. 1, 1998): 36.

Mich, Daniel D., and Eberman, Edwin. *The Technique of the Picture Story*. New York: McGraw-Hill, 1945.

Michel, Ulli, and Reuters ltd. *The Art of Seeing: The Best of Reuters Photography*. London: Pearson Education, 2000.

Middlebrooks, Donald M., Jones, Clarence, and Shrader, Howard. "Access: Scope of Privilege in Gathering News Is Vague and Narrow, Scope of Liability Is Far More Certain." *News Photographer* (Dec. 1981): 10–11, 13–16, 18–19.

Mili, Gjon. *Gjon Mili: Photographs and Recollections*. Boston: New York Graphic Society, 1980.

Miller, Russell. "A Vanishing Vision." *Columbia Journalism Review* 39, no. 2 (July/Aug. 2000): 36–42.

Miller, Russell. *MAGNUM: Fifty Years at the Front Line of History*. New York: Grove Atlantic, 1998.

Moments in Time: 50 Years of Associated Press News Photos. Rev. ed. North Ryde, Australia: Angus & Robertson, 1984.

Mora, Gilles, and Hill, John T. W., eds. *Eugene Smith: Photographs 1934–1975*. New York: Abrams, 1998.

Morgan, Willard D. *Graphic Graflex Photography for Prize Winning Pictures*. 11th ed. New York: Morgan and Morgan, 1958.

Moriarty, Sandra, and Shaw, David. "An Antiseptic War: Were News Magazine Images of the Gulf War Too Soft?" *News Photographer* (Apr. 1995): *VCQ* 4–8.

Morris, Desmond. *Manwatching: A Field Guide to Human Behavior*. New York: Abrams, 1977.

Morris, John G. *Get the Picture: A Personal History of Photojournalism*. New York: Random House, 1998.

Morton, Robert, ed. *Images of Our Times: Sixty Years of Photography from the Los Angeles Times*. New York: Harry N. Abrams, 1987.

Mullen, Lawrence J. "The President's Visual Image from 1945 to 1974: An Analysis of Spatial Configuration in News Magazine Photographs." *Presidential Studies Quarterly* 27 (Fall 1997): 819–34.

Mundt, Whitney R., and Broussard, E. Joseph. "The Prying Eye: Ethics of Photojournalism." Paper presented at the Annual Meeting of the Association for Education in Journalism, Houston, Texas, 1979. ERIC, ED173863.

Murphy-Racey, Patrick. "Pictures of the Month—January: A Case of Situation Ethics." *News Photographer* (May 1988): 30–31.

Mydans, Carl. *Carl Mydans, Photojournalist*. New York: Abrams, 1985.

N

Nachtwey, James, Christian Frei, Christian Frei Filmproductions, Schweizer Fernsehen DRS, Suissimage, and First Run/Icarus Films. "War Photographer." Brooklyn, NY: First Run/Icarus Films, 2001. Videorecording.

Nachtwey, James. "Photojournalism—Photographs." *Nieman Reports* 54, no. 3 (2000): 46.

Nachtwey, James. *Inferno*. London: Phaidon, 1999.

Nachtwey, James. *Deeds of War: Photographs*. New York: Thames and Hudson, 1989.

Natanson, Barbara Orbach. "Spot the Hyphen? Representations of Immigrants and Members of Ethnic Groups in Illustrated Newspaper and Magazine Stories, 1880–1925 (periodicals, illustrations, immigration, photojournalism)." Ph.D. diss., University of Maryland College Park, 1999.

Neubauer, Hendrik, and Black Star Picture Agency. *Black Star: 60 Years of Photojournalism*. Köln: Könemann, 1997.

Newcomb, John. *The Book of Problem Solving: How to Get Visual Ideas When You Need Them*. New York: R.R. Bowker, 1984.

Newhall, Beaumont. *The History of Photography from 1839 to the Present Day*. Rev. & enlgd. ed. New York: Museum of Modern Art, 1964.

Newman, Arnold. *Arnold Newman, Five Decades*. San Diego: Harcourt Brace Jovanovich, 1986.

Newman, Arnold. *Artists: Portraits from Four Decades*. London: Weidenfeld and Nicolson, 1980.

Newman, Arnold. *One Mind's Eye*. Boston: New York Graphic Society, 1974.

Newman, Arnold. *The Great British*. London: Weidenfeld and Nicolson, 1979.

Newton, Julianne H. "The Burden of Visual Truth: The Role of Photojournalism in Mediating Reality." *News Photographer* (Oct. 1998): *VCQ* 4–9.

Newton, Julianne Hickerson. "In Front of the Camera: Exploring Ethical Issues of Subject Response in Photography." Ph.D. diss., The University of Texas at Austin, 1991.

Newton, Julianne Hickerson. *The Burden of Visual Truth: The Role of Photojournalism in Mediating Reality*. Mahwah, NJ: Lawrence Erlbaum Associates, 2000.

Nicol, Mike. *The Invisible Line: The Life and Photography of Ken Oosterbroek, 1962–1994*. Cape Town: Kwela: Random House South Africa, 1999.

Niederpruem, Kyle E. "We Better Step to the Plate on Paparazzi Issue." *Quill* (Chicago, Ill.) 86, no. 5 (June 1998): 42.

Norback, Craig T., and Gray, Melvin, eds. *The World's Great News Photos, 1840–1980*. New York: Crown Publishers, 1980.

Northup, Steve. "Photojournalism— Photographers Can't Hide Behind Their Cameras." *Nieman Reports* 54, no. 3 (2000): 49.

Northup, Steve. "Words on pictures." *Nieman Reports* 53/54, no. 4/1: 177.

Nottingham, Mary Emily. "From Both Sides of the Lens: Street Photojournalism and Personal Space." Ph.D. diss., Indiana University, 1978.

Nowak, Jeffrey R. "Riot Images: Comparing Photographic Coverage of the 1965 and 1992 Los Angeles Riots in Weekly News Magazines." Master's thesis, Marquette University, 1995.

O

O'Brien, Sue. "Eye on Soweto: A Study of Factors in News Photo Use." Paper presented at the Annual Meeting of the Association for Education in Journalism and Mass Communication. Boston, Massachusetts, Aug. 7–10, 1991. ERIC, ED336795.

Olson, Cal. "Fifty Years & Counting ..." *News Photographer* 49 (Aug. 1994): SS1+.

O'Neil, R. M. "Privacy and press freedom: Paparazzi and other intruders." *University of Illinois Law Review*, no. 2 (1999): 703–716.

Oppel, Richard A. "Photography is at the heart of good journalism." *American Editor*, no. 809: 2.

P

Packer, Lori. "Illiterate Morons and Pretty Pictures: Uses and Criticisms of Early Photojournalism in New York's Jazz Age Tabloids." Master's thesis, University of Washington, 1997.

Padgett, G. E. "Let Grief Be a Private Affair." *Quill* 76 (Feb. 1988): 13, 27.

Paine, Richard P. *The All American Cameras: A Review of Graflex*. Houston: Alpha Publishing, 1981.

Panchak, Patricia L. "Issues in Photojournalism Ethics: An Historical Analysis 1865–1987." Master's thesis, Ohio University, 1988.

Paolucci, Christina I. "Visions From Both Sides of the Camera: The Surfacing of Feminism and Photojournalism." Master's thesis, Mankato State University, MN, 1995.

Parrish, Fred S. *Photojournalism: An Introduction*. Belmont, California: Wadsworth/Thomson Learning, 2002.

Pasternack, Steve, and Martin, Don R. "Daily Newspaper Photojournalism in the Rocky Mountain West." *Journalism Quarterly* 62 (1985): 132–35, 222.

Pasternack, Steve, and Utt, Sandra H. "A Study of America's Front Pages: A 10-Year Update." Paper presented at the Annual Meeting of the Association for Education in Journalism and Mass Communication. Atlanta, Georgia, Aug. 10–13, 1994. ERIC, ED376533.

Pasternak, Steve, and Utt, Sandra H. "A Study of America's Front Pages: How They Look." Paper presented at the Annual Meeting of the Association for Education in Journalism and Mass Communication, Corvallis, Oregon, Aug. 6–9, 1983. ERIC, ED232150.

Perlmutter, David D. *Photojournalism and Foreign Policy: Icons of Outrage in International Crises*. Praeger Series in Political Communication. Westport, Conn.: Praeger, 1998.

Peters, Greg. "Ethics: Covering the Klan: Are the Sensational Photos Accurately Portraying the Event?" *4Sight* (Nov–Dec 1993): 10–11.

Peterson, John C. "Toward a Theory of Picture Editing and Use in Printed Publication." Paper presented at the Annual Meeting of the Association for Education in Journalism and Mass Communication. Boston, Massachusetts, Aug. 7–10, 1991. ERIC, ED336791.

Peterson, John Charles. "Reader Acceptance of Complexity and Picture Use in Contemporary Newspaper Design." Ph.D. diss., Ohio University, 1991.

Photojournalism. Rev. ed. Alexandria, Virginia: Time-Life, 1983.

Pictures of the Times: A Century of Photography from the New York Times. New York: Museum of Modern Art distributed by H.N. Abrams, 1996.

Pierce, Bill. "W. Eugene Smith Teaches Photographic Responsibility." *Popular Photography* (Nov. 1961): 80–84.

Pollack, Peter. *The Picture History of Photography*. New York: Abrams, 1969.

Poppy, John. *The Persuasive Image: Art Kane*. New York: Crowell, 1975.

Poynor, R. "The new visual journalism." *Graphis*, no. 325 (2000): 12.

Pozner & Pomeyrol. *Leica Story*. Publisher and date of publication unknown.

Pride, Mike. "Monitor photographers and paparazzi worlds apart." *News Photographer* (June 1998): 21–22.

Professional Photographic Illustration. Rochester, New York: Eastman Kodak, 1989.

R

Rabinowitz, Allen. "Marlene Karas: In a League of Her Own." *News Photographer* (Apr. 1993): 12–16.

Ramos, Betty J. "Digital Imaging, the News Media and the Law: A Look at Libel, Privacy, Copyright and Evidence in a Digital Age." Paper presented to the Association for Education in Journalism and Mass Communication, Atlanta, Georgia, 1994.

Ranck, R. "Get the picture: A personal history of photojournalism." *New York Times Book Review* (1998): 16.

Rayfield, Stanley. *How Life Gets the Story: Behind the Scenes in Photojournalism*. Garden City, New York: Doubleday, 1955.

Reaves, Shiela. "Digital Alteration of Photographs in Magazines: An Examination of the Ethics." Paper presented at the Annual Meeting of the Association for Education in Journalism and Mass Communication, Washington, DC, 1989. ERIC, ED310444.

Reaves, Shiela. "Digital Retouching: Is There a Place for It in Newspaper Photography?" *Journal of Mass Media Ethics* 2 (Spring/Summer 1987): 40–48.

Reaves, Shiela. "Magazines vs. Newspapers: Editors Have Different Ethical Standards on the Digital Manipulation of Photographs." *News Photographer* 50 (1) (1995): VCQ 4.

Reaves, Shiela. "Photography, Pixels and New Technology: Is There a 'Paradigm Shift'?" Paper presented at the Annual Meeting of the Association for Education in Journalism and Mass Communication, Washington, DC, 1989. ERIC, ED310388.

Reaves, Shiela. "Re-Examining the Ethics of Photographic Posing: Insights from the Rank-and-File Members of ASMP." Madison, Wisconsin: University of Wisconsin, 1993. Paper presented at the Annual Meeting of the Association for Education in Journalism and Mass Communication, Visual Communication Division, Kansas City, Missouri, July 1993.

Reaves, Shiela. "The Vulnerable Image: a Hierarchy of Codes Among Newspaper Editors Toward Digital Manipulation of Photographs." Paper presented at the Annual Meeting of the Association for Education in Journalism and Mass Communication. Montreal, Aug. 7, 1992.

Reaves, Shiela. "What's Wrong with this Picture? Daily Newspaper Photo Editors' Attitudes and Their Tolerance Toward Digital Manipulation." *Newspaper Research Journal* Vol. 13/14 (Fall/Winter 1993): 131–155.

Reed, Eli. "Being receptive to the unexpected." *Nieman Reports* 55, no. 3: 32.

Reed, Eli. *Eli Reed: Black in America*. New York: Norton, 1997.

Reed, Pat. "Paparazzo, Meet Ron Galella. Nemesis of Jackie O., Brando, etc." *Houston Chronicle Texas Magazine* (Apr. 15, 1979): 20.

Reese, David. "Photo-Driven Columns." *News Photographer* Oct. 2000: 40.

Reid, Calvin. "Price is no obstacle." *Publishers Weekly* 247, no. 31: 22.

Remole, Mary K., and Brown, James W. "Ethical Issues for Photojournalists: A Comparative Study of the Perspectives of Journalism Students and Law Students." Paper presented at the Annual Meeting of the Association for Education in Journalism, Boston, Massachusetts, 1980. ERIC, ED191022.

Rhode, Robert B., and McCall, Floyd H. *Press Photography: Reporting with a Camera*. New York: Macmillan, 1961.

Riboud, Marc. *Marc Riboud: Photographs at Home and Abroad.* Translated by I. Mark Paris. New York: Abrams, 1988.

Ricchiardi, Sherry. "Photographer on small Indiana daily restores luster to Pictures of the Year." *News Photographer* (Nov. 1996): 32, 34.

Ricchiardi, Sherry. "Getting the Picture: Women are Coming to the Fore in the Long Male-Dominated Field of Photojournalism." *American Journalism Review* 20(1) (1998): 26–33.

Rich, Kathy. "Contact Sheet: Responses of Leading Picture Editors to a Survey to Determine How They Choose Pictures." *Camera 35* (Apr. 1979): 34.

Richards, Eugene. *50 Hours.* Text by Dorothea Lynch. Long Island City, New York: Many Voices Press, 1983.

Richardson, Jim. *High School: U.S.A.* New York: St. Martin's Press, 1979.

Rigger, Robert. *Man in Sport.* Baltimore, Maryland: Baltimore Museum of Art, 1967.

Riis, Jacob. *How the Other Half Lives.* New York: Scribner, 1904.

Ritchin, Fred. "The Web Waits for Photographers, Too." *Nieman Reports* 52 (Summer 1998): 38–39.

Ritchin, Fred. *In Our Own Image: The Coming Revolution in Photography: How Computer Technology Is Changing Our View of the World.* 2nd ed, Writers and Artists on Photography. New York: Aperture, 1999.

Ritchin, Fred. *In Our Own Image: the Coming Revolution in Photography.* New York: Aperture Foundation, 1990.

Roark, Virginia, and Wanta, Wayne. "Response to Photographs." *VCQ* (Spring 1994): 12–13.

Robaton, John, and Smith, Harris. *Photojournalism Basics: An Introduction to Photography for Publication.* Ipswich, Massachusetts: Upper River Press, 1994.

Robin, Marie-Monique, and Sue Rose. *The Photos of the Century: 100 Historic Moments.* Köln: Evergreen, 1999.

Robins, Wayne. "Not picture-perfect." *Editor & Publisher* 135, no. 15: 26.

Robinson, G. "Interview: Donna Ferrato—Photojournalist." *Media Studies Journal* 10 (Fall 1996): 135–136.

Roche, James M. "Newspaper Subscribers' Response to Accident Photographs: The Acceptance Level Compared to Demographics, Death Anxiety, Fear of Death, and State Anxiety." Paper presented at the Annual Meeting of the Association for Education in Journalism and Mass Communication, Corvallis, Oregon, 1983. ERIC, ED234386.

Rodger, George. *Magnum Opus: Fifty Years in Photojournalism.* London: Nishen, 1987.

Roeder, George, Jr. *The Censored War: American Visual Experience During World War II.* New Haven, Connecticut: Yale University Press, 1993.

Rogers, Madeline. "The Picture Snatchers." *American Heritage* 45 (Oct. 1994): 66–73.

Rogers, Michael. "Local News: Tabloid Pictures From the *Los Angeles Herald Express* 1936–1961." *Library Journal* 124, no. 20: 122.

Rogers, Michael. "New York Exposed: Photographs from the Daily News." *Library Journal* 126, no. 20: 117.

Rolling Stone, the Photographs. New York: Simon & Schuster, 1989.

Rose, Bleys W. "Hundreds of readers object to race photos." *News Photographer* (Jan. 1995): 54–55.

Rosett, Jane M. "Photojournalists: Visionaries Who Have Changed Our Vision." *Media Studies Journal* 11 (1997): 39–57.

Rotella, Mark, Charlotte Abbott, and Sarah Gold. "Shutterbabe: Adventures in Love and War." *Publishers Weekly* 247, no. 44: 54.

Rothstein, Arthur. *Words and Pictures.* New York: Amphoto, 1979.

Rotkin, Charles E. *Professional Photographer's Survival Guide.* New York: *American Photo*graphic Book Publishing, 1982.

Rowland, Jack. "Please don't call me paparazzo." *News Photographer* (Nov. 1997): 10.

Rubin, Steven. "A photographer unites generations with his camera." *Nieman Reports* 53, no. 1: 79.

Rubin, Susan Goldman. *Margaret Bourke-White: Her Pictures Were Her Life.* New York: Abrams, 1999.

Rudd, James O'Malley. "Picture Possibilities: An Ethnographic Study of Newspaper Photojournalism." Master's thesis, University of Washington, 1994.

Russial, John, and Upshaw, Jim. "See No Evil? Differing Responses to an Awful Picture." *Columbia Journalism Review* (Jan./Feb. 1994): 9–11.

Russial, John, and Wanta, Wayne. "Digital Imaging Skills and the Hiring and Training of Photojournalists." *Journalism and Mass Communication Quarterly* 75 (Autumn 1998): 593–605.

Russial, John. "Digital Imaging and the Photojournalist: Work and Workload Issues." Paper presented at the Annual Meeting of the Association for Education in Journalism and Mass Communication. Baltimore, Maryland, Aug. 5–8, 1998. ERIC, ED423562.

S

Sajn, Nikolina; Heo, Kwangjun; and Merritt, Sarah. "Framing a War: Photographic Coverage of the Kosovo War in *Newsweek*, *Time*, and *U.S. News & World Report*." Paper presented at the Proceedings of the Annual Meeting of the Association for Education in Journalism and Mass Communication, Phoenix, Arizona, Aug. 9–12, 2000.

Salgado, Sebastião. *Migrations: Humanity in Transition.* New York: Aperture, 2000.

Salgado, S., and Nepomuceno, E. *Workers: An archaeology of the Industrial Age.* New York: Aperture, 1993.

Salgado, Sebastião. *Other Americas.* New York: Pantheon, 1986.

Salomon, Erich. *Portrait of an Age.* New York: Macmillan, 1967.

Santana, Maria Cristina. "Traditional or Digital Photojournalism Education? A Survey of Four-Year Photo Programs and Small Dailies' Photo Needs." *Journal of Educational Technology Systems* 25, no. 4 (1997): 351.

Schlagheck, Carol. "Handling Critics and Controversy: How Some Editors and Ombudsmen Have Dealt with Negative Reader Response." *News Photographer* (July 1993): 17–25.

Schuneman, R. Smith, ed. Photographic Communication: Principles, Problems and Challenges of Photojournalism. New York: Hastings House, 1972.

Schuneman, R. Smith. "The Photograph in Print: An Examination of New York Daily Newspapers, 1890–1937." Ph.D. diss., University of Minnesota, 1966.

Schwartz, Donna. "To Tell the Truth: Codes of Objectivity in Photojournalism." Communication 13 (1992): 95–109.

Sedge, Michael H. *The Photojournalist's Guide to Making Money.* New York: Allworth Press, 2000.

Seelig, Michelle Ivy. "The Social Construction of News Photos: A Case Study of the Photo Editorial-Decision Process at the "Philadelphia Inquirer"." *DAI* 62, no. 02A (2001): 271.

Sentman, Mary Alice. "Black and White: Disparity in Coverage by *Life* Magazine from 1937 to 1972." *Journalism Quarterly* 60 (1983): 501–508.

Shames, Laurence. "Profile: On the Road with Annie Leibovitz, The Queen of Celebrity Photographers Is Quite a Character Herself." *American Photographer* (Jan. 1984): 38–55.

Sharkey, Jacqueline. "The Diana Aftermath." *American Journalism Review* (Nov. 1997): 19–25.

Sherer, Michael D. "A Survey of Photojournalists and Their Encounters with the Law." *Journalism Quarterly* 64 (1987): 499–502, 575.

Sherer, Michael D. "Comparing Magazine Photos of Vietnam and Korean Wars." *Journalism Quarterly* 65 (1988): 752–56.

Sherer, Michael D. "Invasion of Poland Photos in Four American Newspapers." *Journalism Quarterly* 61 (1984): 422–26.

Sherer, Michael D. "Photographic Invasion of Privacy: An Old Concept with New Meaning." Paper presented at the Annual Meeting of the International Communication Association, Dallas, Texas, 1983. ERIC, ED236626.

Sherer, Michael D. "Photojournalism and the Infliction of Emotional Distress." *Communications and the Law* 8 (Apr. 1986): 27–37.

Sherer, Michael D. "Photojournalists and the Law: A Survey of NPPA Members." *News Photographer* (Jan. 1988): 16, 18.

Sherer, Michael D. "Subpoenas Alive: Know Protection." *News Photographer* (Jan. 1999): 22, 29.

Sherer, Michael D. "The Photojournalist and the Law: The Right to Gather News Through Photography." Ph.D. diss., Southern Illinois University at Carbondale, 1982.

Sherer, Michael D. "The Problem of Libel for Photojournalists." *Journalism Quarterly* 63 (1986): 618–23.

Sherer, Michael D. "The Problem of Trespass for Photojournalists." *Journalism Quarterly* 62 (1985): 154–56, 222.

Sherer, Michael D. "Your Photos or Mine: An Examination of the Laws Governing Warranted Searches and Subpoenas for the Photojournalist's Work Product." Paper presented at the Annual Meeting of the Association for Education in Journalism and Mass Communication, Corvallis, Oregon, 1983. ERIC, ED236610.

Sherer, Michael D. *No Pictures Please: It's the Law*. Durham, NC: *National Press Photographers* Association, 1987.

Sherer, Michael D. *Photojournalism and the Law: A Practical Guide to Legal Issues in News Photography*. Durham, NC: *National Press Photographers* Association, 1996.

Sherer, Michael D. "The Photojournalist and the Law: The Right to Gather News through Photography." *DAI* 43, no. 07A (1982): 303.

Sherer, Michael D. "Fake-photo charge, filing of libel suit involve NPPA and its magazine." *News Photographer* (Oct. 1997): 27.

Shiras, George, 3rd. "Photographing Wild Game with Flashlight and Camera." *National Geographic* (July 1906).

Shoemaker, Pamela J., and Fosdick, James A. "How Varying Reproduction Methods Affects Response to Photographs." *Journalism Quarterly* 59 (1982): 13–20, 65.

Simon, Peter. *I and Eye: Pictures of My Generation*. Boston: Bulfinch Press, 2001.

Singletary, M. W. "Newspaper Photographs: A Content Analysis, 1936–76." *Journalism Quarterly* 55 (1978): 585–89.

Six Decades: The News in Pictures: A Collection of 250 News and Feature Photographs Taken from 1912 to 1975 by the Milwaukee Journal Co. Staff Photographers. Milwaukee, MN: Milwaukee Journal Co., 1976.

Skow, Lisa M., and George N. Dionisopoulos. "A Struggle to Contextualize Photographic Images: American Print Media and the 'Burning Monk.'" *Communication Quarterly* 45, no. 4 (Fall 1997): 393–409.

Smith W. Eugene. "W. Eugene Smith Talks About Lighting." *Popular Photography* (Nov. 1956): 48.

Smith, C. Zoe, and Anne-Marie Woodward. "Photo-Elicitation Method Gives Voice and Reactions of Subjects." *Journalism and Mass Communication Educator* 53, no. 4 (Win 1999): 31–41.

Smith, C. Zoe, and Mendelson, Andrew. "The Health of Photojournalism and Visual Communication Education in the Nineties: Cause for Concern or a Bright Future?" Paper presented at the Annual Meeting of the Association for Education in Journalism and Mass Communication, Washington, DC, Aug. 9–12, 1995. ERIC, ED392085.

Smith, C. Zoe, and Mendelson, Andrew. "Visual Communication Education: Cause for Concern or Bright Future?" *Journalism and Mass Communication Educator* 51 (Autumn 1996): 66–73.

Smith, C. Zoe, and Michael Winokur. "Up close and personal." *News Photographer* (Sept. 1996): 42–48.

Smith, C. Zoe, and Woodward, Anne-Marie. "Photo-Elicitation Method Gives Voice and Reactions of Subjects." *Journalism and Mass Communication Educator* 53(4) (1999): 31–41.

Smith, C. Zoe. "An Alternative View of the Thirties: The Industrial Photographs of Lewis Wickes Hine and Margaret Bourke-White." Paper presented at the Annual Meeting of the Association for Education in Journalism. East Lansing, MI, Aug. 8–11, 1981. ERIC, ED204770.

Smith, C. Zoe. "Black Star Picture Agency: *Life*'s European Connection." *Journalism History* 13 (Spring 1986): 19–25.

Smith, C. Zoe. "Dickey Chapelle." *VCQ* (Spring 1994): 4–9.

Smith, C. Zoe. "Emigré Photography in America: Contributions of German Photojournalism From Black Star Picture Agency to *Life* Magazine, 1933–1938." Ph.D. diss., The University of Iowa, 1983.

Smith, C. Zoe. "Great Women in Photojournalism." Parts 1–3. *News Photographer* (Jan. 1985): 20–21; (Feb. 1985): 26, 28–29; (Apr. 1985): 22–24.

Smith, Ron F. "How Design and Color Affect Reader Judgement of Newspapers." *Newspaper Research Journal* 10 (Winter 1989): 75–85.

Smith, W. Eugene, and Smith, Aileen M. *Minamata*. New York: Holt, Rinehart and Winston, 1975.

Smith, W. Eugene, Gilles Mora, John T. Hill, and Gabriel Bauret. *W. Eugene Smith: Photographs 1934–1975*. New York: Harry N. Abrams, 1998.

Smith, W. Eugene. "A Man of Mercy." *Life* (Nov. 15, 1954): 161–172.

Smith, W. Eugene. "Country Doctor." *Life* (Sept. 20, 1948): 115–126.

Smith, W. Eugene. "Nurse Midwife." *Life* (Dec. 3, 1951): 134–145.

Smith, W. Eugene. "Pittsburgh." 1959 *Photography Annual* (1958): 96–133.

Smith, W. Eugene. "Saipan." *Life* (Aug. 28, 1944): 75–83.

Smith, W. Eugene. "Spanish Village." *Life*.

Smith, W. Eugene. *W. Eugene Smith, Master of the Photographic Essay*. Millerton, New York: *Aperture*, 1981.

Smith, W. Eugene. *W. Eugene Smith: His Photographs and Notes*. Millerton, New York: *Aperture*, 1969.

Sobieszek, Robert A. *Arnold Newman*. Englewood Cliffs, New Jersey: Prentice-Hall, 1982.

Solomon, Deborah. "Newman at Work." *American Photographer* (Feb. 1988): 44–55.

Souza, Pete. "Kent Kobersteen: The New Director of Photography at *National Geographic*." *News Photographer* (Summer 1998): *VCQ* 3–8.

Souza, Pete. "White House top photo sparks pro, con on publishing." *News Photographer* (Feb. 1995): 26–27.

Souza, Pete. Unguarded Moments: Behind-the-Scenes Photographs of President Ronald Reagan. Fort Worth, Texas: Summit Group, 1992.

Sparks, Glenn G., and Fehlner, Christine L. "Faces in the News: Gender Comparisons of Magazine Photographs." *Journal of Communication* (Autumn 1986): 70–79.

Spencer, Otha Cleo. "Twenty Years of '*Life*': A Study of Time, Inc.'s Picture Magazine and Its Contributions to Photojournalism." Ph.D. diss., University of Missouri, Columbia, 1958.

Spigel, L. "*Life*'s America: Family and nation in postwar photojournalism." *American Historical Review* 101, no. 4 (1996): 1309–1310.

Spina, Tony. *On Assignment, Projects in Photojournalism*. New York: Amphoto, 1982.

Spina, Tony. *Press Photographer*. Cranbury, New Jersey: A.S. Barnes, 1968.

Spremo, Boris. *Twenty Years of Photojournalism*. Toronto: McClelland and Stewart, 1983.

Spruill, Larry Hawthorne. "Southern Exposure: Photography and the Civil Rights Movement, 1955–1968." Ph.D. diss., State University of New York at Stony Brook, 1983.

Squiers, Carol. "Photojournalism." *American Photo* 9, no. 6 (Nov./Dec. 1998): 64–6+.

Squiers, Carol. "Seeing History As It Happened: A Century and a Half in the Life of the World, As Recorded by Its Most Daring Witness." *American Photographer* (Oct. 1988): 33–44.

Squiers, Carol. "The House of News." *American Photo* 9 (Sept./Oct. 1998): 20.

Squires, Carol. "Diana and the Paparazzi." *American Photo* 8 (Nov./Dec. 1997): 15–16.

Srihari, Rohini K. "Use of Captions and Other Collateral Text in Understanding Photographs." *Artificial Intelligence Review* 8 (Oct–Dec 1994): 409–430.

Staples, Brent. "Photojournalism—the Perils of Growing Comfortable with Evil." *Nieman Reports* 54, no. 3 (2000): 52.

Steele, Bob. "Protocols for Ethical Decision-Making in the Digital Age." *Protocol* 1991: 13–17.

Steichen, Edward. *The Family of Man*. New York: Simon & Schuster, 1955.

Stein, Barney. *Spot News Photography*. New York: Verlan Books, 1960.

Stepan, Peter, and Claus Biegert. *Photos That Changed the World*. Munich; London: Prestel, 2000.

Stepno, Bob. "Staged, faked, and mostly naked: Photographic innovations at the *Evening Graphic* (1924–1932). Paper presented at the Annual Meeting of the Association for Education in Journalism and Mass Communication. Baltimore, Maryland, Aug. 5–8, 1998.

Stern, Bert. *Photo Illustration: Bert Stern*. New York: Crowell, 1974.

Stettner, Louis, and Zanutto, James M. "Weegee." *Popular Photography* (Apr. 1961): 101–102.

Stettner, Louis. *Weegee*. New York: Alfred A. Knopf, 1977.

Stoll, D. C. "Necessary truths: Jean-François Leroy and the Perpignan Festival of Photojournalism." *Aperture*, no. 160 (2000): 2–13.

Stott, William. *Documentary Expression and Thirties America*. New York: Oxford Press, 1973.

Strauss, David Levi. "James Nachtwey: International Center of Photography, New York." *Artforum International* 39, no. 1 (Sept. 2000): 180.

Streitmatter, R. "The Rise and Triumph of the White House Photo Opportunity." *Journalism Quarterly* 65 (1988): 981–85.

Strother, Tracy. "Are We Only Wrong if Someone Gets Caught: A Study of the Credibility of Digitally Altered Photography." Master's thesis, Marquette University, 1994.

Wischmann, Lesley. "Dying on the Front Page: Kent State and the Pulitzer Prize." *Journal of Mass Media Ethics* 2 (Spring/Summer 1987): 67–74.

Wolf, Henry. *Visual Thinking: Methods for Making Images Memorable*. New York: American Showcase, 1988.

Wolf, Rita, and Giotta, Gerald L. "Images: A Question of Readership." *Newspaper Research Journal* 6 (Winter 1985): 30–36.

Wolk, Art. "The Law in Plain English for Photographers." *Library Journal* 126, no. 10: 109.

Woo, Jisuk. "Journalism Objectivity in News Magazine Photography." *VCQ* (Summer 1994): 9.

Woodburn, Bert W. "Reader Interest in Newspaper Pictures." *Journalism Quarterly* 24 (1947): 197–201.

Wooley, Al E. *Camera Journalism*. South Brunswick, New Jersey: A. S. Barnes, 1966.

The World in Photographs 2001. New York: Harry N. Abrams, 2002.

Y

Yang, Daqing. "Image—War's Most Innocent Victim." *Media Studies Journal* 13 (Winter 1999): 18–19.

Yates, Carl. "What to Do When the Law Says, 'No Pictures, Please!,'" *News Photographer* (Nov. 1993): 19.

Yu, Yong-Hoon. "Visual Silences in the American News Media: A Content Analysis of News Photos in *Time* and *Newsweek*." Master's thesis, California State University, Northridge, 1994.

Z

Zarnowski, Myra. "Telling Lewis Hine's Story: Russell Freedman's Kids at Work." Paper presented at the 1997 Annual conference of the National Council of Teachers of English. Detroit, Michigan, 1997. ERIC, ED414574.

Zavoina, S., and T. Reichert. "Media convergence/management change: The evolving workflow for visual journalists." *Journal of Media Economics* 13, no. 2 (2000): 143–151.

Zavoina, S., and Davidson, J. *Digital Photojournalism*. Boston: Allyn and Bacon, 2002.

Zibluk, Jack. "Evaluating Photographs." *Communication: Journalism Education Today* 32, no. 4 (Summer 1999): 22–29.

Zillmann, D., S. Knobloch, and H. S. Yu. "Effects of photographs on the selective reading of news reports." *Media Psychology* 3, no. 4 (2001): 301–324.

Zillmann, Dolf, Rhonda Gibson, and Stephanie L. Sargent. "Effects of photographs in news-magazine reports on issue perception." *Media Psychology* 1, no. 3 (1999): 207–228.

Zimbel, George S, and Maggie Drucker. "Who owns this photograph?" *Columbia Journalism Review* 40, no. 1: 60.

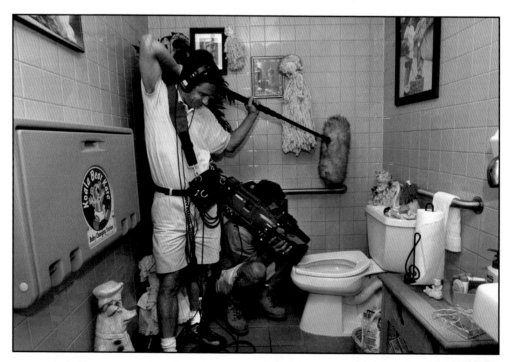

A television news crew goes right to the source—a public restroon rated by travelers as one of the cleanest in the area.

P. Kevin Morley, *Richmond Times-Dispatch*

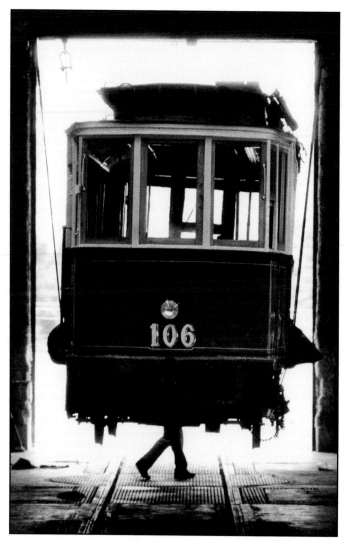

Tom Levy, Honolulu

Limited Warranty

The Publisher warrants the media on which the software is furnished to be free from defects in materials and workmanship under normal use for 30 days from the date that you obtain the Product. The warranty set forth above is the exclusive warranty pertaining to the Product, and the Publisher disclaims all other warranties, express or implied, including, but not limited to, implied warranties of merchantability and fitness for a particular purpose, even if the Publisher has been advised of the possibility of such purpose. Some jurisdictions do not allow limitations on an implied warranty's duration; therefore the above limitations may not apply to you.

Limitation of Liability

Your exclusive remedy for breach of this warranty will be the repair or replacement of the Product at no charge to you or the refund of the applicable purchase price paid upon the return of the Product, as determined by the Publisher in its discretion. In no event will the Publisher, and its directors, officers, employees, and agents, or anyone else who has been involved in the creation, production, or delivery of this software be liable for indirect, special, consequential, or exemplary damages, including, without limitation, for lost profits, business interruption, lost or damaged data, or loss of goodwill, even if the Publisher or an authorized dealer or distributor or supplier has been advised of the possibility of such damages. Some jurisdictions do not allow the exclusion or limitation of indirect, special, consequential, or exemplary damages or the limitation of liability to specified amounts; therefore the above limitations or exclusions may not apply to you.

Recommended System Requirements
256 MB RAM or higher
64 MB or higher Graphics Card
400 MHz or faster processor
16X or faster DVD-ROM drive
Windows 98SE or higher, or
Macintosh OS 9.2 or higher

How to Use This Program

For PC or Mac DVD players:

NOTE: This program works best when played with the InterActual Player.

1. Place the DVD into your PC or Mac DVD player. It should automatically start up with an introductory video play ending with the main menu.
2. If the DVD does not play, then check the age of your DVD player. This DVD may not play in older computer DVD players.

TECHNICAL SUPPORT

Technical support for this product is available between 9 A.M. and 5 P.M. CST, Monday through Friday. Before calling, be sure that your computer meets the minimum system requirements to run this software. Inside the United States, call 1-800-692-9010. Outside the United States, call 314-872-8370. You may also fax your questions to 314-997-5080.

You may also contact Technical Support through e-mail: technical.support@elsevier.com

For access to a list of Frequently Asked Questions (FAQ) and troubleshooting tips please visit our website at http://www.us.elsevierhealth.com/TechSupport

Produced in China